SANTRY BOOKSTORE
DUBLIN CORPORATION PUBLIC LIBRARIES
Withdrawn from Stock
Dublin City Public Libraries
KT-132-398

Iceland, Greenland & the Faroe Islands

31A1

Deanna Swaney

Withdrawn from Stock
Dublin City Public Libraries
DUBLIN CORPORATION PUBLIC LIBRARIES

Withdrawn from Stock
Dublin City Public Libraries

Iceland, Greenland & the Faroe Islands – a travel survival kit
1st edition

Published by
Lonely Planet Publications
Head Office: PO Box 617, Hawthorn, Vic 3122, Australia
US Office: PO Box 2001A, Berkeley, CA 94702, USA

Printed by
Singapore National Printers Ltd, Singapore

Photographs by
Deanna Swaney (DS)
Kjarten Lauring (KL)
David Curl (DC)
Greg Alford (GA)

Front cover: Uummannaq, Greenland (DS)
Back cover: Icebergs near Qaqortoq, Greenland (DS)

First Published
February 1991

Although the authors and publisher have tried to make the information as accurate as possible, they accept no responsibility for any loss, injury or inconvenience sustained by any person using this book.

National Library of Australia Cataloguing in Publication Data

Deanna Swaney
Iceland, Greenland & the Faroe Islands – a travel survival kit.

Includes index.
ISBN 0 86442 092 7.

1. Iceland – Description and travel – 1981–
Guide-books. 2. Greenland – Description and travel –
Guide-books. 3. Faroe Islands – Description and travel –
1981 – – Guide-books. II. Title.

919.4912045

text & maps © Lonely Planet 1991
photos © photographers as indicated 1991

All rights reserved. No part of this publication may be reproduced, stored in a retrieval system or transmitted in any form by any means, electronic, mechanical, photocopying, recording or otherwise, except brief extracts for the purpose of review, without the written permission of the publisher and copyright owner.

Deanna Swaney

After graduating from university, Deanna Swaney made the obligatory European tour and has been addicted to travelling ever since. After a shady career writing funny coded messages to a Basic IV 8000 minicomputer, she dropped out of encroaching yuppiedom and headed south along the gringo trail to write Lonely Planet's *Bolivia – a travel survival kit*. Between wanders around six relatively dry continents, Deanna travelled Oceania – the liquid continent – to research and write LP's *Tonga – a travel survival kit* and *Samoa – a travel survival kit*. This book is the result of a summer in Arctic island paradises and a lifelong fascination with things boreal.

When she's not travelling around the world, Deanna makes her home in the vibrant heart of Anchorage from where she trips around the Alaskan wilderness and loads up on inspiration. She was last seen headed west from Melbourne for 'yet another' exercise in travel survival.

Acknowledgements

Many thanks to Thomas Strack, Heidi Strack, and Evi Weiller in Herxheim, John Roberts of Scanvik Books in Copenhagen, Hauke Wendler & Ulrike in Frankfurt for their help, direction, and hospitality while I was preparing to begin work on the project.

For their friendship and yet more hospitality during my stay in the Faroes, thanks to Lena Mohr, Beinir Kristiansen, Sámal & Bergtóra Kristiansen, Alexander & Caroline Kristiansen, and Jörleif á Dalbö, all of Fuglafjörður, Faroe Islands.

My time in Iceland was considerably enhanced by José & Gloria (Barcelona), Einar Gudjónsson (Reykjavík), Eric Hyppia (Boulder), Heike Robinson (Cleveland), Eugene Smith and Bill Foley (Ísafjörður), Erwin & Angelika Bardli (Graubunden), Dana Sivron (Tel Aviv), and *Die Vier Stöpseln* of that party town Klein Ingesheim 'somewhere around Stuttgart'.

In Greenland, Tage Lauritsen in Qaqortoq, René Nielsen in Nanortalik, Magdalene Pedersen in Maniitsoq, Rikke Bøye Jensen in Narsarsuaq, Peter Bendtzen in Upernavik, Søren Thalund in Narsaq all helped with the finer points of travelling in that country. Thanks also to Max Schmid of Winterthur, Switzerland, and Wenni Wellsandt of Stuttgart for sharing their amazing photographic expertise with a struggling amateur, to Kjartan Lauring for his help with the Disko Island chapter, and to Manfred Ehinger of Qaqortoq for his enthusiastic hospitality.

Finally, love and thanks to Earl Swaney of Santa Clara, CA, and Christy Audette, Dave Dault, and Mark & Josh Delanney of Alaska.

Lonely Planet Credits

This first edition was edited at the Lonely Planet office in Australia by Frith Pike. Designer Vicki Beale was responsible for mapping, illustrations and cover design. Thanks also to Alan Tiller for proofing; Charlotte Hindle for assisting with copy editing; Sharon Wertheim (assisted by Jon Murray) for indexing; Tamsin Wilson, Krzysztof Dydyński and Glenn Beanland for additional mapping; Trudi Canavan, Margaret Jung, Tamsin Wilson and Glenn Beanland for additional illustrations.

Leabharlanna Poiblí Átha Cliath

A Warning & a Request

Things change – prices go up, schedules change, good places go bad and bad places go bankrupt – nothing stays the same. So if you find things better or worse, recently opened or long since closed, please write and tell us and help make the next edition better!

Your letters will be used to help update future editions and, where possible, important changes will also be included as a Stop Press section in reprints.

All information is greatly appreciated and the best letters will receive a free copy of the next edition, or any other Lonely Planet book of your choice.

Contents

GREENLAND

THE FAROE ISLANDS

MAP LEGEND

BOUNDARIES

International Boundaries
Internal Boundaries
National Parks, Reserves
The Equator
The Tropics

SYMBOLS

NEW DELHI ... National Capital
BOMBAY ... Provincial or State Capital
Pune ... Major Town
Barsi ... Minor Town
Post Office
Airport
Tourist Information
Bus Station, Terminal
66 ... Highway Route Number
Mosque, Church, Cathedral
Temple, Ruin or Archaeological Site
Hostel
Hospital
Lookout
Camping Areas
Picnic Areas
Hut or Chalet
Mountain
Railway Station
Road Bridge
Road Rail Bridge
Road Tunnel
Railway Tunnel
Escarpment or Cliff
Pass
Ancient or Historic Wall

ROUTES

Major Roads and Highways
Unsealed Major Roads
Sealed Roads
Unsealed Roads, Tracks
City Streets
Railways
Subways
Walking Tracks
Ferry Routes
Cable Car or Chair Lift

HYDROGRAPHIC FEATURES

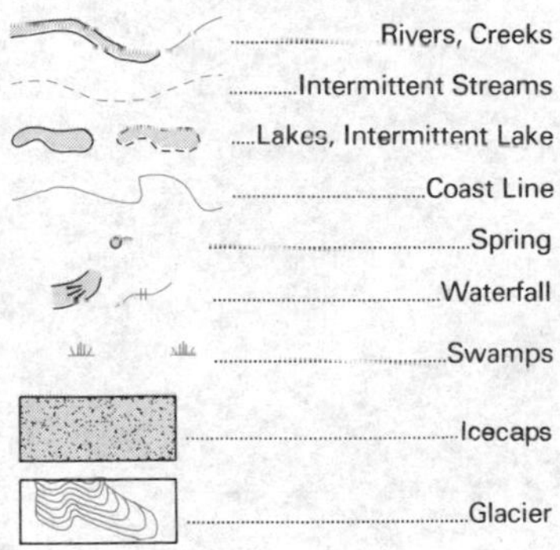

OTHER FEATURES

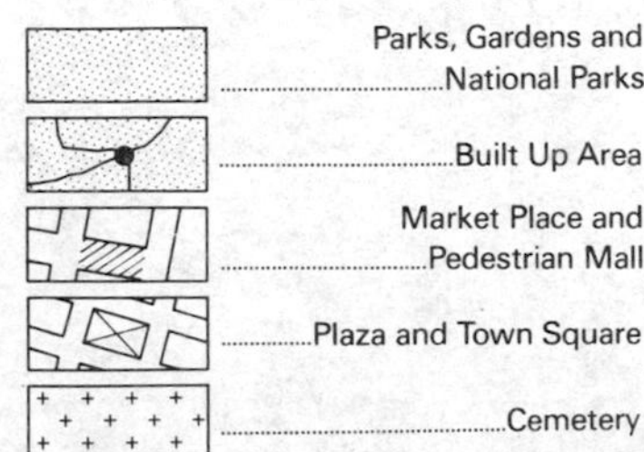

Note: Not all the symbols displayed above will necessarily appear in this book

Introduction

As far as travellers are concerned, the North Atlantic countries have historically been places to fly over quickly or to touch down in briefly while flying between North America and Europe. Few who'd spent a 2-hour stopover gazing at the barren lava fields around Iceland's Keflavík International Airport or looked down on Greenland's seemingly dimensionless icecap could ever have imagined visiting those places on purpose.

To some extent, this is still true but it won't be for long. As more and more visitors spend time seeing the wonders of Iceland, Greenland, and the Faroe Islands, word will get around and many more visitors will keep arriving.

Culturally, Iceland, Greenland, and the

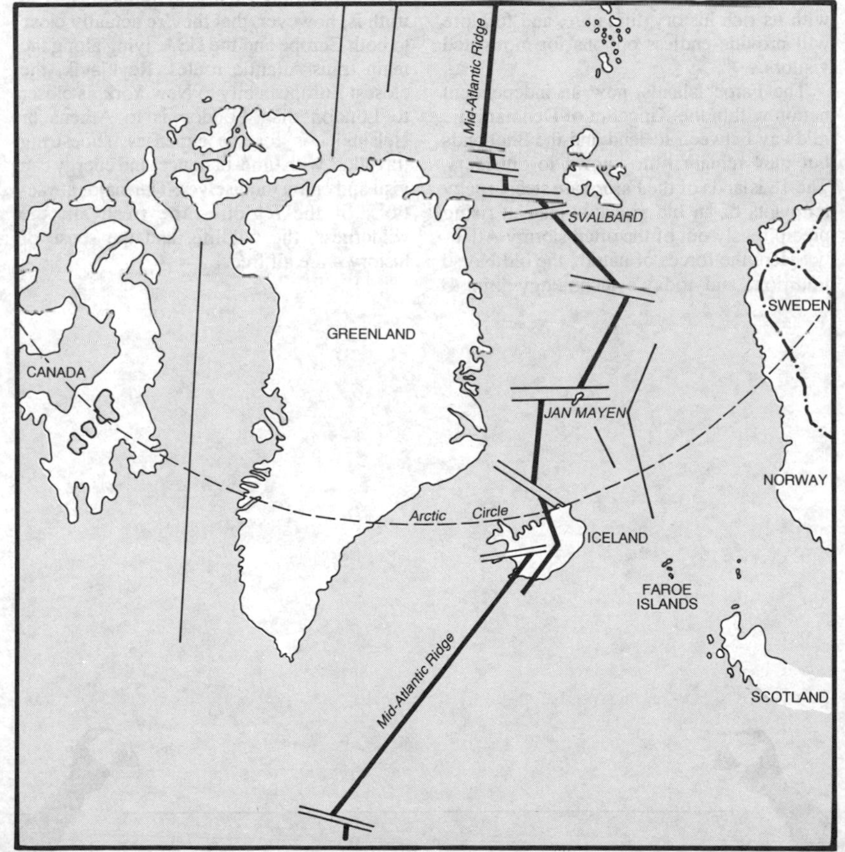

Faroes – collectively known as West Norden – form an arc of stepping stones between Scotland and Canada and provide an intercontinental link as wide as the Atlantic itself. The region is the meeting place of the Inuit peoples who settled from the west and the Norse who arrived (albeit much later) from the east and actually pressed on as far as eastern North America.

Iceland is, of course, the best known and most visited of the three countries due to Icelandair's inexpensive flights between New York and Luxembourg. Its wild volcanic landscapes, its mountains, glaciers, hot springs, geysers, and waterfalls combined with its rich history, literature, and folklore will provide endless options for motivated visitors.

The Faroe Islands, now an independent nation within the Kingdom of Denmark, lie midway between Iceland and the Shetlands but they remain little known to outsiders. The 18 islands of the Faroes are steep, rocky remnants of an old volcanic plateau rising precipitously out of the often stormy Atlantic. Here the forces of nature, the old Norse tradition, and today's technology join to create a part of modern Europe superimposed on a stunning backdrop.

Greenland, the world's largest island, defies description. It also exemplifies what is perhaps the most successful meeting of European and indigenous cultures in the colonial world. Its friendly people, their resourceful and practical traditions, and the haunting beauty of their land will never be forgotten by anyone who's experienced them first-hand.

It seems that seasoned travellers often put off visiting the North Atlantic countries until last due to their perceived remoteness and their reputation as money-munchers. The truth is, however, that they're actually close to both Europe and the USA, lying along the main trans-Atlantic routes. Reykjavík, the closest European city to New York, is closer to London than London is to Athens or Helsinki. As for the expenses, shoestring travellers with time, patience, and energy can visit and enjoy themselves. The major attractions of the region – the fresh air, the wilderness, the wildlife, and the sense of history – are all free.

Facts about the Region

HISTORY

Early Perceptions

Between 325 and 330 BC, the Greek navigator Pytheas embarked upon a voyage from Marseille, through the Gates of Heracles and then northward, to investigate trade routes to the amber and tin markets of northern Europe. In the process, he circumnavigated Britain, 'discovered' the Orkneys (and possibly the Shetlands), and visited the west coast of Norway.

In his report on the journey, Pytheas mentioned the island Ultima Thule, 6 days sailing north of Britain, beyond which the sea congealed into a viscous jelly. This was almost certainly a reference to Iceland. Given the description, it seems unlikely he actually visited the island but it is significant that the Celts or the Norse knew of its existence at such an early date.

Non-Nordic European perceptions of the North Atlantic region both before and after Pytheas' journey, however, were even more shrouded in rumour and myth. The great northern ocean, *oceanus innavigabllls* or the Hyperborean Sea, was a place of maelstrom where the fierce winds of Boreas howled through the Rhipaean mountains and guarded idyllic lands of plenty like Vinland, the Elysian fields, Avalon, the Hesperides and a host of other enigmatic, but mythical, locales. The borders of paradise were inhabited, they believed, by barbaric dog-headed people (the Cynocephali and the Scythians) who ate raw meat and were like bears.

To venture northward, they presumed, would invite all sorts of grisly eventualities. Their fears of the irksome, unknown entities were overcome by economic opportunism when amber and tin deposits beckoned.

The Monks

Some of the myth was dispelled during the 6th century when Ireland was seized by the religious fervour that accompanied its adoption of Roman Christianity; the first Irish monks set sail for fabled lands to the north-west. Some were hermits in search of a solitary environment for religious contemplation. Others undoubtedly observed sea birds flying in from the north-west and concluded that countries awaiting Christian enlightenment lay in that direction.

While some of the Irish zealots were settlers, some were merely voyagers. In the early 6th century the Irish abbot St Brendan embarked upon a voyage for 7 years through the region in a *carraugh*, an open skin-boat. Unfortunately, the account of his journey, *Navigatio Sancti Brendani Abbatis*, wasn't written down until the 9th century and the time lapse surely caused some distortion of fact. Although no conclusive proof of his itinerary has been established, his mention of 'sheep islands', the 'paradise of birds', 'flaming mountains', and 'crystal columns' has been construed as references to the Faroes, Iceland, and the Greenland icebergs. Some traditions state (although they are hardly backed by evidence) that St Brendan and later voyagers pushed on to eastern Canada and even made their way up the St Lawrence toward the North American heartland.

Others brought back to Ireland tales of the land of Thule where there was no daylight in the winter, but on summer nights (according to the clergyman Dicuil in 825) 'whatever task a man wishes to perform, even picking lice from his shirt, he can manage as well as in clear daylight'. This almost certainly describes Iceland and its midnight sun.

To the first monks to permanently settle in the Faroes and Iceland (around the year 700), it would have been apparent that the islands were uninhabited and therefore more suitable as a hermitage than a mission. They built monasteries along the coast and set about their duties. It's likely that some remained in Iceland and the Faroes and mixed with the Norse people who began arriving in the early 9th century although Nordic accounts state that these *papar* ('little fathers') fled during the period of Norse settlement.

The Norse

Although much national pride of the Faroese and Icelandic people is derived from notions that they are 'children of the Vikings', the Nordic settlers of the North Atlantic were actually more ordinary Scandinavian citizens: farmers, herders, merchants, and opportunists. The reasons for this westward expansion were undoubtedly complex but Scandinavian politics and tyranny, population increase, shipbuilding prowess, commercial potential, and even sheer boredom and wanderlust have been cited as catalysts of the Nordic 'explosion' that nurtured both the Viking movements and the westward migrations.

Icelandic tradition, however, officially credits the Norse settlement of Iceland and the Faroes to only one mainland phenomenon. During the middle to late 9th century, the tyrannical Harald Haarfager (Harald Finehair), the king of Vestfold district of south-eastern Norway, was taken over by imperialistic aspirations. In 890, he won a significant naval victory at Hafrsfjord (Stavanger), and the deposed chieftains and landowners chose to flee rather than submit. Many wound up in Iceland and the Faroes, some arriving via the Orkneys and Shetlands which were in turn also conquered by the indefatigable King Harald.

It must be pointed out that much of Europe at this time was being subjected to Nordic mischief. Moving quickly through the British Isles sacking, looting, plundering, and murdering, the Viking hordes struck terror wherever they went and, by the middle of the 9th century, they controlled most of Britain and Ireland. Over the next 200 years, they raided their way across the continent as far east as the Volga and south to the Mediterranean and north Africa. They may have continued in both directions if King Harald Hardraada (Harald Hard-Ruler) hadn't fallen in 1066 at the hands of the Normans.

Throughout the Viking Age (800-1066), particularly violent Norse advances were marked by an exodus into the North Atlantic, not only of Scandinavians but also of Britons, Westmen (Irish), and Scots who had

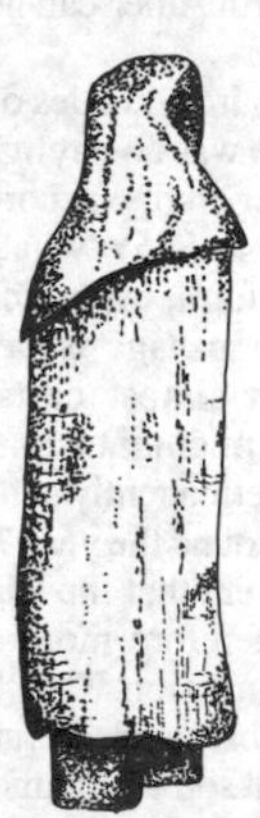

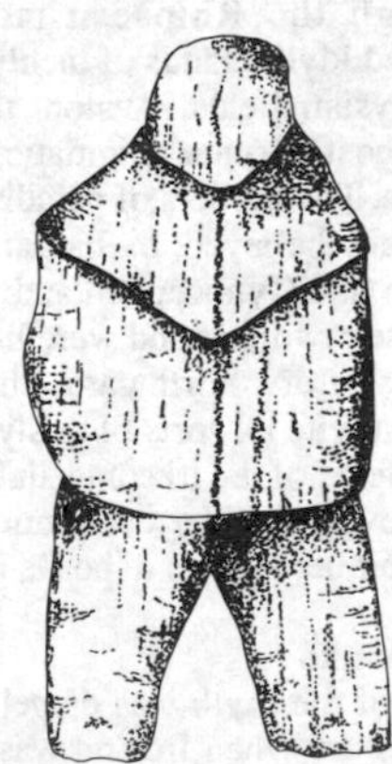

Norsemen portrayed as small wooden dolls by the Inuit people

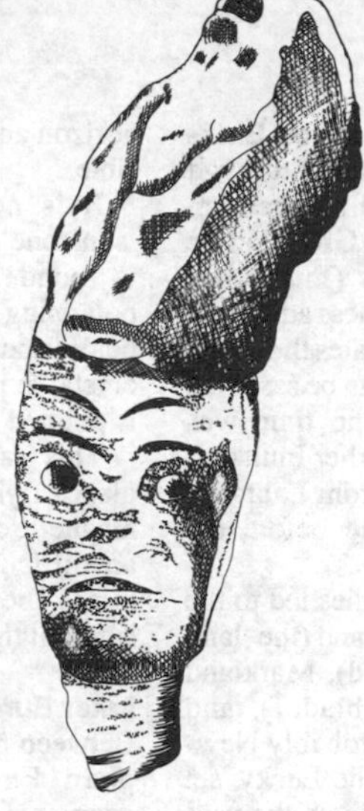

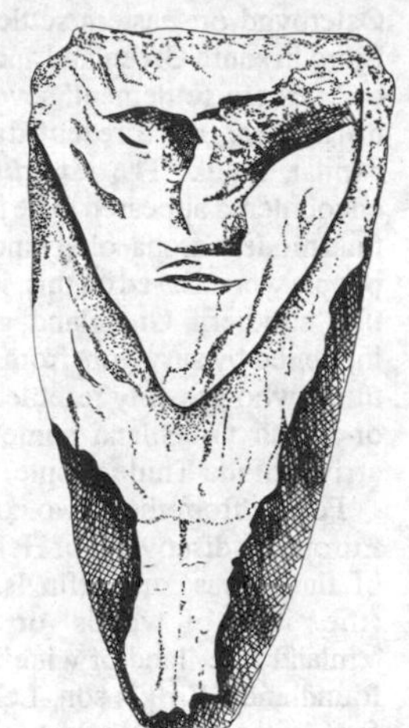

The Norsemen (as they viewed themselves) in figurines of tusk and wood

intermarried with the fleeing victims of Nordic despotism. Slaves and kinsfolk also migrated with these mixed families introducing a heterogeneous stock into Iceland and the Faroes.

The sagas (fact-based literary accounts of the Settlement and subsequent development of these new lands which will be discussed in greater detail in the literature section), penned for the most part after the Viking Age had passed, have much to say about the progression of events in the colonies. The opening lines of the *Faereyingar Saga* are :

There was a man called Grim Kamban. It was he who first colonised the Faroe Islands in the time of Harald Haarfager. There were many people at that time who fled from the tyranny of the King, of whom some settled down in the Faroes and made their abode there; but others sought out other deserted countries.

Another work, the Icelandic *Landnámabók* or *The Book of Settlement*, explains the renaming of Thule far less romantically:

...at a place called Vatnsfjörour on Barðaströnd...the fjord teemed with fish of all kinds...The spring was extremely cold. Flóki climbed a high mountain and looked north towards the coast, and saw a fjord full of drift-ice; so they called the country Ice-land and that has been its name ever since.

In the *Íslendingabók*, the *Book of the Icelanders*, the earliest settlement of that island is also recounted:

A Norwegian called Ingólfur is reliably reported to have been the first man to leave Norway for Iceland...He settled in the south, at Reykjavík.

The Settlement of Greenland by the Norse people is dealt with in two works, the *Saga of Eirík Rauðe* or *Eirík's Saga* and the *Graenlendinga Saga* or *Tale of the Greenlanders*.

The first European contact with Greenland was probably in the 10th century by Norwegian Gunnbjörn Ulfsson. It was first colonised from the east in 982 by Eirík Rauðe, an exiled Icelandic outlaw and murderer. After bestowing the island's lovely name, which has come to be regarded the world's first great real estate scam, he returned to Iceland and enticed 500 other settlers to bring their expertise and livestock and follow him.

They established two settlements, the

Østerbygd or 'eastern settlement' on Eiriks Fjord in south Greenland and the Vesturbygd or 'western settlement' several hundred km north near the present-day Greenlandic capital, Nuuk. The *skraelings* (Inuit) they encountered appeared to be far less advanced than modern archaeology indicates the Thule people were. Based on this, it can be assumed that southern Greenland at the time was inhabited by survivors from earlier Inuit cultures, who possibly resettled from Labrador or North Greenland sometime before the arrival of the Thule people.

Forays from these two colonies led to the European 'discovery' of Helluland (the 'land of flat stones' or Baffin Island), Markland (the 'land of woods' or Labrador), and Vinland (the 'land of wine', probably Newfoundland). Eirík's son, Leif the Lucky, set foot in the New World as early as the year 999. Europeans had reached the Americas, but permanent settlement was thwarted by the skraelings who were anything but welcoming. See also the individual History sections for each country for more details on the Nordic presence.

Nordic Seafaring

Realising the vast distances covered by the early voyagers through difficult seas, one can only wonder what sort of ships and technology the Norse people used to travel so far abroad through uncharted territory.

Archaeological evidence indicates that Viking longboats, low vessels over 30 metres long, were used primarily in war and raiding. The majority of the settlers travelled in smaller cargo boats called *knörrs*. These sturdy little craft, scarcely 18 metres in length with little freeboard, were designed to carry great loads. Journeys in them must have been crowded, uncomfortable and often frightening.

Perhaps the most interesting aspect of these early voyages, however, is the method of navigation employed. The sagas mention a mysterious device known as a *solarstein* which allowed navigation even when the sky was overcast or the sun was below the horizon and celestial navigation was impossible.

It is now generally agreed that the 'sunstone' was a crystal of cordierite which is found in Scandinavia and has natural polarising qualities. When observed from below and rotated, light passing through the crystal is polarised blue when the long axis is pointed toward the source of the sunlight.

This same principle is used today. Jet planes flying over the polar regions, where magnetic compasses and celestial navigation are difficult, use a sky compass which determines the position of the sun by filtering sunlight through an artificial polarising lens.

Later European Exploration

Between the 13th and 15th centuries, European knowledge of North Atlantic geography extended as far north as Iceland. Although Europeans had colonised and occupied Greenland in the late 10th century, the place had been effectively forgotten and, unknown to most people, the Greenland colonies had disappeared. On maps, the world's largest island was normally represented as a vast peninsula connected to the Scandinavian mainland.

Although fishermen from the British Isles were already reaping the harvests of Newfoundland at the time, John Cabot's voyage to that coast in 1497 was considered a mission of discovery. Potential colonies and the possible existence of a North-West Passage to the trading grounds of the East Indies were too much for the Britons to ignore. It didn't take long for much of the rest of Europe – the French, Portuguese, Spanish, and Italians – to show interest in becoming the first to make something of it.

The Portuguese, suspecting that Cabot's landfall may have been east of the Pope's line of demarcation (making it Portuguese territory), sent João Fernandes, a *lavrador* or private landholder, to determine its position. In 1500, he happened instead upon southern Greenland, which he named Lavrador, after himself. Later, a confused cartographer evidently shifted the name south-westward to present-day Labrador. For details of later attempts at conquering the passage see the History section of the Greenland chapter.

GEOGRAPHY

Iceland, Greenland, and the Faroe Islands all lie in the North Atlantic Ocean north-west of Europe and north-east of the North American mainland.

Iceland is just south of the Arctic Circle, roughly three quarters of the distance from New York to London along the Great Circle Route, while the 18 small islands of the Faroes lie about midway between Iceland and Scotland. Greenland, the largest island and most northerly country in the world, is midway between Iceland and the Canadian archipelago.

Geology

The overall character of the North Atlantic landscape is steep and rugged, but the geology of the region displays the most spectacular chronological range on earth. The planet's oldest rock formations, strata at least 3.7 billion years old, exist in the mountains surrounding Nuuk in south-west Greenland. On the other end of the scale, the Icelandic lava fields continue to grow as numerous volcanoes spew new material fresh from the centre of the earth.

In 1620, Sir Francis Bacon glanced at the most recent map of the Atlantic region and noticed that the eastern coast of South America and the western coast of Africa seemed to fit together like two pieces of a jigsaw puzzle. Recently, this curiosity has been conclusively ascribed to plate tectonics, the theory describing the lateral motion of continents on 'plates' of the earth's crust.

The theory attributes plate movement to the creation and destruction of crust along plate boundaries. In zones of thin or weak crust, molten rock (magma) from the core of the earth forces its way upward, spreading the surface plates apart. To compensate, deep-sea trenches form on opposite plate boundaries where one plate is forced to slide beneath another and is destroyed by heat. Most of the earth's vulcanism and seismic activity occur, not surprisingly, on or very near these plate boundaries.

Running the length of the Atlantic Ocean from north to south, the Mid-Atlantic Ridge is one such boundary, a zone extending for 18,000 km. Because of it, the plates containing North America and Eurasia are moving apart at a rate of several cm annually.

In particularly hot spots along the ridge, islands occur. The largest and most notable one is Iceland cleanly cut into north-west and south-east halves by the resulting system of fissures and volcanoes. This zone is so active that one third of all the lava erupted on earth during the last 1000 years is of Icelandic origin. The youngest rocks lie along this rift zone while the east and west coasts are up to 16 million years old.

The Faroe Islands are eroded remains of an old volcanic plateau of the Mid-Atlantic Ridge, subsequently forced away from it as part of the Eurasian plate.

Greenland, on the other hand, consists primarily of rock first deposited as sediment very early in the Earth's history. Subsequent forces of heat, vulcanism, ice, pressure, weathering, and plate motion have tortured and drastically altered both the shape and structure of the land. Most of coastal Greenland today is comprised of gneiss and marble (metamorphosed granite and limestone) and several types of true granite. Due to a pronounced lack of topsoil and vegetation, some extremely dramatic evidence of crustal folding and fracturing is evident.

Beginning 3 million years ago during the Pleistocene epoch, the northern hemisphere experienced a great ice age. On Greenland, it left a vast continental icecap that stretches 2500 km from north to south, 1000 km from east to west, and is over 3 km thick. Its great weight has caused the island's surface to sink to over 3000 metres below sea level. Without the ice, the island would resemble an immense bowl. As a matter of interest, there's so much water in the Greenland icecap, that if it were to melt, the level of the world's oceans would rise at least 6 metres.

Only parts of Iceland's icecaps remain today. They were not formed during the great ice age but in a cool period beginning 2500 years ago and today cover only about 10% of the country. The largest, Vatnajökull, covers 8000 sq km. The Faroe Islands, subject to glaciation in the past, today are ice-free.

Midnight Sun & Polar Night

Because the earth is tilted on its axis, the polar regions are constantly facing the sun at their respective summer solstices and are tilted away from it in the winter. The Arctic and Antarctic circles at 66½° north and south latitude, respectively, are the southern and northern limits of constant daylight on the longest day of the year.

In the North Atlantic, the northern three quarters of Greenland and part of the Icelandic island of Grímsey lie north of the Arctic Circle but, in regions immediately to the south including Iceland and the Faroes, the summer sun is never far below the horizon. Between May and early August, no place in the region experiences true darkness. In northern Iceland, for example, the first stars aren't visible until mid-August. Although many visitors initially find it difficult to sleep while the sun is shining brightly outside, most people quickly get used to it, even if that simply means joining the locals in their summer nocturnal hyperactivity.

Conversely, winters here are dark and dreary with only a few hours of twilight to break the long polar night. In northern Greenland, not even a twilight glow can be seen for several weeks in December and most communities make a ritual of formally welcoming the sun the first time it peeks above the southern horizon. Those who visit during the off season, however, will probably be treated to the following phenomenon that summer visitors miss out on...

The Aurora Borealis

There are few sights as mesmerising as an undulating aurora. Although these appear in many forms – pillars, streaks, wisps, and haloes of vibrating light – they are most memorable when they appear as pale curtains waving in a gentle breeze. Most often, the Arctic aurora is faint green or light rose but, during periods of extreme activity, can change to bright crimson and even yellow.

The visible aurora borealis or northern lights (in the southern hemisphere they're called aurora australis) are caused by streams of charged particles from the sun, the solar winds, flowing past and elongating the earth's magnetic field in the polar regions. Because the field curves downward in a halo surrounding the magnetic poles, the charged particles are drawn earthward. Their interaction with electrons in nitrogen and oxygen atoms in the upper atmosphere (about 160 km above the surface) releases the energy creating the visible aurora (and incidentally the entire spectrum from radio waves to ultraviolet light). During periods of high activity, a single auroral storm can produce a trillion watts of electricity with a current of 1 million amps.

The Inuit people (and nearly everyone else who experiences the lights) attach a spiritual significance to them. Some believe that they represent the capering of unborn children. Some consider them gifts from the dead to light the long polar nights. Others believe that they are a storehouse of events past and future.

Although science dismisses it as imagination, most people report that moving lights are accompanied by a crackling or whirring sound. Don't feel unbalanced if you do hear it. Perhaps it is imagination – that's the sort of sound you'd *expect* to hear during such a dramatic display – but, living in Alaska, I'll vouch that it's a very convincing illusion.

The best time of the year to catch the northern lights in the North Atlantic is in March and October although you may also see them in September and even late August well south of the Arctic Circle. Due to latitude and favourable weather conditions, the best place to observe the most colourful storms is in southern Greenland. Northern Greenland is actually too far north to catch the greatest activity.

Fata Morgana & Mirages

If the aurora inspires wonder, the Fata Morgana and related phenomena common in the polar regions may inspire a visit to a psychiatrist.

The clear and pure Arctic air does not cause distant features to appear out of focus. As a result, depth perception becomes impossible and the world takes on a strangely two dimensional aspect. Distances are indeterminable. An amusing example of distance distortion is described in the excellent book *Arctic Dreams* by Barry Lopez:

> A Swedish explorer had all but completed a written description in his notebook of a craggy headland with two unusually symmetrical valley glaciers, the whole of it a part of a large island, when he discovered what he was looking at was a walrus.

Fata Morgana, a specialised type of mirage, is also common in the vast expanses of sand, ice, and tundra found in the Arctic. Early explorers laid down on maps and charts careful documentation of islands, headlands, and mountain ranges that were never seen again.

Apparently caused by reflections (off water, ice and snow) combined with temperature inversions, Fata Morganas create the illusion of solid, well-defined features where there are none. On clear days along the *sandur* of northern Iceland, I have frequently seen archipelagos of craggy islands resting on the horizon. It was difficult indeed to convince myself, even with an accurate map, that they were not really there.

Also unsettling are the sightings of ships, large cities, and forests where there could clearly be none. While some of these are simply heat mirages, warm air overlying cold water will sometimes cause refraction through and reflection from the upper atmosphere and produce astonishing results. Normal visibility at sea is just under 18 km but, in the Arctic, sightings of islands and features hundreds of km distant have been frequently reported.

Glaciers & Ice

Much of the North Atlantic landscape has been carved and shaped by rivers of ice flowing down from permanent icecaps. In Iceland and Greenland, these icecaps and glaciers are prominent topographical features.

Icecaps are formed as snow piles up over millennia in an area where it never has the opportunity to melt. It is slowly compressed, from bottom to top, into ice. When the weight of the ice becomes so great that the underlying land cannot support it, the land beneath the centre compresses and the ice around the edges begins to flow downward.

When glaciers flow into the sea, they are known as tidewater glaciers. As they are melted by the sea water, chunks break off from the face, some of them immense, and form icebergs which drift throughout the North Atlantic but are concentrated by ocean currents around the southern coast of Greenland.

The following is a list of definitions of glacier-related terms you will hear frequently:

arête – a sharp ridge between two valley glaciers

bergschrund – the crevasse at the top of a valley glacier separating the moving ice from the parent icefield

cirque – an amphitheatre scoured out by a glacier

crevasse – a fissure in moving ice caused by various strains which may be hidden under snow

erratic – a stone or boulder which clearly was transported from somewhere else, possibly by a glacier

firn limit – the highest level on a glacier to which the snow melts each year. The snow that remains above this limit is called *firn.*

glacial flour – the fine, talcum-like silt that flows in glacial streams and is deposited in glacial river valleys. It is formed by abrasion of ice on rock.

hanging valley – a valley formed when a tributary glacier flows into a larger glacier

horn – the sharp peak that remains after glaciers have scoured all sides of a mountain

icecap or *icefield* – a stable zone of accumulation and compression of snow and ice and a source of valley glaciers. An icecap generally covers a larger area than an icefield. When the entire interior of a landmass is covered by an icecap, it is called a *continental glacier*.

ice floe – small chunk of ice floating in the sea, either a bit of sea-ice drift or a small iceberg
jökulhlaup – a sudden, often violent and catastrophic, release of water from a glacier caused by a broken ice dam or by lifting due to volcanic activity beneath the ice
moraine – deposit of material transported by a glacier. Rock and silt pushed ahead of the glacier is called a *terminal moraine*, that deposited along the sides is a *lateral moraine* and, in the centre of a glacier, it is called a *medial moraine*.
moulin – a pond or a stream in a glacier
nunatak – a mountain peak that protrudes through a glacier or icecap
pack ice – floating ice formed in the sea which generally creates an impenetrable barrier to navigation
piedmont glacier – a slumped glacier at the foot of a steep slope caused by the confluence of two or more valley glaciers
roche moutonée – a glacier-scoured boulder, so named because they often look like sheep grazing on the mountainsides
tarn – a lake in a cirque

CLIMATE

The North Atlantic has the reputation, which it almost lives up to, of having a bad climate. While Iceland and the Faroes aren't almost as cold as one would think, especially in the winter, their tendency towards foul weather can at times surpass most visitors' expectations. This is not to say, however, that a fair number of fine days can't be expected at any time of year.

Thanks to the Gulf Stream that washes the south and west coasts of Iceland and the Faroes and to the prevailing south-westerly winds which bring warm air and moisture northward from the tropics, those countries enjoy mild temperatures year-round. In January, the daily mean temperature at Reykjavík in Iceland is 1°C. In July, it is 11°C. At Tórshavn in the Faroe Islands, average January and July temperatures are 3°C and 11°C.

The most consistently miserable weather is limited to the Faroe Islands and the southern and western coasts of Iceland. Although their temperature variation is more dramatic, the Icelandic interior, the north and east coasts, and most of Greenland fare much better as far as sunshine is concerned.

In Greenland, which is not affected by the Gulf Stream, summer daytime average temperatures range from -5°C in the north to 20°C in the south. During the winter, temperatures of -50°C and lower are not uncommon although the far south may only occasionally experience such extreme cold. These periods of high pressure, dominated by the polar continental air mass, bring the calmest and clearest weather experienced in the North Atlantic.

As a general rule, summer visitors to the Faroes or south-western Iceland should dress as they would for Scotland, the mountains of southern Tasmania or New Zealand, or south-eastern Alaska...and then add another wind- and waterproof layer just for good measure. In northern and eastern Iceland you probably won't need as much clothing but in Greenland, where cold is the main factor but there's also wind and rain, it's a good idea to add an extra layer of insulation.

RELIGION

Inuit Religions

Although the Inuit people believed that Europeans were the product of a union between Inuit women and dogs, this didn't prevent them from accepting the relatively simplistic religion of the wealthy outsiders. The people of southern Greenland were converted to Christianity over 2 centuries ago and most of the rest of Greenland had converted by the early 20th century. Greenlanders continue, however, to mix their Christianity with aspects of their traditional shamanistic religion, especially in times of hardship.

Even before Christianity arrived, the Inuit believed in the existence of a soul or a 'breath', that survived death in one form or another. The breaths of the dead whose bodies lay on the earth were relegated to the sky, a cold and unpleasant place, while those who were thrown into the sea lived on underground in warm, rich hunting grounds. The Middle Eastern notion that hell is a hot place must have inspired both amusement and confusion in Arctic dwellers!

Early Inuit religion was characterised by

belief in familiar spirits who helped or hindered individuals on a regular basis. The Inuit did not fear death but they did fear such spirits including the *toornot*, the spirits of the dead; the *tupilat*, the hideous creatures that populate nightmares; and the *qivittoq*, the glacier spirits which could take possession of a person who reported seeing one.

Hunters believed that the earth and its creatures should be treated with respect believing not that the hunter had conquered the animal, but that it had willingly allowed itself to be killed as a gift to its human brothers. This was monitored by a water spirit, an old woman who sat by the shore. Whenever humans blundered, she would comb her hair over the surface of the water thus preventing seals giving themselves up requiring the spells of an *angaqqoq* or shaman to rectify the situation.

The Inuit also lived in fear of upsetting the *sila*, the delicate natural balance of the universe. Such a blunder would be to kill an animal that had been inhabited by a *toornoq* (singular of 'toornot'). In such a case, only the death of the hunter could restore balance.

All sorts of taboos were associated with mourning the dead and they had to be followed to the letter lest the deceased return to administer justice to the guilty party. They also believed justice was inevitable for anyone who had mistreated or dealt badly with that person when he or she was still alive. Those living in fear of the wrath of the dead often became withdrawn, depressed, and even suicidal.

Menstruating and pregnant women were also burdened with a unique (and quite oppressive) code of behaviour. Those women who had miscarried or borne children prematurely were required to adhere to a special set of rules for a year. Such women were forbidden, for instance, to mention animals or wear boots while eating. Neither could they sleep with their husbands or report the presence of strangers with their voices. All of these restrictions were observed in order to appease spirits and thereby preserve balance.

Sickness was often attributed to the presence of *perlussuaq*, a type of evil spirit that took possession of respiration and upset balance. Medicine, which was provided by an angaqqoq, was fairly simplistic. The angaqqoq would examine the patient, then determine whether they would live or die. Those who were pronounced doomed simply gave up hope and died. The rest followed the angaqqoq's prescriptions, most of which dealt with eating, sleeping, sexual habits and payment for medical services.

Those who are interested in learning more about the traditional customs and religion of the Greenlanders should read *The Last Kings of Thule* by Jean Malaurie, a Frenchman who learned the Greenlandic language and spent several years living among the people.

The Norse Religion

Those who've studied European mythology (or at least read a few Hagar the Horrible comic strips) will be familiar with the pantheon of Norse deities worshipped during the Viking period. Although there were many gods and godlike beings, the Norse trinity consisted of Þór, the king of the Gods; Óðinn, the god of war and poetry; and Freyr, the god of fertility and sensuous pleasure.

Óðinn was the patron god of the Viking hordes and the *skalds* ('court poets'). He was traditionally depicted as a brooding and intimidating presence, the one who doled out both victory in battle and literary talent.

Unlike on the mainland where Óðinn was considered the highest ranking deity, Iceland, Greenland, and the Faroes – not so concerned with war and raiding – revered Þór, the rowdy and rather slow-minded god of the common people. Þór, the god of thunder, wind and storm and natural disasters, provided security against malevolent outsiders. He was depicted as a burly, red-haired, red-bearded dolt (in a film he would be played by Arnold Schwarzennegger!) who rumbled through the heavens in a goat-drawn chariot.

Freyr and his twin sister Freyja, the children of the earth god Njörður, served as the god and goddess of fertility and sexuality. Freyr was the one who brought springtime with its romantic implications to both the human and animal world and was in charge of the perpetuation of all species.

The actual belief system was very simple. It was not overly burdened with theology and not at all with dogma. Even the gods were doomed as far as the Norse were concerned and no salvation was possible or necessary. A sort of immortality only came to those who died in battle. Such a warrior would be gathered up by the Valkyries, the warrior-maids, and carried into Valhalla where he could indulge in mead, feasting, and women until their hosts, the gods themselves, fell in battle.

Although all three countries are officially Christian today, in Iceland the ancient Norse religion is gaining popularity not only as a novelty but as an officially recognised sect known as Ásatrú, the plural of *Áss* (that's 'OWSS'), referring to the Norse godhead.

Led by a modern-day skald, sheep farmer Sveinbjörn Beinteinsson, it focuses on the natural forces and the harmony of nature represented by the ancient gods. Like the early religion, it has no sacred text, no rules and regulations, and no real philosophy about the progression of the human spirit. The sect currently has several hundred followers.

Christianity

According to *Faereyingar Saga*, which was written in Iceland in the 13th century, the Faroe Islands officially converted to Christianity around the year 1000 and the first bishopric was set up at Kirkjubøur on the island of Streymoy. Due to the scanty accounts of this period, however, little is known about the conversion or the church administration there.

In Iceland, the sagas provide a great deal of information about the early religious state. Before the official conversion by government decree, there were still quite a few Christians living in the country, most of them immigrants from the British Isles and the Orkneys.

The story of the first Christian mission in Iceland, which was organised by a farm boy from Stóra-Giljá in north central Iceland, is recounted in the *Tale of Þorvaldur Far-Farer*. Þorvaldur, a sort of Nordic Robin Hood, was a Viking mercenary who donated all his plunder to the poor. He became a Christian in Germany and persuaded Bishop Frederick of Saxony to return with him to Iceland and bring the gospel to the Icelanders.

True to saga form, the Bishop was beset with protestations from the incumbent Icelandic deities and spirits. Icelanders accused him of homosexuality and forced him to return home. Þorvaldur left Iceland on a pilgrimage to Jerusalem and went from there to Constantinople where he was appointed overlord to the kings of Russia by the Byzantine emperor.

In the late 10th century, Denmark peacefully became Christian but Norway's conversion was quite another story. In 994 during the siege of London, the ruthless Viking prince Ólaf Tryggvason, heir to the throne of Norway, accepted the new religion. Upon his return home, he usurped power and mercilessly threatened and tortured his subjects into wholesale conversion. His missionary zeal became a bit extreme when the subjects of his next conversion project, the Icelanders, resisted his coercive tactics. He responded by declaring them all criminals and ordering their execution. A couple of Icelandic Christians pleaded for, and were granted, another chance for their pagan brothers.

Traditionally, the date of the decree that officially converted Iceland has been given as 1000 but research has determined that it probably occurred in 999 and was brought about by politics. In the Icelandic *Alþing* ('parliament'), the Christians and pagans had been polarising into two radically opposite factions threatening to divide the country politically if not geographically. In the session of 999, Þorgeir the Law-speaker appealed for moderation on both sides in the interest of national unity, then lowered the boom.

In the *Íslendingabók*, the account of the early Icelanders, Ari the Learned (Ari Þorgilsson) writes:

It was...decreed that everyone...should be Christian, and that those who had not yet been baptised should receive baptism.

But the old laws should stand...Also, people could make sacrifices [to the old gods] in private if they wished to, but sacrificing would be subject to a criminal sentence if it were done in public before witnesses...

Greenland's conversion by Danish missionaries happened relatively recently. In 1721, the 'Greenland Apostle' Hans Egede set up a mission and trading station in Godthåb in 1728.

His mission and that of a rival church, the Moravian Mission, began operating in 1733 and were enormously successful in converting the Greenlanders. Hans Egede left Greenland in 1736 after his wife, Gertrude Rask, died in an epidemic. His efforts there, however, had toppled the first domino and, 200 years later, all of Greenland was Christianised.

Today, as in mainland Scandinavia, all three North Atlantic countries officially belong to the protestant Lutheran church.

Regional Facts for the Visitor

COSTS

Because nearly everything must be imported, food, accommodation, and transport prices in the North Atlantic are high. In fact, Iceland is generally considered second only to Japan in its ability to deplete travellers' means. While expense-account travellers or those who can happily drop US$500 a day will not encounter any problems, those with finite means who want a stress-free North Atlantic holiday may have to put in some effort.

The lowest average price of a single hotel room in Reykjavík or Tórshavn, for example, is US$95; in Nuuk you'll pay from US$135 to US$170 per night. A restaurant meal including some sort of meat dish, a soup or a salad, a spoonful of tinned vegies and a potato will set you back on average from US$10 to US$15. A bus trip in Iceland will cost about US$10 for an hour and a 15-minute flight in Greenland can cost US$80 while the fare on certain domestic routes will break the US$1000 mark!

If you're willing to give up some comforts and sleep in youth hostels, eat at snack bars, and travel on bus passes, you'll probably be able to keep expenses down to an average of about US$30 per day. Rock-bottom budget travel in the North Atlantic is only possible with near total exposure to the difficult weather conditions. If you want to get by on less than US$10 per day you'll have to camp (at least part of the time away from organised sites), cook your own meals, and hitchhike, cycle or walk the vast distances involved. In roadless Greenland, there is no way to avoid the high transportation costs short of bringing your own sea kayak or just contenting yourself with visiting only one area (getting around by foot or on local ferries in a limited local area).

Europeans bringing a private vehicle to Iceland or the Faroes, especially a campervan or caravan, will be able to enjoy a bit more comfort while still keeping within a reasonable budget. Petrol prices in those countries tend to be higher than expected (over US$1 per litre) so be prepared. Fortunately, the sting of fuel costs can be minimised by sharing rides and expenses with travellers without vehicles.

In most cases, holders of student cards are entitled to hefty discounts on entrance fees and some transport fares. In Iceland, students and holders of Iceland bus passes receive 10% discount on camping-ground fees, ferries fares and, sometimes, even hotel and restaurant charges. It's not advertised, so it pays to ask in each case.

TIPPING

Tipping is not required anywhere in the North Atlantic. Finer restaurants will automatically add a service charge to the bill making further tipping unnecessary. Even so, those who may feel compelled to tip for particularly good or friendly service will not be refused.

GENERAL INFORMATION

Electricity

Outlets in the North Atlantic are 220 volts, 50 cycles AC so North American appliances will require an adapter. It should be noted, however, that prongs on foreign equipment may also have to be adapted before they can be used.

Time

The following charts show the time differences (in hours) between the North Atlantic countries and London, New York, Los Angeles, and Sydney. The time changes normally take place around the 25th of October and March.

From 25 October to 24 March

	London	*NY*	*LA*	*Sydney*
Greenland	+2	-2	-5	+13
Iceland	0	-5	-8	+11
Faroes	0	-5	-8	+11

From 25 March to 24 October

	London	*NY*	*LA*	*Sydney*
Greenland	+3	-3	-6	+12
Iceland	+1	-4	-7	+10
Faroes	+1	-5	-8	+10

Business Hours

Normal weekday-shopping hours are from 9 am to 5 pm, although the odd shop may open at 8 am and close at 4 pm or even remain open later. On Saturdays, shops normally open at 9 or 10 am and close at noon or 1 pm. Petrol stations and kiosks, which are similar to US convenience stores or Aussie milk bars, are normally open on weekday evenings until 10 or 11 pm, Saturday afternoons and Sundays. Tourist-oriented souvenir shops will generally stay open longer than other shops.

Post offices will have varying opening hours, but most are open from 8.30 or 9 am to 4.30 or 5 pm on weekdays. Village post offices in Greenland and the Faroes often close for a 1 to 3-hour lunch break.

Banking hours are between 9 am and 4 pm on weekdays in Iceland and the Faroes and between 10 am and 3 pm in Greenland. Faroese banks stay open until 6 pm on Thursdays and the Landisbanki Íslands foreign exchange desk at the Hotel Loftleiðir in Reykjavík stays open for incoming airport buses until 7 pm daily.

Laundry

Laundrettes are rather thin on the ground in the North Atlantic. The camping grounds in both Reykjavík and Akureyri (Iceland) have machines which can be used by guests but you can plan on waiting a long time in queues to use them. In some places in Greenland, Nuna-Tek (see Accommodation) offers a laundry service. Otherwise, most cities just have expensive laundries which will clean your clothes in 24 hours.

HEALTH

North Atlantic residents enjoy one of the healthiest (although sometimes unpleasant) climates and the most pollution-free environments anywhere. Combine these factors with their excellent health-care systems and you come up with an average lifespan of 80 years for women and 74 years for men, the second greatest in the world. The Japanese have now surpassed this with 81 years for women and 78 years for men.

Travellers will have to concern themselves with very few health hazards and those who suffer an injury or get sick during their visit will have no problem finding medical assistance provided they aren't travelling away from roads or populated areas.

Travel Health Insurance

Iceland and the Faroe Islands have reciprocal health-care agreements; these also extend to citizens of the UK, Norway, Denmark, Finland, Sweden entitling them to free health care. Local rates for ambulance services and prescriptions still apply. Citizens of other countries will be required to pay minimal charges for medical services and non-discounted rates on prescriptions.

Greenland extends free health care to everyone, regardless of citizenship, but dental care is not included and prescription medicines are often unavailable in smaller towns and villages.

Even for those who are entitled to free treatment, it's a good idea to take out a travel insurance policy to cover theft, loss, and medical problems which may be encountered during your trip. There is a wide variety of policies available and your travel agent will make recommendations. The international student travel policies handled by Student Travel Association (STA) or other student travel organisations are usually good value. Some policies offer lower and higher medical expenses options but the higher one is chiefly for countries like the USA with extremely high medical costs. Check the small print:

Some policies specifically exclude 'dangerous activities' which can include mountain climbing, motorcycling, and even trekking. If these activities are on your agenda, you don't want that sort of policy.

You may prefer a policy which pays doctors or

hospitals directly rather than requiring you to pay now and claim later. If you do have to claim later, make sure you keep all documentation. Some policies ask you to call back (reverse charges) to a centre in your home country where an immediate assessment of your problem is made.

Check if the policy covers ambulances or an emergency flight home. If you have to stretch out, you will need more than one seat and somebody has to pay for it!

Medical Kit

Especially for those who plan to venture away from roads and populated areas, a small, straightforward medical kit is a wise thing to carry. A suggested kit list includes:

- Paracetamol (called acetominophen in North America) tablets for pain or fever
- antihistamine (such as Benadryl) – useful as a decongestant for colds, allergies, to ease the itch from insect bites or stings or to help prevent motion sickness
- antibiotics – useful if you are travelling in the wilderness but they must be prescribed and you should carry the prescription with you
- Kaolin and pectin preparation and Imodium or Lomotil for bouts of giardia or stomach upset. Imodium and Lomotil should only be used in emergency situations, such as when you are suffering from diarrhoea and must travel for long periods on public transport.
- rehydration mixture – for treatment of severe diarrhoea. This is particularly important if travelling with children.
- antiseptic, mercurochrome and antibiotic powder or similar 'dry' spray – for cuts and grazes
- Calamine lotion – to ease irritation from bites and stings
- bandages and Band-aids – for minor injuries
- scissors, tweezers and a thermometer – mercury thermometers are prohibited by airlines
- insect repellent, sun block, chap stick, and water purification tablets
- space blanket – to be used for warmth or as an emergency signal

Water Purification

The water from taps in all three countries is safe to drink and, for the most part, surface water is potable except in urban areas. Water from glacial rivers may appear murky but you may drink it, if necessary, in small quantities. The murk is actually fine particles of silt scoured from the rock by the glacier and drinking too much of this has been known to clog up internal plumbing.

Those who are concerned about contamination, however, should purify their drinking water. The simplest way is to thoroughly boil it. Technically this means for 10 minutes although most people can't be bothered to wait that long. Remember that at higher altitudes water boils at lower temperatures so germs are less likely to be killed.

Simple filtering will not remove all organisms so, if you cannot boil water, it may be treated chemically. Chlorine tablets (Puritabs, Steritabs or other brand names) will kill many but not all organisms. Iodine is very effective in purifying water and is available in tablet form (Potable Aqua) but follow the directions carefully and remember that too much iodine can be harmful.

If you can't find tablets, tincture of iodine (2%) or iodine crystals can be used. Two drops of tincture of iodine per litre of clear water is the recommended dosage. The water should then be left to stand for 30 minutes. Iodine crystals can also be used to purify water but this is a more complicated process as you have to first prepare a saturated iodine solution. Iodine loses its effectiveness if exposed to air or damp so keep it in a tightly sealed container. Flavoured powder or lemon juice will disguise the taste of treated water and is an especially good idea if you're hiking with children.

Giardia

Despite the fact that most unpopulated lands in Iceland, the Faroes, and far southern Greenland serve as sheep pastures, there seems to be very little giardia and, although most people have no problems drinking untreated surface water, there is still a possibility of contracting it.

Giardia, sometimes called 'beaver fever', is an intestinal parasite that lives in the faeces of humans and animals. Drinking water which has been exposed to it can cause stomach cramps, nausea, a bloated stomach, as well as watery, foul-smelling diarrhoea and frequent gas. Problems can start several weeks after you have been exposed to the parasite. The symptoms may sometimes go away for a few days and then return; this can to on for several weeks or even longer. Metronidazole, known as Flagyl, is the recommended treatment but it should only be taken under medical supervision. Antibiotics are of no use in treating giardia.

Sunburn & Windburn

Sunburn and windburn should be primary concerns for anyone planning to spend time trekking or travelling over snow and ice. The sun will burn you even if you feel cold and the wind will cause dehydration and chafing of skin. Use a good sunblock and a moisture cream on exposed skin, even on cloudy days. A hat provides added protection and zinc oxide or some other barrier cream for your nose and lips is recommended if you're spending any time on ice or snow.

Reflection and glare from ice and snow can cause snow blindness so high-protection sunglasses should be considered essential for any sort of glacier visit or ski trip.

Hypothermia

Perhaps the most dangerous health threat in the Arctic regions is hypothermia. This occurs when the body loses heat faster than it can produce it and the core temperature falls. It is surprisingly easy to progress from very cold to dangerously cold due to a combination of wind, wet clothing, fatigue and hunger, even if the air temperature is above freezing. It is best to dress in layers; silk, wool, and polypropylene are all good insulating materials. A hat is important as a lot of heat is lost through the scalp. A strong, waterproof and windproof outer layer is essential since keeping dry is of utmost importance. Carry basic supplies including food containing simple sugars to generate heat quickly and be sure that plenty of fluids are always available.

Symptoms of hypothermia are exhaustion; numb skin (particularly toes and fingers); shivering; slurred speech; irrational, confused or violent behaviour; lethargy; stumbling; dizzy spells; muscle cramps and violent bursts of energy. Irrationality may include sufferers claiming they are warm and trying to remove clothing.

To treat hypothermia: first get out of the wind and/or rain; if possible, remove wet clothing and replace with dry, warm clothing. Drink hot liquids, not alcohol, and eat some high-calorie easily digestible food. This should be enough for the early stages of hypothermia but, if it has gone further, it may be necessary to place the victim in a warm sleeping bag and get in with them.

Do not rub the patient, or place them near a fire, or remove wet clothing while they're exposed to wind. If possible, place them in a warm (not hot) bath but, if that is not available, remember that the body heat of another person is immediately more important than medical attention so do not leave the victim alone under any circumstances.

Rabies

Rabies exists in Greenland and is caused by a bite or scratch by an infected animal. Dogs are a noted carrier. Any bite, scratch or even lick from a mammal should be cleaned immediately and thoroughly. Scrub with soap in running water, and then clean with an alcohol solution. If there is any possibility that the animal is infected, medical help should be sought immediately. Even if the animal is not rabid, all bites should be treated seriously as they can become infected or can result in tetanus. A rabies vaccination is now available.

Bugs

In its sheer density of bugs and pests, the Arctic rivals the Amazon. What the bug season lacks in length, it makes up for in sheer numbers. Especially in Greenland, tundra bogs turn into nurseries for zillions of mosquitoes. If you venture outdoors in less than 20 knots of wind, you may be overwhelmed by the scourge of the Arctic. (In Alaska, caribou have been driven to insanity and death by the whining swarms.)

Don't be caught out without some sort of protection! Long sleeves and trousers are not enough. Mozzies are perfectly happy to drill anywhere and through anything. A few hardy individuals have even been known to penetrate denim jeans. Some hotels in Greenland sell head-nets but, to protect the rest of your body, the best solution is something containing over 90% diethylmetatoluamide (DEET) which is nasty stuff to put on your skin but eminently better than the mosquitoes settling on you.

Sexually Transmitted Diseases

Nowhere in the North Atlantic is there a negative stigma attached to sexual promiscuity and, in Greenland, the custom of 'wife-swapping' is happily practised. A male Greenlander will in some cases present his wife for a night as a gift to another man and may be rather offended if the intended receiver refuses his hospitality. Those who would accept such offers should be aware, however, that sexually transmitted diseases are rampant in Greenland and precautions should be taken.

Gonorrhoea and syphilis are the most common sexually transmitted diseases and, while abstinence is the only 100% preventative, use of a condom is also effective. Symptoms can include sores, blisters, or rashes around the genitals and discharges or pain when urinating. These symptoms may be less marked or not observed at all in women. Often the symptoms of syphilis, in particular, will eventually disappear completely but the disease continues and can cause severe problems in later years. Treatment of gonorrhoea and syphilis is with antibiotics.

There are numerous other sexually transmitted diseases most of which have effective treatments. There is currently no cure for herpes or for AIDS. The latter is most often spread by male homosexual intercourse, blood transfusions, and injections with shared needles. There is no place in the North Atlantic which yet has problems with AIDS or unsanitary medical equipment, but due precautions are still advised.

Motion Sickness

Since a great deal of North Atlantic travel will be done by boat or ship and much overland travel is on rough, unsurfaced roads, motion sickness can be a real problem for those prone to it.

Eating very lightly before and during a trip will reduce the chances of motion sickness. If you know you are likely to be affected, try to find a place that minimises disturbance – near the wing on aircraft, close to midships on boats, and near the centre on buses. Fresh air almost always helps, but reading or cigarette smoking (or even being around some else's smoke) normally makes matters worse.

Commercial motion-sickness preparations, which can cause drowsiness, have to be taken before the trip – after you've begun feeling ill it's too late. Dramamine tablets should be taken 3 hours before departure and scopolamine patches (which are available only by prescription in most places) should be applied from 10 to 12 hours before departure. Ginger can be used as a natural preventative and is available in capsule form.

WOMEN TRAVELLERS

Women travelling alone in Iceland, Greenland and the Faroe Islands will most likely have fewer problems than they would travelling in their home country. Women, accompanied or not, who venture into an Icelandic disco should be prepared to witness and participate in some fairly unrestrained behaviour. Women hitchhikers, especially those on their own, will not encounter any difficulties if they use common sense and aren't afraid of saying no to lifts.

DANGERS & ANNOYANCES

In Iceland, Greenland and the Faroe Islands where petit larceny merits front-page headlines, police don't carry guns (police aren't even visible most of the time); parents park their children in prams on the street while they shop; and most people are too reserved to even speak to strangers let alone hassle them – there are few dangers and annoyances to contend with. In fact, Iceland actually lets its prisoners go home on public holidays.

Although (or because) it's strictly controlled in Iceland and the Faroes and marginally regulated in Greenland, alcohol is a problem in all three countries. On Friday and Saturday nights you'd be hard-pressed to find someone unaffected by it but alcohol-related violence is almost unheard of. The one exception to this seems to be in east Greenland around the villages of Ammassalik and Ittoqqoortoormiit where serious violence seems to erupt with some frequency. At such times, visitors would do well to keep a low profile.

FILM & PHOTOGRAPHY

Photographers worldwide sing the praises of the magical Arctic light. The crystalline air combined with the long, red rays cast by a low sun create excellent effects on film. Add to that spectacular scenery and colourful human aspects and you have a photographer's paradise. In this region there are quite a few tour companies that offer photography tours and instruction so check with your travel agent or a tourist office if you're interested.

Film, photographic equipment and camera repairs, especially in Iceland, are quite expensive. A 36-exposure roll of Kodachrome 64, for instance, will cost US$18 in Reykjavík, US$14 in Nuuk, and around US$12 in Tórshavn so it would be wise to bring a supply from home (twice as much as you plan to need!) and use as much restraint as possible in the face of celluloid-swallowing scenery.

Film is readily available only during shopping hours in Reykjavík, Akureyri and Tórshavn. In Greenland and in smaller villages, supplies and variety of film will be limited. Film processing is available in Iceland and the Faroes but, for Kodachrome and other films requiring specialised processing, wait until you get home.

Due to the clear Arctic light and glare from water, ice, and snow, photographers should use a UV filter or a skylight filter and a lens shade. In the winter, especially in Greenland, mechanical cameras should be polar oiled so the mechanism doesn't freeze up. In temperatures below about -20°C, electronic cameras may fail altogether.

As usual, subjects for interesting people-pictures are to be found throughout the region and most individuals will enjoy being photographed. As a courtesy, however, it's a good idea to ask before snapping away.

Especially in Greenland, since much of your sightseeing will be done aboard ship and since wildlife normally keeps its distance, it's a good idea to bring a telephoto or zoom lens if you plan to film these things. Conversely, there will also be plenty of opportunities in all three countries to use a wide-angle 28-mm lens for broad vistas, dramatic skies, and urban landscapes.

ACCOMMODATION

Hotels

Every major city and village has at least one up-market hotel. While most of them are fairly sterile and characterless, they are comfortable and have all the amenities including restaurants, pubs, private baths, telephones and television.

Those in need of such creature comforts will, however, pay dearly and the money will go very quickly. The average price of a double room in the Faroes or Iceland will be around US$110 in an average hotel and from US$135 to US$200 in a business travellers' hotel in Reykjavík. The cheapest double rooms in Greenland will set you back about US$90 per night while one of the up-market places in Nuuk will cost over US$150. If it's any consolation, all of these places include a continental breakfast in their rates.

Edda Hotels & Summer Hotels

Edda hotels are a chain of 16 summer hotels operated around Iceland by the Iceland Tourist Bureau. Most of them are school dormitories used as hotels during summer holidays only. All have adjoining restaurants and most have geothermally heated swimming pools. Some offer sleeping-bag accommodation or dormitory facilities in addition to conventional hotel lodging, although many lack private baths.

A double room in an Edda hotel will cost

about US$60 per night and a single US$45. Sleeping-bag or dormitory accommodation, where available, will cost from US$12 to US$16. In addition to the official Edda hotels, there are several other summer hotels around Iceland which also occupy school dormitories.

Seamen's Homes

One form of semi-budget accommodation available in Greenland and the Faroes is the seamen's missions or seamen's homes (*sømandshjemmene* in Danish, *umiartortuq angerlarsimaffii* in Greenlandic, and *sómansheimið* in Faroese). The historical purpose of these missions of the Danish Lutheran church was to provide clean, safe lodging for sailors and fishermen while they were in port.

Since they are religiously oriented, the rules are fairly strict. The staff starts the day with formal prayers and hymn-singing so, if you can accept this and the regulations against alcohol and general carousing, they are a viable alternative to the high-priced hotels.

All of the seamen's homes have a cafeteria which serves a reasonably priced à la carte menu and smørrebrød (open-face sandwiches) all day, and full meals for several hours in the evening. Some rooms have private baths and hot showers; there's also a common TV room open to guests. In Greenland, a double room with/without bath will cost about US$90/70. In the Faroes rooms cost a bit less, about US$75/55.

Guesthouses

There are many types of *gistiheimilið* ('guesthouses') to be found in Iceland and the Faroe Islands. Some are simply private homes which let out rooms to make a little extra cash, others are quite elaborate. Most guesthouses offer single and double rooms with a common bath but some even rent out self-contained flats for up to three or four persons. Some offer hostel-style 'sleeping-bag accommodation' which is just a soft and dry spot (with facilities close at hand) where you can roll out a sleeping bag. In some cases, a continental breakfast will be included in the price of the lodging.

Given the wide range of possibilities, it is difficult to generalise about the prices. Most sleeping-bag accommodation will cost about US$12, double rooms will range from US$45 to US$70, and self-contained units will normally cost somewhere between US$70 and US$90 per night. In Iceland, rooms will always be cheaper if booked in advance through an overseas travel agent. Most guesthouses are only open seasonally.

Farmhouse Accommodation

Exclusive to Iceland, farmhouse accommodation provides a good way to become acquainted with everyday country life. Every farm is named and some of those open to guests date back to Settlement times and are mentioned in the sagas.

A range of accommodation plans is available and most farms offer expensive horse rentals and horse tours. Some offer meals on the side and others just have cooking facilities. During the off-season (from September to May) accommodation must be booked in advance.

Except for the sleeping-bag option, unless you have a large group, farmhouse accommodation cannot really be considered a budget alternative to the hotels although, at times, the conditions will make it seem that way. Don't blame the farmers, though; prices are controlled by the government. Official prices are:

bed & breakfast – US$26 per person
lunch – US$12
dinner – US$16
sleeping-bag accommodation (bed) – US$13 per person
sleeping-bag accommodation (floor) – US$8.50 per person
cottage (six-person weekly rate) – US$400
cottage (four-person weekly rate) – US$340
cottage (six-person daily rate) – US$62
cottage (four-person daily rate) – US$52
bed linen (daily per person) – US$6
child rate – half price
horse rental (hourly) – US$13

One very pleasant option is to participate in the *réttir* or autumn roundup when the farmers ride into the mountains and gather the sheep that have been grazing in the highlands all summer. Those who volunteer to help will normally receive food, accommodation, and some experience of the Icelandic horse *(equus scandinavicus)* to make it worth their while. If you are in Iceland in September and would like to try this, arrangements can be made through tourist offices or directly with individual farmers.

Youth Hostels

Budget travellers will probably be pleased to hear that all three countries have youth hostels. Faroese hostels *ferðafuglaheim* belong to the Danish Youth Hostels Association. Iceland, whose hostels are called *farfuglaheimili* (both the Faroese and Icelandic names translate into something like 'little home for migrating birds'), has its own hostel association. Greenlandic hostels, called *vandrehjemmet* are confined to the southern part of the country and are maintained independently by the villages and tourist offices.

All of the youth hostels offer hot water, cooking facilities, luggage storage, and opportunities to meet other travellers. In some, particularly in Iceland, the 'baby-sitting' role that many European hostels seem to take is in evidence. In both Iceland and the Faroes there are curfews, but in Greenland no such restrictions apply. With a few notable exceptions, such as in Reykjavík, sleeping bags are welcome at youth hostels and guests will not have to provide or rent sleeping sheets.

Those who plan to spend a lot of time in Faroese or Icelandic youth hostels should join the International Youth Hostel Federation (IYHF) and take advantage of the lower rates available to members. Rates in Faroese hostels range from US$8 to US$11 for members and from US$9 to US$12 for non-members. In Iceland, members pay US$11 in all hostels and non-members pay US$13. The least expensive hostels in Greenland charge US$13 and the dearest, at Narsarsuaq, costs US$16 per night. Greenlandic hostels charge the same regardless of hostel association membership but this will change if they are successful in their attempt to join the Danish Youth Hostel Association.

Nuna-Tek Hostels

Nuna-Tek is an instution of the Greenland Home Rule government which is responsible for power plants, telecommunications, shipyards, construction, and mineral investigation in that country. Formerly known as GTO, when it belonged to the Danish government (prior to 1987), it spends about 1.5 billion Danish króna annually on capital projects around Greenland.

Since labour is pooled from all over the country, Nuna-Tek has set up hostel-like accommodation for the workers and any extra space in these places is open to travellers for around US$20 per night. Since there are no youth hostels in Greenland north of Sisimiut, travellers who'd rather not camp have this relatively inexpensive option.

Breakfasts are available for US$4.50 and lunches and dinners for US$10.50, or all three for US$23. They also offer a laundry service at US$3.50 per kg for wash and dry.

Mountain Huts

In Iceland, Ferðafélag Íslands (Icelandic Touring Club – tel 91-19533, Reykjavík) and a couple of smaller local clubs maintain a system of mountain huts *(saeluhús)* in remote areas throughout the country. Although a couple of them, such as those at Landmannalaugar and Þórsmörk, are accessible by 4WD vehicle, most are in wilderness areas and access will require at least a day's walking from populated areas.

Huts along the popular Landmannalaugar to Þorsmörk route must be reserved and paid for in advance through the club office; it's a good idea to book all huts in advance. A few huts offer cooking facilities but accommodation is always dormitory-style and guests must supply their own sleeping bags and food.

The huts are open to anyone. In the more rudimentary ones, Icelandic Touring Club

Symbol of Ferðafélag Íslands, Icelandic Touring Club

members pay US$5 per night while non-members pay about US$7.75. In the posher places, members pay up to US$7.75 and non-members US$11.50. If you are planning to do a great deal of hut-hopping, you should consider club membership. For more information, write to Ferðafélag Íslands, Öldugata 3, Reykjavík, Iceland.

In Greenland, sheep stations maintain mountain huts primarily to bring in extra cash when the station doesn't need to use them. They are limited to the Narsaq, Qaqortoq, and Vatnahverfi districts in the sheep-grazing area of southern Greenland. For *basic* dormitory-style accommodation they charge around US$6.25 per person. Sheep stations are depicted as circles on the DVL-Rejser *Vandrerkort 1:100,000* (Green Tours was formerly known as DVL Rejser) walking map which is essential for trekking in the area.

Sheep-station huts should not be confused with shepherds' huts, basic little shelters where herders sleep during roundup and patrol. The huts are found scattered around the same districts as the sheep stations and can be used by walkers as emergency shelters. In any case, never set off walking in Greenland without a tent; the weather can be positively awful.

There is no hut accommodation in the Faroe Islands.

Emergency Huts

The Icelandic Automobile Association and the government have set up a series of orange emergency huts on high mountain passes, remote coastlines, and other places subject to life-threatening weather conditions. They are stocked with food, fuel, and blankets and are open to anyone in an emergency. Law forbids the use of these huts for any other purpose.

Camping

For those on the strictest of budgets, camping will offer the most effective relief from high accommodation prices in the North Atlantic. Beyond the economic benefits, a tent will offer flexibility not available to those who must confine themselves to formal accommodation. With a tent, you can set up housekeeping beside a particularly appealing lake or stream and stay for a week if you wish.

The necessity of bringing a stable, seam-sealed, well-constructed, and durable tent cannot be stressed enough. One with a four-season rating would be ideal. Most people probably can't imagine the type of destruction that can befall tents in the wrath of a North Atlantic storm. During one particularly fierce bout of weather in Ólafsvík, Iceland, four of the six tents in the camping ground were utterly destroyed. In case you're interested, mine (a Moss Starlight) was one of the two survivors.

Although the sparsely populated North Atlantic countries allow camping almost anywhere, permission is necessary to camp on a farm or private property. There are also organised camping sites (*tjaldstaeði* in Icelandic, *campingpláss* in Faroese, and *campingplads* in Danish) scattered throughout the region. Amenities vary, while some provide washing machines, cooking facilities, hot showers and common rooms, others have nothing but a cold-water tap and a pit toilet.

Charges per night in organised camping sites are dependent upon the number of tents and the size of your group. Normally, you will pay something like US$3 for each tent and *another* US$3 for each person in your group. Some enterprising places charge yet another fee for each car, trailer and even bicycle you may have with you.

The good news is that, in many small Icelandic towns, camping sites are maintained by the local governments to promote tourism and some may be used free of charge. In Greenland, most towns have set aside areas for camping but there are normally no facilities and no charges are made.

Since the North Atlantic is basically treeless, firewood is scarce and those planning to cook must bring their own stove. Butane cartridges for Bluet stoves are available in Iceland and the Faroes. Shellite or white gas is called white spirits and can be purchased at petrol stations. Another fuel that works well in MSR mountain stoves (and with some difficulty in Whisperlites) is called Petroleum (lantern fuel). Methylated spirits for alcohol stoves is available just about everywhere. Kerosene is hard to come by unless you're prepared to buy it in very large amounts; it would make a grimy carbon mess of your equipment, anyway.

WHAT TO BRING

The amount of stuff you'll be required to carry along on a North Atlantic trip will be determined by your budget and your intended activities. Those who want to travel cheaply will unfortunately need to load themselves down with a lot of things that more up-market travellers won't need to worry about – a good case for bringing a vehicle where applicable. Under ideal circumstances, such things as tents, stoves, cooking implements can be divided among members of a group but lone travellers may find themselves struggling beneath a good deal of weight.

Some general items which will be required by just about everyone (except those staying in hotels and eating in restaurants) include a synthetic-fibre sleeping bag preferably rated to at least -10°C, a Swiss army-style knife, a towel, a torch (flashlight), a water bottle (1 litre), lighters or waterproof matches, a couple of thick paperbacks to read during inclement weather (English-language books are very dear there!), a copy of medical and optical prescriptions, and any film or camera equipment that may be needed.

Clothing

Warm clothing will be of utmost importance to everyone. Given the range of weather possibilities, including warm and sunny, the layering method seems to work best. The items on the following list should be sufficient to keep you comfortable anywhere in the region between May and September:

thermal underwear made of polypropylene or similar material
several pairs of thick wool or polypro socks
heavy windproof ski gloves
high-protection sunglasses
wool hat with ear protection
a T-shirt or two
at least one wool pullover
hiking shorts (canvas or polyester)
wool shirt and trousers (jeans are comfortable when dry, but impossible when wet!)
wind- and waterproof jacket and trousers – Gore Tex may not provide sufficient protection. As disagreeable as it can be, treated nylon is probably better although it can trap sweat and cause chills when removed.
strong hiking shoes with ankle support or (preferably) boots
swimsuit – Iceland has many hot springs and thermally heated swimming pools. Greenland has hot springs as well.

Camping Equipment

Apart from the previously mentioned sleeping bag, campers should carry:

a tent – easily assembled (due to wind), sturdy, waterproofed, and preferably free-standing. It's a good idea to get one with some kind of annexe outside for dry storage of wet clothing, boots, and cooking implements.
a light stove and aluminium fuel bottle – an MSR mountain stove, a Whisperlite, or an alcohol stove would be preferable to butane stoves which are rather unstable and don't work well in wind. In Greenland, butane cartridges are hard to come by.
cooking pots, cups and utensils – A nesting kit is probably the best way to go if you want to keep weight and volume to a minimum. If you despise instant coffee and don't want to bring a coffee filter-cup, a very effective one can be made by cutting the top off a 1-litre milk carton and placing a paper filter inside with the spout closed.
waterproof ground cover or space blanket

If you plan on doing any trekking, add the following items:

gaiters
compass and magnetic deviation figures – this is vital in the far north since deviation from magnetic north in the region can be as high as 80°
fishing line, hook and lures for Greenland especially
medical kit (see Health section)
applicable maps

Getting There

AIR

The popularity of the North Atlantic region, especially Iceland, as an adventure-travel destination is mushrooming and the travel industry has scarcely been able to keep up with it. At present there are no earth-shaking bargain fares available to or between points in the North Atlantic. Therefore, the only way to keep transport costs down is to make plans as far in advance as possible, shop around for cheap fares, and purchase airline tickets at least 30 days prior to departure.

The biggest problem travellers face is the scarcity of information especially about the Faroes and Greenland. These places remain off the beaten track and many travel agents can't even find them on a map. To make matters worse, of all the airlines serving the region, only Icelandair and SAS seem to have made their way into the international airline computer networks.

A note of caution: Icelandair, Iceland's national carrier, is quite inflexible when it comes to ticket rescheduling. Unless you're a good actor and can fabricate a really heart-rending sob story, be extremely careful when purchasing an Icelandair ticket if there's any possibility of having to change it.

From Europe

Icelandair serves Reykjavík direct from Luxembourg, Glasgow, London, Paris, Frankfurt, Vienna, Copenhagen, Gothenburg, Stockholm, Oslo, Bergen, and Vágar (Faroe Islands). During high season, the Copenhagen flight operates daily. Four times weekly, it continues on to Narsarsuaq, Greenland. Once weekly, it connects with the flight from Reykjavík to the Faroe Islands.

Since Icelandair promotes its European hub, Luxembourg, with some zeal, they run free buses between that city and Frankfurt, Karlsruhe, Stuttgart, Dusseldorf, and a number of cities en route. They also offer highly discounted bus and train tickets to Amsterdam, Berlin, London, Paris, Madrid, Rome, Zurich, and so forth. If you're flying to Iceland from Luxembourg it might pay to check this out.

The least expensive return ticket to Reykjavík is from Luxembourg which costs US$431 and must be purchased 30 days in advance. You won't save anything by taking the ferry one-way from Denmark to Iceland and returning on the plane – the one-way ticket costs US$517 so you'd do better buying the return ticket and throwing half of it away.

To extend a ticket from Luxembourg to Reykjavík to include a return trip to Narsarsuaq, Greenland, you'll have to pay US$431 extra. This must also be purchased at least 30 days in advance and your stay in Greenland will be limited to 30 days. If you'd rather fly into east Greenland (Kulusuk) and continue on to west Greenland, forget Icelandair – they aren't permitted to carry transit passengers to Kulusuk.

Once a week, Grølandsfly (Greenlandair) flies between Reykjavík and Kangerdlusuaq (Søndre Strømfjord), Nuuk, and Nerlerit Inaat. The latter two depart from Reykjavík City Airport, and the flight to Kangerdlusuaq leaves from Keflavík International Airport. Several times a week in high season and once weekly in winter, Odin Air offers a 'been-there-done-that' day tour from Reykjavík City Airport to Kulusuk for US$350. What it amounts to is 3 hours on the ground but with Odin, those who would like to transit from Kulusuk to some other Greenlandic destination may do so.

Three times weekly, SAS flies directly between Copenhagen and Kangerdlusuaq for US$625 high season (from 15 June to 15 August) return and US$421 low season. One Iceland stopover is permitted with the high-season fare and, if you buy the ticket more than 21 days in advance, the high-season fare will be discounted. SAS also allows you to fly into either Kangerdlusuaq or Nuuk and return to Copenhagen from the other city without extra charge.

Although Icelandair flies to the Faroes, they take a roundabout route through Reykjavík. A better option may be to fly Danair or Atlantic Airways from Copenhagen, the former using Boeing 737s and the latter the British Aerospace high-wing jets.

The price structure of both lines is similar. The discounted 'green price' fare for Copenhagen to Vágar return is US$343 in low season and US$371 high season (from 11 June to 20 August). In order to qualify for this price, you must stay a minimum of 14 days and maximum of 28 days in the Faroes. If you can't comply with this restriction, the non-discounted return fare is US$521.

Other options from Europe include Lufthansa's direct service between Reykjavík and Frankfurt, and Arnarflug's (Eagle Air's) service between Reykjavík and Hamburg, Zurich, Geneva, Milan, Munich, Basel and Brussels.

From North America

During high season (from 24 May to 3 October), Icelandair flies daily between New York and Reykjavík. Since this route caters primarily to those flying to Luxembourg on the cheap, the airline offers a stopover in Iceland (from 1 to 3 days) for no extra charge. Once a week, this flight connects with Icelandair's route from Reykjavík to the Faroe Islands. The fare between New York and Luxembourg is US$388 return with 30-day advance purchase, a minimum stay of 14 days and a maximum of 30 days. Longer stays will significantly increase the ticket price. The return fare between New York and Reykjavík is US$580 with the same purchase and stay restrictions as from New York to Luxembourg.

The easiest way to get to Greenland from North America is to fly to Reykjavík or Copenhagen and work out your route from there (see 'From Europe'). The only other option is to get yourself to Eqaluit on Canada's Baffin Island (Air Canada flies there – at a premium) and then take First Air's once-weekly flight to Nuuk which costs US$480 return.

From Australasia

Since the North Atlantic is on pretty much the other side of the world from Australasia, there is no direct or easy way of travelling there. You'll have to go to either the USA or Europe and continue from there. At the present time, the best way is to purchase a RTW (round-the-world) ticket that passes through New York or Europe and then add a side trip to Iceland, Greenland, or the Faroes. To my knowledge, there are no RTW tickets that include destinations in any of those countries as part of the package.

These RTW tickets have become very popular in the last few years. The official airline RTW tickets are usually put together by a combination of two airlines and permit you to fly anywhere you want on those airlines' routes as long as you do not backtrack. Other restrictions usually include pre-booking the first leg making that sector of the journey subject to cancellation penalties. There may also be restrictions on your number of stops. Tickets will be valid for a year after the first sector is used.

Typical prices for RTW tickets range from A$2000 to A$3000. In Australia and New Zealand, STA (Student Travel Association) seems to put together the cheapest packages.

SEA

Ferry

A very pleasant way to travel between Europe proper and Iceland or the Faroes is by ferry although it takes a bit more time and isn't really economically advantageous to do so. If you want to bring your own vehicle, it's your only option.

The only ferry that stops in Iceland is Smyril Line's *Norrøna* (in Danish) or *Norröna* (in Icelandic), operating from mid-May to mid-September out of Hanstholm in north-western Denmark. Passengers travelling with Smyril from Hanstholm are provided with inexpensive transport to that port city from Copenhagen on the day of departure.

The *Norröna* sails from Hanstholm on Saturdays and arrives in Tórshavn, Faroe Islands, on Monday morning. There, all Iceland-bound passengers must disembark while the ship continues back to Lerwick, Shetland Islands, arriving Monday night. On Tuesday night it is in Bergen, Norway, picking up more passengers. It arrives back in Tórshavn on Wednesdays, gathers up those heading for Iceland, and sails overnight to Seyðisfjörður on the east coast. On the return journey, it sails back to Tórshavn, arriving Friday morning, and then returns to Hanstholm for another circuit.

It is important to note that Iceland-bound passengers cannot remain on board while the ship sails to Shetland and Norway so they will be required to spend 2 nights in the Faroe Islands en route. Those who wish to spend more time in the Faroes, however, will have to break their journey there and pay for two sectors. The normal deck fare from Hanstholm to Seyðisfjörður (which includes a couchette or sleeper) is US$280 one-way. Hanstholm to Tórshavn is US$188 and from Tórshavn to Seyðisfjörður is US$164, adding up to US$352 for the entire trip. Substantial discounts are available to holders of student cards.

The cost of transporting a vehicle up to 5 metres long will be about 75% of the deck-class passenger fare. Above deck class, there are three classes of cabins and a luxury suite. The ship also has a bar, cafeteria, restaurant, disco, casino, and duty-free shops.

For further information, schedules, and fare lists, contact: Smyil Line (tel 01-93-90-97, in Copenhagen), Vester Farimagsgade 6, DK1606 Copenhagen, Denmark.

Those coming from the UK can take Strandfaraskip Landsins' ferry, the *Smyril*, which sails weekly from Scrabster, Scotland, to Tórshavn. From there, it's possible to connect with the *Norröna* and continue on to Iceland. For information contact: Strandfaraskip Landsins (tel 298-14550, Tórshavn), Yvri við Strønd 6, Postbox 88, FR 110, Tórshavn, Faroe Islands.

The third ferry to the North Atlantic is DFDS Scandinavian Seaways' ship MS *Winston Churchill* operating between Esbjerg in south-west Denmark and Tórshavn from mid-June to mid-August. It leaves Esbjerg on Mondays at 9 pm and Tórshavn on Wednesdays at 9.30 am. It is also a car-ferry and prices and services are similar to those on Smyril Line. Their address is DFDS Scandinavian Seaways (tel 298-11511 in Tórshavn), Winthers Gøta 3, PO Box 28, FR-100 Tórshavn, Faroe Islands.

Cargo Ship

The Icelandic cargo-shippers Eimskip, whose vessels *Laxfoss* and *Brúarfoss* sail between Reykjavík, Immingham (UK), Antwerp, Rotterdam and Hamburg, have six cabins for passengers on each ship. Each cabin will accommodate two adults and two children and costs US$1200 between Hamburg and Reykjavík (a bit less from the other cities). For further information contact Eimskip (tel 91-687100 in Reykjavík), Posthússtraeti 2, IS-101, Reykjavík, Iceland.

Faroe Ship Cargo & Passenger Line operates between Fredericia and Copenhagen (Denmark), Lysekil (Sweden), Stavanger (Norway), and Tórshavn weekly throughout the year. Contact them at Eystara Bryggja (tel 298-11225), PO Box 47, FR-100 Tórshavn, Faroe Islands.

To Greenland, there are only two ships per year which accept passengers, both operated by KNI Shipping from Ålborg, Denmark. The Greenland coastal ferry *Kununguak* leaves Ålborg about 10 days before it's set to begin its runs in mid-March. Its sister ship, the *Disko*, leaves Denmark about 10 days before it is scheduled to begin operating (normally sometime in mid to late May). Passage on either ship must be booked in advance through KNI Shipping, Grønlandshavnen, Rederiafdelingen, Ålborg, Denmark.

Iceland

Facts about the Country

INTRODUCTION

While travelling in or reading about Iceland, you'll hear the country frequently introduced as the 'Land of Fire & Ice' so I won't dwell on that cliché. What should be said, however, is that the island with the chilly name is rapidly becoming one of Europe's hottest destinations. Once you've seen Iceland, you won't wonder about its popularity.

Nowhere on earth are the forces of nature more evident than in Iceland. You've got glaciers, hot springs, geysers, active volcanoes, icecaps, tundra, snowcapped peaks, vast lava deserts, waterfalls, craters, and even Mt Snaefell, Jules Verne's gateway to the centre of the earth. On the high cliffs that characterise much of the coastline are some of the most densely populated sea bird colonies in the world and the lakes and marshes teem with waterfowl.

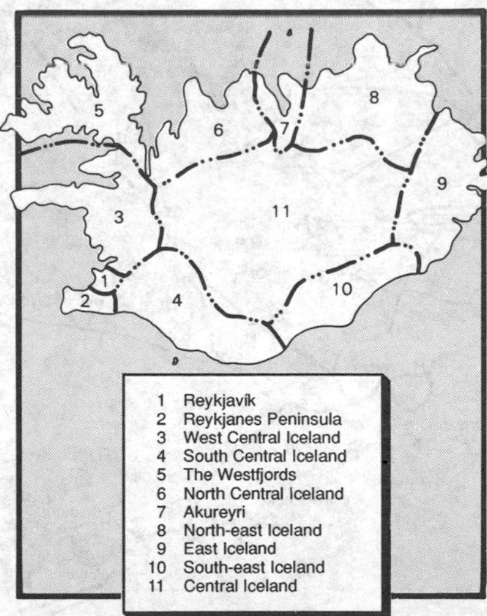

Iceland Chapter Divisions

Superimposed on all this wilderness is a tough and independent society, descendants of the farmers and warriors who fled the tyranny of medieval Scandinavia to settle a new and empty country.

The island also provided a backdrop for the sagas, considered by literature enthusiasts to be the finest of all Western medieval works. Iceland has been inhabited for over 1100 years and the tales of battle, love, revenge and counter-revenge come to life in locales that have changed little since the days of Egill Skallagrímsson and Auður the Deep-Minded.

If it all sounds appealing, there's one catch; Iceland's prices are Europe's highest. That doesn't mean it can't be visited on a shoestring, but it does mean that travellers will have to put in some effort. If you allow yourself lots of time and don't mind camping, it's possible to spend an entire summer in Iceland and spend little more than you would in such traditional budget destinations as Thailand or Morocco.

Iceland's Top 15

The following ranking is designed specifically for those who are unfamiliar with Iceland but would like to enjoy the highlights within strict time constraints. I realise taste is subjective, so if you feel the ranking should be different, write and let me know. In the next edition I'll re-order them (or change them altogether) based on readers' feedback.

After each attraction, the relevant chapter is included in brackets.

1 Mývatn & Krafla (North-East Iceland) – examples of nearly all the island's geological phenomena are represented at Mývatn. Its centrepiece is a lovely blue lake teeming with bird life. What's more, the weather is the finest in Iceland.

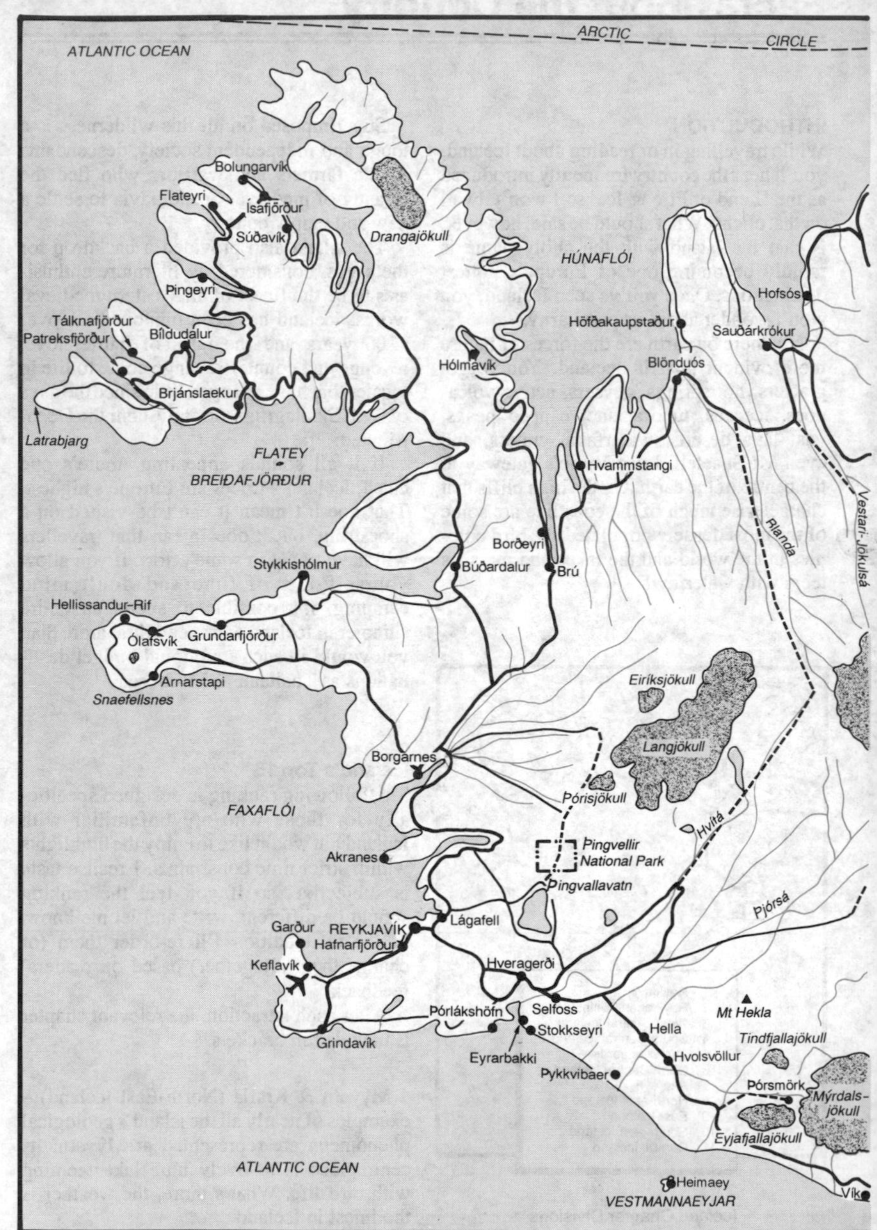
ARCTIC
CIRCLE
ATLANTIC OCEAN
Bolungarvík
Flateyri
Ísafjörður
Súðavík
Drangajökull
HÚNAFLÓI
Þingeyri
Hofsós
Tálknafjörður
Patreksfjörður
Bíldudalur
Höfðakaupstaður
Sauðárkrókur
Hólmavík
Blönduós
Brjánslaekur
Latrabjarg
FLATEY
Hvammstangi
BREIÐAFJÖRÐUR
Vestari-Jökulsá
Rlandá
Borðeyri
Stykkishólmur
Búðardalur
Brú
Hellissandur-Rif
Grundarfjörður
Ólafsvík
Arnarstapi
Eiríksjökull
Snaefellsnes
Langjökull
Borgarnes
Þórisjökull
FAXAFLÓI
Hvítá
Akranes
Þingvellir
National Park
Þingvallavatn
Lágafell
Þjórsá
Garður
REYKJAVÍK
Hafnarfjörður
Keflavík
Hveragerði
Selfoss
Mt Hekla
Þórlákshöfn
Stokkseyri
Hella
Grindavík
Tindfjallajökull
Eyrarbakki
Hvolsvöllur
Þykkvibaer
Þórsmörk
Mýrdals-
jökull
Eyjafjallajökull
ATLANTIC OCEAN
Heimaey
VESTMANNAEYJAR
Vík

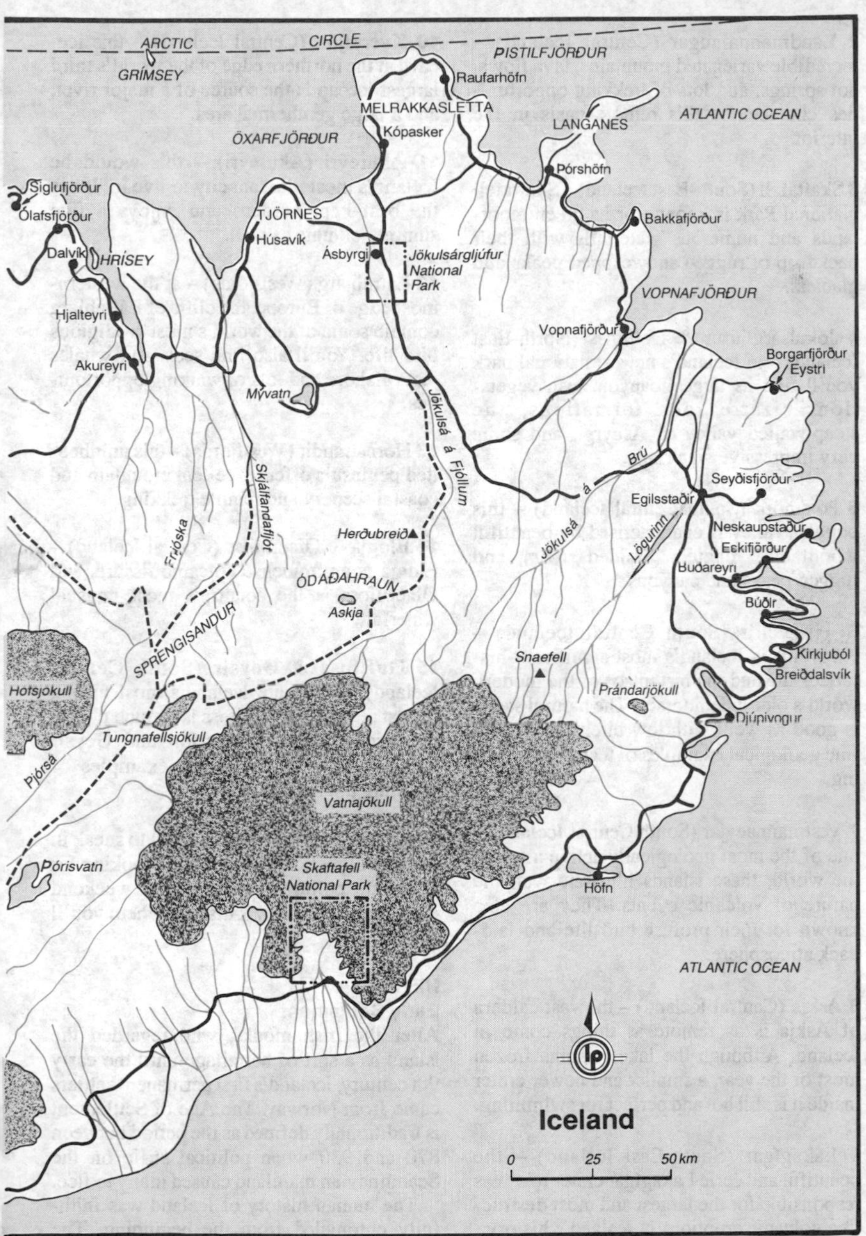
ARCTIC CIRCLE
GRÍMSEY
PISTILFJÖRÐUR
Raufarhöfn
MELRAKKASLETTA
ATLANTIC OCEAN
LANGANES
ÖXARFJÖRÐUR
Kópasker
Þórshöfn
Siglufjörður
Ólafsfjörður
TJÖRNES
Bakkafjörður
Húsavík
Dalvík
HRÍSEY
Ásbyrgi
Jökulsárgljúfur National Park
VOPNAFJÖRÐUR
Hjalteyri
Vopnafjörður
Akureyri
Borgarfjörður Eystri
Mývatn
Jökulsá á Fjöllum
Skjálfandafljót
Jökulsá á Brú
Seyðisfjörður
Egilsstaðir
Fnjóska
Herðubreið
Neskaupstaður
Lögurinn
Eskifjörður
Búðareyri
ÓDÁÐAHRAUN
Askja
Búðir
SPRENGISANDUR
Kirkjuból
Snaefell
Breiðdalsvík
Hotsjökull
Þrándarjökull
Djúpivogur
Tungnafellsjökull
Þjórsá
Vatnajökull
Þórisvatn
Skaftafell National Park
Höfn
ATLANTIC OCEAN
Iceland
0
25
50 km

2 Landmannalaugar (Central Iceland) – incredible variegated mountains, lava flows, hot springs, and lots of trekking opportunities characterise this remote oasis in the interior.

3 Skaftafell (South-East Iceland) – Skaftafell National Park is known for its green moorlands and numerous waterfalls with their backdrop of rugged snowcapped peaks and glaciers.

4 Jökulsárgljúfur & Dettifoss (North-East Iceland) – in Iceland's newest national park you'll find its largest canyon, lush vegetation, bizarre rock formations, the steep-walled valley of Ásbyrgi, and some very impressive waterfalls.

5 Þórsmörk (South Central Iceland) – this popular valley is characterised by beautiful woodlands, glaciers, braided rivers, and rugged peaks and canyons.

6 Þingvellir (South Central Iceland) – Þingvellir is Iceland's most significant historical site and the birthplace of the modern world's oldest democracy. The natural scene is good as well, with low birch forests and fine geological examples of tectonic spreading.

7 Vestmannaeyjar (South Central Iceland) – one of the most geologically active areas in the world, these islands illustrate well the nature of volcanic events. They are also known for their profuse bird life and laid-back atmosphere.

8 Askja (Central Iceland) – the vast caldera of Askja is as remote as things come in Iceland. Although the lake remains frozen most of the year, a smaller and newer crater inside it is still hot and perfect for swimming.

9 Lakagígar (South-East Iceland) – the beautiful and eerie Lakagígar crater row was responsible for the largest and most destructive volcanic eruptions in Iceland's history.

10 Kverkfjöll (Central Iceland) – this ice-cave at the northern edge of the world's third largest icecap is the source of a major river, and a large geothermal area.

11 Akureyri (Akureyri) – this would be Iceland's most pleasant city to live in. It has the best kept gardens and enjoys a fine summer climate as well.

12 Látrabjarg (Westfjords) – at the westernmost edge of Europe, the cliffs of Látrabjarg contain some of the world's most prodigious bird life. You'll also find seals and whales just offshore and lots of walking opportunities.

13 Hornstrandir (Westfjords) – this uninhabited peninsula offers excellent mountain and coastal scenery and remote trekking.

14 Eldgjá & Ofaerufoss (Central Iceland) – Eldgjá is an immense volcanic fissure, and Ofaerufoss is the country's most unusual waterfall.

15 Gullfoss & Geysir (South Central Iceland) – these are Iceland's most visited tourist attractions. Gullfoss is a much photographed two-tiered waterfall and Geysir contains the country's best examples of spouting hot springs.

Disco (Reykjavík) – I'm tempted to sneak in an extra attraction here. If you're looking for a unique cultural experience, a weekend evening in a Reykjavík disco is where you'll find it.

HISTORY

Early Settlement

After the Irish monks, who regarded the island as a sort of hermitage until the early 9th century, Iceland's first permanent settlers came from Norway. The Age of Settlement is traditionally defined as the period between 870 and 930 when political strife on the Scandinavian mainland caused many to flee.

The human history of Iceland was faithfully chronicled from the beginning. The

Íslendingabók, which was written by a 12th-century scholar, Ari Þorgilsson (Ari the Learned), about 250 years after the fact, provides an historical narrative. The more detailed *Landnámabók*, a comprehensive account of the settlement probably compiled from several sources also by Ari the Learned, provides us with a wealth of information about that era.

It's likely the Norse accidentally discovered Iceland after being blown off course en route to the Faroes. The first arrival, the Swede Naddoddur, landed on the east coast around 850 and named the place Snaeland ('snowland') before backtracking to his original destination.

Iceland's second visitor, Garðar Svavarsson, came in search of Naddoddur's Snaeland. He circumnavigated it then settled in for the winter at Húsavík on the north coast. When he left in the spring, some of his crew remained at Húsavík, probably involuntarily, thereby becoming the island's first residents.

Around 860, the Norwegian Flóki Vilgerðarson uprooted his farm and family and headed for Snaeland. He navigated with ravens which, after some trial and error, led him to his destination. This odd practice provided his nickname, Hrafna-Flóki or 'Raven's Flóki', by which he has been known ever since.

Hrafna-Flóki sailed to Vatnsfjörður on the west coast but quickly became disenchanted with the place. Upon seeing icebergs floating in the fjord, he renamed the place Ísland ('Iceland') which he perhaps considered even less flattering than 'Snaeland' and returned to Norway. Apparently, he reconsidered his position at some point because he did return to Iceland some years later and settled in the Skagafjörður district on the north coast.

Credit for the first intentional settlement, according to the *Íslendingabók*, goes to a Norwegian called Ingólfur Arnarson who set up house in 874 at a place he called Reykjavík ('smoky bay') because of the steam from thermal springs there.

Ingólfur was a true Viking who had had his day in the British Isles; he and his blood-brother Hjörleifur had to flee Norway to escape some social difficulties they'd encountered there. Hjöleifur settled near the present town of Vík but was soon murdered by his servants.

Ingólfur's homestead site was determined by the custom of the day; intending settlers would toss their high-seat pillars, a symbol of authority and part of every good Norseman's pagan paraphernalia, into the sea as they approached land. Tradition and prudence required them to build their homes at the place where the gods chose to bring the pillars ashore. At times, settlement required years of searching the coastline for stray pillars.

Statue of Ingólfur Arnarson

While Ingólfur Arnarson and his descendants came to control the entire south-western part of Iceland, others arrived from the mainland. By the time Ingólfur's son Þorsteinn was grown up, the island was dotted with farms and people began to feel the need for some sort of government.

The Alþing

After rejecting the political strife at home, Icelanders were decidedly against monarchy so they set up a democratic parliamentary system of government. It's significant that such a structure had never proved itself before but they reasoned it could only be better than the fearful and oppressive setup on the mainland.

Þorsteinn Ingólfsson founded Iceland's first district assembly near Reykjavík, placing himself in a strong political position. In the 920s, the self-styled lawyer Úlfljótur was sent to Norway to prepare a code of law for Iceland.

At the same time, Grímur Geitskör was commissioned to find a suitable location for the Alþing, the National Assembly. Bláskógar near the eastern boundary of Ingólfur Arnarson's estate with its beautiful lake and wooded plain seemed ideal. Along one side of the plain was a long cliff with an elevated base (the Mid-Atlantic Rift) from where speakers and representatives could preside over, and be heard by, the people gathered below.

In 930, Bláskógar was renamed Þingvellir, the 'parliament plains'. Úlfljótur was designated the first *lögsögumaður* (law-speaker) and Þorsteinn Ingólfsson received the honorary title *allsherjargoði* (supreme chieftain).

The actual power of legislation was held by 39 elected *goðar* (chieftains), nine titular goðar, and the lögsögumaður, who was required to memorise and annually recite the entire law of the land. In addition, 96 advisors served the central assembly. Judicial power was divided between four local courts around the country and the Supreme Court met during the Alþing's annual convention.

At the convention of 999 (some maintain it was 1000), the decree that made Iceland a Christian nation was read. Although the conversion came under extreme pressure from Norwegian King Ólaf Tryggvason, it provided Iceland with a semblance of national unity at a time when squabbles were arising among the country's leaders and allegiances were being questioned. The government held, however, and the first bishoprics were set up at Skálholt in the south-west and Hólar in the north.

During the following years, the 2-week national assembly at Þingvellir became the social event of the year. Single people came looking for mates, marriages were contracted and solemnised, business deals were finalised, and the Supreme Court handed down judgements on disputes and offences that couldn't be resolved in lower courts. One such judgement, the pronouncement of exile upon outlaw Eirík Rauðe, led to the Norse colonisation of Greenland.

During its first century of existence, corruption developed in the Alþing. The goðar began accepting bribes and gifts in exchange for certain favours but even so, the system worked fairly well. Icelandic society established itself and its agrarian economy with little unrest. Schools were founded at the two bishoprics and elsewhere. This educational awareness prepared the way for the great Literary Era to come.

The Literary Era

The first literature to emerge from Iceland was poetry. Most of the early themes probably came from mainland Scandinavia even before the settlement of Iceland but weren't actually written down until the period of literary awareness in the 12th century.

The body of Icelandic poetry was divided neatly into two categories: Eddic poetry, actually more like free-metre prose, and Skaldic poetry, written by court poets employing a unique and well-defined syntax and vocabulary.

Eddic poetry dealt primarily with two themes, the Heroic and the Mythical. The Heroic Eddas are based on Gothic legends and German folktales while the Mythical

Eddas are derived primarily from stories of Nordic gods and their antics.

It's assumed that Skaldic poetry was composed by Norwegian court poets to celebrate the heroic deeds of the Scandinavian kings. Perhaps the most renowned of the skalds was Egill Skallagrímsson, a Viking who had run foul of King Harald Haarfager's eldest son, King Eirík Blood-Axe of York. After being captured and sentenced to death at York in 948, Egill composed an ode to the king. The work is now called *Höfuðlausn*, or 'head ransom', because the flattered King Eirík released Egill unharmed.

During the Saga Age of the late 12th and early 13th centuries, epic tales of early settlement, romance, dispute, and development of Iceland were recorded and sprinkled liberally and artistically with dramatic licence. They provided both entertainment and a sense of cultural heritage for Icelandic commoners. Through the difficult years to come, especially on cold winter nights, Icelanders gathered in farmhouses for *kvöldvaka*, or 'evening wake', a time of socialising and saga reading. While the men spun horsehair ropes and women spun wool or knitted, a family member would read the sagas and recite *rímur*, or impromptu poetry.

Early Icelandic literature will be discussed in more detail in the Literature section later in this chapter.

The Decline

By the early 13th century, the enlightened period of peace that had lasted 200 years in Iceland came to an end and the country entered the infamous Sturlung Age, a tragic era graphically recounted in the tragic three-volume *Sturlunga Saga.* Competition between politicians turned into violent feuds and power struggles and the system began to collapse. Viking-like private armies ravaged the countryside. Even if it had wanted to do so, the failing government was powerless to protect the rights of individuals.

The opportunistic Norwegian King Hákon Hákonarsson regarded the strife as his invitation to take control of the situation. The Icelanders, who saw no alternative, dissolved all but a superficial shell of their government and swore their allegiance to the king. An agreement of confederacy was made in 1262. In 1281, a new code of law, the *Jónsbók*, was introduced by the king and thereby, Iceland was absorbed.

Norway immediately set about appointing Norwegian bishops to Hólar and Skálholt and imposed excessive taxes. Contention flared anew as former chieftains quibbled over high offices, particularly that of *járl* (earl), an honour that fell to the ruthless scoundrel Gissur Þorvaldsson who later murdered Snorri Sturluson, Iceland's best known historian and writer. The governorship of Iceland was actually leased for 3-year periods to the highest Norwegian bidder and with that office came the power to extract revenue in any efficient manner.

To add insult to injury, in 1300, 1341 and 1389, the volcano Mt Hekla in south Iceland erupted violently causing death and destruction of property. Recurring epidemics plagued the country throughout the century and the Black Death that struck Norway in 1349 effectively cut off trade and supplies from the mainland.

The Kjalmar Union of Norway, Sweden and Denmark at the end of the 14th century brought Iceland, still a province of Norway, under Danish rule. Disputes between church and state resulted in the Reformation of 1550. The Danish government seized church property and imposed Lutheranism. When the stubborn Catholic bishop of Hólar, Jón Arason, resisted and gained a following, he and his two sons were taken to Skálholt and executed.

Toward the end of the 16th century, Iceland was devastated by still more natural disasters. Four consecutive years with severe winters led to widespread crop failure; 9000 Icelanders starved to death while thousands more were uprooted from their homes.

In 1602, the Danish king imposed a trade monopoly whereby Swedish and Danish firms were given exclusive trading rights in Iceland for 12-year periods. This resulted in large-scale extortion, importation of spoilt or inferior goods, and yet more suffering for the Icelanders.

Throughout the 17th and 18th centuries, disaster continued to reign in the form of British, Spanish and Arab piracy of Iceland-bound trading ships and natural catastrophes. Mt Hekla erupted continuously for 7 months during 1636 and then again in 1693; Katla erupted violently in 1660 and 1755; and Öraefi erupted in Vatnajökull in 1727.

In 1783, Lakagígar (Laki) erupted continuously for 10 months and devastated much of south-east Iceland resulting in a poisonous haze that destroyed pastures and crops. Nearly 75% of Iceland's livestock and 20% of the human population died in the resulting famine. Furthermore, earthquakes destroyed farms and a spell of particularly bad winters ruined crops and prolonged the suffering.

Independence

Five centuries of oppression under foreign rule had taken their toll on the Icelanders. By the early 1800s, a growing sense of Icelandic nationalism was perceived in Copenhagen, but an ongoing liberalisation process in Europe prevented Denmark's tightening its grip. Jón Sigurðsson, an Icelandic scholar, successfully lobbied for restoration of free trade in 1855. By 1874, Iceland draughted a constitution and was at last permitted to handle its own domestic matters without interference from the mainland.

The Act of Union, which was signed in 1918, effectively released Iceland from Danish rule making it an independent state within the Kingdom of Denmark with Copenhagen retaining responsibility for defence and foreign affairs. The Act of Union was to be valid until 1940 when the Alþing could request a review of Iceland's status.

On 9 April 1940, Denmark was occupied by Germany. Since the Kingdom was in no position to continue overseeing Iceland's defence and foreign affairs, the Alþing took control of its own foreign relations. A year later on 17 May 1941, the Icelanders requested complete independence. The formal establishment of the Republic of Iceland took place at Þingvellir on 17 June 1944.

Recent Times

After the occupation of Denmark and Iceland's declaration of sovereignty in 1940, the island's vulnerability became a matter of concern for the Allied powers. They knew Iceland had no military forces whatsoever and was unprepared to defend its strategic position in the case of German aggression. Britain, which would have been most vulnerable to a German-controlled Iceland, sent in forces to occupy the island.

Iceland grudgingly accepted this help but was pleased to find that British construction projects and spending bolstered the economy. When the British troops withdrew in 1941, the government allowed American troops to move in, presumedly only for the remainder of the war but they stayed on and, in 1946, asked to be allowed 99-year leases on three bases in Iceland. The far-seeing Alþing rejected the request but innocently consented to US use of Keflavík International Airport as a refuelling and staging-point for cargo aircraft flying between Europe and North America.

When the North Atlantic Treaty Organization (NATO) was formed in 1949, Iceland was pressured into becoming a founding member by other Scandinavian states but only on the condition that under no circumstances would foreign military troops be based there during peacetime.

By 1951, however, the US military had completely taken over Keflavík International Airport with no intention of budging. They justified their actions by indicating that Iceland required US protection from the Soviet troops that had invaded North Korea. The Alþing, however, wasn't notified of their intentions until the camel had settled comfortably in the tent, so to speak.

When the Icelanders realised what was happening, they were predictably unhappy but were powerless to evict the Americans whose numbers and military technology at Keflavík continued to increase over the next

4 decades. Currently, growing numbers of Icelanders are becoming more adamant in their demands that the 'Yankees go home'.

Since recent developments in Eastern Europe could potentially weaken the influence of both NATO and the Warsaw Pact, they may soon have their way. The selection of Reykjavík for the 1986 summit between Mikhail Gorbachev and Ronald Reagan was enthusiastically accepted by Icelanders as a sign of warmer relations between the superpowers.

Current Trends

Iceland's only international disputes to date have concerned fishing rights. Collectively known as the Cod Wars, they involved British fishing vessels violating Iceland's increasing self-declared territorial waters. In 1901, Britain and Denmark reduced the extent of the country's offshore fishing rights to less than 4 miles.

In 1952, Iceland increased the limit to 4 miles offshore but expanded it to 12 miles in 1958, 50 miles in 1972, and finally 200 miles in 1975. The wars were characterised mainly by clashes between Icelandic gunships and British warships and in 1976, a stop-gap agreement was made with Britain. Since then British fishing boats have respected the 200-mile limit, and no new violence has erupted. There have, however, been clashes between environmental organisations, especially Greenpeace, and the Icelandic whaling industry which continues unabated in the face of world opposition.

Natural disasters, like those of the 16th and 17th centuries, continue in modern Iceland but better communications and a more urban population have reduced their impact considerably. In 1963, the island of Surtsey appeared out of the sea in a submarine eruption just south-west of Vestmannaeyjar (the Westman Islands). Ten years later, the island of Heimaey, also in Vestmannaeyjar, experienced a terrible eruption that created a new mountain, buried most of the village of 5200 people, and threatened to cut off the harbour. In a matter of hours, the island was evacuated and the cleanup begun. Also in this century, Mt Hekla has erupted and the Krafla fissure north of lake Mývatn has experienced a lot of volcanic activity. At present, Krafla is behaving ominously and is considered the most likely site of the next major eruption.

GEOGRAPHY

With an area of 103,000 sq km, Iceland is the second largest island in Europe. The south-east coast is 798 km from Scotland, the eastern end is 970 km from Norway, and the Westfjords lie 287 km east of Greenland.

The main island, which extends 500 km east to west and 300 km north to south, is roughly duck-shaped. Although no part of the mainland extends north of the Arctic Circle, the island of Grímsey off the north coast actually straddles it.

Most of Iceland, a real juvenile among the world's land masses, is characterised by desert plateaus (52%), lava fields (11%), sandur, or 'sand deltas' (4%), and glacial icecaps (12%). Over half the country lies above 400 metres, which is more significant than it sounds given the northerly latitude. The highest point, Hvannadalshnúkur, rises 2119 metres beneath the glacier Öraefajökull. Only 21% of the land, all near the coast, is considered arable and habitable. The bulk of Iceland's population and agriculture is concentrated in the south-west between Reykjavík and Vík.

Volcanoes

Volcanic and geothermal features – geysers, thermal springs, fumaroles, lava flows, mudpots, craters, calderas, and igneous plugs – figure prominently in the landscape. Currently active volcanoes include Eldfell and Surtsey in Vestmannaeyjar, Hekla in the south-west, Katla beneath the glacier Mýrdalsjökull, Grimsvötn and Öraefi (in Öraefajökull) beneath Vatnajökull, and Krafla at lake Mývatn. In addition to the volcanoes themselves, Iceland has around 250 geothermal areas with a total of around 780 individual hot springs with average water temperatures of about 75°C.

Since volcanic and geothermal terminology will be used throughout the Iceland chapters and visitors will be bombarded with it throughout the country, some explanation may be in order. Here is a rundown of the most frequently used terms:

aa – sharp, rough and chunky lava from gaseous and explosive magma. In Icelandic, it is known as *apalhraun*.

basalt – a rock material that flows smoothly in lava form. Some of the most interesting rock formations in Iceland are columns of basalt cooled into rosette patterns and polygonal shapes.

bombs – chunks of volcanic ejecta that are cooled and solidified in mid-flight

caldera – the often immense depression formed by the collapse of a volcanic cone into its magma chamber

dyke – a vertical intrusion of igneous material up through cracks in horizontal rock layers

fissure – a break or fracture in the earth's crust where vulcanism may occur

graben – a valley formed by spreading and subsidence of surface material

hornitos – small vertical tubes produced in lava by a strong ejection of gases from beneath

laccolith – a mushroom-shaped dome of igneous material that has flowed upward through rock layers and the spread out horizontally often causing hills to appear on the surface

lava cave or *lava tube* – a tunnel or cavern caused by a lava stream flowing beneath an already solidified surface. The Icelandic word is *hellir*.

magma – molten rock before it reaches the surface and becomes lava

obsidian – naturally formed volcanic glass

pahoehoe – ropy, smooth-flowing lava derived from non-gaseous magma. In Icelandic, it's called *helluhraun*.

pillow lava – lava formed in underwater or sub-glacial eruptions. It is squeezed out like toothpaste in pillow-like bulbs and solidifies immediately.

plugs – material that has solidified in volcanic vents and is revealed by erosion

pseudocraters – small craters formed by steam explosions when molten material flows into a body of water

pumice – solidified lava froth. Pumice is so light and porous it will float on water.

rhyolite – light-coloured acid lava solidified into beautifully variegated rock

scoria – porous and glassy black or red volcanic gravel formed in fountain-like eruptions

shield volcano – flattish cones of oozing pahoehoe lava. The name was derived from the classic example, Skjaldbreiður (meaning 'white shield'), near Þingvellir.

sill – a finger or vein of molten material that squeezes between existing rock layers and solidifies

table mountain – the result of an eruption inside a glacier which subsequently retreats or melts. Material flows upward and solidifies as in a mould, giving many table mountains their characteristic 'birthday cake' shapes. In Icelandic they're called *móberg* or *stapi*.

tephra – a collective term for all types of materials ejected from a volcano and transported through the air

CLIMATE

The warm waters of the Gulf Stream and the prevailing south-westerly winds from the tropical Atlantic combine to give the southern and western coasts of Iceland milder winter temperatures than those of New York or Zurich.

The unfortunate side of this incoming warmth is that it combines with relatively cold polar seas and mountainous coastlines to form condensation and, alas, rain. In January, Reykjavík enjoys an average of only 3 sunny days. In July, 1 fine day is the norm. Periods of fierce, wind-driven rain (or wet snow in winter) alternate with partial clearing, drizzle, gales, and fog to create a distinctively miserable climate. It's mostly a matter of 'if you don't like the weather now, wait 5 minutes – it will probably get worse'.

Don't despair, however. As you move north and east in Iceland, the chances of fine weather increase. It's sunniest around Akureyri and lake Mývatn in the central north and warmest around Egilsstaðir in the east. Neither place, however, seems to be free of the relentless wind that makes even 25°C weather feel uncomfortably chilly.

While they're more prone to clear weather than the coastal areas, the interior deserts experience other problems. Blizzards may occur at any time of year and icy, shrieking winds whip up dust and sand into swirling, gritty and opaque maelstroms. Similar conditions can occur on the sandur of the northern and southern coasts. Especially if you're trapped out-of-doors, which is often the case in these remote regions – such times do not pleasant memories make!

Average Rainfall and Temperature

City	Precipitation (mm) Annual	Jan	July	Temperature (°C) Annual	Jan	July
Reykjavík	799	68	51	4.3	-0.9	10.6
Stykkishólmur	756	64	50	3.6	-1.8	10.1
Akureyri	470	53	28	3.4	-2.4	10.7
Vík	2300	179	162	5.3	0.9	10.7
Heimaey	1713	145	89	4.8	1.1	9.6

FLORA & FAUNA

One of the first things visitors notice about Iceland is the absence of trees. An old and tired witticism (that I will nevertheless perpetuate) advises anyone finding themselves lost in the Icelandic forest to stand up.

Iceland has a few stands of scrubby birch (the trees are actually little more than shrubs) and reafforestation projects bring a bit of relief but the days of widespread forests in Iceland seem to be gone forever. Early settlers decimated the slow-growing trees and added insult to injury by importing sheep which loved the tender new shoots of young trees. Without vegetation to hold soil in place, subsequent erosion left nothing but dusty desert.

Lava flows in southern and eastern Iceland are first colonised by mosses while those in the east and at higher elevations by numerous types of lichen. The coastal areas are characterised by low grasses, bogs and marshlands. At higher elevations, the ground is covered with both hard and soft or boggy tundra, the latter occurring in areas of standing water where vegetation grows in odd tussocks.

The only land mammal indigenous to Iceland is the Arctic fox. Polar bears, which occasionally drift across from Greenland on icebergs, would be indigenous if they weren't considered undesirable immigrants. Bears in Iceland have a very short life expectancy thanks mainly to trigger-happy sheep farmers.

Introduced animals include the reindeer, the mink, the field mouse, and several species of rat. Icelandic seas are rich in marine mammals including the common and grey seals and 17 species of whale.

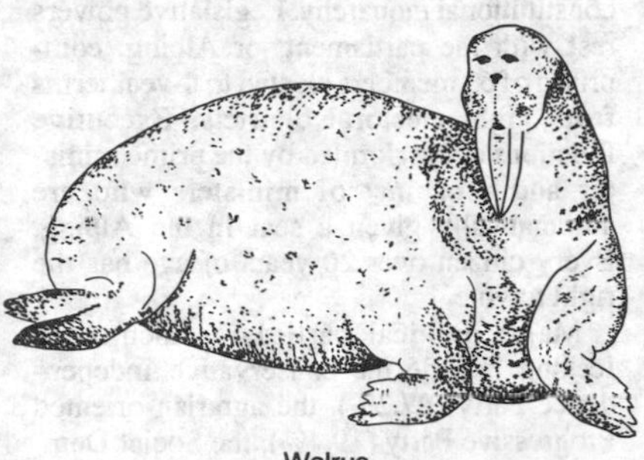

Walrus

Birds are the real wealth of Icelandic fauna. In addition to many species of ducks, gulls, and wading birds there are the rock ptarmigan, the white-tailed eagle, two species of owl, and the gyrfalcon. Most impressive are the sea-bird colonies – gannets, guillemots, razorbills, kittiwakes, fulmars and puffins – that reach saturation point on high coastal cliffs.

Freshwater fish are limited to eels, salmon, trout, and Arctic char. The seas around Iceland, which provide the country with most of its export income, are rich in

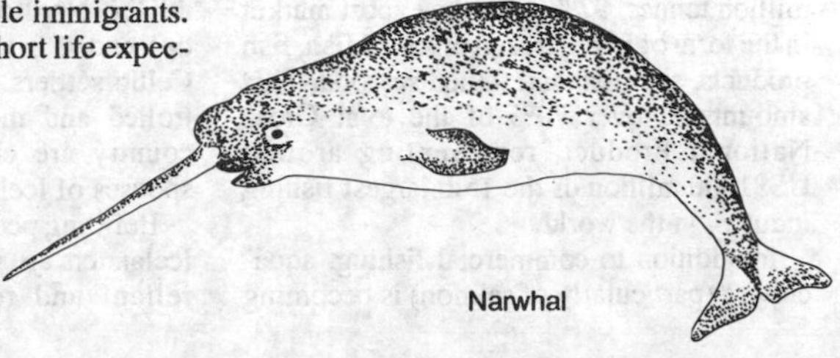

Narwhal

cod, halibut, shrimp, lemon sole, herring, lobster, haddock and whiting, to name but a few.

GOVERNMENT

Since 1944, Iceland has been a democratic republic with a president elected to 4-year terms by majority vote. Presidential duties are similar to those of the monarch in a constitutional monarchy. Legislative powers rest with the parliament, or Alþing, comprised of 63 members elected to 4-year terms from eight electoral districts. Executive functions are performed by the prime minister and a cabinet of ministers who are automatically given a seat in the Alþing. Every citizen over 20 years of age has the right to vote.

Major political parties represented in Iceland include the conservative Independence Party (27.2%), the agrarian-oriented Progressive Party (19.4%), the Social Democratic Party (15.2%), the socialist People's Alliance (13.4%), the Social Democratic Alliance (0.2%), the Women's Party (10.1%) and the Citizens' Party (10.9%). It is significant to note that support for the dominant Independence Party is rapidly declining. In the past 5 years it has lost seven seats in parliament.

Ms Vigdis Finbogadóttir, the first woman ever elected to the presidency of a democratic country, has held the office since 1980.

ECONOMY

Iceland's economy is more or less dependent on fish. A nationwide fleet of 900 vessels employs 5% of Iceland's workforce while fish processing occupies another 8%. Of the total annual catch, which averages about 1.6 million tonnes, 97% is for the export market in the form of fresh, frozen or salted fish, fish products, shellfish and tinned seafood. This amounts to over 70% of the total Gross National Product, representing around US$1000 million or the 15th largest fishing industry in the world.

In addition to commercial fishing, aquaculture (particularly of salmon) is becoming increasingly important. Trout farming comes in a distant second.

Export agriculture is limited to animal products, primarily lamb and wool although some cheese is exported. All agricultural exports combined, however, represent less than 2% of the GNP excluding manufactured woollens.

Other significant industries include geothermal power, aluminium manufacturing, diatomite mining and processing, manufacturing of fishing and fish-processing equipment.

Tourism, of course, is an important source of foreign revenue. The number of tourists visiting Iceland each year is increasing and the industry hasn't really been able to keep abreast of it. Although official arrival figures are higher because returning Icelanders and transit passengers are counted, it is estimated that 130,000 foreigners visited Iceland in 1987 and double that in 1989. From all indications, their numbers will double again by 1991.

Historically, inflation has been a problem in Iceland but in recent years it's been kept down to about 16% annually. Unemployment only runs to about 2%, however, and there is actually a labour shortage. Many people choose to work two or more jobs in order to maintain a high standard of living and Icelandic children normally start their first job around the age of 8 years. During summer school holidays, children are employed in construction, public maintenance and gardening. The government requires half their income be put away for future educational purposes.

POPULATION & PEOPLE

Iceland is the least purely Scandinavian of all the Nordic countries. Most people are descended from the early Scandinavian and Celtic settlers. Immigration is strictly controlled and most foreigners living in the country are either temporary workers or spouses of Icelandic citizens.

Befitting people living on a remote island, Icelanders are generally self-confident, self-reliant and reserved – qualities which gregarious visitors may often find difficult to cope with. Once the icy barrier has been broken, however, they are quite friendly and on Friday and Saturday nights, watch out. Many visitors are astounded by the transformation that takes place in Reykjavík pubs and discos when Icelanders decide to party!

The population, just over 250,000, is increasing by only about 1½% annually. Nearly 150,000 people, well over half the total population, live in the Reykjavík metropolitan area which is growing at a rate of about 3% annually, mostly due to continuous migration from the countryside. About 25,000 Icelanders live on farms scattered around the country while the rest live in cities and villages of 200 or more people.

Statistically, everyone is literate and the average life expectancy is the second highest in the world. The birth rate is 17.2 per thousand and because of a lack of social stigma regarding such things, over 70% of Icelandic firstborn children are to unmarried parents.

Icelandic Names

Icelanders' names are constructed using the patronymic system. That is, a person receives a Christian name from their parents and their surname is constructed from their father's (or on occasion, their mother's) Christian name. Girls add the suffix *dóttir*, meaning 'daughter', to the patronymic and boys add *son*. Therefore, Jón, the son of Einar, would be called Jón Einarsson. Guðrun, the daughter of Halldór, would be called Guðrun Halldórsdóttir. Icelandic telephone directories are alphabetised by Christian name rather than patronymic so the aforementioned Guðrun would be listed before Jón rather than the other way around.

Only about 10% of Icelanders actually have family names, most of them dating back to early Settlement times. They are rarely used, however, and the government is trying to do away with them altogether in hopes of homogenising the system. Currently, nobody is permitted to take a new family name nor can they adopt the family name of their spouse. It is also illegal to bestow non-Icelandic or foreign-sounding names.

LITERATURE

Although there was no written literature in Iceland prior to the 12th century, the bulk of medieval Icelandic literature consists of either Scandinavian poetry composed before Settlement of Iceland or works based upon historical events during the first 250 years of Icelandic history.

Although traditional Norwegian poetry eventually disappeared in its country of origin, the most popular works were carried to Iceland by early settlers and were preserved and written down during the great Literary Age of the 12th and 13th centuries.

Eddic Poetry

Early poetic works were one of two types, Eddic or Skaldic (see the Literary Era in this chapter). The Eddic poems are further subdivided into three classes: the Mythical, the Gnomic and the Heroic. It is assumed that the name of the genre originated with the title of Snorri Sturluson's compilation, the *Snorra Edda*. Some scholars believe it was derived from Oddi, the place where Snorri was educated. Others more logically see it taken from the word *óðr* which means simply 'poetry'.

The Eddic poems were composed in free variable metres with a structure very similar to that of early Germanic poetry. Mythical poetry was based on the dialogue and wisdom of the Nordic gods and was likely promoted as an intended affront to growing Christian sentiments in Norway. Gnomic poetry consists of one major work, the *Hávamál*, which both promotes and optimistically extols the virtues of the common life. The Heroic Eddas are similar in form, subject matter, and even characters to early Germanic works such as the *Nibelungenlied* and *Beowulf*.

Skaldic Poetry

Skaldic poetry, which was developed and composed exclusively in Scandinavia, has a better defined structure than Eddic. It probably first appeared in western Norway, composed by skalds ('court poets') to praise and celebrate the acts of the kings. Over the years, as the genre grew in popularity, other themes were introduced.

The Skaldic poems are far more descriptive than the Eddas which are predominantly dialogue and concern themselves more with the graphic details of battle, an element lacking even in the Heroic Eddas. They also employ *kennings*, vocabulary and descriptions that add colour and interest to the prose. Blood, for instance, is referred to as 'wound dew'. An arm may have been described as a 'hawk's perch' and eyes as 'jewels of the head'. The battle itself was frequently referred to as 'the Valkyries' glorious song'.

The Sagas

Without doubt, the most popular early works to come out of Iceland were the sagas. Literally translated into Old English, the word *saga* means 'saw', referring to something said (as in 'an old saw'), and is from the same root as 'sage'.

There were several types of sagas written in medieval Europe but Iceland was primarily concerned with 'family sagas', tales of early Icelandic settlers and their struggles, battles, heroics, human relations, religion, and occupations. While they are obviously derived from nearly equal parts of fact and fabrication, the historical information and the entertainment they have provided over the ages have set them apart as the most developed form of medieval European literature.

One of the best known, *Egills Saga*, is a biography of the Viking skald, Egill Skallagrímsson. It has been attributed to Snorri Sturluson, Iceland's greatest historian. Other favourite works include the saga of Grettir the Strong, *Grettirs Saga*, about a superhuman outlaw; the *Laxdaela Saga*, the tragic account of a family in north-west Iceland; and *Njálls Saga*, whose relatively lovable characters make it the most popular of all.

The family sagas were originally written in Old Norse, the common language of Scandinavia at the time. While Norwegian, Danish, and Swedish have developed through the centuries and felt the influence of other languages, Icelandic has hardly changed since Viking times. For that reason, Icelanders of all ages read the sagas in their original form for both their historical and entertainment value. Imagine an average English speaker being able to read and enjoy Chaucer's works as easily as a magazine.

Snorri Sturluson Like the Eddas and unlike the Skaldic poems, most of the sagas were written anonymously. Egills Saga, however, has been attributed to Snorri Sturluson of Reykholt in Borgarfjördur, one of the greatest figures in Icelandic literary history. Snorri, who was born in 1179, descended from the famous Snorri Godi of Helgafell, the Sturlungs (who lent their name to the violent and chaotic period of Icelandic history between 1200 and 1262), and the notorious Viking skald, Egill Skallagrímsson himself.

He was reared and educated at Oddi around Borgarfjörður and married the heiress of Borg, the estate of Egill Skallagrímsson. At the age of 36 he was appointed the lögsögumaður of the Alþing and gained wealth and power travelling abroad. On one trip, he came into favour with Scandinavian royalty and made the unfortunate mistake of accepting the task of using his power to actively promote royal interests in Iceland.

Upon returning home to Reykholt, Snorri was again appointed lögsögumaður but found himself so busy writing he couldn't be bothered to turn up at the annual political conventions. During this period he was most prolific, turning out a large body of work which included the *Snorra Edda* and, it is presumed, *Egills Saga*.

Unfortunately, Snorri had apparently forgotten the deal he'd made with the Norwegian king. He'd unofficially given up his position of influence in the government and was unable to keep his side of the bargain, anyway. The king had not forgotten, however, and sent out a decree demanding Snorri's return to Norway – dead or alive. The ambitious jarl Gíssur Þorvaldsson, who aspired to the governorship of Iceland, visited Reykholt, with a contingency of 70 armed men on the night of 23 September 1241. Aware of the danger, Snorri hid. A priest who had been assured that no harm would come to the writer, revealed his whereabouts to the jarl who found him and hacked him to death.

Modern Literature

Currently, Iceland publishes the greatest number of books per capita in the world – mostly translated works of foreign authors – in hopes of keeping its language alive. It also has made some significant contributions to modern literature. During the late 1800s, Jón Sveinsson (Nonni), a priest from Akureyri, wrote a vast body of juvenile literature in German that was subsequently translated into 40 languages. Just after him, Jóhann Sigurjónsson wrote *Eyvind of the Hills*, the biography of the 18th-century outlaw Fjalla-Eyvindar which was later made into a film.

Halldór Laxness

The best known Icelandic writer of the current century is Nobel Prize winning Halldór Laxness. He was born in Reykjavík in 1902 but, at the age of 3 years, moved with his family to the farm Laxness, from which he took his nom de plume.

In 1919, he began the travelling that was to characterise much of his later life. After wandering and writing around Scandinavia he went to Germany, converted to Catholicism, and joined a monastery in Luxembourg. There he wrote his first novel, *Under the Holy Mountain*. After becoming disillusioned with life as an ascetic, he meandered slowly back to Iceland and then to Italy where he wrote of his disaffection with the church and his increasingly leftist leanings in *The Great Weaver from Kashmir*.

When the work reached Iceland, it was highly acclaimed but, by this time, Laxness was in Canada. At this stage he decided to visit Hollywood and have a go at the fledgling film industry. There he wrote *Salka-Valka*, one of his greatest works, as a screenplay. After seeing the suffering caused by the Great Depression of the 1930s in America, he became a Communist sympathiser. Under threat of deportation he bought a ticket to Germany and fled the USA.

Laxness became so taken with the Communist party that he attended the 1937 purge trials in Moscow and deliberately misrepresented them in his writings (by his own later admission) because he could not bring himself to defame the system in which he had placed all his hope and trust.

Most of Laxness' works deal with everyday life in Iceland or thinly disguised autobiographical details. *Independent People* describes the harsh conditions under which the average Icelanders lived, especially the common folk on the farms and in fishing villages. Quite a few Icelanders disputed his observations, but their complaints were primarily motivated by national pride and their reluctance to publicise Iceland's relative backwardness.

His other major novels based on Icelandic life include *The Fish Can Sing* and *The Atom Station*. The former is an exposé of life on the farm and the latter, written almost prophetically in 1948, is about American military presence in Iceland, conflicting political ideologies, and the threat of nuclear proliferation. In 1955, Laxness won the Nobel Prize for Literature.

In 1962, he wrote *A Poet's Time*, which recanted everything he'd ever written praising the Communist party. By this time, he had resettled in Reykjavík and apparently had been mellowed by his wealth of experience with fanaticism on both ends of the spectrum.

MUSIC

The pop music world was astounded in 1986 when the Icelandic band the Sugarcubes arrived on the scene. Iceland? Wasn't that where tinned fish came from? But anyone who'd visited Iceland in the previous 5 years wouldn't have been so surprised since from the early '80s, there were lots of spiky-topped teenagers with multicoloured hair wandering in the streets of Reykjavík. Many seemed to be members of some garage band or other, and frequently put on fairly wild shows in little halls. All this activity certainly wasn't listed as one of the country's prime tourist attractions. Eventually though, it all came together in the form of the Sugarcubes.

Icelandic pop music can be sampled (before you go to Iceland) on the compilation *World Domination or Death*, try to get to some garage performances while you're there. You never know, you might just catch the successors to the Sugarcubes in action!

HOLIDAYS & FESTIVALS

Icelandic Public Holidays

The public holidays in Iceland include:

1 January
New Year's Day
March or April
Maundy Thursday
Good Friday
Easter Sunday
Easter Monday
21 April
First Day of Summer
1 May
Labour Day
12 May
Ascension Day
May
Whitsunday
Whitmonday
17 June
Independence Day
First week in August
Shop & Office Workers' Holiday
9 October
Leif Eiríksson Day
24 December (afternoon)
Christmas Eve
25 December
Christmas
26 December
Boxing Day
31 December (afternoon)
New Year's Eve

Festivals

Pre-Lenten celebrations include *Bolludagur*, the Monday before Shrove Tuesday, when children receive cream buns by pestering adults with coloured sticks. Shrove Tuesday (Mardi Gras) itself is called *Sprengidagur* but instead of pigging out on junk food, Icelanders serve a traditional meal of salted mutton and pea soup. On Ash Wednesday children are again given licence to menace adults, this time by sneaking up and tying sacks of ash on their backs.

The largest nationwide festival of the year is Independence Day on 17 June, the day in 1944 on which Iceland gained full independence from the Danish crown. The biggest celebration is in Reykjavík where there are parades, street music and dancing, outdoor theatre, colourful costumes, and general merriment. Tradition has it that the sun is not supposed to shine on this day, perhaps a psychological concession to what normally happens anyway.

Icelandic independence is also celebrated on a smaller scale on 1 December to commemorate the day in 1918 when Iceland initially became an independent state within the Kingdom of Denmark.

Sometime during the first week in June, Icelanders celebrate *Sjómannadagurinn*, or Sailors' Day, which is dedicated to seafarers. Sailors all take a holiday and the Seamen's Union sponsors celebrations in every port city. In smaller coastal towns, this is often the greatest party of the year (surpassing even Independence Day – probably because it comes first!). Participants compete in rowing and swimming contests, tugs-of-war, sea rescue, etc, and medals are awarded for the past year's rescue operations.

Midsummer is celebrated on 24 June in Iceland but at a decidedly lower level than on the Scandinavian mainland. It's still another excuse for drunken partying and few miss the opportunity. As tradition has it, the Midsummer Night's dew has magical healing powers and that to roll naked in it will cure 19 different health problems. If you plan to try it, however, be warned that it never gets dark in Iceland on Midsummer Night so you could be open to public scrutiny.

Around Midsummer, the founding of the ancient bishoprics of Skálholt and Hólar is marked in those locations with solemn commemorative services.

Interestingly, the first day of summer, or

home or visit Greenland or the Faroes and wait for results. Employers can sometimes convey a sense of urgency that will help hasten the procedure.

The highest paying jobs are on fishing boats; these are hard to come by and normally go to friends and relatives of the fisherfolk. Most foreigners will probably find themselves slopping fish guts 8 hours a day for wages only slightly higher than could be earned doing similar jobs in western Europe, Australia, or the USA (and well below what the average Icelander earns). Some companies include food and/or accommodation in the deal which, given Icelandic prices, will at least double official earnings.

CUSTOMS

Visitors are permitted to bring up to 10 kg of food provided it doesn't include meat products, eggs or milk. Anyone bringing recreational fishing equipment, including rubber boots and waders, must present a certificate from a veterinarian in their home country stating that the equipment has been disinfected by immersion, for at least 10 minutes, in a 2% formaldehyde solution. Alternatively, customs officials can disinfect it upon arrival in the country. In theory, this is to prevent contamination of Icelandic waters by foreign fish diseases.

Travellers over 20 years of age can import duty-free 1 litre of spirits (less than 47% alcohol content) and 1 litre of wine (less than 21%) or 6 litres of foreign beer (instead of wine or spirits). Those aged over 15 years can bring in 200 cigarettes or 250 g of other tobacco products.

If you are bringing a motor vehicle to Iceland, you must present registration, proof of international insurance, and a driving licence. A motor vehicle permit will be issued for the time of your stay but vehicles cannot be sold in Iceland without payment of import duty. Those who are employed in Iceland must pay the duty regardless of the length of stay.

Icelandic customs forbid the importation of firearms, narcotics, telephones or live animals and plants without special permission. In the case of firearms, permission must be granted from the Chief of Police. Plant importers must carry a plant hygiene certificate for each plant from the country of origin as well as a permit from the Icelandic Ministry of Agriculture. Animals will only be admitted with permission of the Ministry of Agriculture's long-term quarantine.

MONEY

The Icelandic unit of currency is the *króna* (Ikr) which is equal to 100 *aurar*. Notes come in 100, 500, 1000, and 5000 króna denominations. Coins come in 1, 5, 10, and 50 króna, and 5, 10 and 50 aurar denominations which are practically worthless. Inflation is about 16% annually and, although the devaluation seems to be slowing, prices throughout the Iceland section of this book will be given in US$.

Foreign Exchange

Foreign-denomination travellers' cheques, postal cheques, and banknotes may be exchanged for Icelandic currency at any bank. A commission of about US$2.50 will be charged for any such transaction, regardless of the amount changed. Any leftover króna may be exchanged for foreign currency before you leave but, occasionally, a bank will ask you to produce exchange receipts for the amount desired.

After-hours banking is available at Keflavík International Airport daily between 6.30 am and 6.30 pm and at the Hotel Loftleiðir (Reykjavík City Airport) daily from 8.15 am to 7 pm (except Sundays in winter). During non-banking hours, hotels will also exchange foreign currency but they are likely to charge a higher commission than the bank.

Major credit cards (Visa, MasterCard, Diners Club, American Express, Eurocard, etc) will be accepted at most places. Icelanders are plastic mad and use cards even for buying groceries and other small purchases. Credit cards can also be used at banks to purchase cash. Eurocard (tel 91-685499), Visa (tel 91-671700), American Express (tel

91-26611), and Diners Club (tel 91-28388) all have service offices in Reykjavík.

The exchange rates at the time of writing were approximately:

A$1	=	Ikr45
C$1	=	Ikr48
Dkr1	=	Ikr9.6
DM1	=	Ikr36
US$1	=	Ikr55

Tax

Sales Tax Icelandic sales tax is 15% and is included in marked prices. New legislation passed in 1988, however, relieves foreigners of some of the sting if the items purchased amount to at least US$55 (Ikr3000) per sales ticket. They must be bought in specially designated shops and exported within 30 days of purchase. Participating shops will have a sign saying *Iceland Tax-Free Shopping*.

In order to collect the 13% to 15% refund, you must fill out a refund voucher at the time of purchase including your name, address, and passport number. Present all items purchased (except woollens which may be packed in your luggage) and your refund vouchers at the Keflavík International Airport duty-free shop at your time of departure. The refund will be made in Icelandic króna.

Those leaving from any other point of departure should show their items and voucher to the customs official who will arrange to have the refund sent to you in your home currency within 3 months.

Departure Tax Iceland levies a airport departure tax of US$17 (Ikr950) which is paid when airline tickets are issued.

TOURIST INFORMATION

Tourist Offices

The Icelandic tourist information offices are very helpful and can load you down with more booklets, brochures and maps than anyone would want to cart around. Employees will normally speak Scandinavian languages, English, and German and there

will be at least one person who speaks French as well. All information and services are free although a small charge may be made for telephone calls made on your behalf. National park brochures and commercial maps are sold at bookshop prices.

In addition to providing information, they will book tours, sell bus passes, and make advance hotel and transport reservations. There are official information offices in Reykjavík (two locations), Vík, Kirkjubaejarklaustur, Höfn, Seyðisfjörður, Mývatn (Reykjahlíð), Húsavík, Akureyri, Sauðarkrókur, Ísafjörður, Stykkishólmur, and Akranes. The camping ground in Reykjavík offers much of the same services but with more emphasis on the budget end of the market.

For information before you leave home, contact one of the following government information centres:

Iceland Tourist Board
    Laugavegur 3, 101 Reykjavík, Iceland
Tourist Information Centre
    Ingólfsstraeti 5, 101 Reykjavík, Iceland
Iceland Tourist Board 655 Third Avenue, New York, NY 10017 USA
Isländisches Fremdenverkehrsamt
    Brönnerstrasse 11, 6000 Frankfurt-Main, Germany

Foreign Embassies & Consulates

The following is a partial listing of representatives of foreign governments in Reykjavík:

Austria
    Austurstraeti 17 (tel 91-24016)
Belgium
    Hverfisgata 6 (tel 91-20000)
Brazil
    Hverfisgata 4 (tel 91-11500)
Canada
    Skúlagata 20 (tel 91-25355)
China (PRC)
    Víðimelur 29 (tel 91-26751)
Denmark
    Hverfisgata 29 (tel 91-621230)
Finland
    Vatnagarðar 4 (tel 91-85044)
France
    Grundarstígur 12 (tel 91-20222)
Germany
    Túngata 18 (tel 91-19535)
Greece
    Reynimelur 62 (tel 91-19621)
Irish Republic
    Þverholt 17-21 (tel 91-26300)
Israel
    Sundagarðar 4 (tel 91-685300)
Italy
    Rauðarárstígur 1 (tel 91-11644)
Japan
    Síðmúli 39 (tel 91-82800)
Mexico
    Garðastraeti 6 (tel 91-27977)
Norway
    Ánanaust, Grandagarður (tel 91-28855)
Portugal
    Sundaborg 42 (tel 91-686166)
Spain
    Laugavegur 170-172 (tel 91-211240)
Sweden
    Lágmúli 7 (tel 91-82022)
Switzerland
    Austurstraeti 6 (tel 91-24210)
United Kingdom
    Laufásvegur 49 (tel 91-15883)
USA
    Laufásvegur 21 (tel 91-29100)
USSR
    Garðastraeti 33 (tel 91-15156)

When to Visit

Every year on 15 August, someone puts on the brakes and Icelandic tourism grinds slowly to a halt. Hotels close, youth hostels and camping grounds shut down and buses stop running. Many late summer travellers are disappointed to find that all the most popular attractions are practically inaccessible by 15 September and, by 30 September, it seems, the country has gone into hibernation.

Although it's safe to predict that this will change in coming years – there are still a lot of foreign stragglers running around in September – at present it's a good idea to plan your holiday with this in mind.

GENERAL INFORMATION

Post

The Icelandic postal system is both reliable and efficient and rates are comparable to those in other western European countries.

Poste Restante is available in all cities and villages but the central post office on Pósthússtraeti in Reykjavík is best set-up to handle it. Tell potential correspondents to capitalise your surname and send mail to Poste Restante, Central Post Office, Reykjavík, Iceland.

Telephone

Public telephone offices are affiliated with the postal system in Iceland as Póstur og Simí. Both services normally occupy the same buildings. You'll wait about 5 minutes for an international call from any telephone office and can make reverse-charge calls to many countries.

Direct dialling is available via satellite to Europe, North America and elsewhere. After dialling the international access code (90 from Iceland), dial the country code, area or city code, and the telephone number. If you're calling from elsewhere, Iceland's international country code is (354). Other countries' codes are listed in Icelandic telephone directories. If you need operator assistance in Iceland, dial (09). The number for directory assistance is (08).

Telefax services are available at communications offices in Reykjavík and most other places around the country. The telefax number in Reykjavík is 91-25901.

MEDIA

The catalyst for the development of Icelandic radio and television was American propaganda, broadcast from Keflavík as early as 1961. It bombarded the people with the US military's one-sided view of the world and was so effective at manipulating public opinion, that the Icelandic government decided to offer more objective, alternative broadcasting.

Until 1988, Iceland had only one radio station and one television station, both state-operated, but now there are several competing independent stations. On radio, a variety of formats is broadcast on FM at 93.5 and 99.9 (both state stations), and at 98.9 and 102.2. The US military radio is at AM 1485.

During June, July, and August daily at 7.30 am, station 93.5 FM broadcasts an English language news translation. A recorded version of this broadcast is available by phoning (tel 91-693690).

There are two television stations operating during some afternoon and evening hours. Many of the programmes deal with Icelandic themes but subtitled British and American programming dominates prime time.

The only English language newspaper, *News From Iceland*, is published monthly primarily for the benefit of second and third generation Icelandic emigrants to Britain, the USA, and Canada. If you're interested in subscribing, write to Höfdabakki 9, PO Box 8576, 128 Reykjavík, Iceland. The annual subscription rate is US$24.

A variety of German and English-language periodicals, including the news magazines *Time*, *Newsweek* and *Der Spiegel*, is available at Eymundsson's in Reykjavík and at Bókaverslunin Edda in Akureyri.

FOOD

You can minimise the sting of Iceland's food prices by self-catering and eating seafood products. The least expensive prepared foods are available at petrol stations and snack kiosks. For a light meal of chips and sausage with trimmings you'll pay around US$3.50.

Self-Catering

Every town and village has at least one *kaupfélagi*, or cooperative supermarket, your key to inexpensive dining in Iceland. The most economical chain is Hagkaup in south-western Iceland.

Since the country produces so few of its own consumer goods, Icelandic groceries come from all over the world. Consequently, expect to pay about twice what you would in the USA, Australia, or Britain and three times what you'd pay in Germany. You could live on tinned fish and coffee – they're cheap!

Icelandic greenhouse produce is very good but imported vegies are normally already past their peak when they hit the supermarkets. Street stands seem to offer the best value for fresh fruit and vegetables.

Supermarkets are open during normal shopping hours. In the evenings, on Saturday afternoons, and on Sundays you'll have to resort to smaller and higher priced convenience stores. Petrol stations normally sell basic groceries, also.

Youth hostels nearly always have a 'common food' shelf where you can use leftovers donated by onward-bound travellers. For those in dire financial straits, these can provide condiments, macaroni, margarine, and powdered soup mixes (but, of course, only hostel guests are welcome to partake).

Fast Food

Apart from the Pizza Hut in Reykjavík and a couple of Kentucky Fried clones in Akureyri, fast food hasn't really caught on in Iceland. You will find numerous snack bars and kiosks where you can grab some instant sustenance and, in smaller towns, the least expensive eateries will invariably be at the petrol stations which serve chips, sausages, sandwiches, doughnuts, ice cream, and coffee.

In larger towns and cities, you'll find street kiosks selling the same things as well as pizza, pastries, and other pre-packaged-pop-it-in-the-microwave sort of items.

Smorgasbord

In Reykjavík and Akureyri, a couple of good-value restaurants offer all the bread, soup, and salad you can eat for around US$12. Iceland caught on to US-style salad bars when greens-starved foreigners resorted to nibbling on the grass. Although Icelanders still aren't big salad fans, these places are growing more popular with young people and travellers seem to flock to them.

Cafes & Pubs

Reykjavík and a couple of other towns have small and intimate pub-style cafes where you can drink beer, eat a relatively cheap meal, or just sit, talk, and drink coffee for hours on end without attracting comment. Some may seem a bit pretentious, but they nearly always have interesting decor and you can expect to hear 60s and 70s music playing in the background. They serve some of the best food available in Iceland and you'll pay only about US$12 for a filling meal with juice or a soft drink.

Restaurants

The word 'restaurant' in Iceland refers to an up-market establishment. Nearly every town has at least one restaurant but, in smaller places, it's normally associated with the hotel and is drab.

An average restaurant meal in Iceland will consist of some meat dish (beef, lamb, chicken or fish), boiled potatoes bathing in an anonymous sauce, tinned vegetables, a brothy soup (I couldn't find any difference between curry soup, cream of chicken, or the ubiquitous cream of asparagus). If you're lucky, there'll also be some kind of cabbage-based salad.

Lunches, especially in hotel restaurants, are often served cafeteria-style and offer a choice of only one 'daily special' and a limited selection of salads, fruit, breads and pastries on the side.

Icelanders display very little imagination

when it comes to pepping up their food. About the only spices you're likely to encounter are paprika (on the chips) and a sprinkle or two of dried parsley. As you can imagine, such fare is not exactly bursting with flavour. If you're looking for something a bit more exciting, you'll have to either prepare it yourself or spend a lot of money in ethnic restaurants.

In Reykjavík, there are some foreign restaurants including Italian, Spanish, Japanese, Indian and Chinese but, even then, the flavours you'd normally associate with such foods are toned down. Icelanders just don't seem to like spicy foods.

For a restaurant meal anywhere in Iceland, don't plan on spending any less than US$30 per person. If you order wine, the price will spiral even higher and, after the service charge is added, will be halfway into orbit.

Traditional Foods

Although most of Iceland's traditional delicacies may remind foreigners of the nightmare feast in *Indiana Jones and the Temple of Doom*, they really aren't as bad as they sound and a few are even quite good.

The one glaring exception is *hákarl*, putrefied shark meat that has been buried in sand and gravel for 3 to 6 months to assure sufficient decomposition. Even birds that usually eat carrion won't touch this stuff so it can be buried anywhere. It reeks like a cross between week-old 'road kill' and ammonia cleaner and most foreigners fail to appreciate its appeal. After I got past the smell and managed to swallow a microscopic chunk, I wasn't surprised to find it as repulsive as expected. Don't take my word for it, though. After trying the hákarl you'll be able to enjoy almost anything.

So how about *hrútspungur*, rams' testicles pickled in whey? Or *svið*, singed sheep's head (complete with eyes!) sawn in two, boiled, and eaten either fresh or pickled? And then there's *blóðmör*, sheep's blood pudding packed in suet and sewn up in the diaphragm or stomach. In one variation, *lifrapylsa*, sheep's liver rather than blood is used.

Moving toward the less bizarre, Icelanders make a staple of *harðfiskur*, haddock which is cleaned and dried in the open air until it has become dehydrated and brittle. It is torn into strips and eaten with butter as a snack. On Christmas Day, they traditionally serve *hangikjöt*, smoked lamb, and *flatkökur*, unleavened bread charred on a grill or griddle without fat. Traditional Christmas Eve fare is *rjúpa*, tough, well-ripened ptarmigan served in milk gravy.

Icelanders also eat broiled *lundi*, or puffin, which looks and tastes like calves' liver. (Puffins are those charming but awkward little birds that look like a cross between a penguin and a toucan.)

Whale blubber, whale steaks, and seal meat are also available from time to time but you'll have to be on the lookout for them if you haven't any objections to trying them.

The unique Icelandic treat is *skyr*. It was originally brought from Scandinavia at the time of Settlement and has become an institution with both Icelanders and visitors. Few dislike this yoghurt-like concoction made of pasteurised skim milk, and a bacteria culture similar to that used to make sourdough. Despite its rich and decadent flavour, it's actually low in fat. It is often mixed with sugar, fruit flavours, and milk to give it a creamy, pudding-like texture.

Dairy Products

One problem many travellers seem to share is the inability to identify the numerous dairy products available. It seems they are all packaged similarly and the Icelandic words printed on them bear little resemblance to their English counterparts. Non-Icelandic speakers often buy three milk-carton shaped containers before they find one actually containing milk. If you'd prefer to avoid that experience, the following list may help:

nymjólk – whole milk
lettmjólk – low-fat milk
undan renna – skim milk
syrmjólk – thick, smooth sour milk
skyr – yoghurt-like concoction made from yeast culture, sometimes mixed with fruit flavours

rjómi – cream
rjómaskyr – skyr mixed with cream
jógúrt – yoghurt
ab mjólk – acidophilus/bacillus milk
mysa – whey
sýrdur rjómi – sour cream
ídýfa – sour-cream dip
smámál – 'small meal' similar to yoghurt
kotasaela – cottage cheese
smjör – butter
smjörvi – low-fat butter mixed with oil to make it creamy
smjörliki – margarine

DRINKS

Coffee & Alcohol

A 500 g bag of good coffee in Iceland costs about US$2. A cup of coffee will cost anywhere between US$1 and US$2 but you'll normally get at least one refill without extra charge.

Alcohol is another matter. The only type of beer that's both readily available and inexpensive (US$1.30 per can) is the weak 2.2% swill. You can't drink it fast enough to feel it.

Beer, wine, and spirits are available from licensed bars, restaurants and *áfengisbúðs*, or State Monopoly shops, around the country. These are open for very limited hours: from 2 to 6 pm Monday to Thursday, 11.30 am to 6 pm on Fridays, and not at all on weekends. There are four shops in Reykjavík and others in Akranes, Ólafsvík, Akureyri, Ísafjörður, Sauðárkrókur, Siglufjörður, Seyðisfjörður, Vestmannaeyjar, Selfoss, and Keflavík. You must be aged 20 or over to buy alcohol anywhere.

The following sample alcohol prices should give you some idea of what you're up against in pubs and restaurants: a glass of house wine costs between US$4.50 and US$5. A 350-ml bottle of beer costs the same on average but can go as high as US$6 in some trendy pubs. The same goes for a shot of spirits. A 350-ml bottle of red table wine costs a minimum of US$14.50 and the cheapest 750 ml bottle will be over US$30.

Fortunately, you're allowed up to 8 litres of domestic beer or 6 litres of imported beer duty-free when entering the country. Imported wines and liquors are available for a quarter of the pub price in the áfengisbúð.

The traditional alcoholic brew is called *brennivín* (meaning 'burnt wine'), an Icelandic schnapps made from potatoes and flavoured with caraway. Its nickname *svarti dauði*, or 'black death', may offer some clues about its character. It tastes a bit like vodka and is at least as potent. This can be a blessing since it's normally administered therapeutically to those who manage to choke down a bite of the previously mentioned hákarl. Even light brennivín consumption has been known to cause excruciating after effects so exercise restraint if you have something important to do the next day.

BOOKS & BOOKSHOPS

Iceland enjoys 100% literacy and, since most people speak both English and German as well as Icelandic, Icelanders have access to much of the world's literature. Reykjavík, it seems, has a bookshop on every corner. Akureyri, home to 14,000 people, has three. Every other settlement of any size will have at least one place to buy books.

The good news is that these places all sell some foreign-language titles. The bad news is that books, even paperbacks, are very expensive in Iceland, costing more than they would in the USA, Britain, or Australia. A couple of shops around the country sell second-hand books, including one in Reykjavík where paperback titles in any language cost from US$1 to US$4.

Since Iceland publishes more books per capita than any other country and imports many foreign publications, a good variety of books is available. You can spend hours perusing the Iceland-related publications alone.

History & Society

Many titles dealing with history and society are available in Iceland, many in English, but the following may be found overseas.

Northern Sphinx – Iceland & the Icelanders from the Settlement to the Present by Sigurður A Magnússon (McGill Queen's University Press, 1977). Although it's a bit dated, this is the most easily digestible of the several books dealing with Icelandic people, places, history, and issues.

Daughter of Fire – A Portrait of Iceland by Katherine Scherman (Little, Brown, & Co, 1976). This is a creatively written and loosely organised description of Iceland and its history in travelogue format.

Iceland Saga by Magnús Magnússon (The Bodley Head, 1987). This is an entertaining and unpretentious introduction to Icelandic history and literature by the host of the British TV quiz *Mastermind.* It identifies and explains saga events and settings in English and will prove a valuable source of information for travellers.

Letters from High Latitudes by Lord Dufferin (The Merlin Press London, 1989). This account of the voyage of the sailing schooner *Foam* to Iceland, Jan Mayan, and Spitsbergen in 1856 is a fascinating and entertaining read. It was written in a state of wide-eyed wonder that still seems to absorb travellers through the region. This book, in particular, would help renew your enthusiasm if you're holed up on a dreary day!

Last Places – A Journey in the North by Lawrence Millman (Houghton Mifflin Co, Boston, 1990). In a successful attempt to transplant Bruce Chatwin's *In Patagonia* to the North Atlantic, this book loses some credibility – so many wonderful things just don't happen to one person on a 4-month trip – but Millman is one of the best writers around and the book is entertaining and side-splitting reading. The quirky personalities so masterfully described throughout certainly brought back memories for me!

Literature

A few of the sagas, the great historical novels of medieval Iceland, are available in translation. Since they are officially anonymous works, they're found in card catalogues and bookshops under the names of their translators, in most cases Magnús Magnússon, Hermann Pálsson, or both. Available titles include *Hrafnkels Saga*, *Egills Saga*, *Laxdaela Saga*, *King Haralds Saga*, *Grettirs Saga*, and *Njálls Saga*.

Iceland's Nobel Prize-winning author Halldór Laxness has written a great body of work, much of which has been translated into English and other European languages. The most highly acclaimed of his novels are *The Atom Station*, *Salka-Valka*, *The Fish can Sing*, and *Independent People*.

The best overall book about Icelandic literature is *The History of Icelandic Literature* by Stefán Einarsson (John Hopkins Press, 1957).

Another book which Iceland-bound travellers may enjoy is Jules Verne's *Journey to the Centre of the Earth*. It includes descriptions of Reykjavík and Snaefellsjökull, the ice-covered volcano which was the gateway to the centre of the earth.

Souvenir Books

The shelves of Icelandic bookshops are packed with glossy coffee-table books on any Icelandic subject from churches and rivers to historical sites. The magazine *Iceland Review* publishes a series of picture books (with captions in 10 languages!) on the Icelandic horse, the Golden Circle, the Icelanders, Route 1 Around Iceland, and Reykjavík. Örn og Örlygur Press does a similar series covering Þingvellir, Mývatn, President Vigdis, Akureyri, Akranes, and *The Flowering Plants & Ferns of Iceland.*

Several general photography books feature the country's unusual light and landscapes. In my opinion, the nicest ones are *Iceland – A Portrait of Land & People* and *Hvitá* ('White River') both by Hjalmar Bjarðarsson, and *Iceland – the Exotic North* by Swiss photographer Max Schmid.

Most of these publications are available only in Iceland and are therefore very expensive but they make good gifts and mementoes of the country.

Guidebooks

Most descriptions of Iceland in travel guides are limited to a few pages in an overall Scandinavia guide with Iceland invariably getting last billing. Several good guidebooks are available in German, French, and Danish but in English, your choices are limited.

Iceland – The Visitors' Guide by David Williams seems to have good contents. It is geared exclusively toward those sightseeing from private vehicles which is lucky because it's a huge textbook-sized hardback and you'd need a vehicle just to lug it around.

Iceland Road Guide by Einar Guðjohnsen and Pétur Kidson Karlsson (Örn og Örlygur Press, 1988). This English translation of the popular Icelandic guidebook *Vega* is a road guide and deals only with attractions on or near the road system. The format is confusing but once you get used to it, a wealth of interesting information can be gleaned. It's primarily for those travelling by private vehicle but bus travellers will also enjoy reading titbits about farms and natural features along the way.

The Visitor's Guide to Iceland by Don Philpott (Moorland Publishing Co, 2nd edition, 1989). Its size and weight are convenient and it has lots of nice, enticing colour photos. However, it seems to be aimed primarily at those travelling in their own vehicles, and the material is disorganised and lacks solid information.

Natural Elements

Guides to nature and outdoor activities include:

Field Key to Flowering Plants of Iceland by Pat Wolseley (Thule Press, 1979). This is the best all-around field guide to Icelandic flowers.

Guide to the Geology of Iceland by Ari Trausti Guðmundsson and Halldór Kjartansson (Örn og Örlygur Press). This is an excellent introduction to the complex geological forces at work in Iceland. It explains in lay terminology the geological history and composition of Iceland's most prominent attractions.

Iceland – A Handbook for Expeditions by Tony Escritt (Iceland Information Centre of London, 1985) This is a preparation and procedure guide for those doing wilderness expeditions, technical climbs, and glacier travel.

Iceland Breakthrough by Paul Vander-Molen (Oxford Illustrated Press, 1985). This is the book version of the *National Geographic* video about a kayak and ultralight trip down the Jökulsá á Fjöllum. The river descent, however, which is referred to as 'exploration', is through an easily accessible area frequently negotiated by tour buses. It's good reading nevertheless.

Gönguleiðir á Íslandi by Einar Guðjohnsen (Örn og Örlygur Press). This series of walking and trekking guides to Iceland is now being translated into English. Mr Guðjohnsen is particularly knowledgeable about walks in the Reykjavík area. Those who'd like to explore around Mt Esja would do well to pick up a copy – even in Icelandic – for the maps if nothing else. The best information source on the progress of the translation is Eymundsson on Austurstraeti in Reykjavík.

MAPS

The Landmaelingar Íslands (Iceland Geodetic Survey) has pretty much a monopoly on map production in Iceland. Their maps are of high quality and they offer topographic sheets and a wide variety of thematic maps.

Most travellers use the *Ferðakort 1:500,000* (touring map), the best general map of the country. If you buy it directly from Landmaelingar Íslands you'll get it for about US$6 but, in a shop, it will cost up to US$12. Other maps of theirs which may prove useful to visitors are the 1:5000 map of Reykjavík, the 1:25,000 map of Skaftafell and Þingvellir, the 1:50,000 map of Hekla, Mývatn, and Vestmannaeyjar, and their 1:100,000 coverage of Hornstrandir and the trek from Þórsmörk to Landmannalaugar to Skógar.

There are three series of topo sheets – 1:25,000, 1:50,000 and 1:100,000, which cover all of Iceland and will be useful for anyone wanting to set off on foot.

Touring atlases and maps with emphasis on population distribution, geology, vegetation, and hydrography are also available. For a catalogue, pricelist, and order form, write to Iceland Geodetic Survey (tel 354-1-681611), Laugavegur 178, PO Box 5060, 125 Reykjavík, Iceland. Maps are available from their office or at the Mál og Menning bookshop at Laugavegur 18 in Reykjavík.

ACTIVITIES

Fishing

The glossy tourist brochures like to make a big deal about salmon fishing in Iceland but they all omit one significant detail: the Icelandic salmon privately caught are among the most expensive fish on earth. A licence for one day of salmon fishing on some rivers costs – sit down, fish fans! – US$1950. That's per *day* and doesn't include a guide, transportation, or equipment hire, just the licence. The least expensive salmon rivers, under some circumstances (such as when there are no fish around!), cost around US$700 per day.

Those whose tastes (and finances) don't run so high, however, can fish for rainbow trout, sea trout, and Arctic char on a more reasonably priced voucher system. Some lakes and streams produce more fish and are therefore dearer than others. Much of the fishing done in Iceland is on privately owned farms and fishing time should be booked in advance. A good source of information is the *Veiðiflakkarinn* (Iceland Fishing Guide) which is available through Icelandic Farm Holidays (tel 354-1-623640), Baendahöllin v/Hagatorg, 107 Reykjavík, Iceland.

For further general information on fishing in Iceland, you can contact the Angling Club of Reykjavík at (tel 354-1-686050), Háaleitisbraut 68, 103 Reykjavík, Iceland.

If you're bringing fishing equipment from overseas, don't forget the disinfection requirement outlined in the Customs section in this chapter.

Hiking & Trekking

Most visitors to Iceland agree that the best way to see the country is on foot, whether on an afternoon hike or a 2-week wilderness trek. Those with the proper equipment and maps will find trekking opportunities unlimited. If the weather proves a nuisance at times, it's all part of facing Iceland on its own terms.

The best months for walking in the highlands are July and August. Earlier or later, some routes will be impassable without skis and complete winter gear. Even during the summer the weather can change in minutes and snow may fall all year round at higher altitudes. For a list of recommended equipment, see the What to Bring section in the Regional Facts for the Visitor chapter.

Lava fields can be very difficult to negotiate but strong boots will help. Ordinary sneakers or running shoes can be torn to shreds on the rough, jagged rock. When walking with children, especially in fissured areas like Mývatn and Þingvellir, beware of even small cracks in the earth which can be hundreds of metres deep.

Mountaineering

Unfortunately for rock climbers, Iceland's crumbly rock formations don't lend themselves well to technical rock climbing. There are, however, lots of opportunities for mountaineering and ice climbing but of course technical expertise and equipment are essential. Crampons, ropes, and ice axes are needed for any walk on glacial ice. Dangerous crevasses can be hidden under snow bridges and even innocent-looking snowfields may overlie rock and ice fissures. Clothing should be sufficient to withstand extreme conditions, especially on alpine climbs.

Before setting off on an expedition, check weather conditions and forecasts before leaving. Leave details of your planned itinerary and estimated time of return with a hut warden, a camping site attendant, or with the Ferðafélag Íslands (tel 91-19533), Öldugata 3, Reykjavík. Report your arrival after completing your trip and, if your plans change, notify them as soon as possible.

When travelling in the wilderness, carry a large-scale map of the applicable area, a compass, a medical kit, and a space blanket in addition to sufficient food and warm clothing.

Crossing Streams

Trekkers and mountaineers in Iceland will invariably find themselves face to face with unbridged rivers but in most cases they needn't be put off. Most streams are crossable, especially those glacier-fed braided ones that wander across the interior of the country.

Remember that constricted rivers passing through narrow passages run deep, so the widest ford is likely to be the shallowest. The swiftest and strongest current is found near the centre of straight stretches and at the outside of bends. Observe the character of the water as it flows and choose a spot with as much slack water as possible.

Never try to cross just above a waterfall and avoid crossing streams in flood – identifiable by dirty, smooth-running water carrying lots of debris and vegetation. A smooth surface indicates that the river is too deep to be crossed on foot. Basically, just use common sense – anything over thigh deep (and even that in some cases) shouldn't be considered crossable without a lot of experience and a more sophisticated technical setup.

Before attempting to cross deep or swift-running streams, be sure that you can jettison your pack in midstream if necessary. Put anything that can't get wet – camera, sleeping bag, and dry clothing – inside sturdy plastic or a waterproof stuff-sack. Unhitch the waist belt and loosen shoulder straps, remove any bulky clothing that will inhibit swimming if necessary, and remove long trousers to prevent drag against your legs and a wet heavy load afterwards. Remove your socks then replace your boots or wear running shoes brought specifically for such occasions.

After crossing, replace your socks and dry your footwear as much as possible. Since more 'legs' offer greater stability, lone hikers should use a hiking staff to probe the river bottom for the best route and to steady themselves in the current.

When crossing, face upstream and look down as little as possible or you'll be mesmerised by the current and possibly lose your balance. If there's more than one hiker, you should cross forming a wedge pointed upstream, with the people behind holding the waist and shoulder of the people at the head of the wedge.

If you do fall while crossing, don't try to stand up. Remove your pack (but don't let go of it), roll over onto your back, and point your feet downstream, then try to work your way to a shallow eddy or to the shore.

Camping

Only a small amount of land in Iceland is privately owned. If you'd like to camp on a private farm, ask the owner's permission before setting up. Apart from nature reserves, where camping is either restricted to certain areas or forbidden altogether, you're free to camp anywhere you like. Take care to keep toilet activities away from streams and surface water and use biodegradable soaps for washing up.

Due to natural fuel shortages and the long-term environmental impact, Iceland tries to discourage campfires so don't wander into the wilderness without a stove and enough fuel for the whole trip.

Swimming

Thanks to Iceland's abundance of geothermal heat, swimming is a national institution and every city and village has at least one public swimming pool (*'sundlaug'* or *'sundhöll'*). In addition, alongside all the swimming pools are jacuzzis varying in temperature from warm to near scalding. It goes without saying that many cold, rainy and windy afternoons are passed in swirling warm waters with a good book or good company.

A session in the pool and/or jacuzzi will

normally cost about US$2. A shower costs about US$1.50.

Skiing

Skiers who enjoy out-of-the-way slopes will find some pleasant no-frills skiing available in Iceland. In the winter, Nordic skiing is available throughout the country and in highland areas it continues until early July. The greatest drawbacks are the lack of winter transport in rural areas and a nearly incessant wind that can make temperatures feel much lower than they actually are.

Both Reykjavík and Akureyri have winter resorts for downhill skiing and a summer ski school operates at Kerlingarfjöll near Hofsjökull in central Iceland.

The Icelandic Horse

Although it's introduced, the Icelandic horse (*equus scandinavicus*) has been prominent in the development of the country and continues to play an important role in the autumn sheep round-up. It's small (about 133 cm high) and weighs between 390 and 400 kg, but it's a sturdy animal perfectly suited to the rough Icelandic terrain.

The first horses were brought by the early settlers. Since no other horses have been imported recently, the breeding stock remains pure. From the first years of settlement to the early part of this century, these horses were the primary form of transportation in the country. Horsefights were organised as a source of entertainment and horsemeat was banned by the church. The meat had been used in pagan rituals and consumed as a staple.

Although the utilitarian value of Icelandic horses has diminished in recent years, they are still used recreationally. Like some Mongolian breeds, they have a fifth gait called the *tölt* which is so smooth and steady that the rider barely notices any motion.

Farmhouse accommodation, tour agencies, and individual farmers rent out horses and lead horse-riding expeditions for those who'd like to see the countryside with relatively little effort. Icelandic horses are gentle by nature and even those who haven't ridden before should have no problems.

Horse tours normally cost about US$100 per day including tent or hut accommodation. If you'd rather hire a horse for a few hours riding, the standard price is US$13 per hour. Remember, if you're visiting in September, you can volunteer to help with the sheep round-up. The job normally provides room and board as well as an interesting experience working with the Icelandic horse.

THINGS TO BUY

One souvenir everyone seems to end up with is a warm and woolly Icelandic jumper (sweater, pullover, jersey...). It's often said you can identify tourists in the street because few Icelanders actually wear them as everyday attire.

The jumpers come in hundreds of different colours and patterns. The traditional ones are thicker and come in white and blue, violet, or earth tones. Not surprisingly, the demand for these is highest and they are therefore more expensive than more delicate pastel fashion sweaters.

An entire street in Reykjavík is devoted to getting woollens onto the backs of tourists.

All shops offer tax-free shopping (see the Customs section in this chapter) and competitive prices. Expect to pay about US$75 (after the tax refund) for a traditional patterned sweater of good quality. All city tours stop at the Álafoss factory outlet which is generally a bit cheaper than the tourist shops.

The Handknitting Association of Iceland has a shop at Skólavörðustígur 19 in Reykjavík and their prices are lower still, at around US$65 for a traditional sweater. Most of their merchandise is handknitted by locals earning extra money in their spare time.

Rock-bottom prices, however, can be found in the street stalls on Austurstraeti. Although quality is not consistent, you'll be able to find some garments that are as good as those in the shops for US$50 to US$55. The best indication of high-quality work is the tightness of knit around the underarm area which should not separate when the sleeve is raised. If you don't mind buying seconds, most of which have only minor flaws, you can pick them up at the airport duty-free as you enter or leave for less then US$20.

A good place to buy other souvenirs and Icelandic kitsch, if you're into such things, is Þorvaldsens Bazar at Austurstraeti 4 in Reykjavík. All their profits benefit charity.

Getting Around

AIR

Iceland's domestic airline is called Flugleiðir which means, oddly enough, 'airline'. It has operated jointly with Icelandair since 1973 and provides the country's only reliable winter transport. Due to snow and ice, most overland transport stops in winter and supplies must be carried air freight. Flugleiðir has even carried entire herds of sheep from remote pastures to winter corrals.

In summer, Flugleiðir has daily flights between Reykjavík and Akureyri, Egilsstaðir, Grímsey, Höfn, Húsavík, Ísafjörður, Sauðárkrókur, and Vestmannaeyjar. They serve small towns and villages from two to six times a week. Some flights offer discounted seats but don't advertise this, so enquire before paying the full fare. Since inclement weather can postpone or cancel flights, flexibility is essential. Don't book a flight back from Vestmannaeyjar to Reykjavík, for instance, the afternoon before you're scheduled to fly to Denmark. If the flight is cancelled, which it frequently is, you won't have time to return on the ferry and will miss your connection.

For the distances involved, domestic flights are rather expensive but, when you compare their cost with bus fares or consider the time you're saving, they look better and better. The regular airfare between Reykjavík and Akureyri, for example, is less than twice the bus fare and the flight takes 1 hour compared to 10 rough hours on the bus.

Some gaps in Flugleiðir's schedule are filled by a second airline Arnarflug (Eagle

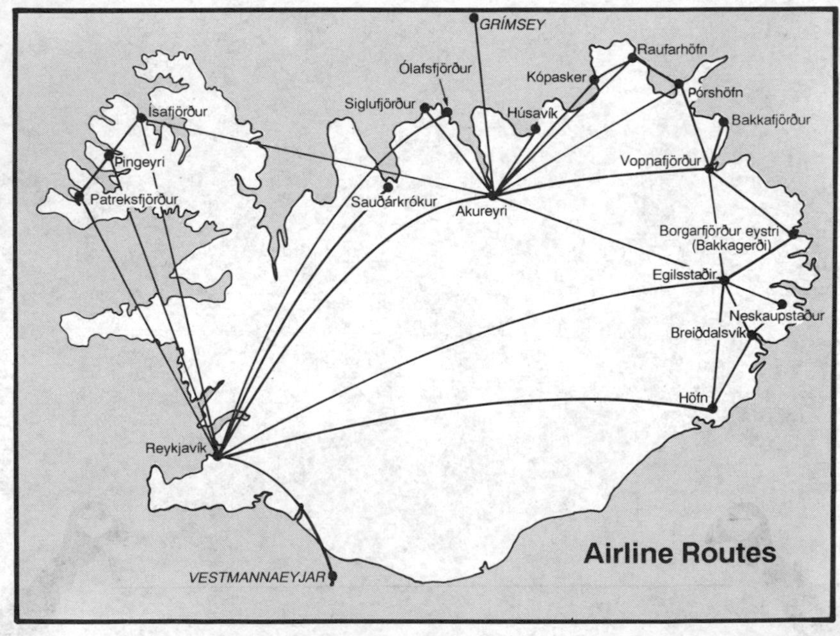

Air) which links Reykjavík with Snaefellsnes and the Westfjords.

Those travelling in larger groups may want to check out charters with Odin Air (tel 354-1-610880, Reykjavík) which operates seven, nine, and 15-passenger charter flights anywhere in the country.

BUS

Although Iceland is small and has a well developed public transport system, the interior is undeveloped and much of National Highway 1, the 'Ring Road', remains unsurfaced. There are no railways and the highway system is the least developed in Europe. In fact, the National Highway was completed as recently as 1974 (in celebration of the 1100th year of Settlement) with the bridging of the river Skeiðará near Skaftafell.

Bifreiðastöd Íslands Umferðarmiðstöðin (just BSÍ if you're in a hurry), a collective organisation of Iceland's long-distance bus lines, does a good job of covering the country in feasible, but often inconvenient ways. On the Ring Road, it's possible to travel roughly one quarter the distance around the country every day in the summer but, on minor routes, you may sometimes have to wait several days for connections.

Over half the buses stop running on 15 September and don't resume until the beginning of June. Interior routes rarely open before July but, in years of high snowfall, some don't open at all. Most are closed again by early to mid-September.

BSÍ offers two bus passes, the *Hringmiði* ('Ring Pass' or Full-Circle Pass) and the *Tímamiði* ('Time Pass' or Omnibuspass). The Full-Circle Pass is valid in the summer and enables you to do one full circuit of the Ring Road in either direction stopping anywhere you like. It costs US$170 which isn't much less than the normal fare but it entitles you to 10% discount at camping grounds, farmhouses and sleeping-bag accommodation, on ferries, and on buses not covered by the pass. It also allows small discounts on some organised tours. Discounts are not advertised or encouraged so you'll have to ask or miss out.

The Omnibuspass is good for 1 to 4 weeks and allows unrestricted travel on all but interior bus routes and a few other special routes. Some bus tours are included and significant discounts are offered on others. It's also good for the same ferry and accommodation discounts as the Full-Circle Pass.

With the 1 and 2-week passes, you'd have to do a lot of travelling to get your money's worth but the 3 and 4-week passes are good value. A 1-week pass costs US$200, 2 weeks cost US$250, 3 weeks cost US$320 and 4 weeks cost US$365.

Bus travellers can pick up a copy of the *Leiðabók* (the timetable) free of charge at any tourist office.

TAXI

Taxis which carry up to five passengers and an English, German or Scandinavian-speaking driver may be hired for sightseeing at an average cost of US$0.50 per km. They can be arranged with any Reykjavík taxi service.

BOAT

Ferry

Major ferries operating in Iceland include the *Akraborg* which connects Reykjavík and Akranes, the *Herjólfur* between Þorlákshöfn and Vestmannaeyjar, the *Baldur* between Stykkishólmur, Flatey, and Brjánslaekur, the Hrísey ferry on Eyjafjörður, and the *Fagranes* operating between Ísafjörður, Jökulfjörður, Ísafjarðardjúp, and Hornstrandir. The first three are car ferries and only the *Fagranes* does not operate year-round.

All ferry trips are relatively smooth except the Vestmannaeyjar route on which some sort of motion sickness preparation would be advisable for those who are prone to getting sick. On rough days, the Hornstrandir trip may also present problems.

Ferry schedules, which are designed to coincide with bus arrival and departure times, are outlined in detail in the *Leiðabók* timetable. Holders of bus passes and student cards are entitled to a 10% discount on fares.

DRIVING

Private Vehicles

It's easy to bring a vehicle – a car, caravan, or motorcycle – on the ferry from Europe and many long-term visitors do. Drivers must carry the vehicle's registration, insurance valid in Iceland, and a driving licence from their home country. After the vehicle is inspected, a temporary import permit will be issued if the driver isn't employed in Iceland. Vehicles can't exceed 2.5 metres in width or 13 metres in length. Those which carry 15 or more passengers aren't permitted to tow trailers.

Most Icelandic roads and highways aren't suitable for high-speed travel so it's better not to be in a hurry. You can get up to about 90 km/hour on surfaced roads but gravel will slow you down considerably. Due to excessive dust and flying rocks, some sort of headlight and radiator protection is advisable. Seat belt use, in the front seats, is compulsory in Iceland.

Those planning to travel in the interior of the country must have a 4WD vehicle and should keep in mind that there are no petrol stations or repair services anywhere on the F-numbered (interior) highway system. A suggested spares or repair kit includes extra oil, brake fluid, extra petrol, sealing compound for the radiator and petrol tank, a distributor cap, a rotor arm, a condenser, a fuel filter, a fan belt, at least two spare tyres and a puncture repair kit, spark plugs, insulated wire, fuses, and headlights.

Tool kits should include a tow rope, a shovel, a crow bar, applicable sockets and wrenches, a jack, a torch, batteries, flares, a fire extinguisher, and emergency rations. And of course, you'll need the expertise to identify all this stuff and fix any mechanical problems.

In the interior, the greatest threats are posed by unbridged rivers and drifting sand. Glacial rivers change course frequently and fords will change. Warmer days may cause excessive glacial melting and placid rivers will turn into torrents without warning.

Tyre marks leading into the water don't mean that a river can be crossed. It's a good idea to wade out into the river before attempting to cross it and check the depth and condition of the riverbed. Carry a pole to steady yourself in the current and face upstream while wading. Only cross where there are rocks or gravel, never sand. Remember that the narrowest fords are normally the deepest.

Before entering the water, remove the fan belt from your vehicle, cover the distributor and ignition system with a woollen rag, and switch off the headlights. While crossing, don't stop in midstream unless you're sure you cannot continue and want to reverse out.

While driving through areas susceptible to sandstorms (the entire interior!), it's best to travel with another vehicle and a good tow rope. Tracks become indistinguishable and even 4WD vehicles can get bogged down in a sand drift. You'll also need large-scale maps, a compass, extra rations, a shovel, as well as a means of protecting your eyes and skin from wind-driven sand.

Car Rental

The Sultan of Brunei would think twice before renting a car in Iceland. First of all, the cheapest vehicles available, compact eastern-European models, cost US$32 per day which seems reasonable until you add US$0.32 per km, 25% sales tax, compulsory insurance, and some of the world's dearest petrol to the price. Anything with 4WD will cost twice that much. Still, a lot of rental agencies in Iceland make a lot of money.

You must be at least 23 years old to rent a car from most of the following agencies:

Ás Car Rental (tel 91-29090), Skógarhlíð 12, Reykjavík
InterRent (tel 91-86915), Skeifan 9, Reykjavík
InterRent (tel 96-21715), Tryggvabraut 14, Akureyri
Arnarflug (tel 91-29577), Síðumúli 12, Reykjavík
Icelandair (tel 91-690200), Flugvallarvegur, Reykjavík
B & J (tel 91-681390), Skeifan 17, Reykjavík
Bílaleiga RVS (tel 91-19400), Sigtúni 5, Reykjavík
Geysir (tel 91-688888), Suðurlandsbraut 16, Reykjavík
ALP Bílaleigan (tel 91-43300), Hlaðbrekku 2, Kópavogur
ALP Bílaleigan (tel 91-17570), Central Bus Terminal, Reykjavík

BICYCLE

In Iceland, the wind is incessant, roads are unsurfaced, hills are steep, river crossings can be hazardous, horrid weather and sandstorms are frequent, and intimidating vehicles howl past in clouds of dust and gravel. Although Iceland doesn't lend itself well to bicycle travel, an increasing number of visitors are trying it anyway.

The first time I looked out a bus window and saw cyclists pushing their heavily loaded bikes through drifted and blowing sand in freezing 100 km/hour winds, I decided they were either masochists or uninformed about the conditions before setting out. Hard-core cyclists will find a challenge in Iceland but those after a pleasant experience should come prepared to pack up their bikes and travel by bus when the going gets this miserable.

In areas better suited to cycling such as Mývatn or urban Reykjavík and Akureyri, bicycles can be hired for around US$13 per day plus deposit. Bicycles may be carried on long-distance buses if there is space available (and there nearly always is).

HITCHING

Summer hitching in Iceland is possible but inconsistent. If there is traffic, you'll almost certainly get a ride eventually but long waits are common in the Westfjords and Snaefellsnes where the normally inclement weather often drives even the hardiest hitchers onto buses. Generally, the thinner the traffic, the higher your chances of getting a ride. Also, remember that Icelandic cars are small and most drivers are on trips themselves so it's best not to hitch in groups of more than two people. Naturally, a lot of visible luggage will put people off stopping for you.

Many tourists complain about the indifferent reception they received from Icelanders but hitchhikers are never among them. Hitching is the best way of becoming acquainted with the normally reserved locals. You'll meet some interesting and down-to-earth people on the road, especially as you move away from Reykjavík.

Anyone planning to hitch in Iceland should be equipped with the whole gamut of warm, windproof and waterproof clothing. A backpack (as opposed to 'luggable' luggage), a sleeping bag, food, and a tent are essential if you'll be hitching in remote areas.

TOURS

After observing obnoxious behaviour in some tour groups, many travellers find the idea of joining a group rather disagreeable. In Iceland, however, most of the nicest sights are in remote locations where no public transport is available. If you don't have a hardy vehicle and don't want to walk, endure difficult hitching conditions, or attempt cycling, the tours will provide the only access.

The word 'tour' is used very loosely here. Yes, a number of private operators offer hundreds of all-inclusive packages but lower-profile options are available. The least expensive and most loosely organised tours are done by BSÍ Travel, the long-distance bus company, in association with small local operators. They are run much like an ordinary bus service but stops are made at points of interest for photos and walks. Sometimes a tour guide is included. Anyone wanting to leave the tour and strike out on their own may do so at any time. Participants may leave and rejoin the tour as many times as they'd like as long as pickup arrangements are made in advance.

Those wanting to undertake some physical activity but who would rather not make their own arrangements may enjoy a hiking, trekking, horsepacking, or photography tour. There are more up-market guided bus tours in which participants sleep in tents and huts instead of hotels to keep costs to a minimum. And then, of course, there are the whirlwind deluxe tours which are 1st class in every respect except perhaps the quality of the experience.

The following operators offer some of the more adventurous and interesting tours available:

Icelandic Highland Travel (tel 91-22225), Laekjargata 3, PO Box 1622, Reykjavík. Strenuous highland expeditions and skiing, geology, mountain-biking, and trekking tours.

Guðmundur Jónasson Travel (tel 91-83222), Borgartún 34, 105, Reykjavík. High velocity bus camping tours with light hiking.

Green Tours, Kultorvet 7, DK-1175, Copenhagen, Denmark. Formerly DVL Rejser, Green Tours is a backpackers' travel agency which organises budget hiking and camping tours around Iceland and other Scandinavian countries.

Ferðafélag Íslands (tel 91-19533), Öldugata 3, 101 Reykjavík. The Icelandic Touring Club leads summer trekking trips along the most interesting tracks and routes around the country. Accommodation is in mountain huts and tents.

Úlfar Jacobsen Travel (tel 91-13499), Austurstraeti 3, PO Box 886, 101 Reykjavík. Bus-camping tours in southern Iceland with light hiking.

Dick Phillips Tours (tel 44-498-81440, Great Britain) Whitehall House, Nenthead, Alston, Cumbria, CA9 3PS, England. Hiking and bus tours to places overlooked by other companies as well as adventure-oriented tours to popular attractions.

Útivistarferðir (tel 91-14606), Grófinni 1, Reykjavík. Known in English as the Outdoor Life & Touring Club, this excellent organisation promotes outdoor appreciation in Iceland. Their 'tours' are actually more like friendly trekking trips and cover just about every corner of Iceland. They're highly recommended.

Reykjavík

Iceland's capital Reykjavík, home to 150,000 of the country's 250,000 people, is unlike any other European city. Not only is Reykjavík the world's northernmost capital, it's also one of the newest. Historically and architecturally, it's not very exciting but politically, socially, culturally, economically, and psychologically it dominates the country. Basically, everything that happens in Iceland happens in Reykjavík.

Many of the residents of Reykjavík and its environs came from somewhere else. Only 100 years ago, most of the population lived and worked on family farms. The shift from predominantly rural to decidedly urban happened very quickly.

Like some smaller American and Australian cities, Reykjavík is unconsolidated reflecting problems in city planning and coping with higher population densities. Construction, renovation, and modernisation continue. On any summer's day, footpaths are more like tunnels through scaffolding platforms and the street sounds are a cacophony of the pounding, digging, and grinding of machinery. If the trend toward urbanisation continues unabated and Reykjavík keeps expanding at its current rate of about 2,000 people annually, it should usurp even more of Iceland's identity in coming years.

History

Reykjavík was the first place in Iceland to be intentionally settled. The original settler, Ingólfur Arnarson, tossed his high-seat pillars overboard in 874, and built his farm at the place where they washed ashore, between the small lake Tjörn ('the pond') and the sea, where Áðalstraeti now intersects with Suðurgata. He called the place Reykjavík, or 'smoky bay', due to steam rising from nearby geothermal features. Ingólfur claimed the entire south-west corner of the island then set about planting his hayfields at Austurvöllur, the present town square.

As other settlers arrived, Reykjavík grew and Ingólfur's descendants multiplied. In 1226, an Augustinian monastery was constructed on the offshore island of Viðey and began to accumulate land and power. The manor farm of Bessastaðir, now the official residence of Iceland's head of state, became crown property when Iceland was absorbed by Norway in 1262 and, by 1613, when the government took over the Viðey monastery, a small fishing village had already begun to develop.

In the mid 1700s, sheriff and businessman Skúli Magnússon decided to establish local industries in the hope that Iceland could overcome the trade barriers imposed by the Danish Trade Monopoly of 1602. In 1752, he set up weaving, tanning, rope-making, and wool-dyeing factories which attracted labour from surrounding farms.

On 18 August 1786, when the Royal Danish government granted Reykjavík a charter as a market town, it had a population of 167. After the rural bishoprics were abolished and Iceland was made subject to the protestant Danish church, Reykjavík became the theological centre of Iceland. The stone Lutheran cathedral was completed in 1796 and, shortly after that, the Alþing was moved from Þingvellir to Reykjavík.

Skúli Magnússon built his home and weaving firm in Reykjavík and laid out

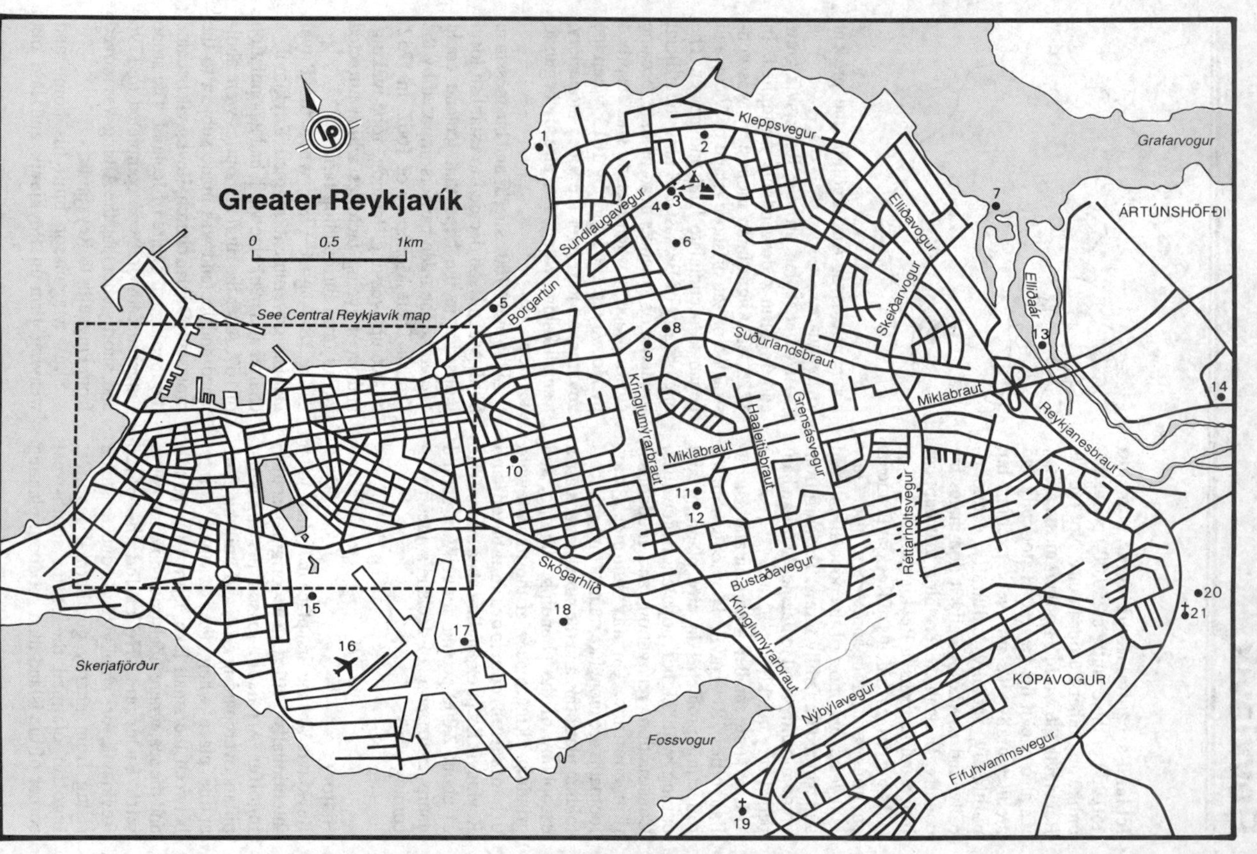
Greater Reykjavík
0
0.5
1km
See Central Reykjavík map
Kleppsvegur
Grafarvogur
ÁRTÚNSHÖFÐI
Sundlaugavegur
Elliðavogur
Skeiðarvogur
Elliðaár
Borgartún
Suðurlandsbraut
Miklabraut
Reykjanesbraut
Kringlumýrarbraut
Haaleitisbraut
Grensásvegur
Miklabraut
Réttarholtsvegur
Skógarhlíð
Bústaðavegur
Kringlumýrarbraut
Skerjafjörður
KÓPAVOGUR
Nýbýlavegur
Fossvogur
Fífuhvammsvegur
1
2
3
4
5
6
7
8
9
10
11
12
13
14
15
16
17
18
19
20
21

1 Sigurjón Ólafsson Museum
2 Cinema
3 Camping Ground & Youth Hostel
4 Laugardalur Swimming Pool
5 Höfði House
6 Laugardalur Sports Centre
7 Pleasure Boat Port
8 Askur Restaurant
9 Hotel Esja & Pizza Hut
10 Kjarvalsstaðir
11 Kringlan Centre (Hard Rock Cafe & Hagkaup Supermarket)
12 Borgarleikhúsið (City Theatre)
13 Salmon Jumping (in season)
14 Árbaejarsafn (open air museum)
15 Nordic House
16 City Airport
17 Hótel Loftleiðir (bus to Keflavík & International Airport)
18 Hot Water Tanks & Restaurant
19 Kópavogskirkja (Church)
20 Cinema
21 Breiðholtskirkja (Church)

Aðalstraeti, the city's first street. His businesses eventually failed but his weaving shed still stands (it burnt down and was rebuilt in 1764) and now houses the cosy, if expensive, restaurant Fógetinn.

Over the next century, Reykjavík firmly established itself as Iceland's capital. A prison and the Supreme Court were built. Danish trading companies and the bourgeoisie settled in. By the late 1800s, the population had grown to over 2000. When the University of Iceland was established in 1911, the population was around 12,000 and, at the time of Icelandic independence in 1944, it had grown to 45,000.

Despite the origins of its name, Reykjavík is now known as the 'smokeless city' thanks to its incessant winds and reliance on geothermal heat. It now boasts a symphony orchestra, theatre, ballet, and opera companies, and all the other trappings of a modern European city like hotels, museums, restaurants, discos, cinemas and pubs. Neat rows of painted concrete houses with brightly coloured roofs climb the hills of Reykjavík-proper and reach out into nondescript suburbs such as Hafnarfjörður, Kópavogur, Mosfellsbaer, Garðabaer, Seltjarnarnes, and Bessastaðahreppur.

Orientation

Modern Reykjavík still stands between the Tjörn and the harbour and many old buildings remain. Nearly everything in the city is within walking distance of the old settlement. Although the town square, Austurvöllur, is the official heart of town, it's more of a quiet city park than a buzzing town square. Most meeting and lounging activity takes place in Laekjartorg and the adjacent pedestrian shopping street, Austurstraeti.

The shopping district extends east along Laugavegur from Laekjargata to Hlemmur bus depot. Most of the souvenir and tourist shops are found near the intersection of Aðalstraeti and Hafnarstraeti. Newer developments, the city airport, the central bus terminal, and the Kringlan Centre shopping mall stretch out along Hringbraut-Miklabraut, the closest thing to an expressway to be found in Iceland.

Information

Tourist Office The main tourist information office is at Ingólfsstraeti 5 near Laugavegur. It's open from 1 June to 15 September from 8.30 am to 7 pm weekdays, 8.30 am to 4 pm Saturdays, and 10 am to 3 pm Sundays. They have an enormous amount of literature and information about Reykjavík and Iceland. If they don't have the answer to your question, they'll go out of their way to find it. Currency exchange is available at the office during regular banking hours and on Saturdays from 10 am to 2 pm.

A second helpful tourist information office is found at the BSÍ long-distance bus terminal on Vatnsmýrarvegur. The Central Youth Hostel on Laufásvegur and the camping ground on Sundlaugavegur offer tourist information services as well. To keep abreast of events like concerts and exhibitions, pick up a copy of *What's on in Reykjavík*, published monthly during summer.

Information on shopping and services is

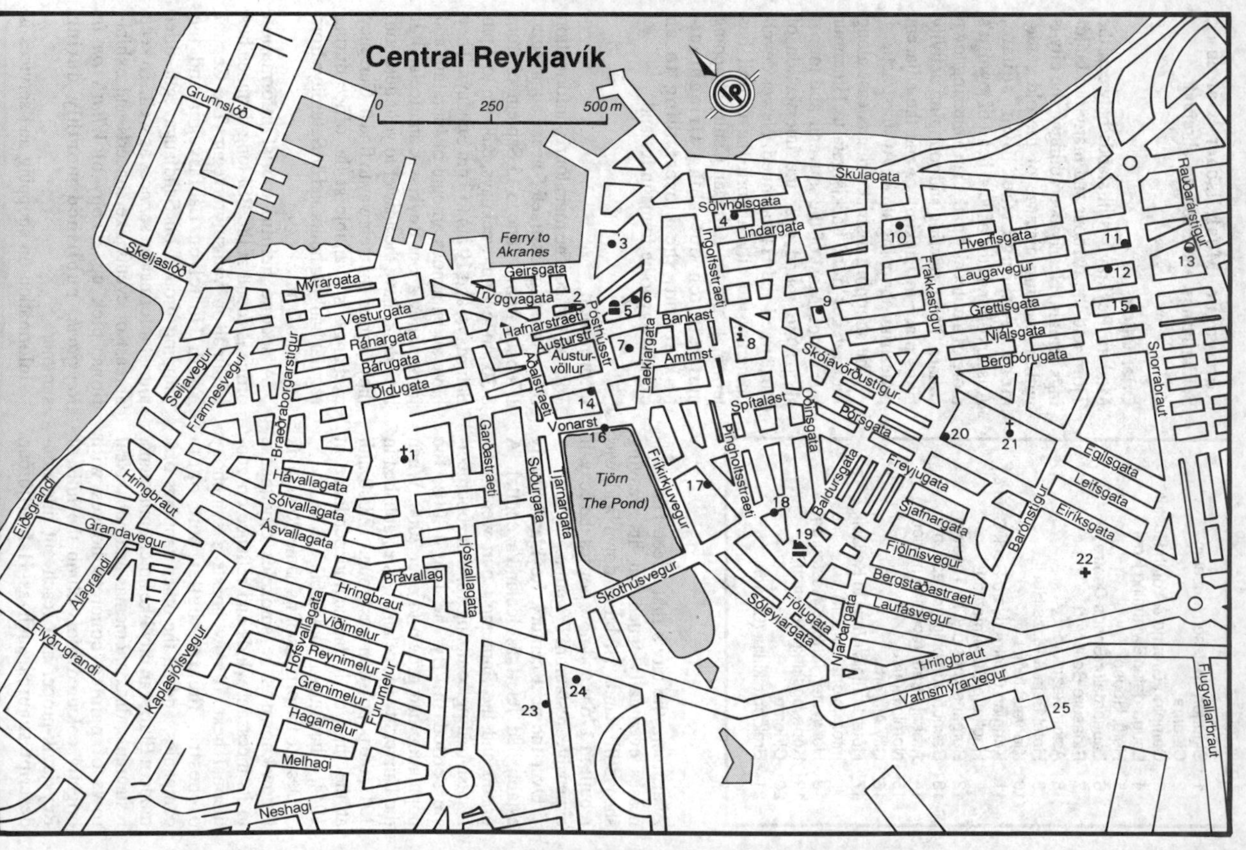
Central Reykjavík
0
250
500 m
Ferry to Akranes
Tjörn
The Pond)
Grunnslóð
Skeljaslóð
Mýrargata
Geirsgata
Tryggvagata
Vesturgata
Ránargata
Bárugata
Öldugata
Hafnarstraeti
Austurstr
Pósthússtr
Austur-völlur
Aðalstraeti
Vonarst
Laekjargata
Bankast
Amtmst
Sölvhólsgata
Lindargata
Ingolfsstraeti
Skúlagata
Hverfisgata
Laugavegur
Grettisgata
Njálsgata
Bergþórugata
Frakkastígur
Rauðarárstígur
Snorrabraut
Skólavörðustígur
Spítalast
Óðinsgata
Þórsgata
Pingholtsstraeti
Baldursgata
Freyjugata
Sjafnargata
Fjölnisvegur
Bergstaðastraeti
Laufásvegur
Barónstígur
Egilsgata
Leifsgata
Eiríksgata
Fríkirkjuvegur
Skothúsvegur
Sóleyjargata
Fjólugata
Njarðargata
Hringbraut
Vatnsmýrarvegur
Flugvallarbraut
Garðastraeti
Suðurgata
Tjarnargata
Ljósvallagata
Brávallag
Seljavegur
Framnesvegur
Braeðraborgarstígur
Hávallagata
Sólvallagata
Ásvallagata
Hringbraut
Grandavegur
Eiðsgrandi
Álagrandi
Flyðrugrandi
Kaplaskjólsvegur
Hofsvallagata
Víðimelur
Reynimelur
Grenimelur
Furumelur
Hagamelur
Melhagi
Neshagi

1 Landakotskirkja
2 Gaukur á Stöng
3 Kolaportið Flea Market
4 National Library & National Theatre
5 Central Post Office
6 Café Torg
7 Kaffi Straeto, Icelandair Office, Tunglið Disco & Café Opera
8 Tourist Office
9 One Woman Vegetarian Restaurant
10 Cinema
11 Natural History Museum
12 Cinema
13 Hlemmur Bus Terminal
14 The Alþing
15 Cinema
16 Reykjavík Theatre Company
17 Listasafn Íslands (National Museum of Art)
18 Volcano Show
19 Central Youth Hostel
20 Einar Jónsson Museum
21 Hallgrímskirkja
22 National Hospital
23 University
24 National Museum
25 BSÍ Bus Terminal

available from the Talking Yellow Pages (tel 91-623045).

Post & Telephone Poste Restante and the long-distance telephone office are both at the main post office on the corner of Posthússtraeti and the Austurstraeti pedestrian mall. The post office is open on weekdays from 8.30 am to 4.30 pm. The sub-station in the BSÍ terminal is open from 9 am to 7.30 pm on weekdays and 8 am to 3 pm Saturdays. The telephone exchange is open weekdays from 9 am and 7 pm and on Sundays from 11 am to 6 pm.

Airline Offices All domestic flights as well as Odin Air's flight to Greenland and Icelandair's flight to the Faroe Islands depart from Reykjavík City Airport. International flights depart from Keflavík International Airport 40 km west of the city. Holders of student cards, who may be eligible for substantially discounted airline tickets, should visit Student Travel at the University Bookshop on Hringbraut before purchasing a ticket elsewhere.

You'll find airline offices at the following addresses:

Icelandair
Laekjargata 2 (tel 91-690100)
Hotel Esja, Suðurlandsbraut 2
Kringlan Centre shopping mall
Arnarflug (Eagle Air)
Lágmúli 7 (tel 91-84477)
Grønlandsfly
Reykjavík City Airport (tel 91-641620)
Odin Air
Reykjavík City Airport (tel 91-10880)

Bookshops & Libraries The widest variety of English and German-language publications is at Sigfús Eymundsson's in Austurstraeti and Mál og Menning (which also sells topographic maps) at Laugavegur 18. Bókaverslun Snaebjarnar, at Hafnarstraeti 4, also has a large selection. The second-hand bookshop on Tryggvagata, one block west of Posthússtraeti, sells hardbacks and paperbacks (mostly English). A variety of classical literature and textbooks is available at the University Bookshop on Hringbraut near Tjarnargata.

The Icelandic National Library near the National Theatre is open from 9 am to 7 pm weekdays and 10 am to noon on Saturdays. Reykjavík also has a city library, at Þingholtsstraeti 29, and a university library on the campus.

There are five international libraries for foreigners wanting to catch up on news from home:

Alliance Française (tel 91-23870), Vesturgata 2, open from 2 to 7 pm weekdays
American Center Library (tel 91-621022), Neshagi 16, open from 11.30 am to 5 pm weekdays
Goethe Institut (tel 91-16061), Tryggvagata 26, open from 3 to 6 pm from Tuesday to Thursday
Nordic House Scandinavian Library (tel 91-17030), Hringbraut at the university campus, open from 11 am to 6 pm daily except Mondays
USSR Library (tel 91-17928), Vatnsstígur 10, open by appointment

Emergency Services The following numbers are useful to have:

Police (tel 91-11166)
Ambulance & Fire Brigade (tel 91-11100)
Search & Rescue (tel 91-27111)

Emergency medical help is available on weekdays from 8 am and 5 pm (tel 91-696600). From 5 pm to 8 am and on weekends dial (tel 91-21230).

Dispensaries, listed under *apótek* in the telephone directory, have a roster for 24-hour openings. To learn which one currently has the shift, check daily papers or phone the Talking Yellow Pages (tel 91-623045).

Film & Photography Kodak photo shops sell a variety of film and camera equipment on Laugavegur near Þingholtsstraeti and in the Kringlan Centre shopping mall. On Sundays, you can buy film in the BSÍ terminal's kiosk.

Laundrettes The Icelandic word for self-service launderette is *Þrottahús*. The most convenient one in Reykjavík is Þvioð Sjálf Laundrette at Barónsstígur 3. The camping ground in Laugardalur also has self-service machines but you'll probably wait in a long queue to use them.

Left-Luggage The left-luggage storage at the BSÍ terminal is open weekdays from 7.30 am to 9.30 pm, Saturdays from 7.30 am to 2.30 pm, and Sundays from 5 to 7 pm. The youth hostel on Laufásvegur offers a left-luggage service for guests and charges US$0.35 (Ikr20) per day to look after your things.

Outdoor Equipment Climbing, camping and fishing gear and repairs are available from Skátabúðin (tel 91-12045) at Snorrabraut 60, a 15-minute walk east of Laekjartorg.

All types of camping equipment suitable for Icelandic weather conditions may be rented from Tjaldaleigan (tel 91-13072), at Vatnsmýrarvegur 9 beside the BSÍ long-distance bus terminal.

Things to See & Do

Although Reykjavík is Iceland's big smoke, it's not exactly a pulsating hotbed of activity. There is, however, the usual gamut of museums, churches, and cultural activities befitting a capital city and visitors should find enough here to keep them occupied for at least 5 or 6 days.

Unfortunately for Reykjavík, most visitors come to see glaciers, waterfalls, geysers, and mountains, not an overgrown village. Fortunately for Reykjavík, nearly everyone has to pass through it at least once and maybe have to stay overnight several times waiting for onward transport. After weeks of facing the elements in the great outdoors, the idea of spending time at the cinemas, discos, coffee shops, and of warm, dry days visiting museums begins to sound appealing even to die-hard nature freaks.

Old Town

Old Town includes the area bordered by Tjörn, Laekjargata, the harbour, and the suburb of Seltjarnarnes, including the east bank of Tjörn and both sides of Laekjargata.

The Harbour During the 18th century, Hafnarstraeti ran alongside the harbour but as the city grew, land was reclaimed and Tryggvagata and new piers were added. The houses on the south side of Hafnarstraeti were originally used by Danish traders during the trade monopoly from 1602 to 1855.

Along Hafnarstraeti, tourist shops sell woollens, pottery, and souvenirs. The Icelandic Handicrafts Centre contains carved wooden falcons which commemorate the real ones captured by the Danish king for gifts to friends and nobles. The birds were stored in this building awaiting shipment to the mainland.

Often, schooners and other restored or replica wooden ships moor in the harbour and add interest and colour to this rustic area.

Dómkirkjan In 1796, the Danish king Christian VII abolished the Catholic bishoprics at

Hólar and Skálholt; he replaced them with a Lutheran diocese centred in Reykjavík. He built this rather ordinary stone structure to serve as the new heart of Christian Iceland, but it has since undergone several renovations and become a bit drabber over the years, especially after the addition of corrugated iron sides. It's open to visitors from 9 am and 5 pm daily except Wednesdays and Saturdays.

Tjörn Its name means simply 'the pond', but old Reykjavík grew up around this pleasant lake in the centre of town. Over 40 species of birds frequent the area, including the original intrepid traveller, the Arctic tern. It's a relaxing place to read or feed the ducks and geese. The pleasant park at the southern end of Tjörn has jogging and bike trails, a fountain, and gardens planted with colourful flowers. The octagonal gazebo is called Hljómskálinn and was built in 1922 as a rehearsal hall for the Reykjavík Brass Band.

National Museum A visit to the National Museum on Hringbraut near the university should be considered obligatory for anyone interested in Norse culture and Icelandic history. You may be put off lingering over the exhibits by the bored guards who scrutinise visitors as if they were all potential perpetrators of the next great museum heist.

On the upper floor are religious and folk relics and tools dating from the period of settlement. The most renowned is the church door from Valþjófsstaður in eastern Iceland which was carved around 1200 and depicts a Norse battle scene. In the basement are nautical and agricultural tools and models including fishing boats and a variety of ingenious early farm implements.

Unfortunately, the lack of explanations in foreign languages will limit non-Icelandic speakers' appreciation of the place. It's open daily except Mondays from 11 am to 4 pm between 15 May and 15 September. The rest of the year, it's open during the same hours on Tuesdays, Thursdays, and weekends. Admission is free.

Árni Magnússon Institute If you're interested in the sagas, don't miss the Árni Magnússon Institute, behind the National Museum.

In the late 17th century in Copenhagen, Árni Magnússon became the secretary of Royal Archives in Copenhagen and, in 1701, he was appointed Professor of Danish Antiquities. In 1702, when collecting Icelandic vellums was all the rage, the king sent him to Iceland for 10 years to track down, beg, and buy every scrap of vellum he could find for the Danish government. His uncanny abilities resulted in a massive collection which he carried back to Copenhagen and deposited in university storerooms. The great fire of Copenhagen on 20 October 1728, threatened the university, but he personally saved as many vellums as possible from the flames. Despite his efforts, however, most of the collection was lost and he died only 15 months later, lamenting his failure to preserve all the manuscripts.

On 21 April 1971, the remaining works, including most famous ones like the *Landnámabók*, the *Íslendingabók*, and *Njálls Saga*, were graciously returned from Denmark to independent Iceland – a cause for national celebration. Most were placed in the Árni Magnússon Institute which was built specifically to house them. The institute is open from 2 to 4 pm on Tuesdays, Thursdays, and Saturdays. There is another small vellum display in the foyer of the National Library.

Kirkjumunir This small museum at Kirkjustraeti 10 displays Icelandic textiles and religious paraphernalia. It's open from 10 am to 5 pm weekdays.

Kolaportið Flea Market Between 10 am and 4 pm on Saturdays, this parking garage on the east side of Laekjargata beneath the National Bank of Iceland turns into the nation's premier flea market. Anyone who wants can set up a booth and sell just about anything they'd like. Travellers needing inexpensive additions to their wardrobes will probably find something here. You'll also find a variety of second-hand stuff ranging from books and phonograph records to lampshades and ashtrays.

Stjórnarráðið The plain white building across Laekjargata from Laekjartorg contains the offices of the president and prime minister. It is one of Reykjavík's oldest buildings, originally built as a goal in the 1700s. Uphill from there on Árnarhóll, or 'eagle hill', is a statue of the first settler, Ingólfur Arnarson.

The Alþing The plain grey basalt building south of Austurvöllur, built in 1881, houses the Alþing, or parliament. Although it lost its legislative powers in 1262 when Iceland joined the Kingdom of Norway (and subsequently Denmark) and didn't regain them until 1845, the Alþing wasn't actually abolished. It was first moved from Þingvellir to Reykjavík in 1798. The Alþing is now comprised of 63 members from six political parties and serves as the national law-making body.

The present building is too small for the growing government and a new building is soon to be constructed nearby.

Austurvöllur The old town square (the 'eastern field') of Reykjavík is where Ingólfur Arnarson grew his hay. His track down to the harbour followed the same route as present-day Aðalstraeti. Today, it is a quiet grassy park surrounded by small restaurants and shops. In the square, there's a statue of Icelandic nationalist and scholar Jón Sigurðsson who lobbied in Copenhagen in 1855 for the restoration of free trade and set the ball rolling toward Icelandic independence, eventually achieved in 1944. The date of independence, 17 June, was selected because it was his birthday.

Fógetinn The small and popular restaurant at Aðalstraeti 10 is housed in Fógeti ('sheriff') Skúli Magnússon's weaving shed, the oldest building in Reykjavík, which was constructed around 1752. Skúli's competitive businesses helped to break the Danish Trade Monopoly which caused so much economic strife in Iceland. Although the shed burnt down in 1764, it was immediately replaced using the same foundation.

New Reykjavík

Most of modern Reykjavík has sprawled eastward from Old Town across the low hills and beyond Elliðaar, the salmon stream that brings an outdoor feeling to Iceland's only cloverleaf junction.

Hallgrímskirkja The immense church at the top of Skólavöðustigur was unashamedly designed to resemble a mountain of basaltic

Statue of Jón Sigurðsson

lava. Although it was originally begun in the late 1940s, it was only recently completed; already the process of renovation is underway. Although the word 'tacky' springs to mind when you see it, Hallgrímskirkja is undoubtedly Reykjavík's most imposing structure. On the lawn is a statue of Leif Eiríksson, called 'Son of Iceland, Discoverer of America', a gift from the USA on the occasion of Iceland's 1100th anniversary of Settlement in 1974.

The rather bland interior of the church is offset by the superb view from its 75-metre-high tower. The elevator to the top costs US$1.80 (Ikr100) per adult. In the summer, it's open daily except Mondays from 10 am to noon and from 2 to 6 pm.

Ásmundur Sveinsson Gallery of Sculpture Ásmundur Sveinsson, born in rural Iceland in 1893, came to Reykjavík to learn woodcarving and ended up in Copenhagen and Paris studying sculpting instead. Most of his themes were derived from Icelandic sagas and folklore and interpreted in massive, but graceful, concrete abstractions.

The gallery devoted to his work is an unusual place. Most visitors first experience this place on bus No 5 between the camping ground and the city centre and most wonder what the hell it is. This igloo-shaped building on Sigtún was designed and built by the controversial sculptor. You wonder who is responsible for the igloo-shaped bus stop shelter in front of it! The exhibit is open daily in the summer from 1 to 4 pm. Opening times change, however, so check current tourist literature before making a special trip out there to see it.

Ásmundur Sveinsson House Not to be confused with his gallery, this house at Freyjugata 41 opposite Hallgrímskirkja is owned by the Association of Icelandic Architects and used for artistic exhibitions. It was designed in 1933 by the artist himself in collaboration with architect Sigurður Guðmundsson. Although avant garde in its day, the building is now considered unobtrusive. It's open weekdays from 4 to 10 pm and weekends between 2 and 10 pm. Admission is free.

National Gallery of Iceland The National Gallery is in the modernistic building behind Fríkirkjan church near Tjörn. The standing collection is rather sparse – only a small percentage of their 5000 pieces are on display – but visiting exhibitions by Icelandic artists make the museum worthwhile. It's open daily except Mondays from 11 am to 5 pm. Admission is free.

Labour Unions' Art Gallery The museum sponsored by Icelandic labour unions at Grensásvegur 16 isn't what you'd call earth-shaking but it's worthwhile for those interested in amateur – and occasionally inspired – artwork. Visiting exhibitions often add interest. It's open daily except Mondays from 11 am to 5 pm. Take bus Nos 8, 9, 10, 11, or 12 from Hlemmur terminal or bus Nos 6 or 7 from Laekjargata.

Kjarvalsstaðir Jóhannes Kjarval is undoubtedly Iceland's most popular artist. He was born in 1885 and, while young, went to work on a fishing trawler. Some of his co-workers recognised his potential as an artist and organised a lottery to pay for his study abroad. Although he was rejected by the Royal Academy of Arts in London, he absorbed the master works in British museums and was accepted to the Academy of Fine Arts in Copenhagen.

The surrealistic style that characterises his work is derived from the ethereal nature of the Icelandic landscape. When observed at close range, it appears to be nothing more than unintentional globs of paint on canvas but seen from a distance of 10 metres or so, the magic appears.

The museum dedicated to his work is in Miklatún park on Flókagata. It's open from 11 am to 6 pm daily. A second hall is used for visiting exhibitions. Admission is free.

Einar Jónsson Museum Near Hallgríms-kirkja on Njarðargata is the cube shaped Einar Jónsson Museum, a worthwhile exhibit of work by Iceland's foremost modern sculptor. The building itself, which was designed by Jónsson in 1923 and subsidised by the government as a gift to him, reflects the mysticism that characterises his work. He created his fantastic art, mostly dealing with political and religious themes, in a self-imposed state of seclusion which he believed necessary for his preferred sort of inspiration. His only non-mystical work, a statue of Jón Sigurðsson, stands in Austurvöllur square.The museum is open on Saturdays and Sundays from 1.30 to 4 pm.

Nordic House Iceland's Nordic House, south of Tjörn, designed by architect Alvar Aalto, serves as a Scandinavian cultural centre. It offers travelling exhibitions, concerts, lectures, films based on Nordic themes, and a library of Scandinavian literature. The cafeteria is open everyday but the exhibition hall and library are only open from 11 am to 6 pm daily except Mondays.

Sigurjón Ólafsson Museum Born in 1908, Sigurjón Ólafsson studied in Denmark and became a sensitive, if not prolific, sculptor and portraitist. A standing collection of his work is on display on Héðinsgata, a couple of blocks seaward from Laugardalur and the city camping ground. It's open Mondays, Wednesdays, and Thursdays from 8 to 10 pm and weekends from 2 to 5 pm. Concerts catering for a wide range of musical tastes are held on Tuesday evenings at 8.30 pm.

Natural History Museum If you're going to Vestmannaeyjar, save your enthusiasm for their museum. The Reykjavík Natural History Museum at Hlemmtorg (Hlemmur bus depot) isn't the most exciting museum in Iceland and it is only worth a brief look if you're very keen on Icelandic geology, fauna, and flora. It's open on Sundays, Tuesdays, Thursdays, and Saturdays from 1.30 to 4 pm.

Numismatic Museum Set up as a joint project by the National Bank of Iceland and the Central Bank of Iceland, this museum at Einholt 4 near Kjarvalsstadíir houses a collection of Icelandic and other notes and coins. It's open from 2 to 4 pm on Sundays.

Höfði House The Höfði House, used for official receptions and city social functions, looks across the bay at 914-metre Mt Esja. In 1986, it was catapulted to dubious fame as the official meeting place of the superpowers in the non-eventful Reagan-Gorbachev summit. It's now referred to in Reykjavík as the 'Reagan-Gorbachev House' and is believed to be haunted by ghosts of the Icelandic past. Those who'd enjoy face to face encounters with history may want to check it out.

Ásgrímur Jónsson Museum Ásgrímur Jónsson, born in 1876, was the first great Icelandic landscape painter. He was educated in Copenhagen and showed so much promise that the Icelandic parliament voted him a grant to study painting in Italy. There he was attracted to the Impressionism that was reflected in the rest of his work. In his will, he bequeathed about half his art to the Icelandic government which set up this display in his former home at Bergstaðastraeti 74. Summer hours are from 1.30 to 4 pm daily except Mondays. Admission is free.

Árbaejarsafn Also known as the Open Air Museum, Árbaersafn is a 12.5 hectare historic farm set up as a museum in 1957. It also includes a collection of old homes and buildings moved from various places to illustrate life in early Iceland.

Árbaejarsafn was first mentioned in literary sources in the mid-15th century. It was originally purchased by the city in 1906 in order to secure rights to the Elliðaár river valley and was an inn until the 1930s.

Besides the farm, there are exhibits outlining the development of public services, transport systems, and emergency services in Reykjavík. There's also a turf church dating back to 1842 which was moved to the museum from Skagafjörður in 1960. In front of the farm is the sculpture 'Woman Churning Milk' by sculptor Ásmundur Sveinsson.

In the summer, it's open daily except Mondays from 10 am to 6 pm. In September, opening hours are from 10 am to 6 pm on weekends only. Take bus Nos 10 or 100 from the city centre.

Botanic Gardens Although they're not the largest in Iceland, these small botanic gardens which contain 65% of all plant species occurring naturally in the country are good for a pleasant evening stroll for those staying at the nearby camping ground. The relief carving is a portrait of Eiríkur Hjartarson, who owned the area and began planting trees there in 1929. It was bought by the city of Reykjavík in 1955.

Volcano Show Don't be put off this place by its outwardly tacky appearance. If you see it before you visit Vestmannaeyjar or lake Mývatn, you'll be able to better appreciate those places and their histories. In addition, it offers insight into the volcanic spectre under which Icelanders live.

For over 40 years, Vilhjálmur and Ósvaldur Knudsen have rushed to the scenes of major volcanic eruptions in Iceland and filmed the greatest action, including the award-winning *Birth of an Island* about Surtsey in Vestmannaeyjar.

The 2½-hour show is at 10 am, 3 pm, and 8 pm daily in the summer. From September to May, it plays Tuesdays, Thursdays, and Saturdays at 8 pm. Shows are normally in English, but French or German presentations can be arranged in advance. Some of the films are available on videotape. The theatre is at Hellusund 6a near the Central Youth Hostel. Admission is expensive at around US$10 per person.

Öskjuhlið Visitors to Reykjavík wondering why their hot showers smell a bit sulphuric will learn why at Öskjuhlið. This group of tanks, east of the city airport, stores hot water fresh from the centre of the earth. A new restaurant is being built on top in order to extract as much tourist interest and value as possible from this non-attraction.

Elliðaár This is Reykjavík's salmon river – in early August, you can watch the leaping salmon making their way upstream to spawn. If it weren't for the noisy cloverleaf junction nearby, it would be easy to forget you're in the city while you sit, relax on the grass, and watch the tumbling water. It's about a 45-minute walk from central Reykjavík. You can also take bus No 10 from Hlemmur or bus No 100 from Laekjargata.

Places to Stay

Finding a place to stay in Reykjavík in late summer, particularly in a youth hostel or inexpensive guesthouse, can be difficult. Bring a tent or book accommodation in advance if you'd rather not risk literally being left out in the cold.

Places to Stay – bottom end

Budget travellers have exactly three choices in Reykjavík: the Salvation Army, the youth hostels, or camping.

The *Salvation Army Guest House* (tel 91-613203) at Kirkjustraeti 2 near Austurvöllur in the city centre offers pleasant and clean private single/double rooms for US$26/38.

Youth Hostels A second youth hostel has recently opened near the camping ground in Reykjavík to take the pressure off the old one. It hasn't made much difference, though; *both* are full all summer now.

If you must stay in the hostels, book at least a month in advance but if you have another option, such as a tent, you can turn up in the evening and hope there's been a cancellation. IYHF members pay US$11 per night and non-members US$13. The midnight curfew, however, precludes enjoyment of Reykjavík's weekend nightlife which is just winding up when the hostel is locking up. Breakfast is available for an extra fee.

The crowded *Central Youth Hostel* (tel 91-24950) is at Laufásvegur 41, just 7 minutes walking from Laekjartorg and 5 minutes from the BSÍ terminal. It has a common room with a TV, a kitchen, hot showers, a travel agency, and left-luggage facilities.

The *Laugardalur Youth Hostel* (tel 91-38110) at Sundlaugavegur 34 offers the same facilities but has a less claustrophobic feeling than the central hostel. It's a 15-minute bus ride (bus No 5) from Laekjartorg and a US$7 taxi ride from the BSÍ terminal. Daily at 7 am during summer, a free shuttle service leaves from the nearby camping ground for the BSÍ terminal. This hostel normally closes down on 15 September but opens to accommodate off-season overflows at the other hostel.

Camping The Reykjavík camping ground is in Laugardalur on the same property as the youth hostel. At the height of summer, you'll be lucky to find enough space for a tent on this immense piece of real estate. There are cooking and laundry facilities, tourist information, and hot showers but be prepared for crowds and queues. Despite the chaos, the attendants maintain a mellow attitude and one can only admire their friendly patience with questions they must hear hundreds of times a day.

The camping ground is open from 1 June to 15 September and costs US$2.50 per person plus US$2.50 per tent. Every day at 7 am a shuttle bus runs from the camping ground to the BSÍ terminal.

Places to Stay – middle

The most up-market middle-range place to stay is the *Hotel Óðinsvé* (tel 91-25640) at Þorsgata 1 which costs US$65/89 for singles/doubles. It's followed by a number of *gistiheimilið*, or 'guesthouses', charging between US$45 and US$60 per night for comfortable, but hardly elegant, accommodation. They include the central *Borgarstjarnan* (tel 91-621804) at Ránargata 10 near the harbour, the *Guesthouse #1* (tel 91-623477) at Miklabraut 1 near Miklatún park, the *Svanurinn Guesthouse* (tel 91- 25318) at Lokastígur 24, the *Matteu Guesthouse* (tel 91-33207) at Bugðulaekur 13 in Laugardalur, *Guðmundur Jónasson* at Borgartún 34, *Snorra* at Snorrabraut 61, and a number of others. For a complete list of guesthouses and private homes which let out rooms (all middle-range), contact the tourist office (tel 91-623045) at Ingólfsstraeti 5.

Places to Stay – top end

Although most of Reykjavík's accommodation would be considered top-end anywhere else, this section includes only up-market hotels charging over US$100 per night for a double room.

The nicest is the *Hotel Saga* (tel 91-29900) at Hagatorg 1. It offers a view over the city and all the trappings of an international hotel – a swimming pool, penthouse restaurant, health club, two bars, shops, convention facilities and so on – but a double room starts at US$145 per night.

Rooms at the *Hotel Esja* (tel 91-82200) cost just US$2 less than at the Hotel Saga. It's at Suðurlandsbraut 2 and isn't central. When I went in to speak with them, I suppose looking too much like a backpacker, they couldn't be bothered helping. Budget travellers who'd like to splurge on a night of luxury may want to look elsewhere.

The *Hotel Loftleiðir* (tel 91-22322) at the city airport is convenient for those catching early morning buses to Keflavík International Airport. It has a swimming pool, massage room, sauna, bank, restaurants and shops, and conference facilities. Double rooms start from US$143 per night.

Also worth mentioning is the *Hotel Holt* (tel 91-25700) at Bergstaðastraeti 37. Even if you're not in the market for a room, it merits a visit to the restaurant to see the collection of Icelandic artwork decorating the lobby and hallways. Rooms start at US$115/132 per night for singles/doubles.

The *Holiday Inn Reykjavík* (tel 91-689000) at Sigtún 38 is Reykjavík's newest and most expensive luxury hotel but it's a considerable distance from the city centre. Double rooms begin at US$155.

Other up-market hotels include the *Hotel Geysir* (tel 91-26477) at Skipholt 27, the *Hotel Borg* (tel 91-11440) at Pósthússtraeti 11, the *Hotel Lind* (tel 91-623350) at

Rauðarárstígur 18, and *the City Hotel* (tel 91-18650) at Ránargata 4a. Their prices range from US$100 to US$130 per night for a double.

Places to Eat

Dining out in Reykjavík is expensive but some places are definitely better value than others. Tourists will see advertisements for the *Sumarréttir*, or tourist menu, a gimmick designed to take some of the sting out of dining at some high-priced restaurants. They offer special scaled-down menus at lower prices for budget-conscious visitors (from US$10 to US$12 for lunches and US$15 to US$20 for dinner). The fact is, many less pretentious places often serve better food for similar prices.

Self-Catering The least expensive supermarket chain in Reykjavík is *Hagkaup* with stores in the Kringlan Centre and on Laugavegur near Snorrabraut. The former has an inexpensive salad bar (small for US$1.50, large for US$2.50!) right in the store and the latter is particularly good for fresh produce. Both are open only during normal business hours, however. Later at night or on weekends, you'll have to resort to the higher-priced convenience stores scattered through residential areas of the city.

There are four State Monopoly stores in the area, at Álfabakki 14, Lindargata 46, Snorrabraut 56, and the Kringlan Centre, which sell beer, wine, and spirits.

Snacks & Fast Food For a quick bite on the run, nothing beats the snack kiosks on Laekjartorg and the Austurstraeti mall. You can buy chips, sausages, pizza, soft drinks, and other snacks to fill you up for around US$4. Along Laugavegur and elsewhere in the business district you'll find similar establishments in more permanent buildings but the food costs slightly more due to higher overheads.

Fried chicken, fish & chips, burgers, etc are offered at *Svarta Pannan* at Hafnarstraeti 17, expect to pay from US$6 to US$8 for a meal. Deli meals are available at the unassuming *Hlölla Deli* at Austurstraeti 1. It's great for deli snacks and a variety of sandwiches.

For a change from the same old snack foods, try the pita sandwiches at *Pítan*, Skipholt 50. Reasonable pizzas are served at *Puzzahúsið* at Grensásvegur 10 and at *Jón Bakan*, Nýlbýlavegur 14. The well-known US chain *Pizza Hut* at the Hotel Esja offers a self-serve salad bar, pizzas, pasta, beer and wine. You only need spend US$20 for a meal with alcohol included. This place is always overflowing with locals who seem to love the concept.

Unless you want to pay US$7 for a small, gristly burger, avoid the American-looking hamburger joint *Tommahamborgarar* on the corner of Hafnarstraeti and Laekjartorg.

A number of small cafeterias around town, many in museums, offer limited à la carte snacks and rich desserts for the hefty prices that can be expected in such bohemian settings. The one exception is the cafeteria at the BSÍ terminal which charges down-to-earth prices.

Smorgasbord There are a couple of places in Reykjavík that have caught on to the need for good, all-you-can-eat sort of soup and salad bars for around US$12. These turn out to be especially attractive to lower budget travellers who the owners hope will return when it's time to splurge and order something from the regular menu.

If you're staying at the camping ground, check out *Askur* at Suðurlandsbraut 4 which specialises in fish and lamb dishes. In addition to the daily soup and salad bar, they have a Sunday smorgasbord.

Both Eldvagninn at Laugavegur 75 and *Potturinn og Pannan* at Brautarholt 22 have lunchtime soup and salad specials. In the evening they serve fish, lamb, and beef dishes for around US$25 without alcohol.

The *Café Opera* upstairs at the corner of Laekjargata and Laekjartorg offers a weekend all-you-can-eat lunchtime smorgasbord for US$23 per person. If you're up to it, this is a good place to try some of the more unusual traditional Icelandic dishes.

Cafes & Pubs For most budget travellers, nothing will beat Reykjavík's small pub-style cafes for good food and lively, friendly atmosphere. After 10 pm on weekends, expect to wait in a queue and, if there's live music playing, you'll also have to pay a cover charge of about US$12 per person. If you want action don't bother to arrive until 11 pm at the earliest. If you want to drink a pint, plan on a major expenditure but if you prefer a cocktail, well one tourist brochure seems to sum it up best: '...don't be surprised when you get a bill the size of a Third World country's defence budget'.

The most popular place, and rightfully so, is *Gaukur á Stöng* at Tryggvagata 22. It's said that this is where Iceland's famous vodka-spiked beer originated and it's become almost legendary for its daring. On Friday or Saturday nights things start winding up at about midnight and maintain fever pitch until closing time at 3 am. Sometimes even weeknights get interesting.

For a much quieter time, try the *Djúpið* at Hafnarstraeti 15 in the cellar of the *Hornið* pizzeria. It's open only on Friday and Saturday nights offering a less rollicking time but a better place for a chat.

By day, *Café Hressó* on Austurstraeti and Laekjartorg is an inexpensive cafe with a coffee shop, cafeteria, pub, bakery, and garden area. At 3.30 pm, it begins serving beer and the full bar opens at 6 pm. On weekdays, it stays open until 12.30 am and on Fridays and Saturdays until 3 am.

Adjacent to the Café Opera is the *Kaffi Straeto* which serves American and European coffee specialties during the day. Its casual bohemian atmosphere and nostalgic 'Transit-Authority' decor make it a favourite of the afternoon crowd. They specialise in stuffed pancake dishes for around US$10. You can choose between anything from Mexican to Neapolitan. Just one is more than an average-sized stomach can manage. At night, they're licensed to serve wine and beer.

If you fancy yourself as an intellectual (or pseudo-intellectual), check out the *Geirsbúð* at Vesturgata 6. This is the hangout of politicians, journalists, government workers, and others in charge of telling Iceland how to think. It can get interesting.

Although it's not licensed, the *Café Torg* overlooking Laekjartorg is one of the friendliest places in town to drink morning coffee and eat a pastry or light meal. Once you go in and get caught up in the warmth of the place, you'll keep coming back. Lunches cost less than US$5 and it's a good vantage point from which to observe the goings-on in Laekjartorg, where just about everything that happens in Reykjavík happens.

At the Kringlan Centre there's Reykjavík's *Hard Rock Cafe*. If you're 'collecting' Hard Rock Cafes, the best thing to do is go out there, buy the T-shirt, and get away as quickly as possible. This pretentious place rides its trendy reputation as far as it can and has been known to clean people out of their life savings in exchange for the dubious privilege of saying they'd been eating or drinking there.

Foreign Cuisine For a city of its size, Reykjavík has a fair number of restaurants serving reasonable examples of ethnic cuisines. Due to local distaste for spicy foods, normally hot or strong dishes are generally toned down. Most of these restaurants are expensive – plan on spending at least US$30 per person for a dinner without alcohol – but several offer lunch specials or smorgasbords for as little as US$10.

The *El Sombrero* at Laugavegur 73 is a Spanish, not Mexican, restaurant so don't be tempted to go in looking for a taco. In addition to paella and a few chicken-based dishes, they serve bland pizzas and pasta dishes.

The only place to get a taco in Iceland is the international kiosk in the Kringlan Centre. It also serves Italian and Vietnamese-style fast food at unreasonable prices. A taco will cost around US$5; a plate of rice with an egg roll and sweet & sour chicken will be about US$10.

The most genuine Italian fare in Iceland is found at *Ítalía* at Laugavegur 11. They offer lunch specials for less than US$16. An odd combination, the *Taj Mahal Tandoori & Sushi Bar* at Laugavegur 34a serves mild Indian curries, tandoori dishes, and Japanese sushi, sashimi, and tempura. Indian or Japanese lunch specials are available on weekdays for US$10 but portions are small.

Sjanghae at Laugavegur 28 serves Mandarin Chinese dishes similar to those available in other Western countries. Their lunch prices are very reasonable. Soup, salad, a spring roll, and coffee cost US$10 while soup, coffee, and the special of the day is only US$11. Dinners will, of course, be a lot more pricey. Chinese food is also available at the *Peking* at Hverfisgata 56 (dinner only) and at the *Mandarininn* at Tryggvagata 26.

Vegetarian Reykjavík has an excellent vegetarian restaurant known simply as the *One Woman Vegetarian Restaurant* at the corner of Laugavegur and Klapparstígur. It has a pleasant atmosphere and is popular with travellers. They serve both macrobiotic and standard vegetarian fare.

Fine Dining Reykjavík has no shortage of up-market wining and dining places. Given the climate, a cosy fireplace-in-the-farmhouse or nautical sort of atmosphere gets a lot of mileage. One of the nicest and best is *Jónatan Livingstone Mávur* at Tryggvagata 4-6 near the harbour. They specialise in seafood and French dishes.

Another popular place is the *Fógetinn*, worthwhile mainly because it is housed in Skúli Magnússon's weaving shed, the oldest building in Reykjavík. They specialise in lamb, ptarmigan, duck, and seafood; there's live music 5 nights a week. Overall, it's pleasant venturing into the realms of high finance.

Laekjarbrekka near the intersection of Bankastraeti (lower Laugavegur) and Laekjargata is another up-market restaurant in an old building. It was originally built in 1834 as the home of shipping merchant P C Knudtzon of Copenhagen. It was used alternately as a bakery and a home until 1980 when it was renovated and converted into a restaurant. If you'd like to have a look at the place but not spend a fortune, the old bakery is open for coffee and pastries in the afternoon.

For steaks and other beef dishes, try the *Eldvagninn* at Laugavegur 73. They pride themselves on their 'American salad bar' and home-baked bread, so if you just crave a salad, it may be worthwhile.

One of the best seafood restaurants in Reykjavík is the *Restaurant Naust* on Vesturgata near the harbour. It offers what appears to be the greatest variety of seafood and some of the more bizarre traditional Icelandic dishes as well. The decor is extremely nautical. In the evening, they have live music and dancing.

All of the big hotels prepare elegant but relatively plain seafood, lamb, and beef dishes, much like those meals you'd find in all the big hotels everywhere.

Entertainment

Cinemas Reykjavík has five cinemas and there's another in nearby Kópavogur. Daily newspapers list shows and showtimes. Films are always screened in their original language with Icelandic subtitles. Admission costs about US$6 per person.

You'll find cinemas at the following addresses:

Bíóborgin (tel 91-11384), Snorrabraut 37
Bíóhöllin (tel 91-78900), Álfabakki 8
Háskóbíó (tel 91-22140), Hagatorg
Laugarásbíó (tel 91-32075), Laugarás
Regnboginn (tel 91-19000), Hverfisgata 54
Stjörnubíó (tel 91-18936), Laugavegur 94

Cultural Activities Reykjavík has several theatre groups, an opera, a symphony orchestra, and a dance company. Information on current events will be available in the daily papers or at the box offices of the following :

Reykjavík Theatre Company (tel 91-16620), Vonarstraeti, open daily from 2 to 7 pm
National Theatre and Icelandic Dance Company (tel 91-11200), between Hverfisgata and Lindargata, open daily (except Mondays) from 1.15 to 8 pm

Frú Emilía Theatre Group (tel 91-678360), Skeifan 3C, book by phone at any hour
The Icelandic Opera (tel 91-11475), Ingólfsstraeti, open daily from 3 to 7 pm
Iceland Symphony Orchestra (tel 91-622255), Hagatorg, box office at Gimli, Laekjargata, open Monday to Friday from 9 am to 5 pm
Alþýðuleikhúsið Theatre Group (tel 91-15185), Vesturgata 3, book by phone

Light Nights This show, staged for tourists and performed in English, is an easily digested account of the sagas and Icelandic Settlement. It focuses a bit heavily on the Vikings but this seems to be what the tourists want.

Performances are held through the summer at Tjarnargata 10e from Thursday to Sunday at 9 pm. Bookings (tel 91-19181) can be made from 8.10 pm on the night of the performance. Tickets can be bought in advance at the hotels Esja, Loftleiðir, and Saga. Discounts are available for groups and holders of student cards.

Discos These provide the most excitement Reykjavík has to offer but they aren't for the destitute. All impose a cover charge from US$13 to US$15 per person. You'll have to queue to get in on a Friday or Saturday night, especially during rush hours from 11 pm to 3 am. If you plan to drink yourself into a stupor, you'll need the better part of US$100 for one person. An unwritten rule requires men to dress up a bit – even a tie wouldn't be out of line – but foreigners get away with being more casual if they're obvious travellers. Women face no real dress restrictions. As for social restrictions, standards are very pleasantly European but conservative foreigners may begin to feel uncomfortable with the liberal attitudes that surface after just a couple of drinks.

Reykjavík's wildest disco used to be the *Hollywood* at Ármúli 5 in Laugardalur. It's toned down now thanks to yuppie influences but is still one of the 'four-in-one' specials which offers admission to four discos under a single cover charge. Others are at the *Hotel Ísland*, also on Ármúli, and the *Hotel Borg* at Pósthússtraeti 11. The fourth is the immense *Broadway* at Álfabakki 8 near the boundaries of Kópavogur (take bus No 11).

The most frantic and popular disco in town these days is the *Tunglið* at Laekjargata 2. If you like it loud but trendy, this is the place to go. Other popular spots include *Abracadabra* at Laugavegur 116, *Casablanca* at Skúlagata 30, *Utopia* at Suðurlandsbraut 26, and *Cuba* at Borgartún 32.

Activities

Sports You can play squash and racquetball at Veggsport (tel 91-19011) at Seljavegur 2, open on weekdays from 11.30 am to 1.30 pm and from 4 to 10 pm. Games cost US$7 per person including the use of their sauna, gym, and training room. Bowling is available at Keilusalurinn Öskjuhlíð (tel 91-621599) beside the Hotel Loftleiðir. It's open daily from noon to 12.30 am.

In August, the city stages a marathon, half-marathon, and a 7.5 km fun run which follow courses through Reykjavík and Seltjarnarnes. The full marathon is open to entrants over 18 years old and costs US$18 to run. Half-marathon runners must be over 16 and pay US$15. The fun run has no age limits and costs US$13. Pre-registration is mandatory. For more information, contact Úrval Travel Bureau (tel 354-1-28522), Reykjavík Marathon, PO Box 1630, 121 Reykjavík.

Football is Iceland's most popular spectator sport. Local and international competitions are played at the Laugardalur Sports Centre. For information on upcoming events, watch the sports sections of Reykjavík newspapers.

Swimming Admission to pools in Rekjavík costs US$1.50 for adults and half-price for children under 12 years old. Towels and swimsuits can be rented at the pools. Most inter-city and national swimming events take place at the Laugardalur pool. You'll find the following information useful if you like swimming:

Top: Icelandic flag at Aðalvík, Hornstrandir, Iceland (DS)
Bottom: Reykjavík, Iceland (GA)

Top: Panicking gulls, Borgarfjörður Eystri, Iceland (DS)
Bottom: Borgarfjörður Eystri, Iceland (DS)

Laugardalur
Sundlaugavegur near the camping ground, from Monday to Friday 7 am to 8.30 pm, Saturdays 7.30 am to 5.30 pm, Sundays 8 am to 5.30 pm
Vesturbaejar
Hofsvallagata, from Monday to Friday 7 am to 8.30 pm, Saturdays 7.30 am to 5.30 pm, Sundays 8 am to 5.30 pm
Sundhöll Reykjavíkur
Barónsstigur, from Monday to Friday 7 am to 8.30 pm, Saturdays 7.30 am to 5.30 pm, Sundays 8 am to 3 pm
Fjölbraut Breiðholt
Austurberg 5, from Monday to Friday 7 am to 8.30 pm, Saturdays 7.30 am to 5.30 pm, Sundays 8 am to 5.30 pm
Seltjarnarnes
Suðurströnd, Monday to Friday 7.10 am to 8.30 pm, Saturdays 7.10 am to 5.30 pm, Sundays 8 am to 5.30 pm

Getting There & Away

Air Reykjavík City Airport serves all domestic flights, Odin Air flights to and from Kulusuk (Greenland) and flights to the Faroe Islands. See also the following Airport Transport section.

Bus Long-distance buses use the BSÍ terminal (tel 91-22300) at Vatnsmýrarvegur 10. During the summer months, there is a daily service between Reykjavík and Akureyri, Skaftafell, Höfn, Akranes, Snaefellsnes, Þorlákshöfn, and Reykjanes. There is also a twice-weekly service to the Westfjords. Travellers between Reykjavík and eastern Iceland must spend the night in either Höfn or Akureyri before they can make connections to their destination.

BSÍ offers a variety of tours during the tourist season, some departing daily. The most popular, the Golden Triangle tour (Gullfoss, Geysir, Þingvellir) offers hotel pick-up service for those with bookings. Although you can join a tour by turning up at BSÍ at the posted time of departure, it's best to book so they'll know in advance how many people to expect. Specific tours will be described in more detail in sections on individual destinations. Pamphlets providing brief outlines and fares are available in German and English at both the BSÍ terminal and the central tourist office.

Ferry The car-ferry *Akraborg* (tel 91-16420) does at least four trips daily between Reykjavík and Akranes. It leaves from Reykjavík's Reykjavíkurhöfn (harbour) at 9.30 am and 12.30, 3.30, and 6.30 pm, with extra sailings on weekends. It leaves Akranes at 8 am (except on Sundays in the off-season), 11 am, 2 pm, and 5 pm, again with extra weekend departures. The one-way fare is US$7.75 per person, US$13.75 for a car and driver, or US$15.50 for two passengers and a car.

For information on the Viðey ferry, see Getting There & Away under Viðey in the Around Reykjavík section.

Getting Around

Airport Transport The Flybus to Keflavík International Airport leaves the Hotel Loftleiðir in Reykjavík exactly 2 hours prior to every international departure stopping en route at Kópavogur and Hafnarfjörður, if passengers are waiting. Buses from Keflavík airport to the Hotel Loftleiðir depart about 45 minutes after arrival of an international flight. The fare in either direction is US$6.30 (Ikr350).

Bus Reykjavík's city bus system is excellent. Services begin at 6 am and end at 1 am, although the last bus will pass a given stop anytime between midnight and 1 am. Buses pick up and drop passengers only at designated stops which are marked with the letters *SVR*.

The two central terminals are at Hlemmur near the intersection of Laugavegur and Rauðarárstígur and at Laekjargata near Laekjartorg. Buses to Hafnarfjörður and Garðabaer use the Laekjargata terminal while those to Kópavogur and Mosfellsbaer stop at Hlemmur. Hafnarfjörður buses also stop at Hlemmur en route.

The standard fare per ride is US$0.90 (Ikr50) . If you don't have exact change or a pre-purchased ticket, you lose. Drivers are not permitted to give change. Discount tickets cost US$0.80 (Ikr45). They're available at either terminal, at the intersection of Grensásvegur and Miklabraut, at Borgartún

35, and at the Reykjavík camping ground. If you need to change buses, ask the driver for a *skiptimiði* or transfer which is valid for up to 45 minutes from the time of issue.

Taxi Although Reykjavík is small enough for you to walk around, taxis will come in handy if you have a lot of luggage or have to catch the 5 am airport bus (all flights to Europe leave Keflavík International Airport at around 7 am). Fortunately, taxis aren't inordinately expensive and since there's no tipping, they work out cheaper than in the USA or most of Europe. Between the Hotel Loftleiðir and the camping ground, for example, you'll pay US$7.75 for up to three people and luggage. From the Central Youth Hostel to the Loftleiðir costs only about US$5.

There are five taxi stations around Reykjavík: Hreyfill (tel 91-685522), Baejarleiðir (tel 91-33500), BSR (tel 91-11720), BSH (tel 91-51666), and Borgarbíll (tel 91-22440).

Around Reykjavík

HAFNARFJÖRÐUR

Of all Reykjavík's suburbs, Harnarfjörður is the only one that stands on its own as a picturesque and interesting place to visit. The village is the butt of Icelandic humour and one senses that the people are almost proud of the distinction it brings.

The red and white striped tower that serves as a minor trademark of Hafnarfjörður belongs to the Swiss-operated aluminium factory at Straumsvík. Across the road on Kapelluhraun ('chapel lava') are the ruins of a chapel and a statue of St Barbara indicating that the site dates from pre-Lutheran times.

Hafnarfjörður is built on the rugged and cave-riddled Búrfell lava formation which was spewed out 7000 years ago. It arcs around a beautiful natural harbour formed by the Hamarinn cliffs and used in the early 1400s as an English trading centre. Germans took over in the early 16th century and dominated until the imposition of the Danish Trade Monopoly in 1602. As Reykjavík developed during that tumultuous period, Hafnarfjörður relaxed into relative obscurity. Today it has 15,000 people.

Hafnarborg

When the town celebrated the 75th anniversary of its municipal charter in 1983, local chemist Sverrir Magnússon and his wife, Ingibjörg Sigurjónsdóttir, donated their home at Strandgata 34 as an Institute of Culture and Fine Art. Now called Hafnarborg, the project finally opened to the public during the summer of 1988. It serves as an exhibition hall for Icelandic artists during the summer months and is used for concerts in the winter. Studio space and living quarters are available at the institute for visiting Icelandic artists working at the centre.

Hafnarborg is open from 2 to 7 pm daily except Tuesdays. The coffee shop, which has a nice view of the harbour, is open daily.

Hellisgerði

This beautiful park in the lava near the town centre preserves a bit of Hafnarfjörður's underlying natural element and offers opportunities for exploration.

Post & Telecommunications History Museum

This interesting collection of artefacts at Austurgata 11 tells the story of communications in Iceland from early Settlement days through the development of the postal and telephone systems. It's open Sundays and Tuesdays from 3 to 6 pm. At other times, phone (tel 91-54321) and they'll open it for you.

Maritime & Folk Museums

The Maritime Museum at Vesturgata 8 is in a house built around 1865. It contains nautical artefacts outlining Hafnarfjörður's history as an important fishing and trading village. In the summer, the museum is open from 2 to 6 pm daily except Mondays. In winter, it's open only on weekends. Next door at Vesturgata 6 is the town folk museum open during the same hours. Admission to either museum is US$1.80 (Ikr100) per person.

Places to Stay & Eat

There are a couple of rather elegant restaurants in Hafnarfjörður which emphasise the town's quaintness in hopes of drawing patrons away from Reykjavík. The restaurant *A Hansen* is in a house built in 1880 by the Danish merchant P C Knudtzon. It's cosy and inviting, but predictably expensive. It's open for both lunch and dinner. On weekends, the bar closes at 3 am. At Strandgata 50 is the equally expensive *Fjaran* which specialises in freshly caught fish and seafood.

Campers tired of the crowds at Reykjavík camping ground may want to shift to the more picturesque site on Flókagata in Hafnarfjörður.

Getting There & Away

Buses for Hafnarfjörður leave Laekjargata bus station in Reykjavík every half-hour.

KÓPAVOGUR

With around 16,000 inhabitants, Kópavogur is Iceland's second largest community. The name means 'seal pup inlet' after the wildlife the early settlers encountered there. The only seals you'll see there today are the stuffed ones in the Natural History Museum at Digranesvegur 12 which is open on Saturdays from 1.30 to 4.30 pm.

Under threat of death, Icelandic leaders were forced to sign a decree pledging allegiance to Denmark in 1622. Today a small memorial stands at the western end of the inlet south of Kópavogur to recall this event.

The distinctive church which sits on a small hill on the west side of town looks more like an opera hall than anything else. The stained-glass work is by Icelandic sculptor Gerður Helgadóttir. It compares the course of a human life to the passage of a single day from dawn to dusk.

The view disc on the hill Vighóll identifies features of the surrounding panorama.

Getting There & Away

To get there, take any bus marked 'Kópavogur' from either the Laekjargata or Hlemmur bus terminal.

GARÐABAER

Built on the lava from the Búrfell eruption of 7000 years ago, Garðabaer is another Reykjavík suburb. The town contains numerous lava caves and formations. Historically, it has been considered the elite suburb but, given Iceland's nearly classless society, it isn't exactly obvious.

Originally, the Garðabaer area consisted of two farms, Skúlástaðir and Vífilsstaðir, and a church, all mentioned in the *Landnámabók*. Just 3 decades ago, Garðabaer was a rural community. To get there, take the bus from Hlemmur terminal.

MOSSFELLSVEIT

Sometimes known as Mosfellsbaer, Mossfellsveit is one of Iceland's fastest growing towns but as a suburb it lacks any sort of character. The main tourist draw is the Álafoss woollens plant and factory outlet where Icelandic knitwear may be purchased at marginal discounts. There are also hot springs in the area which have provided Reykjavík with much of its hot water supply since 1933.

Buses to Mossfellsveit leave from the Hlemmur terminal.

BESSASTAÐAHREPPUR

This town with only 900 inhabitants, on Álftanes ('swans' peninsula') between Hafnarfjörður and Garðabaer, was originally a manor farm. It was taken over by the Augustinian monastery at Viðey in the mid-13th century but in 1262 became crown property when Iceland surrendered to the king of Norway. During Norwegian and Danish rule, the estate served as the official residence of royal governors general. In the early 19th century, the parochial school that had been based at Skálholt moved briefly to Bessastaðahreppur before relocating permanently in Reykjavík in 1845. Today, the estate is the official residence of the Icelandic head of state.

SELTJARNARNES

The small suburb of Seltjarnarnes occupies the western end of Reykjavík's peninsula. Most visitors to Seltjarnarnes are either going to the swimming pool – one of the area's nicest – or to the Rauða Ljónið, a pub on Eiðistorg which claims to be the largest pub in the world. It's actually just a large glass-domed square which will accommodate thousands as long as they don't want to sit in a chair.

Seltjarnarnes also offers nice sunset views when the weather is cooperating, and on clear days you can even see Snaefellsjökull. At the pond Bakkatjörn there's a small nature reserve with abundant bird life.

Getting There & Away

To reach Seltjarnarnes either walk 1½ km west from the centre of Reykjavík or take bus No 3 from Laekjargata bus station.

VIÐEY

Viðey, the 'wood island', is only 1 km north of Reykjavík's Sundahöfn harbour (near Laugardalur). Although it's small, 700 metres from east to west and 1700 metres from north to south, it's the largest island in Kollafjörður and has figured prominently in the history of Reykjavík and Iceland.

History

Viðey is the remnant of a volcano that died some 2 million years ago and eroded into little more than a low hill. The island was part of the estate claimed by Iceland's first settler Ingólfur Arnarson and there is evidence of habitation as early as the 10th century. Viðey probably served as a minor religious centre through the 12th century, but its importance increased with the consecration of an Augustinian monastery in 1226 by Þorvaldur Gissurarson and the renowned Snorri Sturluson.

The monastery operated until 1539 when Dietrich van Minden, an aide of the Danish king, took over the island and drove the monks away and proclaimed Viðey a royal estate. It was restored in 1550 by Jón Árason, the last Catholic bishop of Iceland, and the fort Virkið was constructed to defend the island from further aggression.

In 1751, the government presented Viðey to businessman-sheriff Skúli Magnússon and constructed the Viðeyjarstofa for his personal residence. It was designed by Nicolai Eigtved, the architect who also designed Amalienborg (the royal palace in Copenhagen built from local basalt and sandstone blocks). Completed in 1755, it is the oldest original building in Iceland. In 1774, the Viðey church was completed and consecrated. It is the second oldest church in Iceland and its interior furnishings are original. Skúli Magnússon died at Viðey in 1794.

In 1817, the island was bought by the Supreme Court president Magnús Stephensen who also brought Iceland's only printing press to Viðey. Until 1844, he operated it in a small shed near Skúli Magnússon's old residence. Stephensen's descendants owned the property until 1901 when it was purchased by seminary instructor Eiríkur Briem who established a farm there. A fishing interest called the Million Company was established on the eastern side of the island and the community grew to about 100 people but it was deserted before Icelandic independence in 1944. Subsequent owners donated the property to the city of Reykjavík on the 200th anniversary of its municipal charter in 1986.

Things to See & Do

Most visitors to the island just eat at the Viðeyjarstofa restaurant and return to Reykjavík. If you have more time, there's a camping site and barbecue facilities at Viðeyjarnaust west of the ferry landing.

The walking tracks on the island are outlined on the map but you can walk wherever you'd like. Virkið is about 300 metres west of the landing site. From there, follow the track south-east past the restaurant to the church and over the low pass Gönguskarð to reach Danadys (the Danes' grave) and Minnismerki Skúla (the Skúli Magnússon

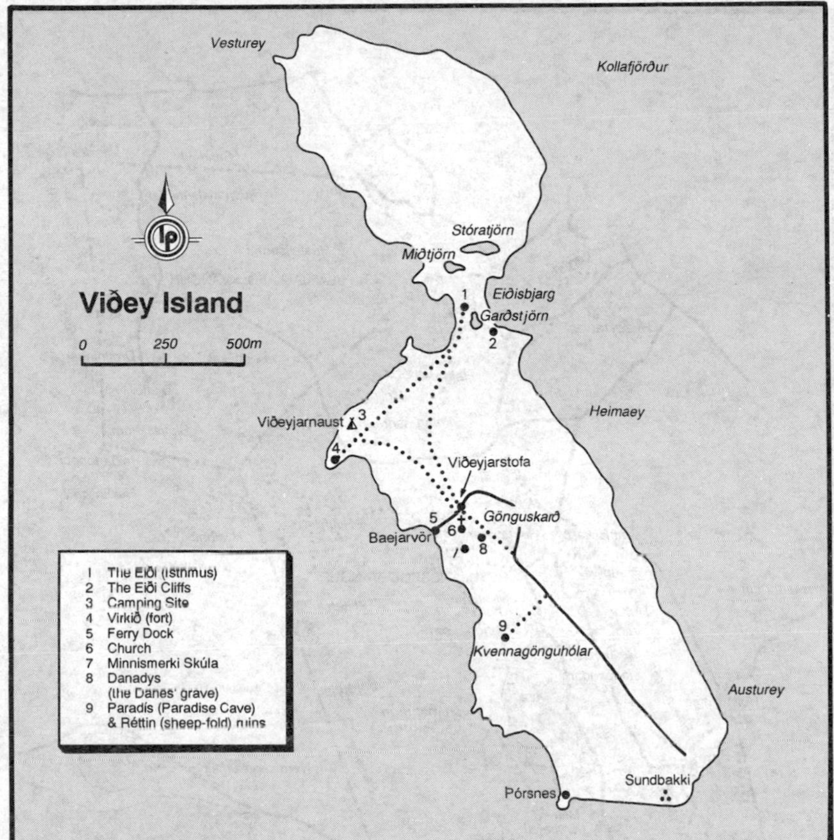

memorial). The next low hill toward the south-east is called Kvennagönguhólar where you'll find some ruins of the sheep-fold Réttin and Paradís, ('paradise cave').

It's also worthwhile to continue to the old Sundbakki village site where only an old school house still stands, or walk to the isthmus and see the ponds, the low cliffs of Eiðisbjarg, and the beautiful basalt columns of the Vesturey area.

Getting There & Away

The Viðey ferry is run by Hafsteinn Sveinsson (tel 91-20099). It leaves at 6, 7, 7.30, and 8 pm from Sundahöfn and from Viðey island at 10, 11, 11.30 pm, and midnight. If you'd like to go at any other time, contact Mr Sveinsson or ask for help at the tourist office. The trip from Sundahöfn to the island takes about 5 minutes.

LUNDEY

Lundey (the 'puffin island'), is the only place around Reykjavík to see puffins. Two-hour cruises to the tiny island leave from the Sundahöfn ferry dock at 5 pm on summer weekday afternoons. They cost around US$22 per person and are arranged through

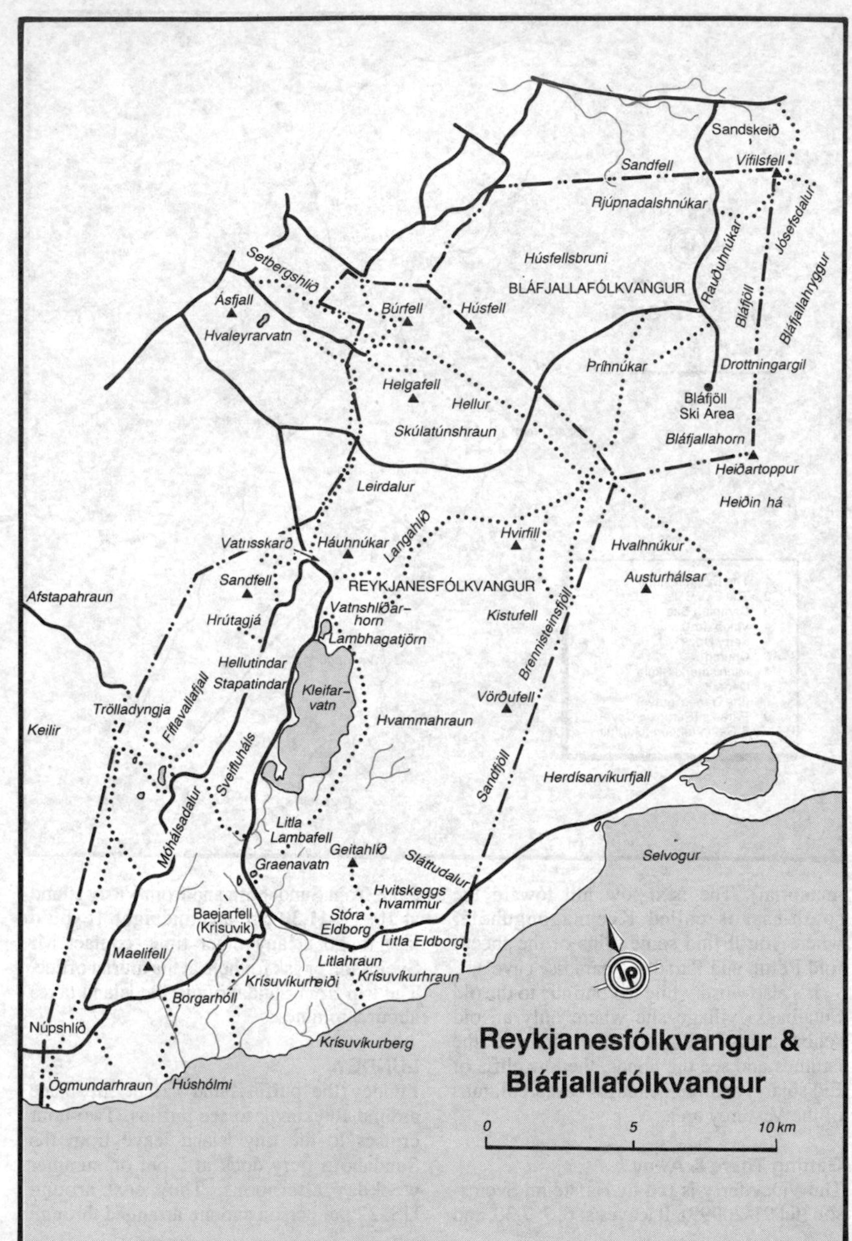

Reykjanesfólkvangur & Bláfjallafólkvangur

the tourist office at Ingólfsstraeti 5 in Reykjavík or Travel City (tel 91-623020) at Hafnarstraeti 2.

BLÁFJÖLL SKI AREA

Iceland's premier ski area is in the 84 sq km Bláfjallafólkvangur reserve just south-east of Reykjavík. It has two chair lifts, 10 rope lifts, and three cross-country ski trails of up to 10 km in length. It's normally open between mid-November and early May. Lifts operate from 10 am to 6 pm Friday to Monday and from 10 am to 10 pm Tuesday to Thursday. The service centre at Bláfjallaskáli has a snack bar and a ski-hire shop.

Daytime lift tickets cost US$7.75 per person and night skiing costs US$6. A season pass costs US$86 – not bad for 5 months. During the summer, Bláfjallafólkvangur offers many km of hiking trails right in Reykjavík's backyard.

Getting There & Away

When the ski area is open, buses leave at least once daily from BSÍ in Reykjavík and stop at Garðabaer, Hafnarfjörður, and Kópavogur. For specific departure information, phone BSÍ (tel 91-22300). The adult one-way fare is about US$5.

There is no public transport to the area in the summer so without a private vehicle you'll have to hitch, but finding rides may be difficult.

Reykjanes Peninsula

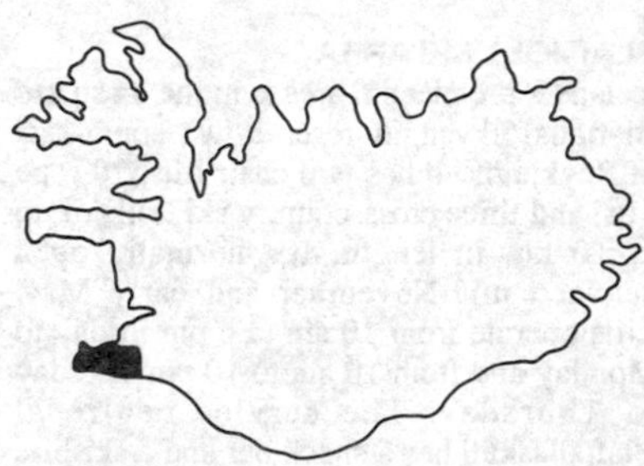

The Reykjanes peninsula is often the first bit, sometimes the only bit, of Iceland visitors see. On the way from the airport to Reykjavík they are normally either intrigued by the stark but grand barrenness or are kicking themselves for being misled into visiting such a horrid moonscape.

Old lava flows dominate the landscape of Reykjanes particularly along the corridor between Reykjavík and Keflavík. The southern half of the peninsula contains the geothermal fields of Svartsengi and Krísuvík (Baejarfell). The western end meets the Atlantic in low, wave-battered bluffs. Bird life is abundant all around the shoreline.

REYKJANESFÓLKVANGUR

Although it's not a fully fledged national park, the 300-sq km Reykjanesfólkvangur was established in 1975 as a national reserve to protect the bizarre lava formations, just a few km from Reykjavík. (See the Reykjanesfólkvangur & Bláfjallafólkvangur map at the end of the Reykjavík chapter.) The main attractions are the geothermal zone at Krísuvík and the extensive network of walking tracks around the park's fascinating topographical features.

It's fairly quiet in the park which is a pleasant escape from Reykjavík, especially when the weather is cooperating (which it rarely is). The most popular walks include the climb up 338-metre Helgafell, the loop past the remote Krísuvíkurberg cliffs, and the walk from Krísuvík around the eastern side of Kleifarvatn.

Kleifarvatn This eerie 10-sq km lake reaches a depth of 97 metres. Until recently, it was considered a 'dead' lake but it's been stocked with trout which are doing well. Some of the lava that flowed across Búrfellshraun and into Hafnarfjörður around the time of Settlement came from the craters around the pass Vatnsskarð, north of the lake.

Krísuvík This area offers steaming vents, fumaroles, mud pots, clay, and sulphur deposits. There was once a church and a few farms but today it's abandoned. Although the church was reconsecrated in 1964, it's too remote to be used regularly. The area is being considered for geothermal exploitation and several experimental bores have been drilled.

Just east of the road at Krísuvík is Graenavatn, a 44-metre deep crater with a lake in the bottom. Across the road is a smaller one, Gestsstaðavatn. Between the old settlement and Kleifarvatn is Austurengjar, an area of fumaroles that became more active after an earthquake in the 1920s.

East of Krísuvík are the craters Stóra and Litla ('big' and 'little') Eldborg. From Stóra Eldborg a rough 10-km walking route leads to the sea-bird cliffs of Krísuvíkurberg where puffins, guillemots, and other birds nest in the summer.

Brennisteinsfjöll This low range along the eastern boundary of the park was the source of most of the lava which flowed through the reserve to the sea. It was first thought to be of pre-Settlement origin but archaeology has revealed transportation routes beneath the lava layers. The abandoned sulphur mining operation at Brennisteinsnáma can be visited by an obscure walking route from either the Bláfjöll ski area or the long way around on the track from the main road north of Kleifarvatn.

Getting There & Away

Access is difficult on public transport. You'll have to take the bus to Hafnarfjörður or Garðabaer and either walk or hitch from there. The quickest access to the trail system is south of Garðabaer at the northern end of the park. Route 42, the best access to Krísuvík, turns off the main Reykjanes Highway (Route 41) just west of Hafnarfjörður.

If you want to visit the southern end of the park without a vehicle, be sure to carry a tent and food because it won't be possible in a single day from Reykjavík without a lot of luck hitching. Since this is a porous volcanic area, surface water will not be available between lakes.

Getting Around

Reykjanes Tour BSÍ does a 4½-hour bus tour of the Reykjanes highlights at 1.30 pm daily from June to August for US$31. Stops include Bessastadahreppur, Hafnarfjördur, and Grindavík. The tour returns to Reykjavík via the Krísuvík geothermal area. If you want to leave the tour anywhere en route, you can rejoin on another pre-specified day.

Tours

For US$150, you can take a taxi tour through the reserve from Reykjavík or, for US$31, the 4½-hour Reykjanes bus tour (see the following Getting Around section). Every Tuesday in summer, Sagaland Travel (tel 91-627144), at Bankastraeti 2 in Reykjavík, offers easy half-day guided hiking trips through Reykjanesfólkvangur. Tours alternate between five different routes.

GRINDAVÍK

With a population of 2100, Grindavík is a friendly and picturesque fishing village near the end of the peninsula. Although there's no

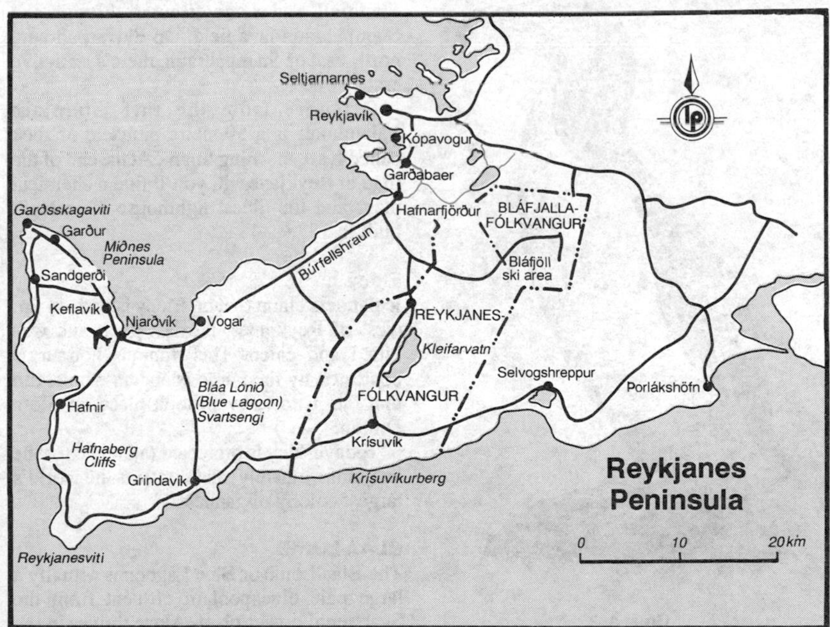

particular must-see attraction, those with time on their hands may enjoy staying for a few days to explore the coastline and volcanic topography. Grindavík's heating comes exclusively from the Svartsengi geothermal power plant just north of town.

Instead of a seamen's monument engraved with names of those lost at sea, Grindavík has erected a monument called *Hope* which unceremoniously depicts a seafarer's family gazing hopefully out to sea.

Places to Stay & Eat

At Hafnargata 17 is the relatively inexpensive *Fiskanes Guest House* which also has a lounge and cafeteria. More up-market accommodation is available, 5 minutes out of town by bus, at the Blue Lagoon. For details, see the following Bláa Lónið section. The camping ground is just east of town.

Great Auk

The most popular place to eat in town is the friendly *Sjómannastofan Vör* overlooking the harbour. Local fishermen hang out there for light meals, snacks, desserts, and coffee. The bus terminal at Hafnargata 6, open daily until 11 pm, sells a variety of general merchandise including groceries, snacks, and souvenirs.

Getting There & Away

In the summer, buses leave BSÍ in Reykjavík daily at 10.30 am, 2 pm, and 6.30 pm. They depart from Grindavík at 1, 5, and 9 pm. In winter, schedules are cut back to two departures daily in each direction. The fare is US$5.

Reykjanesviti

The country west of Grindavík steams with volcanic features. Hot springs, sulphur pools, and mud pots are found around Gunnuhver at the peninsula's south-west corner. There are also a couple of small shield volcanoes, Háleyjarbungar and Skalafell and some fissures through the Stampahraun lava field. On Eldvarpahraun, north-east of Stampahraun, there's an active crater row.

Offshore from the tuff mountain Valahnúkur is a 50-metre pinnacle of rock called Karl, meaning 'man'. At the end of the road at Reykjanesviti you'll find a chemical plant and the oldest lighthouse in Iceland, built in 1878.

Eldey

Icelanders claim that on Eldey island, 14 km west of Reykjanes, the last great auk was killed and eaten. This dubious honour is contested by the Faroe islanders who claim that the historic event took place on Stóra Dímun.

Today Eldey is protected (a bit late for the auk, unfortunately) and contains the world's largest colony of gannets.

BLÁA LONIÐ

The Bláa Lónið or Blue Lagoon is actually a large pale blue pool of effluent from the Svartsengi power plant. Algae thrives in the

20° C-water that emerges from the pipes but, as the water cools in the air, the algae dies leaving a sort of organic soup.

Although it's sometimes known affectionately as the 'chemical waste dump' by visitors, bathing in the lagoon really isn't dangerous. The chemical content of the silica mud combined with dead algae in the lagoon has been known to cure or relieve the effects of psoriasis. The Icelandic surgeon general is currently studying the phenomenon and, although a number of patrons swear by the place, there hasn't yet been any official recognition of its alleged curative value.

A swim in the Blue Lagoon can be an ethereal experience. Great clouds of vapour rise from the water, parting from time to time to reveal the immense stacks and buildings of the power plant and moss-covered lava formations in the background. The bottom is covered with chalky white rocks and slimy white silica mud that feels just as disagreeable as it looks interesting. You'll need to bring enough shampoo to rinse your hair several times after leaving the lagoon or it will be left a brick-like mass.

The bath house is open from 10 am to 10 pm daily in the summer. In the winter, when swimming out of doors would be particularly appealing, it's open Monday to Friday from 2 to 9 pm and weekends from 10 am to 9 pm. Admission costs US$5 per person.

Places to Stay & Eat

The bath house has a snack bar selling soft drinks, chips, and sausages. To stay the night, seek out a camping site in the surrounding lava fields (not an easy prospect), stay in nearby Grindavík, or check into the *Blue Lagoon Motel*. They offer sauna and jacuzzi, a workout room, restaurant, television, and a free shuttle service to Keflavík International Airport. Rooms cost singles/doubles US$80/95 per night including breakfast.

Getting There & Away

From Reykjavík, take the Grindavík bus from the BSÍ terminal. In summer, it leaves at 10.30 am, 2 and 6.30 pm. From the lagoon back to town, it passes at 1.05, 5.05, and 9 pm. The one-way fare is US$5.

Many people catching afternoon flights from Keflavík stop at the Blue Lagoon en route to the airport. Schedules vary so it's a good idea to contact the tourist office to arrange this for you.

MIÐNES & HAFNIR

The sub-peninsula at the north-western tip of Reykjanes is called Miðnes, a flat green thumb fully exposed to the winds and waves of the North Atlantic. Since it has no mountains to trap incoming moisture, a lot of the worst weather by-passes it and comes ashore with full force at Reykjavík instead. At the start of Miðnes is Keflavík International Airport and its associated NATO base.

The Miðnes peninsula was the subject of the first real estate deal made in Iceland. A widowed kinswoman of Ingólfur Arnarson, Steinunn the Old, was offered all of Miðnes free of charge for her own use. For some reason, she doubted Ingólfur's scruples and insisted on paying to ensure the permanency of the transaction. In exchange for the land, part of which would become an American base over 1000 years later, she paid a valuable embroidered cloak.

Although the west coast of the peninsula is rugged and historically has proven hazardous to seafarers, the small towns of Garður and Sandgerði survive by fishing and fish processing. An interesting trip is to the abandoned fishing village and trading centre Bátsendar which was destroyed by an unusually high tide on 9 January 1798. The area is good for birdwatching especially near the lighthouse at Garðsskagaviti north of Garður and the tjörn at Sandgerði.

The pleasant and picturesque community of Hafnir clings to the rocky coastline just south of Miðnes. A half-hour's walk west from the road, 8 km south of Hafnir, will bring you to the beautiful bird cliffs of Hafnaberg.

Getting There & Away

From BSÍ in Reykjavík, buses depart for Keflavík, Garður, and Sandgerði five times daily from Monday to Saturday. Only four buses run on Sundays. From Sandgerði to Reykjavík there are four departures daily from Monday to Saturday and three on Sundays. The fare is US$5.50 each way.

There is only one bus daily to Hafnir at 5.30 pm. From Hafnir, it leaves for Reykjavík daily at 10 am. The fare is US$5.20.

KEFLAVÍK & NJARÐVÍK

These are sibling towns about 40 km west of Reykjavík. Before the Danish Trade Monopoly of 1602, Keflavík was one of Iceland's main trading centres. Although the first official trading licence wasn't issued until 1566 to German merchant Jochim Thim of Hamburg, there is evidence that the English were there as early as 1513. Although some Germans put up resistance after the imposition of the trade monopoly, they were ousted by the Danes.

After the monopoly was lifted in 1855, Keflavík resumed some of its importance as a trading centre but it's now far more prominent as a fishing village. It's the service centre for the unpopular US military base and Iceland's international airport. Keflavík was granted municipal status in 1949 and now has a population of about 7500, several fishing-related industries, and a fishing fleet of 50 or so ships.

Njarðvík was first settled around 1300 but continued as a collection of rural farms until 1889 when it gained municipal status. It was politically united with Keflavík between 1908 and 1942 but is now considered a separate community and currently has about 2500 inhabitants. The village is split by its bay into two parts, Ytri- and Innri-Njarðvík ('northern' and 'inner' Njarðvík).

Things to See & Do

Both Keflavík and Njarðvík have swimming pools (with jacuzzis, saunas, and solariums) open daily. Several of Keflavík's older homes have been renovated into the folk museum Byggðasafn Suðurnesja (tel 92-13155), on Vatnsnesvegur. It's open on Saturdays from 2 to 4 pm and at other times upon request. The stone church at Njarðvík is marginally interesting. Keflavík also has a golf course and two cinemas.

Places to Eat

Quite a few grills and up-market restaurants are strung out along Hafnargata in Keflavík. The rather trendy *Píanóbarinn* ('piano bar', of course) is at Tjarnargata 31 and shares the building with the *Restaurant Brekka* which serves pizza, fish, and salads. The restaurant and pub at the air terminal serves the least expensive drinks in Iceland (although they're technically not *in* Iceland, which is why they are cheap).

There are several supermarkets in the area but the *Hagkaup*, just south-west of Njarðvík has the best prices.

Places to Stay

Neither Keflavík nor Njarðvík has camping grounds but campers shouldn't have any difficulty finding an informal place to set up near the shore outside town.

Three hotels in the area contend for the title of *the* airport hotel. A room at the *Flug Hotel* (tel 92-15222), at Hafnargata 57, in Keflavík will set you back US$130 per night. A similar room at the *Hotel Keflavík* (tel 92-14377), at Vatnsnesvegur 12, costs US$98 and a double at the *Hotel Kristína* (tel 92-14444), at Holtsgata 49 in Njarðvík, costs only US$87. The Hotel Kristína, incidentally, hires out bicycles.

Keflavík International Airport When the British forces pulled out of Iceland in June 1941, American forces moved in and set up the base at Keflavík. Although they weren't particularly welcome after WW II, Iceland agreed to allow them use of the already constructed base at Keflavík as a refuelling and staging post for transport aircraft flying between North America and Europe. In true 'give an inch, take a mile' tradition, the US military used this and the creation of NATO in 1949 to weasel their way into permanent residence there.

Visitors arriving at Keflavík will be welcomed by rows of camouflaged military jets and transport aircraft. Although it all may seem a bit unsettling at times, Icelanders seem to believe assurances that no nuclear hocus pocus is going on there.

In 1987, the new civilian air terminal Flugstöð Leif Eiríkssonar opened to handle increasing international passenger traffic. The terminal has a restaurant, pub, duty-free shopping, airline offices, and banking facilities.

Getting There & Away

The airport bus leaves Reykjavík, from the Hotel Loftleiðir, 2 hours before the departure of international flights and leaves the air terminal about 45 minutes after arrival of international flights. The one-way fare is US$6.

Regularly scheduled buses to Garður and Sandgerði stop at Keflavík city. Between Reykjavík and the airport, two regular buses charging only US$4.65, leave BSÍ daily at 8.30 am and 5.30 pm and depart from the air terminal at 10 am and 5 pm. Local buses between Keflavík and Innri-Njarðvík operate, on an average, every 45 minutes between 7 am and 6 pm and cost US$1. On weekdays, there are four daily runs between Grindavík and Keflavík.

West Central Iceland

West central Iceland extends from Reykjavík and its environs north to the valley Laxárdalur and Kolfningsnes peninsula at the base of the Westfjords. It includes the Akranes and Snaefellsnes peninsulas and the Borgarfjörður area. It is perhaps the richest area of Iceland historically. Most points of interest relate in some way to the sagas – especially the *Laxdaela Saga* and *Egills Saga*.

West central Iceland also has its share of interesting and unusual natural features like the famous Snaefellsjökull and the caves and craters of Borgarfjörður. Visitors' enjoyment of the west central area, however, can be tempered by its often disagreeable weather. Thanks to a natural funnel phenomenon, lots of nasty ocean-borne storm systems are channelled between the Reykjanes, Snaefellsnes, and Westfjords peninsulas. Conditions can get positively awful so, if you're lucky enough to have a sunny day in this region, enjoy yourself. There aren't likely to be two in a row!

HVALFJÖRÐUR

The long and beautiful fjord, just north of Mt Esja, is called Hvalfjörður or 'whale fjord'. Especially in August, up to 17 species of whale can be seen in its waters. At the mouth of Hvalfjörður is the iron silicon smelter at Grundartangi.

Esja

This 918-metre-high landmark, north of Reykjavík, offers many wilderness hiking and climbing routes right in the capital's backyard. The most popular routes to the summit are from the river Mógilsá and the old farm Esjuberg via the 850-metre spur Krehólakambur and 830-metre Kistufell.

The farm at Esjuberg was the site of the first church in Iceland. The *Landnámabók* states that the first settler in this region (Kjalarnes) was Helgi Ketillsson, son of Ketill Flatnose, who received the land as a

gift from Ingólfur Arnarson. When his Christian cousin Örlygur came to Iceland from the Hebrides to settle, Helgi presented him with the estate at Esjuberg. He built a church there in the honour of St Columba. Although no church is to be seen today, the old ruins at the farm are a protected historical site.

Farms

There are two farms and churches called Saurbaer around Hvalfjörður. The southern one, which was raided by English pirates in the 15th century, dates back to Settlement times. Just south of it is the farm Hof where one of the largest pagan temples is said to have existed during Settlement times but excavations haven't revealed any enlightening evidence.

The Saurbaer on the north shore is newer. The church, which contains beautiful stained-glass work, was built in memory of Hallgrímur Pétursson. He was the poor leprous pastor and composer who penned Iceland's most widely known work *50 Passion Hymns* and served there between 1651 and 1669.

Whaling Station

Along with the Soviet Union and Japan, Iceland refuses to impose a moratorium on commercial whaling. Its four-boat whaling fleet annually fills the country's quota of 400 cetacean bodies which are processed at the

Miðsandur US naval station on the northern shore of Hvalfjörður.

Most of the whale products have cheap, easily produced substitutes which can be used for pet food, vitamins, chicken feed, bouillon cubes, and lubricating oil. Iceland, however, refuses to acknowledge that whale numbers are dwindling, citing proudly that it has followed the self-serving regulations of the International Whaling Commission since 1948.

In 1986, two Icelandic whaling vessels were sunk and the processing plant sabotaged by a Canadian protest vessel but the industry doesn't appear to have been fazed. A brochure they distribute to tourists blames Greenpeace for subversive activities and the whales for consuming too much of Iceland's marine biomass which they feel should be left to the commercial fishing industry.

If you have a stomach for ghastly carnage and can muster a group of at least four similarly constituted people, there is a 2½ hour tour that leaves from Akranes on request and costs US$40 per person.

Getting There & Away

To get to Hvalfjörður, take any northbound bus from BSÍ in Reykjavík. Buses between Reykjavík and Borgarnes passing Hvalfjörður leave two or three times daily.

AKRANES

This small town with a population of 5500 is on the peninsula separating Hvalfjörður and Borgarfjörður, cut off from the mainland by the 555-metre-high mountain Akrafjall. Akranes' harbour faces Reykjavík and has been a fishing centre since the Settlement era.

Akranes has a hospital, pharmacy, swimming pool, sports complex, and tourist office. City officials are now encouraging residents to paint their chimneys in bright, arty colours and designs – an attempt to add some character, which is currently lacking – in hopes of attracting tourists.

History

The *Landnámabók* tells us that around 880, the property Garðar (1 km east of Akranes) was settled by Celt Jörundur the Christian and used as a hermitage.

His nephew, Ásólfur, and 11 other Irish monks came to Iceland travelling together emulating the 12 disciples. They originally settled at Eyjafjöll on the south coast but were driven away by greedy neighbours jealous of the ascetics' ability to inspire local streams to teem with fish. Ásólfur and company fled to Akranes and resettled at Innrihólmur, a few km to the east of his uncle Jörundur's Garðar, where both men remained hermits and sages.

After Ásólfur's death, he habitually appeared to friends and acquaintances in dreams, expressing discontent about their choice of his burial site at Innrihólmur. In order to mollify him, a church was built on the prefered site and his remains were placed inside. Although it's not the original, the current church (built in 1891) is worth seeing if you manage to find it unlocked.

Until the 17th century, when the fishing industry boomed and a town began to develop around the harbour, Akranes remained a rural farming and fishing region. It wasn't granted municipal status until 1942. In 1958, the economy diversified with the addition of Sementsverksmiðja Ríkisins (the Iceland State Cement Works). The stacks of this factory dominate the town and can be seen from Reykjavík on a clear day.

The Garðar Folk Museum

Byggðasafnið í Görðum or the Garðar Folk Museum (tel 93-1255), about 1 km east of town, is a combination of indoor and outdoor exhibits. Beside the tower is the old cemetery and a stone, engraved in both Icelandic and Gaelic, commemorating the Irish role in settling Akranes. It was a gift from the Irish Republic in 1974 for Iceland's 1100th anniversary of Settlement.

Its sailing days over, the 1885 cutter *Sigurfari* lies stranded in the sheep pastures near the museum. Inside the newly constructed building are many artefacts ranging from whaling paraphernalia to weapons and

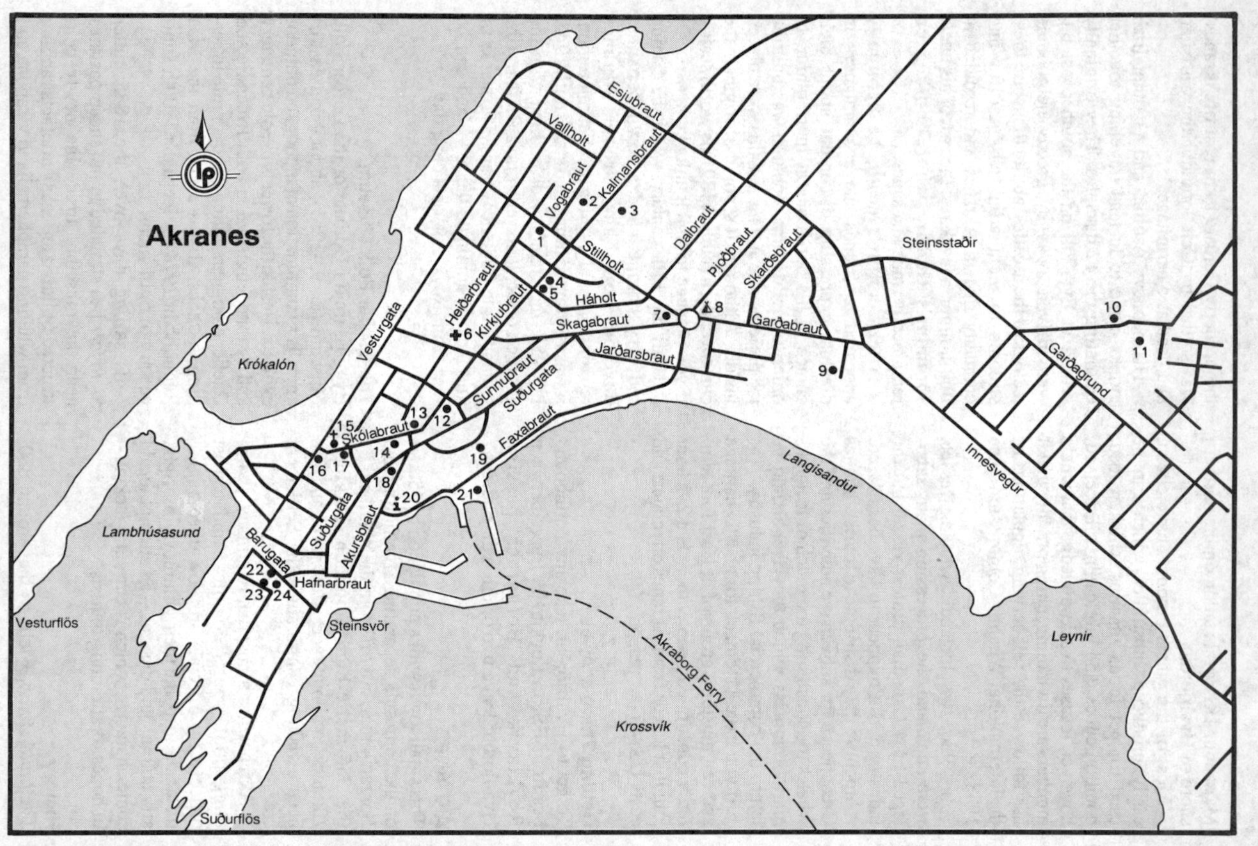
Akranes
Esjubraut
Vallholt
Kalmansbraut
Vogabraut
Stillholt
Dalbraut
Þjóðbraut
Skarðsbraut
Steinsstaðir
Háholt
Heiðarbraut
Kirkjubraut
Skagabraut
Garðabraut
Jaðarsbraut
Vesturgata
Sunnubraut
Suðurgata
Faxabraut
Skólabraut
Garðagrund
Innesvegur
Langisandur
Krókalón
Lambhúsasund
Barugata
Akursbraut
Hafnarbraut
Vesturflös
Steinsvör
Akraborg Ferry
Leynir
Krossvík
Suðurflös
1
2
3
4
5
6
7
8
9
10
11
12
13
14
15
16
17
18
19
20
21
22
23
24

1 Caféteria & Shop
2 Hotel Ósk
3 Supermarket
4 Bakery
5 Bookshop
6 Hospital & Health Care Centre
7 Coach Terminal, Shop, Car Rental & Caféteria
8 Camping Ground
9 Sports Centre & Swimming Pool
10 Folk Museum
11 Monument
12 Police Station
13 Barbró Restaurant
14 National Bank of Iceland
15 Church
16 Bookshop
17 Stjörnukaffi Coffee Shop
18 Bakery
19 Cement Works
20 Tourist Information
21 Akranes-Reykjavík Ferry
22 Restaurant & Pizzeria
23 Pub
24 Hotel (Dancing)

ships used against the British in the Cod Wars.

Between 18 May and 31 August, the museum's open daily except Mondays from 11 am to noon and 2 to 5 pm. The rest of the year, it's open Tuesday to Friday from 2 to 4 pm. Admission is US$2.60 for adults and US$1.50 for children. Tour groups can arrange special visits by phoning in advance.

Langisandur

This sandy south-facing beach, at Akranes, is 1 km long and the nicest beach in urban Iceland. When the sun shines, the sand catches the direct rays. When the wind isn't screaming across the icy water, it's ideal.

Akranes Church

The rather seedy-looking Akranes church was constructed in 1896. It attests to the wonders of corrugated aluminium, a common 'siding' and roofing material in a treeless country.

Arafjall

The 555-metre peak Akrafjall dominating the view in Akranes can be easily climbed in a day. The Berry valley, source of Akranes' water supply, splits the peak in two and provides climbers with an easy route up to either of the summits. It's possible to camp anywhere on the mountain.

Sementsverksmiðja Ríkisins

The cement works in Akranes was established in response to Iceland's lack of natural building materials. Ingredients for the cement come from the seashell beds of Faxaflói, about 20 km south-west of Akranes, and the volcanic rhyolite around Hvalfjörður. There really aren't any tours of the plant but the locals are extremely proud of this industry and anyone interested in the process can probably arrange something informally.

Places to Eat

The new *Strompurinn* (tel 93-12020), in the Hotel Akranes at Barugata 15, is very up-market. It's one of the best places in Iceland to sample some of the more unusual delicacies like ram's testicles, cod chins, and (oh, horrors) hákarl. For the squeamish, they serve more innocuous dishes and even pizza specialties.

At Skólabraut 14 is the reasonably priced *Stjörnukaffi* coffee shop. Even less expensive snacks are found at the several petrol stations around town, but don't expect more than the usual sausages and soft drinks.

There are two *Harðarbakarí* (bakery) outlets, one at Kirkjubraut 56 and the other at Skólabraut 14, and a couple of supermarkets near the town centre. The state liquor store is at Þjóðbraut 21.

Places to Stay

Akranes has two up-market lodgings, the *Hotel Akranes* (tèl 93-12020), at Barugata 15, and the summer *Hotel Ósk* (tel 93-13313), at Vogabraut 4. The latter is cheaper with double rooms for US$74 per night. It has a laundry which non-guests may be able to use for a fee. Dormitory style sleeping-bag accommodation is available from June to August for US$17 per night.

The camping ground is near Garðar on Garðabraut.

Getting There & Away

Bus The two or three daily buses between BSÍ in Reykjavík and the town of Borgarnes pass Akranesvegamót (*vegamót* means 'junction') and connect with Akranes buses. The fare each way between Reykjavík and Akranes is US$10.35.

Ferry The ferry *Akraborg* (tel 91-16420 Reykjavík or 93-11095 Akranes) sails at least four times each day between Reykjavíkurhöfn and Akranes. For fares and schedules, see the Getting There & Away section in the Reykjavík chapter.

BORGARNES

Borgarnes is different because it 's the only Icelandic coastal town which doesn't depend on fishing; it's the trade and service centre for the Borgarfjörður district. Strung out along a narrow 2-km-long peninsula (so that the wind assaults it from all directions), Borgarnes has a beautiful setting, clear weather permitting. Some visitors have been lucky, but go there expecting the worst weatherwise. Who knows? You may be pleasantly surprised.

The town has a welcoming swimming pool with a sauna, a solarium, and jacuzzis that take the depression out of oppressive weather. Women's saunas are available on Thursdays from 5 to 9.30 pm and men's on Fridays during the same hours. There's a cinema on Thursday and Sunday nights.

Things to See

The art, natural history, and folk museum is at Borgarbraut 61, west of the camping ground.

In the park near the centre is the burial mound of Skallagrímur Kveld-Úlfsson, the father of the infamous skald Egill Skallagrímsson of *Egills Saga*. The saga tells us that Egill carried the body of his accidentally drowned 17-year-old son, Böðvar, to this mound and buried him beside his grandfather. On a nearby stone is a very nice relief plaque by Danish artist Annemarie Brodersen which depicts the event.

Places to Stay & Eat

Borgarnes' only hotel is the *Hotel Borgarnes* (tel 93-71119), at Egilsgata 14 near the western end of the peninsula. It's a very sterile-looking place, typical of Icelandic hotels, but has a pleasant dining room. A double costs US$77.

Across town, near Iceland's second longest bridge, is the free camping ground. The nicest place to camp is above the cliffs overlooking the water. When you want to dry off and get tired of sheltering in the toilet, take advantage of one of Iceland's best bargains at the *Esso* petrol station across the street where a bottomless cup of coffee costs only US$0.90 and freshly baked doughnuts are served all day. Both this and the *Shell* station by the bridge have grills as well and are open daily from 8 am to 10 pm. The supermarket is opposite the Hotel Borgarnes in the 'progressive' shopping centre and the bakery is just west of the Esso station.

Getting There & Away

Borgarnes is the hub of all the bus routes between Reykjavík, Akureyri, the Westfjords, Borgarfjörður and Snaefellsnes. There are two bus terminals in town, one at the Hotel Borgarnes and the other at the Esso station. Travellers often have problems working out which services use which terminal. There seems to be no rhyme or reason to it, so ask before making assumptions.

The first service from Reykjavík departs at 8 am (except on Sundays) and from Borgarnes at 10 am. There are also several daily services to Reykholt (Borgarfjörður), Ólafsvík, and Stykkishólmur, and three times weekly to and from the Westfjords. At the height of summer, two daily services between Reykjavík and Akureyri pass through Borgarnes.

Tours

Grand Tour of Borgarfjörður Those with a ready US$80 can arrange to go on the full-day 'Grand Tour' of Borgarfjörður. Ask for details at the Hotel Borgarnes. The itinerary takes in Deildartunguhver (Iceland's largest hot spring), Snorri Sturluson's Reykholt, Hraunfossar, Barnafoss, Húsafell, Surtshellir cave, and the farms Gilsbakki and Svignaskarð.

AROUND BORGARNES

Hafnarfjall This is the crumbly scree mountain that you pass entering Borgarnes from the south. Although it's beautiful to look at, unconsolidated Hafnarfjall would prove difficult to climb. The grainy, light coloured basalt composition is called Flyðrur.

Borg á Mýrum The most famous farm in the country, Borg is the historical equivalent of George Washington's Mt Vernon. Its name means 'rock in the marshes'. The farmsite was determined by Kveld-Úlfur, Egill Skallagrímsson's grandfather, who got on the wrong side of King Harald Haarfager of Norway and fled to Iceland. As they approached land, Kveld-Úlfur became ill and knew he would die. He instructed his son, Skallagrímur Kveld-Úlfsson, to make a coffin for him, place his body in it and throw it overboard. He was to select the site for the family farm where it washed ashore. This happened to be at Borg; Egill's father settled and reared his family there.

While in England, Egill married his brother's widow Ásgerður but domestic life failed to tame him. Twenty years later, in 957, Egill finished his havoc-wreaking spree in Europe and returned to Borg to settle down. Egill's son Þorsteinn built a church on the estate in 1003. His daughter Þorgerður married Ólafur Peacock, a hero of *Laxdaela Saga*, and his other son Böðvar was, of course, buried in the mound in Borgarnes.

In 1197, historian and descendant of the Borg dynasty Snorri Sturluson married the heiress of Borg and thereby acquired the property, but family responsibility ended there as far as Snorri was concerned. He left his wife at Borg and moved to Reykholt further inland.

Today you can see a small church, the large rock that gave the place its name, and an interesting sculpture by Ásmundur Sveinsson. Icelanders say that the old grave on the farm is that of Kjartan Ólafsson (whom the *Laxdaela Saga* reports was buried at Borg) but that's probably only wishful thinking.

Svignaskarð The farm Svignaskarð, about 20 km north-east of Borgarnes along the Ring Road, was once owned by Snorri Sturluson. On the hill Kastalinn above the farm is a view disc for the considerable panorama including cone-shaped Mt Baula, Hafnarfjall, Okjökull, Þorisjökull, Geitlandsjökull, and Eiríksjökull. Near the farm is a small stand of larch and dwarf birch trees – only in Iceland would this rate a mention!

Hítardalur About 33 km north-west of Borgarnes past the river Hítará, is Barnaborgarhraun, a lava field with a couple of impressive craters. Just east is 640-metre Fagraskógarfjall, where the outlaw Grettir the Strong of *Grettirs Saga* hid from the law in a crack in western end of the rock.

Those without a car will find it difficult to reach upper Hítardalur. Their choice is a long 20-km walk or a near-impossible hitch from the main road along Route 539. The secluded mountain lake Hítarvatn, at the upper end of the valley has plenty of trout. South of Hítarvatn there's a region of lava caves and to the north are unusual rock sculptures and formations.

UPPER BORGARFJÖRÐUR

Varmaland

Tentless travellers may want to use Varmaland, which has a youth hostel, as a base for exploring the upper Borgarfjörður area. Although it was originally developed as an educational centre, Varmaland is in a geothermal area and is a resort popular with Icelanders. Tourist facilities include a camping area, snack bar, swimming pool, and stands selling local hothouse vegetables. Basic groceries are available as well.

Accommodation in the youth hostel (tel

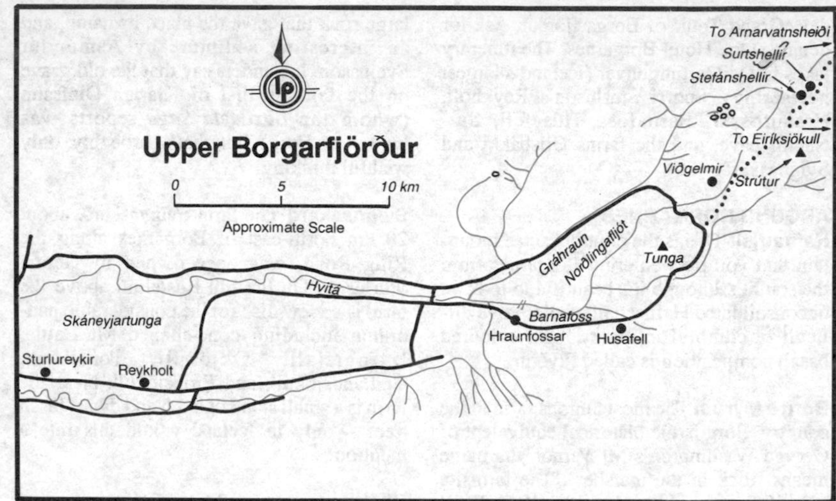

93-51301), open from 15 June to 15 August, costs US$11/13 for members/non-members. Reservations are recommended.

Getting There & Away Those prepared to walk the 5 easy km from the Ring Road to Varmaland should get off the bus from Reykjavík to Akureyri at the farm Haugar, where Route 50 meets the Ring Road. Reykholt-bound buses to and from Borgarnes stop at Varmaland daily except on Saturdays.

Around Varmaland

Munadarnes The farm Munadarnes near Varmaland is a summer camp for Icelandic government employees. It has a grill and a licensed restaurant and reasonably priced food. Those staying at Varmaland may appreciate this option.

Laxfoss This waterfall on the Norðurá, 6 km north-east of Varmaland, makes a pleasant day-hike from the hostel. Fossilised plants can be found in the rocks near the falls.

Flókadalur Upstream from Route 50 along the Flokadalsá river, a tributary of the Hvitá, is the valley Flókadalur . It was named after disenchanted settler Hrafna-Flóki Vilgerðarson, who named Iceland. The wide and grassy valley slopes gently upward to the volcanic 1141-metre-high Ok, capped by the icefield Okjökull. The name wasn't intended as an assessment of the place, but it's appropriate. The best hiking access to the mountain is from Húsafell or from Route F35 where it passes the base of Ok.

Deildartunguhver Iceland's most powerful hot spring, the boiling pool of Deildartunguhver, issues from the earth at a temperature of 100° C and at a rate of 200 litres per second. It supplies Borgarnes and Akranes with hot water. There is a platform at the farm Deildartunga which allows public viewing. It's on Route 522 near the Hvitá crossing, about 15 km by road from Varmaland.

Bifröst

Bifröst, on the Ring Road, consists of a relatively inexpensive hotel and its geologically interesting surroundings. The Hotel Bifröst (tel 93-50000) offers rooms, meals, petrol, and a break in the trip between

Reykjavík and Akureyri. A double room costs US$58 per night but the open countryside around it offers unlimited camping opportunities and, despite the volcanic nature of the area, some sites with surface water available.

Grábrók & Grábrókarhraun The 3000-year-old lava field Grábrókarhraun is unusual because it is covered with moss, lichen, and dwarf birch. It came from the two small craters Grábrók and Grábrókarfell, about 1 km north-east of the Hotel Bifröst. Both can be easily climbed but Grábrókarfell has been damaged by gravel mining. All Borgarfjörður tours include them on the itinerary. Petrol and snacks are available at Hreðavatnskáli beside the craters.

Hreðavatn The beautiful lake Hreðavatn, about 1 km south-west of the Hotel Bifröst along the side road, is a peaceful and colourful place to explore on foot. Lignite (low grade coal) is found north of the lake and the surrounding rocks contain plant fossils. If you'd like to camp on the north shore, ask permission at the Hreðavatn farm .

Hraunsnef Although it's unlikely that it happened so apocalyptically, legend has it that shortly after the settlement of Borgarfjörður, half of the mountain behind Hraunsnef broke away and crashed down into the valley. The event reportedly left the immense heap of alluvium on which the farm is built as well as the 100-metre-high cliff face behind it.

Desey Desey, the broad floodplain across the road from Hraunsnef, was created when the river Norðurá was dammed by lava from Grábrók and formed a lake in this area. The dam subsequently broke leaving the flat marshes there today.

Baula This near-perfect grey rhyolite cone rises 11 km north-east of Bifröst. The 935-metre-high mountain consists mostly of scree but can be climbed easily in a day from the point where Route 60 passes its base. It's a fairly easy hitch from Bifröst but can also be walked in a couple of hours.

Getting There & Away

Bifröst is along the main bus route between Reykjavík and Akureyri. The fare from Reykjavík is US$14.

Reykholt

Although Snorri Sturluson married the heiress of Borg and owned that historic farm just outside Borgarnes, he preferred to leave his family on the coast and live at the educational centre, Reykholt. At this retreat, he lived like a rambunctious bachelor and wrote and copied his greatest works, the *Prose Edda*, *Heimskringla* and *Egills Saga*. Aged 62, he was assassinated at Reykholt by his political enemy, Gissur Þorvaldsson (see Literature in the Iceland Facts about the Country chapter).

Reykholt now is little more than a tiny farming hamlet set amid beautiful truncated hills and geothermal springs. In front of the present school is a statue of Snorri by Norwegian sculptor Gustav Vigeland. It was presented to Iceland as a gift from Crown Prince Ólaf of Norway in 1947 in gratitude for Snorri's writing of *Heimskringla*, the definitive historical account of medieval Norway. There's also a small exhibit of Snorri Sturluson's writings and a collection of written accounts about his life.

This Reykholt shouldn't be confused with the one in Biskupstungur near Geysir where there is a new youth hostel.

Places to Stay & Eat The *Edda Hotel* (tel 93-51260) in Reykholt has a restaurant, pub, and sleeping-bag accommodation. It charges US$45/58 a single/double, and about US$14 for a bed in the dormitory.

Other services include a petrol station and general store. The nearest official camping ground is at Geirsárbakkar in Reykjadalur about 12 km west of Reykholt near the confluence with the Hvitá. As usual, however, camping nearer Reykholt should not be problematic. The hotel should allow you to set up outside and use their facilities for a small charge.

Getting There & Away The bus between Borgarnes and Reykholt runs daily except Saturdays. It leaves Borgarnes at 10 am and Reykholt at noon except on Sundays when it departs Borgarnes at 2.30 pm and Reykholt at 4 pm.

Around Reykholt

Snorri's Pool With the possible exception of Helgafell at Stykkishólmur, no saga site in Iceland is quite as haunting as Snorri's pool. It's a circular bath 4 metres in diameter, lined with stones and fed by a stone aqueduct from the Skrifla hot spring 100 metres away. Sheltered by the low hill Skáneyjarbunga to the north, it could be used all year round. The passage behind the pool is said to have ended in the cellar where Snorri Sturluson was murdered but most of it has been destroyed by building the school and only about 12 metres remain.

Húsafell

Húsafell is the easternmost farm in upper Borgarfjörður. It's in a geothermal area and has become a popular place for individuals and corporations to have summer homes. Húsafell, which sits amid stands of birch by the turbulent river Kaldá, has good views of both lava fields and glaciers. Just west of Húsafell are the excavated ruins of a Settlement-era farm.

Information The small service centre at Húsafell has hot springs, a snack bar, grocery kiosk, petrol station, and a geothermally heated swimming pool. For further information, phone (tel 93-51374).

There are camping sites scattered around and farmhouse accommodation is available at the nearby farms Húsafell (tel 93-51374), Fljótstunga (tel 93-51198), and Bjarnastaðir (tel 93-51426).

Getting There & Away Public access to Húsafell is difficult. There is only one scheduled bus per week (on Sundays) and you may have to resort to hitching in from Reykholt. If you just want a quick visit to the caves, the 'Grand Tour' of Borgarfjörður outlined in the Borgarnes section is your best option.

Around Húsafell

Hraunfossar About 4 km west of Húsafell is a scenic series of cascades and waterfalls where the river Hvitá makes its way through the lava and between trees and boulders.

Barnafoss The waterfall Barnafoss, whose name means 'children's falls', cascades through a ravine just above the Hraunfossar. Its name was derived from a legend about two children who fell into the river from a natural stone span here.

Hallmundarhraun Caves Most foreign visitors to Húsafell want to see the the immense expanses of Hallmundarhraun, a lava flow created by craters in Eiríksjökull and north-western Langjökull. Surtshellir, north of the 4WD road 14 km east of Húsafell, is 1.5 km long and the largest lava tube in Iceland. A smaller cave, Stefánshellir, is 200 metres west of it. The third cave, a large one called Viðgelmir, is best reached from the Fljótstunga, a farm on the road 7 km north-east of Húsafell and 2 km north-west of the cave. Both Viðgelmir and Surtshellir show signs of ancient occupation but don't forget to bring a torch if you want to see anything at all.

All the lava tubes contain cave decorations – stalactites and stalagmites – which are protected by law. Hitching on Hallmundarhraun will prove difficult so carry supplies and plan on walking the entire distance.

Arnarvatnsheiði The lakes of Arnarvatnsheiði ('eagle lake moors'), along with the islands of Breiðafjörður and the hills of Vatnsdalur, make up the three sets of Iceland's legendary 'innumerables'. The vast lake-studded landscape has long been popular for trout fishing but the open and lonely nature of the place appeals to those who are into other-worldly solitude as well.

If you like the Yorkshire dales, you'll love Arnarvatnsheiði!

The area is most easily reached on the 4WD track which continues north-east from Surtshellir. Those with time and energy can walk through the region which extends for 40 km or so north-east of Húsafell.

Horse tours (for up to 9 days) across Arnarvatnsheiði are available from Arinbjörn Jóhannsson (tel 95-1938) in Hvammstangi. His Reykjavík office (tel 91-26482) is at Framnesvegur 20b.

LAXDAELA SAGA COUNTRY

Laxárdalur, the 'salmon river valley', was the setting of the *Laxdaela Saga*, considered the most romantic and entertaining of all the Norse sagas. Although the genealogies get complex, the fairly simple theme revolves around a love triangle involving 'the most beautiful woman in Iceland', Guðrun Ósvífursdóttir; Kjartan Ólafsson, the son of Ólafur Peacock (the illegitimate grandson of the Irish king) and grandson of the warrior poet Egill Skallagrímsson; and Bolli Þorleiksson, Ólafur Peacock's nephew and adopted son.

You'd be hard-pressed to find an Icelander who hasn't read the *Laxdaela Saga* at least once and its complicated genealogies are familiar to all. Although the Laxárdalur landscape isn't the most exciting in Iceland, foreigners who have read the tale may want to visit the settings that are so near and dear to Icelanders.

Búðardalur

The name of this village on Hvammsfjörður at the mouth of the Laxá means 'booth valley'. There Höskuldur Dalakollsson, great-grandson-in-law of Auður the Deep-Minded (more about her later), set up a boat shed and some warehouse booths for his cargo enterprise.

The village with a population of 300 has an undeveloped summer camping site and Skjólshús (tel 93-41322), a basic summer guesthouse at Dalbraut 2. There's a grocery kiosk and a petrol station with a snack bar selling basic groceries as well.

Eiríksstaðir

This now-abandoned farm across the Haukadalsá from Stóra-Vatnshorn church was the home of Eirík Rauðe, before he was exiled as an outlaw and left for Greenland. There his son Leif the Lucky, Leif Eiríksson, was born. The boy, of course, went on to earn his place in history by 'discovering' North America. Some ruins of the farm are still visible but they're nothing to go out of your way for unless you have a particular interest.

Höskuldsstaðir

Höskuldsstaðir farm, 4 km up the Laxá from Búðardalur, was the home of Höskuldur Dalakollsson. Bolli Þorleiksson of the *Laxdaela Saga* love triangle was the son of (this gets confusing) Höskuldur's legitimate son Þorleikur.

Hjarðarholt

Across the river from Höskuldsstaðir is Hjarðarholt, the farm established by Ólafur Peacock in 960. He built an elaborate residence and entertainment hall befitting his name. The feast he held there for his father's, Höskuldur Dalakollson's, funeral reportedly accommodated nearly 1100 guests. The farm is still inhabited and now has a church.

Hvammur in Skeggjadalur

A whole line of prominent Icelanders hail from Hvammur. The farm was originally settled by Auður the Deep-Minded around the year 895. She had moved to Britain from Norway with her father Ketill Flatnose and there married Ólaf the White who became Ólaf Godfraidh, King of Ireland. When he was killed in battle, she set out for Iceland, where her brothers had already settled, marrying off some of her children and grandchildren along the way. In the *Laxdaela Saga*, the Auður character is known as Unnur.

Auður's descendants remained at Hvammur including Hvamm-Sturla, the forbear of the Sturlung clan. In 1179, her most famous descendant, Snorri Sturluson, was born there where there's now a basalt sculpture in his honour. More recently, Árni

Magnússon, the man responsible for rescuing saga vellums from the great fire in Copenhagen, was born and reared at Hvammur.

Krosshólar Across the road, 1 km from Hvammur, is the craggy rock formation Krosshólar. Although the *Laxdaela Saga* maintains Auður the Deep-Minded was a pagan, the *Landnámabók* claims that in Britain she became a Christian – one of the first to settle in Iceland – and prayed daily beside crosses on this hill. There is now a cross on the hill inscribed with the words from the *Landnámabók*:

> She said her prayers at Krosshólar. She set up crosses there, for she had been baptised and was strong in her faith.

Laugar in Saelingsdalur

Laugar, 15 minutes by road north of Buðardalur, is the birthplace of *Laxdaela Saga* heroine, Guðrun Ósvífursdóttir. The word *laugar* means 'hot springs' and is attached to geothermal areas all over Iceland. A stone conduit has been excavated from beneath a rockfall at the farm confirming that this spring was used for bathing and recreation at the time of Guðrun's birth around 973. By the stream at Saelingsdalur farm is Bollatóttir, the ruins of the shepherd's hut where Bolli Þorleiksson was killed to avenge the murder of Kjartan Ólafsson.

In addition to all this history, Laugar now has a small folk museum.

Places to Stay Laugar is a summer resort with a camping ground and an *Edda Hotel* (tel 93-41265). Double rooms cost US$58 and sleeping-bag accommodation, the usual US$14. There is also a licensed restaurant and, of course, a naturally heated swimming pool.

Getting There & Away

The only public access to the Laxárdalur area is by the thrice weekly bus between Reykjavík and Ísafjörður. Northbound, it passes Búðardalur at 11.45 am on Tuesdays and Thursdays and heads south, at 4.30 pm Wednesdays and Fridays and at 6.30 pm Sundays.

Snaefellsnes

The French science-fiction author Jules Verne wrote that the 100-km-long peninsula called Snaefellsnes was 'very like a thigh-bone in shape'. Those with less sophisticated imaginations will probably look at the map and see something else. Jutting out into the Atlantic Ocean between Faxaflói and Breiðafjörður, it's characterised by convoluted mountains rising from a broad coastal plain on the south coast and a narrower one on the north. Near the western end, the plain disappears altogether.

One of Iceland's most renowned landmarks, the 1446-metre dormant volcano Snaefell, is capped by the glacier Snaefellsjökull. Its crater led Professor Hardwigg and his nephew to the centre of the earth in Jules Verne's classic, *A Journey to the Centre of the Earth.*

Most of the population of Snaefellsnes lives in the strip along the sheltered north coast in the villages of Stykkishólmur, Grundarfjörður, Ólafsvík, and Hellissandur-Rif. The south coast has no villages and, once you've seen an average day's weather, you'll be able to work out why.

The bird life on Snaefellsnes is rich, the people are laid-back, the scenery is good, and the weather...well that just has to be experienced.

STYKKISHÓLMUR

Snaefellsnes' largest village, Stykkishólmur, is named for the islet Stykki that partially shelters its harbour. It sits at the end of a complicated sub-peninsula called Þorsnes jutting into Breiðafjörður.

History

For the past 4 centuries, Stykkishólmur with its well-sheltered harbour has been an important fishing, trading, and administrative

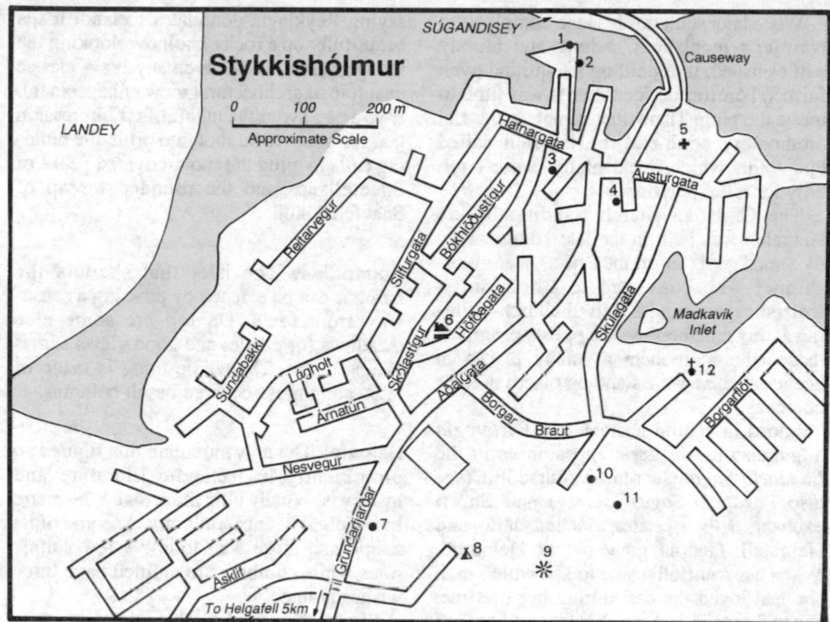

1	Ferry
2	Passenger Boats
3	Norska Húsið ('Norwegian House')
4	Swimming Pool
5	Hospital
6	New Youth Hostel (approximate location)
7	Petrol Station & Grill
8	Camping Site
9	View Disc
10	Hotel
11	Golf Course
12	Church

centre. In its more distant past, however, the area served as a religious centre for both pagan and Christian traditions.

From the time of Settlement, the area has been significant to the worshippers of Þór. According to *Eyrbyggja Saga*, the first settler Þórólfur Mostrarskeggi named the land after his god and transplanted a wooden temple he'd used at his previous home in Norway. The bay west of his farm Hofstaðir ('temple stead') he named Hofstaðavogur ('temple bay').

East of his property was a mountain Þórólfur regarded as holy and called it, naturally, Helgafell ('holy mountain'). His son Þorstein Cod-Biter once reported seeing Helgafell open up into a fiery Valhalla where he witnessed the dead feasting and enjoying themselves immensely. Thanks to an unfortunate fishing accident, Þorstein was able to join them early.

Þórólfur gathered his relatives and formed the first Icelandic þing or government assembly, on the plain near his farm. Lest the holy land around there be defiled in any way during these meetings, Þórólfur set up a toilet area on a small offshore islet which he called Dritsker, the Icelandic equivalent of Shitskerry. No one today knows which islet this was but many have surely gazed out into Hofstaðavogur and wondered.

When later settlers refused to comply with Þórólfur's regulations, a long and bloody battle ensued, thus defiling the ground even further. Þórólfur decided then it was time to move the þing. Thereafter, it met on the flat promontory north-east of Helgafell called Þingvöllur which, incidentally, wasn't too holy for relief purposes.

The Christian church standing beside Helgafell was built in the late 10th century by Snorri goði (Snorri the Priest), a Þór worshipper who converted to Christianity. Iceland experienced a rash of church-building at this time because the priests promised those who built them as many places in heaven as there were standing places in their churches.

Snorri, a central character in *Eyrbyggja Saga*, also makes guest appearances in the *Laxdaela Saga*. Guðrun Ósvífursdóttir (see also *Laxdaela Saga* Country) and Snorri exchanged their estates, Saelingsdalur and Helgafell. Guðrun grew old at Helgafell. When her son Bolli came to ask which man she had loved the best during her lifetime, she understood him to ask which of her four husbands she'd loved the best. When he explained himself, however, she replied, 'I treated the worst the one I loved the most', thereby providing an enigmatic ending for her tragic tale.

Around Town

Stykkishólmur is a picturesque community that could almost be called quaint. In the centre is the Norska Húsið ('Norwegian House'), built by trader Árni Þorlacius in 1829 and recently converted into a museum. It was closed at the time of writing but it may be open again by the time you read this. Near Norska Húsið is another old house called Egills Húsið ('Egill's House'). It now serves as a restaurant, guesthouse, and tourist information office.

On the rocky hill above the camping ground is a view disc for Breiðafjörður and the surrounding landscape.

Church The new church is an odd one. To say that it dominates the town would be like saying Reykjavík dominates Iceland. It sits beautifully on a rocky knoll overlooking the village; some would even say it's a classic example of architectural view enhancement. If you can avoid the natural first impression that it's about to be shot into orbit, the building calls to mind the snow-covered peaks of Snaefellsnes and the rounded icecap of Snaefellsjökull.

Súgandisey The islet that shelters the harbour can be reached by crossing a causeway from town. On top are some nice meadows for picnics and good views across Breiðafjörður. The whole thing is made of interesting moss-covered basalt columns.

Helgafell The holy mountain that figured so prominently in Icelandic literature and history is actually little more than a 73-metre hill. Helgafell apparently retains some of its magic and those who follow a few simple rules while climbing are entitled have three wishes granted.

Firstly, they must climb up the south-west slope to the temple ruins without speaking or glancing backward. Secondly, the wishes must be for good and made with a guileless heart. Thirdly, wishers must descend the eastern slope to the grave and never reveal their wishes to anyone.

Interestingly enough, you may be distracted while climbing the mountain. When I was halfway up, it began to rain. A few moments later there came a panic of quacking ducks on the lake behind me (there *were* no ducks before or after the climb, incidentally). Having wishes granted requires more concentration than you'd expect!

East of the hill is a grave believed to be that of Guðrun Ósvífursdóttir. Snorri goði's church is still there, several renovations later. Until the Reformation there had been a monastery there as well.

To reach Helgafell, walk or hitch the 5 km south of town to the second dirt track turning left after the head of Nesvogur. From there, it's another 1.5 km east past the lake (the one with no ducks) to Helgafell.

Þingvöllur The level place to where Þórólfur moved his assembly is south-east of Stykkishólmur. There are remains of some minor platforms and a block of blue basaltic stone containing deposits of red scoria suggesting blood. According to *Eyrbyggja Saga*, human sacrifices to Þór were held there but historians generally agree that although rape, plunder, pillage, and slaughter figured prominently in the Norse tradition, human sacrifice didn't.

To visit Þingvöllur, walk or hitch to the intersection 5 km south of town where a dirt track turns left near the head of Nesvogur. The site is near the water, 5 km north-east.

Places to Stay & Eat

Buy good snacks, chips, sausages, and coffee at the petrol station near the camping ground. The slightly more up-market cafeteria and snack bar in *Egill's House* is also nice. Near the sports complex, at Nesvegur 1, is a bakery with the supermarket across the street.

The *Hotel Stykkishólmur* (tel 93-81330) has a rather posh dining room and you pay well for the nice view. Double rooms start at US$112 per night. A more pleasant place to stay is *Egillshusið Guest House* (tel 93-81450) where doubles with/without linen are US$54/35. Dormitory sleeping-bag accommodation is available for US$10.

The new *Youth Hostel* in Stykkishólmur is reportedly on or near Skólastígur. Their prices will probably be the same as at other Icelandic youth hostels: US$11/13 for members/non-members.

The free camping ground near the sports complex is one of the nicest you'll come across in Iceland. It has full facilities, a children's playground, barbecues, and drying areas.

Getting There & Away

Air Arnarflug has flights between Reykjavík and Stykkishólmur on Tuesdays, Fridays, and Sundays. The airport is 2 km south of town west of the main highway.

Bus Daily buses operate between Reykjavík and Stykkishólmur and take 4 hours. All buses between Reykjavík, Stykkishólmur, and Ólafsvík meet at an unassuming intersection called Vegamót ('intersection') and passengers sort themselves out according to their destination. What's going on is normally explained only in Icelandic, so stay on your toes.

Ferry The ferry *Baldur* (tel 93-81120) operates between Stykkishólmur, Flatey (Breiðafjörður), and Brjánslaekur (in the Westfjords) at least once daily between 1 May and 30 September. These routes connect with buses to and from Reykjavík on the southern end and Westfjord buses from Brjánslaekur.

The fare to Flatey is US$12 and to the Westfjords is US$14.65. Car and driver pay US$48 across Breiðafjörður. It's interesting to watch the cars (especially if they aren't yours) being loaded into the hold of the ship with a crane.

A new ferry service will run during July and August leaving Stykkishólmur daily at 10 am and 4.30 pm and leaving Brjánslaekur at 1 and 7.30 pm.

AROUND STYKKISHÓLMUR

Breiðafjörður

A popular tourist activity in Stykkishólmur is a trip through the 'innumerable islands of Breiðafjörður', see Arnarvatnsheiði earlier in this chapter. This maze of low, flat, and rocky islets is rich in bird life and, during the proper season, some of the islets are literally covered with nests and eggs. Expect to see kittiwakes, fulmars, gulls, guillemots, puffins, and cormorants, to name a few. Seals are also abundant.

Highlights of the islands include the basalt columns and 'pancake' rocks of Þórishólmur and Purkey; Dímonarklakkar, the highest island in the group; the old fishing station at Bjarney; and Flatey, the only currently inhabited island.

Tours Boat tours of Breidafjördur are offered by Eyjaferdir (tel 93-81450) whose office is in Egill's House in Stykkishólmur.

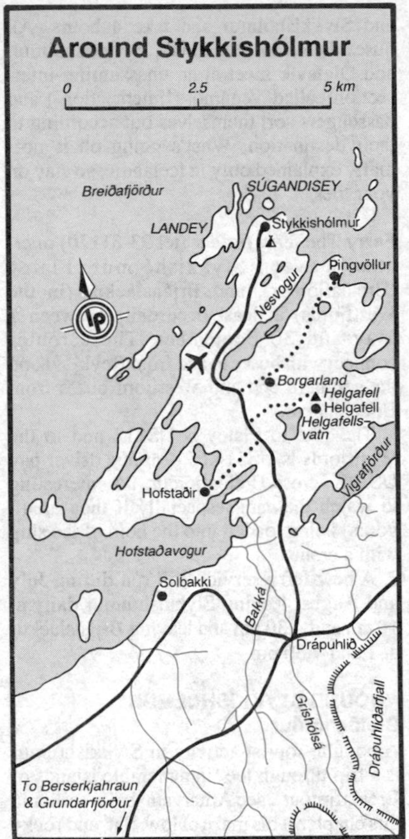

A 2½-hour trip which winds through through the southern islands costs US$25. A longer 4-hour tour which includes Flatey costs around US$31.

Flatey

This island whose name, not surprisingly, means 'flat island', was the location of the film *Nonni and Manny*. If you'd like to explore some of the island's historical buildings or observe its abundant bird life, there's a primitive camping site at Útraekt on the western end. The Vogur Guesthouse (tel 93-81413) in the village offers sleeping-bag accommodation and serves meals and coffee, but you'll have to book in advance so they'll know to cook something up!

Breiðafjörður would be ideal for sea kayaking; you'll have to bring your own equipment because kayaking hasn't yet caught on in Iceland.

BSÍ offers a 3-day tour to Flatey from Reykjavík including transport, meals, a boat tour, and accommodation at the guesthouse for US$215 per person.

Drápuhlíðarfjall

This beautiful and colourful 527-metre-high mountain south-west of Stykkishólmur is composed of sulphur, basalt, jasper, rhyolite, and lignite. As usual around lignite deposits, fossilised plants and petrified wood can be found. Rock hounds who'd like to have a go at climbing or exploring the mountain can hitch or take any bus south from Stykkishólmur to about 2 km east of the intersection with Route 57 (the main Snaefellsnes highway).

Kerlingarskarð

The name of this eerie place means 'witch pass' after a female troll or witch who haunted it until she turned into the stone pillar at the north-west foot of Kerlingarfjall, the mountain forming the eastern side of the pass.

About 5 km west of the southern slope of the pass is Baulárvatn, said to have been the witch's fishing lake. In the 1800s, a local resident reported seeing huge tracks leading into the lake. At least four or five sightings of Loch Ness-style creatures have been reported.

All the buses between Reykjavík and Stykkishólmur travel through the pass. It's possible to camp and explore around the lake but the weather is normally foul. When the clouds swirl down around the mountains and storms howl through, one can imagine how all the strange tales probably surfaced.

Berserkjahraun

The story of the Berserkjahraun, the 'berserks' lava', from *Eyrbyggja Saga* adds interest to this rather ordinary lava field, 15 km west of the intersection of the Stykkishólmur road and Route 57.

The settler Vígastyrr, who lived at Hraun, and his brother Vermundur, who lived across the lava field at the farm Bjarnarhöfn, had to take a long and circuitous route around an impassable lava field in order to visit each other. On one of Vermundur's Viking raids in Norway, he brought back two berserk brothers, Halli and Leiknir, who had been given to him as a gift there.

Berserks were valuable property in those days – the best fighting thugs who were given to excessive, uncontrollable, and often disastrous temper tantrums. Halli, took a liking to Vígastyrr's daughter Ásdís. In desperation, Vígastyrr turned to Snorri goði, the charismatic young district priest of whose power Vígastyrr had always been jealous. Snorri goði advised him to offer his daughter in marriage only if the two berserks could make a passage through the up-till-then impassable lava field.

While the berserks worked like crazy through the lava, Vígastyrr built himself a sauna bath house. After completing the impossible passage, the berserks went for a much needed relax in the sauna and Vígastyrr saw his chance to wriggle out of his agreement. He locked the berserks inside the sauna and tried to scald them. Though they managed to escape, they were soon cut down by their master's brother and buried in a deep pit in the lava. In the end, Ásdís married Vígastyrr's former enemy, Snorri goði.

The berserks' passage through the lava between Hraun and Bjarnarhöfn is still evident. The grave, which is marked by a memorial stone, was excavated in the 1800s to reveal the remains of two men.

GRUNDARFJÖRÐUR

Formerly called Grafarnes, this small village with 800 people was historically a trading centre but is now more reliant on fishing and fish processing. Across the harbour rises the prominent 463-metre-high landmark Kirkjufell, originally called Sukkertoppen ('sugarloaf') by Danish traders.

Behind the town are the steep and forbidding 900-metre Helgrindur, the 'ridges of hell'. Although it has a nice setting, Grundarfjörður doesn't have any specific tourist attraction, so it remains well off the worn routes.

Places to Stay & Eat

Grundarfjörður has a coffee shop *Ásakaffi* at the west end of town and a restaurant in the *Ásafell Guesthouse*. The supermarket is across the street from the harbour.

Farmhouse accommodation is available at *Kverná* (tel 93-86814) by the camping ground and at *Þórdísarstadir* (tel- 93-86866) on the peninsula further east. Otherwise, you can choose between the *Ásafell Guesthouse* (tel 93-86988) or the camping ground at Kverná farm by the river of the same name.

Getting There & Away

In the summer, buses leave Grundarfjörður for Stykkishólmur and Reykjavík daily (except Saturdays) at 5 pm. Coming from Stykkishólmur, buses leave at 1 pm daily except Saturdays and arrive in Grundarfjörður at 2 pm. On Mondays and Fridays, they continue on to Ólafsvík and Hellissandur-Rif.

SNAEFELLSJÖKULL

The document that sent Jules Verne's adventurers into Snaefellsjökull and on their way to the centre of the earth read:

> Descend into the crater of Yocul of Sneffels,
> Which the shade of Scartaris caresses,
> Before the kalends of July, audacious traveller,
> And you will reach the centre of the earth. I did it.
> Arne Saknussemm

This connection is apparently important because local tourist offices have begun to call Snaefellsnes 'Jules Verne Country'. The 1446-metre three-peaked mountain was created when the volcano beneath the glacier exploded and collapsed in on itself forming a caldera. Although there are no reports of its

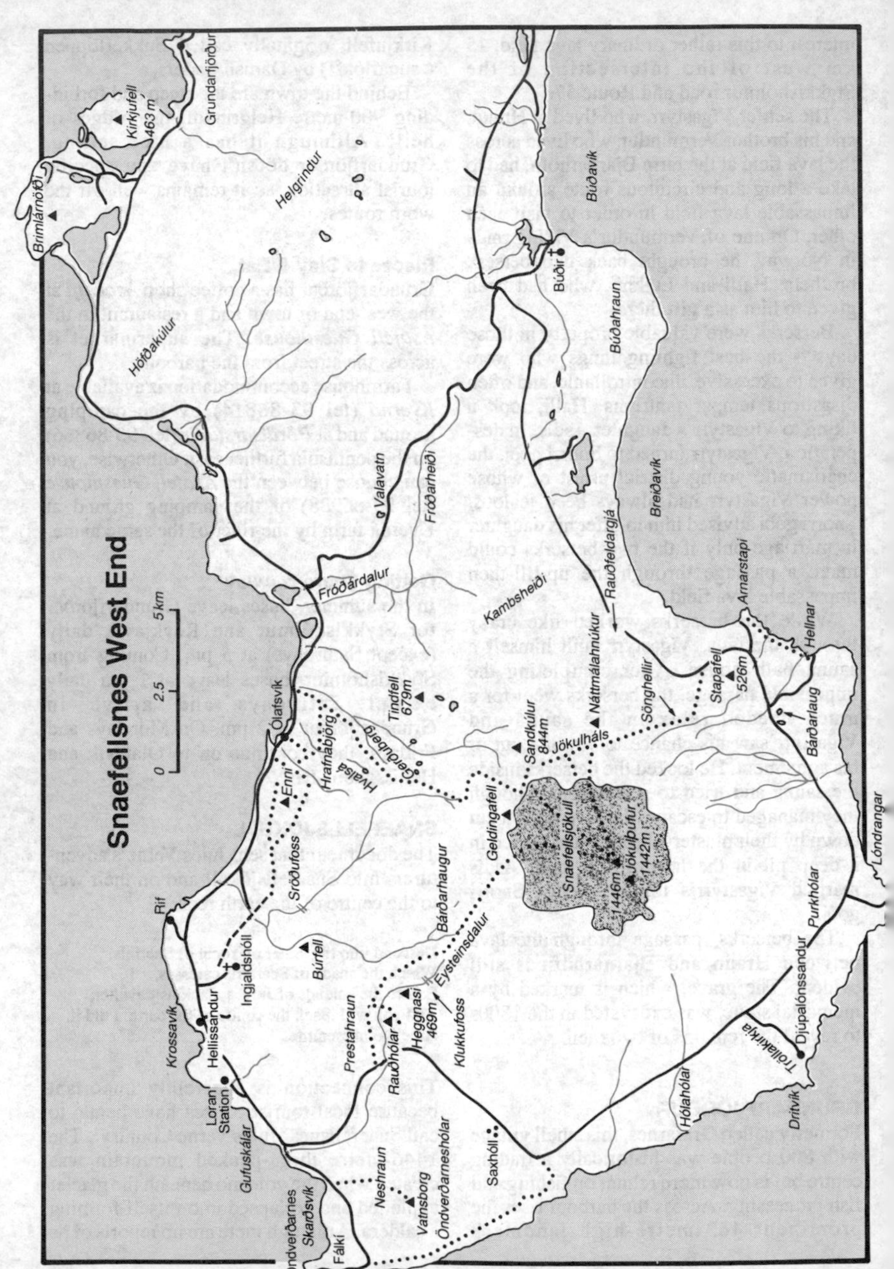
Snaefellsnes West End
0
2.5
5km
Brimlárhöfði
Kirkjufell
463 m
Grundarfjörður
Helgrindur
Búðavík
Búðir
Búðahraun
Höfðakúlur
Valavatn
Fróðárheiði
Breiðavík
Rauðfeldargjá
Kambsheiði
Fróðárdalur
Arnarstapi
Hellnar
Stapafell
526m
Sönghellir
Náttmálahnúkur
Jökulháls
Bárðarlaug
Lóndrangar
Ólafsvík
Tindfell
679m
Hrafnabjörg
Gerðuberg
Hvalsá
Enni
Sandkúlur
844m
Geldingafell
Snaefellsjökull
Jökulþúfur
1442m
1446m
Rif
Svöðufoss
Bárðarhaugur
Búrfell
Eysteinsdalur
Klukkufoss
Heggnasi
469m
Rauðhólar
Prestahraun
Ingjaldshóll
Hellissandur
Krossavík
Loran Station
Gufuskálar
Öndverðarneshólar
Neshraun
Vatnsborg
Saxhóll
Hólahólar
Purkhólar
Djúpalónssandur
Tröllakirkja
Dritvík
Öndverðarnes
Skarðsvík
Fálki

eruptions during the human history of Iceland, it's not yet considered extinct.

Visitors who want to climb the mountain have three options. Walking tracks lead up from Arnarstapi past the north-east flank of Stapafell, and from Route 54 about 1.5 km east of Ólafsvík on the north coast (see Ólafsvík). The longest and most interesting route is from the west side along Móðulaekur, which passes near the red scoria craters of Rauðhólar, the waterfall Klukkufoss, and through the scenic valley Eysteinsdalur.

Whatever route you choose, prepare for harsh weather conditions and carry food and a stove to melt snow for water. At times, ice conditions will require use of crampons and ice axes to reach the summit. Don't hesitate to turn back if conditions worsen – most people can't imagine how awful it can get up there.

With 4WD vehicles, you can drive in some 4 km on the Móðulaekur route and nearly three quarters of the way to the summit on the other routes, snow conditions permitting. From either Ólafsvík or Arnarstapi, in good weather, allow at least 4 hours for the climb. The western approach will take much longer and you'll have to stay overnight on the icecap.

Ólafsvík

Ólafsvík gives easy and direct access to Snaefellsjökull. It also has a sort of New Age following because the mountain is considered one of the world's great 'power centres'. There is power, certainly, but it is mostly in the form of wind and rain. Ólafsvík, for me, holds the distinction of having the most consistently vile weather I've seen anywhere in the world.

It began as a trading village. In 1687, it became the first place in Iceland to be issued with a trade licence. In 1844, the Old Packing House, now the town's oldest building, was constructed by the Clausen family, which owned the leading trading firm in town.

Olafsvík sits along the main highway just west of the river. The most prominent ship to call in there, the *Swan of Ólafsvík* sailed the route for 116 years until she ran onto an offshore rock reef in 1893.

Besides the obvious attraction of the glacier, there is a pretty waterfall, a nice arc of beach, an unusual church which was finished in 1967, and lots of hiking routes through the mountains between Snaefellsjökull and the coast. The nautical museum advertised in some brochures was closed up and abandoned when I was last there.

Places to Stay & Eat The hotel dining room never sees much activity but there are a couple of inexpensive places to eat in Ólafsvík. *Hafnarkaffi*, by the harbour, serves soup and salad for US$5 each. The grill place by the hotel has burgers, sausages, chips, and lunch specials; there's a bakery in the same building. Alternatively, pick up a snack at the petrol station. There is one supermarket nearby and a kiosk close to the swimming pool. The state liquor store is on Mýrarholt above town.

Accommodation in Ólafsvík is relatively good. The *Hotel Nes* offers comfortable doubles for US$58 and it has sleeping-bag accommodation for US$12 per person. The camping ground, north of the road and 1 km east of town, is the historic site where I was trapped in my tent for 3 days by a hurricane-force storm. Most of the tents in the camping ground were smashed and their occupants had to take refuge in the toilet block, unable to even stand up outside. Prospective campers may want to take this into consideration. The camping site costs US$3 per person and US$3 per tent and fees are collected regardless of the weather.

Campers who want a bit of relief are permitted to use the TV lounge at the hotel but they like it if you buy at least a cup of coffee.

Getting There & Away There are twice weekly buses between Hellissandur-Rif and Stykkishólmur which pass through Ólafsvík. Between Ólafsvík and Reykjavík or Borgarnes, buses leave the village at 5.30 pm daily except Saturdays. Northbound, they leave Borgarnes at 10.45 am.

Ólafsvík shares an airport with Hellissandur-Rif so flight details are the same as theirs.

Route to Snaefellsjökull The track up Snaefellsjökull, which begins 1 km east of the camping ground, is negotiable by 4WD part of the way. On foot, the climb will take at least 4 hours one way. Camping and hiking on the glacier will be cold and wet; there is normally lots of fog so carry a good map and a compass. In summer, skiing is possible but the glacier buzzes with snow machines. Crampons and ice axes are recommended, steer away from any sags or cracks in the snow which may hide crevasses. This is no way to reach the centre of the earth!

If you're interested in 'doing' the glacier the easy way, 4WD glacier tours (tel 93-61490 or 93-61527) are conducted every clear summer midnight. Since darkness is never an issue during the Icelandic summer, they travel at night because the snow is firmer and there is less recreational traffic on the glacier.

HELLISSANDUR-RIF

Hellissandur-Rif, the westernmost village on

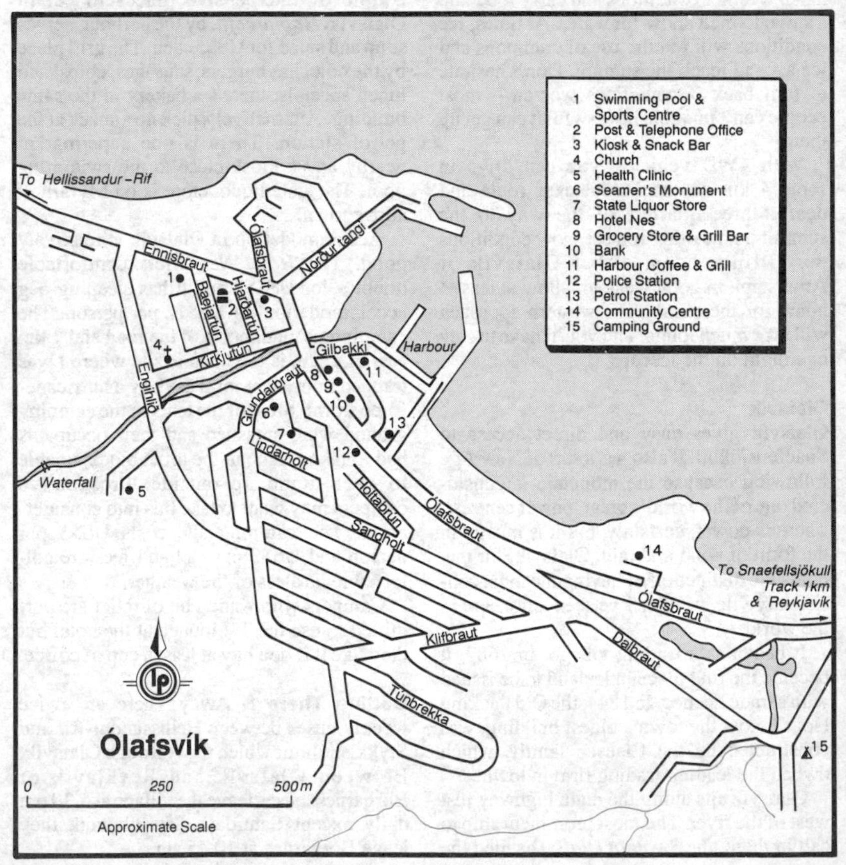

Left: Strokkur geyser, Geysir, Iceland (DS)
Right: Clam boat at Hornvík, Hornstrandir, Iceland (DS)
Bottom: Fishing nets, Akranes, Iceland (DS)

Top: Puffins, Iceland (DC)
Bottom: Arctic cotton, Skaftafell National Park, Iceland (DS)

Snaefellsnes, is actually two communities just over 2 km apart. The original fishing village of Hellissandur, sometimes known as just Sandur, had no harbour and was exposed to the open sea. A new harbour has been constructed nearby at a settlement of 100 people called Hávarif. The name was shortened to Rif which means 'reef' and the community grew around it.

There are a couple of fish-processing and freezing plants in town but there is really nothing specific to see except perhaps the small nautical museum and a view disc between them. The towns are primarily useful as a base for visits around the western end of Snaefellsnes.

Places to Stay & Eat

The *Gimli Guesthouse* (tel 93-66825) near the shore in Hellissandur is the only formal accommodation available. It's good news for campers who want to come in out of the rain and wind because it has sleeping-bag accommodation and cooking facilities and meals. Hellissandur has a camping site, of course, but don't bring a wimpy tent – this far out on the peninsula, campers are probably in for some punishment.

There is a snack bar, the *Virkið*, in Rif and the supermarket is in Hellissandur.

Getting There & Away

Buses to Grundarfjörður and Stykkishólmur leave at 4 pm from Mondays and Fridays. To Reykjavík via Ólafsvík they leave at 5 pm daily except Saturdays and at 7.45 am on Saturdays. Arnarflug has flights between Hellissandur-Rif and Reykjavík six times weekly (again, not on Saturdays) leaving the capital at 5 pm and the Hellissandur-Rif airport at 5.40 pm.

SOUTH-EAST COAST

All the weather systems moving into Iceland from the south-west come ashore on the broad coastal plain of southern Snaefellsnes and run into the east-west mountain barrier yielding predictably diluvian results.

Eldborg

The prominent crater of Eldborg, an easy half-hour walk from the road, rises 100 metres above Eldborgarhraun. The *Landnámabók* mentions an eruption here during the early Settlement era.

Gullborgarhraun

The large lava field from the crater Gullborg on Heggstaðir farm is riddled with unusual lava caves. The farmers require visitors to obtain permission before wandering in at will but access is difficult because no bus passes along this route. You'll have to get off the Ólafsvík or Stykkishólmur buses at Kolbeinsstaðir and walk or hitch the 9 km from there to Heggstaðir.

WEST END

Few visitors ever reach the western end of Snaefellsnes because there is no public transport beyond Buðir in the south or beyond Hellissandur-Rif in the north. Tours can be arranged through the Gimli Guesthouse in Hellissandur and the Hotel Buðir at Buðir. Hitching is possible but long waits should be expected and may become unpleasant because of the climate.

Búðir

If it weren't for the weather, the former fishing village of Buðir, abandoned in the early 1800s, would be more popular as a resort. It's within walking distance of some wonderful natural features, and pleasant facilities make it ideal for those willing to bet on the long shot with the elements.

The Hotel Buðir (tel 93-56700) has a licensed restaurant and a general store. The naturally hot outdoor pool at Lysuhóll, 5 km west, is open daily except Tuesdays from 2 pm. The camping site offers basic facilities but a *sturdy* tent is essential if you plan to take this route.

The sandy beach along Breiðavík, west of Buðir, is nice but could create a dilemma; it would be difficult to choose between hiking or lazing on the beach should a fine day happen along. West of the hotel is the leprechaun-infested lava field Buðahraun and its prominent 88-metre crater Buðaklettur. The large lava tube beneath Buðahraun is said to be a gold-paved tunnel to Surtshellir in Borgarfjörður.

Arnarstapi
The former fishing village of Arnarstapi is a small service centre with farmhouse accommodation, the *Arnabaer Cafe*, a camping ground, and a general kiosk. Here the coastline is riddled with arches, caves, basalt cliffs, and blow holes. The best-known feature is a circular arch called Gatklettur.

Stapafell
Stapafell, the 526-metre-high mountain behind Arnarstapi, reputedly shelters leprechauns. Along the mountain face, 3 km north-east of Stapafell, is the deep gash of Rauðfeldargjá. Higher up on the mountain north-west of Stapafell is the cave Sönghellir which contains some old inscriptions. It is best reached by the walking track that skirts the north-east base of Stapafell and continues up toward Snaefellsjökull.

Hellnar
A short 2.5-km walk south-west from Arnarstapi at Hellnar is the large sea-level cave Baðstofa. At high tide, it emits a blue luminescence. It's chockablock with birds but approach quietly or the ensuing panic will hinder your observation.

Between Hellnar and the main highway is Bárðarlaug, supposedly the bathing pool of the demigod Bárður Snaefellsás who, according to local legend, makes his home in Snaefellsjökull and works as its appointed protector.

Lóndrangar
The two rock pillars of Lóndrangar, the higher of which is 75-metres high, are remnants of an ancient basalt cinder-cone. They're only a 15-minutes walk from the main road about 5 km west of the Hellnar turn-off.

Dritvík & Djúpalón
There is a track leading 1.5 km west from Route 574 to the coast at Djúpalón or 'deep lagoon', a sea-filled rock basin surrounded by rugged formations. On the beach you'll find four 'lifting stones' where fishermen working at the former fishing station at Dritvík would prove their strength. The smallest is Amloði at 25 kg, next is Hálfdraettingur at 50 kg, Hálfsterkur at 140 kg, and the largest, Fullsterker weighs 155 kg. Hálfdraettingur marked the border of wimphood and any man who couldn't pick it up was considered unsuitable for the local version of polite society.

Just south is the crater Purkhólar which has some interesting lava caves.

Hólahólar
This crater cluster, about 100 metres west of the road, can be be explored quickly. Its primary attraction is the crater Berudalur – you pass through a crack in the side to enter a natural amphitheatre.

Gufuskálar
Gufuskálar boasts the highest structure in Iceland, the prominent 412-metre mast of the US Loran Station. The Írskibrunnur or 'Irish well' south-west of the station was built by Irish monks before the Norse people arrived in Iceland. The surrounding area is dotted with ruins of hundreds of medieval stone huts constructed by early Scandinavian settlers as fish-drying sheds when Iceland was supplying much of Europe with fish.

The small creek flowing through Gufuskálar is called Gufuskálamóða, meaning 'steam basin river'. Given its size, it would be more appropriately called Gufuskálalaekur or 'steam basin creek', but legend has it that a huge underground river flows beneath its course, hence the name.

Öndverðarnes
Önaverðarnes is the westernmost cape of Snaefellsnes and, in fair weather, it's worthwhile spending a day exploring the area on foot. It was once inhabited but now all that

remains is a lighthouse and an abandoned stone well called Fálkí. Lazing seals are often seen on the pebble beach and, south of the cape, are the bird cliffs of Svörtuloft which are carved into sea arches and caves by the constant pounding of Atlantic breakers. Skarðsvík, the bay east of the cape, has a nice sandy beach backed by a steep escarpment.

A walking track leads from Skarðsvík across the Neshraun lava flow to the crater Vatnsborg between the road and the sea. Saxhóll, one of its prominent craters, can be easily climbed in a few minutes and offers a good view of Neshraun and the sea beyond.

West End Tour

BSÍ offers a 2-day tour from Reykjavík to Stykkishólmur and around the western end of Snaefellsnes. It departs from Monday to Friday at 9 am in July and August and costs US$185 per person including transport, a night's accommodation at the Hotel Stykkishólmur, a boat tour of Breiðafjörður, and breakfast.

South Central Iceland

South central Iceland is known in the local tourist industry as the 'Golden Triangle' referring to Gullfoss, Geysir, and Þingvellir, the 'Big Three' destinations for Icelandair's stopover visitors. Whirlwind day-tours packed with wide-eyed new arrivals cruise out of Reykjavík in the morning, squeeze in all the biggies and a few other sights as well, and still leave time for a long and leisurely lunch, coffee and biscuits in the afternoon, and a 45-minute shopping spree in Eden, the original tourist trap. They wobble back into Reykjavík, heads spinning, wondering what happened!

If you're one of those unfortunates who have only 3 days at their disposal in Iceland, you won't have time to be lured far off the beaten track so this trip is probably the best way to go. It's tiring and you're bound to experience scenic overload at some stage but you'll never forget the experience.

Note also that south central Iceland isn't all tour buses and clicking cameras. Beyond the well trampled route, you'll find many other worthwhile natural phenomena and historical sites. Beyond the volcanoes, glaciers, geysers, and hot springs are broad, sandy beaches, buried settlements, spectacular highlands, and an archipelago of rugged new islands teeming with bird life.

HVERAGERÐI

East of Reykjavík along the Ring Road, the first town you reach is Hveragerði ('hot springs foliage'). It sits against the mountains in a nice valley with steaming hot springs. Numerous greenhouses take advantage of the geothermal heat giving Hveragerði its nicknames 'the flower town' and the 'greenhouse village'. It boasts about 40% of the country's greenhouse agriculture.

Hveragerði's population is about 1500 but it's growing and is expected to someday become a satellite city for Reykjavík commuters. Earthquakes and crustal shifting have caused new hot springs and fissures to emerge and old ones to close. All this geothermal power is harnessed for heat and electricity. Hiking is good around the town and the place is worth a visit for a day or so.

Information

There is a laundry at Reykjamörk 1 and a tourist office at Breiðamörk 10 which also serves as an Icelandair agency and a car rental office. The swimming pool, near the mountains by the horticultural college, is open Monday to Friday from 7 am to 8.30 pm, Saturdays from 9 am to 5.30 pm and Sundays from 9 am to 4.30 pm.

1. Horse Rentals
2. Grýla Geyser
3. Church
4. Youth Hostel
5. Hotel Ljósbrá
6. Post Office
7. Camping Ground
8. Swimming Pool
9. NLFÍ Clinic
10. Tourist Office
11. Hotel Örk
12. Eden Tourist Shop
13. Tivoli Amusement Pavilion
14. Long-Distance Bus Stop

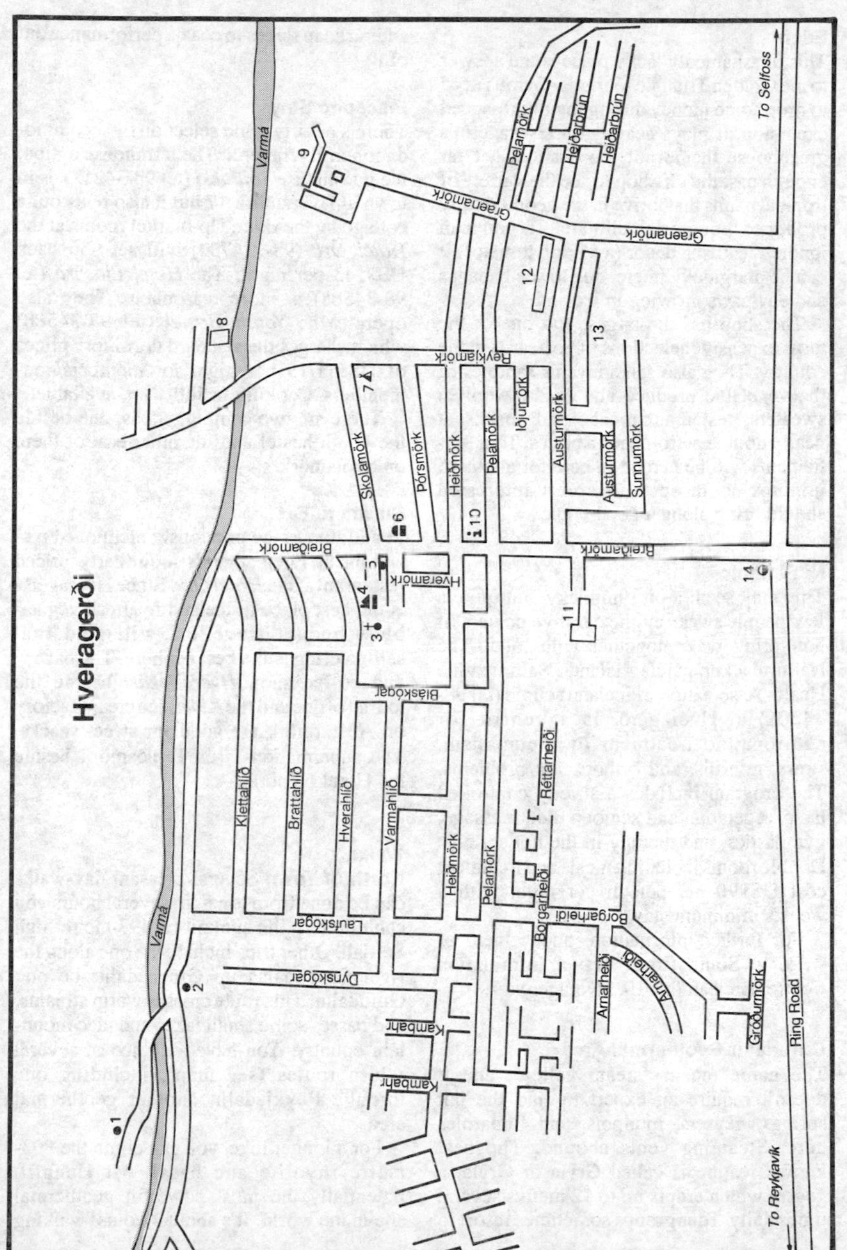
Hveragerði
Varmá
Varmá
To Selfoss
To Reykjavík
Ring Road
Grænamörk
Grænamörk
Þelamörk
Heiðarbrún
Heiðarbrún
Reykjamörk
Iðjumörk
Austurmörk
Austurmörk
Sunnumörk
Skólamörk
Þórsmörk
Heiðmörk
Þelamörk
Breiðamörk
Breiðamörk
Hveramörk
Bláskógar
Klettahlíð
Brattahlíð
Hverahlíð
Varmahlíð
Heiðmörk
Þelamörk
Réttarheiði
Borgarheiði
Borgarheiði
Arnarheiði
Arnarheiði
Gróðurmörk
Laufskógar
Dynskógar
Kambahr
Kambahr

Eden

This unashamedly tacky place is the answer to the Golden Triangle tourist's obvious need to drop some money during their high-speed excursion. It plays heavily on Hveragerði's greenhouse theme but few visitors get far enough past the giftshop to see the variety of tropical plants that thrive in the geothermally produced equatorial climate. If you can ignore the kitsch decor (a Viking tomato!) it can be marginally interesting to see bananas and pawpaws growing in Iceland.

The shop has the largest and one of the most expensive selections of postcards in the country. They also sell souvenir samples of the vegetable produce and seeds, woollen sweaters, restaurant meals, and snacks at nearly double petrol-station prices. Tour participants will be herded in here for about 45 minutes so those who aren't interested should bring along a good book.

NLFÍ Clinic

This may seem a bit gimmicky, but quite a few people swear by the curative powers of hot-spring water together with mud. The Náttúrulaekningafélag Ísland (Naturopathic Health Association of Iceland) clinic (tel 98-34201) at Hveragerði is a centre for naturopathic treatment of rheumatism, stress, arthritis, and orthopaedic problems. The program includes a strictly controlled lacto-vegetarian and seafood diet, massage, gymnastics, and therapy in the hot springs. Double rooms including meals and treatment cost US$90 per person per night with a week's minimum stay.

For further information, phone them or write to South Coast Travel Information Centre, Breiðamörk 10, Hveragerði.

Gufudalur Geothermal Area

The name means 'steam valley', and it doesn't require an expert to find the hot springs, geysers, mudpots, and fumaroles here. Steaming vents abound. The best known feature is called Grýta or Grýla, a geyser which erupts up to 12 metres several times daily. Tour groups sometimes resort to adding soap flakes to coax a performance out of it.

Places to Stay

There's a fairly good selection of accommodation in Hveragerði. The farmhouse option, the guesthouse *Sólbakki* (tel 98-34212), is in town at Hveramörk 17 but it also rents out a cottage by the river. Up-market rooms at the *Hotel Örk* (98- 34700) will set you back US$143 per night. The *Hotel Ljósbrá* (tel 98-34588) is more reasonable. They also operate the *Youth Hostel* (tel 98-34588) which charges the standard dormitory prices of US$11/13 per night for members/non-members. Cooking facilities are available.

There are two camping areas, one beside the youth hostel and the other east of there on Skolamörk.

Places to Eat

In addition to the previously mentioned restaurant at Eden, there's a similarly priced restaurant at the *Hotel Örk*. Since Hveragerði is the best place in Iceland for fresh vegetables, budget travellers will find that self-catering is the best bet here. The bakery and coffee shop *Hverabakarí* beside the tourist office and the *Kjöris* ice cream factory on Austurmörk are good for sweet snacks. The supermarket is on Breiðamörk beside the Hotel Ljósbrá.

Walks

North of Town Several pleasant day-walks can be done from town. In several hours you can climb to the summit of 497-metre-high Selfjall. Other trips include the one along the river Graendalsá up Graenadalur beyond Gufudalur. This route crosses warm streams, and passes some small lakes and nice mountain country. You have a choice of several return routes (see map), including one through Reykjadalir, another geothermal area.

For a longer hike, you can climb the 803-metre rhyolite and basalt Mt Hengill, potentially the most powerful geothermal site in the world. It's about 4 hours' walking

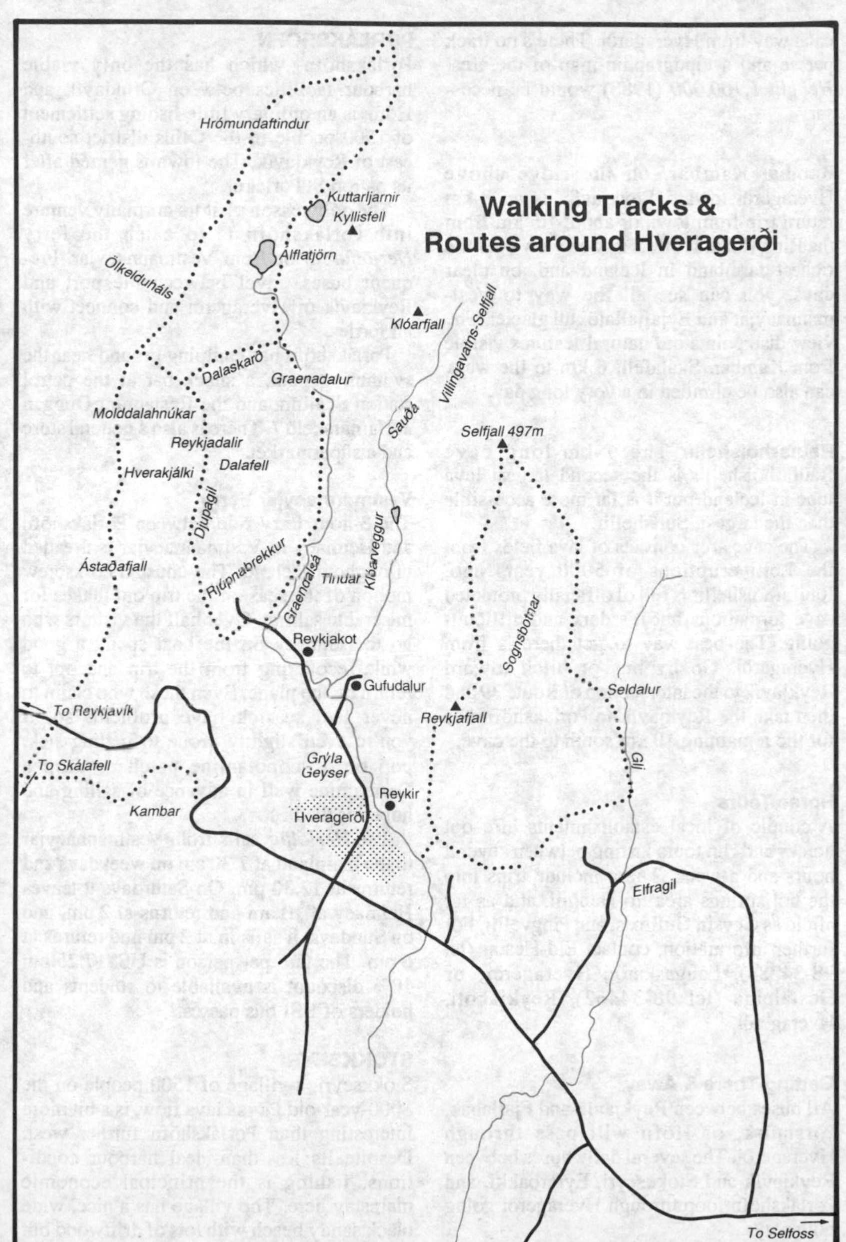
Walking Tracks &
Routes around Hveragerði
Hrómundaftindur
Kuttarljarnir
Kyllisfell
Álflatjörn
Ölkelduháls
Klóarfjall
Villingavatns-Selfjall
Dalaskarð
Graenadalur
Sauðá
Molddalahnúkar
Selfjall 497m
Reykjadalir
Dalafell
Hverakjálki
Djupagil
Klóarveggur
Ástaðafjall
Rjúpnabrekkur
Tindar
Graendalsá
Sognsbotnar
Reykjakot
Gufudalur
Seldalur
To Reykjavík
Reykjafjall
To Skálafell
Grýla
Geyser
Gil
Reykir
Kambar
Hveragerði
Elfragil
To Selfoss

each way from Hveragerði. There's no track per se and a topographic map of the area, *Hengill 1:100,000* (1988) would be necessary.

Kambar Kambar, on the ridge above Hveragerði toward Reykjavík, is an 8-km return trip from town or about 1.5 km from the Ring Road. It offers a good view over the richest farmland in Iceland and, on clear days, you can see all the way to Vestmannaeyjar and Eyjafjallajökull glacier. The view disc points out natural features visible from Kambar. Skálafell, 6 km to the west, can also be climbed in a very long day.

Raufarhólshellir The 1-km-long cave Raufarhólshellir is the second largest lava tube in Iceland but it is far more accessible than the largest, Surtshellir.

The cave area consists of lava fields from the Leiti eruptions of 5000 years ago. Raufarhólshellir is full of officially protected cave formations but it's dark and difficult-going. The best way to get there is from Hveragerði. Go by bus or hitch toward Reykjavík to the intersection of Route 39 and then take the Reykjavík to Þorlákshöfn bus for the remaining 10 km south to the cave.

Horse Tours

A couple of local establishments hire out horses and run tours lasting between several hours and a week. These include trips into the hot springs area, to Hengill, and as far afield as Geysir, Gullfoss, and Þingvellir. For further information, contact Eld-Hestar (tel 98-34884), Laugaskarði, Hveragerði, or Hestaleiga (tel 98-34462), Reykjakoti, Hveragerði.

Getting There & Away

All buses between Reykjavík and Fjallabak, Þórsmörk, or Höfn will pass through Hveragerði. The several daily buses between Reykjavík and Stokkseyri, Eyrarbakki, and Þorlákshöfn loop through Hveragerði going both ways.

ÞORLÁKSHÖFN

Þorlákshöfn, which has the only viable harbour facilities between Grindavík and Höfn, is an ordinary little fishing settlement of 1500 people in the Ölfus district southeast of Reykjavík. The town is named after its patron St Þorlákur.

The only reason visitors normally venture into Þorlákshöfn is to catch the ferry *Herjólfur* to or from Vestmannaeyjar. Frequent buses travel between the port and Reykjavík or Hveragerði and connect with all ferries.

Þorlákshöfn has camping ground near the swimming pool, a snack bar at the petrol station Skálinn, and the Restaurant Duggan at Hafnarskeið 7. There is also a general store and a supermarket.

Vestmannaeyjar Ferry

The 3-hour ferry ride between Þorlákshöfn and Heimaey in Vestmannaeyjar is dreaded throughout Iceland. The unusual corkscrew motion of the seas on the trip out makes for miserable sailing. Over half the visitors who go to Heimaey on the boat spend a good while recovering from the trip and opt to return on the plane. Even those who claim to never feel seasick have problems so, if you're even slightly prone to getting sick, pop on a scopolamine patch or drop a Dramamine well in advance of sailing and hope for the best.

The *Herjólfur* sails from Vestmannaeyjar to the mainland at 7.30 am on weekdays and returns at 12.30 pm. On Saturdays it leaves Heimaey at 10 am and returns at 2 pm, and on Sundays, it sails in at 2 pm and returns at 6 pm. The fare per person is US$17.25 but 10% discount is available to students and holders of BSÍ bus passes.

STOKKSEYRI

Stokkseyri, a village of 1500 people on the 8000-year-old Þjórsá lava flow, is a bit more interesting than Þorlákshöfn further west. Despite its less-than-ideal harbour conditions, fishing is the principal economic mainstay here. The village has a nice, wide black sandy beach with lots of driftwood but the weather rarely allows you to fully appreciate it. In the 1790s a seawall was constructed west along the coast to the mouth of the Öfulsá lagoon in response to the Básenda or 'Great Flood'.

An old fishermen's hut, Þuríðarbúð, has been turned into a small museum which is named after Þuríður Einarssdóttir (1777-1863) the female captain of an old oarboat based there. Another museum is housed on the Baugsstaðir dairy farm, east of town on the Hróarholtslaekur stream. The village church dates back to 1886.

The village has a general store and a snack bar at the petrol station but there's no official camping site. Camping is possible on the beach (above the high tide line) weather permitting. There is farmhouse accommodation at Fljótshólar (tel 91-77268) on the Hróarholtslaekur, 13 km east of town.

Buses run between Reykjavík and Stokkseyri at least four times daily.

EYRARBAKKI

The wild, sandy coastline around Eyrarbakki is a beautiful place to observe bird life and the dramatic pounding of the surf on the broad beaches. Although its harbour is abysmal, Eyrarbakki was historically the primary trading centre on the south coast. Today some 550 people there continue to make a living from the sea. The interesting sculpture at the state prison on the Lítli Hraun lava field east of town is Krían or 'the Arctic tern'.

Things to See

Eyrarbakki's wooden buildings and quaint main street hasn't changed much for the past century. The church dates back to 1890. One of Iceland's oldest structures, the Husið built in 1765, housed early Danish traders. Their clerks lived in the home just west of it. The same seawall that started in Stokkseyri passes through Eyrarbakki near the Husið. A new nautical museum was opened in 1989 and exhibits various maritime artefacts including an ancient Danish oarship called *Farsaell.*

Places to Stay & Eat

Guðlaugur Pálsson's friendly general store is open in the mornings. *Ólabúð* and *Ásinn* (the petrol station) are open later hours. The nearest formal accommodation is in Selfoss, but there is beach camping here similar to that in Stokkseyri.

Getting There & Away

All buses between Stokkseyri and Reykjavík also pass through Eyrarbakki.

ÞJÓRSÁRDALUR

The long, broad valley of the big river Þjórsá, meaning 'bull river' winds its way south-west from the glacier Hofsjökull in the heart of Iceland to the Atlantic west of Hella. The area referred to as Þjórsárdalur includes the bit along Route 26, between Skarð and the intersection of Route F22.

Nearly all of Þjórsárdalur lies beneath lava fields and lava desert created by eruptions of Hekla, Iceland's most famous volcano. Around 8000 years ago, a river of lava swept over the landscape covering 800 sq km on its way to the Atlantic. In 1104, the first Hekla eruption witnessed by settlers rendered all of south-west Iceland uninhabitable. Today there are only two farms in the area but ruins of 20 have been excavated.

Hekla

Visitors must be lucky to see the near perfect cone of Hekla ('the hooded') because of the almost perpetual bank of cloud that shrouds it. Its current altitude is 1491 metres, over 40 metres higher than before the big eruption in 1947. It erupted again in 1970 and all signs indicate it's not extinct yet.

The account of St Brendan's voyages says a great flaming mountain existed in Thule. Just prior to Settlement in the early 9th century, it erupted but the settlers failed to recognise the danger it posed and established farms and homesteads in the beautiful, inviting green valley.

In 1104, however, disaster struck and everything within a radius of 50 km was destroyed, buried beneath a metre of solid ejected matter or tephra. Since that devastating eruption, the mountain has blown its top 14 times. In 1300, it split open and spewed ash across more than 83,000 sq km over the next year.

By the 1500s, mainland Europe had decided that vile Hekla was the entrance to hell. Literature of the day reported that the skies around it were black with vultures and ravens and the howls and moans of the condemned inside could be heard. The brush-off of the day all over Europe was, 'Go to Hekla'.

In 1947, after over 100 years of inactivity, Hekla belched a mushroom cloud of ash that rose over 27 km into the air and spread as far as the Soviet Union. The eruption continued for 13 months and destroyed farms and fields then the mountain lay dormant for 23 years. In the last eruption, in 1970, nearly 50 million tonnes of ejecta spread out across the landscape and again destroyed crops.

Hekla is a relatively easy mountain to climb, the best route is up the northern ridge but, as you may suspect, it's not entirely safe.

Places to Stay

There is a *Youth Hostel* and farmhouse accommodation (tel 98-76591), 10 km from the mountain at Leirubakki on route 26. They also have a camping site with running water and facilities.

Getting There & Away

In the summer, there's a daily BSÍ tour over the Fjallabak Route between Reykjavík and Skaftafell leaving at around 8 am. The whole trip costs US$63 but you can stop as often as you'd like along the way and resume the tour later or you can have them charge pro rata for the length of time you're on the tour. BSÍ tours across Sprengisandur and the one through Þjórsárdalur also pass by here.

Stöng

The farm of Gaukur Trandilsson – the Reykjavík pub Gaukur á Stöng was named after him – was buried under the devastating Hekla eruption of 1104. His holdings at Stöng were excavated in 1939 by a team of Scandinavian archaeologists. Although the comparison may be a bit strained, Icelanders refer to Stöng as the 'Northern Pompeii'.

In 1974, to mark 1100 years of Settlement, Iceland decided to reconstruct a farm, on the site a few km away at Þjóðveldisbaer, to exactly match the original. Builders paid meticulous attention to detail. The construction materials, layout, building techniques, and indoor furnishings resemble those of a medieval Norse farmstead.

Details of construction methods and materials as well as a room plan are outlined in a pamphlet, *The Reconstructed Medieval Farm in Þjórsárdalur*, available at Þjóðveldisbaer and at the National Museum in Reykjavík.

While you're at Stöng, it's also worth visiting the gorge Gjáin with its interesting rock formations and waterfalls upstream along the Rauðá from the farm ruins. Also, several hours' walk up the Fossá valley west of Stöng is Iceland's second highest waterfall Háifoss which plunges 122 metres from the escarpment above. You can camp anywhere in this valley.

More farm ruins can be found at Skeljastaðir between Þjóðveldisbaer and Stöng. By the power station is another beautiful waterfall called Hjálparfoss.

Getting There & Away The easiest way to see Stöng is to take the Þjórsárdalur tour outlined at the beginning of this section. It goes to both the ruins and the reconstructed farm.

Otherwise, without a car or a bike, it will be tricky but hitching isn't impossible. By bus, you can only get as close as Búrfellsvirkjun power plant. From there, the farm ruins are 12 km away by the shortest route. The reconstructed farm, however, is only about 3 km from the power plant. Buses leave Reykjavík at 9 pm on Sundays, 5.30 pm on Tuesdays, and 6.30 pm on Fridays and return at 5 pm Sundays, and at 9 am Tuesdays and Fridays.

Tröllkonuhlaup The name of this falls means 'troll woman's run'. It was once believed that trolls lived in the mountains around Hekla: a male troll in Búrfell and his sister in Bjólfell. They set out to catch a farmer called Gissur of Laekjarbotnar for a meal but the intended victim heard of their plot and escaped across the river. They followed him through the stepping stones at Tröllkonuhlaup but never got him into the stewpot.

These falls are actually more of a cascade than a proper falls but are nice on a clear day. All the tours passing through stop for a break here. Otherwise, don't go out of your way to see it.

Tours

Þjórsárdalur Tour BSÍ offers a day-tour twice weekly for US$45 around the highlights of the valley. It visits Gullfoss and Geysir as well as the excavated farm Stöng, and some waterfalls and caves.

Horse Tours

Hekla and Þjórsárdalur are favourite horse-trekking areas and lots of farms operate tours. Some run from Þjórsárdalur to Stöng, Háifoss, Gullfoss, and even up to Hofsjökull glacier and Borgarfjörður. For further information, contact:

Fákar Hestar (tel 99-6028), Steinsholti, Gnupverjahreppur (this is near the Búrfellsvirkjun power plant)
Saga Hestar (tel 98-78138), Miðhúsum, Hvolsvöllur
Hekla Hestar (tel 99-5598), Austvaðsholt, Landmannahreppur (this is on Route 271 not far from Laekjarbotnar)

BISKUPSTUNGUR

The Biskupstungur or the 'bishop's tongue' technically takes in the district between the river Hvítá on the east and Brúará on the west, split in two by the Tungufljót. For convenience, I'm also including the approaches to it along Route 35. This is the heart of Golden Triangle country so, thanks to lots of traffic, hitching is pretty good.

Kerið & Seyðishólar

Kerið, a 55-metre-deep explosion crater, which contains a forbidding green lake, was formed 3000 years ago in a crater swarm known as Tjarnarhólar. About 3 km north-east across the road is the red-sided Seyðishólar crater group which produced most of the surrounding lava field. There are lots of nice places to camp nearby and a surface stream west of the craters but, at times, the wind can get fierce.

Reykholt

Independent travellers wanting to spend time in the Biskupstungur can make their base at Reykholt which has both a youth hostel (tel 98-68831) and a camping ground. If you plan to stay at the hostel, advance reservations are recommended.

This settlement of 100 people is in the middle of a geothermal area and occupies itself with greenhouse agriculture and tourism. The main attraction is the geyser Reykjahver which erupts five or six times per hour. Services include a general shop, a petrol station, and a naturally heated swimming pool.

For details on public transport to Reykholt, see Getting There & Away in the Skálholt section.

Skálholt

Between 1056 and 1796, Skálholt served as one of the two bishoprics and theological centres in Iceland. Until the Reformation, when Catholic Christianity was ousted in favour of Danish Lutheranism as the official state religion, it was site of a great deal of religious drama.

History Skálholt was the homestead of Gissur the White, the lobbyist who railroaded the Christianisation of Iceland through the Alþing. Realising that the future of Iceland would be greatly determined by Christianity, he constructed a church at Skálholt and sent his son Ísleifur to Germany to study for the priesthood. Ísleifur returned in 1030 and established a parish on his late father's estate and, in 1053, was unanimously appointed Bishop of Iceland.

Ísleifur Gissurarson was one of the best loved but least heeded religious figures in Icelandic church history. Though troubled by his ineffectiveness, he managed to win friends for Iceland in Rome and Germany and it was said that he performed miracles.

Ísleifur Gissurarson's son (celibacy for the clergy was introduced in France during the previous century but hadn't yet become doctrine in Iceland) Gissur followed in his father's footsteps. To ease the church's financial difficulties, he introduced the tithe and divided the resulting revenues equally between the priests, the poor, the church building fund, and the bishopric.

Skálholt was by this time the undisputed theological centre of Iceland. In the 12th century, an elaborate timber cathedral was constructed to replace Gissur's humble church and a seminary was organised, establishing Skálholt as the nation's educational centre as well.

In 1550, when Iceland was experiencing religious turmoil, Jón Arason, the best-known of all the historical bishops, and two of his sons were executed at Skálholt for actively opposing the Reformation brought about by the Danish government (see the History section of the Iceland Facts about the Country chapter). The Lutheran bishopric remained at Skálholt until it was moved to Reykjavík in 1797, when the old timber church was completely dismantled.

In 1954, when the cornerstone was being laid for the new commemorative church, they discovered the coffin of another early bishop, Páll Jónsson who served from 1196 to 1211. According to *Páls Saga*, a biography of his life, he was the nephew of St Þórlakur and promoted both culture and learning within the church. The story goes that his death brought about great earthquakes and storms and he was universally mourned by his constituents. As the coffin was being opened, the heavens suddenly cut loose with such a deluge that excavators began to wonder whether they were doing the right thing.

Bishop Páll Jónsson's coffin is still kept in the new church but the real attraction of Skálholt is the beautiful mosaic by Nina Tryggvadóttir on the wall above the altar.

Places to Stay All Golden Triangle tours stop at Skálholt for 5 minutes. If you want more time, there's farmhouse accommodation at Sel (tel 98-64441), within 3 km of the site, and the youth hostel at Reykholt is only 10 minutes away by vehicle.

Getting There & Away In the summer there are daily buses from Reykjavík leaving BSÍ at 11.30 am, passing Sel and the Skálholt turn-off at about 1.35 pm northbound and 2.50 pm southbound (toward Reykjavík). These buses also stop at Reykholt which is less than 10 minutes north-east of Skálholt along Route 35.

Gullfoss

If Iceland has a star attraction, Gullfoss is it. Oddly enough, it only became known to foreigners in this century, having been completely overshadowed by the waterworks at nearby Geysir. Here the river Hvitá drops a total of 32 metres in two falls. The canyon above and below them is 70 metres deep and 2.5 km long. When the sun is shining, you're likely to see a rainbow through the ample spray that forms.

The nearby farm Brattholt (tel 98-68941), where farmhouse accommodation is now available, formerly included part of Gullfoss. In the middle of this century, this attraction was going to be sold to foreigners for hydroelectric development but the farmer Tómas Tómasson and his daughter Sigríður Tómasdóttir opposed the sale. Sigríður walked all the way to Reykjavík to lobby her cause, threatening to throw herself into the falls if they were to be destroyed. The government purchased the site and set it aside as a national monument. There is now a monument to Sigriður above Gullfoss.

Getting There & Away The daily bus service to Gullfoss and Geysir from Reykjavík passes through Laugardalur instead of the Biskupstungur. The Skálholt and Reykholt buses on Tuesdays also go on to Gullfoss. On Sundays, Tuesdays, and Fridays, you can get as far as Geysir, 10 km down the road, from where you can hitch to the falls.

Haukadalur
Haukadalur ('hawk valley') lies upstream from the geothermal phenomena at Geysir. It was originally established as one of the three great centres of learning of southern Iceland. Its most famous graduate was Ari the Learned (1067-1148), the author of the *Íslendingabók*, and the *Landnámabók*.

Over the years, the farm was eroded and abandoned. The church, originally built in 1842 (the ring on the church door is said to be from the staff of Bergþór, the troll of Bláfell), was renovated in 1939 after the site was purchased by Danish philanthropist Kristian Kirk. He bequeathed the site to the Icelandic Forestry Commission (yes folks, there really is one!). They have curbed the erosion by planting over half a million trees. This area is not on the Golden Triangle tour but it lies just a short walk up the Beiná valley from Geysir.

Geysir
All the world's spouting hot springs were named after this, the 'Great Geysir', which first began erupting in the 1300s and ceased earlier this century after thousands of tourists tried to set it off by pouring in loads of rocks and dirt. When the water level inside the geyser was artificially lowered, it resumed activity for awhile, spouting up to 60 metres, but now it only erupts on specially engineered occasions.

Eruptions are caused when boiling water deep in the spring, trapped by cooler water on the surface, explodes and spews out everything above it. Every 17 June, Icelandic Independence Day, tonnes of soap are poured into the Great Geysir sufficiently lowering the surface temperature and tension of the water to cause an eruption.

Luckily for the Icelandic tourist industry, the Great Geysir has a faithful stand-in. Nearby Strokkur (the 'butter churn') spouts and sprays up to 20 metres every 3 minutes. Photographers will have to be quick or they'll miss the eruptions which normally last only a couple of seconds. While tourists make a lot of fuss over Iceland's geysers, some locals maintain that the famous fountains are just another variation on Icelandic rain – hell, it falls in every other direction there.

Around the site are numerous beautifully coloured hot springs, steaming vents, warm streams, and psychedelic algae and mineral deposits. The Golden Triangle tour won't allow you time to see more than a single eruption of Strokkur before directing you over to the hotel for the snack you've already paid for. Although you can't camp on the site itself, there are plenty of spots in the surrounding hills and valleys. It's worthwhile climbing up nearby Laugarfjall where there is a view disc.

Places to Stay & Eat Geysir has a summer hotel, the *Hotel Geysir* (tel 98-68915), with a beautiful dining room but food and accommodation are very up-market. If your means are more limited, the petrol station beside the hotel has a great snack bar.

Getting There & Away Details on getting to Geysir by public transport are outlined in the Gullfoss section.

Tours
If you do opt for a tour, it's best to adopt a mellow attitude. So many daytrippers are processed through here every summer day that groups are normally falling over each other at the major stops. The biggest drawback is that so many sights are packed into a day and there isn't time to absorb any of it. The real intent of the tours seems to be getting you into the coffee shops and restaurants for as long as possible. You get 8 minutes at Geysir, for example, and 45 minutes at the hotel across the street for cakes and coffee. As usual, though, you have the option to leave the tour at any time and rejoin later.

The standard route includes a long stop at Eden in Hveragerði, the crater at Kerið, the southern bishopric at Skálholt, lunch, Gullfoss, Geysir, a snack, and finally Þingvellir (for just enough time to whet your appetite to return and stay a week!). The tour leaves Reykjavík at 8 am daily in the summer and costs US$51 without lunch. If you're booked, they'll collect you from your hotel or the central youth hostel.

LAUGARVATN

On summer weekends, the resort village of Laugarvatn buzzes with activity. On Friday nights, hundreds of Reykjavík families flee urban pressures and flock to this pretty lake to spend a couple of days camping, barbecuing, sailboarding, and enjoying the thermal springs.

Laugarvatn is an educational centre and has a number of schools. Historically, the hot spring Vígðalaug served as a site for early Christian baptisms.

Information

Today the area has all the trappings of a major resort. There are lots of nice walks in the mountains behind Laugarvatn, horse rental (tel 98-43420), sailboard rental, steam baths, and naturally heated swimming pools.

The farm Miðdalur (tel 98-61169), 5 km east of Laugarvatn, offers horse tours from there into the interior.

Places to Stay & Eat

Two Edda hotels, the *Húsmaeðrask* (tel 98-61154) and the *Menntaskóla* (tel 98-61118) provide accommodation. A double room in the former costs US$83 and in the latter only US$58. At the Menntaskóla, sleeping-bag accommodation is also available. The Edda hotels have restaurants and there is a supermarket at the Esso station in the village . The *Stjörnusamlokur*, a fast-food restaurant, serves hamburgers, sausages, and snacks.

The camping site is across the highway and about 400 metres north-east of the village. In the summer, especially on weekends, it is extremely crowded but no one goes there expecting solitude. The Icelanders are generally very courteous campers but the odd television or stereo system does find its way in and makes itself an integral part of the experience for everyone.

Getting There & Away

Golden Triangle tours pass Laugarvatn and will drop passengers. Public buses on the Laugardalur route between Reykjavík and Gullfoss pass here daily at 11 am eastbound and 5.45 pm westbound.

SELFOSS

Selfoss ('barn falls'), with over 4000 inhabitants, is the largest town in southern Iceland. It lies in the richest farming district in the country and is the home of Scandinavia's largest dairy operation.

Selfoss is a singularly uninteresting town and there's little there to draw tourists unless they're interested in the dairy industry. It's central, however, and has some inexpensive accommodation so you could use it as a base in south central Iceland.

Places to Stay & Eat

There are sleeping-bag accommodation and cooking facilities at the hostel-style *Gistiþjónustan Selfossi* (tel 98-21765). The farm *Hjarðarból* (tel 98-34178) offers farmhouse accommodation and cooking facilities but has no dormitory.

The *Hotel Selfoss* with an attached restaurant, cafeteria, and bar (tel 98-22500) has doubles for US$80. Slightly cheaper is the *Hotel Þóristún* (tel 98-21633) at Þóristún 1 which charges US$58 for a double room. Selfoss also has a camping site.

The restaurant *Inghóll* has been recommended but seems expensive. Those with less ready cash will probably have to resort to the petrol station or the supermarket.

Getting There & Away

All of the buses between Reykjavík and Höfn, Skaftafell, Fjallabak, Þórsmörk, and Vík pass through Selfoss. You'll have at least four options daily but there are the Fjallabak and Þórsmörk buses and the more expensive BSÍ tours.

Ingólfsfjall

According to legend, Iceland's first settler Ingólfur Arnarson is buried in Inghóll, a mound on top of 551-metre Ingólfsfjall. Since the peak is solid rock, it's doubtful that anyone is actually buried in it and more reliable sources place Ingólfur's grave in Reykjavík. At the foot of the mountain near the intersection of the Ring Road and the Biskupstungur Highway (Route 35) is the buried farm Fjallastún which is reputed to have been Ingólfur Arnarson's first permanent winter home.

It you're in town and feeling restless, it's a nice day-hike to Inghóll. The best route up begins 3 km west of Selfoss along the Ring Road.

HELLA

Like Selfoss, Hella is not a terribly interesting place but it does lie within close range of quite a few scenic attractions. On a clear day, there's a good view of the Hekla volcano.

Hella was established in in 1927 and developed from a single shop into a modest trading and agricultural village with 700 residents.

Aegissíða

Less than 2 km from Hella on the western bank of the river Rangá is the farm Aegissíða with a camping ground, a pleasantly rural alternative to camping in town. In the fields are ruins of 12 artificial caves believed to have been constructed by early Irish monks and hermits.

Places to Stay & Eat

The tourist centre in Hella is the *Mosfell Guesthouse* (tel 98-75828) at Þrúðvangi 6 which has private rooms, sleeping-bag accommodation, and a camping ground beside the river Rangá. If you have limited time and want to 'do the sights' quickly, South Iceland Tours Escorted (tel 98-34178) offers informal Mosfell Guesthouse-based package tours including airport transfers, meals, a week's accommodation and daily tours out from Hella to all of south-west and south central Iceland. For more information, contact them at PO Box 124, 802 Selfoss. Besides the restaurant at the Mosfell Guesthouse, there is a snack bar at the petrol station.

Getting There & Away

Details are the same as for Selfoss. The fare from Reykjavík is US$9.

Oddi

The name of this farm and church, 10 km by road south of Hella, means 'triangle', in reference to the land between the angular confluence of the Þverá and the Ytri-Rangá rivers. Oddi used to have a wealthy monastery and boarding school for children of the aristocracy. Of the priests who served as instructors at Oddi, six went on to become bishops.

Numerous scholarly works were written by Oddi residents including the *Elder Edda* and the *Prose Edda* by Saemundur Sigfússon and Snorri Sturluson (who was brought up at Oddi). Some believe the word 'Edda' itself is a corruption of 'Oddi'.

To look at it now, you'd never suspect the early importance of this place but the church does retain some relics of the Literary Era of the 1300s. To get there, take any bus east from Hella or west from Hvolsvöllur, get off at the intersection of Route 266 and walk or hitch the final 4 km to the church.

Njálla Country

The valleys of Þórsmörk and Fljótsdalur and the surrounding area are known to Icelanders as Söguslóðum Njálu or *Njálls Saga* country. The plot and events of this saga are far too complicated for a detailed description to be useful here. The brief outline that follows will be helpful to those who wish to recognise the saga sites and know something about the events associated with them.

Geographically, the area is a transition zone between the country's richest agricultural area and the spectacular Fjallabak region. It encompasses green farmlands, scrubby forests, canyons, and rugged glaciated peaks and valleys.

Njálls Saga

The story of Njáll has three parts. The first is

the saga of Gunnar Hámundarson of Hliðarendi and his wife Hallgerður, the daughter of Höskuldur Dalakollsson of the *Laxdaela Saga*. Hallgerður had a quarrel with Bergþóra, the hot-tempered wife of saga hero, Njáll Þorgeirsson of Bergþórshvoll, and the stage was set for the ultimate downfall of everyone involved.

When their feud was well and truly underway, Hallgerður and Bergþóra took to murdering each other's slaves and employees. One of Hallgerður's victims was the godfather of Njáll's three sons. One of those involved in the killing was Hallgerður's son-in-law, Þráinn Sigfússon. Provided with a motive for revenge, Njáll's sons became embroiled in the killing. Suspicion and ill-will escalated with the number of people involved and the killings became more matters of vindictive malice than of familial pride and honour.

The obnoxious Hallgerður again flew into a killing rage over an emotional disagreement with a local farmer-merchant who refused to sell her produce. In revenge, she employed a slave to steal food from him. Gunnar, trapped between his honour and his difficult wife, grew angry and slapped her, he then offered the farmer compensation for Hallgerður's foolishness.

The farmer refused to settle the matter peaceably, however. Gunnar was obliged to kill him, resulting in attempted revenge, and further killing. Gunnar was pronounced an outlaw. He planned to flee Iceland, but his love of farm and country was so great that he chose to remain and face his fate.

When a bloodthirsty vigilante group (led by the evil Mörður Valgarðsson – a new character – who had incited many killings) came looking for him, Gunnar asked Hallgerður for a lock of hair to repair his bowstring so he might have a chance against Mörður. She refused, recalling the time he'd insulted her by slapping her. Gunnar replied with one of the most oft-quoted lines in the sagas: 'To each his own way of earning renown...You shall not be asked again'. Although he fought bravely and wounded many, Gunnar finally fell.

The second part of the story is sometimes called *The Burning of Njáll*. Through all the turmoil, Njáll and Gunnar managed to remain friends. Gunnar's death had been avenged by his son Högni and Skarp Héðinn, Njáll's eldest and beefiest son. After a Viking spree on the mainland, Njáll's other sons, Grímur and Helgi, accompanied by Skarp Héðinn and their brother-in-law Kári Sölmundarson, ambushed and murdered Þráinn Sigfússon, whom they held responsible for their godfather's death at Stóra Dimon.

In order to forestall further violence, Njáll adopted Þráinn's orphaned son, Höskuldur, and offered him anything his heart desired. The boy had a saintly disposition, however, and had no intention of joining the violence and bloodshed to avenge his father's death. Mörður Valgarðsson, however, convinced Njáll's sons that Höskuldur would do just that. Of course, it wasn't long before Höskuldur was also dead.

Again Njáll was placed in a desperate situation but, as an upstanding citizen, he chose to try settling peaceably. A member of the offended family, Flosi Þórðarson of Svínafell, pleaded Njáll's case. He tried to persuade his kin to put the matter in the hands of the Alþing or be done with all the killing but was rejected and taunted into joining the violence himself. In a dramatic climax, Njáll and his family, who were weary of all the craziness and bloodshed, allowed themselves to be burned to death in their home at Bergþórshvoll. The only survivor of the fire was Njáll's son-in-law Kári.

The anti-climactic third part of the saga involves an epic judicial case, the murders of the arsonists, and the ultimate reconciliation of Flosi Þórðarson and Kári Sölmundarson. In the end, Kári was betrothed to Höskuldur's widow, Hildigunnur, as a peace offering between the families.

HVOLSVÖLLUR

This small service centre of 700 people is mainly a stop for tourists and travellers en route between Reykjavík and Þórsmörk or south-east Iceland. There's a swimming pool two blocks from the bus terminal. Horse rentals and tours through *Njálls Saga* country can be arranged with Söguhestar (tel 98-78138) at Miðhus on Route 262, about 1 km from the bus terminal.

Places to Stay & Eat

Most of the activity in Hvolsvöllur centres on the roadhouse-style *Hliðarendi Esso* which has a petrol station, grill, restaurant, supermarket, camping ground, and bus terminal. Campers en route to Þórsmörk should pick up their last-minute supplies here. The *Shell* station across the street also has a snack bar and is a bit less chaotic than the Hliðarendi complex.

The *Hotel Hvolsvöllur* (tel 98-78187) charges US$58 for double rooms. It also has a dining room and offers tourist information.

Getting There & Away

Access to Hvolsvöllur is the same as to Selfoss and Hella. During the summer, the bus from Þórsmörk back to Hvolsvöllur leaves the Húsadalur hut daily at 3.30 pm.

Bergþórshvoll

In the Landeyjar ('land islands'), a region of low knolls and marshes near the coast south of Hvolsvöllur, is Bergþórshvoll ('Bergþóra's knoll'), the farm which belonged to Njáll Þorgeirsson, hero of *Njálls Saga*, and his wife, Bergþóra. The farm sits on a low hill above the surrounding fields.

It was, of course, the site of the burning of Njáll and his family in the year 1011. The family was entirely aware of what was coming but, tired of the seemingly neverending cycle of revenge killings, they submitted to their dramatic fate. Njáll, who decided not to attempt escape, asked his sons to remain with him. The women and children, whom the arsonists would have permitted to leave the building, also elected to remain, Bergþóra stating that her husband's fate was also her own.

In 1951, archaeology revealed that a fire did destroy the building and radio-carbon dating has since determined that it took place in the 11th century. Unfortunately for saga fans, Bergþórshvoll is not easily reached by public transport but there's not much to see, anyway. The nearest bus stop is at Hvolsvöllur, 20 km away by road, and hitching may prove difficult.

Hvolsvöllur to Þórsmörk

Stóra Dimon This monolithic mountain near the intersection of the Ring and Þórsmörk (Route 249) roads was known in *Njálls Saga* as Rauðuskriður (the 'red scree'). It was the site of several events in the saga including reciprocal murdering of slaves by Bergþóra and Hallgerður and the ambush and murder of Þraínn Sigfússon by the sons of Njáll including Skarp Heðinn.

Gígjökull The tortured-looking mountains bordering the Markarfljót valley along Route 249 are characterised by rugged outcrops, deep gashes and high waterfalls. Along a small spur south of the main route, the steep glacier-tongue Gígjökull flows headlong into the small lake and fills it with calved icebergs. All the eastbound bus tours to Þórsmörk stop here for about 5 minutes and the place resounds with creaking ice and clicking shutters.

Steinholtsjökull Another tongue of Eyjafjallajökull, this glacier flows into a small pond higher on the mountainside and is the source of Stakksholtsá, a short river which has carved a sheer-sided 100-metre-deep gorge, Stakksholtsgjá. The eastern fork of the canyon can be explored on foot and is a spectacular 2-hour return walk from the road.

Húsadalur Although the Þórsmörk buses used to actually go into Þórsmörk, they now stop in Húsadalur where there's a dormitory hut, a common hut, and a tiny shop owned by the bus company (see the map 'Landmannalaugar to Þórsmörk & Skógar Trek' on page 287). Getting there involves fording several large channels of the Markarfljót and should be done only in a 4WD vehicle.

On the hill behind the Húsadalur hut is the cave Sönghellir. From there, a maze of confusing walking tracks leads through the scrubby birch forests – over the hill to Þórsmörk, a half-hour walk from Húsadalur.

If you're planning to stay at the hut, prepare for a crowded experience. It costs US$10.35 per person per night and reservations are necessary. You have to bring your own sleeping bag and food. Cooking facilities are available, although you'll probably have to wait in a queue to use them.

Basic snacks are available at the shop which is open only a couple of hours a day. The sauna in the common hut costs US$5 per half-hour. It's closed on weekends because it can't accommodate weekend crowds. Campers are herded into a designated site away from the hut so your best bet is to wander over the mountain to the beautiful grassy valleys at Þórsmörk where you can spread out a bit.

For reservations and information, contact Austurleið (tel 98-78145), 860 Hvolsvöllur or enquire at the BSÍ terminal's tourist office in Reykjavík.

ÞÓRSMÖRK

The valley of Þórsmörk (the 'woods of Þór'), is one of the most beautiful in Iceland. Imagine a forested glacial valley full of flowers, braided rivers, and clear-running steams surrounded by snowy peaks and glaciers and you'll have an idea of what you can expect here. The area's been protected since 1921 by the Icelandic Forestry Department but hasn't gone unnoticed. On a sunny summer weekend, it can be more crowded than central Reykjavík. This is probably because a good proportion of central Reykjavík is in Þórsmörk. It's packed with tour buses, 4WD vehicles, and hundreds of tents. All-terrain vehicles buzz everywhere playing havoc with the landscape and no one seems to go walking in groups of less than 15. It's frantic, but still worthwhile. If you want to experience anything resembling solitude, go during the week or when it's raining.

Places to Stay

All the grassy lawns and valleys around Þórsmörk are open to camping and, although it's obviously not an environmentally sound policy, it currently seems to be the only way to accommodate the hordes that descend on the place. If it gets much more littered and trodden than now, however, expect them to set aside a formal camping area and fill it to elbow-knocking maximum density.

In my opinion, staying at the main hut would be an exercise in endurance. Not only is it packed but all the campers wander in and out, especially when it's raining, and it gets claustrophobic. There are cooking facilities available but it wouldn't hurt to bring your own stove anyway, especially if you're there on a weekend.

If you want to stay at the hut, book in advance through the Ferðafélag Íslands (tel 91-19533), Öldugata 3, Reykjavík. Guests must supply their own food and sleeping bags. Club members/non-members pay US$7.75/10.35 per night. Hot showers cost US$3.

Þórsmörk to Skógar Walk

The relatively short, but at times difficult, walk between Þórsmörk and Skógar begins with the ascent described in the Goðaland section (see also the map on page 287). From the Fimmvörðuháls pass between Eyjafjallajökull and Mýrdalsjökull, which was itself once covered with glacial ice, there's a rough jeep track all the way down to Skógar. Although the walk from Þórsmörk to Skógar can be done in a long day, most hikers prefer to break it up and spend a night at the hut south of Fimmvörðuháls pass.

This walk also is a welcome option for those who've just come off the crowded Landmannalaugar trek and are ready for more walking. Both segments appear on the Landmannalaugar to Þórsmörk topographic sheet. Due to snow conditions, the route is normally open for hiking only from the middle of July to the end of August.

The map and description of the popular Landmannalaugar to Þórsmörk trek are included in the Fjallabak section of the Central Iceland chapter.

Getting There & Away

During the summer, the Þórsmörk bus leaves the BSÍ terminal in Reykjavík daily at 8.30 am and arrives at Húsadalur at around noon. It departs Húsadalur for Reykjavík at 3.30 pm. On Friday nights, there is a special weekenders' bus that departs Reykjavík at 8 pm. The return fare is US$52.

Around Þórsmörk

Opportunities for hiking and exploration abound. Although there are lots of trails and tracks, some of the most rewarding trips will be cross-country and it is advisable to carry topographical sheets and a compass. The best map is *Þórsmörk/Landmannalaugar 1:100,000* (1987) which is sometimes available at the Þórsmörk hut. Be prepared, also, for sudden and dramatic changes in the weather.

Valahnúkur The summit of 458-metre-high Valahnúkur, immediately west of Þórsmörk, is a popular climb from the Húsadalur and Þórsmörk huts. The view disc on top identifies all the mountains, valleys, and glaciers within the far-ranging vista. The return trip can be done easily in a couple of hours from either side of the mountain.

Goðaland Goðaland or 'land of the gods' encompasses the rugged area along the Þórsmörk to Skógar walking track between the Bólfell hut (across the river Krossá from Þórsmörk) near Básar and the pass between Eyjafjallajökull and Mýrdalsjökull.

The return walk to the pass can be done in a long day from the hut or you can continue over the pass, past a series of impressive waterfalls to connect with the Ring Road at Skógar. It's also possible to spend a day wandering through Goðaland. To reach it from Þórsmörk, cross the pedestrian bridge about 1 km downstream and then walk back upstream for 2 km along the southern bank of the Krossá. You can cross directly from Þórsmörk to Básar in a high-clearance 4WD vehicle but the water is fast and deep; due caution should be exercised. Don't try to cross on foot.

Útvist (tel 91-14606, Reykjavík), the trek-

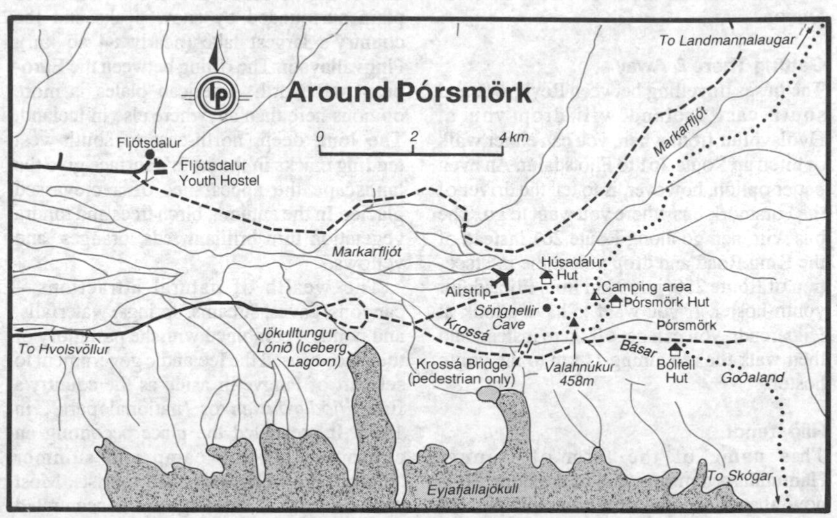

king company that owns the hut runs day-tours of the region on Sundays and Wednesdays at 8 am in the summer. If you'd like to join a tour or stay in the hut, contact them for a reservation.

FLJÓTSDALUR

The farm at Fljótsdalur is in the heart of *Njálls Saga* country. Most travellers go to Fljótsdalur to stay in the small and cosy sod-farmhouse youth hostel (tel 98-78498). Since the hostel is the headquarters of Dick Phillips Tours it is booked by groups for many nights during the summer. Other youth hostels in Iceland keep a listing of dates when Fljótsdalur is unavailable.

The warden is English and keeps a library of English-language books for guests who want to vegetate for a while in the pristine setting. Since the hostel is so small, advance booking is advised.

Only 10 km north is 1462-metre Tindfjallajökull, a small icecap which can be reached on foot from the youth hostel. The 4WD track passing Fljótsdalur continues into the interior and provides access to the Landmannalaugar to Þórsmörk trek. The only other foot access to Þórsmörk from Fljótsdalur is via the river bridge at Stóra Dimon.

Getting There & Away

The buses travelling between Reykjavík and south-east Iceland will drop you at Hvolsvöllur from where you can either walk or hitch up Route 261 to Fljótsdalur. An even better option, however, is to tell the driver of the Þórsmörk bus where you want to go. The bus will then go along Route 261 instead of the Ring Road and drop you at the intersection of Route 250, just 9 km from Fljótsdalur youth hostel. If you want to have a look at Hliðarendi, you can get off there instead and then walk the remaining 11 km to the youth hostel.

Hliðarendi

This name of the farm of Gunnar Hámundarson means 'end of the slope'. It is now abandoned and only some dilapidated buildings remain. The setting is lovely and you can imagine the dismay Gunnar must have felt at the prospect of leaving it after being declared an outlaw. Riding toward the river Markarfljót to leave his home forever, his horse stumbled. Gunnar had the opportunity to turn and look at the scene saying:

> How lovely are the hillsides more lovely than they have ever seemed before, with their golden cornfields and new-mown hay. I am going home and will not go away.

It was, of course, a fatal decision for Gunnar, but he realised that and accepted what he considered his fate.

What remains of Hliðarendi lies just 11 km west of Fljótsdalur.

ÞINGVELLIR

Þingvellir (the 'plains of parliament') has been the most significant historical site in Iceland since the Alþing was established there in 930. The site was selected because of its topography, acoustics, and proximity to most of Iceland's population.

Þingvellir is more than a setting for historical drama, however. It is also geologically interesting, a broad fissured and forested plain surrounded by snow peaks and the country's largest lake (nearly 84 sq km), Þingvallavatn. The rifting between the European and North American plates is more obvious here than anywhere else in Iceland. The long deep, north-east to south-west tending cracks in the earth's surface give the landscape the appearance of a crevassed glacier. In the autumn, birch trees and tundra vegetation turn brilliant reds, oranges, and yellows.

The wealth of natural attractions – canyons, caves, streams, springs, waterfalls, and ponds – combined with the past glory of the place caused the Icelandic government to set part of Þingvellir aside as the country's first *Þjóðarðurinn* or 'national park', in 1928. It prevented the place becoming an enormous holiday camp and summer 'suburb' for weekenders and tourists. Most of the historical buildings are concentrated

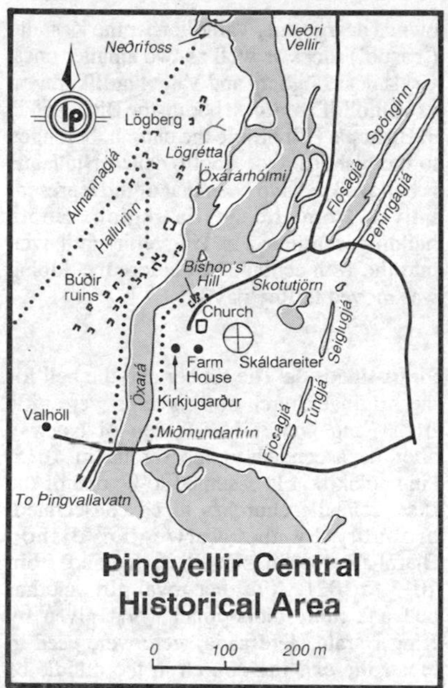

Þingvellir Central Historical Area

in one small area, having been moved there from around the park; the remainder is left pretty much to nature. A maze of hiking trails crisscrosses the plain and leads through the woods to points of interest or simply through scenic areas.

History

The descendants of Ingólfur Arnarson, Iceland's first settler, established the Alþing at Þingvellir, the eastern edge of his property. This site was selected for the Alþing because the great fissure of Almannagjá above the surrounding plain provided the ideal open-air podium for the representatives and legislators who would arbitrate disputes and formulate laws for the young country.

It cannot be overstressed that the annual summer convention of the Alþing was the event of the year and everyone who could attend did so. Nearly everything that happened in Iceland until 1271 had some connection with the Alþing and the history of the country coincides for the most part with the history of Þingvellir. There the courses of human lives were determined: legal disputes were settled, marriages were arranged, business contracts were drawn up, executions were carried out, and laws were made.

Christianity was accepted as the national religion and subsequent issues such as the establishment of the bishoprics at Hólar and Skálholt and the introduction of tithes were sanctioned. There Gunnar of Hliðarendi met and married Hallgerður Long-Legs, the woman who orchestrated the downfall of half of south central Iceland in *Njalls Saga*. There Snorri Sturluson became known to his countrymen as lögsögumaður, and there Iceland surrendered itself to Norway in 1262, bringing about the Alþing's loss of power in 1271. It was dissolved completely in 1800, just after being moved to Austurvöllur in Reykjavík and, when it reorganised and regained power in 1843, Iceland was already on its way to independence. Þingvellir's importance as the seat of government became little more than a novelty as Reykjavík took over both the government and Iceland itself.

On the 1000th anniversary of Settlement in 1874, Christian IX of Denmark became the first king to attend the assembly and many Icelanders turned up for the show. In 1930, Þingvellir hosted 30,000 guests, including King Christian X, in celebration of the 1000-year anniversary of the Alþing. On 17 June 1944, around 30,000 people witnessed the birth of the republic. In 1974, in honour of Iceland's 1100th anniversary of Settlement, 60,000 Icelanders turned up at Þingvellir for the biggest party the country has ever known.

For more details of the Alþing's history, see also the History section of the Iceland Facts about the Country chapter.

Things to See & Do

The primary attraction of Þingvellir is the ease with which you can stroll around its interesting landscapes. Well maintained footpaths, good for several day-hikes, wind throughout the historical and scenic areas. The more adventurous can venture off into the surrounding mountains or around the lakeshore.

Walkers can pick up a copy of the topo sheet *Þingvellir 1:25,000* (1974) which is available at map shops in Reykjavík (see the Reykjavík chapter for locations).

Almannagjá Almannagjá is the greatest rift at Þingvellir. It formally included the crack between Kárastaðastígur, the track leading in from the south, and Öxarárfoss (the 'axe river falls') where the Öxará flows into it from the north. Geologically, however, it runs all the way to Ármannsfell in the north and Þingvallavatn in the south. According to legend, the falls of Öxarárfoss were created artificially by diverting the course of the river in order to enhance the scenic value of the parliament's backdrop.

There is a broad track through the gorge today bordered by high stone cliffs on the west and lower rock outcrops on the east.

Lögberg The Lögberg or 'law rock' served as the official podium during sessions of the Alþing from 930 to 1271. After Iceland's conversion to Christianity, this was moved from Spönginn, east of Flosagjá, to its present site on the slope east of Almannagjá. There the lögsögumaður annually recited the laws of the land and presided over the parliament. Active geological forces have caused the rock podium to subside into a grassy mound, but the site of its disappearance is marked by a flagpole.

Búðir The Búðir or 'booths' were owned by the goðar, parliamentary representatives and used as shelters and meeting places. Some were large and some served only temporary businesses where visitors could buy ale, writing vellum, weapons, shoes, and food. One dispute at the Alþing reportedly resulted in a person being dumped head-first into a boiling cauldron at such a concession.

The remains of many booths can still be seen along Almannagjá. Snorri Sturluson owned a large one, Valhöll, near the Kastalar ('castle') rocks as well as two smaller ones, Grýla near Lögberg and Valhallardilkur west of Valhöll. The largest booth, the Biskupabúð at Bishop's Hill beside the church, belonged to the bishops. One booth, called Njállsbúð is believed to have been that of the representatives from the Njálla region. Booth building continued at Þingvellir until well into the 18th century just before the Alþing was moved to Reykjavík.

Þingvallakirkja The timber and the bell for the original church at Þingvellir were gifts from King Ólafur Haraldsson of Norway after he ascended to the throne in 1015. Þingvallakirkja is assumed to be one of the first Icelandic churches to be consecrated, probably by the Norwegian Bishop Bjarnharður who stayed in Iceland from 1016 to 1021. A further royal gift, another bell and more Norwegian wood given by King Harald Hardraada, were were used to repair the existing church in the middle of that century.

When the royal church collapsed in 1118, the Þingvallabaer farmer's private church came into general use. It was enlarged and became St Ólafur's, the main church at Þingvellir. It was prone to flooding, however, and in 1523 was moved to the site of the present church, which was built in 1859.

The current church has three bells: one of the originals, one from 1698, and one cast on the occasion of Iceland's independence in 1944. The pulpit dates back to 1683. Ófeigur Jónsson's *The Last Supper* was painted in 1834 and served as the altarpiece until it was sold in 1899 and replaced by a more modern painting of Christ healing the blind man.

The old work, purchased by Englishwoman Mrs Disney Leith, was installed in her family church on the Isle of Wight. It was ingeniously tracked down and returned to Iceland in time for the 1974 festivities.

If you want to see the interior of the church and find it locked, contact the national park warden at the office in the Þingvallabaer farmhouse.

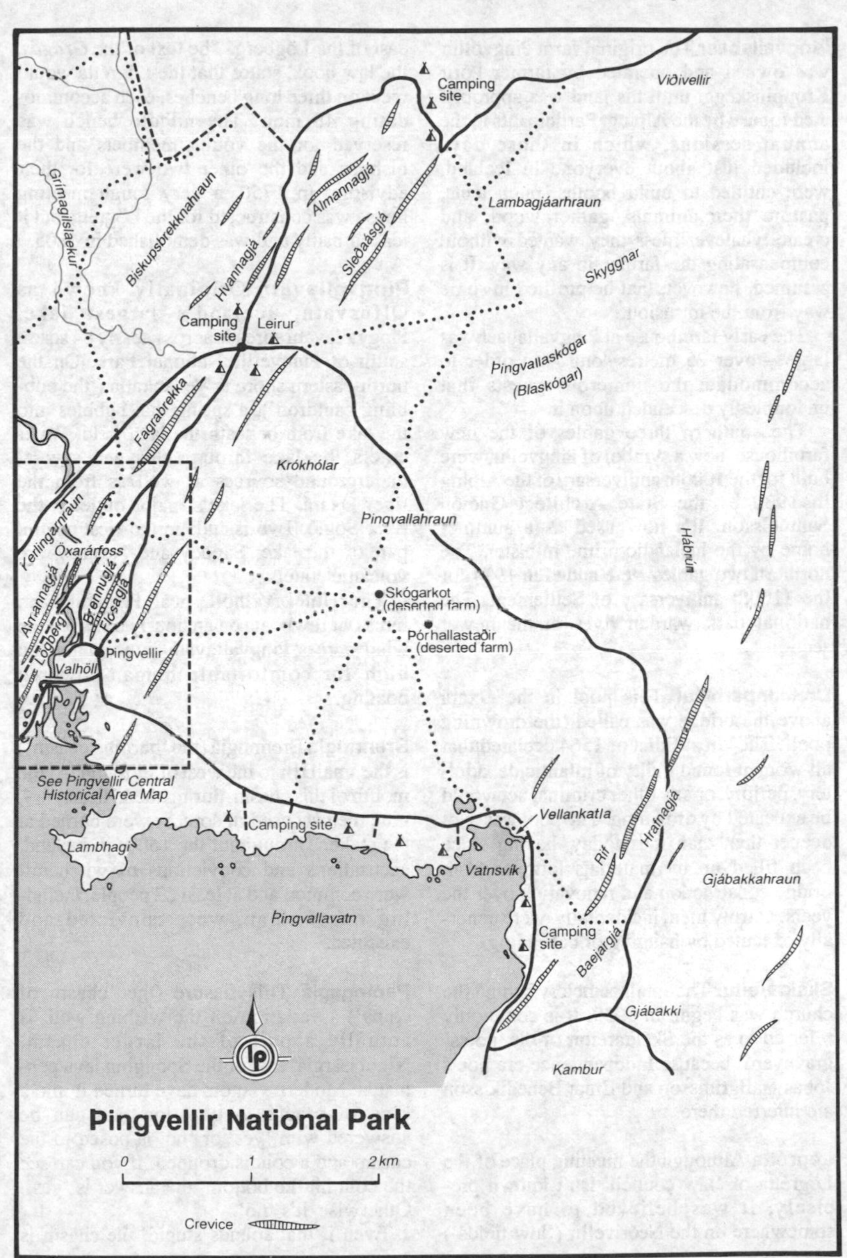

Camping site
Viðivellir
Grímagilslaekur
Biskupsbrekknahraun
Almannagjá
Lambagjáarhraun
Hvannagjá
Sleðaásgjá
Skyggnar
Camping site
Leirur
Fagrabrekka
Þingvallaskógar
(Bláskógar)
Krókhólar
Þingvallahraun
Hábrún
Yerlingarhraun
Öxarárfoss
Almannagjá
Brennugjá
Flosagjá
Lögberg
Skógarkot
(deserted farm)
Þórhallastaðir
(deserted farm)
Þingvellir
Valhöll
See Þingvellir Central Historical Area Map
Camping site
Lambhagi
Vellankatla
Rif
Hrafnagjá
Vatnsvík
Gjábakkahraun
Þingvallavatn
Camping site
Baejargjá
Gjábakki
Kambur
Þingvellir National Park
0
1
2 km
Crevice

Þingvallabaer The original farm Þingvöllur was owned and operated by farmer Þórir Kroppinskeggi until his land was appropriated for use by the Alþing. Participants in the annual sessions, which in those days included just about everyone in Iceland, were entitled to build booths, pitch tents, pasture their animals, gather wood, and create whatever mess they wanted without compensating the farmer in any way. It is assumed, however, that he profited in some way from the intrusion.

The early farmhouse at Þingvallabaer was large – over 25 metres long – in order to accommodate the numerous guests that undoubtedly descended upon it.

The southern three gables of the new farmhouse, now a symbol of Þingvellir, were built for the 1000th anniversary of the Alþing in 1930 by the State Architect Guðjón Samúelsson. It's now used as a summer home by the Icelandic prime minister. The northern two gables were added in 1974 for the 1100th anniversary of Settlement. The national park warden lives in the newer section.

Drekkingarhylur This pool in the Öxará above the bridge was called 'the drowning pool'. The Great Edict of 1564 declared that all women found guilty of infanticide, adultery, perjury, or any other criminal act would be executed by drowning. The pool was a lot deeper then than it is today, having since been filled up by materials leftover from bridge construction and renovation over the years. Unruly men, incidentally, were generally executed by hanging or beheading.

Skáldareitur The small cemetery behind the church was begun in 1939. It is commonly referred to as the Skáldareitur or the 'poets' graveyard' because Independence-era poets Jónas Hallgrímsson and Einar Benediktsson are interred there.

Lögrétta Although the meeting place of the Lögrétta or 'law council' isn't known precisely, it was believed to have been somewhere on the Neðrivellir ('low fields') east of the Lögberg. The text of the *Grágás*, the law book, states that the Lögrétta would meet on three long benches, each accommodating 48 men. The middle bench was reserved for the voting members and the bishops and the other two were for their advisors. In 1750, a very rough meeting house was constructed for the Lögrétta but it leaked badly and was demolished in 1805.

Þingvallavatn Originally known as Ölfusvatn, Iceland's largest lake, Þingvallavatn spreads across nearly 84 sq km south of Þingvellir National Park. On the north-eastern shore is Vellankatla ('the bubbling cauldron'), a spring that bubbles into the lake from beneath the lava field. Water enters the lake through this and several underground sources as well as from the river Öxará. The lake's major outlet is the river Sogið. Two islands in the west central part of the lake, Sandey and Nesjaey, are volcanic craters.

The Hotel Valhöll, near Þingvallabaer, hires out rowboats on an hourly basis but the wind across Þingvallavatn is normally too high for comfortable human-powered boating.

Brennugjá Brennugjá (the 'burning chasm') is the small rift to the west of Flosagjá. At the mouth of this chasm, during the 17th century, nine men accused of sorcery were burned at the stake. Throughout the 1600s in Iceland, accusations and convictions of witchcraft were common and at least 22 people, including one woman, were convicted and executed.

Peningagjá This fissure (the 'chasm of coins') a variation on the wishing well, is actually a part of the larger chasm, Nikulásargjá, east of the Spönginn lava peninsula. Modern visitors have turned it into a kind of oracle. A question that can be answered with 'yes' or 'no' is posed to the chasm and a coin is dropped. If you can see the coin hit the bottom, the answer is 'yes'. Otherwise, it's 'no'.

Even if that sounds stupid, the chasm is

worth seeing. Its eerie depths of sapphire-blue water glow with reflected light from the thousands of coins in it creating an effect reminiscent of the milky way.

Flosagjá This chasm, west of Spönginn, is named after Flosi Þórðarson of *Njálls Saga*. It's significant because you can see into the water for an incredible 70 metres.

Skógarkot Most of the walking tracks through the Þingvellir plains converge at Skógarkot, an abandoned farm site below the small hill Sjógnarhóll. It was occupied until 1936. Just south-east lie the ruins of another farm, Þórhallastaðir where, during 13th-century conventions, ale was brewed and served to Alþing participants.

Ármannsfell Ármannsfell, the prominent mountain immediately north of Þingvellir, is named after the giant Ármann Dalmansson who is considered in folk legend to be the benevolent guardian spirit of Þingvellir.

Skjaldbreiður Although not in the park itself, Skjaldbreiður can be plainly seen from Almannagjá on a clear day. Its name means 'broad shield' and is the namesake for all the 'shield' volcanoes in the world – the volcanoes of Hawaii, for example, are of this type. Its distinctly shield-like shape was created by slow-building, oozing lava. If you're tired of the level terrain around the park, the mountain makes a fascinating walking trip from Þingvellir which takes several days. Use the *Hengill 1:100,000* topographic sheet.

Places to Stay & Eat

There are several camping grounds around the park. The most popular one is at the park headquarters at Leirur, which also has a petrol station, shop, and snack bar and lies within walking distance of the central historical area. Other camping sites can be found along the lakeshore, east of Hvannagjá, and at the extreme northern end of the park (see map).

The *Hotel Valhöll* (tel 98-34700), across the Öxará from the church, offers fairly elegant accommodation for US$83 a double per night. Its three dining rooms serve meals for those with more sophisticated tastes than the petrol station can accommodate.

Getting There & Away

Tours to Þingvellir rarely stay more than a half-hour and normally include only a quick stroll along Almannagjá past the lower waterfall and the Lögberg. Few tour participants are satisfied with the amount of time allotted to them there.

Public buses travel between Þingvellir and Reykjavík once or twice daily between 1 June and 15 September. At other times, including the autumn when the foliage is wonderful, you'll have to take the Golden Triangle tour. Þingvellir is the last stop, however, so you'd have to endure the rest of it, too, and pay the full tour price. Try hitching!

Mossfell

Mossfell is a farm and a mountain on the Þingvellir road, 4 km east of Mosfellsbaer. It was the last home of the poet Egill Skallagrímsson who, when he was old and almost senile, requested to be taken to the Alþing. Here he planned to mock the materialistically corrupt proceedings by flinging two chests of silver coins (which had been given him by the king of England) from the Lögberg to watch the violence and greed with which the crowd would surely react.

His family refused his request, of course, so one night when they were all at Þingvellir, he set out with some slaves, a horse, and the two chests. The next day, he was found wandering senseless but neither the slaves nor the coins were ever found. Legend has it that Egill buried his treasure somewhere on the mountain.

Across Route 36 from Mossfell is Reykjahlið, a geothermal area which is the source for some of Reykjavík's hot water supply.

Skálafell

Skálafell is a small ski area between

Reykjavík and Þingvellir. The mountain is 770 metres high and offers good cross-country skiing with tows and ski cabins. The season is the same as that for Bláfjöll, from mid-November to early May, but Skálafell isn't as popular or crowded.

Nesjavellir

South-west of Þingvellir is the Hengill geothermal area. At the foot of the mountain is the field of boreholes which Reykjavík people hope will be the future site of the 400 mega-watt Nesjavellir power plant. Approaching these boreholes, you begin to get some idea of kind of power we're talking about here. The temperature in one of the 2000-metre deep bores is 400°C and the steam pouring out sounds like a high-speed freight train. The plant is scheduled to be completed soon and should be included on a tour route or two.

Skógar

Skógar, a small settlement just north of the Ring Road, is a summer resort that normally buzzes with tourist activity. Above the village are the white heights of 1666-metre-high Eyjafjallajökull and its craggy green foothills. Although the weather is normally disagreeable, you may be lucky. If so, Skógar is an excellent spot to relax and explore the extreme south of Iceland. There's a folk museum in an old sod-roofed farmhouse.

Places to Stay & Eat In the summer, an *Edda Hotel* (tel 98-78870) operates offering doubles for US$58 as well as sleeping-bag accommodation for US$13.75. There is a licensed restaurant, a swimming pool, a shop, horse rental (tel 98-78860), and a snack bar in the settlement. The camping ground is near waterfall.

Getting There & Away To get there, take any bus between Reykjavík and Höfn or Vík. If you're going to Skógar, they'll drive you there.

Around Skógar

Skógafoss About 200 metres west of Skógar is 60-metre-high Skógafoss, the lowest in a series of over 20 waterfalls along the hike to the mountain hut at Fimmvörðuháls pass. There is a legend that an early settler named Þrasi hid a chest of booty somewhere near Skógafoss but it's never been found, not for the lack of searching, I'm sure.

Fimmvörðuháls Pass It's possible to walk to the pass and back in a day. A further 1 or 2 hours of walking will take you to the edge of the Eyjafjallajökull icecap but go prepared for a night at the hut or to campout. You can also continue north to Þórsmörk, a trip which is best done in 2 days.

Drangshlíð The farm Drangshlíð, beneath the 478-metre mountain Drangshlíðarfjall, is 3 km west of Skógar. The interest lies in the big rock in the field, part of an extinct volcano, which contains caves now used as stables. Ask permission at the farm before having a look around, however.

Ásólfsskáli The farm at Ásólfsskáli was originally settled by Ásólfur, the missionary who ended up resettling with his uncle at Akranes because he was driven out of the Eyjafjöll district. Wherever he went, the rivers filled with fish. His greedy neighbours were jealous and drove him away.

Eyjafjallajökull Although it's small by Icelandic standards, Eyjafjallajökull icecap covers about 100 sq km. Deep under the ice is an active volcano which erupted in both 1612 and 1822 and is not yet extinct. The easiest way to reach the edge of glacier is via the jeep track from near Skógafoss.

Another less travelled route to the glacier (requiring technical climbing equipment) begins at Seljavellir, which has a swimming pool and camping site. It lies 1.5 km north of the Ring Road and if you're relying on the buses, you'll have to walk. From the intersection take any bus between Reykjavík and Vík or Höfn.

Hamragarðar Around the abandoned farm Hamragarðar, 29 km west of Skógar along the Ring Road, are several interesting sights. The most prominent is Seljalandsfoss, actually on Seljaland, the next farm west. This high and wispy falls is one of the most unique in Iceland. Another interesting falls, Gljúfurárfoss tumbles from the same cliff just north-west of Seljalandsfoss into a wrap-around canyon and half of it is hidden from view. Interestingly enough, its name means 'canyon river falls'.

West of Hamragarðar near the farm Fit, you'll find the cave Paradíshellir whose name can be deciphered easily enough. Folk legends report that it was a hideout for the 16th-century outlaw Hjalti Magnússon. There is an easy track up from the sheep corral close to the Ring Road.

Jökulsá á Sólheimassandur This braided glacial river flowing from the tongue of Sólheimajökull is also sometimes known as Fúlilaekur or 'stinking creek'. It emits a strong smell of sulphur, apparently due to springs flowing into it. It crosses the Ring Road 6.5 km east of Skógar from where the tongue of the glacier Sólheimajökull is plainly visible.

VÍK Í MÝRDAL

Although it's the rainiest spot in Iceland, there's no denying that Vík, at the southern tip of Iceland, is beautiful. The full name, which is equally enchanting, means 'bay of the marshy valley'. The broad, sandy beaches of the south coast are punctuated here by craggy cliffs and headlands teeming with bird life and pounded by high surf. Above the green hills rises the Mýrdalsjökull icecap under which lies Katla, one of Iceland's most notorious volcanoes.

The town started out as a fishing village but the harbour conditions were so bad it was abandoned early on. It received a trading charter in 1887. In 1906, a cooperative society was formed and still serves as the town's primary employer. Vík remains small – with only about 500 people – and the surrounding area has many interesting places to explore.

The church is in an ideal setting but it's normally locked up so you probably won't have the chance to look inside. The tourist information office is at the Víkurskáli petrol station where the bus stops.

Places to Stay & Eat

Vík has one lodging, the *Kaupfélag Skaftfellinga Guesthouse* (tel 98-71193), commonly known as just *KS Guesthouse* at Víkurbraut 24a. They only serve breakfast, but there's a supermarket in the same building.

The *Reynisbrekka Youth Hostel* (tel 98-71243) is 9 km from town and they will come to the bus stop and fetch you if you like. The place is owned by the only police officer in south Iceland so don't be too alarmed when the police car arrives to pick you up. The youth hostel charges the standard prices, US$11/13 for members/non-members.

Farmhouse accommodation is available at the farm *Ytri Sólheimar* (tel 98-71322) which offers both cooking facilities and sleeping-bag accommodation 23 km west of town.

Höfðabrekka (tel 98-71208) is 5 km east of town but has no sleeping-bag accommodation. The farm is reputed to be haunted by Höfðubrekkujóka, the ghost of a former farmer's wife who came back to annoy the farmhand who got her daughter pregnant. One of the farm's corrals is in a cave and the place is surrounded by nice moss-covered cliffs and waterfalls. Höfðabrekka was moved up the slope for awhile after the 1660 eruption of Katla caused flooding down there. It moved back to the flats in the early 1960s.

The camping site in Vík is in a pleasant spot but it's the most expensive place in Iceland to pitch a tent and the attendants are a pretty sour bunch. Perhaps they're just tired of campers complaining about the price and the rain.

At the bus terminal, which doubles as the petrol station, is a nice big snack bar but it fills beyond capacity and gets frantic when a bus is passing through.

Getting There & Away

Vík is on the bus routes between Höfn and Reykjavík. Buses depart from Reykjavík at 8.30 am daily and Höfn at 9 am passing through Vík at 12.15 pm eastbound and at 3.15 pm westbound. Another service leaves Reykjavík at 5 pm from Monday to Friday and at 8.30 pm Sundays and leaves Vík at 7.30 am from Monday to Saturday. This bus does not travel east beyond Vík.

Around Vík

Without a vehicle, it will be difficult to get around outside of Vík because there are few tours and the infrequent public buses keep to the Ring Road. If you want to visit the sights, in other words, you'll have to resign yourself to long walks (mostly along roadways) or to hitching.

Reynisfjall The abandoned Loran station, on top of 340-metre Reynisfjall west of Vík, affords a magnificent view out to sea if the weather is cooperating. The cliffs provide nesting sites for numerous sea birds including puffins.

The long sandy peninsula west of Reynisfjall encloses a shallow lagoon, Dyrhólaós. When the waves aren't too high, the beach is great for camping (you'll have to bring water from elsewhere, however). At Garðar is Iceland's southernmost farm and nearby are lots of caves, beaches, and interesting rock formations to explore.

Reynisdrangar The oft-photographed sea stacks (the higher of which rises 66 metres) are a favourite subject for postcards. They are Vík's trademarks dominating the view out to sea. Their cliffs are simply squawking with activity.

Kerlingardalur The 'witch valley', Kerlingardalur lies in the green hills above Vík providing hiking opportunities from the Reynisbrekka youth hostel.

Hjörleifshöfði The prominent peak rising from the sand flats south of the Ring Road is named after Hjörleifur, Ingólfur Arnarson's blood brother. Hjörleifur continued on down the coast from Ingólfur's settlement and set up his farm near Vík but, after a short time, he was murdered in a slave uprising. On top of the 221-metre summit is a stone monument and some modern grave sites.

The headland used to be at the shore but now 3 km of sandy beach and some rock pillars that were once sea stacks stand between it and the water. Directly south of Hjörleifshöfði is Kötlutangi, the southernmost point in Iceland. The cliffs of the mountain are covered with nesting birds and behind the rescue hut on the seaward side is a large cave formed by wave action.

Dyrhólaey This long spur of rock, 120 metres high and cut into a natural arch by Atlantic breakers, stands in water deep enough to allow boats to have passed through, hence its name ('door hill island'). Njáll's son-in-law Kári had his farm here. There is a lighthouse on top of this nesting site for eider ducks and far-ranging Arctic terns. The sea stacks off the coast are called Háidrangur.

Eider Duck

Unless you're up for a 6-km walk from Skeiðflötur farm on the Ring Road, the only way to reach Dyrhólaey is with the relatively expensive youth hostel-run tour which costs US$20 per person and operates when there's enough interest.

Laufskálavörður The curious little stone mounds along the rough desert stretch of Ring Road, from 35 to 45 km east of Vík, are a mystery to most visitors. Early travellers would build cairns as they passed through, believing it would bring good luck as well as mark the track. By the looks of things, modern-day travellers have taken up the tradition. There'd better be an awful lot of good luck floating around out there.

East of Laufskálavörður, note the contrast in vegetation between grazed and ungrazed hillsides. Before the arrival of sheep, much of the non-forested landscape of Iceland looked like this.

Hafursey & Mýrdalssandur Like a green island, Hafursey rises 582 metres above the 700-sq km desert Mýrdalssandur. There's a jeep track leading 12 km north to its base from the Ring Road at Hjörleifshöfði. The glacial sands of the Mýrdalssandur desert were deposited by braided rivers and jökulhlaups caused by the Katla volcano beneath Mýrdalsjökull.

Álftaver The small Álftaver region is between the Ring Road and the Kúðafljót river. Its 50 inhabitants have been able to stay here because the Vellustrompur pseudocrater field shelters them from flooding caused by Katla's eruptions. At the farm Þykkvabaejarklaustur, 8 km east of the Ring Road on Route 211, a basalt monument commemorates the monastery which operated from 1168 until 1550 (during the Reformation). The current church was built in the 1800s. There is a small area of woodland near the farm and a lava field at Skálmarbaer.

This area is so far from service centres that the only really practical way to explore it is in a private vehicle. The very game can try hitching but, in my opinion, there's not really enough there to justify the effort.

Katla & Mýrdalsjökull

The 700-sq km glacier Mýrdalsjökull, Iceland's fourth largest icecap, rises to 1480 metres and is over 1000 metres thick in places.

The insidious volcano Katla ('cauldron') snoozing beneath Mýrdalsjökull just above the glacier spur Höfðabrekkujökull, is among the most destructive volcanoes in Iceland. When Katla boils over, as it has done 16 times since Settlement, it melts enough of the glacier above it to send devastating walls of water, sand, and tephra to wash away everything in their paths. In fact, the liquid output of a Katla eruption is five times that at the mouth of the Amazon – up to 70,000 cubic metres per second.

The first recorded eruption was in 894 and the mountain has exploded on an average, once every 70 years since. The last eruption was in 1918 and another one is expected during this century.

Vestmannaeyjar

Vestmannaeyjar or the 'Westmen Islands', named for the Irish slaves who unwittingly became the first inhabitants, form one of the world's youngest archipelagos. Most of the islands were formed by submarine volcanoes between 10,000 and 5000 years ago. In 1963, the world witnessed the birth of its newest island, Surtsey, on film. It continued erupting until 1967.

Only the island of Heimaey (the 'home island') with 5000 residents, supports a permanent human population. The other 15 islands are rocky and steep-sided affairs with only the temporary huts of puffin hunters. An unwritten rule requires that only young or non-breeding puffins are to be taken. In the past, puffin down was used as a bedding material in the islands and the meat was a staple of the islanders' diet but it's now more of a delicacy. Occasionally, gannets are also eaten but a disease among fulmars has saved them from the stewpot in recent years.

Sea bird's eggs – mostly those of guillemots and fulmars which are larger than hens' eggs – are gathered from the thousands of nests on the cliffs. The collection of guillemot eggs requires rock-climbing and abseilling skills and, today, egg gathering is considered a 'macho' sport rather than a necessity.

Kelp, another unique item in the Vestmannaeyjar diet, is collected from the northern shore of the Stórhöfði peninsula on Heimaey. Rich in iron, the seaweed is a favourite of the islanders who turn out at low tide to fill their net bags with slimy goodies.

The mainstay of the economy, however, is fishing. Although Heimaey's population is less than 2% of the Icelandic total, Vestmannaeyjar fishing vessels supply 15% of the country's export total. Both net boats and trawlers – 100 vessels in all – catch halibut, cod, sole, haddock, ocean perch, lobster, herring, catfish, and pollock in the rough and rich waters around the islands. Most of the catch is processed at Heimaey but some is exported fresh to Europe.

Visitors normally intend to stay a day or so but invariably wish they'd allotted more time to the islands. When the weather is reasonable (the word is loosely defined here and 'reasonable' weather can include light rain, fog, or overcast skies), there's little chance of becoming bored for at least 4 or 5 days.

History

The first volcanoes began erupting in the area several hundred thousand years ago, but the new land didn't break the surface of the sea until perhaps 10,000 years ago. Heimaey was formed by the joining of several separate volcanoes. The north-western extreme of the island is one volcano, Norðurklettur. East of it are Heimaklettur, Miðklettur, and Ystiklettur, which formed a second island. A third volcano which erupted between 6000 and 5000 years ago formed Stórhöfði. All three islands were joined about 5000 years ago with the eruption of Helgafell.

According to the *Landnámabók* Heimaey was first settled by five Irish slaves belonging to Hjörleifur, blood-brother of Ingólfur Arnarson. After murdering their master near Vík, they fled to the rugged offshore islands, where they were certain no one would pursue them. They were wrong and, 2 weeks later, were tracked down and killed. The entire archipelago was named in their honour.

It is recorded that the first permanent settler was Herjólfur Barðursson who settled on Heimaey in Herjólfsdalur. Although life was difficult on the rocky and stormy island, it was more peaceful than on the feud-ridden mainland. A church was built in 1000 and the islands were placed under its jurisdiction. In 1413, however, an unscrupulous bishop gave the islands to the king of Norway in payment for outstanding debts.

Through the following centuries, Heimaey became a sitting duck for any raiding party that happened by. First came the British privateers who duly repaid the Norsemen for all their improprieties in the British Isles. Heimaey served as their North

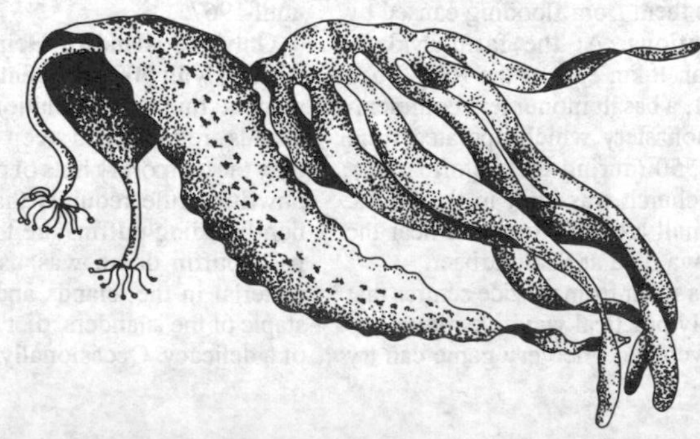

Atlantic headquarters for over 100 years. They built fortifications and ruled by force until they were kicked out by Danish traders in the mid-1500s.

In 1627, Heimaey was raided by Moroccan pirates led by a Dutch renegade, Jan Jantzen, who saw the undefended island as an easy target. Since there was little booty to carry off, they murdered citizens, raped women, and kidnapped 242 people hoping to ransom them to the Danish king. Many died, however. Some of the women were sold as concubines, and a number of the men joined the pirate brigades. The ransom, which was paid, returned only 13 people to Heimaey.

In the following years, disaster followed disaster. The islanders' unbalanced diet of fish, eggs, and sea birds invited scurvy and dysentery. Furthermore, Heimaey's fresh water supply dried up from time to time and, in 1783, a massive volcanic eruption on the mainland poisoned the seawater and killed all the fish around Vestmannaeyjar.

On 23 January 1973, yet another volcano appeared on Heimaey. At 2 am, the eastern slope of Helgafell exploded and over the course of the next 5 months, spewed out over 30 million tonnes of lava and tephra. When all was said and done, Heimaey had grown by 15%. When you see Eldfell now and realise how close it is to the village, you can imagine how vulnerable the island's residents must have felt when the eruption began. Overnight, Heimaey's 5000 inhabitants were evacuated to the mainland and, miraculously, only one person died from inhaling toxic gases.

During the 5 months of eruptions, a third of the town was buried under the lava flow. The most menacing problem, however, was the lava's intrusion into the harbour – the steadily advancing flow threatened to seal off its entrance and thereby destroy the island's economic viability. The hero of the day turned out to be physicist Þórbjörn Sigurgeirsson who suggested firefighters hose cold seawater onto the molten lava in order to slow its advance.

No one is sure whether the tactic worked or the lava flow, which stopped 175 metres short of closing off the harbour, just ran out of steam. Whatever the case, the harbour facilities were actually improved by the increased shelter gained from the flow.

HEIMAEY

(For the purpose of this account, the village of Heimaey and the island of the same name coincide.) Characterised by brightly coloured roofs, Heimaey spreads across about a third of the island. It enjoys a spectacular setting with the *klettur* escarpments rising abruptly behind the well-sheltered harbour basin on one side and the steaming red peak of Eldfell and green Helgafell on the other.

Information

The tourist information office is at Westmann Islands Travel, Kirkjuvegur 65. Heimaey has a swimming pool open weekdays from 7 am to 12 noon and 1.30 to 8.30 pm. There are also two banks, a bookshop at Heiðarvegur 9 selling English-language paperbacks, a golf course in Herjólfsdalur, and a photo shop at Bárustígur 9. You can find the state liquor store at Strandvegur 50.

Things to See & Do

Aquarium & Natural History Museum The Vestmannaeyjar Natural History Museum, founded in 1964, shouldn't be missed. The aquarium with its unique collection of bizarre Icelandic fish is especially good. Also worth seeing is the small but amazing collection of 'landscapes in stone' in the geology room. This is a collection of polished slices of agate and jasper containing magnificent natural landscape paintings. After you see these two items, the rest of the museum, which is probably the best in Iceland seems anti-climactic – just the usual mineral samples and stuffed birds and fish.

The admission price of US$2.50 is collected ostensibly to keep the fish in meals. The museum is open daily from 11 am to 5 pm from 1 May to 1 September. The rest of the year, it's open from 3 to 5 pm on weekends.

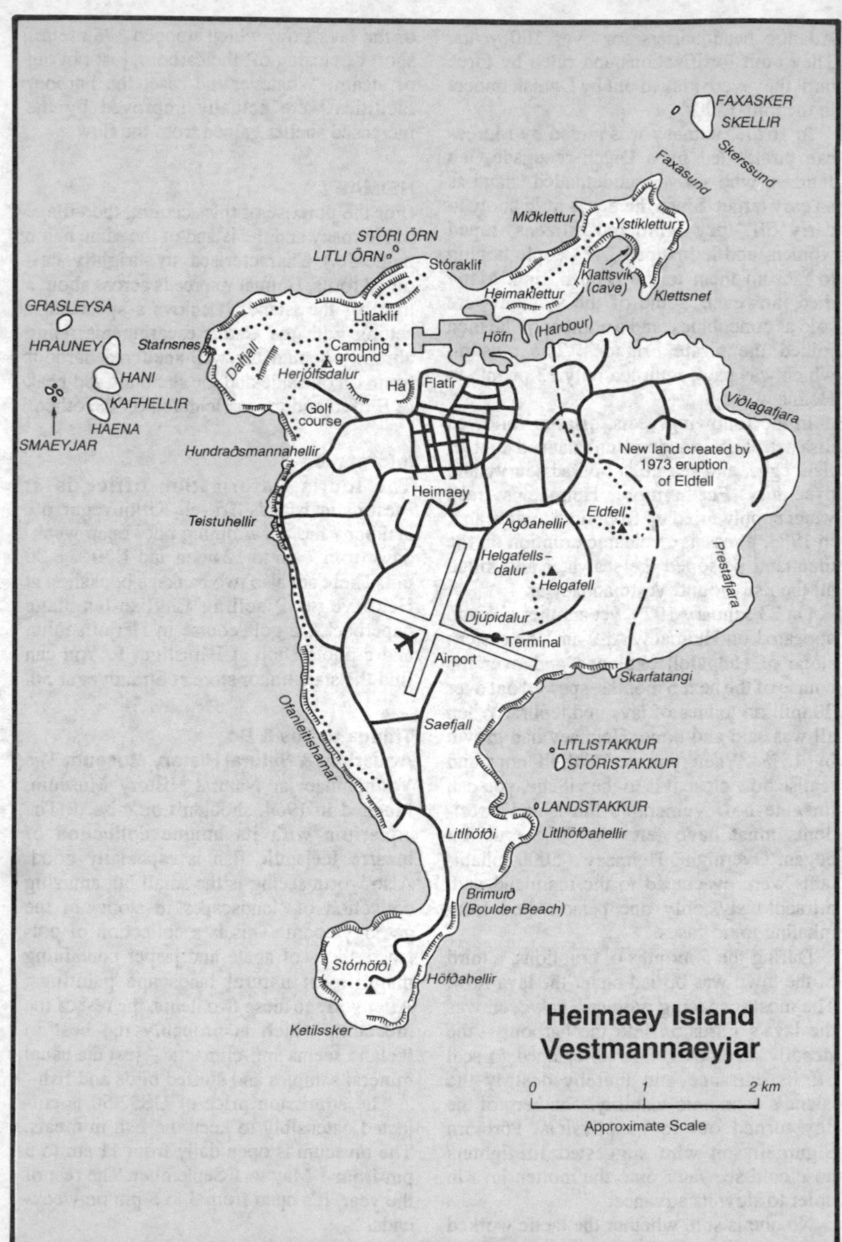
FAXASKER
SKELLIR
Skerssund
Faxasund
Miðklettur
Ystiklettur
STÓRI ÖRN
LITLI ÖRN
Stóraklif
Klattsvík
(cave)
Heimaklettur
Klettsnef
GRASLEYSA
Litlaklif
HRAUNEY
Stafnsnes
Camping ground
Höfn
(Harbour)
Dalfjall
Herjólfsdalur
HANI
Há
Flatír
Viðlagafjara
KAFHELLIR
Golf course
HAENA
SMAEYJAR
Hundraðsmannahellir
New land created by 1973 eruption of Eldfell
Heimaey
Teistuhellir
Agðahellir
Eldfell
Helgafells-dalur
Helgafell
Prestafjara
Djúpidalur
Terminal
Airport
Skarfatangi
Ofanleitishamar
Saefjall
LITLISTAKKUR
STÓRISTAKKUR
LANDSTAKKUR
Litlhöfði
Litlhöfðahellir
Brimurð
(Boulder Beach)
Stórhöfði
Höfðahellir
Ketilsskér
Heimaey Island
Vestmannaeyjar
0
1
2 km
Approximate Scale

Folk Museum The Folk Museum upstairs in the library is well worth a visit. They have a large collection of art with a Vestmannaeyjar theme including a magical painting of the docks on a rainy night. Also, there's a nice relief map of pre-1793 Heimaey for those who are wondering how it looked before Eldfell. Other interesting items include a nearly complete collection of Icelandic stamps, old nautical relics, folk implements and tools, and samples of Icelandic currency through the ages (note the inflation!).

It's open from 1 to 4 pm weekdays in the summer. Admission is free.

Volcano Show Not to be confused with the Volcano Show in Reykjavík, Heimaey's volcano show gives you something to do if it's raining or you've exhausted all other possibilities. One of the films, *Beyond the Limits*, is about the survival of a fisherman who swam over 5 km in icy seas and walked barefoot over the lava to safety after his boat sank and the rest of the crew drowned. The other film is about the salvage operations after the Eldfell eruption in 1973.

The double feature plays daily from 15 May to 15 September at 3 and 5 pm. In July, there's a third showing at 9 pm. Admission is US$4.30.

Eldfell & Helgafell Look at a pre-1973 map or photograph of Heimaey and you'll scarcely recognise it. The island just didn't look the same without 221-metre Eldfell and the surrounding 3-sq km lava field Kirkjubaejarhraun added to it.

The mountain is easily climbed by one of several routes (see the map). The easiest is through the northern entrance into the crater, up to the rim, and then east along the ridge. On the summit there are lots of steaming vents and brilliantly coloured mineral deposits. In places, the ground is still so hot you can melt the soles of your shoes!

The track down the west side of the crater ends at the foot of Helgafell (only 5 metres higher than Eldfell) which was formed in an eruption 5000 years ago. It's best climbed on the track up the south-west slope.

Herjólfsdalur The valley of Herjólfsdalur, the home of Vestmannaeyjar's first intentional settler, Herjólfur, is a green grassy amphitheatre surrounded by the steep slopes of the extinct Norðurklettur volcano. Excavations there have revealed remains of a 10th-century home assumed to have been his. The valley today is occupied by a golf course and the camping site.

From Herjólfsdalur, walk along the sheep tracks down the west coast which is rugged and indented with lava caves like Hundraðsmannahellir and Teistuhellir. The cliffs become increasingly higher as you move southward, then disappear at the bay at Stórhöfði where islanders collect kelp.

On your way to Herjólfsdalur from town, don't miss the large and obtrusive football monument beside the road. It seems to have no apparent purpose apart from providing a subject for photographers.

Stórhöfði This southernmost peninsula of Heimaey, tacked onto the main island by a low narrow isthmus, looks as if it were an afterthought. From June to August, its cliffs are some of the best places to see puffins. On the 122-metre summit is a lighthouse which offers a view across the island.

It's possible to scramble down to the boulder beach at Brimurð, on the east coast of the isthmus, and walk back towards Helgafell above the cliffs and roiling surf that normally pounds on that side of the island.

Puffin Release In August, after adult puffins have stopped feeding them, the juveniles driven by hunger leave their rocky nests in search of food. In Heimaey, thousands of the clumsy birds descend toward the lights of the town and land, sometimes tragically, on the pavement or within range of ferocious cats. On such evenings, the children of Heimaey hurry around with cardboard boxes gathering up such unfortunate birds. They take them home, pamper them overnight, and the next morning, carry them to the sea and fling them into the air. It's assumed that the young birds are able to overcome the trauma of the whole experience and fend for themselves thereafter.

Walks North of Heimaey The nearly vertical slopes of the kletturs can be negotiated with a bit of caution but it isn't possible to reach Ystiklettur without technical equipment. From the harbour a track of sorts allows you to scramble to the Stóraklif radio tower on ropes, cables, and ladders for the best view on the island. Look down the rugged and inaccessible cliffs of the north-east coast at beautiful sea stacks and thousands of nesting birds. On clear days, you can make out Surtsey to the south-west. Some maps show a route down the eastern slope of Stóraklif to the eiði but I wouldn't have attempted it without proper equipment.

From the radio tower, return to the large scree slope you climbed up and cross it. From there, it's possible with some caution to climb Dalfjall and even reach Stafnsnes but these aren't hikes for the dizzy or faint-hearted. Likewise the scramble from the eiði up to Heimaklettur and across to Miðklettur isn't for casual hikers. The slopes are very steep and you'll have to carefully pick your way along the ridges. What everyone seems to wonder is how the sheep got to the top of Heimaklettur.

Festivals

Þjódhátíð This 3-day 'people's feast' is held over a weekend in early August to commemorate the granting of Iceland's constitution on 1 July 1874. Foul weather prevented Vestmannaeyjar people joining the celebration on the mainland so they held their own festival at home a month later. It's been an annual tradition ever since.

Most of the festivities, including an immense bonfire, music, singing, dancing, and drinking take place in Herjólfsdalur. Icelanders and visitors come from all over to participate and Herjólfsdalur fills up with tents and barbecues and even locals move outdoors for the event.

Places to Stay

Most travellers either camp in Herjólfsdalur or stay at the *Vestmannaeyjar Youth Hostel* (tel 98-12915) at Faxastígur 38. The hostel fills up quickly when the ferry arrives so you'll either have to run from the boat or book in advance. It's open from 1 June to 15 September.

In the summer, the islands get a lot of tourists so it follows that there are quite a few hotels and guesthouses in town. If the youth hostel is full, sleeping-bag accommodation is available at the *Heimir Guesthouse* (tel 98-11515), at Heiðarvegur 1 (just look for the mural on the side). They also offer accommodation in private rooms for US$58 per night.

The most up-market hotel is the *Þórshamar* (tel 98-12900), at Vestmannabraut 28, which charges US$110 for a double room. The *Hotel Gestfjafinn* (tel 98-12577), at Herjólfsgata 4, costs US$78 a double. Next down the line is the *Skútinn* (tel-98-11420), at Strembugata 10, which charges US$53 per night. The Þórshamar also has a subsidiary guesthouse called

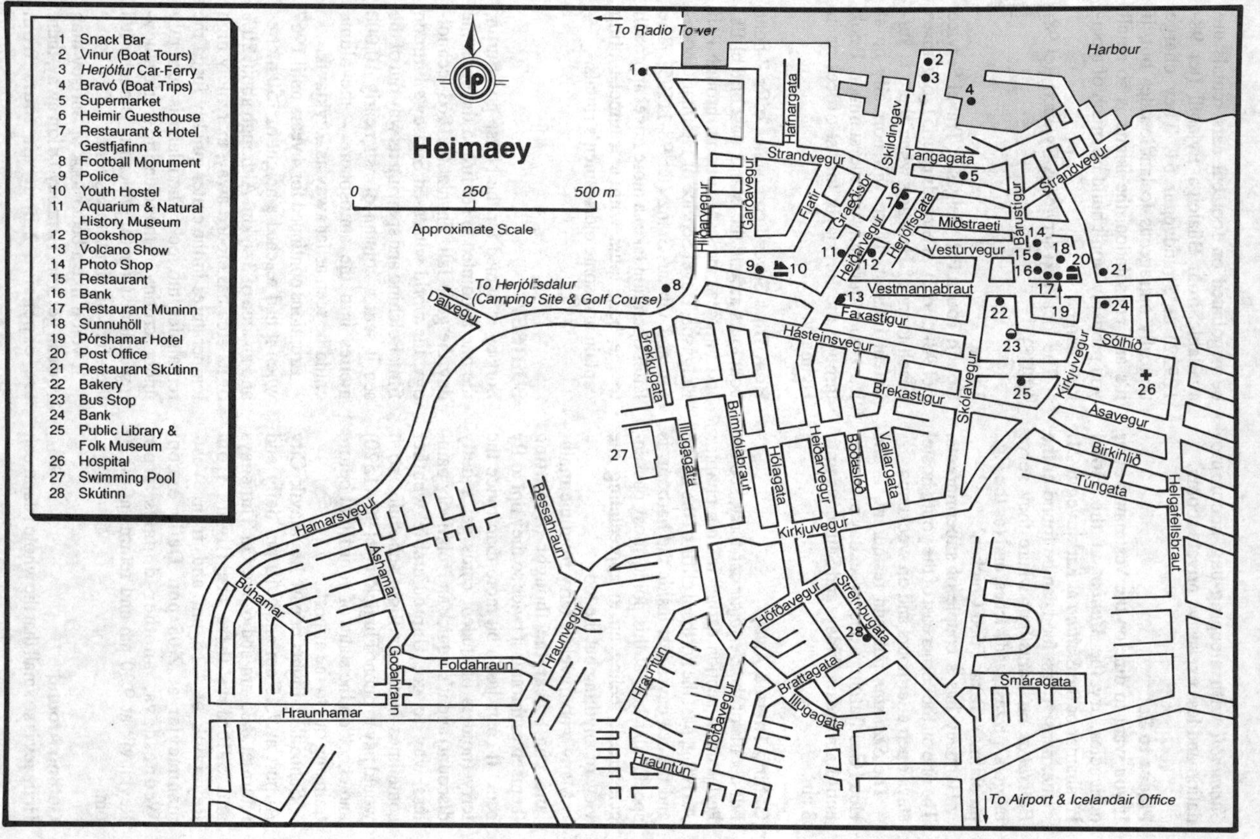

1 Snack Bar
2 Vinur (Boat Tours)
3 Herjólfur Car-Ferry
4 Bravó (Boat Trips)
5 Supermarket
6 Heimir Guesthouse
7 Restaurant & Hotel
Gestfjafinn
8 Football Monument
9 Police
10 Youth Hostel
11 Aquarium & Natural
History Museum
12 Bookshop
13 Volcano Show
14 Photo Shop
15 Restaurant
16 Bank
17 Restaurant Muninn
18 Sunnuhöll
19 Þórshamar Hotel
20 Post Office
21 Restaurant Skútinn
22 Bakery
23 Bus Stop
24 Bank
25 Public Library &
Folk Museum
26 Hospital
27 Swimming Pool
28 Skútinn
Heimaey
0
250
500 m
Approximate Scale
To Radio Tower
Harbour
To Herjólfsdalur
(Camping Site & Golf Course)
To Airport & Icelandair Office
Hafnargata
Skildingav
Strandvegur
Tangagata
Strandvegur
Garðavegur
Flatir
Græðisbr
Herjólfsgata
Heiðavegur
Miðstraeti
Bárustígur
Vesturvegur
Vestmannabraut
Faxastígur
Hásteinsvegur
Sólhlíð
Kirkjuvegur
Skólavegur
Brekastígur
Ásavegur
Birkihlíð
Túngata
Helgafellsbraut
Dalvegur
Brekkugata
Illugagata
Brimhólabraut
Hólagata
Heiðarvegur
Boðaslóð
Vallargata
Kirkjuvegur
Hamarsvegur
Ressahraun
Áshamar
Búhamar
Höfðavegur
Strembugata
Foldahraun
Hraunvegur
Goðahraun
Hraunhamar
Hrauntún
Höfðavegur
Brattagata
Illugagata
Hrauntún
Smáragata

Sunnuhöll with sleeping-bag accommodation and less expensive private rooms.

Places to Eat

If you want to dine on the Vestmannaeyjar delicacies, try the *Muninn* at the Hotel Þórshamar or the *Skútinn* at Kirkjuvegur 21.

Inexpensive fast food can be found at the *Bjössabar* on Bárustígur where they serve burgers, pizzas, sandwiches, and (as the sign proclaims) 'Texas Fried Chicken'.

Heimaey has a couple of supermarkets. The one on the corner east of the youth hostel stays open after hours and on weekends.

The *Skansinn* pub and restaurant, at the Hotel Gestfjafinn, is open weekday evenings until 1 am and on Fridays and Saturdays until 3 am.

Getting There & Away

For details of the *Herjólfur* car-ferry, see the Þorlákshöfn section earlier in this chapter. Arriving, past the northern cliffs of the island and the sea caves just inside the harbour, is spectacular but, at this point, most passengers aren't feeling up to appreciating the view of anything but the loo.

Many who travel by ferry from the mainland can't bear the thought of putting themselves through it twice so they opt to fly back. It costs just a bit more than twice the ferry (holders of student cards get a hefty discount) and it's a quick and relatively painless way to go. Unpredictable weather sometimes interrupts flight schedules so it would pay to phone Flugleiðir (tel 98-11520) and check on the status of your flight before traipsing out to the airport.

Scheduled flights depart Reykjavík City Airport at 7.45 am and 5.10 pm daily and return at 8.35 am and 6 pm. On Thursdays and Saturdays there are flights from Reykjavík at 1.15 pm and from Vestmannaeyjar at 2.05 pm. Daily except Wednesdays, another departs from Reykjavík at 9.30 pm and returns at 10.20 pm.

Getting Around

Heimaey is so small that the whole island can be negotiated on foot but cars rentals are available from Bílaleiga Eyjabíll (tel 98-12922) at Strandvegur 51. They charge typically outrageous Icelandic rates but, if it's any consolation, the island is so small you probably won't build up much of a per-km charge.

The local taxi service is Eyjataxi (tel 98-12038).

Tours

Coach Tours Páll Helgason Travel Service (tel 98-12922), at Strandvegur 51, organises coach tours of Heimaey when there is sufficient interest. There will normally be at least one tour daily in the summer. Book through the Reykjavík tourist offices or in Heimaey.

Boat Trips Several companies offer 2-hour boat tours around the island, past bird cliffs, and into sea caves. Also book through Páll Helgason Travel Service or Hjálmar Guðnason and Ólafur Gränz (tel 98-11195). The latter operation takes a more novel approach to the boat tours with a trumpet-tooting captain and some old seamen's rituals.

SURTSEY

Surtsey is named for the Norse god Surtur, the one appointed to set fire to the earth the day the gods fall. Thanks to 1963-technology, the world witnessed Surtsey's birth on film. Belching and spewing its way out of the sea it sent a column of ash nearly 10,000 metres into the atmosphere – the plume could be seen as far away as Reykjavík.

Eruptions continued for 4 years until 1967 when it had reached a height of 150 metres and an area of 3 sq km. Although about 30% of its area has eroded away, extremely high temperatures in the crater quickly fused the remainder into rock. The island is currently under scrutiny by the scientific world studying colonisation of volcanic islands. It's therefore off limits to visitors.

If you'd like a better look at Surtsey than you can get from Heimaey 18 km away, there are expensive 2-hour air tours from

Reykjavík. For further information, contact Leiguflug (tel 91-28011) at Reykjavík City Airport. Once upon a time, boat tours were available from Heimaey but, at the time of writing, they weren't running. It might pay to check with the tourist office in Heimaey if you're interested.

If you're fascinated by Surtsey, don't miss the film *Birth of an Island* at the Volcano Show in Reykjavík.

The Westfjords

Extending claw-like toward Greenland, the Westfjords peninsula, attached to the mainland by a narrow isthmus, is the most rugged and remote part of Iceland. If Iceland is shaped like a swimming duck, the Westfjords is the head.

Geologically, this is the oldest part of Iceland, a remnant of the basalt Thulean plateau heaved out of the sea 50 million years ago forming a land bridge between Europe and Greenland. When it sunk, it left only minor pieces of land above sea level. The island that formed Iceland's north-western extreme was subsequently flattened and carved by icecaps and glaciers into a convoluted coastline of 50 deep fjords and alternating steep headlands. The largest fjord, Ísafjarðardjúp, nearly splits the Westfjords into two unequal parts.

The central area, inasmuch as the Westfjords have one, consists of high rocky tundra plains, dotted with hundreds of ponds, which average 700 metres above sea level. Drangajökull, the 176-sq km icecap on the northernmost sub-peninsula, is the only remaining glacier in the region.

For the most part, the coastal gravel highways wind energetically around fjords and headlands. In places, you will have to travel along 100 km of road to make 10 km of headway, so it can take a long time to get anywhere by bus.

As in the rest of Iceland, most people work in fishing and related industries. Due to the inhospitable landscape and the slackening fishing industry, the regional population is low and emigration to the cities is reducing it further. The Westfjord's northernmost sub-peninsula, Hornstrandir, was abandoned in the 1950s and remains uninhabited. Icelanders have seized the opportunity to set it aside as a national monument and it isn't far from becoming a major destination for hikers and climbers.

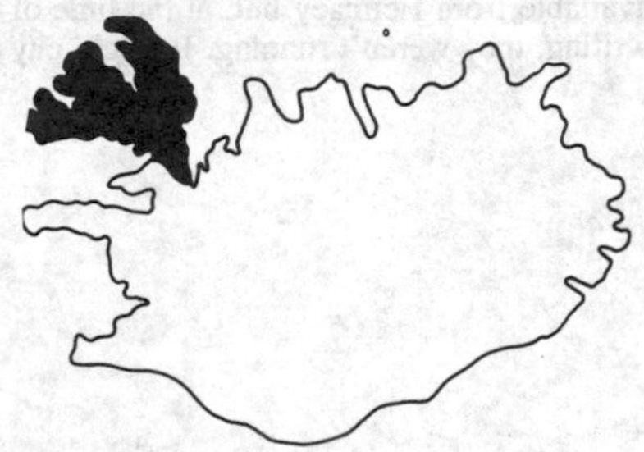

ÍSAFJÖRÐUR

Ísafjörður, the Westfjords' commercial centre, is the region's largest settlement with about 3500 people. Formerly called Eyri ('sandspit'), it appropriately sits on a prominent spit jutting into Skutulsfjörður, a small branch of Ísafjarðardjúp. It is surrounded on three sides by the calm waters of the harbour between steep and towering peaks.

Although Ísafjörður is gaining importance as a tourist destination, access entails either an expensive flight or a long and arduous bus ride over gravel mountain roads; it will probably be a long time before the town experiences a real tourist invasion.

History

The first inhabitants of the Ísafjörður (Skutulsfjörður) area were Norwegian and Icelandic traders who set up temporary summer trading camps on the sandspit, transacted their business, and moved on. In the 1500s, German and English firms established more permanent enterprises. There is mention of a Hanseatic League trading post on the spit as early as 1569. With the Danish Trade Monopoly of 1602, the Danish moved in, usurped the old buildings and constructed new ones. Those still in existence are preserved at the museum in Ísafjörður.

Information

Tourist Office The extremely friendly and helpful tourist office Ferðaskrifstofa Vestfjarða (tel 94-3557) at Aðalstraeti 11 is open from 9 am to noon and 1 to 5 pm weekdays in the summer. They'll help you with planning visits anywhere in the Westfjords and are also happy to help those on more restricted budgets.

The *Hotel Ísafjörður* also offers information and tour bookings but they are primarily concerned with the up-market end of the spectrum.

Books & Film The bookshop on the main street has the lowest book prices I found in Iceland. They have a large selection of titles and tourist publications, many in English and German, as well as maps, photocopies, and Kodak film and processing. Perhaps it's just a matter of inflated prices elsewhere not having caught up there yet, but it was a pleasant surprise to find this place and pick up a couple of cheap reads.

Fuji film and processing are available at the Leo Photographic Studio.

Laundry Laundry services are available at Efnalaugin Albert at Fjarðarstraeti 16.

They're open Monday to Friday from 7 am to 6 pm and normally need 24 hours to finish your washing.

Westfjords Maritime Museum

This museum (tel 94-4418) is one of the finest in Iceland as far as rustic presentation is concerned. It was originally suggested in 1939 by Barður G Tómasson who thought the town should undertake the building of a *sexaeringar*, a six-oared sailing ship used for early transport. The ship *Ölver* was commissioned in the 1930s and completed in 1941 by retired boat builder and ship's captain, Jóhann Bjarnason from nearby Bolungarvík. The rest of the museum grew up around it.

The museum was originally housed in the swimming hall but, in 1988, it was moved to some of the old trading houses at Neðstíkaupstaður at the end of the sandspit. It's full of maritime exhibits, wonderful old photographs, and nautical paraphernalia. The oldest building is the log Tjörnuhús which was originally constructed in 1736. Attached to it is Krambuð which was built in 1761 and used as a shop until early in this century when it was converted into a private residence. The Turnhús, originally used as a warehouse and fish-processing shed, dates back to 1765. The old building nearby is the Faktorshús, the shop manager's residence.

The museum is open Tuesday to Sunday from 1 to 5 pm and during other hours if previous arrangements are made. Admission is free.

Ice House

Just inside the door of the Ice House on Fjarðarstraeti is a group of paintings depicting the history of ice collection in Iceland. They deserve a quick look.

City Park

The city park, east of the summer hotel, has

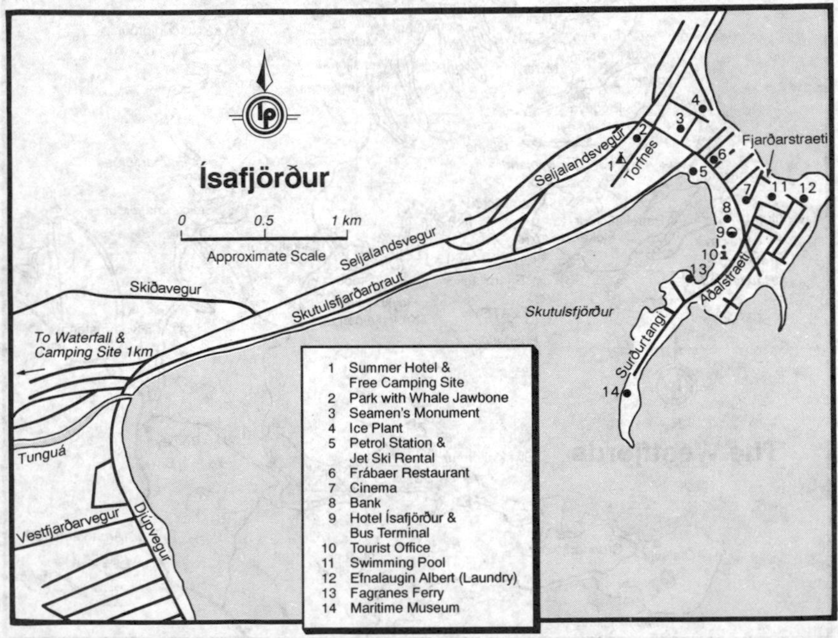

a colourful flower garden. Its centrepiece is a whale jawbone arch which looks a bit tacky but its size is impressive. Across the street is a large lawn where the Ísafjörður seamen's memorial stands.

Tungudalur

This valley begins about 2 km west of town. A further 30-minute walk from the bus stop brings you to the camping ground at Tunguskógar, a secluded retreat with waterfalls and birch trees. The entire walk from town will take an hour so only stay there if you're looking for solitude. There are no facilities except a toilet and washbasin.

Seljalandsdalur

In summer, this valley is a pleasant hill walk but in the winter it's a ski resort. There's a small ski lodge with illuminated slopes of varying difficulty and lots of more level terrain for cross-country skiing.

Hnífsdalur

The small village of Hnífsdalur, administered as part of the city, is 4 km north of Ísafjörður. It lies in a deep valley and in the winter, avalanches pose a serious threat. On 18 February 1910, an avalanche crashed down on the town killing 20 residents.

Places to Stay

The *Hotel Ísafjörður* (tel 94-4111) between the main street and the shore is a typically sterile Icelandic hotel. A double room costs US$110 including a buffet breakfast. They also operate a *Summer Hotel* (tel 94-4485) at the school west of town where a double without private bath costs US$80. Sleeping-bag accommodation costs US$17.25 in a small room or US$10.35 in the dormitory. Breakfast is included for those with private rooms but others pay US$7.

At the unnamed guesthouse (tel 94-4075) at Austurgata 7, a double room without bath costs US$38 and sleeping-bag accommodation is US$10.35.

Besides the previously mentioned free camping site in Tungudalur, the town camping ground, also free, is behind the summer hotel. The only drawback is that the toilet is inside the hotel. In the middle of the night, you have to go to the door, ring the bell, and wait for someone to open it up for you.

Places to Eat

The *Hotel Ísafjörður's* dining room is expensive but the food is good and the breakfast buffet, which costs US$7, is excellent if you're feeling like a splurge.

The snack bar *Hamraborg* is two doors west of the hotel. *Frábaer* in the solarium back toward the summer hotel (where you can fill up with food for less than US$10) serves burgers, chicken and chips, spaghetti, sandwiches, and other fast foods for reasonable prices. The *Seamen's Cafeteria* further out on the spit serves simple inexpensive meals.

Self-catering is also easy, the *Hamraborg Kiosk* is open after hours and on weekends for milk and other staples. The main supermarket is at Austurvegur 2 but several smaller ones are found around town. There are two bakeries in Ísafjörður, *Gamla Bakariið* on the main street and *Óðinn Bakari* on Hafnarstraeti. The state liquor store at Aðalstraeti 20 is open Monday to Friday from 10 am to 6 pm.

Entertainment

Cinema The cinema in Ísafjörður shows new films 5 nights a week at 9 pm. Most are in English with Icelandic subtitles.

Nightlife Although the nightlife in Ísafjörður hardly compares to that of Reykjavík, nearly everyone participates in what's available. In fact, on Friday or Saturday nights, it is difficult to find someone who hasn't been participating. *Gosi* at Mánagata 6 is a pool hall which oddly serves only weak soda beer. *Krúsin*, the local pub at Austurvegur 1 is open in the evenings from Thursday to Saturday and has a disco on Friday and Saturday nights.

Activities

Swimming On your way around town, stroll past the pool building and have a look at the ridiculous statues out the front. The pool is open during very odd and often-changing hours so, if you want to swim or sit in the jacuzzi, check the notice on the door. Aswim costs US$1.75.

Boat Rental Although the area around Ísafjörður would be ideal for sea kayaking, it hasn't yet caught on there. The locals have, however, recognised the popularity of jet-skis and the petrol station at the isthmus hires them for around US$20 per hour. They also rent a canoe and what must be the world's oddest pedal-boat. Wet or dry-suits are included in the rental price.

Getting There & Away

Air Flugleiðir has daily flights between Akureyri and Ísafjörður; the westbound flight departs Akureyri at noon daily and the eastbound flight departs Ísafjörður at 1.20 pm. Between Reykjavík and Ísafjörður, there are both morning and evening flights daily. Unfortunately, schedules often go awry due to weather conditions, so leave yourself a couple of days' leeway.

Bus Westfjords bus schedules are complicated because they are geared to coincide with bus tours where possible and ferry sailings between Brjánslaekur and Stykkishólmur. The following description, although confusing, should give you some idea of what's available.

There are two highway trips per week each way between Reykjavík and Ísafjörður. Sometimes the southbound bus takes the Ísafjarðardjúp route to Bjarkalundur rather than going down the west coast to Flókalundur. When it goes to Flókalundur, it sometimes connects with a bus to Brjánslaekur ferry terminal or to Breiðavík and Látrabjarg. When it goes to Bjarkalundur, it sometimes connects with the bus between Reykjavík and the Strandir coast to Norðurfjörður. BSÍ tours in the Westfjords use some combination of these buses.

If you're going to Akureyri from Ísafjörður, you'll have to either backtrack to Borgarnes or be very lucky to catch the Ísafjörður to Hólmavík bus, connect with a bus to Brú, and then another to Akureyri. In theory, this works in reverse, as well. If you're feeling lost at this point, go to the tourist office and ask when the next bus leaves for your destination!

Between Ísafjörður and Bolungarvík, two buses depart daily Monday to Friday from Ísafjörður at 2 and 6 pm and from Bolungarvík at 1 and 5 pm.

Getting Around

City bus services operate Monday to Friday from 7 am to 7 pm and connect the city centre with the summer hotel and the 'mouths' of Tungudalur and Seljalandsdalur. An airport bus meets incoming and departing flights.

Taxis (tel 94-3418) must be reserved in advance.

Mail Tour

If you'd like to see the Westfjords from the air, join the weekday mail tour which departs Ísafjörður airport, weather permitting, at 1 pm from Monday to Friday. It makes stops in several Westfjord communities before returning in the late afternoon. The trip costs US$67.25 per person. Book through the tourist office or Ernir Air (tel 94-4200). If there is sufficient demand, the same plane does an air tour of the Hornstrandir peninsula on weekends.

AROUND ÍSAFJÖRÐUR

Bolungarvík

Bolungarvík, the second largest city of the Westfjords with a population of 1500, is only 15 km from Ísafjörður. Its impressive setting in a valley beneath high peaks is bringing it into its own as a day-trip from Ísafjörður.

The *Landnámabók* records that Bolungarvík was originally settled by a woman named Þuríður Sundafyllir and her son Völusteinn. She earned her living by collecting a toll from fisherfolk who set out to sea from her farmstead.

Across the bay from Bolungarvík is Óshlíð and the precipitous but scenic route from Ísafjörður. Ösvör, back toward town, is a boat landing and the ruins of a fishing station believed to have been used around the time of Settlement. Restoration was begun in 1988 and there are plans to open the site as a museum.

Places to Stay & Eat The only accommodation in the area around Bolungarvík is *Meiribakki Guest House* (tel 94-7193), 12 km north-west of town, at Skálavík. They have one cottage and free fishing for guests. Sleeping-bag accommodation and cooking facilities are also available. The owner's residence is at Hlíðarstraeti 15 in Bolungarvík. If you're staying at Skálavík, they'll provide transport from town. The camping site at Bolungarvík is beside the sports complex.

Fish & chips, pita sandwiches, burgers, etc are available at *Finnabaer* on Kirkjuvegur. There's also a snack bar at the *Shell* petrol station.

Walks Around Bolungarvík The uninhabited coastal valley at **Skálavík** offers solitude and wilderness camping, 12 km from Bolungarvík along the jeep track from the north-west side of town. There's a guesthouse at Skálavík offering sleeping-bag accommodation (see Places to Stay & Eat).

The **Coast Walk**, a popular Sunday walk for locals, leads 8 km north-west along the Stigahlíð coast to a really great beach and picnic spot.

The **NATO Radar Base**, above town on 636-metre Stigahlíð, is a good day-hike which provides a broad vista of both the sea and the highlands.

Getting There & Around Buses depart Ísafjörður at 2 and 6 pm and Bolungarvík at 1 and 5 pm from Monday to Friday but hitching is easy. The driver of the airport bus lives in Bolungarvík and you can also ride out there with him if he's going home between airport runs.

Charter fishing and sightseeing boat trips to Jökulfirðir across Ísafjarðardjúp from Bolungarvík are offered by Vagn Hrólfsson. Contact (tel 94- 7183) for more information.

Suðureyri

Suðureyri is a small and isolated fishing community on 13-km-long Súgandafjörður. In the late 1800s, the settlement developed around the farm Suðureyri at the foot of Spillir. It became a licensed trading place in 1899 when it had only 11 inhabitants. The population today is around 400.

Things to See & Do At Staðardalur, 2 km south-west of the village around Mt Spillir, is a church dating back to 1886. At Botn, 8 km up the fjord from Suðureyri, researchers are conducting experiments with salmon farming. The area is in a nature reserve with scrubby birch woods, fossilised plants, and lignite deposits. The village has a swimming pool, sauna, and jacuzzi.

Places to Stay & Eat The *Esso* petrol station has both a snack bar and guest rooms (tel 94-6262). There's no formal camping site but you'll find plenty of good places to pitch a tent in Staðardalur where surface water is abundant.

Getting There & Away No public transport goes to Suðureyri and traffic is very sparse so hitching is difficult. You'll have to get off the Ísafjörður bus at the intersection of Routes 60 and 65. From there, it's 16 isolated km to the village.

Súðavík

The small fishing settlement of Súðavík, 22 km south-east of Ísafjörður by road, has a population of 260. At Langeyri, 2 km south along Álftafjörður is the remains of a Norwegian whaling station built in 1882 and operational until the early 1900s. There's an informal camping site near Seljaland at the head of the fjord. You can buy snacks at the Shell petrol station in the village. Once a week, the Reykjavík-bound bus takes the Ísafjarðardjúp road and passes through the village.

Flateyri

Flateyri, a fishing village with 400 residents, on Önundarfjörður, was licensed as a trading place in 1823 although trading had been going on there since the late 1700s. A Norwegian whaling station was begun at nearby Solbakki in 1889 but it burnt down in 1901. At Hóll, at the head of the fjord, is the chimney of another whaling enterprise (from the same period) that never quite got off the ground. There's a whale's pelvic bone in the town square and the village church has lovely stained glass.

The *Vagninn Restaurant* on Hafnarstraeti serves meals and snacks. The camping site is outside of the village.

The Ísafjörður to Brjánslaekur bus will stop at Flateyri if there are interested passengers. Between Reykjavík and Flateyri, Arnarflug has daily flights from Sunday to Friday departing Reykjavík at 1.30 pm and Flateyri at 2.30 pm.

Þingeyri

This scenic village of 500 inhabitants, the oldest trading station in the Westfjords, was once the site of a local parliament mentioned in the *Saga of Gísli Súrsson*. Ruins can still be seen at Valseyri, just south of town.

Þingeyri later became a service centre for Basque whalers and other European and American fisherfolk. It now depends economically upon fishing. Due to its dramatic peaks, the peninsula (on which Þingeyri stands) between Dýrafjörður and Arnarfjörður is sometimes known as the 'north-western alps'.

At the head of the 39-km-long fjord Dýrafjörður is a nature reserve with good camping sites but there's official accommodation in town. Þingeyri lies just 1 km from the intersection of Routes 60 and 622 along the bus route between Ísafjörður and Flókalundur.

Around Þingeyri

Sandafell The 367-metre-high high ridge rising behind Þingeyri is accessible by a 4WD track that turns off Route 60 south of town. The steep climb can also be done in a half-day return trip from the village. On top of the ridge is a view disc and a radio tower.

Haukadalur Further out Route 622 along Dýrafjörður from Þingeyri is the scenic Haukadalur area where the events of the *Saga of Gísli Súrsson* took place. Beyond the end of the road are precarious tracks leading to the Ófaera bird cliffs and the lighthouse at Svalvogar 22 km from Þingeyri. There is no public transport.

Hrafnseyri On Arnarfjörður across the pass from Þingeyri is Hrafnseyri, named after Hrafn Sveinsson, a local chieftain in the late 1100s and the first professional physician in Iceland. Statesman Jón Sigurðsson, the 'father of Icelandic Independence', was born there on 17 June 1811. Displays at the free museum at Hrafnseyri outline aspects of his life.

Gláma These otherworldly moors above the head of Dýrafjörður were formerly covered in ice. From the head of the fjord where you can camp, it's a long day of walking one way up to the 920-metre peak Sjónfrið from where the entire Westfjords peninsula is visible on a clear day. A longer, but easier, route takes off from the high pass between Hrafnseyri and Þingeyri. By either route, you'll need camping equipment suitable for chilly and unpredictable weather conditions.

Kaldbakur The highest peak in the Westfjords, 998-metre Kaldbakur in the rugged heart of the north-western alps, is most easily reached from the high pass between Hrafnseyri and Þingeyri. Be prepared for a long walk over rugged terrain, possible snowfall at any time, and typically foul weather conditions. Camping equipment and good footwear are essential for managing loose and unstable rock surfaces. Use the *Þingeyri 1:100,000* (1989) topo sheet for this trip.

Núpur On the northern shore of Dýrafjörður, 28 km by road from Þingeyri, is the Alfiðra Guest House (tel 94-8229) which offers sleeping-bag accommodation and cooking facilities as well as private rooms and meals.

The price structure is the same as for farmhouse accommodation.

At nearby Mýrar is the largest eider duck breeding grounds in Iceland and possibly in the world.

Dynjandi Sometimes known as Fjallfoss, this broad and unique waterfall drops in a veil-like 100-metre plunge. Below it, five more waterfalls carry the Dynjandi river into Arnarfjörður. The falls, which are all protected in a nature reserve, are only 1 km off the main road and can be seen from the bus. Buses running ahead of schedule sometimes stop at Dynjandi for a 10-minute break. If you want to explore the area more closely, there's an increasingly popular informal camping site there.

Nearby is the Mjólkarvirkjun ('milk river power plant') hydroelectric power station, named after the wild white water that drives it. Informal tours can be arranged upon request.

ÍSAFJARÐARDJÚP

The largest of the Westfjords, 75-km-long Ísafjarðardjúp ('ice fjord deep'), nearly bisects the Westfjords peninsula. When interest is sufficient, the Ísafjörður tourist office operates a weekly speedboat tour of the fjord.

Reykjanes

At the end of the brush-shaped peninsula between Reykjafjörður and Ísafjörður (don't confuse either of these fjords with others of the same name elsewhere in the Westfjords) is the friendly, but rather seedy Hotel Reykjanes (tel 94-4842). This summer hotel in the district school offers meals, a swimming pool and sleeping-bag accommodation. They also operate greenhouses heated by nearby geothermal sources. Between 1770 and 1790, salt was extracted from these hot springs.

Ögur

The manor at Ögur, built around 1850, was once the largest farmhouse in Iceland. The church has some ancient relics.

Vatnsfjörður

Early Saga-era chieftains lived at Vatnsfjörður, the site of a former church and farm. Later, it was converted into a residence inhabited alternately by church leaders and artists. Near the farm there are ruins of sod and stone fish-drying racks built in the 1800s.

Snaefjallaströnd

The stretch of coastline between Jökulfirðir and Kaldalón (the 'snowy mountain coast') was once inhabited as far as the cliffs of Bjarnarnúpur. Nowadays, the entire roadless section is abandoned. The green landscape slopes steeply upward toward the Drangajökull icecap, best reached up the valley at the head of Kaldalón.

Aeðey

Aeðey, or 'eider island', east of Ísafjörður contains one of the Iceland's largest colonies of eider ducks. If you wish to disembark there and camp or look around, get permission from the owner through the tourist office in Ísafjörður.

Vigur

The tiny but pretty island of Vigur at the mouth of Hestfjörður is rich in bird life and contains a single farm. It boasts Iceland's only windmill as well as farming paraphernalia leftover from earlier days. Visitors must have permission from the farmer to camp or walk around there so, before you book a ferry passage, make arrangements through the Ísafjörður tourist office.

Kaldalón & Armúli

The valley at the head of the inlet Kaldalón leads up to a receding tongue of the Drangajökull icecap. The toe of the glacier is level, but only approach it with extreme caution. The newly exposed moraine areas are also interesting to explore.

The closest accommodation is at the Armúli farmhouse (tel 94-4801) south of Kaldalón. They have private rooms, sleeping-bag accommodation, cooking facilities, petrol, and meals. Horse tours are available along the beach from Melgraseyri (tel 94-4856). Access by ferry is via Melgraseyri. You'll have to walk the last 3 km.

Getting There & Away

The *Fagranes* car-ferry cruises through Ísafjarðardjúp from Ísafjörður twice a week leaving at 8 am on Tuesdays and Fridays. The Friday trip takes 4 or 5 hours and stops at the islands of Vigur and Aeðey and the farm Baeir. If there are passengers for Ögur, it stops there also.

The Tuesday cruise takes between 8 and 12 hours depending on the number of stops. Obligatory stops include Vigur, Ögur, Aeðey, Baeir, Melgraseyri, Vatnsfjörður, and Reykjanes. It will also stop at Arngerðareyri and Suðavík (Eyri) if passengers wish.

Trips to Jökulfirðir begin on 30 June and continue through the summer departing at 2 pm on Fridays, stopping at Grunnavík and Hesteyri en route to Aðalvík on Hornstrandir.

Note that you can disembark anywhere along the ferry route but must advise where and when you plan to reboard so they know whether to pick you up. Camping is possible nearly anywhere along the route and Ísafjarðardjúp offers a myriad of hiking possibilities. If you stop in a remote site, however, you'll have to pay double the normal return fare. To any destination along Ísafjarðardjúp, you pay US$10.35 per person and US$26 for a car. To Jökulfirðir, it costs US$23.25 per person.

Further *Fagranes* ferry schedules will be discussed in the section on Hornstrandir.

HORNSTRANDIR

This rugged 580-sq km wilderness occupies the Westfjords' northernmost peninsula. In the 1950s, it was abandoned by its few remaining residents who found the isolation too trying. Remains of their farmsteads are scattered around the valleys and coastlines. In 1975, the government took advantage of the situation and created a national monument for recreation and the preservation of wildlife. There are also 10 emergency huts in various locations around the coastline.

The characteristic landscape includes rugged headlands, sheer sea cliffs, gently undulating uplands, and glacial valleys. Vegetation, for the most part, is limited to grasses and small shrubs. Now unthreatened by grazing sheep, more natural scrubby vegetation is returning. Arctic foxes roam the highlands, seals lounge along the shorelines, and whales are often observed offshore. Sea birds are of course abundant, predominantly along the cliffs of the northern coast.

Given its ominous location in the Greenland Sea just south of the Arctic Circle, travellers expect horrid weather conditions. However, most visitors go to Hornstrandir's north coast where the popular spots are relatively sheltered from the prevailing south-westerly weather systems.

Access to the area is by ferry or long walking routes from Norðurfjörður or Kaldalón, south-east of the reserve. Allow at least a week to walk to the ferry pick-up at Hornvík, north-west from Norðurfjörður. From Kaldalón, it will take 5 or 6 days. Both routes can often be done in less time but bad weather and tempting side trips can slow you down.

There is no accommodation available in Hornstrandir, although some factions are talking about a hotel at Hornvík in order to bring in organised groups. The way things are going, they may be successful in the near future so, if you want to visit Hornstrandir as a wilderness, you'd best hurry.

At the moment, visitors must be self-sufficient, that is carrying a tent, sleeping bag, stove, fuel, and food for the entire stay. Warm wind and waterproof clothing is essential here at the doorstep of the Arctic. Bringing extra food is also advisable should inclement weather delay the ferry pick-up.

Everyone visiting Hornstrandir must also carry a compass and the *Ramblers Map of Hornstrandir 1:100,000* published by Landmaelingar Íslands. The map in this book is designed to give an idea of routes and natural features to aid in planning trips, but it's not sufficient for navigating through the area.

At least 90% of Hornstrandir visitors go to Hornvík. The most popular walk is from

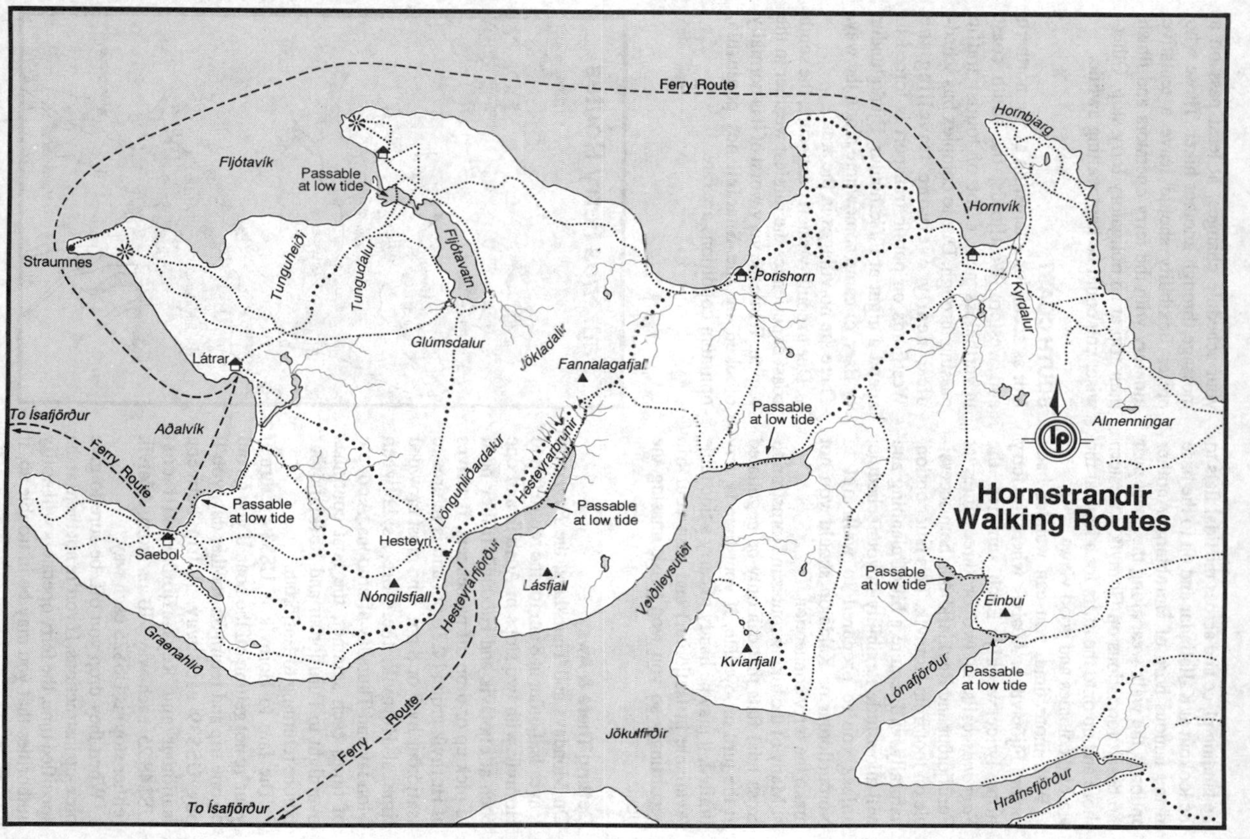
Hornstrandir Walking Routes
Ferry Route
Fljótavík
Passable at low tide
Straumnes
Tunguheiði
Tungudalur
Fljótavatn
Glúmsdalur
Jökladalir
Fannalagafjall
Þorishorn
Hornbjarg
Hornvík
Kyrdalur
Almenningar
Látrar
To Ísafjörður
Aðalvík
Ferry Route
Passable at low tide
Saebol
Lónguhlíðardalur
Hesteyrarbrúnir
Passable at low tide
Passable at low tide
Hesteyri
Nóngilsfjall
Hesteyrarfjörður
Lásfjall
Veiðileysufjör
Passable at low tide
Einbui
Kvíarfjall
Passable at low tide
Lónafjörður
Graenahlíð
Ferry Route
Jökulfirðir
Hrafnsfjörður
To Ísafjörður

the landing place and across the tidal flats to the lookout at Kálfatindar and on to the base of the famous horn of Hornbjarg. Another option is the walk west along the coast past the basalt formations on Hornvík's western shore and up onto the cliffs for a look at the sea bird colonies and good views.

With more time, you can wander back toward Fljótavík or Aðalvík where the ferry stops twice weekly. Each summer, the *Fagranes* calls in two or three times at Furufjörður and Reykjafjörður, both accessible on foot from Hornvík. This latter option, naturally, will require a bit of planning and will allow little flexibility in your schedule, unless you're prepared to walk out to Norðurfjörður or Kaldalón should you not make the ferry connection.

Many of the hiking routes in Hornstrandir cross tidal flats that can only be negotiated at the turn of low tide. If your time is very limited, it may be handy to carry a tide table (available in Ísafjörður) and plan your trip accordingly so you won't risk missing the boat.

Getting There & Away

On Mondays and Thursdays, the *Fagranes* leaves Ísafjörður at 8 am for the return trip to Hornvík with two stops in Aðalvík and one each at Fljótavík and Hlöðuvík if they need to pick up or drop off passengers. It arrives at Hornvík around 2.30 pm and is returns to Ísafjörður by 7 or 8 pm. The most crowded time at Hornvík, therefore, is between Monday and Thursday afternoons. A couple of times each summer, the boat continues overnight to Furufjörður and Reykjafjörður before returning to Ísafjörður.

The fare to Hornvík is US$39 return *if* your're not getting off the boat. If you go out on one trip and return on another day, you'll pay US$39 each way. A trip between Ísafjörður and Reykjafjörður will cost US$48.25 each way. To or from Aðalvík (either stop) is US$25 each way.

When they drop you off, be sure to give pick-up instructions. If you're not there at the specified time, the ferry operators will notify authorities that you may be in trouble so, if your schedule changes, at least pass on a message through another hiker. Those who prefer flexibility should leave a tentative itinerary with the ferry operators and finish their trip at an obligatory ferry stop. Otherwise, you could be kept waiting awhile.

SOUTH COAST

Not as scenic or interesting as the northern and western Westfjords, the south coast nevertheless gets a lot of tourist traffic passing through. Due to complex bus schedules, nearly everyone travelling the Westfjords on public transport is forced to spend a night at Flókalundur, Bjarkalundur or Baer, or camp somewhere along the way. There are no villages in the area.

Due to south-westerly exposure, the south coast experiences the rainiest weather in the region. While the very worst of it is normally blocked by the Snaefellsnes peninsula, optimum conditions are rare.

The fjords of the southern coast are typically shorter and shallower than their northern counterparts so the road along the coast doesn't do quite as much meandering as those around Ísafjörður. The landscape is also gentler and more hospitable, making for easier hiking; the area is also nearer to Reykjavík time-wise.

Reykhólar

The farming settlement of Reykhólar ('smoke hills') is on a small peninsula encircled by hot springs. Historically, it was one of the richest farms in the Westfjords. A factory that processes seaweed Þörungaverksmiðja operates by the shore. Individuals can gather mussels and seaweed from the shore at low tide. Reykhólar has a geothermally heated swimming pool and a shop.

At Staður, in the south-west corner of the peninsula, there's farmhouse accommodation (tel 93-47730) with cooking facilities but no dormitory option. Camp beside the shore or inland on the peninsula, but ask permission before camping on a farm. The bus stop is at Bjarkalundur and from there it's 13 km south to Reykhólar and 23 km to Staður. If you're booked in at Staður, phone from Bjarkalundur and they'll come to fetch you.

Bjarkalundur

Bjarkalundur has a camping site, a service station and the Hotel Bjarkalundur (tel 93-47762) which charges US$58 for doubles and US$12 for sleeping-bag accommodation. Camping outdoors is free. The oddly shaped and easily climbed twin peaks of Vaðalfjöll rise about 6 km to the north. Look for deposits of quartz, jasper, and zeolites which are common in the area.

At the head of nearby Djúpafjörður west of Bjarkalundur is the Djúpadalur geothermal area with hot springs and steaming vents.

Baer

The farmhouse accommodation at Baer (tel 93-47757), 10 km south-east of Bjarkalundur, is an option if the other guesthouse is full (it's often booked up by tour groups). It offers sleeping-bag space and individual rooms in a rural setting overlooking Breiðafjörður. There are nice walks in the hills across the road and down along the shore. The shop sells only pre-packaged snacks so either bring along your own food or resign yourself to paying dearly for their home cooking.

Flókalundur

The Edda Hotel (tel 94-2011) on the abandoned farm Hella is conveniently at the junction of the Patreksfjörður and Ísafjörður roads. Diagonally across the highway is a natural bathing pool and hot springs. The hotel is nice enough but prices are a bit steep at US$83 for a double; it has no sleeping-bag accommodation. The dining room is nothing special. The closest camping site is at nearby Brjánslaekur.

Flókalundur boasts a monument to its namesake, Hrafna-Flóki Vilgerðarson, who was apparently not impressed to see icebergs floating in the fjord as he looked down from the mountain Lónfell. In that moment of disenchantment he called the country 'Iceland'.

If you're bored while the bus is stopped at Flókalundur, walk to the highway intersection and see the curious stone pillar in the small gorge just north of the bridge.

Inland from Flókalundur on the Ísafjörður road is a mysterious anthropomorphic monument of a person resembling a warrior from the New Guinea highlands. I first saw it in oppressive, foggy rain – the sight of a large Melanesian face staring through the mists of Iceland was rather disconcerting. I later learned that it was constructed by some bored highway workers with leftover materials on their hands!

Brjánslaekur

The small farming centre of Brjánslaekur is little more than a ferry terminal between Stykkishólmur, Flatey island, and the Westfjords. Near the settlement is Flókatóttir, supposedly the ruins of a hut built by Hrafna-Flóki Vilgerðarson during the 9th century. If so, they're the oldest Norse ruins discovered in Iceland to date.

Buses between Brjánslaekur and nearby Flókalundur connect with ferry arrivals and departures. There is a camping site at the Brjánslaekur farm where horse rentals are also available.

Vatnsfjörður Reserve

The area around Vatnsfjörður is a nature reserve and the lake Vatnsdalsvatn is a nesting area for harlequin ducks and loons (divers) – both the red-throated and great northern species. The cry of the loon is one of the most incredible sounds in nature and, if you won't be visiting Mývatn where they're relatively plentiful, it's worth setting up camp for a couple of days and listening.

In the gorge Surturbrandsgil above the ruins at Brjánslaekur you can find fossilised plant leaves of species, which are now found in Florida and the Mediterranean area, in lignite deposits. To enter the gorge, you must get a permit from the reserve office in Brjánslaekur.

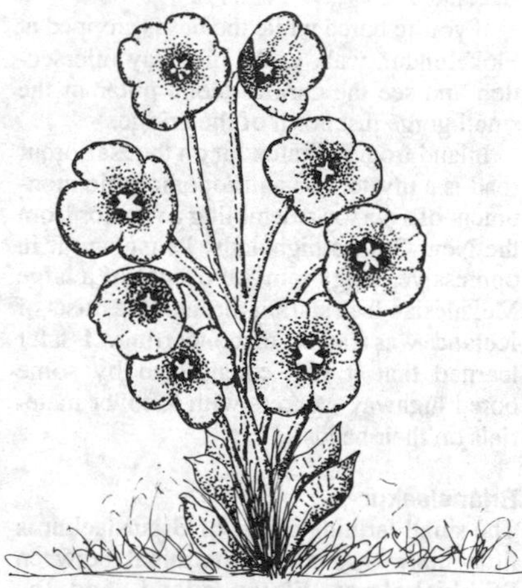

Papaver Relictum - the most common flower in the Westfjords

STRANDIR COAST

The east-facing Strandir coast of the Westfjords is divided by the 30-km-long Steingrímsfjörður. South of there, the land is characterised by low rolling hills and shallow grassy valleys. Northward, the coast grows steeper and more rugged, indented by deep fjords with a backdrop of snowy mountains.

The road and the bus lines only extend as far as Norðurfjörður, north of which all exploration must be done on foot. On the coastline north of Hólmavík, there are no tourist attractions to speak of and few amenities. It's one of the least visited parts of Iceland and therein lies its appeal.

Holmavík

The only settlement of any size in Strandir, the fishing village of Hólmavík with about 450 inhabitants, lies on the southern shore of Steingrímsfjörður. It began as a trading village in 1895. The population increased rapidly, then began to decline, a trend which continues to the present day.

Along the coast are lots of fossils in lignite. The church at Staður, about 17 km north from Hólmavík, contains a pulpit dating back to 1731.

Places to Stay & Eat Accommodation is available at the *Hólmavík Guesthouse* (tel 95-13185) at Höfðagata 1 where rooms cost US$53 per night. The official camping site is beside the supermarket and snack bar. Meals are available at the guesthouse.

Getting There & Away During the summer, there's bus transport between Hólmavík and Brú on the Ring Road five times a week. Between Ísafjörður and Hólmavík, there is one bus a week on Saturdays. It departs Ísafjörður at 8 am and Hólmavík at 1 pm.

Arnarflug flies between Reykjavík, Hólmavík, and nearby Gjögur on Mondays and Thursdays.

Drangsnes

Drangsnes, at the southern end of the Drangsnes peninsula, guards the north shore of the entrance to Steingrímsfjörður. There's really nothing to attract visitors but an overwhelming sense of remoteness. No formal camping site is available but there's a small cooperative supermarket in the village. Southbound, the bus passes at 1 pm Sundays and 8 am Wednesdays. Northbound, it stops at 5.30 pm Fridays if there are passengers to drop off or pick up.

Laugarhóll Laugarhóll (tel 95-3380) is a geothermal resort on Bjarnarfjörður, 19 km north from Drangsnes. There's a hotel with a dining room and sleeping-bag accommodation, a camping site, and a naturally heated pool. The southbound bus passes it at 12.30 pm Sundays and 7.30 am Wednesdays. The northbound bus departs at 6 pm Fridays.

Norðurfjörður

The only reason to visit Norðurfjörður is to use it as a departure or termination point for a backpacking trip to or from Hornstrandir. Although there's no specified camping site, the shop in the village will allow campers to use their facilities. More formal accommodation is available. At nearby Krossnes is a geothermally heated pool. There is one bus a week between Norðurfjörður and Brú to the south. It leaves Brú at 2.10 pm Fridays arriving in Norðurfjörður at 8 pm and returns at 10 am on Sundays.

Djúpavík

The former herring-processing village of Djúpavík, which operated in the 1930s, is now nearly abandoned. The Hotel Djúpavík (tel 95-3037) offers summer accommodation and a restaurant at the school. Sleeping-bag space is available at nearby Finnbogastaðir (tel 95-3031).

SOUTH-WEST PENINSULA

The triton-shaped peninsula between Arnarfjörður and Breiðafjörður is a rugged, sparsely populated but wonderfully scenic region. Poor weather is the norm, but fine days are not as infrequent here as they are across Breiðafjörður. Thanks to the youth hostel at Breiðavík, a growing number of travellers are visiting this westernmost bit of Europe – a highlight of many trips. The beaches are among the nicest and cleanest in Iceland, the cliffs are dramatic, bird life and marine mammals are abundant, and hiking opportunities are rife. It's also the best place to observe the rare white-tailed sea eagle and the Icelandic gyrfalcon. If you'd find it easy to entertain yourself when faced with such things, you could spend a week out here absorbing it all.

Bíldudalur

Bíldudalur, a major supplier of shrimp and the home port of Iceland's first steam-powered fishing boat, has been a trading and fishing centre since the late 1500s.

Further north-west along the road to Arnarfjörður is the historical site of Selárdalur, the home of the 17th-century fanatical pastor Páll Björnsson. Although he was well-educated, spoke many languages and was an accomplished mathematician, throughout his life he was convinced that the district was plagued by witches. When his wife complained that she was a victim of witchcraft, the good reverend had two neighbours burnt at the stake for alleged indiscretions.

Places to Stay & Eat The *Vegamót Guesthouse* (tel 94-2232) has rooms and sleeping-bag accommodation as well as a restaurant and snack bar. There is also a supermarket in the village. Although it has no official camping site, you're welcome to set up a tent anywhere outside of town. There's a popular spot 15 km from the village by the swimming pool in Reykjafjörður.

Graenahlíð (tel 94-2249), 13 km north-west along the fjord from Bíldudalur, offers farmhouse and sleeping-bag accommodation with cooking facilities.

Getting There & Away The Saturday evening tour bus returning from Látrabjarg to Ísafjörður passes through Bíldudalur. Arnarflug has daily flights between Reykjavík and Bíldudalur.

Tálknafjörður

Sometimes called Sveinseyri, the village of Tálknafjörður (with a population of 370) has a swimming pool, a small guesthouse, the Valhöll (tel 94-2599) by the shore, and a snack bar and coffee shop in the Esso petrol station. Five km beyond the village is a small geothermal area. No public transport serves Tálknafjörður but there's little reason to go there, anyway.

Patreksfjörður

Patreksfjörður, with a population of 1000, stands on two low sandspits, Geirseyri and Vatneyri, which form its superb harbour. The fjord and subsequently the town is named after St Patrick of Ireland, godfather of the region's first settler. It has long been a trading place but has become a population centre only during this century. In 1983, a mudslide buried part of the town.

The village swimming pool is on Eyrargata and the cinema at Aðalstraeti 27. Snacks are available at Eyrargrill on Eyrargata which is open after hours and on weekends. Both meals and accommodation can be found at the Erlu Guesthouse (tel 94-1227). Public transport to Patreksfjörður is the same as to Bíldudalur.

Around Patreksfjörður

Above town on the road from Kleifaheiði, you'll see an odd monument similar to the one above Flókalundur. This one reputedly represents the foreman of the crew that built the road. Like the work at Flókalundur, it's the result of bored road workers with leftover time and materials.

On the beach along the southern shore of the fjord near Hnjótur is the oldest steam-powered fishing boat in Iceland. It arrived in this spot by accident and remained. The owner, who prefers to use it as a summer home rather than scrap metal, keeps it in good condition.

A museum at Hnjótur, identified by the Norwegian Viking ship parked outside, is worthwhile visiting. Other displays include examples and drawings of early implements including details of how they were used. If the museum's closed when you arrive, ask a local to find the person with the key. They're always pleased when visitors are interested in this remote place. Admission is US$1.75 but the curators are quick to point out that all visitors receive a free postcard which offsets the expenditure.

Rauðisandur (the 'red sands') is a pink beach with pounding surf, south-west across the mountain from upper Patreksfjörður. Access is difficult without a private vehicle and will probably entail walking the 15 km from the junction of routes 612 and 614. There are a couple of farms and lots of nice places to set up camp. If you have a fine day, this place will prove idyllic.

Breiðavík

Breiðavík, which was once a reform school, has now been converted into a fox farm and tourism complex, but they've definitely gone over the top with the goldenrod paint! If you can ignore that and all the stuffed wildlife in the lounge, the setting could hardly be better. There's a restaurant, guest-house and youth hostel surrounded by a landscape of white sand, crashing surf, green grass, and dusky hills.

If you have a strong stomach, take a look around the fox farm and watch future fur coats dining on fresh seal – it's enough to put you off buying furs should the thought ever have crossed your mind.

The Youth Hostel (tel 94-575) costs US$11 per night for IYHF members and US$13 for non-members. Meals are expensive so budget travellers had best bring their own supplies. In addition to the Saturday tour bus, there are three weekly buses between Brjánslaekur and Breiðavík.

Hvallátur

Between Breiðavík and Látrabjarg is the tiny farming settlement of Hvallátur which prides itself on being the westernmost inhabited place in Europe. Its golden-sand beach is wonderful if you happen to have a sunny day and it's sometimes used as an airport. Around the settlement are some old stone and sod ruins.

Kóngshaeð

The uplands north-east of Breiðavík are called Kóngshaeð ('the king's head') after the shepherd known as the 'mountain king'. Don't look for Grieg's dancing cave-dwelling trolls, however. The name referred to the person overseeing the sheep roundup in the early days. This hill was the best vantage point for finding all the stray ones.

Látrabjarg

The cliffs of Látrabjarg wrap around the western end of the Westfjords. They are home to one of the greatest concentrations of bird life in Iceland, are 12 km long and range from 40 metres to 511 metres high.

Historically, local people lowered themselves over the edge on ropes to retrieve sea birds' eggs right from nests. When the British trawler *Dhoon* foundered off Látrabjarg in 1947, 12 crew members were rescued by the residents of nearby Hvallátur who employed their expertise to haul them up the cliffs. So casual was the procedure that midway up, they fed the sailors warm soup to alleviate some of the chill before taking them to the top.

The following year a film crew, hoping to film a documentary on the rescue, set up a re-enactment of the scene. En route to Látrabjarg, however, they discovered a trawler that had run onto the rocks and several of the crew had already perished. The villagers were obliged to repeat the previous year's rescue, it was captured on film, and there was no need for a re-enactment!

Even with the frequently foul weather it's difficult not to be impressed by this place. In the hour allotted by the tour, you'll only have time to reach about the 80-metre level before scrambling back to the bus. To see the really high cliffs, you'll have to walk the 10 km to the southern shore which will require an early start or camping overnight.

The puffins are normally the main attraction for visitors. Like tiny little men in tuxedos, they pose for photographs apparently unalarmed by the cameras that edge toward Europe's westernmost drop off to capture them on film. Tourists can approach within a metre without so much as a flinch from the trusting little creatures. Even those who aren't into harassing them with a camera will enjoy watching them.

Other birds which flock around the cliffs in screeching clouds include guillemots, cormorants, gulls, and kittiwakes. You'll normally see seals on the rocks north of the

lighthouse barking, lazing, and flopping playfully in the waves. Whales are often observed further out.

Getting There & Away

From Breiðavík, it's 12 km each way to the lighthouse. Hitching isn't impossible but it's best not to count on it. The optimum situation for walkers would be to carry a tent and spend a night somewhere above the cliffs. Be sure to carry all the liquids you'll be needing, however, because surface water is usually unavailable.

It is also possible to catch a ride out with the tour; it passes Breiðavík at around 3 pm on Saturdays but check at the hostel to be sure of the schedule.

Tour

From other parts of the Westfjords, hitching is possible but unpredictable. For those in a hurry, the 2-day BSÍ tour from Ísafjörður is the only reliable option. It is, however, a long and trying affair, especially when you consider it leaves you with only an hour on the cliffs.

The tour departs Ísafjörður on Fridays at 8 am and drops you at either Bjarkalundur or Baer where you have a choice of a hotel room, sleeping-bag accommodation, or the camping site. The following day, it continues to Látrabjarg, stays for an hour, and then begins the long and winding road back to Ísafjörður.

The normal price is US$80 excluding meals and the night's accommodation. Omnibuspass holders need only pay for their meals, accommodation, and US$25 because so much of the tour is along routes covered by their pass.

North Central Iceland

North central Iceland consists of three rugged peninsulas jutting into the Arctic Ocean separated by short bights and braided river deltas and punctuated by less than dramatic fjords. Although the landscape has its moments, most of the scenery along the principal highways is ordinary; to reach anything really spectacular will, with few exceptions, require striking out on foot or horseback. What's more, nearly everything of historical interest is away from the Ring Road and therefore off the bus routes. Only a few sights are accessible on guided tours.

Most travellers between Reykjavík and Akureyri consider the region a place to be passed by quickly. If you're short on time, you may want to employ the same reasoning but, if you're not in a hurry, there is quite a lot to see and, without a vehicle, you'll need time to see it.

Female Ptarmigan

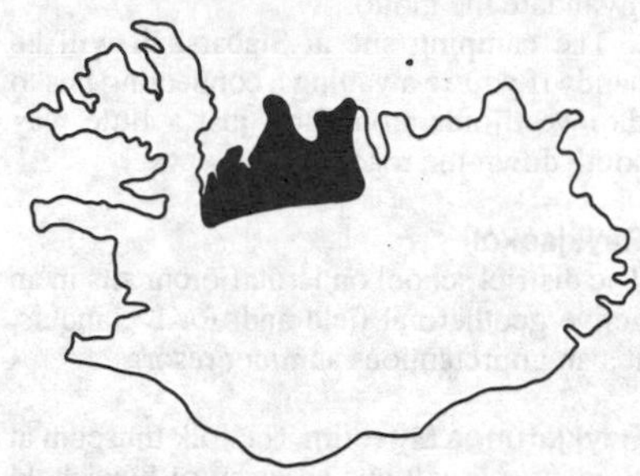

HRÚTAFJÖRÐUR

Hrútafjörður is a long but narrow fjord extending southward from Húnaflói ('bears' bay'). Surrounded by low treeless hills, the landscape is notably unspectacular but birdwatchers will appreciate the opportunity to look for wild swans, ptarmigan, loons, and golden plovers which all live here.

Brú

This tiny junction at the southern end of Hrútafjörður serves mainly as a connection point between north central Iceland and the Westfjords but buses to Hólmavík are infrequent and hitching is slow. If you have to wait overnight for a connection, there's a camping site up the road at Staðarskáli and a youth hostel at Reykjaskóli.

Brú means 'bridge' and that fairly sums up the extent of the place. Well, there is a petrol station and a post & telephone office which was moved from nearby Borðeyri in 1950, but no one actually lives at Brú.

Staðarskáli

The motto of this snack bar-cum-restaurant, guesthouse, petrol station etc is 'Everyone stops at Staðarskáli'. This isn't far off the mark. It's a pretty good replica of a Texas truckstop or an outback roadhouse, so Americans and Aussies might feel at home. The place is pretty tacky; they even give away free postcards of the petrol pumps out front! Not to be left out, all the buses between

Reykjavík and Akureyri stop here so most travellers won't have the opportunity to invalidate the motto.

The camping site at Staðarskáli will be handy if you're awaiting a connecting bus to the Westfjords from Brú, just a little way south down the road.

Reykjaskóli
The district school on Hrútafjörður sits in an active geothermal field and, for Icelanders, it's an unpretentious summer resort.

Reykjatunga Museum The folk museum at Reykjaskóli exhibits an array of household and agricultural implements from early Iceland. Featured are the reconstructed interior of a traditional 19th-century homestead and the old shark-fishing boat *Ófeigur*.

Places to Stay
A stop at the *Saeberg Youth Hostel* will break up the trip between Reykjavík and Akureyri but it's a bit far from anything so it wouldn't make a good base for touring around. If you don't want to walk to Staðarskáli for supplies or spend big bucks at the hotel restaurant, bring your own groceries from elsewhere.

The *Edda Hotel* (tel 95-10004) at Reykjaskóli has a geothermally heated pool and a licensed restaurant. Singles/doubles cost US$45/58 per night. Sleeping-bag accommodation is about US$13 per person but there are no cooking facilities so the youth hostel may be better value.

HVAMMSTANGI
Hvammstangi, a small and non-descript village of 160 inhabitants on the eastern shore of Miðfjörður, has been a licensed trading centre only since 1895. Unfortunately the village lies 6 km off the Ring Road so almost anything that could liven up the place just whizzes past. The economy is based on fishing, primarily for shrimp and molluscs.

Hindisvík, at the northern tip of Vatnsnes peninsula, is the home of the largest easily accessible seal colony in Iceland. If you'd like to visit it or take the Vatnsnes tour (see Getting There & Away in this section) you'll probably end up spending at least a night in Hvammstangi.

Places to Stay & Eat
The *Hotel Vertshúsið* (tel 95-12516) has singles/doubles for US$67/98 and sleeping-bag accommodation; guests receive a free pass to the village swimming pool. Eating establishments are limited to the hotel restaurant and bar.

Laugarbakki, at the junction of the Ring Road and the Hvammstangi road, has an *Edda Hotel* with a geothermal pool, a licensed restaurant and sleeping-bag accommodation. Private rooms cost US$58.

Farmhouse and sleeping-bag accommodation are available at *Melstaður* (tel 95-1955) 13 km south from Hvammstangi or at *Brekkulaekur* (tel 95-1938), 10 km south of Melstaður. Brekkulaekur organises 7 to 13-day horse tours around Arnarvatnsheiði and upper Borgarfjörður. Near Melstaður is Álfhóll, a small hill believed to be inhabited by leprechauns.

The camping site is at Kirkjuhvammur, just north-east of Hvammstangi.

Getting There & Away
There aren't any buses to Hvammstangi. Get off the bus at Hvammstangivegamót (the junction on the Ring Road) and walk or hitch the 6 km north into town.

Vatnsnes Tour
The Hotel Vertshúsið offers tours on Tuesdays between early July and early August. They first visit the village then continue north along the Vatnsnes peninsula to Skarð hot springs and the Hindisvík seal colonies along the way. On the way back, it stops at the outcrop Hvítserkur and the Kerfossar canyon before returning to Hvammstangi.

The tour departs from the Hotel Vertshúsið but will pick-up people at any of the farmhouse accommodation, Laugarbakki, Staðarskáli, or Reykjaskóli. The tour can be arranged by booking in advance. It costs US$19 per person.

BLÖNDUÓS

With a population of about 1100, Blönduós is a trading centre and a shrimp and shellfishing community at the mouth of the river Blandaá. Its lack of harbour facilities prevent it becoming populous but, since it is on the Ring Road, it sees some activity in the summer.

The first bridge across the river Blandaá was built at the village in 1963. The river starts in the Hofsjökull icecap, deep in the interior of Iceland, and residue scoured out along the way clouds up Húnafjörður several hundred metres out from the river mouth. The river offers excellent salmon fishing but the price of a 1-day licence is US$2054 or Ikr113,000 – it sounds even more unbelievable in króna! Don't forget your platinum fish hooks and gold-plated sinkers.

Information

Tourist Office The tourist information office and booking services are at the Hotel Blǫnduós on Aðalgata south of the river.

Hrutey

The islet of Hrutey just upstream from the river bridge is a nature preserve and the site of a reforestation project. A foot bridge crosses to Hrutey from the camping site.

Textile Museum

This small, but unique, display of local textile work and handicrafts (tel 95-4153) is open Tuesdays and Thursdays from 2 to 4 pm. If you're there at any other time and want to have a look, phone and arrange a special opening.

Church

Similar to Hallgrímskirkja in Reykjavík and the new church at Stykkishólmur, the Blönduós church is consistent with the geological theme dominating modern religious architecture in Iceland. This new structure was unashamedly designed in the shape of a volcanic crater. It's amusing, anyway.

Places to Stay

The *Hotel Blönduós* (tel 95-4126), at Aðalgata 6, has both private rooms for US$58 a double and sleeping-bag accommodation at youth hostel prices.

The free camping site, which has a very pleasant setting, is a short way upriver from the northern end of the Ring Road bridge. Three farms in Húnafjörður offer accommodation. Sleeping-bag space is available at *Víðigerði* (tel 95-1592), *Hnausar* (tel 95-4484), and *Stóra-Giljá* (tel 95-4294). The first two offer private rooms as well and Stóra-Giljá has a camping ground. Hnausar rents horses and has cooking facilities.

Places to Eat

Apart from the relatively plush dining room at the hotel, there are two petrol stations with coffee shops and snack bars. At the *Esso* station you can get chips, burgers, sausages, and chicken. The *Krútt Kökahús*, at Aðalgata 8 near the hotel, serves bakery goods, snacks, and coffee between 8 am and 6 pm.

The supermarket is opposite the camping site.

Activities

Horse Rental Horse rentals are available between 1 July and 15 August at the Hestaleiga Blönduós (tel 95-4126).

Swimming The pool, by the Ring Road north of the river, is open Tuesday to Friday from 10 am to noon and 2 to 9 pm and on Saturdays and Sundays between 1 and 4 pm.

Getting There & Away

Air Arnarflug flies between Reykjavík and Blönduós on Tuesdays, Fridays, and Sundays. The airline agent is at the Esso station (tel 95-4598). There's also an airline office (tel 95-4289) at the airport.

Bus All the buses between Reykjavík and Akureyri stop at the Esso petrol station in Blönduós. In summer, a bus departs Reykjavík daily at 8 am and Akureyri at 9.30 am. From early June to mid-August, there's a second bus on Sundays, Tuesdays, Thursdays, and Fridays leaving either end at 5 pm.

Northbound buses pass Blönduós at 1.30 pm and southbound buses stop at 12.10 pm.

Tour

The Hotel Blönduós does a 4-hour US$19 tour on Wednesdays at 1.30 pm from the end of June to the first week in August. It includes a quick tour of the village then heads north to Skagaströnd and beyond to the 50-metre-high basalt bird cliffs of Króksbjarg. Next it continues to Hafnir, a seal breeding area at the northern end of Skagaströnd, and to Ketubjörg and the rock pillar Kerling before returning to Blönduós. The tour provides the only public transport to the Skagaströnd peninsula.

HÚNAFJÖRÐUR

The upper Húnafjörður area has a surprisingly diverse array of interesting natural features and historical sites, but few are along the Ring Road bus routes so they're difficult to reach without a vehicle.

Vatnsdalshólar

Another of the great 'innumerables' in

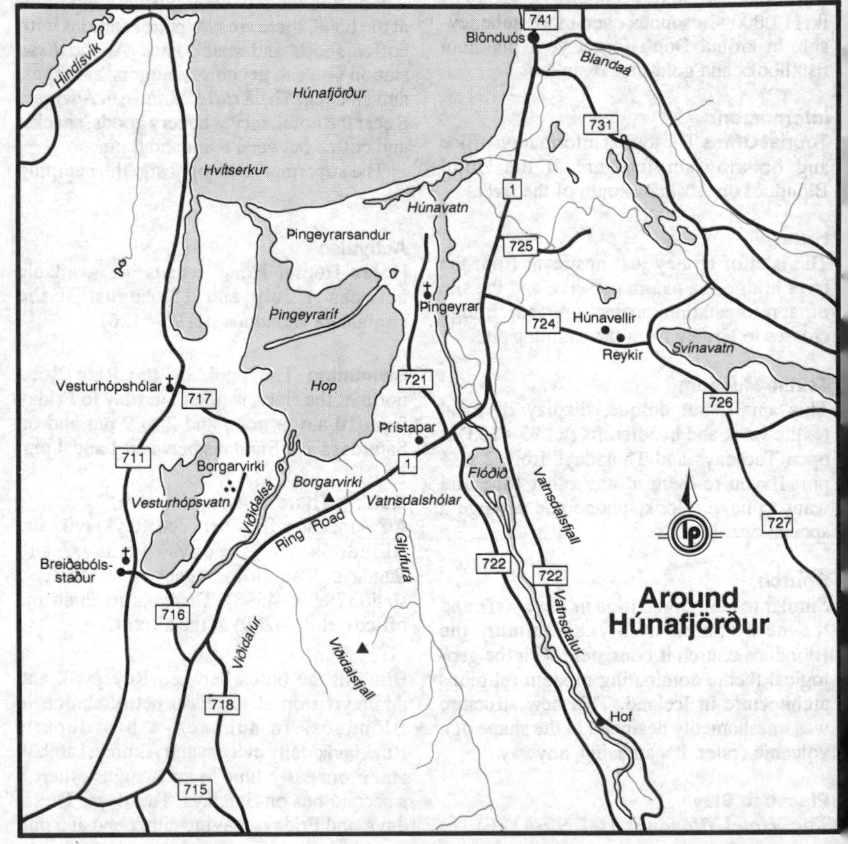

Iceland, the grassy hills of Vatnsdalshólar covering about 4 sq km were formed by the collapse of part of Vatnsdalsfjall around 10,000 years ago. Here Vigdís, wife of Ingimundur the Old of *Vatnsdaela Saga*, gave birth to their daughter Þórdís and thereby started the settlement of the valley (see the following Hof section). There's now a copse and a plaque commemorating the birth.

In October 1720, a great landslide dammed up the river Vatnsdalsá south of the present Ring Road to form the lake Flóðið. Across the Ring Road from Vatnsdalshólar are the three smaller hills of Prístapar where the last execution in Iceland took place on 12 January 1830.

If you'd like to camp out or walk around and lose yourself in the innumerable hills of Vatnsdalshólar, the best access is from Blönduós 20 km away. All the buses travelling between Reykjavík and Blönduós pass the area.

Hof

Hof ('temple') was the farm of the pagan Ingimundur, the hero of the *Vatnsdaela Saga*, a work which was later condensed for publication in the *Landnámabók*. Ingimundur was the son of a Norwegian chieftain and was reared in a Viking household. As a supporter of King Harald Haarfager, he was awarded a silver charm depicting the Norse god Freyr.

Ingimundur was told by a medium that his charm had disappeared and been transported to an Icelandic grove where he and his family would settle and be happy. Although he'd had no plans to emigrate, he accepted his fate and sailed to Iceland in search of the missing charm. At the spot where his wife gave birth to their first child, he realised the countryside fitted the description of his future homestead. He wandered further up the valley to build a temple to the Norse gods. As he was excavating a foundation for the pillars, he found the charm and named his farm Hof.

On the hill Goðhóll at Hof, 20 km up Route 722 from the Ring Road, you can see evidence of Ingimundur's temple although it's never been excavated. Unless you have a vehicle or you're an especially keen saga buff it's probably not worth the effort it will take to get there walking or hitching.

Hvítserkur

Hvítserkur is a 15-metre-high sea stack eroded by wave action into a bizarre and whimsical rock formation that looks like an animal. Legend tells us Hvítserkur was a troll caught by the sunrise while attempting to destroy the Christian monastery at Þingeyrar. Like all trolls caught by the sunrise, he was turned to stone.

I don't see a troll in it but there is a grazing Brahma bull – or an American bison, or an Asian elephant with a howdah on its back, or...

Hvítserkur is just offshore near the northern end of the Vatnsnes peninsula. There's no public transport except the tour from Hvammstangi so the car-less will have to cycle or hitch.

Hóp

At high tide, Hóp is the fifth largest lake in Iceland at 44 sq km. At low tide, it shrinks to 29 sq km. Although it's large, Hóp is a singularly uninteresting body of water except for the curious spit Þingeyraríf which nearly bisects it. The spit is 10 km long and just a few metres wide. Those into unusual geographic phenomena may want to walk out to the end and back.

Þingeyrar

Þingeyrar, south of Blönduós and at the base of Þingeyraríf, is one of Iceland's greatest historical places. It was the site of a district assembly or þing, and there Jón Ögmundarson, the original Bishop of Hólar, founded Iceland's' first monastery in 1112.

Hoping to alleviate some of the famine and crop failure that had been plaguing northern Iceland, the bishop vowed to build a church on the site.

With his own hands, he cleared the foundations of the church and less than a week later, the land became productive again. The bishop interpreted the miracle as a divine go-ahead for the construction of a Benedictine monastery on the site, an institution which was to become the greatest centre of literary production in the country. During the late 12th century, the monks wrote, compiled, and copied histories and sagas, including those of the Norwegian kings and *Jóns Saga Helga*, the biography of Bishop Jón himself.

The monastery no longer stands but on the site there's a wonderful stone church constructed entirely by the owner of Þingeyrar between 1864 and 1877. The pulpit from Holland dates back to the 17th century. Its 15th-century altarpiece was made in England and set with alabaster reliefs from the original monastery. Most impressive are the replicas of the oak statuettes of Christ and the apostles which were carved in the 1500s in Germany and stood in the church until the early 1900s when they were sold and then donated to the National Museum in Reykjavík.

Outside the church is an ovoid outline of an outdoor enclosure known locally as the Lögrétta, believed to be the remains of the meeting place of a district legislative body prior to the establishment of the monastery.

Visiting Þingeyrar can be a bit tricky without a car but it's worth the effort. Basically, it's a matter of getting to the intersection of the Ring Road and Route 721, then walking the 6 km nòrth to the site.

Gljúfurá

The river Gljúfurá crosses the Ring Road 2 km west of Vatnsdalshólar. It flows through a scenic gorge below and further down into lake Hop.

Húnavellir

The site of an Edda hotel (tel 95-24370), Húnavellir, or the 'bear plains', sits on the shores of Svínavatn (named 'pig lake' after the swines of *Vatnsdaela's* Ingimundur). The hotel has a naturally heated swimming pool, a licensed restaurant, as well as private rooms and sleeping-bag accommodation. Singles/doubles cost US$45/58.

Borgarvirki

On a 180-metre hill near Vesturhópsvatn are the ruins of Borgarvirki, a fort-like circular stone enclosure above 10 metre-high basalt columns. Inside are the remains of a well and some dwellings or huts. It was renovated in 1950 but archaeologists really don't know its original purpose. Legend says that it was used as a lookout and defence post against attack from the south. There is a view disc on top which points out the features around upper Húnafjörður.

To get there, go to the intersection of the Ring Road and Route 716 and turn right onto the latter. After 6 km, you'll come to a 'T' intersection where you should again turn right onto Route 717. Walk or hitch the remaining 11 km to the site which lies just west of the road, 5 km north of that intersection.

Blandavirkjun

On the upper Blandaá is the 1150 kilowatt per hour Blandavirkjun hydro plant which will be the fourth largest in Iceland. The reservoir to be created will drown the present Kjólar Road and the power authority will be obliged to build a new road within a couple of years.

Interestingly enough, everyone agrees Iceland doesn't need more power but once Blandavirkjun is completed, an aluminium plant can be constructed to provide jobs and slow the emigration to Reykjavík and Akureyri. Unfortunately, the whole project spells ecological disaster for the region. Farmers will have to be compensated for flooded pasture and farmland by the government and immense areas of hitherto undeveloped land will be planted with non-native species to provide pasture for displaced sheep.

Skagaströnd

One of the oldest trading centres in northern Iceland, Skagaströnd began as a German and English merchant town in the 1500s. It's now primarily a fishing village and has a population of less than 700.

There's a new hotel, the Dagsbrún (tel

95-22730), and a camping ground just south of the town. The only public transport to Skagaströnd is the weekly bus tour from the hotel in Blönduós. (See the Blönduós section in this chapter for more information about this tour and the northern part of the peninsula.)

Kyrpingsfjall About 25 km north of Skagaströnd is a series of gravel hills less than 100 metres high. The southernmost of these is called Gullbrekka, the 'golden hillside', below which is the bog Gullkelda. It's said that the farm Gullbrekka which once existed on this site sunk Atlantis-style into the bog and neither it nor its inhabitants were ever seen again.

SKAGAFJÖRÐUR

This area includes roughly the eastern coast of the Skagi peninsula, the islands in Skagafjörður, and the delta area at the head of the fjord which is about 40 km long and 30 km wide at the mouth.

Varmahlíð

Varmahlíð ('warm slope'), a village of 100 people, is named after the geothermal sites around it. It has developed only recently as a service centre around the intersection of the Ring Road and the Sauðárkrókur highway. It now has a bank and a swimming pool as well as tourist facilities.

The easy walk to the summit of 111-metre Reykjahóll affords a good view over the town and surrounding green countryside.

Places to Stay & Eat The village has a supermarket, a petrol station with a snack bar, and the *Hotel Varmahlíð* (tel 95-6170) which has a camping site and sleeping-bag accommodation for US$12 and double rooms for US$58. The food at the hotel restaurant is very marginal in quality. The *Shell* petrol station snack bar is cheaper and infinitely better.

Quite a few farmhouses offer rooms, meals, sleeping-bag accommodation, and horse tours and rentals.

On the Ring Road, west of town, is *Stóra Vatnsskarð* (tel 95-6152) and south on Route 752 in Tungusveit are *Varmilaekur* (tel 95-6021), *Steinsstaðdaskóli* (tel 95-6812), and *Bakkaflöt* (tel 95-6245). The latter two have camping sites as well as rooms and dorms. East of Varmahlíð along the Ring Road is *Úlfsstaðir* (tel 95-6228) offering only private rooms.

Getting There & Away Since it's on the Ring Road, all the buses between Reykjavík and Akureyri pass through Varmahlíð.

Around Varmahlíð

Reynisstaður The church and farm 14 km north of Varmahlíð is another former monastery site. This one operated between 1295 and 1552. The present church at Reynisstaður was built in the 1800s.

Vatnsskarð The Ring Road crosses Vatnsskarð, or 'lake pass', between the Húnafjörður and Skagafjörður watersheds. At the eastern foot of the pass near Varmahlíð is the hill Arnarstapi where there's a monument to the Icelandic-Canadian poet Stephan G Stephansson, the 'Rocky Mountain Bard', and a view disc.

At the western foot of the pass, the clear-water river Svartá ('black river') joins the milky white glacier-fed river Blandaá and creates an interesting 'meeting of the waters'.

Víðimýri Just west of Varmahlíð along the Ring Road is the old chieftain's residence at Víðimýri. The turf-covered church, which has been considered architecturally superior to other similar 19th-century structures in Iceland, is worth a look as you're passing by.

Glaumbaer Parts of the old turf farm at Glaumbaer, one of the best remaining examples of early Icelandic building techniques, were built in the 1700s. The interior has been converted into the Skagafjörður folk museum. It is believed that Þófinnur Karlsefni, the first European born in North America, is buried at Glaumbaer where he lived after returning from Vinland to his parents' native Iceland. Museum hours are from 10 am to noon and 1 to 5 pm daily between 1 June and 1 September.

The bus is pretty useless here because it travels from Varmahlíð to Siglufjörður on Mondays, Wednesdays, and Fridays and returns on Sundays, Tuesdays, and Thursdays. Luckily, hitching isn't that difficult along relatively well-travelled Route 75.

Sauðárkrókur

With 2500 inhabitants, Sauðárkrókur is the second largest town in north Iceland but since it's not on the Ring Road and gets only three buses a week from Reykjavík, it hasn't really seen much tourism. Although it obtained a trading licence on New Year's Day 1858, the first settler arrived in 1871 and Sauðárkrókur received its municipal charter in 1947. It's supported economically by fishing, trading, a wool tannery and factory (Loðskinn), and the hydroelectric station Gönguskarðsárvirkjun ('trail pass river power plant').

The village church was built in 1892 and is open daily to visitors during the summer months. At the library is a small local art and folk museum.

Information The tourist office is the front desk of Hotel Áning (tel 95-36717). On the hillside above town is a nine-hole golf course. Other services include banks, a laundry, a swimming pool, and horse rentals.

Places to Stay Both the summer hotel, *Hotel Áning*, and the *Hotel Maelifell* (tel 95-35265) at Aðalgata 7 charge US$58 per night and offer sleeping-bag accommodation for US$12. A third choice is the *Torg Guesthouse* (tel 95-35940). The camping site is beside the swimming pool, the laundry and the Faxatorg museum. On weekends, the Hotel Maelifell holds a disco.

Places to Eat All hotels serve meals of varying quality. The restaurant and pub *Saelkerahúsið* is fairly up-market. Better value are the snack bars at *Ábaer* near the supermarket and *Bláfell* across from the camping site. The state liquor store in Sauðárkrókur is at Smáragrund 2 but it's a matter of luck to ever find it open.

Getting There & Away Three buses per week connect Sauðárkrókur with the Ring Road at Varmahlíð to the south and Siglufjörður to the north. The southbound

Glaumbaer

bus runs on Tuesdays, Thursdays and Sundays, and the northbound bus runs on Mondays, Wednesdays, and Fridays.

Flugleiðir (tel 95-5630) flies between Reykjavík and Sauðárkrókur at least once daily except Saturdays. The weather is stable enough this far north that airline schedules are fairly reliable.

Tindastóll

The 989-metre Tindastóll is a prominent Skagafjörður landmark. It extends for 20 km along the coast north of Sauðárkrókur. The mountain and its caves are believed to be inhabited by an array of supernatural beings – sea monsters, trolls, giants – one of which kidnapped the daughter of an early bishop of Hólar. At its northern end is a geothermal area, Reykir, which was mentioned in *Grettirs Saga*. Grettir supposedly swam ashore from the island of Drangey in Skagafjörður and, not surprisingly, one of the hot springs at Reykir is named Grettislaug, or 'Gretti's bath'.

North of the peninsula where Reykir stands is the cove of Glerhallavík where you'll find a beach covered with surf polished stones. There is also an old wishing-well which contains a magic stone believed to float to the surface on Midsummer's Day.

The summit, of course, affords a spectacular view across all of Skagafjörður but it's difficult to climb from the eastern slope. It's much easier from the higher land along Route 745 west of the mountain.

Trölli Hut Across Route 745 from the south-western foot of Tindastóll, you can walk to Trölli mountain hut which lies about 8 km south-west of the farm Tunga. It has 18 beds but no cooking facilities. Use the *Skagaströnd 1:100,000* topo sheets for the walk.

Drangey

The rocky island of Drangey in Skagajörður is a flat-topped mass of tuff rising abruptly 200 metres above the water. The cliffs serve as nesting sites for thousands of sea birds and have been used historically for egg collection and bird netting. *Grettirs Saga* says that both Grettir and his brother Illugi lived on the island and were slain there.

From the landing place, a steep path leads to the summit. Icelanders maintain that it's necessary to pray before ascending, however, because only part of the island was blessed by the early priests and that the north-eastern section remains an abode of evil. The superstitious locals will only collect birds or eggs from the bits stamped with the greater powers' official seal of approval.

Half-day boat trips to the island can be arranged through the Hotel Áning in Sauðárkrókur (tel 95-36717) or through the farmer at Fagranes (tel 95-6503) (near Tindastóll) or Vatn (tel 95-6434). Normally they only operate on weekends.

Málmey

Málmey, the other Skagafjörður island and home to an abundance of sea birds, is 2½ sq km in area. It isn't as foreboding as Drangey and rises to just over 150 metres. It's been uninhabited by humans since 1951. There is currently no public transport to Málmey although private farmers will sometimes take people over. If you're interested, try the farm Vatn (tel 95-6434) in Höfðaströnd.

TRÖLLSKAGI

Both the topography and climate of the Tröllskagi make it ideal hiking country. The rugged peninsula between Skagafjörður and northern Iceland's longest fjord, Eyjafjörður, is a maze of mountains, rivers, and even some small glaciers. This bit of Iceland has good weather and a mild summer climate. Unless you can find a suitable windbreak, however, conditions aren't ideal for sunbaking.

The Tröllskagi's best known attraction is Hólar, the northern bishopric. Parts of the peninsula, especially around the village of Ólafsfjörður, are reminiscent of the Westfjords. In the southern part of the peninsula climbers will find some of Iceland's most challenging peaks, ridges, and spires within easy walking distance of the highway system.

Hofsós

Hofsós, a small village of about 280 people, is north-east of Sauðárkrókur and has been a trading centre since the 1500s. The 18th-century log warehouse, Bjálkahús, is owned and preserved *in situ* by the National Museum. South of town are some unusual basalt formations and near Grafarós, the mouth of the river Grafará, are the remains of a trading post from the 1800s. The farm Gröf, 2 km south of the river, has an old turf church, renovated and re-consecrated in 1953.

The only accommodation in the area is at the farm Vatn (tel 95-6434), 7 km north of town, but no sleeping-bag accommodation is available. They do hire horses and will organise excursions to Málmey island if there is sufficient interest. The farm Hof (tel 95-6444), a couple of km upstream from the village, arranges longer horse tours.

Snacks are available at the Esso petrol station in town. The Siglufjörður-bound bus (see Getting There & Away in the Sauðárkrókur section) passes through Hofsós.

Hólar

The northern bishopric of Hólar was the ecumenical and educational capital of northern Iceland between 1106 (when it was founded) and the Reformation. It continued as a religious centre and the home of the northern bishops until 1798.

The first bishop of Hólar was Jón Ögmundarson, nominated for sainthood by his Icelandic constituency. The canonisation was never recognised by Rome but a monk at the monastery of Þingeyrar (see the Around Húnafjörður section) called Jón's biography *Jóns Saga Helga*, or 'The Saga of St John'.

Bishop Jón constructed the first timber cathedral at Hólar of Norwegian wood, replacing the small turf church that had previously been in use. Until 1135, when the Skálholt cathedral was completed, 14 years after the first bishop's death, it was the world's largest wooden church. He also established a highly successful school at Hólar, required church attendance and memorisation of sacred recitations, and promoted books he considered edifying.

He officially abolished any sort of fun and mischief that he thought might detract from students' and parishioners' religious education or moral values. Public dances, love songs, frivolous celebration, and anything that could be construed as paganism or sorcery was banned throughout his jurisdiction. He even managed to change the names of days of the week from those named after Nordic gods (those now used in English) to the more general ones used in Icelandic today. In short, Bishop Jón's word was law in northern Iceland.

The current red sandstone church, now whitewashed, was built in 1757 of materials from Hólabyrða, the mountain forming its backdrop. It was financed by donations from Lutheran congregations all over Scandinavia.

The altarpiece was donated by the last Catholic Bishop of Hólar, Jón Arason, in 1522. After he and his son were executed at Skálholt for opposition to Danish Reformation, his remains were brought to Hólar and entombed in the bell tower. The most unusual item in the church, however, is a bizarre mosaic of modern-day astronauts fraternising with seductive Roman nymphs – not the sort of artwork you'd expect to find in such a historically conservative place! The church is open to the public daily in summer between 2 and 6 pm.

Access to Hólar is difficult unless you join a day-tour from Akureyri. Otherwise, travel on the Varmahlíð to Siglufjörður bus to the intersection of Routes 76 and 769. From there it's an 11-km walk up to Hólar. There's a camping site at the tree nursery at Hólar and a small coffee shop at the agricultural school which conducts research on fish and tree farming.

Víðvík

Not far from the intersection of Route 76 and

Ólafsfjörður, Iceland (DS)

Top: Laugahraun, Landmannalaugar, Iceland (DS)
Left: Church at Húsavík, Iceland (DS)
Right: Dwarf birch forest at Höfði, Mývatn, Iceland (DS)

the two Hólar access roads (one on either side of the river Hjaltadalsá) are the farm and church at Víðvík. Þórbjörn Öngull, the character from the *Grettirs Saga* who was responsible for Grettir's death, lived there. The altarpiece at the church dates back to the early 1700s, but the church is unfortunately locked most of the time.

Reykir

The uppermost farm of Hjaltadalur is, as its name would suggest, a geothermal site. Its two hot springs, Vinnufólkslaug and Biskupslaug, are reputed to have been the bathing place for the bishops and other personnel at Hólar.

Siglufjörður

This town, with less than 2000 people, enjoys a beautiful setting beside a small fjord of the same name on the northern Tröllskagi. Originally known as Þormóðseyri after its sandspit, Siglufjörður gained municipal status in 1918. At the height of activity in its herring fishery during the early 1940s, Siglufjörður had a population of over 3000 but, when herring disappeared from the northern coast of Iceland, it declined and has never recovered its former status.

In the winter, a ski lift operates in Skarðsdalur above town.

Siglufjarðarskarð Since the 800-metre tunnel Strákagöng through Strákar mountain was opened, the road over the 630-metre-high pass between Siglufjörður and Fljótavík has been abandoned. From early July to late August, it's open to foot traffic. You can walk up to the pass and continue north along the ridge to Strákar (above the tunnel) for some wonderful views.

Places to Stay & Eat The *Hotel Höfn* (tel 96-71514), the only formal accommodation in town, charges US$53 for a double room. They have a licensed dining room which is open all day. On weekends, there's music and dancing in the bar. There's no sleeping-bag accommodation so the only budget option is the camping site south of town. Groups can book the cabin at *Höll Sports Centre* (tel 96-71284). It's a bargain if you split the cost between enough people.

The *Veitingastofan Restaurant* near the hotel is open from 8.30 am to 8.30 pm daily. The state liquor store at Siglufjörður is found at Eyrargata 25 in the town centre.

Getting There & Away For details on reaching Siglufjörður by bus, see the Sauðárkrókur Getting There & Away section. Arnarflug (tel 96-71162) has flights to Siglufjörður from Reykjavík departing at 10 am weekdays and 6.30 am weekends. They return to the capital at 11.30 am weekdays and 8 pm on weekends.

Akureyri

Most travellers agree that Akureyri, the 'meadow sandspit', offers the best of urban Iceland. The setting is superb, and sunny days are the norm in this small and tidy town which has nearly all the amenities of Reykjavík. It's at the head of Eyjafjörður ('island fjord' named after the island of Hrísey in the middle) beneath perpetually snow-capped peaks.

Akureyri's climate supports diverse vegetation. Locals put a lot of effort into planting and maintaining trees and gardens to improve on the town's already lovely appearance, and the results are exhilarating. Along the streets, in flower boxes, and in private gardens grow some of the most beautiful and colourful blooms you'll ever see, and the clear air is filled with the fresh scent of sticky birch. In the botanic gardens, you'll find species from Africa, the Mediterranean, and China growing beside Alaskan, Greenlandic, and indigenous specimens, all outdoors. You'd never guess you were just a stone's throw south of the Arctic Circle.

Akureyri's population is now around 14,000 and its appeal is drawing immigrants not only from the countryside but from Reykjavík as well. Its only aesthetic downfall is the characterless high-density housing projects in the newer residential areas away from the city centre.

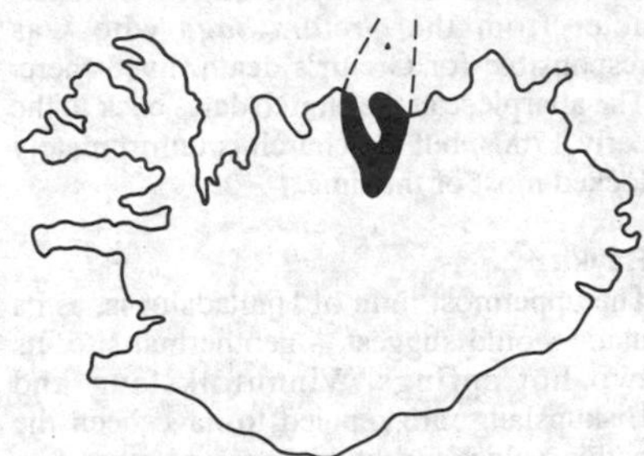

History

The first permanent settler in the Eyjafjörður area was Norwegian Helgi Magri, or 'Helgi the Lean', so named because of an unfortunate period of nutritional deficiency during his youth in the Orkneys. He seemed to take a cover-all-the-bases attitude toward religion. Although he worshipped Þór and tossed his high-seat pillars into the sea to locate a homestead in Iceland, Helgi named the place where they washed up Kristnes or 'Christ's peninsula' and established his farm there, 7 km south of present-day Akureyri.

Akureyri began as a trading centre just before the Danish Trade Monopoly of 1602 came into effect. Although the town was used for commercial enterprises, no one actually lived there because the settlers all maintained rural farms and homesteads.

Although business had been booming for a century and a half, Akureyri's first actual residence was that of Danish trader Friðrik Lynge in 1777. By the late 1700s, the town had accumulated a whopping 10 residents, all Danish traders. Population expansion didn't begin in earnest until Akureyri received its official municipal charter on 29 August 1862, when it had 286 people. The first cooperative society, Gránufélagsins, was established in 1870 at Oddeyri, the spit that juts out into Eyjafjörður from the current town centre.

In 1890, Akureyri's population had grown to 602 and, by the turn of the century, 1370 people were living there. By this time, the original cooperative had begun to decline but it was quickly replaced in 1906 by the Akureyri Cooperative Society (KEA) whose ubiquitous insignia still graces many of the city's businesses.

The Akureyri Fishing Company is Iceland's largest. Akureyri's shipyard is also the country's largest. Prior to the decline of the herring stock in northern Iceland the town's primary industry was herring salting. Fishing remains important, but now the emphasis is on trawling, canning, and freezing of larger fish. Currently, Akureyri's industrial base is expanding to include such diverse enterprises as brewing, food processing, and tourism.

Orientation

Akureyri is small, so you can get around it on foot. Most of the shops, restaurants, and businesses are concentrated along the shore between the bus terminal and the football stadium. Most activity centres on the pedestrian shopping street Hafnarstraeti and the industrial area on the Oddeyri spit. Most residential sections as well as the camping site, church, swimming pool, botanic gardens, and medical centre are found on the prominent bluff rising above the city centre.

Information

Tourist Information The tourist information office (tel 96-27733) in the BSÍ bus terminal at Hafnarstraeti 82 is one of the most helpful in the country. They can help you with planning trips around the city, and tours to surrounding areas including Jökulsárgljúfur National Park, lake Mývatn, Grímsey island, and even into the interior highlands. They will also reserve and arrange accommodation for you anywhere in Iceland. The office is open between 8 am and 7 pm Monday to Friday and from 8 am to noon on weekends.

Post & Telephone The Postur og Simi is at Hafnarstraeti 102 on the pedestrian mall. The telephone office is open from 9 am to 6 pm Monday to Friday and on Saturdays from 9 am to noon. The post office is open weekdays from 9 am to 4.30 pm.

Banks Akureyri has five banks and, since the city sees so much tourism, they are well set up for foreign exchange. If it's any sort of recommendation, the Landsbanki on Ráðhústorg (the town square) offers free coffee while you wait in the queue.

Books & Bookshops It seems amazing that a city the size of Akureyri can support three bookshops. Two of them are on the pedestrian mall and the other is just around the corner on Skipagata. All three sell a variety of souvenir books in English, French, and German as well as popular foreign language paperbacks and Icelandic titles. The Bókaverslunin Edda at Hafnarstraeti 100 specialises in foreign language periodicals.

Emergency Services The fire brigade and ambulance services (tel 96-22222) and the Akureyri police (tel 96-23222) are available 24 hours a day. The hospital is just south of the botanic gardens on Spítalavegur.

Film & Photography There are two film and camera shops on the pedestrian mall which offer film, film processing, and camera repairs, all at typically outrageous Icelandic prices. Kodak processing is available at Pedromyndir at Hafnarstraeti 98.

Outdoor Equipment For fishing, camping equipment, and sporting goods, try Eyfőrð at Hjalteyrargata 4 east of the city centre on Oddeyri spit.

Things to See & Do

A walking tour around the museums and churches in Akureyri will take at least a day. Add the botanic gardens and Kjarnaskógur wood and you'll keep yourself occupied for 2 days. Even those who aren't interested in museums and churches will probably enjoy just strolling around Akureyri and seeing the beautiful gardens and trees that make the city unique in Iceland.

Churches

Akureyri Church It's easy to see that this church was designed by Gudjón Samúelsson, the architect of Hallgrímskirkja in Reykjavík. The geologic look that seems to be common to the newer Icelandic church architecture has not been lost on Akureyri. Less blatantly 'basalt' than Hallgrímskirkja, Akureyrarkirkja is basalt, nonetheless. Most visitors aren't overly impressed with the exterior but the interior is certainly interesting and worthwhile seeing.

Built in 1940, it contains a large and beautiful 3200-pipe organ and a series of

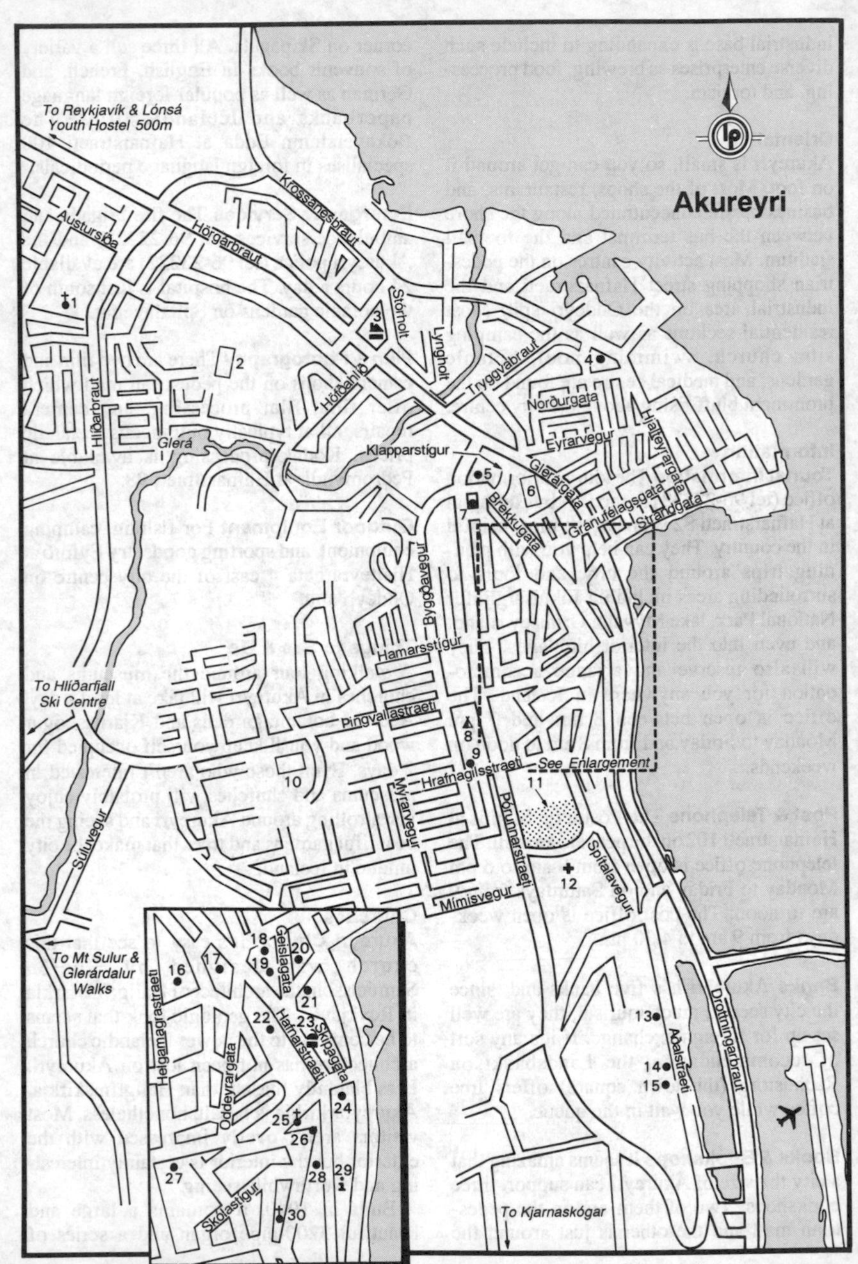
Akureyri
To Reykjavík & Lónsá Youth Hostel 500m
Austursíða
Hörgárbraut
Krossanesbraut
Stórholt
Lyngholt
Höfðahlíð
Tryggvabraut
Norðurgata
Eyrarvegur
Hjalteyrargata
Hlíðarbraut
Glerá
Klapparstígur
Glerárgata
Brekkugata
Gránufélagsgata
Strandgata
Byggðavegur
Hamarsstígur
Þingvallastræti
Hrafnagilsstræti
See Enlargement
Mýrarvegur
Þórunnarstræti
Spítalavegur
Mímisvegur
Súluvegur
To Hlíðarfjall Ski Centre
To Mt Sulur & Glerárdalur Walks
Drottningarbraut
Aðalstræti
To Kjarnaskógar
Helgamagrastræti
Oddeyrargata
Geislagata
Hafnarstræti
Skipagata
Skólastígur
1
2
3
4
5
6
7
8
9
10
11
12
13
14
15
16
17
18
19
20
21
22
23
24
25
26
27
28
29
30

1 Glerá Church
2 Sports Stadium
3 Youth Hostel
4 Hagkaup Supermarket
5 View Disc & Helgi the Lean Statue
6 Sports Stadium
7 Police
8 Camping Ground
9 KEA Supermarket
10 Sports Stadium
11 Botanic Gardens
12 Hospital
13 Friðbjarnarhús
14 Nonnahús
15 Akureyri Folk Museum
16 Davíðshús
17 Library & Archives
18 Cinema
19 Bank & Foreign Exchange
20 Bank & Foreign Exchange
21 Uppinn Pizzeria & Bar
22 Bank & Foreign Exchange
23 Post & Telephone Office
24 Bautinn Restaurant
25 Akureyri Church
26 Natural History Museum
27 Swimming Pool
28 Matthías Jochumsson Memorial Museum (Sigurhaeðir)
29 Tourist Information Office & Bus Terminal
30 Catholic Church

rather untraditional reliefs of the life of Christ. There's also a very interesting painting of the crucifixion. The centre window in the chancel is from Coventry cathedral in England which survived when that church was destroyed in WW II.

The angel was done by the Danish sculptor Bertel Thorvaldsen, renowned for his intricacy with clothing detail. The ship hanging from the ceiling represents the old Icelandic and Faroese tradition of invoking a deity for the protection of loved ones at sea.

The church is open daily from 9.30 to 11 am and 2 to 3.30 pm. During the summer, services are held at 11 am on Sundays.

Catholic Church The Catholic chapel in Akureyri is a nice old house at Eyrarlandsvegur 26. It was built in 1912 and acquired by the church in 1952. On the nearby roundabout is Einar Jónsson's sculpture *Útlaginn* or 'The Outlaw'.

Glerá Church The new Glerá church being constructed in the heart of the blocks of flats north of the river adds a bit of character, albeit grey, to the otherwise characterless scene. It was designed to resemble the outline of Mt Sulur, a prominent peak in Akureyri's background, but it's difficult to work out how this is so. At any rate, the church wasn't completed at the time of writing so perhaps the mountain has yet to emerge.

The Glerá church will replace the parish church at Lögmannshlíð.

Lögmannshlíð The centre of the old northern Akureyri parish, this little country church at Lögmannshlíð high above the town near the river Lónsá was built in 1861 but, according to Settlement records, a religious structure has existed on this site since the 11th century. Inside are artefacts dating back as far as the 1600s. The church is mostly reached by the walk up from the Lónsá youth hostel. Before visiting, it's a good idea to determine whether it's unlocked or not. The tourist office will be able to help you, or you can phone the church caretaker (tel 96-24637).

Museum Church The small church beside the folk museum is constructed in typical 19th-century Icelandic style. It was originally built at Svalbarðseyri on the eastern shore of Eyjafjörður and moved to its present site in 1970. It was used as a storage shed by the British during WW II but is now re-consecrated and is used for weddings and social functions. The garden beside it was begun as a nursery in 1898, and there's been some sort of garden there ever since.

Museums

Akureyri has quite a few museums but most of them are the homes of 'local boys done good'. It's to the Icelanders' tribute that they remember their artists, poets, and authors rather than their generals and politicians but, unless you have a particular admiration for their work, many of the museums will probably prove to be of limited interest if you're not an Icelander.

Matthías Jochumsson Memorial Also known as Sigurhaeðir, this memorial museum on Hafnarstraeti was the home of the Icelandic poet laureate and dramatist Matthías Jochumsson. He was born in 1835 and wrote the noted play *The Outlaws* in 1861 and the Icelandic national anthem, *Iceland's 1000 Years*, in 1874. He was also responsible for translating Byron, Shakespeare, and German poetic works into Icelandic.

The house was built in 1902 and Jochumsson lived there until his death in 1920. The museum contains his collection of works and his personal property. The US$1.50 admission charge goes to the upkeep of the property which is open daily from 15 June to 15 September from 2 to 4 pm.

Nonnahús Probably the most interesting of the artists' homes, Nonnahús at Aðalstraeti 45b, was the childhood home of Reverend Jón Sveinsson (nicknamed 'Nonni') who lived from 1857 to 1944. This cosy old home, built in 1850, is one of Iceland's best examples of early village dwellings.

Jón Sveinsson was born south of Akureyri at Möðruvellir in 1857 and moved to Akureyri at the age of 8 years. He was invited to the Latin School at Amiens, France, by a French nobleman. En route, he visited Denmark and converted to Roman Catholicism. In 1878, he joined the Jesuit order and continued his theological education around western Europe before accepting a teaching post in Ordrup, Denmark, in 1883. After just a few years there, he went to England and was ordained a priest, then returned to Denmark and continued teaching for 20 years until ill health forced him to retire to a more sedate literary life. Nonni died in Germany in 1944.

It was during his later years that he wrote his most famous works, the *Nonni and Manni* children's adventures about his youth in Iceland and travels around the world. Originally written in German, the books have been translated into 40 languages, including Icelandic, and many of the original copies as well as numerous illustrations can be seen in the museum today. Perhaps the most interesting aspect of the house, however, is its cramped, lived-in atmosphere and simple furnishings. It tells much about life in 19th-century Iceland that museums normally fail to convey. It's open daily from 15 June to 31 August between 2 and 4.30 pm. Admission is US$1.75.

Laxdalshús At Hafnarstraeti 11 near the bus terminal is Laxdalshús, the oldest building in Akureyri. It was constructed in 1795 as a Danish trading house. It wasn't open to the public when I was last there but it's worth a look from the outside.

Friðbjarnarhús Unless you are especially interested in the service club the International Organisation of Good Templars (IOGT), you can give this museum a miss. It was established to commemorate the founding of Iceland's first chapter on 10 January 1884, and most of the items displayed relate to their activities. At Aðalstraeti 46, in the 1856 home of early book merchant Friðbjörn Steinsson, the museum is open on Sundays in July and August from 2 to 5 pm. Admission is US$1.50.

Akureyri Folk Museum At Aðalstraeti 58, this museum houses a large and interesting collection of art and items of practical use during the development of Iceland right through to the present day. Particularly amusing are the collection of Icelandic milk cartons, the typewriters complete with Icelandic characters, and the early television set. Admission is US$2.60. The museum is open daily from 1.30 to 5 pm between 1 June and 15 September.

Natural History Museum At Hafnarstraeti 81, you'll find the rather ordinary Náttúrugripsafnið, or Natural History

Museum. It's worth a quick visit on a rainy day, however. It was founded in 1951 and houses a complete collection of stuffed Icelandic birds and their eggs. There are also stuffed fish and mammals and a variety of native shells, insects, fungi, lichen, and flora. The geological display is somewhat interesting but the best item in the whole museum is the stuffed great auk (extinct for 100 years) which isn't a great auk at all but a reasonable facsimile constructed from parts of other species. It's pretty well done, considering.

Admission to the museum is US$1.50. It's open from 1 to 4 pm daily except Saturdays from 1 June to 10 September.

Davíðshús This tidy little house at Bjardarstígur 6 was built in 1944 by the poet, novelist, and playwright Davíð Stefánsson who became an Icelandic poet laureate. His most notable poetic work was the volume *Black Feathers* published in 1919 and his most famous play was *The Golden Gate*, a tale of a woman who saved her worthless husband's rambunctious and unpenitent soul by packing it up in a bag and smuggling it into heaven after all other methods had failed.

The museum was created upon the artist's death in 1964 and, as a respectful tribute, all of his books and belongings remain exactly as he left them. The place has a particularly scholarly air about it but it's a bit of a shame to see such an extensive library of books untouched and unavailable for use.

It's open from 15 June to 15 September from 3 to 5 pm daily. Admission is US$1.50.

Library & Archives

The public library at Brekkugata 17 was first established in 1827 and houses over 80,000 volumes as well as the district historical archives. It's open Monday to Friday from 1 to 5 pm.

Botanic Gardens

The Lystigarður Akureyrar, the botanical gardens on Eyrarlandsvegur, was first opened in 1912. This happened 2 years after a group of local women founded the Akureyri Park Society to provide a place for family recreation. The society arranged purchasing of the land and the planting and landscaping of an old hay field. Gifts of land increased the size of the park to its current 3.4 hectares.

The municipality took over management in 1955 and, in 1957, bought a private collection of Icelandic plants to create a botanical garden. It now includes every species indigenous to Iceland and an extensive collection of high-latitude and altitude plants from around the world.

The flora are meticulously labelled with scientific names and the countries of origin. It seems that Akureyri is proud of its comfortable microclimate. The locals are happy to point out that plants from New Zealand, Spain, and Tanzania can grow there without the aid of a greenhouse. If you're not into plants, however, the park lawns are sheltered from the wind and provide a nice place to just crash in the sun. You'll also see statues of the poet Matthías Jochumsson and of Margrethe Schiöth who voluntarily managed the park for 30 years.

It's open from 1 June to 30 September from 8 am to 10 pm weekdays, and opens at 9 am on Saturdays and Sundays.

Kjarnaskógur

Just an hour's walk south from the centre of town is Iceland's most visited 'forest', Kjarnaskógur woods, an area of bushland south of town. It has a 2.2 km athletic course, short tracks through birch woods, picnic tables, a very amusing and original children's playground and some unusual fitness-testing devices. It's a great place to spend a few hours on a sunny day but camping is no longer permitted. The nursery and greenhouses at Grodvarstöð, just to the east of the park, sell fresh vegetables and are open from 8 am to 6 pm on weekdays.

Helgi the Lean Statue

On the hill north-east of Klapparstígur (a 5-minute walk from the city centre) is a statue of Helgi the Lean, the first settler in the Akureyri area, and a view disc.

Places to Stay – bottom end

Apart from the sleeping-bag accommodation described in the section on guesthouses, budget accommodation in Akureyri is limited to two youth hostels.

The main one is *Akureyri Hostel* (tel 96-23657) at Stórholt 1, a 15-minute walk from the city centre. It's a friendly place but there are often language difficulties between English-speaking guests and the management. Those who know German or Danish will have no problem but, it can get to be a good-natured comedy of errors otherwise. It is essential to book in advance if you want to stay here, but sometimes miscommunication occurs and reservations are lost. A *laissez-faire* attitude will go a long way here.

The *Lónsá Youth Hostel* (tel 96-25037) is about 3 km from the city centre near the river Lónsá. If you arrive after 5 pm and plan to stay, phone and they will come and fetch you in town. Alternatively, the Akureyri city bus stops within several hundred metres of the hostel.

Both hostels charge US$13 per night for non-IYHF members and US$11 for those with hostel cards. Both have cooking facilities. The hostel in town is open all year and Lónsá opens between 1 June and 1 October.

The camping ground is in two parts, one beside the swimming pool and the other across Þórunnarstraeti in a big open, grassy lawn. They're nice but the place can get very crowded and sometimes noisy. It costs US$4.30 per person per night. Free coffee is available in the office (on the swimming pool side) every morning and there is a washing machine that sees a lot of activity.

Places to Stay – middle

All the middle-range accommodation in Akureyri is guesthouse-style. Some places are small family-owned private homes and others are a bit more commercial.

The one that is consistently recommended is the *Salka Guesthouse* (tel 96-22697) in the centre of town at Skipagata 1. It's small and friendly, offering singles/doubles for US$27.50/38 and sleeping-bag accommodation for US$12. They have cooking facilities and serve as a convenient, but unofficial, youth hostel.

Nicer, but less ideal for budget travellers, is the nearby *Ás Guesthouse* (tel 96-26110) at Skipagata 4. This one offers bed and breakfast, but only private rooms are available. Singles/doubles cost US$38/US$53.50.

Other guesthouses in Akureyri all have the same price structure, singles/doubles cost US$27.50/38. They include the *Brauðstofan* (tel 96-23648) at Skólastígur 5, the *Dalakofinn* (tel 96-23035) at 20 Lyngholt, Þórunnarstraeti 93 (tel 96-21345), and *13 Gilsbakkavegur* (tel 96-26861). All but the last offer sleeping-bag accommodation for US$12.

Places to Stay – top end

Predictably, Akureyri has quite a few hotels catering to up-market tourists. The most expensive is the *Hotel Kea* (tel 96-22200) run by the KEA cooperative below the church at Hafnarstraeti 89. It's a nice, plush hotel which proudly advertises a mini-bar in every room but the cheapest doubles start at US$128. Of course they also have a bar, a cafeteria, and a dining room but, surprisingly, it's not the best place to eat in town.

Lower in price is the *Hotel Norðurland* (tel 96-22600) at Geislagata 7. Doubles here with/without bath cost US$100/US$77.50.

Slightly cheaper is the *Hotel Stefanía* (tel 96-26366) at Hafnarstraeti 85. It's quite a bit lower key than the Hotel Kea. Singles/doubles here cost US$65/95. The *Hotel Akureyri* (tel 96-22525) at Hafnarstraeti 98 charges US$69/50 for a double with/without bath. The *Edda Hotel* (tel 96-24055), up on the bluff at Hrafnagilsstraeti 98, is similarly priced. Only a couple of rooms here have private baths so, if you'd like one, book well in advance.

Places to Eat

Self-Catering Thanks to KEA, Akureyri has a wealth of supermarkets and kiosks competing for business, therefore, keeping prices under control. They're all very well-stocked and convenient. There is a particularly good supermarket at the camping ground that's open evenings and weekends. The *Hagkaup*, at Norðurgata 62 on Oddeyri, is good value but a bit of a walk from the city centre. *Einars Bakery*, at Tryggvabraut 22 east of town not far from the river, sells fresh bread and cakes. The state liquor store is found at Hólabraut 16, near the cinema.

Snacks Along the pedestrian shopping mall there are quite a few small kiosks selling mostly the old stand-bys sausages and chips, burgers, sandwiches, and soft drinks. *Turinn*, the schoolhouse painted with a Coca-Cola motif is actually an ice cream shop. It's open during shopping hours.

The small kiosk *Naetursalan* at Geislagata 1 on Ráðhústorg is a snack bar serving hamburgers, sausages, chips, and soft drinks to those on the run. On Friday and Saturday nights, it's open until 4 am.

Fast Food *Crown Chicken* at Skipagata 12 claims to be the only fast-food restaurant in Akureyri but, actually, it's the only one in the city centre. You can get a burger, sausage, or chicken with chips there for around US$8. It's open from 11 am to 11.30 pm daily in the summer.

Across the street from the Stórholt youth hostel is *Vegemesti Southern Fried Chicken*, a near-perfect replica of a US fast-food drive-in, complete with stars and stripes decor. Icelanders think this is quite a novelty and it seems to be pretty successful, probably because it's close to the youth hostel.

On Ráðhústorg is *Uppinn Pizzeria*, a pizza restaurant and bar which is more expensive than the chicken places but you can buy a cold brew if you're into splurging. It's open between 11.30 am and 1 am weekdays and until 3 am on Fridays and Saturdays. *Elefant Disco* on the shopping street also has a pizzeria and is open similar hours.

Restaurants Those who are planning to splurge only once on a meal in Iceland would do well to save it for Akureyri. As restaurants go, the *Bautinn* in the city centre is probably the best bargain in the country. What's more, it serves items that travellers are generally craving by the time they get this far. The solarium atmosphere is cosy and relatively elegant but not the least bit stuffy. They don't embrace the 'rip-em-off' attitude that seems so prevalent among businesses catering to visitors. Here you can get all-you-can-eat soup and salad-bar food for US$10.25. If you buy a complete meal (main dish, potato dish and vegetable dish) which averages about US$15, the soup and salad are thrown in free.

The Bautinn is licensed and they keep alcohol prices down to a minimum, lower than in most pubs. Daily specials, which are posted at the door, sometimes include such things as puffin, whale, seal, other Icelandic delicacies, and vegetarian fare. In the afternoon, they offer a coffee buffet.

Next door to the Bautinn, the *Smiðjan* (under the same management) provides a posh alternative for those who can't escape the expense-account mentality. All the big hotels have elegant and expensive dining rooms but, if your means are limited, these are best given a wide berth. The *Hlóðir*, at Geislagata 7, is a Spanish and Italian restaurant which is also very expensive but I've heard the food is quite good.

Entertainment

There are a couple of pubs or discos on the pedestrian street which are open until 3 am on Friday and Saturday nights and they can get nearly as wild as those in Reykjavík. The previously mentioned Uppinn Pizzeria on Ráðhústorg has live music and dancing on weekends. It's open from 11.30 am to 1 am Sundays to Thursday and 11.30 am to 3 am Friday and Saturdays.

The cinema on Hólagata has two *salur* and each shows two films per night. To find out what's playing and at what time, try to work it out from the advertising on the windows or ask at the tourist office.

Activities

Glerárdalur/Mt Sulur Walks A good, but potentially exhausting, day-walk from Akureyri is up the Glerá valley and to the summit of 1144-metre Mt Sulur. It's a long but easy climb and there's a road part of the way up. To get there, walk up Glerárdalur to the level of the ski area but stay on the south side of the river. The route up the mountain will be pretty obvious – just follow the north-east pointing ridge.

If you have more time, you can continue on up to the Baugasel mountain hut and turn it into a 2-day trip. Near this hut and higher up in the Glerárdalur there are sites of ancient forests; petrified wood may be found in small quantities. It's also possible to cross the river and visit the small glacier Vindheimajökull (see Öxnadalur in the Around Akureyri section). The hut has a gas stove but no cooking implements.

For all these walks, use the *Akureyri 1:100,000* topo sheet.

Jet-Ski Rental If you'd like to buzz around the harbour on an oversized bathtub toy, jet skis may be rented at Strandgata on Oddeyri spit. They charge around US$20 per hour and are open from 11 am to 11 pm daily.

Swimming The swimming pool is on the bluff beside the camping ground. It's one of the nicest in Iceland and is open long and convenient hours. There are tennis courts and a solarium in addition to the usual sauna and jacuzzis.

The solarium must be booked in advance (tel 96-23260) and is open weekdays from 7 am to 9 pm. The sauna is available to women on Tuesdays and Thursdays from 1 to 9 pm and on Saturdays from 8 am to noon. Men may use it on Mondays, Wednesdays, and Fridays from 1 to 9 pm and on Sundays from 9 am to noon. The pool and jacuzzis are open to everyone from Monday to Friday between 7 am and 9 pm, Saturdays from 8 am to 6 pm, and on Sundays from 8 am to 3 pm.

Golf Akureyri has what claims to be the world's northernmost 18-hole golf course and advertises that golfers are able to play around the clock during the endless summer daylight. Golf fans may want to be in town during the annual 36-hole Arctic Open which is played overnight in late June. For more information, contact the Akureyri Golf Club (tel 96-22974), PO Box 896, Akureyri.

Beside the swimming pool there is a miniature golf course which is open from 10 am to 10 pm.

Skiing At Hlíðarfjall, just a 10-minute drive from Akureyri, are Iceland's best downhill ski slopes. There are five lifts open from 8 am to 10 pm between January and May, and cross-country ski routes are open whenever snow cover is sufficient. The longest run is 3 km with a vertical drop of about 500 metres. Due to nearly perpetual darkness in winter, ski runs are floodlit. Buses go out to the site three times daily during the winter.

At the ski hill is the Skíðastaðir Lodge (tel 96-22930) and restaurant. A ski school offers both individual and group instruction. You can hire equipment.

Horse Rentals The only horse rentals available are from farms in the outlying districts. The most notable one is probably Pólar Hestar (tel 96-33179) at Grýtubakka near the village of Grenivík. It offers 3-day trips through the wilderness north of there. Other horse rentals and tours are found at Pétursborg (tel 96-25925) north of Akureyri and Alda (tel 96-31267) south of the city.

Things to Buy

Souvenirs Akureyri has a subsidiary of the Álafoss woollens factory where jumpers and other woollen goods can be purchased at prices comparable to those at the Reykjavík outlet. It's open from 9 am to 6 pm Monday to Friday and on Saturdays between 10 am and noon. The shop is in the residential area about five blocks north of the camping ground, just a block north-west of the view disc.

On Hafnarstraeti, several shops offer duty-free goods using the same confusing scheme available in Reykjavík. For details, refer to the section on tax in the Iceland Facts for the Visitor chapter.

Getting There & Away

Air Flugleiðir (tel 96-22000) has up to seven

flights daily between Akureyri and Reykjavík in the summer. The first one departs Reykjavík at 7.30 am and returns at 8.50 am. There are other northbound flights at 10.15 am and 9.45 pm daily except Saturdays which return to Reykjavík at 11.35 am and 11.05 pm. Other daily flights leave Reykjavík at 1 and 4 pm and Akureyri at 2.20 and 5.20 pm. For further information and ticketing, contact Akureyri Travel Bureau (tel 96-25000) on Ráðhústorg.

Bus Between Akureyri and Reykjavík, there are buses departing at 9.30 am year round and additional departures at 5 pm from 15 June to 31 August. Buses travelling over the Kjölar Route through the interior to Reykjavík leave on Wednesdays and Saturdays at 8 am in July and August.

Buses to Egilsstaðir in east Iceland run from 19 May to 31 August. Between 19 June and 31 August, they do the run daily at 8.15 am. All buses to Egilsstaðir pass through Mývatn. During July and August, there is a second bus to Mývatn weekdays at 8 pm. From 17 May to 30 September, buses from Mývatn to Akureyri depart at 4.30 daily and, during July and August, there are two additional departures at 8 am and 7.30 pm from Monday to Friday.

There is a bus to Húsavík from Monday to Friday at 4 pm and on Sundays at 9 pm during the summer. From Húsavík, buses depart to Akureyri on Mondays, Wednesdays, and Fridays at 8 am; Tuesdays and Thursdays at 1.15 pm; and on Sundays at 7 pm. On Tuesdays and Thursdays, there is a bus to Vopnafjörður. There are also buses to Vopnafjörður via Ásbyrgi on Mondays and Wednesdays at 4 pm, returning on Tuesdays and Thursdays at 8 am.

Buses to Dalvík, the Hrísey ferry, and Ólafsfjörður leave the terminal in Akureyri from Mondays to Friday at 11 am and on Tuesdays and Fridays at 5.45 pm. To Dalvík, there are additional departures on weekdays at 5.45 pm. From Ólafsfjörður, southbound buses depart at 8.30 and 2 pm from Monday to Friday, passing through Dalvík.

Getting Around

City Bus Akureyri has a regular city bus service which costs about US$1 per ride.

Car Rental There are two rental agencies in Akureyri: Inter-Rent (tel 96-21715) at Tryggvabraut 14 and Bílaleiga Örn (tel 96-24535) at the airport. The absolute minimum charge for an Eastern-European model sedan is US$40 per day plus US$0.40 per km, insurance, tax, and petrol. From there, the charges rise to well over US$100 per day for a 4WD vehicle and over US$1 per km plus all the trimmings. These charges climb into the ozone range fairly quickly so keep in mind that hitching around the relatively well-populated area of Akureyri isn't all that difficult.

It's also possible to arrange to pick up a car here and drop it off in Reykjavík or vice versa.

Taxi The BSO Taxi (tel 96-22727) is available for bookings 24 hours a day.

Bicycle Once you get up the steep slope behind the centre and onto the bluff, cycling around Akureyri is very easy. The tourist information office at the bus terminal rents bicycles for around US$15 per day.

Tours

In the summer, BSÍ offers sightseeing tours around the lake Mývatn area departing at 8.30 am daily for US$48. With the Omnibuspass, it's only US$17. The tour stops at Goðafoss waterfall, and then continues to the lake for a quick tour around the shore stopping briefly for the highlights, before visiting the Krafla area and returning to Akureyri. This is a quick and painless way to visit Mývatn but once people have seen the place, they'll kick themselves for having spent so little time there. Unless you're extremely rushed, forego this option and give Mývatn a week. You won't regret it.

There's also a midnight-sun tour nightly in the summer at 7 pm which includes Hrísey island, Dalvík, and Ólafsfjarðarmúli. See the Around Akureyri section for more details.

In addition to the BSÍ tours, a vast number of companies offer tours of lake Mývatn, the Húsavík area, Grímsey island, and Jökulsárgljúfur National Park. The best sources of information on these tours are the bus terminal tourist office or the Akureyri Travel Bureau (tel 96-25000).

Around Akureyri

ÓLAFSFJÖRÐUR

The fishing village of Ólafsfjörður, north of Akureyri, is a beautifully situated village. The snow-topped mountains rising immediately from the edge of town reach 1200 metres and, south of the town, is the large lake Ólafsfjarðarvatn which is connected to the town's namesake fjord by a short tidal channel.

The valley was an exclusively agricultural area until a village began to grow up around the fishing port in the late 1890s. Ólafsfjörður was granted trading rights in 1905 and became a municipality in 1944. Just under 2000 people live there now.

Ólafsfjarðarmúli

This is one of the best vantage points for observing the midnight sun in midsummer. This beautiful 400-metre-high headland above the village of Ólafsfjörður is high enough to allow you to see beyond the Arctic Circle and experience the real midnight sun for several weeks around the end of June. The island of Grímsey, through which the Arctic Circle passes, is clearly visible from here in fine weather. There's no easy route to the top; the hillsides of loose scree material are steep and rather hazardous climbing so most people do their viewing from the high point along the road.

A new 3.2-km tunnel which is being built through Ólafsfjarðarmúli is scheduled for completion in 1991.

Drangar

The old trail over Drangaskarð is very steep and not easily negotiated. It leads up the hill from Bustarbrekka just up valley from Ólafsfjörður, climbs precipitously over the ridge and ends up at Karlsá on Eyjafjörður, an indirect but exceptionally scenic route of about 10 km each way. From Karlsá, it's possible to hitch or catch the bus back to Ólafsfjörður or Akureyri.

Places to Stay & Eat

For those with tents who'd like to spend a day or so out of Akureyri, Ólafsfjörður is ideal. It has a free camping site beside the swimming pool and the weather is excellent for over half the time in the summer.

The *Hotel Ólafsfjörður* (tel 96-62400) has rooms for US$83 per night, a bit steep for the sterile facilities, but the coffee shop/cafeteria is good and offers reasonable lunch specials. There's a supermarket that's open a few hours on weekdays and the *Shell* petrol station has a grill and snack bar but that's the extent of the food scene. There's also a cinema in the village centre which shows films several times a week.

Getting There & Away

If you just want to visit Ólafsfjörður for a couple of hours, the bus leaves Akureyri at 11 am and arrives at 12.30 pm on weekdays. It leaves Ólafsfjörður at 2 pm, stops for an hour in Dalvík, and then arrives back in Akureyri at 4 pm. The fare each way from Akureyri is US$7.75.

DALVÍK

On the mainland directly west of the island of Hrísey at the mouth of the valley Svarfaðardalur, the village of Dalvík has long been a fishing station but only during the past century has it become a proper village. Its harbour is excellent and, naturally, the emphasis here is on fishing. In 1934, an earthquake destroyed or damaged 77 homes leaving nearly half the inhabitants homeless.

The scenery around Dalvík is superb and provides some inviting hiking routes but keen hikers short of time would do better to continue northward to the Ólafsfjörður area which is more impressive for day-hiking.

The church in the village is unusual and has on display a Bible published in 1584. Dalvík's current population stands at just under 1500.

Heljardalsheiði

A popular walk or horseback tour from Dalvík is over Heljardalsheiði. It begins at the end of Route 805 (20 km up-valley from the village) and traverses the Tröllskagi to the northern bishopric at Hólar. There's no public transport to the end of the road so you'll either have to walk or hitch. Hitching is difficult, but people have been lucky.

The walk is a wilderness backpacking trip, more of a route than a trail, but it passes through some of the best mountain scenery in Iceland. Allow at least 2 days for the walk and more time if you'd like to wander up and have a look at the small glaciers Þverárjökull and Tungnahryggsjökull along the way. It's also best to allow yourself some extra time in case of foul weather.

Another option between Hjaltadalur and Eyjafjörður is the route across Hjaltadalsheiði. It's a 2 to 3-day walk across the moors between Hólar and the upper end of Route 814. You can also opt for the more difficult route up Kolbeinsdalur and via the huts Tungnahrygg and Lambi (Barkárdalur) through the pass between the glaciers.

These routes are covered by the topo sheets *Eyjafjörður 1:100,000*, *Akureyri 1:100,000* and small parts of *Skagaströnd 1:100,000* and *Víðimýri 1:100,000*. Before July and after August, snow will be a concern.

Places to Stay & Eat

Dalvík has one summer hotel, the *Víkurröst* (tel 96-61405), with a restaurant, the *Saeluhúsið*. Double rooms cost US$58 per night and sleeping-bag accommodation can be arranged as well. The camping site is beside the hotel but, in the valleys behind Dalvík, camping opportunities are unlimited.

The village has a well-stocked supermarket in its small shopping complex and, across the street near the harbour, there is a wonderful bakery and coffee shop with a patio for sunny days.

Getting There & Away

Buses between Akureyri and Dalvík depart Akureyri at 11 am and 5 pm weekdays and leave Dalvík at 9 am and 3 pm. The fare each way is US$5.85.

ÁRSKÓGSSTRÖND

Árskógsströnd, the western shore of Eyjafjörður north of Akureyri, is a rich agricultural area. As far as tourism is concerned, the area really has little to recommend it except as a jumping-off point for visits to Hrísey island. There are a number of tiny and non-descript fishing settlements along this shore including Hauganes, Hjalteyri, and Lítla Árskógssandur all with less than 100 people each. The Hrísey ferry terminal is at Lítla Árskógssandur. Buses from Akureyri connect with some of the arrivals and departures of the ferry.

At Syðri Hagi (tel 96- 61961) and Ytri-vík (tel 96-61982) you can find farmhouse accommodation, horse rentals, sleeping-bag space, meals, and cooking facilities. Syðri Hagi also has a rowing boat available to guests. Ytri-vík hires both rowing boats and sailboards.

HRÍSEY

This low-lying island in Eyjafjörður is about 7 km long and 2½ km wide. It's the second largest island off the Icelandic coast and has a population of around 300.

Its beaches are backed in places by low sea cliffs and caves and the bush areas have reverted to a natural state, untouched by wandering sheep for the past few years.

The tourist literature makes a lot of fuss about Hrísey being an ideal spot for viewing the midnight sun in midsummer. Unfortunately, the best vantage points are off limits. Much of the island north of the village is tied up in a privately owned sanctuary for ptarmigan and eider duck; visitors are forbidden to leave the road or the nature track without permission. I've heard that such permission isn't easy to get but those who want to have a go can get the owner's name and number at the front desk of the Hotel Brekka in the village.

Those who want to see the real midnight sun – all of Eyjafjörður is south of the Arctic Circle so the sun actually does set when viewed from sea level – should climb Ólafsfjarðarmúli near Ólafsfjörður. There you can get high enough to see beyond the Arctic Circle and not experience any sunset in midsummer.

Places to Stay
The *Hotel Brekka* (tel 96-61751) is a very popular spot during the summer but it's rather expensive. Sleeping-bag accommodation can be found at the school and should be booked in advance through the hotel which also hires out bicycles for around US$15 per day. Campers are obliged to stay at the official camping site beside the bank in the village.

Places to Eat
The Hotel Brekka's licensed dining room offers 'Galloway Beef' as its specialty. Originally imported from Scotland, the beef is now raised in Iceland only on Hrísey. Those who'd rather not lay out a fortune for gourmet cow, however, will have to resort to the supermarket.

Getting There & Away
During the summer, the *Saevar* ferry departs Hrísey daily at 9 am and 1, 4, 6, and 10 pm; it returns from the mainland a half an hour after each departure.

Buses from Akureyri arrive at the ferry terminal at 11.35 am and 6.20 pm on weekdays only. They leave for Akureyri at 9.20 am and 2.50 pm, also on weekdays only.

There's a lot of traffic along the road from Akureyri so it's really no problem to hitch at least between the city and the Lítla Árskógssandur turn-off.

Midnight Sun Tour
During the summer, BSÍ offers a tour around Eyjafjörður on Mondays, Wednesdays, and Fridays which departs Akureyri at 7 pm. It includes a quick tour around the city, then visits Hrísey for dinner at the Hotel Brekka (dinner isn't included in the price of the tour). You continue on to Dalvík and Ólafsfjörður, reaching Ólafsfjarðarmúli in time to view the 'non-sunset'. With a bus pass or a student card, the tour costs US$41; otherwise, it's US$46.

ÖXNADALUR
The most impressive natural scenery along the Ring Road between Reykjavík and Akureyri is along Öxnadalur at the base of the Tröllskagi, a deep and narrow valley through which the road passes for over 30 km. The highest point along this road is 540 metres. The whole area is excellent mountaineering country and the weather is as fine as you're likely to encounter anywhere in the Icelandic mountains.

Hraundrangi
The imposing and 1075-metre-high spire of Hraundrangi and surrounding peaks of Háafjall are the most dramatic in Iceland. Early settlers considered the summit of Hraundrangi inaccessible and perpetuated legends of a hidden cache of gold that awaited the first climber to reach the top. It was finally climbed in 1956 but the treasure seemed to have gone missing sometime before that.

Steinsstaðir
Across from this farm, within view of Hraundrangi, is a view disc which identifies some of the rugged features of the surrounding ranges.

Baegisá
The beautiful valley of Baegisá is accessible up the valley between the farms Ytri-Baegisá and Syðri-Baegisá. At the head of the valley is the 'remnant' glacier Baegisájökull surrounded by high peaks and steep rock walls. This area is ideal for more technical mountaineering but casual hikers and trekkers can also enjoy most of it.

Vindheimaöxl

East of the road above the farm Neðri-Vindheimar is the steep and rocky ridge of Vindheimaöxl, above which is the tiny remnant of the glacier Vindheimajökull. There's lots of loose scree making for slow-going in places. Although it's more easily reached by going up past the ski area in Akureyri, climbers may prefer to take the much steeper and more challenging route from the west.

Barkárdalur

A pleasant wilderness trekking trip takes off westward from the Ring Road at the farm Ytri-Baegisá. From there, it's a fairly short walk across the river Hörgá. Pass the first road on your left and take the second, a small track which leads up into the valley Barkárdalur 5 km to Lambi hut. A further climb up the ridge from there will take you to Tungnahrygg hut in the second largest glacial area in northern Iceland. For alternative routes back, see Heljardalsheið in the previous Dalvík section.

Lambi hut has six bunks and an oil stove but Tungnahrygg, with 12 bunks, is little more than a shelter.

GRENIVÍK

This tiny village of 300 didn't get started until 1910. It grew to 20 families by 1935, and the population has gained steadily since a harbour and a fish-freezing plant were opened. For tourists, the village has a supermarket, a camping site, and a petrol station.

The main reason for visiting Grenivík would be to participate in one of the Pólar Hestar horse tours from the farm Grýtubakki II (tel 96-33179) over the mountains to the Fjörður area at the northern end of the peninsula, deserted since WW II. These 3-day treks depart every weekend during July and early August. They're popular and should be booked in advance. For further information, contact Pólar Hestar, Grýtubakka II, Grenivík.

There are no public buses between Akureyri and Grenivík. Take the lake Mývatn or Egilsstaðir bus to the intersection of the Ring Road and Route 83, then hitch. From there, it's 22 km north to the village.

Laufás

One of the more unkempt of Iceland's farmhouse museums Laufás, south of Grenivík, is only worthwhile if you're already in the area. It originally served as an elite manor farm and vicarage. The turf farmhouse there dates back to 1850 and contains the usual household and agricultural implements used by the gentry during that period and earlier. The church was built in 1865. During the summer, the museum is open from 10 am to 6 pm daily except Mondays.

There is no public transport to Laufás so you'll either have to take a tour (see the Akureyri Travel Bureau or the tourist office for a list of those available) or hop on the eastbound BSÍ service toward Mývatn and get off at the intersection of the Ring Road and Route 83 on the eastern shore of Eyjafjörður then walk or hitch the 10 km north to the site.

Svalbarðseyri

This is a small settlement only 11 km by road from Akureyri on the eastern shore of Eyjafjörður. It's little more than a tiny harbour, a petrol station, swimming pool and the Smáaratún Guesthouse (tel 96-25043). Singles/doubles here cost US$24/41.50. They also have a small snack bar and kiosk.

GOÐAFOSS

One of Iceland's most notable and easily accessible waterfalls is Goðafoss (the 'waterfall of the gods'). It was formed by the glacial waters of the Skjálfandafljót river cutting through the 8000-year-old Bárðardalur lava field from the Trölladyngja crater near Vatnajökull far to the south.

The falls' romantic name wasn't derived from any reference to aesthetics. After meditating for 24 hours on the issue of a national religion, Þorgeir (the lögsögumaður of the Alþing) declared publicly that Iceland would thenceforth be a Christian nation and would forbid the open practice of paganism. On his way home to Ljósavatn, he passed the familiar horseshoe-shaped waterfall near his farm Djúpá ('deep river') and tossed into it all his carvings of the Norse gods, thus bestowing its name.

Most of the buses passing Goðafoss, including the tour buses, stop at the Fosshóll petrol station for a 10-minute break, allowing enough time for travellers to snap a photo or two before moving on. Those who'd like to spend some time contemplating or exploring will have to catch a later bus onward. It's possible to camp at the site but, apart from the petrol station, there aren't any formal facilities.

Stórutjarnir

The name of this Edda hotel (tel 96-43221), 9 km west of Goðafoss, means 'big pond' – presumably it was named after the lake Ljósavatn. It's situated near scenic birch woods and is only a short walk from the lake. The outdoor pool is geothermally heated. Singles/doubles here cost US$45/58, and sleeping-bag accommodation is US$12 per person. There's a licensed restaurant but no inexpensive place to eat so sleeping baggers would be wise to bring their own food and stoves.

Vaglaskógur

Just south of the Ring Road midway between Akureyri and Goðafoss is Vaglaskógur, a 300 hectare area of birch woods up to 13 metres high. This would be notable only in Iceland, of course, but for those craving some interaction with real trees may enjoy spending a night or so in the camping site here on the eastern side of the river Fnjóská. To get there, get off the Akureyri to Mývatn bus at the intersection of the Ring Road and Route 832 then walk southward to Route 836, a total distance of about 3 km.

GRIMSEY

The northern part of the island Grímsey constitutes Iceland's only bit of territory north of the Arctic Circle. For this reason, it has become a 'been-there-done-that' sort of tourist destination. The island lies 41 km north of the mainland and the only real interest that could be inspired by the place is in its extensive bird colony which is said to be home to at least 60 different species. The island's one human settlement has a population of just 104.

Historically, it has been known as the home of the most avid chess players in Iceland and many a poor performance at this sacred pastime has resulted in the blunderer flinging himself into the sea. On Grímsey, a failure in chess was a failure in life.

The island is also known for its rather unconventional American benefactor, Daniel Willard Fiske, who set himself up as its protector after hearing about its passion for the game of chess. During the late 1870s, he sent badly needed firewood (as well as chess supplies!) to the remote island, financed its tiny library, and bequeathed part of his estate to this forgotten Arctic island without ever visiting it. For the complete story, which is quite amusing, read Lawrence Millman's account of a visit to the island in his book *Last Places – A Journey in the North*.

Places to Stay

Camping is possible nearly anywhere away from the village and sleeping-bag accommodation can be arranged in the community centre if you phone in advance (tel 96-73111).

Getting There & Away

Access to Grímsey is by air. The airline Flugfélag Norðurlands operates flights from Akureyri at 8.15 pm on Tuesdays, Thursdays, and Sundays and returns at 10 pm. Other days, flights depart Akureyri at 10 am and return at 11 am. All these flights connect with Flugleiðir services to and from Reykjavík. The evening trips cost US$90. They include a midnight-sun tour of the island and a certificate stating that you've crossed the Arctic Circle which bisects the Grímsey airfield. Omnibuspass holders pay only US$80. It's no problem to leave the tour on the island and return to Akureyri on another day.

UPPER EYJAFJÖRÐUR

Möðruvellir

North of the Hörgá is the large farm Möðruvellir. It was the site of an early monastery founded in 1296 and the birthplace of the author Jón Sveinsson, subject of the Nonnahús museum in Akureyri. The current church at Möðruvellir was built in 1868.

Gaesir

A former trading post, Gaesir lies on the fjord side of Route 816 south of the estuary of the river Hörgá. It was once the largest port in northern Iceland and dates back to the Saga Age. Some protected ruins remain on the site including the foundation of a medieval church, a graveyard, and some grass-covered outlines where port trading offices once stood. To get there, head north from Akureyri along the Ring Road, turn east on Route 816, 6 km from town, and then continue another 5.5 km to the site. It's manageable as a daywalk from the Lónsá youth hostel but it may be more pleasant to hitch than to walk along the road.

Hrafnagil

Just 12 km south of Akureyri is Hrafnagil, or 'ravens ravine', the home of Bishop Jón Arason of Hólar. Today, there's an Edda hotel (tel 96-31136), a cafe, greenhouse, and a summer camping site. Doubles cost US$58. No sleeping-bag space is available here but the camping facilities are good, an option for those who prefer more serenity than the Akureyri camping ground can offer. There is, of course, a geothermally heated pool at the hotel.

Grund

The church at Grund was built by the farmer Magnús Sigurðsson in 1905. Its Romanesque style seems out of place in Iceland but, earlier in this century, it was one of the most impressive churches in the country. If you want to have a look inside, ask for a key at the farmhouse.

Leyningshólar

Leyningshólar is a cluster of hillocks and moraines formed by ancient landslides dating back 7500 years. They provide nice camping sites but no facilities are available so campers should be self-sufficient. The hills are marginally interesting to walk around especially when you combine them with the surrounding native birch woods, the only original stand in the Eyjafjörður area.

Saurbaer

The Saurbaer farm, 27 km south of Akureyri along Route 821, has an interesting old turf and stone church (built in 1838) which is now under national protection.

Kristnes

Kristnes, 7 km south of Akureyri, was the original Eyjafjörður settlement. At Pollurinn (the 'puddle') near the head of the fjord, Helgi the Lean found his high-seat temple pillars washed ashore and looked after all possibilites by naming his farm after Jesus Christ. The hospital on the site today was the first large public building in Iceland to be geothermally heated.

Torfufell

The farm Torfufell (tel 96-31296) at the head of Eyjafjörður 42 km south of Akureyri has private rooms, sleeping-bag accommodation, and cooking facilities. You'll find good walking in the area, including the trip up Torfufell and a hike along the track up the canyon of Torfufellsá.

Getting There & Away

There is no public transport into upper Eyjafjörður except for the Sprengisandur tours between Reykjavík and Akureyri. They leave Reykjavík on Mondays and Thursdays at 8 am in July and August. They don't do the route southbound so the only access from Akureyri is by hitching or private vehicle.

North-East Iceland

Beyond Mývatn and Jökulsárgljúfur National Park, the north-eastern corner of Iceland is rarely visited. Here the Ring Road takes a short-cut across the interior desert missing a large area of practically uninhabited upland moors, wild coastal country, and barren desert. In fact, more tourists visit the empty interior of Iceland than venture up to Raufarhöfn or the Langanes peninsula. There are few facilities for tourists, traffic is scarce away from the Ring Road, and public transport even scarcer. If you venture off the beaten track here, allow some time for 'hoofing it' or being delayed in out-of-the-way places.

On the other end of the spectrum, lake Mývatn is considered one of the natural wonders of the world. It's a highlight of any trip to Iceland and most visitors wish they'd allowed it more time. As Icelandic tourism grows and more people discover Mývatn, the available facilities are being strained beyond capacity.

Newly popular is tongue-stifling Jökulsárgljúfur National Park. Here is Iceland's 'Grand Canyon', the Jökulsá á Fjöllum, and its myriad waterfalls. Other attractions include the basalt sculptures of Vesturdalur and the impressive cliffs of Ásbyrgi. It has only recently been 'discovered' but before long, it may catch up with Mývatn in popularity.

HÚSAVÍK

With a population of over 2500, Húsavík is the main town of north-east Iceland. Its setting beside a good harbour and beneath snow-capped peaks is quite picturesque but it's the sort of place that could win a contest for the most 'typical' Icelandic town. Fishing and fish processing are Húsavík's primary activities. The numerous fish-drying racks, just south of town, and the wheels of dried fish at the harbour make interesting subjects for photos.

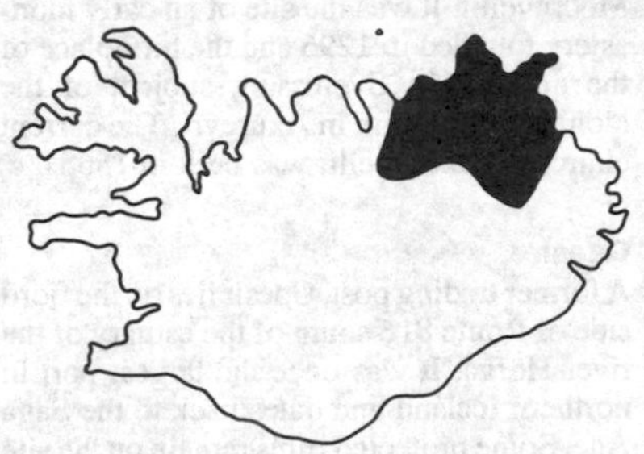

History

Although the honours normally go to Reykjavík and Ingólfur Arnarson, Húsavík was the site of the first Nordic settlement in Iceland. A Swedish Viking, Garðar Svavarsson, who set off in around 850 bound for mysterious Thule or Snaeland ('snowland'), was actually responsible for Iceland's first permanent human settlement.

After a brief stop at Hornafjörður in the south he arrived at Skjálfandi ('shivering gulf') on the north coast and built a settlement which he called Húsavík or 'bay of houses'. Modestly renaming the country Garðarshólmur ('Garðar's island'), he dug in for the winter. When spring arrived, he prepared to depart but some of his slaves were left behind. These castaways were actually the first permanent settlers on the island but history hasn't given them credit because their 'settling' was probably unintentional.

Húsavík's history as a mercantile centre and Iceland's primary sulphur exporting port goes back a long way. The historic general store of the Kaupfélag Þingeyinga cooperative, one of the first in Iceland, still stands on the main street. Despite this town's early roots and economic importance, it only received municipal status in 1950.

The curious grass-roofed housing complex in the centre is a free retirement community for Icelandic senior citizens.

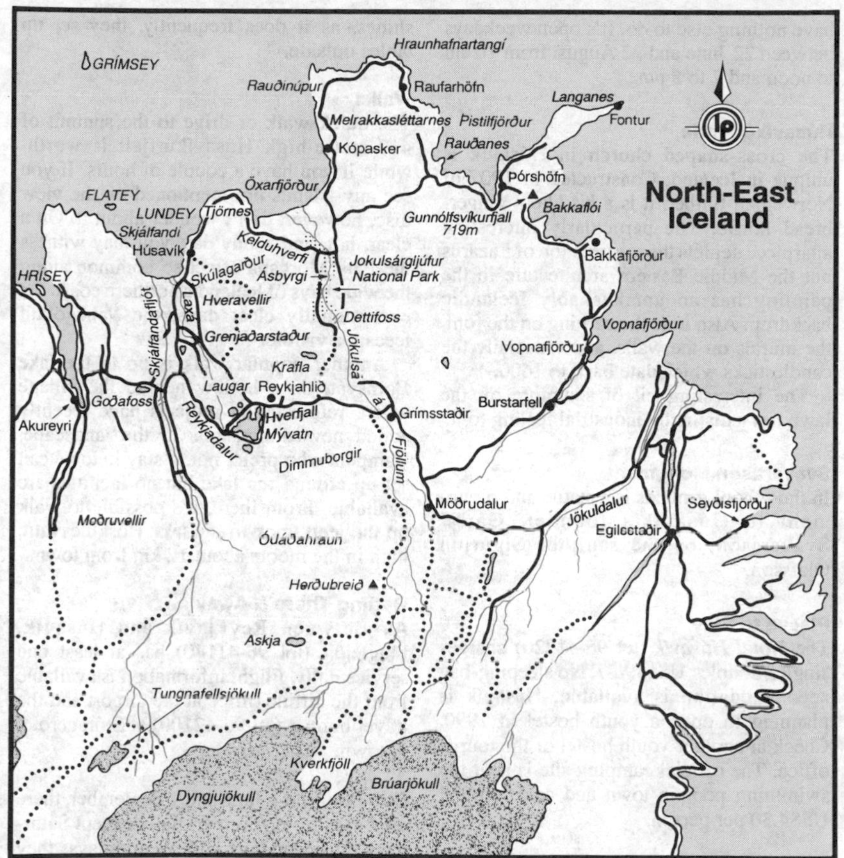

Information

Húsavík has a swimming pool, a golf course, a car rental service, a hotel, restaurants, banks, and a camping site. There are also two ski lifts north-east of town which operate through the long winter. Camping equipment is available at the Kaupfélag cooperative. The bookshop opposite the church has souvenir books and novels in both German and English.

Safnahúsið

The Safnahúsið (village museum) was founded in 1980. It has a combination folk, art, and natural-history exhibition containing a wealth of photographs, paintings, and books including a copy of a Bible printed in 1584. Other paraphernalia includes numerous 16th-century weapons, dried plants, stuffed birds and animals, and a large collection of Icelandic minerals. The town's pride and joy, however, is the stuffed polar bear which was welcomed to Grímsey in 1969 by a bullet in the head – such humiliation after a long cruise from Greenland on an iceberg.

Admission to the museum costs US$1.50 but it's not all that interesting unless you have nothing else to do. It's open weekdays between 22 June and 22 August from 10 am to noon and 2 to 5 pm.

Húsavíkurkirkja

The cross-shaped church in Húsavík is unique in Iceland. Constructed in 1907 of Norwegian timber, it is a bit like a gingerbread house. The particularly interesting altarpiece depicts the resurrection of Lazarus but the Middle Eastern architecture in the painting has an unmistakably Icelandic backdrop. Also note the carving on the font, the murals on the walls, and especially the candlesticks which date back to 1600.

The interesting bit of sculpture on the lawn has a distinctly industrial feeling to it.

Svavarsson Monument

In the school grounds is a statue and monument to Húsavík's founder, Garðar Svavarsson, by the sculptor Sigurjón Ólafsson.

Places to Stay

The *Hotel Húsavík* (tel 96-41220) charges singles/doubles US$59/87. No sleeping-bag accommodation is available. Húsavík is planning to open a youth hostel in 1990. Check at another youth hostel or the tourist office. The official camping site is near the swimming pool in town and costs around US$4.30 per person.

Places to Eat

The hotel restaurant and the pleasant *Bakinn* are predictably expensive but self-catering will be a joy in Húsavík, anyway. In addition to the cooperative supermarket, there's a fresh-fish market at the harbour. Locally grown vegies and some of the cheapest hardfiskur in Iceland are available at the flea market across from the church. You'll find greenhouses selling local produce 18 km down the road in Hveravellir.

Both the *Esso* and the *Shell* petrol stations have snack bars and coffee shops selling ice cream, sausages, burgers, sandwiches, cakes, coffee, and pizza. When the sun shines, as it does frequently, they set up tables outside.

Walks

The quick walk or drive to the summit of 417-metre-high Húsavíkurfjall is worthwhile if you have a couple of hours. If you see any islands not mentioned on the view disc, however, don't wonder about it. On a clear, hot, and sunny day, you may witness the Fata Morgana effect so common along the wide bays of Iceland's northern coast. On exceptionally clear days, the Vatnajökull icecap is visible.

Another popular walk is up to the lake Botnsvatn in a hollow behind the village where reforestation projects have recently added new dimensions to the landscape. Campers who prefer not to stay in town can set up around the lake but no facilities are available. From there, it's possible to walk up the jeep track to the lake Höskuldsvatn, high in the moors about 12 km from town.

Getting There & Away

Air Between Reykjavík and Húsavík, Flugleiðir (tel 96-41140) has at least one service daily. Flight information is available from the airline office at the airport and the travel bureau (tel 96-42100) at Stóragerði 7 in town.

Bus Between 1 June and 1 September, there are buses from Akureyri daily except Saturdays. On Mondays and Wednesdays, they connect with an onward bus to Ásbyrgi, Raufarhöfn, and Vopnafjörður. An Akureyri bus leaves at 8 am Mondays, Wednesdays, and Fridays, at 1.15 pm on Tuesdays and Thursdays, and at 7 pm on Sundays.

From Vopnafjörður, the bus leaves for Húsavík at 8 am on Tuesdays and Thursdays. There are two or three departures daily to Mývatn but be warned that some of them are tours and will cost more than the regularly scheduled services.

Tours

If you're headed into the nether lands between Húsavík and Vopnafjörður, but still want to quickly 'do' the tourist sights, Húsavík would provide an ideal base. Otherwise, it would be better to use Mývatn as a staging point.

On Tuesdays and Thursdays, there are BSÍ tours to Tjörnes, Jökulsárgljúfur National Park, and Dettifoss for US$54.50 (US$50 with Omnibuspass). In July and August, 3-day tours to faraway Kverkfjöll ice cave in the Vatnajökull icecap depart Fridays at noon and cost US$170 (without food) or US$153 with Omnibuspass. Accommodation is in huts or tents so participants must provide their own warm sleeping bag.

The trip to Vopnafjörður is regarded as a tour in the brochures but no guide is provided and it's actually a scheduled service covered by Omnibuspass. Otherwise, the fare is US$39 each way.

Lundey & Flatey

The two small islands of Lundey and Flatey are in Skjálfandi near Húsavík. Lundey, the 'puffin island' is a breeding ground for puffins, fulmars, and other species of sea birds. It rises dramatically from the sea in a series of high nest-covered cliffs.

Flatey or 'flat island' lives up to its name, rising only a couple of metres above sea level. As recently as 1942 it had a population of over 100 but is now abandoned. To arrange boat trips to the islands or around Skjálfandi, contact Húsavík Travel (tel 96-42100) at Stóragerði 7.

Tjörnes

The stubby peninsula Tjörnes, north of Húsavík, divides Skjálfandi from Öxarfjörður. On the 50-metre cliffs along the east coast are puffins and other sea birds' colonies. Near the northern end is a lighthouse where clear weather allows a good view of Grímsey island on the Arctic Circle.

From the farm Syðritunga an old 20-km-long track crosses the mountains and moors of the Tjörnes' interior to Fjöll on Öxarfjörður. This can be walked in a long day but it's more pleasantly spread over 2 days.

Ytritunga From the farm Ytritunga, a track leads down to the sea. In the cliffs on either side of the Hallbjarnarstaðaá river mouth you'll find alternating layers of fossil shells and lignite. The oldest layers, which were laid down about 2 million years ago, are about 12 metres above sea level. The current water temperature along Iceland's Arctic coast is about 4°C. The creatures that inhabited the shells are now found only in waters 12°C or warmer in mainland Europe, an indication that the sea has cooled over the past 2 to 3 million years. The newer layers at Ytritunga contain fossil shells of cold-water molluscs still living around Iceland.

Mánáreyjar Háey and Lágey, two small islands 10 km off the north coast of Tjörnes are called Mánáreyjar or 'moon river islands'. They are remnants of old volcanic plugs.

KELDUHVERFI

Like Þingvellir, low-lying Kelduhverfi reveals some of the best visible evidence that Iceland is spreading from the centre. Beside the drowned estuary of the Jökulsá á Fjöllum, the North Atlantic Ridge enters the Arctic Ocean in a series of odd cracks, fissures, and grabens up to 6 or 7 metres deep. Most of those visible today were formed by earthquakes during Krafla eruption of 1977 which caused dramatic fissuring and subsidence. Locals were literally rattled but most of them were happy to find that their farms had actually increased in size overnight.

Kelduhverfi Lakes North of the highway at Kelduhverfi is the estuarine lake, Víkingavatn. The nearby farm of the same name has been occupied by the descendants of the original farmer for nearly 4 centuries. Between Víkingavatn and Lón, the lagoon to the west, is a large and interesting tree. Anything to do with a large tree would be notable in Iceland but this one appears to be devouring a house. It's worth a glance as you pass, anyway.

East of Víkingavatn is Skjálftavatn, a new

lake formed by surface subsidence, which hasn't yet made it onto most maps. It is currently used for freshwater fish-farming. Continued spreading may someday result in the entire area being flooded with seawater, similar to the process taking place in Ethiopia where Africa's Great Rift enters the Red Sea.

Places to Stay

Two farms, *Hóll* (tel 96-52270) and *Skúlagarður* (tel 96-52280) offer farmhouse accommodation and horse rentals. The former rents rooms on a weekly basis while the latter is actually an informal youth hostel set up in a school. Meals are sold but there are no cooking facilities. Both are on Route 85 but Hóll is closer to Ásbyrgi and the national park.

REYKJADALUR

The Laxá and Skjálfandafljót valleys, south of Húsavík, are gentle and grassy separated by green moors which belie the area's significant geothermal value. Reykjadalur ('smoky valley') is actually only one of several parallel valleys separated by low and non-descript hills.

Aðaldalshraun

The distinctive birch and scrub-covered lava field Aðaldalshraun covers an area of nearly 100 sq km. Near the farm Knútsstaðir, between Route 85 and the river Laxá, are some strange caves and hollow hills formed when steam lifted the surface of the lava into bubbles that hardened before breaking. The driver of the bus from Húsavík to Akureyri will tell you where to get off if you'd like to have a look at them.

Hveravellir

The source of part of Húsavík's hot water supply, Hveravellir, is a very active geothermal site. At the farm are three geysers, the most active of which, Ystihver, is just 300 metres east of the road. It spouts up to three metres every 2 or 3 minutes. The farm sells fresh vegies from its geothermally heated greenhouses. All buses travelling between Mývatn and Húsavík pass it and the Jökulsárgljúfur tours from Mývatn also spend a few minutes at the geyser.

Laugar

This Laugar or 'hot springs', north-east of the Ring Road on Route 846, is often referred to as Laugar í Þingeyjarsýsla to distinguish it from the numerous other 'Laugars' in Iceland. The school there operates as the Hotel Laugar (tel 96-43120) during the summer. It was built in 1924 and the following year received Iceland's first indoor swimming pool.

Singles/doubles cost US$45/58. Other facilities include a snack bar, a kiosk, a petrol station, and a camping site. All the buses from Akureyri to Mývatn pass within 1 km of the hotel and will drop you at the intersection.

Grenjaðarstaður

This wealthy old farm beside the Laxá served as a church and vicarage during the last century but the graveyard contains a stone with runes dating back to medieval times. The turf farmhouse, which was constructed in 1876, now houses a low-profile folk museum which is open daily from 1 June to 31 August from 10 am to 6 pm. It's difficult to reach on public transport, however, and you may not deem it worth the effort it would take to get there. If you'd like to try anyway, get off the Húsavík to Mývatn bus at the intersection of Routes 87 and 853. Walk 2 km west, turn left on Route 854, and walk the remaining 3 km to the farm.

Þverá

The stone church at Þverá was dates back to 1878. The turf farmhouse was the original home of Iceland's first cooperative organisation, Kaupfélag Þingeyinga, founded in 1882. Þverá now belongs to the National Museum in Reykjavík and may be opened for display in the future.

It's at the confluence of the Laxá and Þverá rivers, 7 km up-valley from the Laxá bridge, on Route 856.

Places to Stay

Two farms in Reykjadalur, *Bláhvammur* (tel 96-43901) and *Hraunbaer* (tel 96-43595) provide farmhouse accommodation but neither offers sleeping-bag space. The former has cooking facilities, a geothermal pool, and a geyser-heated sauna which is quite a novelty.

JÖKULSÁRGLJÚFUR NATIONAL PARK

The nearly unpronounceable name (try 'YEW-kl-sour-GLYU-fr') of this impressive new national park means 'glacial river canyon'. The name belies the fact that within its borders are other varied and wonderful natural features.

Jökulsárglúfur is sometimes called 'Iceland's Grand Canyon' in tourist literature, perhaps in order to lure visitors with a sense of the familiar, but the park is also known for its diverse birch forests, unusual rock formations, and Ásbyrgi, the impressive result of a natural catastrophe 200 km away. Just outside the park boundaries is Dettifoss, Europe's largest waterfall, known predictably as the 'Niagara of Europe'. You won't, however, find any kitsch wax museums or coloured floodlights at this one – just nature at its finest.

The heart of the park is the 25-km-long Jökulsárgljúfur which averages 100 metres deep and 500 metres wide. In the uppermost reaches of the canyon is a series of waterfalls which includes Selfoss, Dettifoss, Hafragilsfoss, Réttarfoss, and Vígabjargsfoss. The last, which just about disappeared when the Jökulsá á Fjöllum changed course in 1940, is in the luxuriant Hólmatungur region. Further north is Vesturdalur with lots of caves and some of the most unusual and interesting basalt formations in Iceland. Near the northern end of the park is Ásbyrgi, a verdant forested plain enclosed in ruddy canyon walls. The northernmost thumb of the park, Landgraeðslusvaeði, is part of the Jökulsá á Fjöllum's alluvial delta.

History

Most of the land now protected within the park belonged historically to the Ás estate,

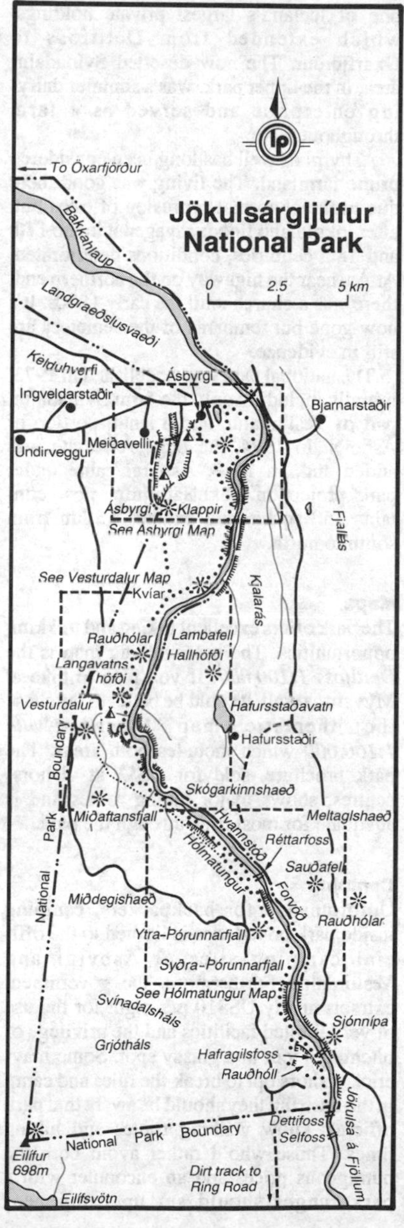

one of Iceland's largest private holdings, which extended from Dettifoss to Öxarfjörður. The now deserted Svínadalur area, in the upper park, was a summer dairying enterprise and served as a farm throughout 1946.

Ásbyrgi as well has long been considered prime farmland. The living was good there due to the abnormal profusion of trees but, after jökulhlaup floods ravaged it in the 17th and 18th centuries, conditions deteriorated. At Ás, near the highway on the northern end, there was a church until the early 1800s. It's now gone but remnants of the cemetery are still in evidence.

The national park was established in 1973, initially including only the farm Svínadalur, part of Vesturdalur, and a small portion of Ásheiði. In 1974, the huge Ás estate was added and, in 1978, Ásbyrgi came under park protection. Jökulsárgljúfur now contains 150 sq km and extends 35 km from south to north.

Maps

The park offers excellent hiking and trekking opportunities. The best walking map is the *Dettifoss 1:100,000*. If you plan to hike at Mývatn as well, it could be better to purchase the thematic map *Húsavík-Mývatn 1:100,000* which includes both areas. The park brochure, sold for US$1 at visitors' centres, shows major hiking routes and is adequate for most trips through the park.

Camping

Unfortunately for backpackers, camping inside park boundaries is limited to the official camping sites at Ásbyrgi and Vesturdalur. Furthermore, the government extracts nearly US$10 per night for the use of very limited facilities and the privilege of pitching a tent in a grassy spot. Some maverick visitors opt to break the rules and camp in the bush but they should be aware that park officials know walking routes and hiking times. Those who'd rather avoid both the outrageous prices and an encounter with a park ranger should set up camp near Dettifoss or elsewhere outside park boundaries.

Jökulsá á Fjöllum

The second longest river in Iceland, the Jökulsá á Fjöllum ('glacial river of the mountains') starts in the Vatnajökull icecap and flows 206 km to the Arctic Ocean at Öxarfjörður. Its 30-km long canyon through Jökulsárgljúfur National Park was formed by numerous jökulhlaups – a minor one on an average of every 10 years and a major one once or twice a century.

Ásbyrgi

Just south of the highway Route 85 is the lush horseshoe-shaped canyon of Ásbyrgi. It extends 3.5 km from north to south and averages about 1 km in width and 100 metres in depth at its southern extremity. Near the centre of the canyon is the protruding outcrop Eyjan whose name appropriately means 'island'.

There are two stories about the creation of Ásbyrgi. The early Norse settlers believed that Óðinn's normally airborne horse, Slaettur, accidentally touched down on earth

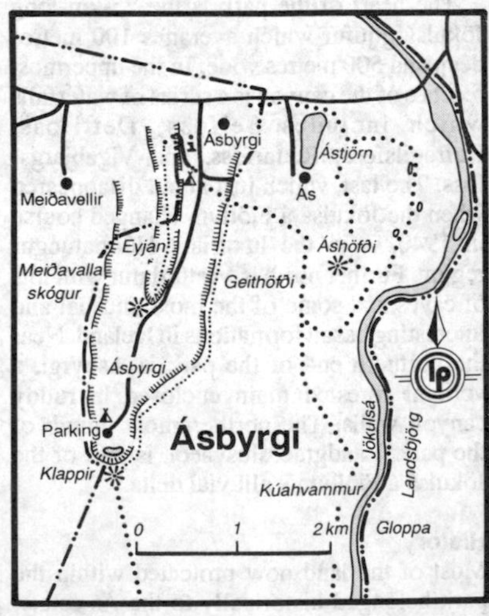

and left one hell of a hoofprint to prove it. Once you've seen Ásbyrgi, it's not difficult to imagine how this explanation surfaced.

The other theory, though more scientific, is equally incredible. Geologists believe that the canyon was created apocalyptically by an eruption of the Grímsvötn caldera beneath distant Vatnajökull. It released an immense jökulhlaup which ploughed northward down the Jökulsá á Fjöllum and gouged out the canyon in a matter of 2 days or less. After flowing through Ásbyrgi for 100 years or so, the river shifted eastward to its present course. There is evidence that sometime during its history, Ásbyrgi was flooded with sea water.

Thanks to being protected from sheep and the windbreak provided by the canyon walls, the vegetation of Ásbyrgi is profuse. The canyon is forested with birch trees up to about 8 metres in height.

From the parking lot, at the end of the road, you'll find several short walks. The eastern one leads to a spring near the canyon wall, the western one climbs to a good view across the valley floor, and the one leading straight ahead ends at a small lake at the head of Ásbyrgi.

Those with more time can climb to the summit of Eyjan or ascend the cliffs at Tófugjá. From there, a loop track leads around Áshöfði past the gorges. Alternatively, follow the rim right around to Klappir, above the canyon head, from where it's possible to continue southward to Kvíar and return via the river. For a longer trip, carry camping supplies and continue from Klappir to Vesturdalur (4 hours), Hólmatungur, and Dettifoss in 2 days, camping at the Vesturdalur site.

Places to Eat The snack bar, supermarket, and petrol station at the Ásbyrgi farmstead on Route 85 is really the only place to purchase supplies. It's 1 km from the main camping ground at the mouth of the canyon.

Camping Ásbyrgi has camping grounds near the mouth of the canyon and at the upper end. The latter is nicer as far as vegetation goes but the one nearer the main highway has a tourist information centre and is closer to long-distance trailheads and facilities at the Ásbyrgi farmstead.

Vesturdalur

The diversity of the Vesturdalur ('west valley') area makes it one of Iceland's nicest off-the-beaten-track attractions. The bushy scrub and grassy lawns around the camping site give way to the cave-riddled pinnacles and rock formations of Hljóðaklettar. In addition, you get the Rauðhólar crater row, the ponds of Eyjan (not to be confused with the Eyjan at Ásbyrgi), and the canyon itself.

Numerous tracks crisscross the area and you could spend several days exploring and absorbing the natural surroundings. Vesturdalur's appeal can be especially frustrating to those who visit, as most people do, on a day-tour from Húsavík or Mývatn. Although the tours provide the only public transport into this relatively remote site, they allow only about 45 minutes of breathless elbow-to-elbow sightseeing. For information on the tours, see the following Getting There & Away section.

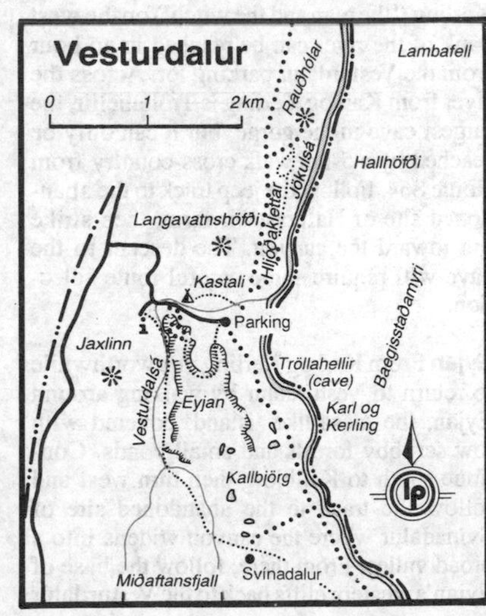

Hljóðaklettar The swirls, spirals, rosettes, honeycombs, and columns in the Hljóðaklettar ('echo rocks') basalt formations are unique in the world. It's a surprising place and well worth the effort of visiting. The Vesturdalur parking area is surrounded by intriguing patterns but the best formations are found north-east of the parking area along the river.

It's difficult to imagine what sort of volcanic activity produced Hljóðaklettar. Polygonal basalt columns are normally formed in instantaneously cooled lava perpendicular to direction of flow but there seems to be no rhyme or reason to these.

The formations are riddled with lava caves, as well. The largest, on the western side of the river, is in a pit about a 15-minute walk from the parking lot.

Rauðhólar The Rauðhólar or 'red hills' crater row, immediately north of Vesturdalur, spawned the Hljóðaklettar basalt. They can be explored on foot but they're a 2-hour return walk from the parking area so tour participants can't reach them in the allotted time.

Karl og Kerling The formation Karl og Kerling ('the man and the witch') on the west bank of the river can be reached in an hour from the Vesturdalur parking lot. Across the river from Karl og Kerling is Tröllahellir, the largest cave in the gorge, but it can only be reached by a 5-km walk cross-country from Route 864. Follow the jeep track to the abandoned site of Hafursstaðir farm, then strike out toward the canyon. The descent to the cave will require some careful route selection.

Eyjan From Karl og Kerling, it's worthwhile to return to Vesturdalur by walking around Eyjan, the mesa-like 'island' covered with low scrubby forests and small ponds. Continue south to Kallbjörg then turn west and follow the track to the abandoned site of Svínadalur where the canyon widens into a broad valley. From there, follow the base of Eyjan's western cliffs back to the Vesturdalur parking area. The entire circle will take about three hours but allow time for distracting side trips. Another shorter walk is from the camping area up onto the inviting Eyjan plateau which can be easily explored away from the established route.

Hólmatungur

The lush Hólmatungur area is a 3-hour walk south of Vesturdalur by hiking track but, since there are no overnight camping facilities there, it must be seen on a day-walk from either Vesturdalur or Dettifoss or you could have lunch there en route between the two.

The real attraction of the place is its peaceful greenery. At the mouth of the spring-fed Holmá the harsh lines of the canyon soften a bit and provide several nice waterfalls – Holmáfoss on the Holmá and Vígabjargsfoss and Réttarfoss on the Jökulsá á Fjöllum. A good view over Hólmatungur can be had from the hill Ytra-Þórunnarfjall 1 km south of the parking lot. Below Hólmatungur, halfway to Vesturdalur, is the Gloppa cave from which you can look at the river through a natural window in the cliff.

The Hólmatungur parking lot is a 4-hour

walk from Dettifoss. Hitching is very difficult into Hólmatungur and should probably be considered hopeless so the best access with is the Monday, Wednesday, and Friday tours from Mývatn which stop just long enough for a walk to Ytra-Þórunnarfjall.

Eilífur The 689-metre-high Eilífur peak at the south-western corner of the park is a móberg or what geologists would call an hyaloclastite mountain. It was formed when lava flowed into the glacier, melted a cavity inside it, and filled it with igneous material. When the glacier melted, the odd moulded mountain remained. This area can be explored on foot from the jeep track along the river's west bank but there is no road leading into it. Fresh water is available at lake Eilífsvötn, 2 km outside the park to the south.

Dettifoss Dettifoss, the largest waterfall in Europe, is a real power house. It's only 44 metres high, but 500 cubic metres of water per second send up a plume of spray which can be seen a km away and form brilliant double rainbows above the canyon. All the tours stop at Dettifoss for about an hour but it can probably be better appreciated without the resulting crowds. Since the falls aren't actually inside park boundaries, wilderness camping is possible almost anywhere in the vicinity.

The Monday, Wednesday, and Friday tours from Mývatn visit the western bank while tours on other days stop at the more heavily visited eastern bank. It's difficult to determine which is the better vantage point although most people who've seen the western bank cast a vote in its favour, probably because highway sightseers don't want to face the poor road leading to it.

Hafragilsfoss In one of the deepest parts of the canyon, 2 km downstream from Dettifoss, 27-metre-high Hafragilsfoss cuts through the Raudhólar crater row and exposes the volcanic dyke that formed it. There's a good view down the canyon from the small hill just north of the Hafragilsfoss parking area. On the canyon rim, east of the falls, are numerous red scoria cones and craters.

Selfoss Only 11 metres high, Selfoss is a broad but nevertheless impressive waterfall about 30 minutes walk upstream from Dettifoss. Since it's outside park boundaries and few visitors bother to walk up there, it would be a more private camping site than Dettifoss.

Getting There & Away

Day-tours to some of the sights in Jökulsárgljúfur operate from Húsavík twice weekly at 10 am and from Mývatn six times weekly. The tours which take in Dettifoss, Hafragilsfoss, Ásbyrgi, and Hljóðaklettar cost US$53 (US$47 with Omnibuspass) and are run by Jón Árni Sigfússon (tel 96-44196) at Reykjahlíð (Mývatn). The Eldá (tel 96-44220) tours, also from Reykjahlíð, visit the western side of Dettifoss and Hólmatungur in addition to the other sights and cost a bit more.

Besides the bus from Húsavík to Vopnafjörður, which passes Ásbyrgi, the tours provide the only public transport to the park. As usual participants may leave the tour at any time and rejoin later at another place provided arrangements are made in advance.

Hitching isn't recommended along the very lightly travelled road, north of the Ring Road 22 km west of Grímsstaðir. The worst scenario and probable outcome of such a venture would be a 20-km walk on the unsurfaced Dettifoss road before you could get onto the park trail system.

KOPASKER

This tiny village with 150 residents, on the eastern shore of Öxarfjörður, became an official international trading port in 1879. Today it's involved in agricultural trade and the shrimp industry. There's really not much to see in the immediate area of Kópasker but it's a point of entry into the wilds of Iceland's far north-east.

On 13 January 1976, Kópasker suffered a

severe earthquake which caused the damage and destruction of a number of buildings and cracked the wall of the harbour. Rockslides and fissuring were violent and evidence of the seismic activity can still be seen near Presthólar, about 5 km south of town.

Snartarstaðir

If you're in Kópasker anyway, it may be worthwhile to have a look at this early district assembly site and the church built in 1928, just east of Route 85 near the village. At the original schoolhouse there is a small county museum. To arrange a visit, make enquiries at the petrol station in town.

Places to Stay & Eat

The KNÞ cooperative has a grocery kiosk, a snack bar, and automobile services. Beside it there is an official camping site. Rooms or sleeping-bag accommodation may be arranged there as well.

Getting There & Away

Air From Akureyri you can fly to Kópasker at 12.15 pm on Mondays, Tuesdays, Thursdays, and Fridays. Flugleiðir flights return to Akureyri at 1 pm on the same days.

Bus Two buses run weekly in each direction between Húsavík and Vopnafjörður via Kópasker. Eastbound, they depart Húsavík at 6.15 pm on Mondays and Wednesdays and pass through the village at 7.45 pm. From Vopnafjörður, they leave at 8 am Tuesdays and Thursdays and arrive in Kópasker at 11 am.

Rauðinúpur

The Melrakkasléttarnes peninsula between Öxarfjörður and Þistilfjörður is characterised by low-lying flatlands, marshes, and many ponds. In its far north-western corner is extinct 73-metre-high crater Rauðinúpur and a cliff-girt headland occupied by nesting sea birds. A 5-km jeep track turns off to Rauðinúpur from the Húsavík to Vopnafjörður bus route, 18 km north of Kópasker. It's a remote and scarcely visited place which can only be reached on foot or in a private vehicle.

RAUFARHÖFN

It is believed that Raufarhöfn has been used as a port since the Saga Age and possibly has the finest harbour in north-east Iceland. This harbour is formed not by a sheltered bay or fjord but by the small Ásmundarstaða islands just offshore. The town's economic high point was during the herring fishing boom, early this century. The land surrounding this village of 450 people is flat and relatively uninteresting but the wide beaches nearby are covered with driftwood. Bird life is profuse.

Places to Stay & Eat

The *Hotel Norðurljós* (tel 96-51233) charges US$58 for a double room and does offer sleeping-bag accommodation when space permits. The new official camping site is beside the swimming pool. There is a restaurant at the hotel and a grocery kiosk in the village.

Getting There & Away

The Húsavík to Vopnafjörður bus passes through Raufarhöfn eastbound at 8.30 pm on Mondays and Wednesdays and westbound at 10.15 am Tuesdays and Thursdays.

The Flugleiðir flights between Reykjavík and Kópasker continue on to Raufarhöfn, arriving at 1.10 pm on Mondays, Tuesdays, Thursdays, and Fridays and return at 1.25 pm the same days.

Hraunhafnartangi

If the northernmost point of the Icelandic mainland Hraunhafnartangi were a few hundred metres further north, it would lie within the Arctic Circle and its novelty value would increase dramatically for tourists. Even so, it seems the Arctic Circle hype can't be avoided. Visitors staying at the Hotel Norðurljós, in nearby Raufarhöfn, who make it out there will receive a certificate stating they've at least approached the magic line.

Hraunhafnartangi is the site of a lonely lighthouse, a Saga-Age landing site, and the burial mound of saga character Þorgeir Hávarsson, who killed 14 enemies before being struck down in battle.

To get there, walk approximately 2 km north from Route 85 at lake Hraunhafnarvatn. It's possible to camp anywhere on this remote headland. The nearest formal accommodation is in Raufarhöfn, 12 km to the south-east.

Rauðanes

About midway between Raufarhöfn and Þórshöfn, a jeep track leads northward from Route 85, south of Viðarfjall, to scenic Rauðanes. This small peninsula is endowed with steep bird-cliffs full of caves, beautiful offshore sea stacks, and an exposed rock face called Stakkatorfa where a large part of the peninsula has collapsed into the sea. If you'd like to walk around or camp in this interesting area, walk about 4 km to the farm Vellir at the end of the jeep track. From there it's less than 2 km north-east to the cape.

LANGANES

Shaped like a goose with a very large head, the foggy Langanes peninsula is a remote, lonely corner of Iceland. The highway ends only 17 km along the 50-km-long peninsula. Access out to Fontur at the tip of the 'beak' is along a jeep track on foot or by private 4WD vehicle. Most of the peninsula is flat or undulating and rich in marshland and Arctic and alpine flora. The outermost coasts are characterised by sea cliffs up to 130 metres high. The southern extreme of Langanes is mountainous; the tallest peak is Gunnólfsvíkurfjall is over 700 metres high. There are lots of abandoned farms throughout the area.

Visitors seeking a quiet and remote place (far from the beaten tourist track) to camp, hike, and explore couldn't do better than Langanes. Drinking water is plentiful everywhere but there are no facilities beyond Þórshöfn so carry everything you'll need. Allow about a week to walk from Þórshöfn to Fontur and back, especially if you want to spend any time exploring away from the jeep track.

Þórshöfn

Although it's served as a busy port since Saga times, all of Þórshöfn's growth has occurred during the last century. It became a recognised trading site in 1846 but had no permanent residents until 1875. In the early 20th century a herring-salting station was established. Although the herring fishery has now all but disappeared, the village of 410 inhabitants remains reliant on fishing.

Places to Stay & Eat Þórshöfn is the best base to use if you're heading out to Langanes. There's a camping site just south of town and the *Hotel Jórvík* (tel 96-81149), at Langanesvegur 31, provides formal accommodation and meals. Snacks are available at the *Esso* station bus terminal.

Getting There & Away The bus from Húsavík to Vopnafjörður passes eastbound on Mondays and Wednesdays at 9.40 pm and westbound on Tuesdays and Thursdays at 9 am.

Brekknaheiði

The moors at the base of Langanes form a tundra plain of lakes, marshes, and low hills. It's pleasant and unchallenging walking country.

Fontur

The fogbound cliffs at the north-eastern tip of Langanes have long proved dangerous to passing ships. There's a lighthouse at the cape which dates back to 1910 and a monument to some shipwrecked English sailors who died of hypothermia after ascending the ravine there now called Engelskagjá or 'English gorge'.

Skoruvík

Along the bay Skoruvík between the head and the beak of Langanes is a major breeding ground of the peripatetic Arctic tern. There's a lighthouse and a beach below with lots of driftwood.

Skálabjarg

The Látrabjarg of the east, Skálabjarg is a

long and impressive bird cliff on the wild south coast of Langanes. Now little more than ruins, the abandoned farm of Skálar to the north-east of the cliff served as a fishing village at the turn of the century.

BAKKAFJÖRÐUR

A fishing settlement where a harbour is currently being constructed, Bakkafjörður, on the southern shore of Bakkaflói, is home to less than 150 people and offers only limited services for visitors. There is no designated camping site but camping is possible either at Skeggjastaðir church or near the river just above town. Groceries are available at the cooperative kiosk in the village.

Skeggjastaðir

The church at Skeggjastaðir estate farm, 6 km from Bakkafjörður, was originally built of wood in 1845 but has since been radically renovated. The pulpit was crafted in Denmark during the early 1700s. It is possible to camp at Skeggjastaðir and visit the church, both with permission of the proprietor. Just offshore, 1 km north-west of the farm, you'll find the unusual sea stack Stapi.

VOPNAFJÖRÐUR

Vopnafjörður can claim the dubious distinctions of being the hometown of a former Miss Universe and the site of some of Prince Charles' angling holidays. The current population of this fishing village and former trading centre on the Kolbeinstangi peninsula is around 930 and increasing. The setting is very nice with beautiful mountains and shores but attempts at promoting tourism are thwarted a bit because there's no bus through to Egilsstaðir. Visitors who arrive on public transport from Húsavík must backtrack along the meandering north coast route at least to Ásbyrgi before they can make connections to anywhere else.

Places to Stay & Eat

South of Vopnafjörður for 8 km on Route 917, travellers can find farmhouse accommodation with horse rentals, cooking facilities, and sleeping-bag space at *Syðri-Vík* (tel 97-31449). In town, the *Hotel Tangi* (tel 97-31224) offers both private rooms and sleeping-bag accommodation and sometimes hires motorboats for excursions on the fjord. There's a camping site in the village as well.

The only restaurant is the hotel dining room but there is a supermarket for self-catering.

Getting There & Away

As far as the bus lines are concerned, Vopnafjörður is a dead end. The bus from Húsavík arrives at 11 pm on Mondays and Wednesdays and returns to Húsavík at 8 am Tuesdays and Thursdays.

Flugleiðir has flights from Reykjavík to Vopnafjörður via Akureyri daily (except Saturdays) at 1 pm, returning at 4 pm. Flights from Egilsstaðir depart Mondays at 9.30 am and Thursdays and Fridays at 4.20 pm. They return on Tuesdays at 10.40 and Mondays, Thursdays, and Fridays at 5.30 pm. Most of the Egilsstaðir flights connect with other flights to or from Reykjavík.

Bustarfell

At the foot of the mountain Bustarfell, 23 km west of Vopnafjörður, lies the farm with the same name. The folk museum in its gabled turf-farmhouse, which dates back to the 18th century, is considered one of the finest in the country. To the west, the road climbs the mountain and passes two nice lakes on top of it. Across the highway from the first lake, Nykurvatn, is a view disc. There is no public transport to Bustarfell. Too bad because it is Vopnafjörður's only hope of attracting the tourist money it could obviously use. Visitors without private vehicles will have to hitch to and from town. The museum is open daily between 15 June and 1 September from 10 am to 7 pm.

NORTH-EAST DESERT

From Egilsstaðir, the Ring Road northward abandons the coastal area and takes a drastic short cut inland across the stark and empty highland deserts of the north-east interior . There's really not much to lure travellers off the Egilsstaðir to Mývatn bus but the loneliness can be an attraction in itself – an eerie and otherworldly place of endless vistas.

Those who aren't planning a trip into the interior can catch a glimpse of it here. The country is dotted with numerous small lakes, the result of melted snowfields (they're melted in the 'right' season, anyway), streams and rivers wander aimlessly and disappear into gravel beds, and sharp peaks skewer passing clouds. In places, the landscape is the dullest grey imaginable yet, in the spring, parts of it are spattered with clumps of tiny purple blooms which have somehow gained root in the gravelly volcanic surface. In other spots, however, even a sprig of dry grass would considerably liven the scene.

Jökuldalsheiði

This vast moorland between Jökuldalur and Möðrudalur along the Ring Road is relatively verdant and was farmed up until 1875 when the cataclysmic explosion of the Askja caldera displaced the inhabitants. Although the former greenery has since returned, the area remains abandoned.

Möðrudalur

An oasis in the desert between an entanglement of streams, isolated Möðrudalur, at 470 metres above sea level, is the highest farm in Iceland. The Egilsstaðir to Mývatn (or vice versa) bus stops here for a half-hour. If you'd rather not be ripped off by the exorbitant prices at the Fjalla-kaffi snack bar there, wander across the road to the church and see the interesting altarpiece. It's a rather untraditional interpretation of the Sermon on the Mount by Jón Stefánsson, the local farmer who also built the church in 1949.

Biskupsháls

Folktales say that two early bishops, one from Skálholt in the south and the other from Hólar in the north, met frequently on top of this tuff ridge, perpendicular to the Ring Road about 10 km south of Grímsstaðir. It is believed they constructed a cairn there to mark the eastern boundary between their two dioceses.

Grímsstaðir

Grímsstaðir is a remote farm at the intersection of the Ring Road and Route 864 near the Jökulsá á Fjöllum. Before a bridge was completed across the river, a ferry operated. Get off the Ring Road bus at the petrol station at Grímsstaðir, if you want to attempt hitching north to Dettifoss and Jökulsárgljúfur National Park. There's a camping site and a small grocery kiosk in the settlement. It's also popular among budget travellers to camp for nothing, north of Grímsstaðir between the Jökulsá á Fjöllum and Route 864, the Dettifoss road.

On a clear day, looking south from here, you can plainly see the distinctive form of Herðubreið, deep in the interior.

Hrossaborg

The name of this 40-metre-high and 500-metre-long crater means 'horse rock' because it is used as a sort of corral by horses seeking shelter from the fierce and icy winds that howl through here. It's situated at the intersection of the Ring Road and the dirt track Route F88 to Herðubreið and Askja in the interior.

Mývatn

In 1974, lake Mývatn ('midge lake') was set aside as a national conservation area although it wouldn't be surprising to find it upgraded to a national park in the future. The pseudocrater field, at Skútustaðir at the southern end of the lake, is preserved as a national natural monument. The Mývatn area is a place where travellers can settle in, spend a week camping, sightseeing and relaxing, and never become bored.

The Mývatn basin sits squarely on the Mid-Atlantic Ridge. Although most of the interesting sights in the region are volcanic or geothermal topographic features, the centrepiece of the reserve is the lake itself. It's a large, shallow body of water 37 sq km in area with an average depth of 2.5 metres. The lake is almost bisected by the Neslangatangi peninsula which separates Ytriflói or 'north gulf' from the even larger Syðriflói or 'south gulf'. Together, they contain over 50 islands and islets, most of which are pseudocraters formed by gas explosions caused when molten lava flowed into the water.

Thanks to its location in the rainshadow of the Vatnajökull icecap, the reserve is statistically the driest spot in Iceland so it's reasonable to expect fine weather. The nearly perpetual icy wind that blows across the lake and surrounding unsheltered landscape, however, may put a minor damper on any warm-weather activities you may be planning.

The other annoyance to contend with is the swarms of midges after which the lake is named. Unprotected campers may well be driven to the brink by these insanity-inspiring nuisances. They're similar in profusion and demeanour to New Zealand sandflies or North American 'no-see-ums', so don't even think of using a tent without an insect screen.

Geology

At the end of the ice age 10,000 years ago, the Mývatn basin was covered by an icecap. The moulded symmetrical mountains that characterise the central deserts south of the lake were formed by volcanic eruptions beneath the ice. Near Reykjahlíð, on the northern end, spur glaciers pushed up terminal moraines. Many of these were later buried beneath lava flows. One of these moraines became the earth dam that formed lake Mývatn from the meltwater of the retreating glaciers.

Immediately after the ice disappeared, so did the lake. Volcanic activity to the east formed the Lúdent tephra complex and, over 6000 years later, another cycle of activity created the Ketildyngja volcano 25 km south-east of Mývatn. The lava from that crater flowed north-west, nearly to the sea along the Laxá valley, creating a lava dam and a new improved lake Mývatn. After another millennium or so, a volcanic explosion along the same fissure spewed out Hverfjall, the classic tephra cone that dominates the landscape around the lake today. Over the following 200 years, activity escalated along the eastern shore and craters were thrown up across a wide region, providing a steady stream of molten material flowing toward Öxarfjörður. The lava dam created during the end of this cycle determined the present Mývatn shoreline.

Between 1724 and 1729, the Mývatnseldar ('Mývatn fires') eruptions commenced in the Krafla area north-east of the lake. Sporadically active since then, the extremely dramatic Krafla fissure has erupted as recently as 1984. During late 1989, sub-surface rumblings were on the increase and experts believed that another major eruption was imminent.

Suggested Itinerary

There is a lot to see at Mývatn. In addition, there are quite a few destinations outside the immediate area such as Jökulsárgljúfur National Park, Kverkfjöll ice cave, and Askja caldera which are best reached from a Mývatn base. Independent travellers who want to see the area thoroughly should plan on staying at least a week with perhaps 4 nights at Reykjahlíð and 2 or 3 at Skútustaðir.

One good day-hike from Reykjahlíð will include climbing Hverfjall crater and a few hours exploring Dimmuborgir. Another will include visiting the Námaskarð geothermal area and climbing Námafjall and a third day might be spent cycling to the waterfowl conservation area west of the lake and climbing Vindbelgjarfjall.

Visiting the Krafla area can, unfortunately, prove problematic. Howling winds and dust storms kick up out there with some regularity making one-speed cycling a potentially unpleasant option. Krafla is best visited by hitching both ways from Reykjahlíð or participating in the 4-hour afternoon segment of the 'Grand Mývatn' tour which visits Námaskarð, Bjarnarflag, Viti, Leirhnjúkur, and the Krafla fissures. Campers prepared to hike up into the hills (carry all the water you'll need) behind the

Top: Ásbyrgi canyon, Jökulsárgljúfur National Park, Iceland (DS)
Bottom: Hverfjall crater, Mývatn, Iceland (DS)

Top: Puffins on Grímsey Island, Iceland (DC)
Left: Leirhnjúkur geothermal area, Krafla, Iceland (DS)
Right: Road sign without road near Askja, Central Icelandic desert (DS)

Viti crater near Krafla, can leave the tour there and rejoin it the next time around but it's forbidden to camp or even wander in the area around the power station.

The features around the southern end of Mývatn, good for 2 days of sightseeing, are best explored on foot from Skútustaðir.

Walking trips to more distant mountains and lava fields such as Lúdent, Þrengslaborgir, or Búrfell will require extra time.

REYKJAHLÍÐ

Mývatn's principal population and service centre, Reykjahlíð, was only one of several Settlement-Age farms in the area. According to the *Landnámabók*, Reykjahlíð's first settler was farmer Arnór Þorgrímsson. The earliest residents of the area found a lush landscape of birch woods and grasslands but overcutting and grazing diminished the greenery and subsequent lava flows finished off the process.

Today, the livelihood of the village is based on the nearby Bjarnarflag diatomite plant, the Krafla power station, and the burgeoning tourist industry. The current population of Reykjahlíð, including surrounding farmsteads, is just under 600.

Information

Tourist Office Tourist information is available at front desk of the Hotel Reynihlíð and at the Eldá guesthouse by the lake. Both will book tours or onward transport and accommodation. The latter also hires rowboats and horses and sells a variety of souvenir publications and pulp-fiction paperbacks in English.

Bank The bank is down the side street between the swimming pool and the eastbound highway. There's no sign out the front

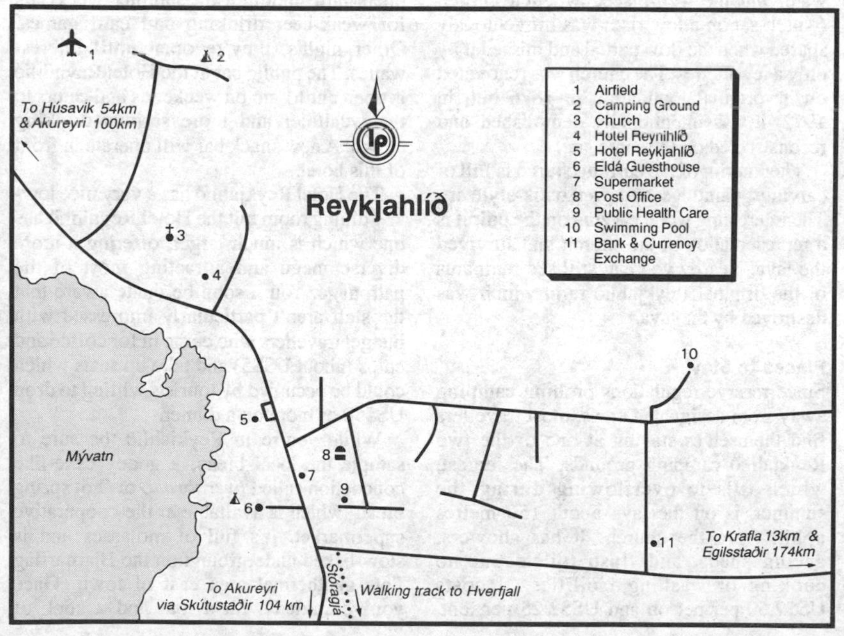

but a local will be able to point it out to you. It's open for currency exchange between 11 am and 2 pm weekdays.

Swimming Pool A stormy day in Reykjahlíð couldn't be better spent than at the outdoor pool and jacuzzi, less than 1 km east of the main village. It's open from 10 am to 8.30 pm on weekdays and 11 am to 7.30 pm on Saturdays and Sundays and costs US$1.75 per person. The *gufubaðið* ('sauna') is open between 4 pm and 8.30 pm on Thursdays to men and the same hours on Tuesdays to women.

Church

During the Krafla eruption of 1727, the Leirhnjukur crater 10 km north-east of Reykjahlíð began an eruption which lasted 2 years and sent streams of lava down through the old glacial moraines and past Reykjahlíð to the lakeshore. On 27 August 1729, the flow ploughed through the village destroying farms and buildings before reaching the water but the well-placed wooden church (which sat on a low rise) was miraculously spared when the flow parted and missed it by only a few metres. The church was renovated on its original foundation in 1876 but, in 1972, it was intentionally demolished and reconstructed on the same site.

The interior of the current church is full of carvings, paintings, and even batik-style art. The interesting wood carving on the pulpit is a representation of the church that survived the lava. Nearby you can still see remnants of the original Reykjahlíð farm which was destroyed by the lava.

Places to Stay

Since reserve regulations prohibit camping away from designated areas, most travellers find themselves staying at one of the two Reykjahlíð camping grounds. The largest, which fills to overflowing during the summer, is on the lava about 150 metres uphill from the church. It has showers, drying sheds, and flush toilets but no cooking or washing facilities. It costs US$2.60 per person and US$2.25 per tent. The other camping site on the lakeshore behind the *Eldá* (tel 96-44220) guesthouse charges US$5.20 per person. Camping outside the reserve will prove difficult due to lack of surface water in the porous and fissured volcanic landscape.

Sleeping-bag accommodation at the Eldá costs a whopping US$14 per night. The *Hotel Reykjahlíð* (tel 96-44142) is a small 12-room hotel on the lakeshore charging US$66 for a double room. The major upmarket tourist lodging is the *Hotel Reynihlíð* (tel 96-44170) which charges US$85/112 for singles/doubles with private bath, both prices include a continental buffet breakfast. The TV lounge and the pub there serve as a sort of community centre and seem always to be crowded.

Places to Eat

Reykjahlíð has two snack bars, one in a kiosk in front of the cooperative supermarket and the other at the petrol station. The latter also serves as a village social centre and stays open until midnight on summer weekends for weak-beer drinking and card games. Other nights, they're open until interest wanes. The public bar at the Hotel Reynihlíð is open until 1 am on weekends and caters to the wealthier and more serious drinking crowd. A new snack bar will operate in front of this hotel.

The Hotel Reykjahlíð has a very nice low-key dining room but the Hotel Reynihlíð has one which is much larger, offering a more diverse menu and attracting most of the patronage. You'll soon be made aware that the staff aren't particularly impressed with budget travellers who come in for coffee and chips (about US$5) and take up seats which could be occupied by tourists willing to drop US$50 or more on a dinner.

While you're in Reykjahlíð, be sure to sample the local bread, a gooey cake-like concoction called *hverabrauð* or 'hot spring bread' which is available at the cooperative supermarket. It's full of molasses and is slow-baked underground on the Bjarnarflag flats geothermal area east of town. Once you've started with a loaf and a stick of butter, it's difficult to stop. Don't buy it at the gift shop in front of the Reynihlíð, however, or you'll pay several times the supermarket price.

Volcano Show

If you missed the Volcano Show in Reykjavík, you can see it here where it will be particularly interesting because some of the footage was taken at nearby Krafla during recent activity there. The cinema is on the street between the village and the swimming pool. Admission is a bit steep, US$10 per person, but the films bring home the reality of volcanic activity in Iceland and are worth seeing once during your stay.

Getting There & Away

Air Flights to Mývatn from Reykjavík go via the Húsavík or Akureyri airports from which shuttle buses carry passengers to and from Reykjahlíð. Mýflug Air operates charter and sightseeing tours in and out of Reykjahlíð airfield. Information and ticketing are handled by the Eldá guesthouse (tel 96-44220).

Bus Reykjahlíð has the main long-distance bus terminal for the Mývatn area although those travelling between the lake and Akureyri also make a stop at Skútustaðir. Buses between Akureyri and Mývatn take less than 1½ hours and, during high season, depart Akureyri daily at 8.15 am and weekdays at 8 pm. From Reykjahlíð, they leave at 8 am weekdays and at 4.30 and 7.30 pm daily. To Egilsstaðir, they depart Mývatn at 8.15 pm daily and return at 4 pm daily. From Húsavík, they run two or three times daily in each direction during the summer months but some of these trips are guided tours which will cost a bit more than normal fare.

The Akureyri bus is the one to use between Reykjahlíð and Skútustaðir on the southern end of the lake.

Getting Around

For travellers without access to a car or bicycle, getting around at Mývatn can be frustrating. The Reykjahlíð tourism industry is notoriously unfriendly toward independent travellers and, so far, local bus and tour companies have successfully fought proposals for an around-the-lake shuttle bus for those not inclined to pay excruciating prices to hire decrepit one-speed bikes or join tours which spend just a few crowded photo moments at major attractions.

There are a few hiking trails around but they can't begin to get you to all the points of interest so you'll have to take to the road from time to time. Watch out for high-speed sightseers who will send so much gravel flying you'll think the place is erupting all over again. Distances are relatively great as well – plan on taking at least 3 hours on foot between Reykjahlíð and Skútustaðir.

Many people try to hitch around to the sights and invariably find themselves walking, anyway. Most of the vehicles travelling around the lake belong to tourists and tour companies, neither of which are normally disposed to picking up dust-covered hitchhikers.

Bicycle If you can afford it and have calm wind and weather, your best option is to hire a bicycle at the Reykjahlíð petrol station. They have many one-speed bikes available but few of these actually work so try several before deciding on one. Cyclists will still have to contend with tour buses and caravans on often rough unsurfaced roads so exercise due caution while riding. Bikes cost US$8.75 to rent for 6 hours, just enough for a quick trip around the lake and a few of its points of interest, or US$13.75 for 12 hours.

Tours

Tourism with a capital 'T' reigns at Reykjahlíð and a number of BSÍ tours are available there.

Those around the immediate area are very popular with day-trippers flying in from Reykjavík and people with very limited time. These tours are not recommended unless you're in a real hurry or you want to get to or from Krafla this way. The 2-hour whirlwind tour around the lake operates daily and allows you only fleeting views of the sights. It departs Skútustaðir daily at 11.15 am and Reykjahlíð daily at 1.30 pm and costs US$17 per person. The Grand Mývatn tour operates from the Hotel Reynihlíð on Tuesdays, Thursdays, and Sundays at 8.30 am and actually consists of two tours. The morning segment is a 4-hour version of the round-the-lake tour and in the afternoon you visit the Krafla area. Segments cost US$22 each.

To Dettifoss, Jökulsárgljúfur National Park, Húsavík, and Reykjadalur there are tours on Mondays, Wednesdays, and Fridays which visit the west side of Dettifoss and Hólmatungur at 8.30 am. On Tuesdays, Thursdays, and Saturdays, they depart at 8 am and visit the eastern side of Dettifoss instead.

Other tours include the long but magnificent day-tour to Herðubreið and the Askja caldera deep in the interior. It goes at 8.15 am on Mondays, Wednesdays, and Fridays in July and August (snow conditions permitting) and costs a well-spent US$70. Many people take this tour and stay at the Herðubreið or Dreki huts for several days of hiking and exploring before catching another tour back.

Another very worthwhile trip is the 3-day camping tour to Kverkfjöll ice cave, the source of the Jökulsá á Fjöllum. It departs weekly on Fridays at 1 pm and costs US$153 from Mývatn excluding food costs, and camping or hut fees.

All of these tours can get extremely crowded so, in order to assure a place, try to book at least a day before departure through the Hotel Reynihlíð.

AROUND THE LAKE

By one-speed bicycle, lake Mývatn is 37 easily negotiated km around by the shortest route. There are a number of walks and side trips away from the main roads so, even with a motor vehicle, it's a good idea to plan at least a day exploring the sights, 2 days if you're including the attractions along the Hverfjall-Dimmuborgir hiking trail system.

Hverfjall & Dimmuborgir Trail

If you allow a day to walk this track from Reykjahlíð to Dimmuborgir and back, it will give you time to explore all the points of interest along the way.

Walk south-east from the intersection of the Ring Road and the round-the-lake route. After a few minutes, the trail will reach a dead end at a pipeline. From here, turn left and walk several hundred metres to the point where the track continues southward toward Hverfjall. It meanders a bit through an overgrown lava field before it reaches Grjótagjá but it's well marked and you should have no trouble following it.

Stóragjá This rather eerie, hidden fissure is found just 100 metres south-east of the Reykjahlíð intersection of the Ring Road and the round-the-lake route. It contains a beautiful and secluded 38°C hot spring which is reached by a ladder leading down from the footpath. From the bottom of the ladder, walk a few metres south and you'll see the pool hidden in a crack between boulders. Bathers will have to lower themselves into the spring on an attached rope. The temperature of the water, however, fosters the growth of potentially harmful algae so it's best to check that you haven't got any cuts first and then to shower when you've finished bathing.

Grjótagjá Along the walking track in a gaping fissure between Reykjahlíð and Hverfjall is another beautiful hot spring, Grjótagjá. Although this was once used for bathing, it has heated up to 60°C in recent years and is far too hot to be bearable. Especially when the sun is out, the light filtering through cracks in the roof creates mesmerising patterns in the steam and the water. The several entrances to this otherworldly chamber are east of the steaming crevice where the track drops 10 metres or so to a rough parking area.

Hverfjall The classic tephra ring Hverfjall stands prominently 163 metres above the vast lava fields east of the lake. It appeared in an cataclysmic eruption of the already existent Lúdent complex 2500 years ago. The 1040-metre-wide crater serves as a Mývatn landmark and is surely one of Iceland's most interesting mountains.

The crater is made up of loose tephra-gravel which is like ball bearings. It's best negotiated along the ready-made tracks where you'll also be least likely to do any damage to this feature. The walking track diagonally ascends the northern slope then continues around the western side of the crater rim to a lookout at the southern end before descending steeply into the Dimmuborgir area. From the rim, several routes descend into the crater itself. The floor has become a sort of hikers' billboard where numerous pictures and messages have been written in light-coloured stone patterns.

Dimmuborgir The convoluted 'black castles' of Dimmuborgir are good for hours of imagination-invoking exploration. It is believed that the oddly shaped pillars and crags were created 2000 years ago by lava from the Þrengslaborgir and Lúdentsborgir

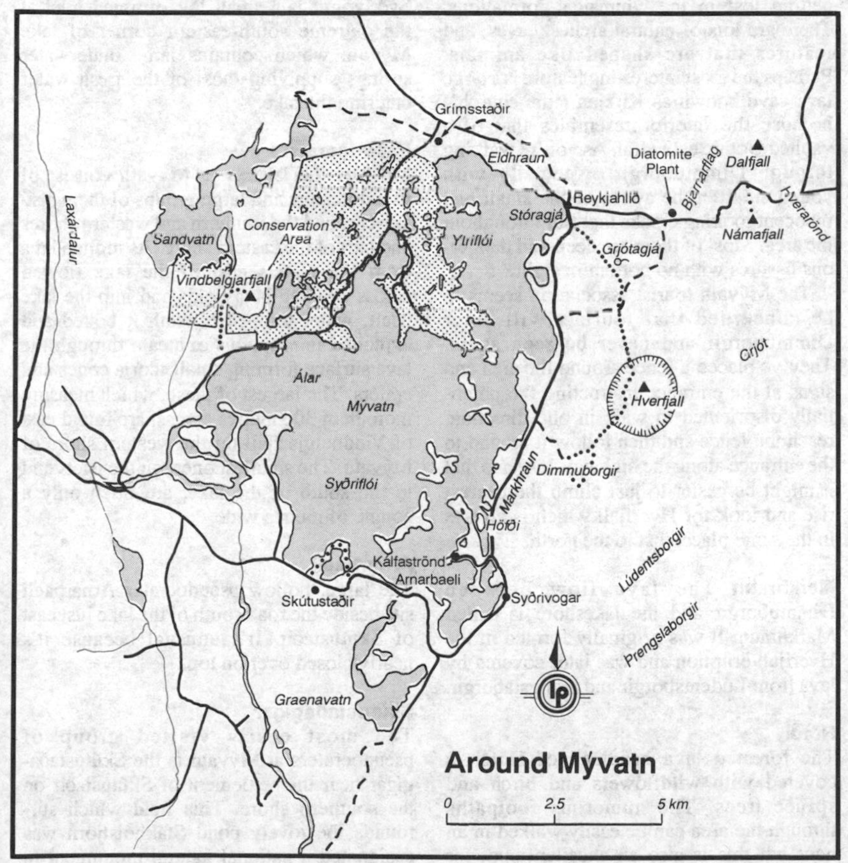

Around Mývatn

crater rows which originally erupted 9000 years ago. The lava flowed across older Hverfjall lava fields and was dammed into a fiery lake in the basin where Dimmuborgir now sits. When the surface of this lake cooled, a domed roof was formed over the still molten material below. It was supported by pillars of older igneous material welded by the heat of the lava lake. When the dam finally broke, the molten lava drained in stages and the odd pillars of Dimmuborgir remained marked with terraces at various surface levels.

It's easy to spend a day intentionally getting lost in the whimsical formations. There are lots of natural arches, caves, and features that are shaped like animals. Perhaps the most interesting feature is a large lava cave known as Kirkjan ('the church') because the interior resembles that of a vaulted Gothic cathedral. As you're walking through Dimmuborgir, especially with young children, be aware of the small and innocent looking cracks that run throughout the area. Most of them are deep and dangerous fissures with no bottom in sight.

The Mývatn tourist association seems to be concerned that tourists will enter Dimmuborgir and never be seen again. They've placed a fence around the area and signs at the entrance instructing the potentially disoriented to walk in one direction, reach the fence and then follow it around to the entrance along the highway. It seems that it might be easier to just climb the nearest rise and look for Hverfjall which is always in the same place, just to the north.

Markhraun The lava flow between Dimmuborgir and the lakeshore is called Markhraun. It was originally formed in the Hverfjall eruption and was later covered by lava from Lúdentsborgir and Þrengslaborgir.

Höfði

The forested lava headland of Höfði is covered with wildflowers and birch and spruce trees. The numerous footpaths through the area can be easily walked in an hour but this is also an excellent spot for picnics and relaxing. In the spring, the fresh scent of the vegetation here is incomparable. Listen to the wild and chilling cries of the loons on the lake and along the shore observe the many small caves, lava pillars, and unusual formations called *klasar*.

Kálfaströnd This coastline on the southern side of the same peninsula as Höfði has some of the most interesting klasar formations anywhere on the lake. It is also a breeding area for loons.

Syðrivogur

Syðrivogur is a small lava-rimmed inlet at the extreme south-eastern corner of lake Mývatn which contains large underwater springs supplying most of the fresh water entering the lake.

Pseudocraters

Most of the islands in Mývatn consist of pseudocraters and large groups of them also exist around the southern and western shores and part of the eastern shore. As molten lava from the craters east of the lake flowed across existing lava fields and into the lake itself, water trapped beneath it boiled and exploded in eruptions of steam through the lava surface forming small scoria cones and craters. The largest of these, which measure more than 300 metres across, are found east of Vindbelgjarfjall on the western shore of Mývatn. The smallest ones, on the islets and to the south of the lake, are often only a couple of metres wide.

Arnarbaeli

The large, hollow pseudocrater Arnarbaeli sits beside the road south of the lake just east of Skútustaðir. It's unusual because it's nearly closed over on top.

Skútustaðagígar

The most easily visited group of pseudocraters at Mývatn is the Skútustaðagígar near the settlement of Skútustaðir on the southern shore. This field which surrounds the lovely pond Stakhólstjörn was designated a national natural monument in

1973. The pond and surrounding boggy marshland are havens for nesting waterfowl. Hiking trails wander between, up, and down the craters; a complete circuit of Stakhólstjörn will take about an hour at a leisurely pace. Since the features are rather delicate, regulations require hikers to remain on marked tracks in the area.

Skutustaðir

The settlement of Skútustaðir serves as a secondary service centre on Mývatn. It was originally owned by a notorious character called Vigaskúta or 'Killer Skúta' who was known for his ruthlessness and was marked for assassination by his neighbours. He was clever, however, and more often than not turned the tables on those who threatened him. The only real point of interest in the village is the church at the eastern end which contains a nice painting of the Last Supper and enjoys a quiet and shady vantage point over the surrounding area.

Places to Stay & Eat Skútustaðir has a swimming pool and a general store, a cafeteria, and a snack bar at the petrol station. Sleeping-bag accommodation is available at the school and costs US$8.60 per person. Private doubles cost a very reasonable US$11.20 per person. The camping site beside the pool costs US$4.80 per person. The *Skútustaðir Farm Guest House* (tel 96-44212) has both private rooms, cooking facilities, and sleeping-bag accommodation.

Laxá

One of the numerous 'salmon rivers' in Iceland, the Laxá flowing toward Öxarfjörður from the western end of lake Mývatn is one of the best and most prohibitively expensive salmon-fishing rivers in the country. It is, however, a beautiful stream of clear turbulent water which rolls across the tundra and past numerous mid-channel islets. Brown trout fishing is also available and a little more affordable. Permits may be purchased at Eldá in Reykjahlíð.

Vindbelgjarfjall

The easy climb up 529-metre Vindbelgjarfjall, west of the lake, will take about an hour up and half an hour down. Because it's so close to the lake, the summit offers one of the best views across the water, pseudocraters, and protected wetlands along the north-western shore. Like most of the other peaks near the lake, it's made of unconsolidated volcanic slag.

Conservation Area

The bogs, marshes, ponds, and wet tundra along the north-western shore of Mývatn are a high density waterfowl nesting zone. Offroad entry is restricted between 15 May and 20 July when the chicks are hatching but overland travel through this soggy area would be pretty difficult, anyway.

Most species of waterfowl present in Iceland are found here in their greatest numbers and the area is world-famous among birdwatchers. Included are 15 species

Grebe with chick

of duck consisting of nearly 10,000 breeding pairs. Three of these species, the scoter duck, the gadwall, and Barrow's golden eye breed nowhere else in Iceland. Incredible numbers of eider ducks, harlequin ducks, mergansers, mallards, tufted ducks, goosander ducks, shovellers, whooper swans, grebes, loons, gulls, ptarmigans, great skuas, several species of geese, ravens, falcons, plovers, snipe, whimbrels, wheatears, and heaps of other species are also present. Mink and Arctic fox are occasionally seen taking advantage of the large numbers of birds for them to prey on.

Eldhraun

Eldhraun, which unimaginatively means 'fire lava' is the field which lies along the northern shore of the lake and includes the bit that nearly engulfed the church at Reykjahlíð. It was belched out of Leirhnjúkur during the Mývatnseldar in 1729 and flowed down the channel called Eldá ('fire river'). With some slow scrambling, it can be explored on foot (or on protected hands and knees) from Reykjahlíð.

Hlíðarfjall

The prominent 771-metre-high mountain, 4 km north of Reykjahlíð, is sometimes called Reykjahlíðarfjall. It's made of volcanic rhyolite and is a long but pleasant day-hike from the village. The summit affords a spectacular view across the lake to the south-west and out to the Krafla lava fields to the north-east.

Arctic fox

Harlequin duck

BJARNARFLAG

The flats at Bjarnarflag, west of Námafjall 3 km east of Reykjahlíð, overlie an active geothermal area. During this century, it has been the site of numerous economic ventures. Early on, farmers tried growing potatoes there but they sometimes emerged from the ground already boiled (yes, really!) and only a couple of fields remain. In 1938, a sulphur mine was opened at Bjarnarflag. It was closed down shortly after because of a boiler explosion. During the early 1950s, attempts were made to extract sulphur from the solfataras or volcanic vents which dot the area but the project proved uneconomical and was quickly abandoned.

A cinder-brick factory has been set up to manufacture building materials from the volcanic ash found there. Near the brick factory is the underground oven where hverabrauð is packed into milk cartons and slowly baked for 22 hours into delicious cake-like loaves. Look for the small, round glass doors that open into the ground but don't disturb the bread.

During the late 1960s, 25 test holes were bored at Bjarnarflag to see if it was feasibile to construct a geothermal power station in the area. The most accessible hole, just south-east of the 'bakery', has become a sort of tourist attraction and all the tour buses stop there. This particular bore is 2300 metres deep and the steam roaring out of the pipe is emitted at 200°C. Standing beside it, you can begin to imagine the magnitude of the power potential we're talking about here.

Kísilgúrverksmiðja The most prominent and unusual enterprise at Bjarnarflag today is the geothermal diatomite plant. Diatoms are tiny microfossils, the skeletal remains of a type of single-celled algae. Although they are only about 0.00005% the size of a sand grain, the layer is 15 metres deep on the floor of lake Mývatn and increasing in thickness at a rate of 1 mm annually. Near the northern shore of the lake, a barge gathers sediment from the bottom and pipes it to the shore where it is strained and placed in holding ponds and allowed to settle. It is then transported to the plant and treated with fire and steam to remove further impurities before it is exported. Diatomite is used as a filler in fertilisers, paints, toothpaste, and plastics and as a filtering agent for oil, pharmaceuticals, aviation fuel, beer, and wine.

In September 1977, a series of earthquakes occurred at Mývatn. The holding ponds were destroyed, the bore holes that served as its power source were blocked with new lava, and the plant was damaged. It was closed for several years while repairs were made and didn't re-open until 1980.

Unfortunately, the environmental impact of all this is fairly serious. The collection barge infringes on the significant waterfowl breeding grounds at Mývatn, increasing the water depth there, and preventing some bird and fish species getting food from the lakebed. In addition, if the extraction of diatomite continues at its present annual rate of 25,000 tonnes, supplies from the northern lake-bed will be exhausted within 10 years and operations will have to move into now unspoilt areas in order to supply the plant.

Námafjall

Produced by a fissure eruption, the pastel coloured Námafjall ridge lies south of the Ring Road, 6 km east of Reykjahlíð. It sits squarely on the spreading zone of the Mid-Atlantic Rift and contains numerous steaming vents. A short trail leads from the highway at the pass Namaskarð to a view disc at the summit, a climb of less than 20 minutes which provides a grand vista over the steaming surroundings. North of the pass is another ridge, Dalfjall, which sports a large and growing notch, dramatic evidence that the mountain is literally being split in two.

Hverarönd

The impressive geothermal field immediately east of Námafjall is called Hverarönd. It's full of mudpots, steam vents, sulphur deposits, boiling springs, and fumeroles – some of them real dynamos. Unlike in such areas in other countries, visitors here are pretty much allowed to roam freely. They will risk serious injury and damage to the natural features if they venture onto lighter coloured soil or past the ropes placed around the more enticing (or intimidating, depending upon your disposition) features.

KRAFLA

Krafla is the name of a mountain 7 km north of the Ring Road. This name has come to signify the entire caldera as well as a geothermal power station and the series of eruptions that created Iceland's most beautiful and awe-inspiring lava field.

While it's possible to ride a bicycle to Krafla, most people will find that the howling winds, sandstorms, and steep hills don't make this particularly appealing. There's lots of tourist traffic during the summer so hitching shouldn't be too difficult. Thrice-weekly afternoon tours from Reykjahlíð offer another alternative.

Those who are prepared to melt into the hills will be able to camp in the area but otherwise, camping is prohibited anywhere in the vicinity of the power station.

Kröflustöð

The idea of constructing a geothermal power station at Krafla was conceived in 1973 and preliminary work commenced with the drilling of 24 test holes, including the oft-visited one at Bjarnarflag, to determine the feasibility of the project and to provide steam sources should the plan be given the green light.

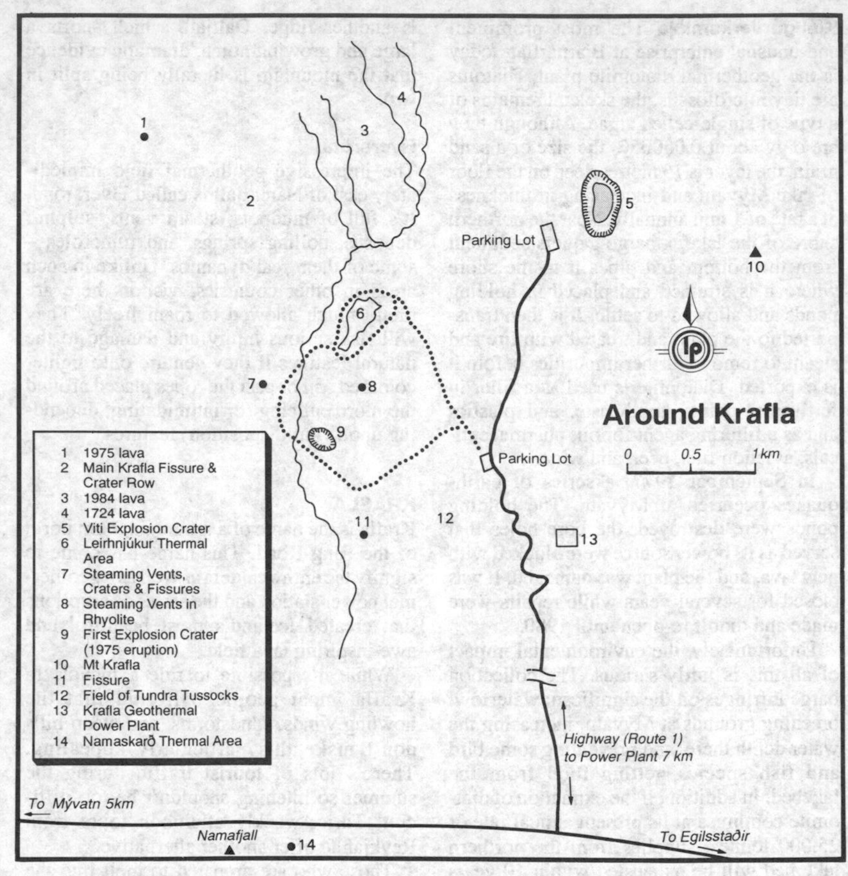

On 20 December 1975, however, after a rest of several hundred years, the Krafla fissure unexpectedly burst into activity with the first in a series of nine eruptions and 20 cases of surface subsidence. Although this significantly lowered the projected geothermal potential of the site and nearly deactivated Leirbotnar, one of the primary steam sources, the project was completed in 1978. The current operation utilises only one of its two 30-megawatt generators and 11 of the bore holes. Unfortunately for power plant fans, the Krafla station is off limits to visitors.

Viti

The name of this impressive 320-metre-wide explosion crater means 'hell' (not to be confused with the similar crater of the same name at Askja in central Iceland). This is the centre of the fairly non-descript Krafla caldera where the destructive Mývatnseldar began in 1724. It set off a series of eruptions nearby that continued steadily for 5 years. Activity has continued in spurts to the present day, but Viti itself is now inactive.

Behind the crater are the 'twin lakes', boiling mud springs which are marginally interesting but not included in the guided tours so you'll have to get there on your own to see them. During the Mývatnseldar, they were known to shoot mud up to 10 metres into the air but now they're down to a simmer.

Leirhnjúkur & Kröfluöskjunni

Safety It's as if no one heeds the horrendous red warning sign that forbids visitors entering the Leirhnjúkur and Kröfluöskjunni areas. Postcards and glossy tourist brochures extol it and organised tour groups, cyclists, grandparents, and young children flock into this hazardous volcanic zone as if going to a fun fair. It's one of the country's most impressive – albeit potentially risky – tourist attractions and no one is going to keep tourists out.

To be on the safe side, however, avoid the lighter coloured soil around the mudpots, snowfields which may overlie hidden fissures, loose sharp lava chunks, and slopes of scoria. As mentioned before, the Krafla complex is expected to go off again sometime soon and there will naturally be some risk involved if you're there at the time. At the first sign of an eruption, however, I'd expect the entire tourist population of Iceland to descend on the place rather than follow official advice and get the hell out of there.

Leirhnjúkur The impressive and colourful crater at Leirhnjúkur is the primary attraction of the Krafla area. It originally opened up in August 1727, as a lava fountain which spouted molten material for 2 years before calming down. After a minor burp in 1746, it became the menacing sulphur-encrusted mudhole that tourists love today. It was lava from Leirhnjúkur, incidentally, that flowed through Reykjahlíð destroying farm buildings and threatening the church.

To get there, enter the field of tundra tussocks at the intimidating red warning sign and continue north-westward below some steaming vents on the pastel coloured rhyolite mountain to the west. The pit of Leirhnjúkur lies to the north of this mountain, which you can circle for a fairly comprehensive tour of the area's points of interest (see map).

Kröfluöskjunni The source of the layers of lava at Kröfluöskjunni is the north-south tending fissure which bisects the Krafla caldera. From the rim above Leirhnjúkur, you can look out across flows from the original Mývatnseldar and from the 1975 eruptions, all overlain in places by the still steaming 1984 lava. Parts of the field, west of Leirhnjúkur, remain so hot that they feel like a natural sauna. The impressive crater on the western slope of the rhyolite mountain, south of Leirhnjúkur, was the explosion crater that in 1975 set off a series of eruptions known as the 'Krafla fires'– a continuation of the Mývatnseldar of the early 1700s.

OUTLYING AREAS OF MÝVATN

If you have a lot of time and an inclination to walk longer distances over rugged terrain, there are quite a few scattered mountains and geological features to explore in the deserts south and east of the main lake area.

Lúdentsborgir

The Lúdentsborgir crater row to the east of Mývatn is part of the same 8-km-long fissure system as Þrengslaborgir. The landscape there was assumed to closely resemble that of the moon and, in 1968, the area of the Lúdent crater was used as a training ground for lunar-bound astronaut Neil Armstrong.

The craters in this row rise an average of 100 metres above the surrounding lava desert. The largest, Lúdent, measures nearly 1 km in diameter and 70 metres deep.

Those with a bit of extra time will find it worthwhile but don't miss Krafla or Dimmuborgir for the sake of seeing this. To get there, follow the light track which rounds the southern base of Hverfjall and continues south-eastward for 5 more km through the Lúdentsborgir row to Lúdent itself.

Þrengslaborgir

The Þrengslaborgir crater row lies 5 km due east of the southern extreme of lake Mývatn. It's part of the 8-km-long Lúdent complex which erupted between 9000 and 6000 years ago. If you're visiting the Lúdentsborgir area and have a little extra time, you may want to wander south along the crater row to have a look at it.

Bláfjall

About 15 km south-east of Graenavatn, near the southern shore of Mývatn, is 1222-metre-high table mountain Bláfjall or 'blue mountain'. Like all the other table mountains of central Iceland, it was formed in a sub-glacial volcanic eruption during the last ice age.

There are no marked routes into the area. Getting there from Graenavatn is tough-going through marshes and across ropy, chunky lava fields so only the adventurous need attempt it. A longer but easier route is around the lava field from the farm Baldursheimur south of Skútustaðir. Hikers going into this region should be self-sufficient. Surface water is available in some places but those opting to cross the lava field should carry water with them.

Búrfell

Another table mountain which can be reached with some difficulty across formidable lava fields is 953-metre-high Búrfell, 12 km south of the Ring Road and 15 km east of the lake. It's a beautiful symmetrical peak but, unless you're a masochist or a climber keen on difficult going, it's probably not worth the effort it will take to get there.

Búrfellsheiði between the mountain and the Ring Road is popular with Icelandic ptarmigan hunters who enjoy a great deal of success here – procuring the main course of their traditional Christmas Eve dinner.

Sellandafjall

The third major table mountain visible from Mývatn is 988-metre Sellandafjall which is a manageable 12-km hike south of Baldursheimur farm, itself 8 km south of the Ring Road. It's the most eroded of the three and is therefore the most easily climbed. From the intersection of the Ring Road and Route 849, allow yourself at least 3 days for the return trip to the summit. Although it's a relatively easy walk, this is considered a cross-country wilderness trek and careful preparations should be made.

East Iceland

Due to its distance from the spreading zone along the Mid-Atlantic Ridge, eastern Iceland is an old and geologically stable region. The main attraction here is the sunshine; visitors can expect cool but clear summer weather with the odd rainy day thrown in just to keep things interesting. Iceland's largest forest and longest lake are found here as well as a wealth of rugged and remote peaks and headlands, and some very nice waterfalls.

If you prefer your travels to be quiet and unstructured, you'll probably appreciate eastern Iceland. Travellers arriving at Seyðisfjörður on the ferry from the Faroe Islands are normally impressed by the steep snow-topped peaks and rugged coastline, deep fjords, and lightly populated farmlands that characterise Iceland's eastern extremes. Even so, most of them quickly shoot off to Mývatn or Skaftafell without having appreciated the appeal of this largely tourist-free corner of the island.

EGILSSTAÐIR

Egilsstaðir, which began as a large farm in the late 1800s, is now the transport and commercial hub of eastern Iceland. It sits in the Lagarfljót valley farming district beside the lake Lögurinn, the 'smooth one'. The town is a small and rather sterile-looking place but everyone arriving from Europe on the Seyðisfjörður ferry will probably have to spend a night there. Additionally, there are quite a few places of interest in the area and the town serves as a good base for day-trips into the scenic and extensive hinterland.

As far as the village is concerned, the monotony of box-like houses is broken only by the church which dominates the scene, attempting to look like its mountain backdrop. It's actually one of Iceland's nicer 'geological' churches.

Just east of the camping ground, a rocky hill with a view disc on top provides a good excuse for a trip up to laze in the sun.

Information & Orientation

Except for the post office (which is just up the hill) and the bus terminal, the tourist complex beside the camping ground contains nearly everything that may be of interest to travellers. There's a cafeteria, petrol station, bank, and supermarket. The tourist information office, Ferðamiðstöð Austurlands (tel 97-11510), is open weekdays during business hours.

Places to Stay

Surprisingly, there is no youth hostel in Egilsstaðir so most budget travellers end up at the camping ground which is one of the nicest in Iceland. It has hot showers for one thing and is, to my knowledge, the only one in the country that has semi-private camping sites for those staying in a tent while the caravans are forced to park in a large common area. It's cheap as well – only US$5.50 for two people in a tent. If even that seems expensive, there are several small rocky outcrops around town where you can camp free.

The large and boring *Hotel Valaskjálf* (tel 97-11500) charges US$63/81 for a single/double and has a cinema which may be appreciated if it's raining.

More reasonable for those interested in a roof over their head is the *Farm Guesthouse* (tel 97-11114) beside the lake. It offers horse rental, private rooms, and sleeping-bag accommodation at official farmhouse prices.

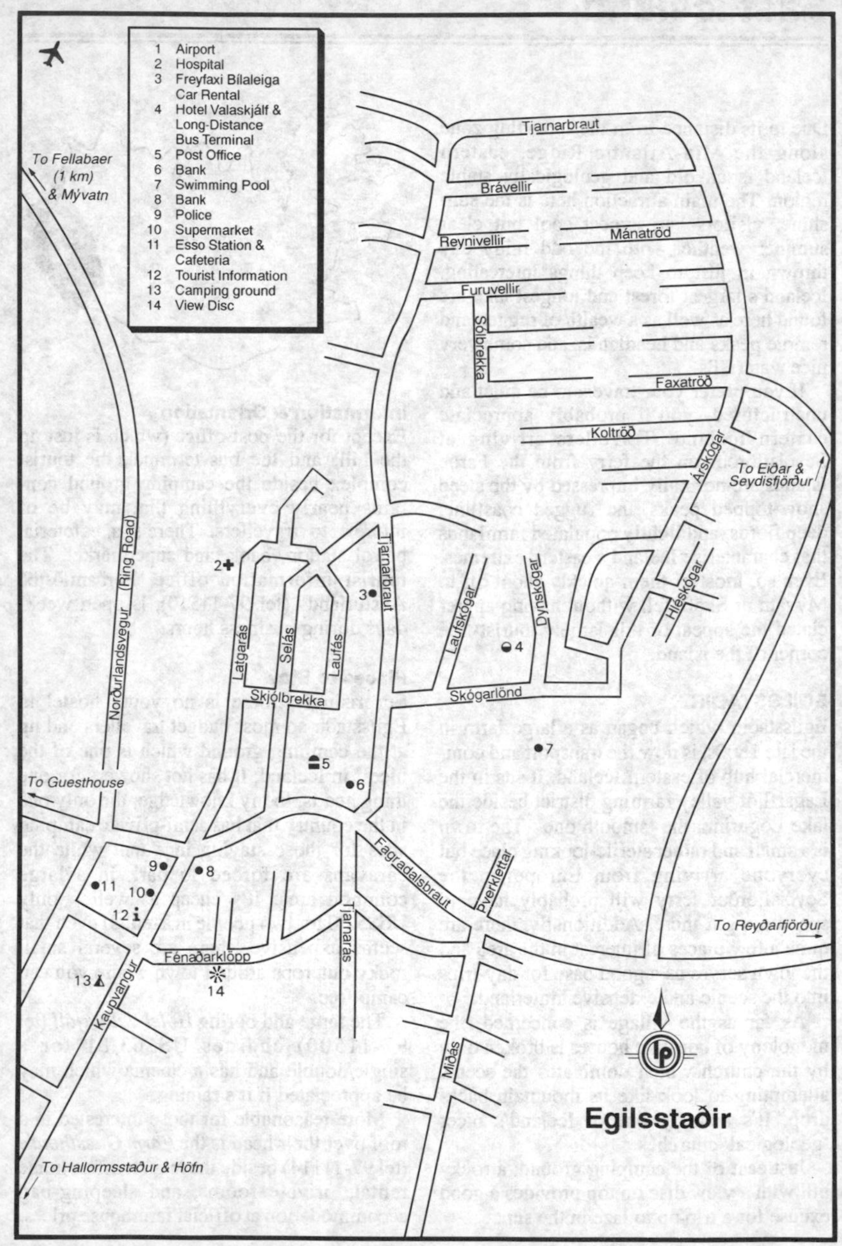
1 Airport
2 Hospital
3 Freyfaxi Bílaleiga Car Rental
4 Hotel Valaskjálf & Long-Distance Bus Terminal
5 Post Office
6 Bank
7 Swimming Pool
8 Bank
9 Police
10 Supermarket
11 Esso Station & Cafeteria
12 Tourist Information
13 Camping ground
14 View Disc
To Fellabaer (1 km) & Mývatn
Tjarnarbraut
Brávellir
Reynivellir
Mánatröð
Furuvellir
Sólbrekka
Faxatröð
Koltröð
Árskógar
To Eiðar & Seydisfjörður
Norðurlandsvegur (Ring Road)
Tjarnarbraut
Latgarás
Selás
Laufás
Laufskógar
Dynskógar
Hléskógar
Skjólbrekka
Skógarlönd
To Guesthouse
Fagradalsbraut
Tjarnarás
Þverklettar
To Reyðarfjörður
Fénaðarklöpp
Kaupvangur
Miðás
Egilsstaðir
To Hallormsstaður & Höfn

Other farmhouse accommodation in the vicinity includes *Miðhús* (tel 97-11324) north-east of town and *Skipalaekur* (tel 97-11324) at Fellabaer across the bridge from Egilsstaðir. The latter has a camping site and sleeping-bag accommodation as well as private rooms.

Places to Eat

Your culinary choices are fairly limited in Egilsstaðir. Apart from the bland dining room at the Hotel Valaskjálf and the cafe at the Farm Guesthouse, all you have are the cafeteria and the supermarket in the tourist complex. In season, a farm market on the grassy area just north-east of the bank sells produce, smoked salmon, and snacks.

Getting There & Away

Air Flugleiðir has several flights daily between Reykjavík and Egilsstaðir.

Bus Egilsstaðir is a hub city and one of the four 'corner stones' of the Ring Road so there are no bus connections through town. Those travelling between Höfn and Mývatn or Akureyri will have to spend the night there before continuing. Travellers should note that buses use the Hotel Valaskjálf as a depot and do not stop at the tourist complex.

During the summer months, there are two buses weekly between Egilsstaðir and Eiðar. Buses also go once daily from Monday to Friday to Hallormsstaður; daily except Saturdays to Reyðarfjörður, Eskifjörður, and Neskaupstaður; and daily from Monday to Friday to Fáskrúðsfjörður, Stöðvarfjörður, and Breiðdalsvík. On Fridays there is a bus which leaves Egilsstaðir for Dalatangi at 11.20 am and returns at 4 pm.

On Mondays, Tuesdays, Thursdays and Fridays the bus from Egilsstaðir to Seyðisfjörður bus departs Seyðisfjörður at 10 am and leaves Egilsstaðir at 11.15 am. On Wednesdays, the bus does three runs in either direction in order to accommodate passengers travelling on the ferry *Norröna* to or from mainland Europe and the Faroes. They depart from Egilsstaðir at noon, 4.15 and 8.40 pm, and leave Seyðisfjörður at 10.45 am, 2.45, and 7.40 pm.

During the summer, the bus to Höfn departs daily at 9 am and leaves Höfn for Egilsstaðir at 4 pm. There is also a daily bus from Egilsstaðir to Akureyri and Mývatn at 4 pm.

Car Rental The Freyfaxi Bílaleiga (tel 97-11318) hires vehicles at typically steep Icelandic prices.

LAGARFLJÓT

The 'smooth river', Lagarfljót, starts in the Vatnajökull icecap. For much of its length, it isn't a river at all but rather a long narrow lake, Lögurinn. Like long narrow lakes elsewhere, Lögurinn is reputed to have a resident monster, Lagarfljótsormurinn, which makes an occasional appearance just to stir up excitement (and promote tourism?).

The lake is 24 km long, less than 2 km wide and reaches a depth of 112 metres. Around its perimeter are several points of interest, but access for those without vehicles will be difficult south of Hallormsstaður on the eastern shore and Fellabaer on the west. You may be lucky hitching, particularly on weekends but, if you want to attempt a circuit of the lakeshore, plan on walking much of the 56 or so km between those two places.

Those with vehicles should note that the bridge across Bessastaðaá on the south-western shore was washed out in a flood in 1989. Until repairs are made, a project which is apparently not a high priority with public works, the river can be crossed only on foot (with extreme caution – refer to the Stream Crossing section in the Iceland Facts for the Visitor chapter) or in a high-clearance 4WD vehicle.

Hallormsstaður

Believe it or not, Iceland has a forestry commission and Hallormsstaður on the eastern shore of Lögurinn is its showcase. In addition to protecting the native dwarf birch and mountain ash it is planting spruce, Alaskan poplar, and Siberian larch, most unfortunately, in neatly ordered rows. Still, these

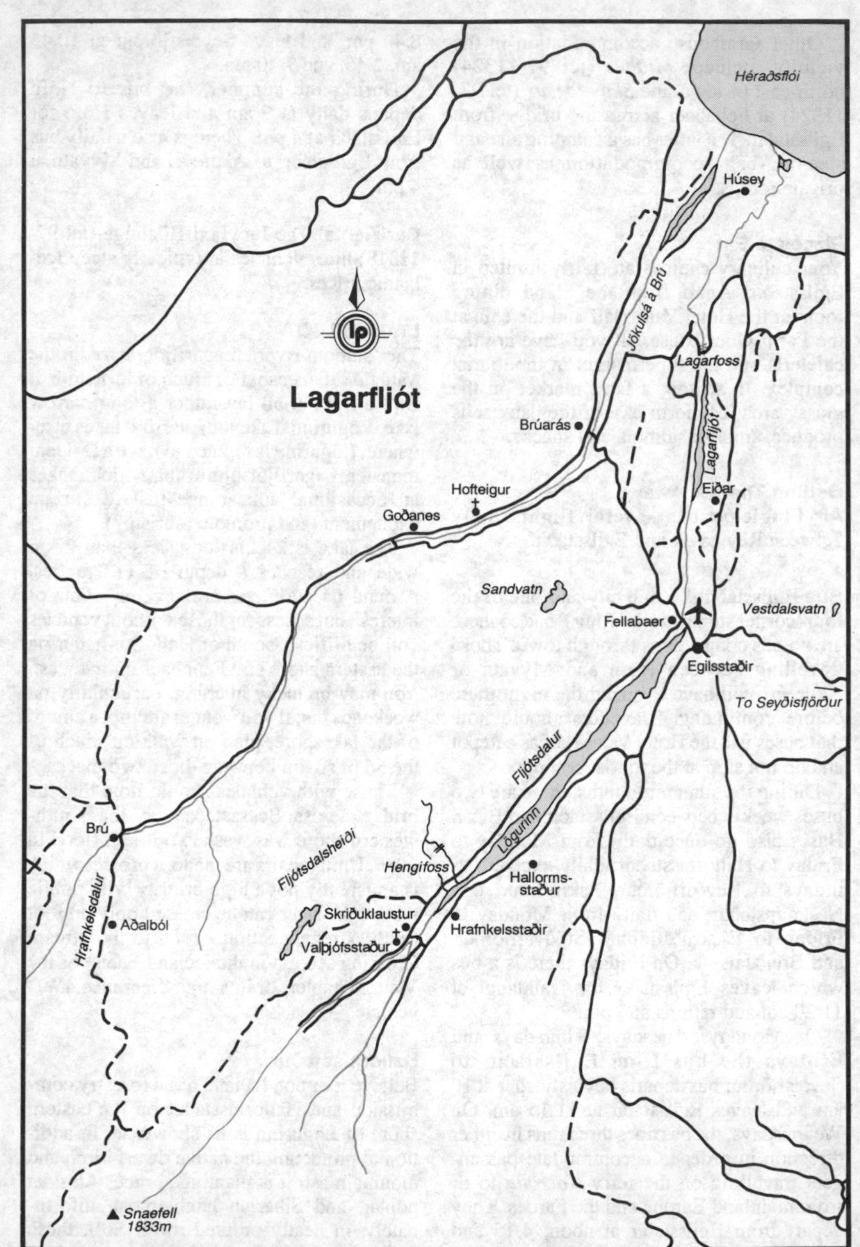

Lagarfljót
Héraðsflói
Húsey
Jökulsá á Brú
Lagarfoss
Lagarfljót
Brúarás
Hofteigur
Goðanes
Eiðar
Sandvatn
Fellabaer
Vestdalsvatn
Egilsstaðir
To Seyðisfjörður
Fljótsdalur
Lögurinn
Brú
Fljótsdalsheiði
Hengifoss
Hallormsstaður
Skriðuklaustur
Hrafnkelsstaðir
Aðalból
Valþjófsstaður
Hrafnkelsdalur
Snaefell
1833m

trees seem heartily welcome to the normally tree-starved Icelanders who flock to this place. Lots of travellers seem to enjoy it as well.

Formerly a large farm, Hallormsstaður covers about 800 hectares. It was the home of Guðmundur Magnússon, Iceland's prominent 18th-century publisher and translator.

Places to Stay Hallormsstaður boasts an *Edda Hotel* (tel 97-11705) with a restaurant and sleeping-bag accommodation but no swimming pool. Down the hill, near the lakeshore at Atlavík, is a beautiful but very noisy camping ground. It is extremely popular on summer weekends and may be full so try to arrive early.

Hrafnkelsstaðir

Above the head of Lagarfljót, about 10 km south-west of Hallormsstaður, is the farm Hrafnkelsstaðir where the reformed Hrafnkell Hallfreðarson Freysgoði of saga fame fled after being tortured and forced to leave his ancestral farm Aðalból in Hrafnkelsdalur. For more history, see the Hrafnkelsdalur section later in this chapter.

Valþjófsstaður

The tiny and unassuming church at Valþjófsstaður at the head of Lögurinn is worth a look inside, if you're nearby. The door, which depicts an ancient battle scene, is a replica of the famous one carved at Valþjófsstaður around 1200. (The original is on display at the National Museum in Reykjavík.) The farm on which it sits also dates back to the 13th century.

Skriðuklaustur

Just a few km north of Valþjófsstaður along the road is the unusual stone building at Skriðuklaustur. It served as a monastery from 1493 until the Reformation, then as a church until 1792. It's now used as an agricultural and sheep research institute and interested visitors can have a look around if there's someone there.

Hengifoss

While the Icelanders love Hallormsstaður, the primary attraction for foreign travellers along Lögurinn seems to be Hengifoss ('the hanging falls') – the third highest falls in Iceland and one of the more unusual. It sounds like a 747 taking off as the water

Wood carving on the church door, Valþjófsstaður

plummets 120 metres into a brown and red-striped gorge.

It can be reached by a fairly well-defined track (once a sheep trail) leading up from the south end of the first bridge south of the farm Brekka and north of Bessastaðagerði on the western shore of Lögurinn. Allow an hour for the climb up (although it will probably take less) and half that coming down. Halfway up, the smaller falls Litlanesfoss are surrounded by spectacular basalt columns.

Fljótsdalsheiði & Snaefell

The expanses of Fljótsdalsheiði ('the river valley moors') stretch away westward from Lögurinn into the interior. The extinct volcano Snaefell ('snow mountain') the 1833-metre-high peak at the southern end of Fljótsdalsheiði, is the country's highest outside the Vatnajökull massif and is popular for mountaineering. Although it's not difficult to climb, weather can be a concern and proper climbing equipment is essential.

Access to Snaefell is by 4WD and even then only for 2 months or so at the height of summer. It's also possible to walk the 60 or so km from the end of Lögurinn to the mountain. Head along the road leading steeply upward from the Bessastaðir farm near the broken bridge. It winds along for about 8 km onto the moors, an eerie expanse of both wet and dry tundra.

When you see a large mound of stones (with an odd structure that looks like a cross or an antenna which is actually neither and serves no apparent purpose) to your right on top of a hill called Klausturshaeð Þherfall Teigsberg, climb up for an amazing view nearly halfway across Iceland. On a clear day you can see Askja, Herðubreið, Vatnajökull, and Snaefell.

If you keep walking along this road, you will eventually reach Snaefell itself where there is, at an altitude of 800 metres, a mountain hut which will hold up to 60 people. Along this track you'll have a good chance of observing wild, albeit introduced, Icelandic reindeer.

If you'd rather not follow the road's sinuous climb, scramble up to the ridge (just south of the Bessastaðaá and its spectacular gorge) and then meet up with the road as it circles that river's headwaters. It is also possible to climb up the hillside about 1 km south of Valþjófsstaður church. The cliffs are steep and can be dangerous but are negotiable if you're careful. At the top are funny tussocks of wet tundra, boulder fields, perennial snow patches, and numerous alpine lakes.

Lagarfoss

Lagarfoss 'falls' are actually a long, wildly turbulent chute along the Jökulsá á Dal. A power plant there is fed by a 6-metre drop in one small channel and there is also a fish ladder where jumping salmon can be seen in late July and August. It's difficult to reach it without a private vehicle but, if you're really keen, take the BSÍ Borgarfjörður Eystri tour bus (which leaves from Egilsstaðir on Tuesdays at 11.30 am) to the intersection of Routes 94 and 944, then walk south-westward on 944 for 10 km to the falls. You'll probably have to hitch back which may be a difficult proposition. At this point, you'll probably have realised the trip isn't worth it.

Urriðavatn

The lake Urriðavatn, a couple of km along the Ring Road west of the Lagarfljót bridge, contains the only hot springs used for heating east of the volcanic zone. It is also a source of water for Egilsstaðir.

Eiðar

There's an Edda hotel (tel 97-13803) with a swimming pool, licensed restaurant, and sleeping-bag accommodation at Eiðar, just 12 km north of Egilsstaðir on Route 94. It sits beside a popular trout lake close to Lagarfljót and caters primarily to fisherfolk. Despite the short distance, only two buses weekly go to Eiðar because most people have vehicles. You'd probably be better off trying to hitch.

Héraðsflói The shores of the bight Héraðsflói form an intriguing landscape of sand dunes, basalt outcrops, and marshes at the mouths of Lagarfljót and Jökulsá á Brú. This is also one of the best places in Iceland to observe the Fata Morgana that on bright, sunny days augment the view out to sea with beautiful fictitious rocky islets.

Húsey

Húsey, near the shores of Heraðsflói, is a farm and 20-bed youth hostel. It's fairly isolated and is an excellent spot to observe seals (the farmers hunt, tan, and eat them by the way), geese, and waders, and provides a good opportunity to learn about Icelandic farming. Camping is available as well.

To reach Húsey, take the Egilsstaðir to Mývatn bus to the eastern side of the Brúarás bridge about 20 km north-west of Egilsstaðir along the Ring Road. If you've booked in advance, the hostel wardens will fetch you from here. Unfortunately, the Húsey hostel was recently marked for possible closure so check at the tourist office in Egilsstaðir before making plans.

JÖKULSÁ Á BRÚ

The name means 'glacial river of the bridge'. The river originally was spanned by a natural bridge (which has since collapsed) at the farm Brú, 28 km upstream from the Ring Road. The river is 150 km long, the longest in eastern Iceland. It is an extremely silty and turbulent watercourse. Each hour it deposits, in Heraðsflói, nearly 1 tonne of Icelandic real estate for each km of its length. Folktales say that during the 16th century another of those Nessie-style monsters was observed in the river near the bridge where the Ring Road now crosses.

Farmhouse accommodation with sleeping-bag option is available at Brúarás (tel 97-11046) near the Ring Road bridge.

Goðanes

The stretch of the Jökulsá á Brú along the present Ring Road is said to be haunted not only by monsters but also by mischievous leprechauns and bloodthirsty Norse deities. The outcrop called Goðanes lies about 3 km west of the farm Hofteigur and was the site of an ancient pagan temple where some ruins are still visible. A nearby iron-stained spring is called Blóðkelda ('blood spring') because, as legend has it, the blood of both human and animal sacrifices flowed into it.

HRAFNKELSDALUR

This side valley, south of the Jökulsá á Brú above the farm Brú, is full of Saga-Age ruins. The farm Aðalból was the home of Hrafnkell Hallfreðarson Freysgoði, the priest of Freyr and hero of the popular *Hrafnkels Saga*.

There's a 4WD track that continues up the valley and connects with the Bessastaðir track offering Snaefell-bound mountaineers the choice to follow a loop. For anyone else, there's not really anything that justifies the considerable effort getting there will require but, if you're a saga buff, you may take exception to that assessment.

Hrafnkels Saga

One of Iceland's most popular sagas and one which has been translated into English is the saga of Hrafnkell, a priest of the Norse war god, Freyr. Hrafnkell, a religious fanatic, built a temple to his favourite god on the farm at Aðalból in Hrafnkelsdalur where he held animal sacrifices and offered up half his wealth in veneration of Freyr.

Hrafnkell's prize stallion was called Freyfaxi ('the mane of Freyr') and he swore to the gods to strike down the person who dared ride him without permission. As you would expect, someone did. It seems the stallion himself tempted one of Hrafnkell's shepherds into riding him to find a herd of lost sheep. He returned from the excursion exhausted and covered with mud. Hrafnkell, of course, knew what had happened and wasted no time taking his axe to the errant youth.

In a moment of belated conscience, he offered the boy's father, Þorbjörn, compensation for the loss of his son in the form of foodstuffs and financial help. Proudly, the man refused and the characters were launched into a court battle that ultimately led to Hrafnkell's being declared an outlaw. Responding with a decidedly wait-and-see attitude, he decided to ignore the sentence and return home.

He didn't have long to wait before Þorbjörn's nephew Sámur Bjarnason took the matter into his own hands. Hrafnkell was summarily subjected to the particularly painful and humiliating Norse custom of stringing enemies up by their Achilles tendons until they were prepared to make enough concessions to their torturers.

Hrafnkell had given up his estates and his priestly authority as a result of the experience. His temple was destroyed and Freyfaxi was weighted with stones, thrown over a cliff, and drowned in the water below. Hrafnkell, apparently convinced by now that his favourite god didn't care about his predicament, renounced his beliefs and moved to a new farm beside Lagarfljót. He vowed to reform his naturally vengeful character and become a kind and simple farmer. So great was his success with the new farm, however, that he gained even more wealth and power than he'd had at Aðalból and it appeared as though history was fated to repeat itself.

One day, Sámur's brother Eyvindur came by en route to Aðalból. As he passed Hrafnkelsstaðir, Hrafnkell's maid saw him and reminded her employer of his responsibility to take his revenge. Something snapped in Hrafnkell. Abandoning his vow to reform, he set out in pursuit of the troublesome brothers. He made quick work of dispatching Eyvindur before tackling Sámur and forcing him to flee the ill-gotten Aðalból. Hrafnkell thereby regained his former estates and, as far as anyone knows, lived there happily ever after.

Getting There & Away

No public transport (and scarcely anything mobile) finds its way into Hrafnkelsdalur so, again, those without a sturdy vehicle should expect to follow literally in Hrafnkell's footsteps and hoof the 73 km from the Ring Road to Snaefell. This will require about 4 days each way under optimum conditions. Weather on this high and lonely plateau is extremely changeable so come prepared for winter at any time of year.

BORGARFJÖRÐUR EYSTRI

The village of Borgarfjörður Eystri (Borgarfjörður East), sometimes known as Bakkagerði, probably doesn't receive as much attention as it should. Beneath a stunning backdrop of rugged rhyolite peaks on one side and the spectacular Dyrfjöll mountains on the other, the town enjoys the best setting in eastern Iceland. Iceland's best-known artist, Jóhannes Kjarval who lived at the nearby farm Geitavík, was inspired by the place and it seems that its relatively few visitors are as well.

Awkwardly nicknamed 'the paradise of the mineral enthusiast', it is popular with rock hounds who come to search for jasper, zeolite, obsidian, basalt, and agate. Some of the best and most accessible hunting grounds are found near the beach east of town. The sandy spit across the estuary serves as a nesting and roosting site for thousands of gulls. The slightest disturbance results in panic and an explosion of flapping wings and feathers. It's good entertainment, if you have time to sit and watch awhile.

In the village itself is a well maintained and often-photographed historic sod-covered home but, since it is still inhabited, it isn't open to visitors.

Lots of mountain walks are easily reached from town. Walk around the estuary to Geitfell and Svartfell if you're interested in scrambling around on the rhyolite peaks. Away from vegetation, use extreme caution because the material is unconsolidated and, at times, makes for an experience akin to walking on thousands of tiny ball bearings.

Church

The pride of the village seems to be the beautiful altarpiece in its church – a Kjarval painting depicting the Sermon on the Mount with Dyrfjöll in the background and a typically Icelandic sky above.

Álfasteinn

This rock shop, strictly for the tourists, seems to make a fortune collecting the semi-precious stones lying around everywhere, polishing them up, gluing them into kitsch forms, and selling them to tourists at premium prices. They do have a few high-quality items for sale here but most of them have been imported from Brazil. It's worth a look around, anyway. The shop is open Monday to Saturday from 10 am to noon and 1 to 6 pm and on Sundays from 1 to 6 pm only. The name, by the way, means 'elf stone'.

Álfaborg

The name of this small mound and nature reserve near the camping ground means 'elf rock'. On top there is a view disc and a fabulous vista. In the spring, the surrounding fields are white with blooming Arctic cotton. This is the 'borg' that gave Borgarfjörður Eystri its name.

Places to Stay & Eat

Sleeping-bag accommodation can be found at the *Fjarðarborg* (tel 97-29920) hall for US$8.75 per person. At the farm *Stapi* (tel 97-29983), about 500 metres south of town along the coast, it costs US$13 per person. Stapi also offers normal farmhouse accommodation, private rooms and camping.

The only enterprise that resembles a hotel is the *Greiðasalan Borg* (tel 97-29943), a bed & breakfast on the main street.

The camping site beside the church has sinks and flush toilets and can be used free of charge.

Horse Trips

Short excursions on horseback through the Borgarfjörður Eystri district or longer trips across the Loðmundarfjarðarleið are available from Guðmundur Sveinsson at the farm Bakki (tel 97-29987) immediately south-west of the village.

Getting There & Away

The only public transport to Borgarfjörður Eystri is the BSÍ tour that operates from Egilsstaðir on Tuesdays at 11.30 am. The tour spends a great deal of time in the

Álfasteinn rock shop. The normal price for this tour is US$40, but those with the Omnibuspass can join it free. Chances of hitching to or from Egilsstaðir could be rated as poor to medium.

AROUND BORGARFJÖRÐUR EYSTRI

Staðarfjall

Staðarfjall is the colourful 621-metre-high rhyolite mountain, about 8 km south-east of Borgarfjörður Eystri, which is nice for day-walks. The best access is up the ridge from the farm Desjamýri across the estuary from the village. Legend has it that a troll is buried in the gravel near the foot of the mountain there.

Dyrfjöll

One of Iceland's most rugged ranges, the Dyrfjöll mountains rise precipitously to an altitude of 1136 metres between the valley of Lagarfljót and Borgarfjörður Eystri. The name means 'door mountain' due to the large and conspicuous notch in the highest peak – Iceland's answer to Sweden's famous Lapporten. The range is composed of heavily glaciated basalt, tuff, and rhyolite. There are no actual tracks through the range but day-hikes and longer trips are possible from Borgarfjörður Eystri just a couple of km from its base.

Njarðvíkurskriður

This dangerous bit of scree-slope, near Njarðvík en route to Borgarfjörður Eystri from Egilsstaðir, was the site of numerous tragic accidents in ancient times. All of these were blamed on a nuisance ghost believed to reside in a cave at sea level beneath the slope.

In the early 1300s, the ghost was exorcised by the proper religious authorities and, in 1306, a cross was erected on the site bearing the inscription *Effigiem Christi qui transis pronus honora* which means 'You who are hurrying past, honour the image of Christ'. The idea was that travellers would repeat a prayer when passing the danger zone and therefore be protected from malevolent powers. The cross has been replaced several times since but the current one is still inscribed with the original prayer.

Walking in the Eastfjords

Although not so large nor so rugged as their counterparts in north-west Iceland, the Eastfjords nonetheless provide a lot of scenic value for visitors. Villages are all small and quiet and everywhere walkers will find opportunities to explore. Most trekking in the area will also entail route-finding so topo sheets and good navigational skills will be essential for any off-track forays.

With some careful planning, it is possible to follow old riding and walking routes through the mountains all the way from Borgarfjörður Eystri in the north to Breiðdalsvík in the south, passing through Seyðisfjörður and Reyðarfjörður for supplies en route. It's not an easy walk, however, and will require some scree-sliding, snow-walking, boulder-hopping, and bog-slogging so come prepared.

LOÐMUNDARFJARÐARLEIÐ

Although it's scarcely known at the moment, I suspect that this route up over the mountains between Borgarfjörður Eystri and Loðmundarfjörður will become increasingly popular with backpackers in years to come.

Although the route follows a 4WD track up over the pass, there are lots of opportunities for further exploration in more pristine surroundings. The trip begins at the farm Hvannstöð, 9 km south of Borgarfjörður Eystri, and continues for 30 km over Húsavíkurheiði from which a side track leads down to the small bay of Húsavík and the deserted Loðmundarfjörður. From there, the really keen can follow the route that continues from there up Hjálmárdalur and across to Seyðisfjörður, another 30 km of much harder going. The map required for this walk is *Dyrfjöll 1:100,000* (1986).

The usual warning to carry clothing for adverse weather conditions holds true here also. Of course walkers will need to carry a tent and be self-sufficient in food, cooking equipment, and fuel. As usual, it's also a good idea to bring along several days' extra supply of food in case the weather is bad or the scenery distracts you.

Along Loðmundarfjarðarleið

Hvítserkur This unusual mountain that rises to an altitude of 775 metres above Húsavíkurheiði is composed of rose-coloured rhyolite shot through with impressive basalt dykes.

Húsavík This small bay and deserted farm site is a 6-km-return side trip. It isn't particularly interesting but may be a nice trip down to the shore if the weather is fine.

Nesháls This pass, between Víkurá and Loðmundarfjörður, is 435 metres above sea level. Just to the west is the 830-metre peak Skaelingur, sometimes called the 'Chinese temple' but I suspect that 'Tibetan lamasery' would more accurately describe it.

Loðmundarfjörður This relatively short but beautiful fjord was once well-settled with at least 10 farms occupying the upper basin. It seemed uneconomical to build all-season roads into sparsely populated areas and, when coastal supply vessels stopped sailing, habitation became too difficult in such remote corners of Iceland. Except for the summer house at Stakkahlíð where sleeping-bag accommodation may be arranged, the entire valley is now deserted.

Karlfell This 925-metre-high symmetrical peak stands out prominently above Loðmundarfjörður and dominates the view from the head of the fjord.

Stakkahlíð This recently abandoned farm above the head of Loðmundarfjörður lies near the foot of rhyolite deposits fallen from the hill Flatafjall. In this area you can also find deposits of petrified wood signifying that this was once forested country.

SEYÐISFJÖRÐUR

Seyðisfjörður, the terminal for ferries from the European mainland, is a pleasant introduction to Iceland for many travellers. It's an architecturally interesting town surrounded on three sides by mountains and on the other by a deep, 16-km-long fjord. Travellers expect to feel the pinch in Iceland, but Seyðisfjörður greets them with some of the highest prices in the country before they get a real feel for the situation. Grocery prices are noticeably higher here than in Egilsstaðir, the hotel restaurant is very expensive and even an innocent postcard costs US$0.90. If you're concerned about cash, it's best to save optional purchases for Egilsstaðir and beyond.

Seyðisfjörður started in 1834 as a trading centre and, thanks to its sheltering fjord, grew over the next few decades into eastern Iceland's largest settlement. During this period of prosperity most of the town's beautiful and unique Norwegian-style wooden buildings were constructed. Seyðisfjörður attained municipal status in 1895.

In summer, the Smyril Line ferry *Norröna* arrives from Hanstholm (Denmark), Tórshavn (the Faroe Islands), Lerwick (the Shetland Islands), and Bergen (Norway) on Thursdays at 8 am and departs 3 to 4 hours later. Obligingly, local residents hold an art & craft market on Wednesday afternoons and Thursday mornings in order to inspire last minute souvenir frenzies.

At last reports, fishing without a permit was possible in the river Fjarðará above town, but check locally to see whether the situation has changed.

Information

Tourist Information The tourist information desk is found in the Smyril Line building at the ferry dock. They stock an overwhelming number of brochures dealing with attractions all over the country and will book your onward accommodation free of charge.

Post & Telephone The post & telephone office is on the eastern shore, 1 km from the ferry dock toward the small boat harbour.

Bank The bank is on Oddagata, 300 metres from the dock. When the boat comes in, however, it becomes a crowd scene with disembarking passengers struggling to change currency. If you'd rather avoid that, buy enough Icelandic currency in Europe or the Faroes to get you through to Egilsstaðir. 'Enough', incidentally, is probably best defined as twice what you expect to need.

Consulates There is a German consulate at the Norröna dock. The Danish consulate is found in the Smyril Line office and the Swedish consulate is opposite the small boat harbour.

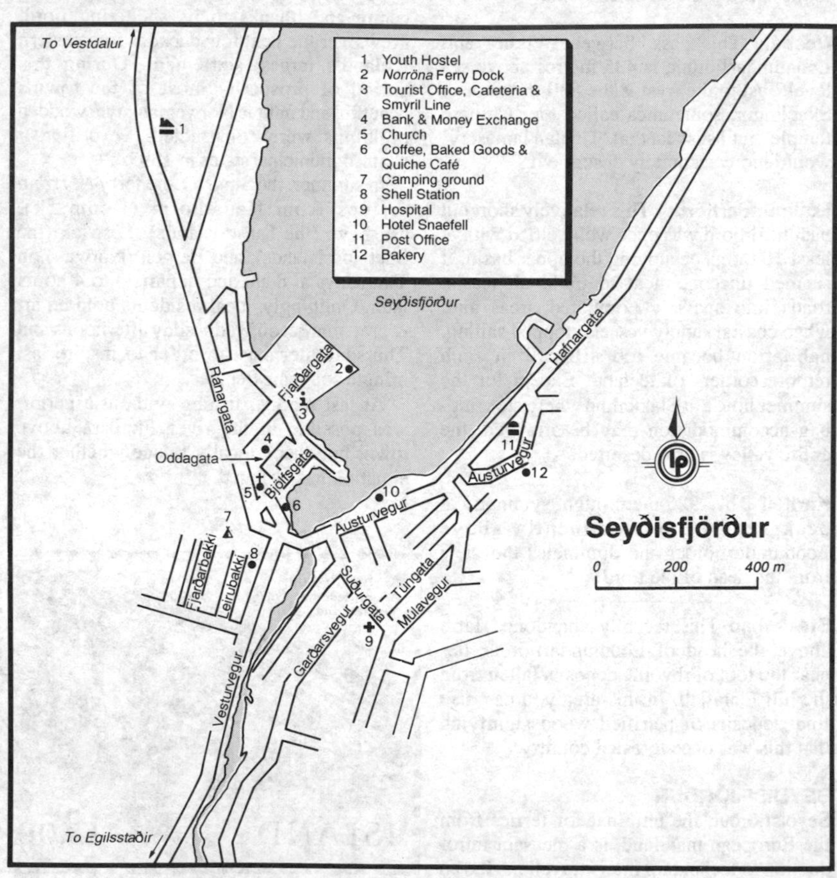

Places to Stay

Predictably, Seyðisfjörður has a *Youth Hostel* (tel 97-21410). It's been recently renovated and is a clean and cosy place to crash before or after a normally rough boat ride. Since it's frequently full of departing passengers on Wednesday nights and new arrivals on Thursday nights, advance bookings are advised if you plan to stay there on either day.

Farmhouse accommodation can be found at *Þórsmörk* (tel 97-21324). They offer sleeping-bag space so, if the hostel is full, there is another budget option.

The pleasant and well located *Hotel Snaefell* (tel 97-21460) costs singles/doubles US$61/81. This is quite reasonable considering it costs half that for a meal in their dining room!

The camping site is beside the Shell petrol station in the town centre. Alternatively, excellent (and free) camping sites are found below the first waterfall in Vestdalur less than an hour's walk from town. What's more, they're out of range of the unpleasant fishy smell that pervades Seyðisfjörður.

Places to Eat

The only fully fledged restaurant in town is at the *Hotel Snaefell*. It seems to be one of the dearest in the country, but the food isn't anything special. It probably should be given a miss unless you're prepared for a financial blow-out.

On the corner by the bridge is a very pleasant and reasonably priced coffee shop which also serves home-baked goods, quiche, and specials. It's open weekdays and Saturdays from 2 pm, and on Friday mornings between 9 am and noon.

There are two supermarkets, both closed between 12.30 and 1.30 pm. The kiosk, however, is open for lunch. Light snacks are available at the Smyril Line office near the ferry dock.

Vestdalur Walk

A wonderful introduction to walking in Iceland is the popular trip up the Vestdalur valley and around Mt Bjólfur to the Seyðisfjörður to Egilsstaðir road. It makes an

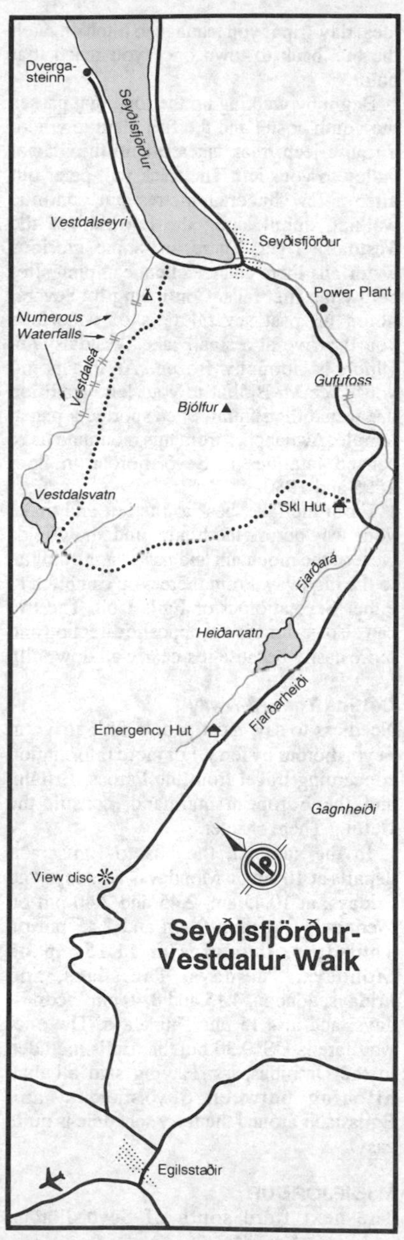

ideal day-trip if you manage to hitch or catch the bus back to town once you reach that point.

Begin by walking up the road that passes the youth hostel and the fish plant to where a rough jeep track takes off up the glacial valley to your left. The track will peter out after a few hundred metres but continue walking uphill along the left side of the Vestdalsá river. There are some glorious waterfalls there and excellent camping sites below the first falls. Continuing for several hours up past several tiers of waterfalls you'll arrive at a small lake, Vestdalsvatn, which is normally frozen. At this point, you'll see Mt Bjólfur to your left. Tradition has it that the summit once sported a pagan temple. Avalanches from this mountain have caused fatalities in Seyðisfjörður in both 1895 and 1950.

From the lake, bear to the left and make your way across the tundra and snowfields west of the mountain and past a small ski hut to the highway. From there, you can hitch to either Seyðisfjörður or Egilsstaðir. The trip can also be done in the opposite direction and more easily because it's nearly all downhill.

Getting There & Away

Needless to say, most people first arrive in Seyðisfjörður by ferry. For more information concerning travel from the Faroes, Britain, and the European mainland, consult the Getting There chapter.

In the summer, the bus to Egilsstaðir departs at 10 am on Mondays, Tuesdays and Fridays; at 10.45 am, 2.45 and 7.40 pm on Wednesdays; and at 9 am and 2.45 pm on Thursdays. It returns at 11.15 am on Mondays, Tuesdays, Thursdays, and Fridays; at noon, 4.15 and 8.40 pm Wednesdays; and at 4.15 pm Thursdays. The one-way fare is US$9.30 but the trip is included in the Omnibuspass. Having said all that, hitching between Seyðisfjörður and Egilsstaðir around the ferry schedule is quite easy.

MJÓIFJÖRÐUR

The next fjord south of Seyðisfjörður, Mjóifjörður is well off the tourist circuit. In fact, the district, which has a population of only 35, is well off anyone's circuit. Despite that, Mjóifjörður is flanked on both sides by spectacular cliffs and it's generally considered the most beautiful fjord in Iceland. It is a very interesting region with many abandoned turf farmsteads and a nice 19th-century wooden church at Brekkuþorp. The best known attraction, however, is the ruin of the Dalatangi lighthouse, the oldest in the country. The new lighthouse and nearby vegetable and flower gardens are also of interest. Asknes on the southern shore was the site of a Norwegian whaling station early in this century.

Due to the lack of sheep in some areas, parts of the valley are covered with blueberries ripe for the picking in early autumn (late August or early September).

Places to Stay & Eat

There used to be a youth hostel at Brekkuþorp but it seems to have gone. Given the current popularity of Iceland as a backpackers' destination, however, it may be worthwhile checking at the tourist information office in Egilsstaðir to see if the situation has changed.

The former hostel is now occupied by a small guesthouse (tel 97-60002) which offers sleeping-bag accommodation. Out the back is a camping site as well, but you can camp almost anywhere in this valley.

Limited groceries are available at the shop in Brekkuþorp.

Getting There & Away

Hitching into Mjóifjörður is as near to hopeless as you're likely to get. From Egilsstaðir, there is one bus a week that goes to Dalatangi, departing Egilsstaðir at 11.30 am Fridays and returning at 4 pm the same day. The trip leaves little time for anything but a buzz around the lighthouse. Those who wish to have a better look will probably be in for a 47-km walk from Dalatangi back to Route 92 where it's possible to catch a bus to Egilsstaðir or Neskaupstaður daily from Monday to Friday.

Alternatively, those with a couple of extra days can make their way eastward along the southern shore of Mjóifjörður and ascend the Reykjaá valley to 1100-metre Goðaborg before descending to Kirkjuból, 8 km west of Neskaupstaður. From there, it's fairly easy to get a bus out to Egilsstaðir. If you haven't already worked it out, you can also enter Mjóifjörður by this route.

ESKIFJÖRÐUR

Stretched out along a short side fjord of Reyðarfjörður, the village of Eskifjörður looks across the water at the majestic 985-metre peak of Hólmatindur. The peak is beautiful, residents agree, but it's a bit of a nuisance in that it severely limits their day-light hours; the village receives no sunlight at all between September and April. In addition, the slopes behind the town, down which four rivers tumble, pose serious avalanche threats during the winter.

Although Eskifjörður was a recognised trading centre as early as the late 1700s and its herring fishery reached its height in the late 19th century, the village didn't receive municipal status until 1974. About 1100 people live there currently.

Maritime Museum

The Maritime Museum of East Iceland is housed in an old general store constructed in the early 1800s. There you can see 2 centuries of history of the east coast fishing and whaling industries. It's open daily between 15 June and 1 September from 2 to 5 pm.

Helgustaðir

At Helgustaðir, about 9 km south-east of Eskifjörður, are the remains of the largest Iceland spar (silfurberg) mine in the world. It began operating in the 1600s but is now abandoned. Geology buffs will probably want to have a look but it probably won't provide much interest for anyone else. Incidentally, the mines are now a national preserve so absconding with anything that may be of interest is officially a no-no.

Places to Stay & Eat

The only official lodging in town is the *Hotel Askja* (tel 97-61261). Camping is available at the abandoned farm Byggdarholt, about 1 km outside the village.

Apart from the hotel dining room, which serves meals and light snacks, the only food options are the supermarket or the grill and snack bar at the petrol station.

Getting There & Away

During the summer, there is a bus between Egilsstaðir and Neskaupstaður daily Monday to Friday. Westbound, it leaves Neskaupstaður at 8.30 am and passes through Eskifjörður at 9.10 am. Eastbound, it leaves Egilsstaðir at 11.10 am and passes here at noon.

REYÐARFJÖRÐUR

Reyðarfjörður, formerly known as Búðareyri, sits at the head of the largest fjord along the eastern coast. It's a relatively new settlement, having become a trading place early in this century. During WW II, it was one of several allied bases in Iceland.

Above the fjord, about 2 km east of town, there is a view disc and, of course, a broad vista. The extremely energetic can make the 985-metre climb up Hólmatindur which rises behind the town. It's a far easier proposition from this side than from Eskifjörður.

Places to Stay & Eat

The *Hotel Búðareyri* (tel 97-41378) and the *KHB Guesthouse* provide formal accommodation but budget travellers will have to resort to the camping site near the west end of town. For food, there are a couple of small shops in the village and both hotels have restaurants.

NESKAUPSTAÐUR

Sometimes known as Norðfjörður, Neskaupstaður (with a population of1700) is the largest settlement in the Eastfjords. The highway approach to Neskaupstaður crosses 632-metre Oddsskarð which is the highest mountain pass in Iceland. The summit is by-passed through a narrow 626-metre tunnel.

Like most villages along the coast, the settlement began as a trading centre. The first merchants arrived in 1882 and, by 1900, Neskaupstaður had 100 residents. Again, like most villages in the area, it prospered when the herring fishery reached its peak around the turn of the century.

Backed by steep slopes, Neskaupstaður is prone to avalanches and, in 1974, a large one tumbled down on the village and killed 12 residents.

There's a fairly nice natural history museum, Náttúrugripasafnið í Neskaupstað, in the village centre which is open from 4 to 6 pm Monday to Friday and 3 to 6 pm on weekends. Apart from that, there's nothing in particular to attract visitors to this generally scenic area unless they're interested in fine out-of-the-way trekking.

One of the more popular routes is the one up 1100-metre Goðaborg from the farm Kirkjuból, 8 km west of town. From the summit, it's possible to descend into Mjóifjörður on the other side of the ridge. Unfortunately, this is a relative dead end as far as transport is concerned (see the Mjóifjörður section in this chapter) and the best way out will often be back the way you came. Allow 2 days for the trip across since much of it involves steep ups and downs. This is best attempted only during the height of summer due to late snows at higher altitudes.

Another possible route is from Oddsskarð along the ridges eastward to the deserted fjords of Hellisfjörður and Viðfjörður. These routes can be found with the aid of the *Gerpir 1:100,000* (1986) topo sheet. It's difficult to get to Gerpir, the easternmost point of Iceland with steep cliffs along the southern edge.

Places to Stay & Eat

The hotel *Gistheimilið* (tel 97-71179), or 'guesthouse', is the only formal accommodation since the farmhouse at Kirkjuból seems to no longer accept guests.

Snacks and coffee can be found at *Hafnarkaffi* on Hafnarbraut.

Getting There & Away

In the summer, there is a bus from Egilsstaðir daily from Monday to Friday at 11.10 am. From Neskaupstaður, it departs on the same days at 8.30 am. It costs US$15.50 each way.

FÁSKRÚÐSFJÖRÐUR

The village of Fáskrúðsfjörður was originally settled by French fishermen during the late 1800s. It is sometimes known as Búðir, meaning 'booth', and the current population is around 800.

From Dalir above the head of the fjord, it's possible to walk the old route up over Stuðlaheiði to Reyðarfjörður. Near the mouth of the fjord are two small islets. Andey, or 'duck island', has a large colony of eider ducks and the other, Skrúður, contains a colony of gannets and a large cave which is believed to be the home of a giant. Neither islet is accessible by public transport.

Above the southern shore of Fáskrúðsfjörður is the laccolithic mountain Sandfell, a part of the volcanic system that existed in the Eastfjords during the Tertiary geological period. It's one of the best visible examples of this kind of igneous intrusion in the world.

Places to Stay & Eat

The *Hotel Snekkjan* (tel 97-51298) charges US$60 a double. The only other option is the camping site near the centre of the village. The only restaurant is operated by the hotel but it serves grill snacks as well as proper meals.

Getting There & Away

There is a bus that runs daily from Monday to Friday between Fáskrúðsfjörður and Egilsstaðir during the summer. It departs Fáskrúðsfjörður at 8.40 am and returns from Egilsstaðir at 11.10 am. You can travel to Stöðvarfjörður and Breiðdalsvík at 12.40 pm on the same days.

STÖÐVARFJÖRÐUR

This small village on the fjord of the same name is sometimes known as Kirkjuból, not to be confused with the farm Kirkjuból near Neskaupstaður. It has a population of only 350 and derives most of its income from fishing.

The best and frankly the only reason to visit Stöðvarfjörður is to see Steinasafn Petru (tel 97-51834) at Fjarðarbraut 21, a private collection of impressive stones and minerals assembled by resident Petra Sveinsdóttir. It's best to phone in advance to arrange a visit.

Places to Stay & Eat

The only accommodation is the camping site a few km to the west of the village. Limited snacks are available from the grill on Fjarðarbraut.

Getting There & Away

To get to Stöðvarfjörður, take the Breiðdalsvík bus from Egilsstaðir which departs Monday to Friday at 11.10 am arriving at 1.20 pm. To Egilsstaðir, the bus leaves Monday to Friday at 8 am and, to Breiðdalsvík, at 1.20 pm.

BREIÐDALSVÍK

This very young village has a population of only 260. It is beautifully situated but its primary claim to fame is that it was attacked by a German bomber in 1942. Coincidentally, the farm Snaehvammur also suffered damage during WW II when a mine exploded on the beach there in 1940.

There is a difficult walking route from Snaehvammur across the unconsolidated slopes to the fjord Stöðvarfjörður.

Places to Stay & Eat

Accommodation, camping, and meals are all available at *Hotel Bláfell* (tel 97-56770) where double rooms cost US$58. Their award-winning restaurant is highly acclaimed in Iceland and may be worth checking out. Sleeping-bag accommodation, meals, and laundry services can be found at the farm *Fell* (tel 97-56679) about 6 km up the fjord from the village.

Getting There & Away

The bus to Egilsstaðir operates during the summer departing at 7.30 am from Monday to Friday. It arrives at 10 am then turns around and leaves for Breiðdalsvík at 11.10 am.

AROUND BREIÐDALSVÍK

Breiðdalur

This valley, nestled beneath beautifully coloured rhyolite peaks, is traversed by the Ring Road as it returns to the coast from its inland jaunt through Egilsstaðir and the north-eastern deserts. On Breiðdalsheiði, near the head of the valley, you can often see reindeer from the highway. At Þorgrímsstaðir, a bit further down valley, is a 250-metre waterfall harnessed for electricity and at the abandoned farm Jörvík is a forestry reserve containing native birch and aspen woodland.

Berunes & Berufjörður

The first fjord south of Breiðdalur along the Ring Road is Berufjörður, a longish steep-sided fjord flanked by rhyolite peaks and dominated by the 1069-metre mountain Búlandstindur above the south-western shore. There are several historical walking routes which may still be negotiated through the steeply rugged terrain. The best known of these climbs from the head of the fjord at the farm Berufjörður, crosses the 700-metre pass Berufjarðarskarð then descends into Breiðdalur.

Places to Stay A good staging point for exploring the district is the *Berunes Youth Hostel* (tel 97-88988) with 25 bunks and a camping site. The hostel building dates back to 1907 and the neighbouring church was used during the previous century. There's no shop at Berunes, so you'll have to bring supplies from elsewhere, but cooking facilities are provided. Breakfast is available at the hostel for an additional charge.

The farm *Eyjólfsstaðir* (tel 97-88971) on the south-western shore of Berufjörður offers private rooms, camping, and sleeping-bag accommodation. The nearby river Fossá is riddled with cascading waterfalls.

Either of these places can recommend hiking routes and advise you on current conditions.

Getting There & Away All buses between Egilsstaðir and Höfn pass through Berunes.

DJÚPIVOGUR

Djúpivogur at the mouth of Berufjörður is the oldest trading centre in the Eastfjords. It has served as a commercial port since the 16th century and thrived through the inception and heyday of the Danish Trade Monopoly. Today, it survives as a quiet fishing village with 450 residents.

Places to Stay & Eat

The *Hotel Framtíð* (tel 97-88887) is small and very nice as Icelandic hotels go. With only nine rooms and a small restaurant specialising in fresh locally caught fish and seafood, it's a comfortable and pleasant sort of place. Singles/doubles cost US$43/54 but, if they're not full, sleeping-bag accommodation can be arranged.

Alternatively, there is a camping site at Hermannastekkur near the intersection of the Ring Road and Route 98.

Getting There & Away

Like Berufjörður, Djúpivogur is on the Ring Road so all buses travelling between Egilsstaðir and Höfn stop there. During the summer, there's a daily bus that leaves Höfn at 9 am and stops at the hotel in Djúpivogur at 11 am. Southbound, the bus leaves Egilsstaðir at 4 pm and passes Djúpivogur at 8.15 pm.

AROUND DJÚPIVOGUR

Búlandstindur

This obtrusive peak on the south-western shore of Berufjörður rises to 1068 metres. The westernmost part is called Goðaborg, or 'God's rock'. When Iceland officially converted to Christianity in either 999 or 1000, locals supposedly carried their pagan images to the top of this mountain and threw them over the cliff.

The tourist literature says that it's an easy climb to the top but I suspect that's a bit optimistic. You be the judge.

Teigarhorn

At the farm Teigarhorn, just 4 km from Djúpivogur, is the finest deposit of zeolite in Iceland. Rock hounds shouldn't get any ideas about collecting, however, since the geology is now officially protected. If you're interested in seeing the farmer's collection, make enquiries at the hotel in Djúpivogur.

Djáknadys

This odd heap of stones beside the Ring Road, about 12 km west of Djúpivogur on the northern shore of Hamarsfjörður, is said to be the result of a battle between two early ecumenical authorities who fought and killed each other on this spot. It has since been determined that passing travellers who toss three stones on top of the pile will prevent any unfortunate events happening on their journey.

Just 5 km west at the farm Bragðavellir, at the head of Hamarsfjörður, two Roman coins were unearthed in 1952. This led to speculation that a lost Roman ship might have happened along at some time in the dim and distant past. It is far more likely, however, that the coins were merely plundered souvenirs from Britain or other lands ravaged by the Vikings.

Geithallar

Although it's nothing spectacular, the farm Geithallar is historically significant because it's on the site where famous first settler Ingólfur Arnarson and his chum Hjörleifur spent their winter holiday on their initial visit to Iceland in the 860s.

PAPEY

The name of the offshore island, Papey ('friars island'), indicates it was probably a hermitage for the Irish monks that inhabited Iceland before the arrival of the Norse and then fled in the face of Settlement. This tranquil island was once a farm but it is now inhabited only by nesting sea birds.

Getting There & Away

You can arrange a boat trip to Papey by contacting the Hotel Framtíð (tel 97-88887) in Djúpivogur.

STAFAFELL

Although it isn't exactly a town, the former manor farm of Stafafell, south-west of Djúpivogur, is a good place to settle in for a while and avoid the high costs of travelling around Iceland. The scenery is spectacular and there are enough hiking routes in the vicinity to keep anyone tramping over the hills for a few days.

Stafafell is situated between high rainbow-hued rhyolite peaks and Lónssandur, the delta of Jokulsá í Lóni. It functioned as a remote parsonage until 1920, and the present church contains some interesting old artefacts including an original altarpiece. For travellers, the farm operates a youth hostel (tel 97-81717), guesthouse, and camping ground.

Getting There & Away

There is a daily bus between Höfn and Egilsstaðir during the summer which departs Höfn at 9 am and passes Stafafell at around 9.20 am. The returning bus from Egilsstaðir departs at 4 pm and passes Stafafell at 9.30 pm. If you're planning to board the bus at Stafafell, have the youth hostel wardens book it for you or it could go whizzing past without stopping.

AROUND STAFAFELL

Lón

The name, which is pronounced 'lone' and means 'lagoon', fairly sums up the nature of this shallow bay enclosed by two long spits and sandwiched between the Austurhorn and Vesturhorn. To the north-west is the delta of Jökulsá í Lóni, a breeding ground for swans. Boat tours can be arranged through the youth hostel at Stafafell. Alternatively, you can just walk for hours along the empty sandspits and enjoy the loneliness (pun more or less intended) of the place.

Austurhorn

Like most other peaks in the area, the mountain Austurhorn at the eastern end of Lón is batholithic. That is, it was formed as an igneous intrusion beneath the surface and was then thrust up and revealed through erosion of the overlying material. It is primarily granite.

Beneath the walls of Austurhorn is the farm Hvalnes where there is a lighthouse and a former fishermen's landing. If you're into strolling on sandspits, this is the best access to the Fjörur spit which encloses the eastern portion of Lón.

Þórisdalur

This farm on the western bank of Jökulsá í Lóni was the home of the Skálholt clergyman Þórður Þorkelsson who lived there during the late 17th and early 18th centuries. In addition to being a physician and naturalist, he wrote a definitive work on glacial geology which was published posthumously in Germany.

To Þórður were attributed all sorts of supernatural powers including the ability to detect and intercept *utilegumenn* ('outlaw spirits') as they passed into the district over Almannaskarð and send them packing back to where they'd come from.

Trekking

The youth hostel can arrange horse tours and 4WD excursions into the rugged and colourful interior of the Lón area but these are not cheap so those on a budget will have to engage their feet in order to appreciate its appeal. Some of the walks in the area are day-trips so even those without camping equipment can reach many of the points of interest. For these walks you will need some combination of the following topo sheets: the *Hornafjörður 1:100,000* (1986), *Hamarsfjörður 1:100,000* (1987) and *Snaefell 1:100,000* (1988) .

Tröllakrókur This trip begins with a 20-km walk along the 4WD track that crosses Kjarradalsheiði to Illikambur. From there,

Walking Areas

1 Tröllakrókur & Geldingafell Hut
2 Illikambur-Víðidalur
3 Hnappadalur & Jökulgílstindar
4 Dalsheiði-Hoffellsdalur
5 Laxárdalur í Lóni-Hoffellsdalur
6 Hvanngíl
7 Reyðarártindur (Circuit)
8 Endalausidalur-Laxárdalur í Hornafirði
9 Vesturhorn (Circuit)

it's a 6-hour walk to Tröllakrókur, an area of impressive wind-eroded pinnacles beneath the tongue of Öxarfellsjökull, the eastern extreme of the Vatnajökull icecap. If you can't arrange transport to and from the end of the road, it's best to allow a minimum of 3 days for the return trip.

As a side trip (6 hours return) you can cross the ridge north of Kollumúli (see the Around Stafafell map) into Viðidalur along the Jökulsá í Lóni as it flows below the small icecaps of Tungutindar and Hofsjökull.

Geldingafell Those prepared for serious trekking can do the 3-day (each way) trip to Geldingafell mountain hut which is situated beneath the north-eastern edge of Vatnajökull between the Lónsöraefi and Fljótsdalur headwaters. The trip starts with the previously mentioned Tröllakrókur route and continues up the same valley onto the lonely moors south-east of Snaefell mountain. The hut, at 820 metres elevation, accommodates 10 persons.

Reyðarártindur This 3-hour walk which begins 7 km east of Stafafell goes up the Reyðará valley and around the peak Reyðarártindur. It returns to the Ring Road via the Ossurá valley, 11 km east of Stafafell. Across the Ring Road near the start of this walk is a view disc which names some of the surrounding natural features.

Vesturhorn It's possible to walk around this impressive 575-metre peak and its companion Brunnhorn which form a cape between Skarðsfjörður and Papafjörður. The route begins just west of the river Fjarðará and follows it until it empties into Papafjörður. Continue from there out to the cape at Papós and follow the coastline around to the Stokksnes track. From there, you can either return to the Ring Road just below Almannaskarð or continue out to the lighthouse and NATO radar station on the Stokksnes spit.

The area of Papafjörður, which used to be a fishing station and trading centre, is worth exploring if you have the time. Ruins of the settlement of Syðri-Fjörður, which was abandoned in 1899, are still visible. Just to the south are the more intriguing ruins of Papatóttir with the remnants of buildings constructed by the Irish monks who inhabited the region prior to Norse settlement.

In order to leave time for exploring, it's best to allow an entire day for this trip even though actual walking time will be only a few hours. You may also encounter difficulties hitching back and forth from Stafafell. Carry all the water you'll be needing since surface water has a tendency to disappear into the sands in this area.

Jökulgilstindar This 2 or 3-day trip will take you up to the small 1313-metre icecap Jökulgilstindar. Begin by walking from Stafafell up the 4WD track along the eastern bank of Jökulsá í Lóni then continue up the valley through the woods Austurskógar toward Hnappadalur. You can either keep going up to the headwaters of Hnappadalur or climb Jökulgilstindar to the base of the glacier.

Hvanngil A short day-walk from Stafafell goes up the ravine Raftagil and Hvanngil, down Hvannadalur, and returns via the 4WD track down the east bank of Jökulsá í Lóni.

Other Routes Other walking routes in the area include the 1 or 2-day trip up Endalausidalur from the western foot of Almannaskarð (on the Ring Road) and down the Laxárdalur í Hornafirði. Other possibilities are the 2-day trip up Laxárdalur í Lóni through Reipsdalur and down Hoffellsdalur back to the Ring Road and one which includes Dalsheiði and Hoffellsdalur. The youth hostel at Stafafell can provide both information and directions regarding these and other hikes and routes in the area.

South-East Iceland

The topography of Iceland's south-eastern quarter is dominated by the vast icecap Vatnajökull, the world's third largest after those of Antarctica and Greenland. Most of the region's population lives in the towns of Höfn and Kirkjubaejarklaustur or on farms strung out along Vatnajökull's southern flank.

Nature reigns supreme here, and the area includes Iceland's most violent and destructive volcano, the 30-km-long Lakagígar (Laki) fissure, which caused famine and destruction across the country in the late 18th century.

Similarly, beneath the Vatnajökull system lie the temperamental craters of Grímsvötn and Öraefi. These volcanoes cause more damage locked beneath the ice than they would if allowed to spout. During an eruption, some of the covering ice melts and pressure from the heat and steam actually lifts the icecap releasing devastating floods that spread out across surrounding lowlands.

The residue from these jökulhlaups, combined with the effective scouring action of ice against rock, has formed the great deserts of glacial detritus known as the sandur. These are characterised by sandy plains, long empty beaches, and shallow lagoons enclosed by sandspits and barrier islands.

Travellers through south-eastern Iceland normally spend the bulk of their time at Skaftafell National Park, a pristine enclave between the southernmost extensions of Vatnajökull. Although it's very popular with Icelanders and foreigners alike, those willing to strike out on foot will normally be able to escape the crowds.

Most visitors also take the time for an excursion onto the icecap itself either by tour bus or on foot. The glacier is popular with skiers and climbers.

KIRKJUBAEJARKLAUSTUR

Many tongues have been tied in knots trying to wrap themselves around this one but it really isn't so difficult – at least there aren't any accented letters. Try breaking it into bits: *Kirkju* meaning 'church', *baejar* meaning 'farm', and *klaustur* meaning 'convent'. If it's still a problem, just say 'Kirkju' ('KEERK-ya') and everyone will know what you mean. Currently, Kirkjubaejarklaustur has a population of 300.

Kirkju certainly isn't a must-see sort of destination but it has a surprisingly pleasant setting and a few reasonably interesting sights. If you have the time, it's worth breaking your journey between Reykjavík and Skaftafell to spend a day having a look around here.

History

Originally the town was known as Kirkjubaer. The 'klaustur' bit was added in 1186 when a convent for Benedictine nuns was established there. Although it was abandoned in 1550 with the Reformation, the name has stuck.

According to the *Landnámabók*, this tranquil place between the cliffs and the river Skaftá was first settled by papar, the Irish monks who used Iceland as a retreat before the coming of the Norse.

The first Icelander to move in was an early Christian, Ketill Fíflski or Ketill the Foolish whose genealogy was impressive. He was the nephew of Auður the Deep-Minded (Unnur) of *Laxdaela Saga*, the son of Jórunn

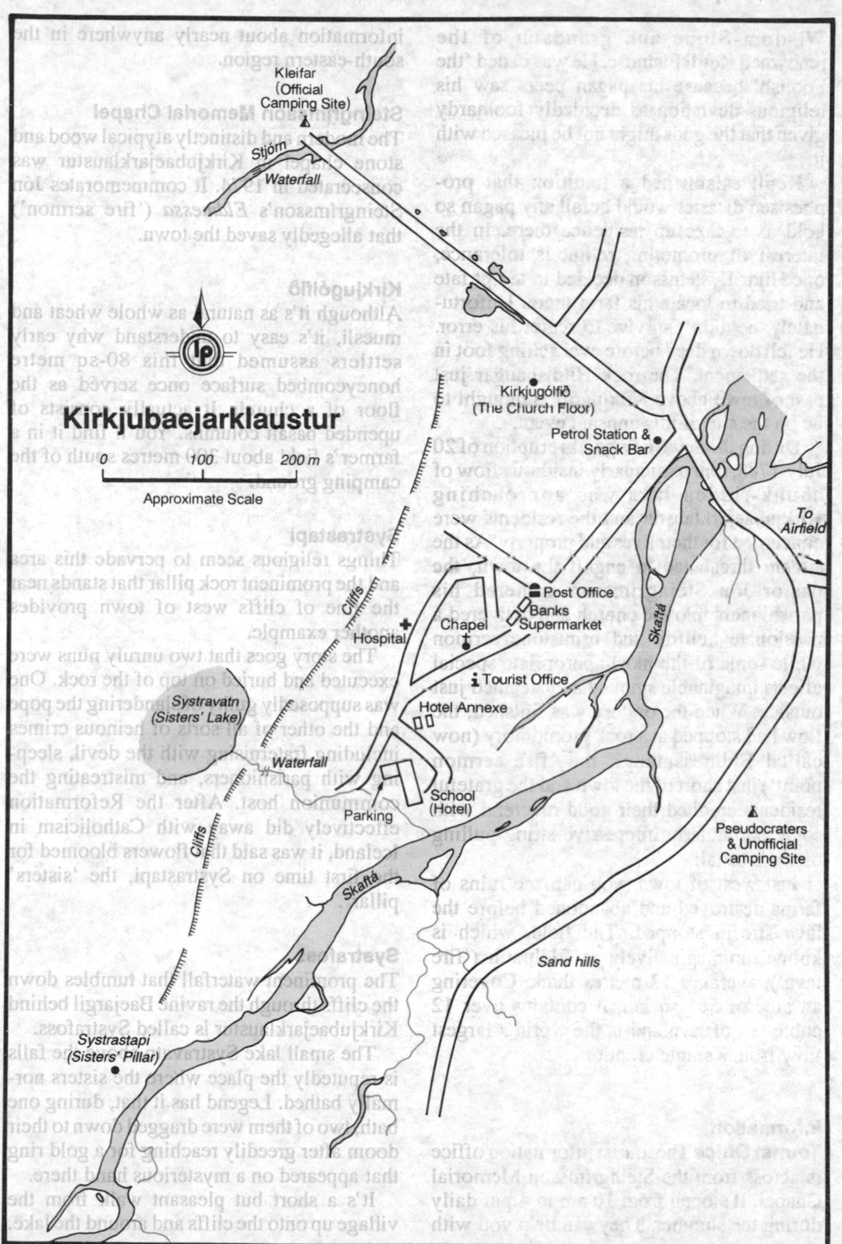
Kirkjubaejarklaustur
0
100
200 m
Approximate Scale
Kleifar
(Official
Camping Site)
Stjórn
Waterfall
Kirkjugólfið
(The Church Floor)
Petrol Station &
Snack Bar
To
Airfield
Post Office
Banks
Supermarket
Chapel
Hospital
Cliffs
Tourist Office
Hotel Annexe
Systravatn
(Sisters' Lake)
Waterfall
School
(Hotel)
Parking
Skaftá
Pseudocraters
& Unofficial
Camping Site
Cliffs
Skaftá
Sand hills
Systrastapi
(Sisters' Pillar)

Wisdom-Slope and grandson of the renowned Ketill Flatnose. He was called 'the Foolish' because his pagan peers saw his religious deviation as decidedly foolhardy given that the gods might not be pleased with it.

Ketill established a tradition that prophesised disaster would befall any pagan so bold as to take up residence there. In the interest of promoting religious tolerance, one Hildr Eysteinsson decided to tempt fate and tried to locate his farm there. Unfortunately, he didn't survive to regret his error. He fell down dead before ever setting foot in the settlement. The rock Hildishaugar just east of town above Kirkjugólf is thought to be on the site of this unusual event.

During the devastating Laki eruption of 20 July 1783, one particularly insidious flow of chunk-ridden lava was approaching Kirkjubaejarklaustur and the residents were concerned for their lives and property. As the stream threatened to engulf the town, the pastor Jón Steingrímsson gathered his parishioners into the church and delivered a passionate hellfire and brimstone sermon while some of the most appropriate special effects imaginable smoked and steamed just outside. When the oratory was finished, the flow had stopped at a rock promontory (now called Eldmessutangi, the 'fire sermon point') just short of the town and the grateful residents credited their good reverend with some particularly impressive string-pulling on their behalf.

Just west of town, you can see ruins of farms destroyed and abandoned before the lava stream stopped. The field, which is known unimaginatively as Eldhraun ('fire lava'), averages 12 metres thick. Covering an area of 565 sq km, it contains over 12 cubic km of lava and is the world's largest flow from a single eruption.

Information

Tourist Office The tourist information office is across from the Steingrímsson Memorial Chapel. It's open from 10 am to 4 pm daily during the summer. They can help you with information about nearly anywhere in the south-eastern region.

Steingrímsson Memorial Chapel

The modern and distinctly atypical wood and stone chapel in Kirkjubaejarklaustur was consecrated in 1974. It commemorates Jón Steingrímsson's *Eldmessa* ('fire sermon') that allegedly saved the town.

Kirkjugólfið

Although it's as natural as whole wheat and muesli, it's easy to understand why early settlers assumed that this 80-sq metre honeycombed surface once served as the floor of a church. It actually consists of upended basalt columns. You'll find it in a farmer's field about 300 metres south of the camping ground.

Systrastapi

Things religious seem to pervade this area and the prominent rock pillar that stands near the line of cliffs west of town provides another example.

The story goes that two unruly nuns were executed and buried on top of the rock. One was supposedly guilty of slandering the pope and the other of all sorts of heinous crimes including fraternising with the devil, sleeping with parishioners, and mistreating the communion host. After the Reformation effectively did away with Catholicism in Iceland, it was said that flowers bloomed for the first time on Systrastapi, the 'sisters' pillar'.

Systrafoss

The prominent waterfall that tumbles down the cliffs through the ravine Baejargil behind Kirkjubaejarklaustur is called Systrafoss.

The small lake Systravatn above the falls is reputedly the place where the sisters normally bathed. Legend has it that, during one bath, two of them were dragged down to their doom after greedily reaching for a gold ring that appeared on a mysterious hand there.

It's a short but pleasant walk from the village up onto the cliffs and around the lake.

Landbrot

This vast area of pseudocraters south of the Ring Road was formed during the Laki eruptions of 1783 when the steam explosions occurred in the lava-heated marshes there. It's now used as a rather informal camping area.

Foss á Siðu

On the farm Foss á Siðu is a nice waterfall which normally tumbles down from the cliffs 12 km east of Kirkju. When it's windy, however, it actually tumbles up. Don't go out of your way to get there but it's worth noticing as you pass on the Skaftafell-bound bus.

Across the road is the outcrop Dverghamrar which contains some classic basalt columns. Just 4 km east of Foss is Brunahraun, the easternmost flow of the Skaftáreldar lava which flowed down from Lakagígar in 1783.

Places to Stay & Eat

Most travellers stay at the official camping area at Kleifar 1 km north-west of the petrol station and 300 metres past Kirkjugólf. It's a substantial walk from the bus stop if you have a lot of luggage but you will be rewarded with a serene lawn beside a beautiful waterfall. What's more, it's free.

In town there is an *Edda Hotel* (tel 98-74799) which is the centre of all activity. There's lots of sleeping-bag accommodation for about US$15 and the standard rates of US$45/58 apply for single/double rooms. The hotel has a restaurant and coffee shop as well as a nice swimming pool.

Grill snacks and basic groceries are available at the petrol station/bus stop near the camping ground turn off. The supermarket is just east of the chapel.

Farmhouse Accommodation It seems there is a glut of farmhouse accommodation nearby. The only one which caters to budget travellers is *Nýibaer* (tel 98-74678) which is west of town just across the river.

Hunkabakkar (tel 98-74681) on the Laki Road, *Efri-Vík* (tel 98-74694) on Route 204 about 6 km from town, and *Geirland* (tel 98-74677) out past the camping site all offer private rooms and meals. Efri-Vík has fishing and horse rentals as well.

Entertainment

The Kirkjuhvoll Community Centre sometimes stages dances on weekends. Check at the tourist office for information.

Getting There & Away

All the Reykjavík to Höfn buses pass through Kirkju. During the summer, they run daily departing Reykjavík at 8.30 am and arriving in Kirkju at 1.30 pm. Westbound buses depart Höfn at 9 am and also arrive at 1.30 pm.

The Skaftafell-bound tour bus which comes from Reykjavík via the Fjallabak Route passes anytime between 5.30 pm and 6 pm from 15 July to 31 August. It stops at the hotel so you can board there if space is available.

If you'd like to join the westbound Fjallabak tour, it passes Kirkjubaejarklaustur at around 9.30 am daily also between 15 July and 31 August. The price of the entire tour is US$60 but holders of the Full-Circle Pass (provided they haven't yet used this section of the Ring Road) and Omnibuspass pay only US$32.

LAKAGÍGAR

The Laki eruptions of 1783 were among the most catastrophic volcanic events in human history and easily the most devastating Iceland has ever known. The Laki itself is extinct and hasn't erupted at all in modern times but it nonetheless gives its name to the volatile row of craters that begins at its base. The Skaftáreldar ('shaft river fires'), as the eruptions are often called, originated in the 25-km-long Lakagígar fissure 40 km north of Kirkjubaejarklaustur. It is suspected that this crater system is interconnected with the Grímsvötn volcano beneath Vatnajökull.

During the activity, which began in the spring of 1783 and continued for 10 months, the volcano spewed out 30 billion tonnes of lava and 90 million tonnes of sulphuric acid. Farms and fields throughout the island were devastated and well over half the livestock succumbed to starvation and poisoning. Some 9000 people – 20% of Iceland's population – were killed while the remainder faced the *Moðuharðindi*, the period of famine that followed. Traces of ash from the Laki eruptions have been found around the world. Of all the misfortunes that befell Iceland during the Norwegian and Danish regimes, the Skaftáreldar brought the most suffering.

From the parking area, Laki can be climbed in under an hour for a fantastic view along the intimidating fissure and across surrounding lakes and peaks. For the easiest climb, keep to the left of the crest that leads up to the first plateau.

The crater row itself is fascinating to explore, particularly the one nearest Laki itself which contains a nice lava cave. Another cave, which is a 2 hour walk south of the parking area, shelters a lake but, if you're on the tour, you won't get there and back in the allotted time so you'll have to spend the night and return to Kirkju the following day. The area is also riddled with black sand dunes and lava tubes, some of which contain tiny stalactites.

The lava field itself belies the apocalypse that spawned it just over 200 years ago. The sharp, black boulders are overgrown with soft and spongy moss which oddly resembles relief maps of imaginary landscapes. On a dry day this appealing natural cushion is also ideal for a nap but don't snooze too long or you'll miss the bus back to Kirkju!

Lakagígar Road

The 4WD road from just west of Kirkjubaejarklaustur to the Lakagígar crater row is passable after July in a normal year. There are lots of puddles and big rivers to ford so, after rain, it could prove treacherous to low-clearance vehicles.

Fjaðrágljúfur This unusual canyon along the Fjarðrá, a tributary of the Skaftá that flows past Kirkjubaejarklaustur, lies just 3.5 km north of the junction of the Laki and Ring roads. It's very interesting with lots of steep rock walls and chunky promontories. A walking track begins at the mouth of the canyon and follows the southern rim for a couple of km to some wonderful views into the canyon's impressive depths.

Not far away, near the farm Holt, is the small Holtsborg nature reserve. This is the only place in Iceland where wild roses are found growing naturally.

Fagrifoss This impressive and relatively little known falls on the Geirlandsá lies just east of the Laki Road hidden from view by a low rise. Look for the turn-off about 20 km north of the Ring Road.

The Hole Not far from Fagrifoss, there is a very deep hole in a small slump crater just east of the Laki Road. It doesn't seem to have any particular name – although it may – everyone just calls it 'the hole'. Locals will tell you it's the back door to hell (Hekla is the front door). In 1989, an impromptu French expedition, the Groupe Speleo Gaillard, went down into the hole and ran out of rope at 45 metres with lots of hole left beneath them. Visitors normally just like to toss stones into it and never hear them hit bottom.

This place is so unassuming – its entrance is just 35 or so cm across and hidden in a cleft in the rocks – that it's unlikely you'll find it without someone to point it out for you. If you'd like to have a go anyway, it's just a couple of metres east of the Laki Road about midway between the craters and the Ring Road.

Getting There & Away

The only public transport to the Lakagígar reserve is the BSÍ bus tour from Kirkjubaejarklaustur which operates daily at 9.30 am from 15 July to 15 August and costs US$24/27.50 with/without Omnibuspass. It's one of the few tours that allows adequate time at points of interest and most participants say it's exceptionally good value. Stops include all the previously mentioned attractions along the Laki Road and best of all, it allows over 3 hours of unstructured exploration at the craters themselves. The operators will even encourage you to camp out at Laki and return to Kirkjubaejarklaustur on another day in order to allow you time to fully appreciate the place.

If you'd like to join the tour, they collect people from the Edda Hotel and the camping ground in Kirkjubaejarklaustur between 9 and 9.30 am. If you're staying at one of the farmhouses, have your hosts ring and book in advance so they'll know to fetch you.

It's probably best to forget hitching along this road unless you're prepared to entertain yourself for awhile – it just doesn't have much traffic.

Southern Vatnajökull

Vatnajökull, or 'water glacier', is by far Iceland's greatest icecap. It rests on top of 8400 sq km of otherwise rugged territory and, in places, is 1 km thick. Scores of smaller valley glaciers flow down from the central icecap in crevasse-ridden rivers of sculpturing ice. Two of the largest ones, Skeiðarárjökull and Breiðamerkurjökull, flow southward in broad and spreading sheets that can be easily observed from the Ring Road. The most visited is probably Skaftafellsjökull, a relatively small glacier that ends within a few hundred metres of the Skaftafell camping ground.

THE SANDUR

The broad desert expanses that sprawl out along the south-eastern coast of Iceland are called sandur. 'Sandur' is another Icelandic word that has come to be used worldwide to describe a specific topographic phenomenon – the deposits of silt, sand, and gravel scraped from the high peaks by glaciers and carried in glacial bursts and braided rivers to the shore.

For cyclists, the sandur can become a nightmare when the wind is blowing. The fine sand and talcum-like glacial flour whips up into abrasive clouds, drifts across the road, and reduces visibility. Cyclists tell tales of being blown off the road and into sand drifts with no shelter from the stinging clouds. Be prepared.

If you're driving a vehicle across the sandur in high winds, place a strip of cardboard between your grill and radiator. There's no way to avoid the sandblasting a vehicle will suffer in a windstorm there but it may help to rinse the car with water (don't wipe it) once you're across.

Meðallandssandur

This sand desert in the Meðalland district south of Eldhraun and east of the river Kuðafljót is so flat and featureless that a number of ships have run aground upon its coast, apparently unaware they were nearing land. There's now a lighthouse in case someone still hasn't learned their lesson.

Lómagnúpur

This immense landmark rising like an island 668 metres above the sandur can be seen plainly from Kirkjubaejarklaustur, 35 km to the west, and from the Öraefi far to the east. Its name means 'loon peak'.

Núpsstaður

Beneath the cliffs of Lómagnúpur you'll find this small 17th-century turf church which has now been restored by the National Museum. Núpsstaður means 'peak church estate'. Early on, a battle was waged between private landowners and the church overseers regarding control of the estate.

The nearby farm with the turf building is one of the few still in use in the country.

Skeiðarársandur

The sprawling expanse of Skeiðarárjökull ('the wandering glacier') is Europe's largest valley glacier and covers an area of 1600 sq km. Its effective scouring action combined with numerous Grímsvötn jökulhlaups is responsible for this 600-sq km glacial delta, the largest of Iceland's sandur.

The sandur Skeiðarársandur is currently growing and, since Settlement, has swallowed a considerable amount of farmland. The area was once well populated (for Iceland, anyway) but, in 1362, the volcano Öraefi beneath Öraefajökull erupted and the subsequent jökulhlaup laid waste the entire district, covering it with sand and silt.

The Ring Road across Skeiðarársandur was finished in 1974, the last segment of the National Highway to be completed. Long gravel dykes have been constructed in strategic places to channel floodwaters away from this highly susceptible artery.

Ingólfshöfði

The promontory of Ingólfshöfði rises 76 metres above a sandy barrier island, about 8 km across a shallow tidal lagoon from the mainland coast. It was here that Iceland's first settler, Ingólfur Arnarson, stayed on his original winter visit to Iceland; there's a monument on the cape to that effect. When Ingólfur was there, however, it was greener and more pleasant than today. Camping is possible but, since Ingólfshöfði is exposed to the weather and lacks fresh water, it may not be ideal.

A 4WD track goes out there from the farm Fagurhólsmýri near the Ring Road but, even in a jeep, it's rough going and easy to get bogged down in the muck. If you're walking, plan on getting your legs wet. Access to the headland is up a sandy ramp on its northern side.

Hof

The tiny settlement of Hof ('temple') contains a peat-brick and wooden church originally built in the 1300s on the foundation of a temple dedicated to Þór. It was reconstructed in 1884 and now sits pleasantly in a thicket of birch and ash with flowers growing on the grassy roof. Nearby are the ruins of Gröf, a farm which was destroyed in the jökulhlaup caused by the 1362 Öraefi eruption.

If you're passing by you may enjoy having a look around but, if you'd like to linger awhile in this quiet place, there's farmhouse and sleeping-bag accommodation at Hof (tel 97-81669). Meals are available as well but the nearest shop and snack bar is at the Fagurhólsmýri airstrip 5 km away.

Breiðamerkursandur

The easternmost of the big sandurs, Breiðamerkursandur is the home and main breeding ground of Iceland's largest colony of great skuas, the original dive bombers, which nest in the tufts of grass on top of low mounds there. Beware of aerial attack while wandering through here!

Njálls Saga ends with the remaining protagonist, Kári Sölmundarson, coming to this idyllic spot to 'live happily ever after':

> ...Flosi gave to Kári in marriage his niece Hildigunn, the widow of Höskuld Hvitanesgóði. To begin with, they lived at Breiða.

Kári's farm Breiða was destroyed by the glacier in the 17th century but that was long after Kári and Hildigunn would have had any use for it.

Above this sandur today, you'll see an impressive panorama of glacier-capped mountains with deep lagoons in front of them. The 742-metre-high mountain Breiðamerkur was once a nunatak enclosed by Breiðamerkurjökull and Fjallsjökull but the glaciers have since retreated and freed it. At the foot of the peak is the glacial lagoon Breiðárlón which is normally crowded with icebergs calved from the glacier. Though similar, it's less touristy than nearby Jökulsárlón and is worth the short walk to see it.

Graenalón & Núpsvötn

The glacial river Núpsvötn is formed by the confluence of the Núpsá and Hvítá which flow out of Vatnajökull and join as they fall into the same canyon.

It is possible, but fairly difficult, to pick your way up the ridges and valleys west of the immense glacier Skeiðarárjökull to Graenalón ('green lagoon'). This ice-dammed lake above the headwaters of the Hvítá and Núpsá is known for its ability to drain like a bathtub. The 'plug' is the western edge of Skeiðarárjökull and when pressure builds to breaking point, the glacier is lifted and the lake lets go. It has been known to release up to 2,700,000 cubic metres of water at 5000 cubic metres per second in a single burst.

To get there from the Ring Road, make your way up the Núpsá valley and up to Eggjar, the ridge just south of Graenalón. This return trip can be done in 2 days but you will have to cross some glacial rivers and mountain streams, so seek local advice before you go. The topo sheet to use for this trip is *Lómagnúpur 1:100,000* (1986).

JÖKULSÁRLÓN

The 100-metre-deep 'glacial river lagoon', Jökulsárlón, is more or less an obligatory stop for travellers between Skaftafell and Höfn. It's full of large icebergs that have calved from the glacier Breiðamerkurjökull.

The area almost appears to belong at the North Pole – it was interesting enough to some locations coordinators that parts of the James Bond film *A View to a Kill* were shot there.

The glacier seems to advance and retreat with some frequency; go to the small restaurant east of the lagoon and compare their aerial photos taken in 1945 and 1982. It has retreated considerably even since 1982 – much of the tongue shown in the photo is now gone.

If you have a spare US$10, you can cruise through the icebergs to better appreciate their imaginative shapes and shades. Cruises last about 30 minutes and leave from the dock whenever there's a boatload waiting.

Places to Stay & Eat

At the *Hali Restaurant* near the lagoon you can buy fast food or a sticky snack.

A lot of travellers camp out at Jökulsárlón but the camping site keeps being moved. It should be fairly obvious, however, where to set up camp.

Getting There & Away

Assuming that most passengers will be chaffing at the bit to snap a few photos of Jökulsárlón, all public buses stop for 10 minutes or so. Those on the BSÍ glacier tour from Höfn will have about an hour, leaving enough time for a cruise.

Öraefajökull & Hvannadalshnúkur

This area, the southernmost spur of Vatnajökull, isn't a glacier but actually a separate icecap covering the immense Öraefi caldera. Part of Öraefi's crater rim protrudes through the ice. This nunatak is called Hvannadalshnúkur. At 2119 metres elevation, it's the highest point in Iceland

Mountaineers wishing to climb Hvannadalshnúkur will find the best access from the abandoned farm Sandfell about 12 km south-east of Skaftafell. Climb up onto Sandfellsheiði above the farm. You'll reach the tricky crevasse-laden edge of the glacier at about 1300 metres and climb another 400 metres before it levels off and smooths out. Hvannadalshnúkur rises 200 metres (a technical climb) above the icefield 4 km away. Expeditions should be well versed in glacier travel and should allow at least 4 days for the return trip in case they're held up by inclement weather.

The Ferðafélag Íslands (tel 91-19533 in Reykjavík) at Öldugata 3, Reykjavík, will be able to provide further information and guidance.

Svínafell & Svínafellsjökull

The farm Svínafell, 8 km south-east of Skaftafell, was the home of Flosi Þórðarson, the character who burned out Njáll and his family in *Njálls Saga*. It was also the site where Flosi and Njáll's family were finally reconciled:

> It was snowing furiously...They walked to Svínafell through the snowstorm. Flosi was sitting in the main room. He recognised Kári at once and jumped up to welcome him, embraced him, and sat him on the high-seat beside him. He invited Kári to stay the winter and Kári accepted...

Thus ended one of the bloodiest feuds in the history of Iceland.

During the 1600s, the glacier Svínafellsjökull almost engulfed the farm but it has since retreated. This glacier has a particularly prominent terminal moraine. From the road it's a short walk over the moraine to the snout of the glacier or, from Skaftafell, only 5 km along the side roads.

Getting There & Around

Glacier Tour A quick and painless way to get up above the valley glaciers to the vast Vatnajökull icecap is to take the BSÍ glacier tour which departs from the hotel in Höfn daily at 9 am from 20 June to 31 August. This day-trip stops for an hour at Jökulsárlón when returning and costs US$14/26 with/without Omnibuspass. It can be booked through your place of accommodation anywhere in Höfn or the surrounding area.

The tour takes you past the Smyrlabjörgvirkjun power plant and up a twisting 4WD road to the edge of Skálafellsjökull, a broad spur of Vatnajökull, where there's a ski hut and a parking lot full of paraphernalia used for glacier travel. Budget travellers best resign themselves to walking around on the ice, however, since snow machines cost an extortionate US$33 to rent for 2 hours. A trip in the *thiokols* ('glacier buggies') for a similar time costs US$41 per person.

Walkers are cautioned not to wander beyond the red poles planted in the ice about a km from the hut without technical equipment and expertise. There are lots of snow-bridged crevasses and the danger is extreme. White-out conditions are common and the poles are spindly, widely spaced, and hard to see. If you come across a long narrow depression in the snow, steer clear of it and don't continue any further up.

Those who'd like to do longer expeditions on Vatnajökull can depart from here but don't even consider it unless you have experience in glacier travel, orientation, equipment, and rescue procedures.

If you'd like to spend more time on the glacier than the tour allows, sleeping-bag accommodation is available in the ski hut near the edge of the ice for US$10 per night. It's possible to rejoin the tour when you're ready to return to Höfn.

SKAFTAFELL NATIONAL PARK

Few travellers in Iceland fail to at least put in an appearance at Skaftafell, the nation's second largest national park. In fact, few Icelanders can keep away from it through an entire summer either, so during the height of the season, it's very popular. On long summer weekends, you're looking at a mob scene with tent-fly-to-caravan-door camping conditions, a cacophony of boombox stereo systems, raucous all-night parties, and at least an hour's queue at the toilets (no exaggeration!). I wouldn't have been surprised if Skaftafell were the second most populous place in Iceland the weekend I spent there!

It can be a lot of fun but it may be disappointing if you've come to appreciate the beauty of the place. Time your visit according to your preferences or go elsewhere to commune with nature.

History

Historically, Skaftafell was a large farm centred west of the camping site at the foot of the hills. A build-up of sands in the area forced the farm to be moved to a more suitable site 100 metres higher up the hill. Three other farms were established on the moor after it. Another farm and a church are known to have existed near the foot of Jökulfell (across Morsárdalur from Skaftafell) in the early 1300s but all the farms in the district were destroyed by the Öraefi eruptions of 1362. It was at this time that the Herað Milli Sandur ('land between the sands') district was renamed Öraefi, meaning 'waste land'. After the vegetation returned, Skaftafell was rebuilt in its former location.

The modern park was jointly founded in 1967 by the Icelandic government and the World Wildlife Fund. It originally contained only the area cradled between Skeiðarárjökull and Skaftafellsjökull and included Skaftafellsheiði ('shaft mountain moors'), the valley Morsárdalur, and the Skaftafellsfjöll range. In June 1984, the park was expanded to include about 20% of the Vatnajökull icecap. Sheltered as it is by mountains, Skaftafell enjoys decidedly better weather conditions than the surrounding area.

Maps

The Landmaelingar Íslands publishes a thematic map of Skaftafell National Park showing the non-glacial area of the park at 1:25,000 and the Öraefi district at 1:100,000. It's available in Reykjavík (see the Maps section in the Iceland Facts for the Visitor chapter) or from the shop at Skaftafell. You can also use the *Öraefajökull 1:100,000* (1986) topo sheet.

The map on the national park pamphlet is adequate for day-hiking near the service centre as is the one included in this book.

Hiking & Trekking

Skaftafell, as ideal a place as you're likely to find for easy day-walks, provides a breathtaking backdrop; it's also good for longer and more involved trekking through the park's wilderness regions. It's a safe bet that 90% of Skaftafell's visitors never wander beyond the popular routes of Skaftafellsheiði, and most of the others are only headed as far as the hot springs at Baejarstaðarskógur. In short, if you want solitude at Skaftafell it's available but you need a bit of time, motivation, and effort to attain it.

Trekkers should keep in mind that all the flora, fauna, and natural features of the park are officially protected. Open fires are prohibited and all rubbish must be carried out. In the high-use area around Skaftafellsheiði, hikers are requested to keep to the tracks so as not to damage the delicate plant communities that characterise this region.

Of course, advice not to approach or climb on glaciers without proper equipment and training applies double here. The average ice berg calving off Skaftafellsjökull, for instance, would crush anyone within a few metres of the face so use common sense.

Skaftafellsjökull One of the most popular walks in the park is the effortless 1-hour return walk to the glacier Skaftafellsjökull. The track starts from the service centre and leads right to the glacier face where you can experience first-hand evidence of glacial activity – bumps, groans, and flowing water as well as the brilliant hues of the ice itself.

Svartifoss If Skaftafell has an identifying feature, it is Svartifoss, a nice waterfall flanked by unusual overhanging basalt columns. An extremely well used walking track leads up from the camping ground. Plan on spending about an hour for the return trip. It's also worthwhile to continue westward from Svartifoss up the short track to Sjónarsker where there is a view disc and a magnificent view across Skeiðarársandur.

Skaftafellsheiði Loop If you have a fine day, the loop walk around Skaftafellsheiði is highly recommended. It begins by climbing from the camping ground up past Svartifoss and Sjónarsker and continues across the moor to 610-metre-high Fremrihnaukur. From there, follow the edge of the plateau to the next rise, 706-metre Nyrðrihnaukur, where you'll get an excellent view of Morsárdalur, Morsárjökull, and the iceberg-

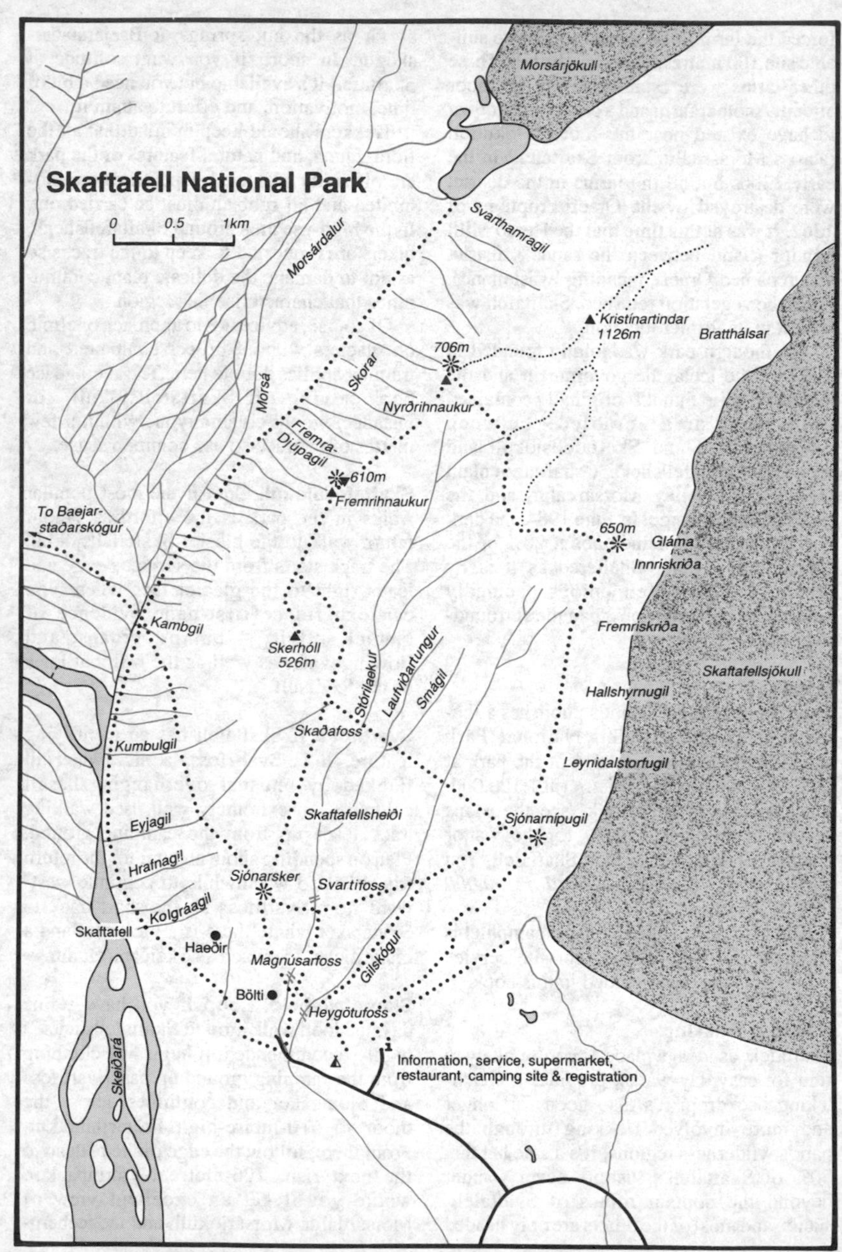
Skaftafell National Park
0
0.5
1km
Morsárjökull
Morsárdalur
Svarthamragil
Kristínartindar
1126m
Bratthálsar
706m
Skorar
Morsá
Nyrðrihnaukur
Fremra-
Djúpagil
610m
Fremrihnaukur
To Baejar-
staðarskógur
650m
Gláma
Innriskriða
Kambgil
Skerhóll
526m
Fremriskriða
Stórilaekur
Laufviðartungur
Smágil
Skaftafellsjökull
Hallshyrnugil
Skaðafoss
Kumbulgil
Leynidalstorfugil
Skaftafellsheiði
Eyjagil
Sjónarnípugil
Hrafnagil
Sjónarsker
Svartifoss
Kolgráagil
Skaftafell
Haeðir
Magnúsarfoss
Gilskógur
Bölti
Heygötufoss
Information, service, supermarket,
restaurant, camping site & registration
Skeiðará

choked lagoon at its base. If you're interested, the glacier contains a textbook example of a medial moraine.

The track then turns south-west, past the slopes of Kristínartindar, and takes you to a point on the cliff above Skaftafellsjökull. From here, you begin to get some idea of the size of this relatively small river of ice! There are good lookouts all along the cliff edge but the rock crumbles easily underfoot so exercise due caution.

Those with more time may want to follow the route up one of several possible ridges to 1126-metre Kristínartindar and, from there, along the ridge for even better views of the upper reaches of Skaftafellsjökull as well as Morsárdalur and the sandur below.

Morsárdalur & Baejarstaðarskógur The long day-walk from the camping ground to the glacial lagoon in Morsárdalur is fairly ordinary but enjoyable, if you have the time. Plan on about 7 hours for the return trip.

Alternatively, you can cross the Morsá (the bridge is broken) at the ford which is near the point where Kambgil ravine comes down from Skaftafellsheiði. From there, make your way across the many rivulets in the gravel to the birch woods at Baejarstaðarskógur. The trees here reach a whopping 12 metres and there are 80°C-springs which flow into heavenly Heitulaekir ('hot stream') just to the west in Vestragil. The return walk to Baejarstaðarskógur will take about 6 hours. Add at least another hour if you'd like to visit the hot springs. In all cases, ask about river-crossing conditions at the park headquarters visitors' centre.

Other Walks Other possibilities include the 7-hour return trip to the foot of Skeiðarárjökull. Since camping is restricted to the organised site at park headquarters, those who'd like to pick a route through the rugged Skaftafellsfjökull or walk up into the remote Kjósarbotn area will have to plan on a very long day of walking. If you're keen on a longer overnight trip, it wouldn't hurt to try and secure a camping permit from the visitors' centre. Also be sure to ask about river crossings before you head out. On hot days and after heavy rains the rivers can become impassable.

Grímsvötn Rumbling quietly beneath a mantle of Vatnajökull ice, the seemingly innocuous crater Grímsvötn has been known to erupt and release massive jökulhlaups. It was Grímsvötn which caused the cataclysmic flood that carved out the Ásbyrgi canyon in just a couple of days. In 1934, it released a jökulhlaup which swelled the river Skeiðará to 9 km in width and caused it to flow at 40,000 cubic metres per second. Large areas of farmland in the Öraefi ('wasteland') district around Skaftafell were laid waste in this fit of temper.

Places to Stay & Eat

Nearly everyone ends up in the camping ground at the park headquarters. This immense, grassy field is broken only by the odd windbreak hedge or barbecue spit. The service area has an information office, coffee shop, cafeteria, supermarket, and toilet block. Prices at the coffee shop/cafeteria are surprisingly reasonable, if you give the alcohol a wide berth.

Showers are available and cost US$1.75 for 5 minutes but, on weekends, plan on interminable waits. There's only one shower room for men and one for women. Queues do back up despite the requirement that you shower two at a time. Tent sites cost US$2.50 per tent and an additional US$2.50 per person.

A very nice place to stay is at the farm *Bölti* (tel 97-81626) on Skaftafellsheiði above the western end of the camping ground. They offer private double rooms and a five-bed dorm with sleeping-bag accommodation. Outside the park, the nearest farmhouse for sleeping-bag accommodation is at Hof (see the Hof section earlier in this chapter) 23 km away.

The *Freysnes Guesthouse* (tel 98-81845), near the foot of Svínafellsjökull, charges US$55/75 for a double room without/with bath. For an extra US$10, they'll serve you breakfast.

Getting There & Away

To reach Skaftafell from Reykjavík, take the Höfn or Fjallabak buses. Both depart at 8.30 am daily. The Höfn bus, which arrives in Skaftafell at 3.30 pm, operates from 1 June to 31 August. The Fjallabak bus, which only runs from 15 July to 31 August, follows the incredibly scenic inland route through Landmannalaugar and Eldgjá rather than the coastal Ring Road. It's slightly more expensive and even holders of Omnibuspass will have to pay an additional US$32. From Skaftafell back to Reykjavík, the Fjallabak bus departs daily at 8 am, but again only from 15 July to 31 August. The bus from Höfn to Reykjavík departs Höfn at 9 am and passes Skaftafell at noon daily.

HÖFN

The name of this town is pronounced exactly like an unexpected hiccup. If you're not prone to hiccups, just say 'hup' while inhaling. That's close enough.

Sprawling across a sandy spit in the lagoon Hornafjörður, Höfn is basically an ugly town with stunning surroundings. Since the completion of the Ring Road allowed straightforward transport to and from the capital (until 1974, Höfn-ites had to drive through Akureyri to reach Reykjavík), its population has swelled to 1600. The town is economically dependent upon agriculture, fishing, and fish processing.

Travellers who aren't planning on taking advantage of Höfn's star tourist attraction, the Vatnajökull glacier tour, may still be stuck here overnight awaiting onward transport to Reykjavík or Egilsstaðir. Try not to arrive on Saturday or Sunday. Höfn may have a hiccup name but its demeanour is definitely a yawn.

Information

There is a tourist information office-cum-produce market in the hut beside the camping ground. It's open from 8 am to 2 pm and 4 to 11 pm daily in the summer.

Regional Museum

This museum, housed in an 1864 trade storehouse, has both nautical and agricultural displays. There is a small section dealing with natural history as well. It's open from 2 to 6 pm daily between 1 June and 1 September.

Places to Stay & Eat

Around Town Travellers normally stay at Höfn's pleasant camping site on Þjoðvegur near the entrance to the town. It's a real bargain at only US$1.25 per person and US$1.25 per tent to camp there.

Those who would prefer a proper roof over their head will find that there is a *Youth Hostel* (tel 97-81736) at Hafnarbraut 8, just a block from the harbour. It's friendly and pleasant, but they lock up the building during the day.

The *Hotel Höfn* (tel 97-81240) is another of those uninspired pre-fab looking hotels that would be at home in the suburbs of Moscow. Singles/doubles cost US$53/78. Their coffee shop isn't bad, if you'd like to grab a cuppa before hopping on the early bus out of town, but otherwise their dining room is very ordinary.

The *Hérinn* restaurant in the Shell petrol station is one of the bargains of Iceland. It's pleasant and inexpensive yet offers a good variety of relatively high-quality food. The *KASK Cooperative* supermarket is on the road between the youth hostel and the restaurant.

Alternatively, try the *Hafnarbúdin* snack bar on Ránarslóð near the harbour. It's open from 9 am to 11.30 pm daily.

Out of Town Nesjaskóli, 7 km from Höfn, is the site of an *Edda Hotel* (tel 97-81470) where you can get a bed in a private room for singles/doubles US$45/58. Sleeping-bag accommodation is also possible. Slightly further afield at *Brunnhóll* (tel 97-81029), 30 km from Höfn, you'll find farmhouse accommodation with sleeping-bag options as well.

About two-thirds of the way between Höfn and Jökulsárlón is the *Guesthouse*

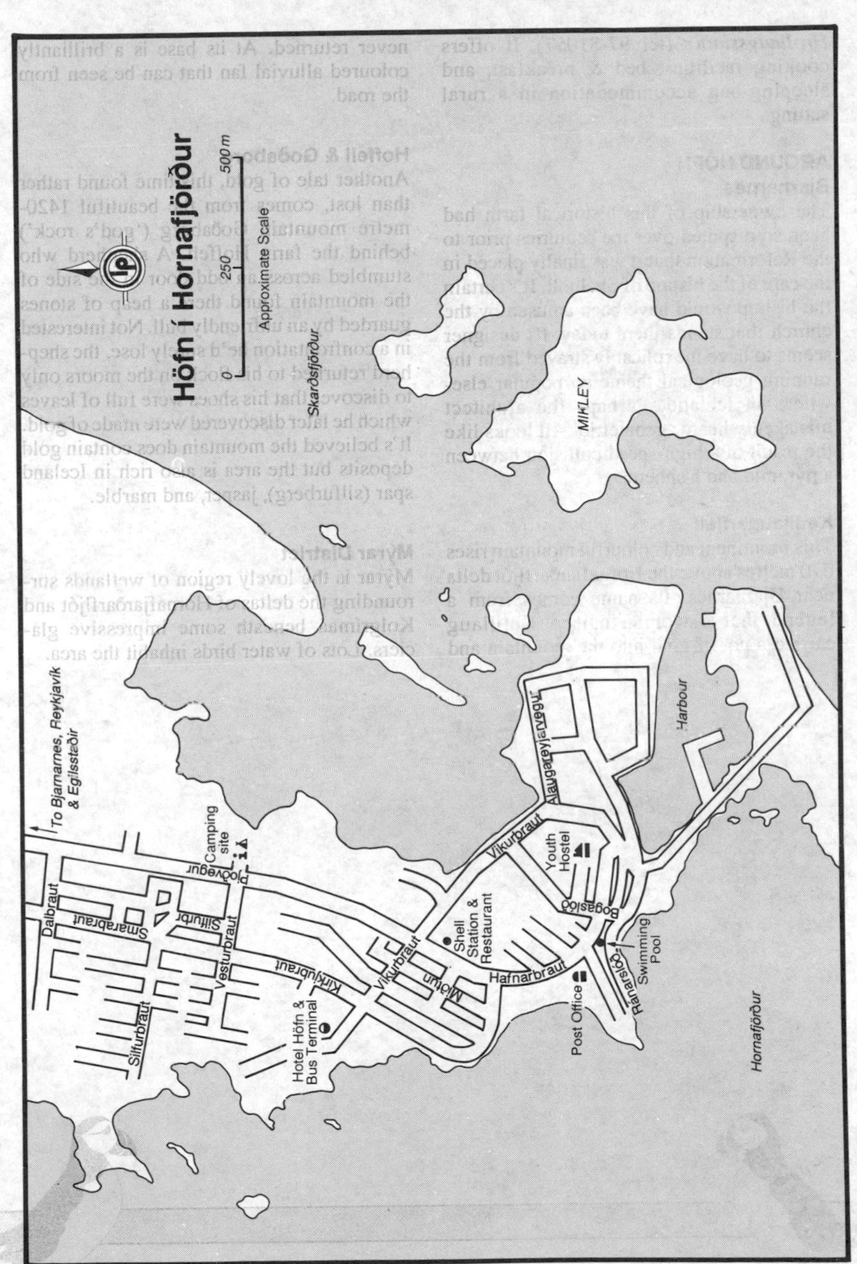
Höfn í Hornafjörður
0
250
500 m
Approximate Scale
Skarðsfjörður
MIKLEY
To Bjarnarnes, Reykjavík & Egilsstaðir
Camping site
Dalbraut
Smárabraut
Silfurbraut
Vesturbraut
Kirkjubraut
Víkurbraut
Miðtún
Hafnarbraut
Hotel Höfn & Bus Terminal
Shell Station & Restaurant
Youth Hostel
Álaugareyjarvegur
Bogaslóð
Ránarslóð
Swimming Pool
Post Office
Harbour
Hornafjörður

Hrollaugsstaðir (tel 97-81057). It offers cooking facilities, bed & breakfast, and sleeping-bag accommodation in a rural setting.

AROUND HÖFN

Bjarnarnes

The ownership of this historical farm had been so disputed over the centuries prior to the Reformation that it was finally placed in the care of the bishop of Skálholt. It's certain the bishop would have been amused by the church that stands there today. Its designer seems to have inexplicably strayed from the running geological theme so popular elsewhere in Iceland. Perhaps the architect mistakenly heard 'geometric' – it looks like the result of a high-speed collision between a pyramid and a sphere.

Ketillaugarfjall

This prominent and colourful mountain rises 670 metres above the Hornafjarðarfljót delta near Bjarnarnes. Its name comes from a legend that a woman named Ketillaug carried a pot of gold into the mountain and never returned. At its base is a brilliantly coloured alluvial fan that can be seen from the road.

Hoffell & Goðaborg

Another tale of gold, this time found rather than lost, comes from the beautiful 1420-metre mountain Goðaborg ('god's rock') behind the farm Hoffell. A shepherd who stumbled across an odd door in the side of the mountain found there a heap of stones guarded by an unfriendly bull. Not interested in a confrontation he'd surely lose, the shepherd returned to his flock on the moors only to discover that his shoes were full of leaves which he later discovered were made of gold. It's believed the mountain does contain gold deposits but the area is also rich in Iceland spar (silfurberg), jasper, and marble.

Mýrar District

Mýrar is the lovely region of wetlands surrounding the deltas of Hornafjarðarfljót and Kolgrímaá beneath some impressive glaciers. Lots of water birds inhabit the area.

Central Iceland

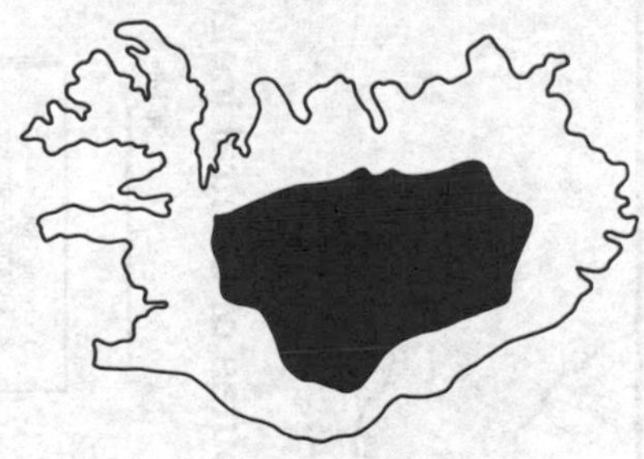

The vast and barren interior of Iceland comprises one of Europe's greatest wilderness areas, and trivia buffs may be interested to know that it's her only desert as well. Gazing across the expanses, you could imagine yourself in Tibet, Mongolia or, as many people have noted, on the moon. The Apollo astronauts even held exercises there in preparation for their lunar landing.

Historically, the routes across the interior were used during the summer months as short cuts between the northern and southern coasts. The mountains, valleys, and broad expanses were the haunt of *utilegumenn*, outlaws fleeing justice.

When it comes to outlaws, people all around the world have tended to embellish their historical exploits into the realms of high (albeit entertaining) fiction and Icelanders are no exception. Perhaps they just reasoned anyone who could survive the Icelandic interior must be extraordinary. The utilegumenn thereby joined the ranks of giants and trolls and provided the theme for the popular and fantastic *Grettirs Saga*.

One particular outlaw, Fjalla-Eyvindar, has become a sort of Icelandic Robin Hood, Ned Kelly, or Butch Cassidy. He had a penchant for sheep rustling which left him decidedly unpopular in the society of the day. Throughout the centre of Iceland you'll find shelters and hideouts attributed to him and hear tales of his ability to survive in impossible conditions while always staying ahead of his pursuers.

In fact, in most cases pursuers feared the outlaws far more than the outlaws feared capture. The traditional sentence for outlaws was simply exile to another country where the guilty party could spend a couple of years bothering someone else – a send-the-kids-to-the-neighbours sort of solution.

Travelling in the Interior

Travelling through the uninhabited centre of Iceland isn't like travelling anywhere else in the country. There are no services, no accommodation, no bridges, and no guarantees should something go awry. In some cases, there isn't even a road.

It's officially recommended that vehicles travel in pairs. If one gets bogged, the other can drag it out or fetch additional help. The officials don't say what to do if both get bogged which is a very real possibility. Carry lots of supplies, especially if you can scarcely afford to take one vehicle, let alone two!

Another concern is weather. Conditions in the centre of Iceland can be fickle and there's even the occasional snow blizzard in July and August. I once visited Askja in July and found myself facing 50-knot winds, blowing sand, and snow. Although I enjoyed the trip, it didn't make for a leisurely experience. Those who spurn the 4WD buses and opt to walk or cycle through the central Iceland should be especially prepared for anything nature may deal out. Particularly important is protection for the face and eyes. The agony caused by gritty, wind-driven sand cannot be exaggerated.

In addition to reading the guidelines in the Driving section of the Iceland Getting Around chapter, those planning to drive their own vehicles may want to obtain a copy of the helpful pamphlet *How to Travel in the Interior of Iceland*. It's written in English, German, French, and Danish and is available by contacting the Iceland Tourist Board, Laugavegur 3, 101 Reykjavík.

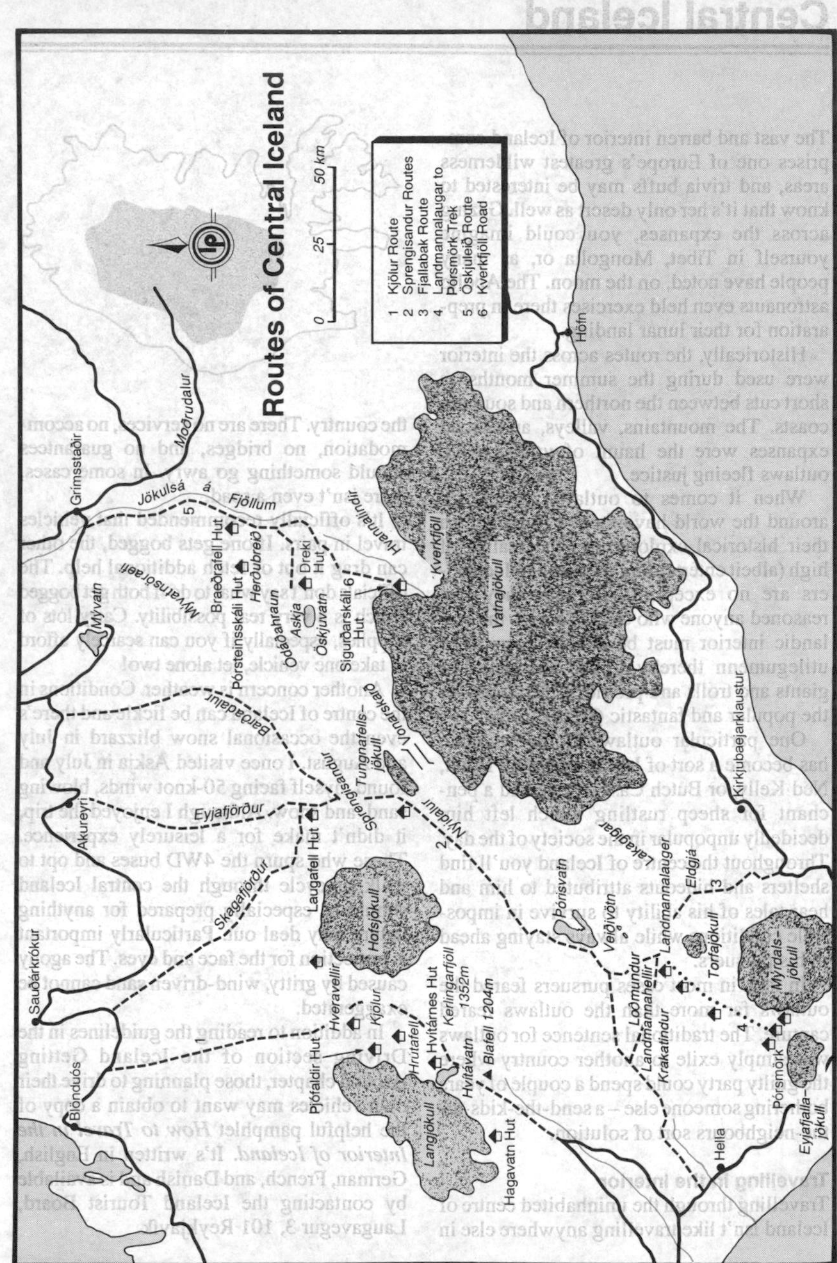
Routes of Central Iceland
1 Kjölur Route
2 Sprengisandur Routes
3 Fjallabak Route
4 Landmannalaugar to Þórsmörk Trek
5 Öskjuleið Route
6 Kverkfjöll Road
0 25 50 km
Blönduós
Sauðárkrókur
Akureyri
Grímsstaðir
Mývatn
Höfn
Kirkjubaejarklaustur
Hella
Þórsmörk
Skagafjörður
Eyjafjörður
Jökulsá á Fjöllum
Möðrudalur
Mývatnsöræfi
Bárðadalur
Langjökull
Hofsjökull
Vatnajökull
Mýrdalsjökull
Eyjafjalla-jökull
Tungnafellsjökull
Torfajökull
Kverkfjöll
Hvannalindir
Sprengisandur
Vonarskarð
Nýidalur
Lakagígar
Þórisvatn
Veiðivötn
Eldgjá
Landmannalaugar
Landmannahellir
Loðmundur
Krakatindur
Hvítárvatn
Bláfell 1204m
Kerlingarfjöll 1352m
Hveravellir
Kjölur
Hrútafell
Hvítárnes Hut
Þjófaldir Hut
Hagavatn Hut
Laugafell Hut
Askja
Öskjuvatn
Ódáðahraun
Dreki Hut
Herðubreið
Braeðrafell Hut
Þorsteinsskáli Hut
Sigurðarskáli Hut

If you plan to stay at any of the numerous mountain huts in the interior, it is recommended that you book them in advance through the Ferðafélag Íslands (Icelandic Touring Club), Öldugata 3, Reykjavík (tel 91-19533).

KJÖLUR ROUTE

The name of this route across the central highland desert means 'keel' which refers to the perceived shape of the topography. Although the Kjölur Route is more interesting, has more grasslands along the way and passes through less inhospitable territory than its counterpart, the Sprengisandur, it was historically the less popular of the two. Potential travellers were often put off by the common belief that it was infested by fearsome outlaws.

At its highest point, the track reaches 700 metres as it passes through the 30-km-wide valley between the Langjökull and Hofsjökull icecaps.

Hveravellir

The primary attraction along the Kjölur Route is Hveravellir, a geothermal area of fumaroles and multi-coloured hot pools at the northern end of the pass. It was reputed to have been one of the many hideouts of the ubiquitous outlaw Fjalla-Eyvindar. On a small mound near the geothermal area are the ruins of a shelter where he is believed to have holed up with his wife, Halla, and their family during one 18th-century winter.

There's a touring club hut there which will accommodate 40 people and, if you have time, it's worth breaking your trip here to explore the area before rejoining the tour southward. This is one of the few huts in the system which has kitchen facilities but you'll still have to bring your own cooking implements. Also, there's a naturally heated pool where you can become intimately acquainted with the hot springs while enjoying the atmosphere.

Hofsjökull

Beneath the 995-sq km Hofsjökull icecap east of Kjölur pass, a caldera, or collapsed magma chamber, has been recently discovered. Hofsjökull is the third largest icecap in the country.

Geirsalda

At 670 metres, not far from the highest point along the route, is a view disc. Beside it is a monument to Geir Zoëga who died in 1959. He served as the president of the Ferðafélag Íslands for over 20 years.

Beinahóll

The rather spooky name of this hill at the edge of the Kjalhraun lava flow near Geirsalda means 'bone hill'. The story goes that in October 1780, a party of four men and a flock of sheep set out to cross Kjölur from Skagafjörður. They realised it would be difficult so late in the year but they decided to have a go anyway. When bad weather set in, they decided to hole up until it passed but 3 weeks went by before there was any change and, by then, all had perished.

Icelanders believe that Beinahóll is haunted by the victims of this unfortunate incident (this presumably includes the sheep). They believe that to remove any of the bones or disturb the site is to invite permanent bad luck and they want nothing to do with it. If you should hear ominous bleating in the night...

Kerlingarfjöll

Kerlingarfjöll (the 'witch mountains') are considered the most 'alpine' of all Iceland's ranges. Until 150 years ago, these mountains were thought to harbour the vilest sort of outlaws. Icelanders believed that in the heart of the range there existed a deep and isolated valley like Shangri-la where these loathsome characters operated a clandestine outlaw society. People were so frightened by the prospect of meeting them that the range wasn't explored at all until the mid 19th century.

A summer ski school with seven rope-tows, a camping site, a petrol station, and mountain-hut accommodation operates at the base of these beautiful rhyolite peaks. It's popular with Icelanders but foreign travellers have scarcely discovered it. If you'd like to have a go at summer skiing, you can rent equipment and ski lessons are available.

Hrútafell

There's a tiny 10-sq km icecap on top of the móberg peak Hrútafell ('ram's mountain'). The prominent peak rises over 700 metres above the surrounding landscape.

Hvítárvatn

The 'white river lake' is the source of the glacial river Hvítá. There is a tongue of Langjökull, Iceland's second largest icecap, which calves into the pale blue lake filling it with icebergs.

In the marshy grasslands north-east of the lake is Hvítárnes hut. Built in 1930, it was the first mountain hut owned by the touring club. It is, oddly enough, another Kjölur site believed to be haunted, this time by the innocuous spirit of a young woman. If a female camper sleeps in one particular bed in the hut, it is said she will dream of the ghost carrying two pails of water.

Despite the tale, don't be put off breaking your trip in this idyllic and isolated setting. The hut has space for 30 people but no cooking facilities and you'll have to walk the 3 or so km from the road.

Mountain Huts

In addition to the previously mentioned Hveravellir and Hvítárnes huts, there are Ferðafélag Islands' mountain huts at Þjófadalir, 10 km south-west of Hveravellir; at Þverbrekkumúli 8 km west of Innri-Skúti hill; and at Hagavatn near the southern end of Langjökull about 15 km from the Kjölur Route. All of these huts have pit toilets but no running water or cooking facilities. The Hagavatn hut has no water available in the area so you must carry water or have the means to melt snow.

Getting There & Away

The Kjölur Route is far better suited to walking or cycling than the Askja Route which is plagued with dunes, lava flows, and sandstorms. Even so, most travellers opt for the much easier and dearer BSÍ tour. It departs Akureyri on Wednesdays and Saturdays at 8.30 am during July and August and arrives in Reykjavík 15 hours later, stopping for lunch at Hveravellir where you can just squeeze in a swim at the hot pool in the time allotted. You then whiz past Hvítárvatn and through the highlights of the Golden Circle – Gullfoss, Geysir, and Þingvellir – before ending in Reykjavík. The tour doesn't operate in the other direction.

The normal fare is US$108 but Omnibuspass holders pay US$71. If you have the Hringmiði (Full-Circle Pass), you can opt to replace the Akureyri to Reykjavík section of the Ring Road with the Kjölar Route and pay only the Omnibuspass fare. When you consider that the stretch between Akureyri and Reykjavík is not the national highway's most interesting section, this option is only marginally appealing.

SPRENGISANDUR ROUTES

The Sprengisandur Route (F28) is probably the least interesting track across the interior but it does offer some wonderful views of Vatnajökull, Tungnafellsjökull, and Hofsjökull as well as Askja and Herðubreið from the western perspective (see the Routes of Central Iceland map).

The broad pass between Tungnafellsjökull and Hofsjökull lies over 800 metres above sea level. The name 'Sprengisandur' refers to the desert moors that lie around the northern end of this 20-km-long saddle. Just a few km to the west of the current route is an another, the Old Sprengisandur, which was historically used.

Skagafjörður Route

The Skagafjörður access (F72) to the Sprengisandur Route goes for 81 km from southern Skagafjörður to connect with the F28, near the lake Fjórðungsvatn just 20 km east of Hofsjökull.

The major point of interest along the way is Laugafell, a 890-metre mountain on whose north-west slope are some nice hot springs. There's a 15-bunk hut belonging to Ferðafélag Íslands and a geothermally heated pool. The hut is open only during the summer and no cooking facilities are available. Near the springs are some stone ruins reputed to be an old dwelling.

Eyjafjörður Route

The road from southern Eyjafjörður (F82) connects up with the Skagafjörður road at Laugafell. The Sprengisandur tour from Reykjavík to Akureyri follows this route and stops at the Laugafell hot springs en route.

Barðadalur Route

The route through Barðadalur from Mývatn is technically the start of F28 itself. The entire track runs for about 240 km across the generally inhospitable territory between Barðadalur and Þjórsádalur. It was used historically by the clergy from the southern bishopric at Skálholt when travelling to visit their flock in eastern Iceland.

Veiðivötn

This beautiful area not far to the north-east of Landmannalaugar (on the Fjallabak Route) is a convoluted entanglement of small desert lakes in a volcanic basin, a continuation of the same fissure that produced Laugahraun in the Fjallabak reserve. It lies 27 km off the southern end of the Sprengisandur Road south of Þórisvatn. There is no public transport from the bus route and easy access from Landmannalaugar is thwarted by the substantial river Tungnaá.

At Tjaldvatn, the 'camping lake' below 650-metre Miðmorgunsalda, you'll find a camping site with huts and a petrol pump. This is a wonderful area to wander around and you can spend a lot of time following the numerous 4WD tracks which wind across the tephra sands between the numerous lakes.

No meals are available in the area so, bring all the food you'll be needing. There's a view disk on the hill to the north-east which points out the various lakes and peaks in the vicinity. The Veiðivötn area appears on the Landmaelingar Íslands' *Þórsmörk/Landmannalaugar 1:100,000* (1986) route map.

Þórisvatn

Iceland's second largest lake, Þórisvatn, covers 82 sq km although it had a surface area of only 70 sq km before the Tungnaá hydroelectric schemes diverted water into it from Kaldakvísl. Þórisvatn is 11 km north-east of the junction between Route 26 and the Fjallabak Route. The Sprengisandur tours pause here briefly to explain the hydro configuration.

Versalir

Iceland's most remote farm, Versalir (tel 985-22161), is just a few km off the Sprengisandur Road north of Þórisvatn. Although farming isn't an easy process here, they do have a petrol pump and offer camping, sleeping-bag accommodation, and a restaurant. If you have a 4WD vehicle or feel up to a long walk up the Old Sprengisandur Route, you can visit the Þjórsáverin nature reserve in the grassy wetlands 25 km to the north.

If you're staying at Versalir be sure to book in advance and advise the bus driver so you can get off at the right place.

Innra-hreysi

At this lonely spot north of the Þjórsárver nature reserve along the Old Sprengisandur Route are some more ruins of the outlaw Fjalla-Eyvindar's shelters – these date back to approximately 1772. They're not under any circumstances worth the long 23-km walk from Nýidalur but, if for some reason you choose to slog or cycle the 48 km along the old route between Nýidalur and Versalir, you'll go right past them.

Nýidalur & Tungnafellsjökull

Those who are going to break their journey across Sprengisandur will most likely end up staying at Nýidalur where there is a camping site and two Ferðafélag Íslands' huts, both of which provide kitchen facilities and cooking implements. Together they accommodate 160 people and are open from 1 July to 31 August. If you're staying at Nýidalur, be sure to bring warm gear. The nights will be particularly chilly here, 800-metres high.

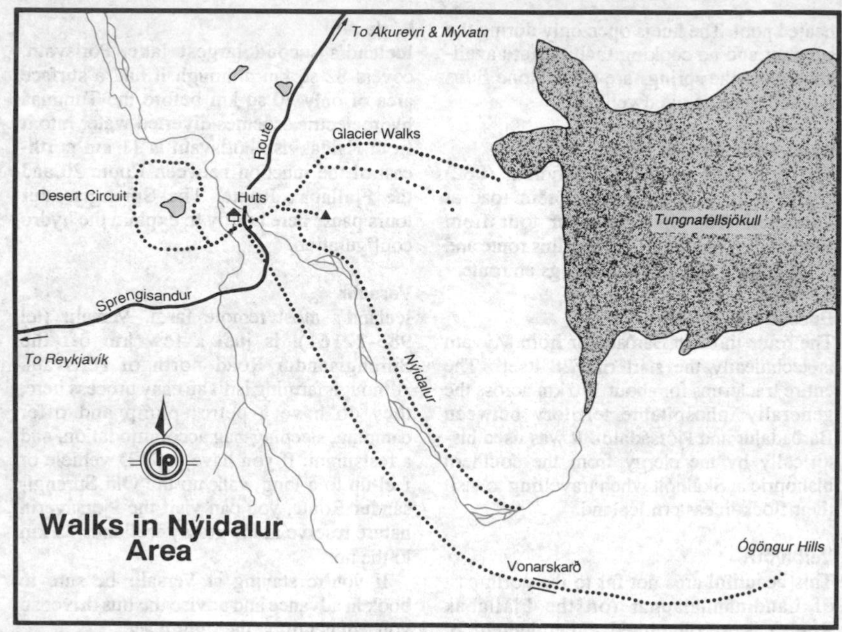

This valley, sometimes known as Jökuldalur, was only discovered in 1845. Although there aren't any tracks, per se, there are quite a few walking routes from the huts. It's a leisurely trip up this relatively lush valley.

Alternatively, there's a day-trip to colourful Vonarskarð pass, a broad saddle 1000-metre-high between the glacier Tungnafellsjökull, the green Ógöngur hills, and the Vatnajökull icecap. It takes you through some remote, active geothermal fields. Other walks include day-trips up to the base of Tungnafellsjökull or across the vast desert landscape east of Nýidalur. You can also wander up the 150-metre hill east of the huts for a wide view across the desert expanses.

Aldeyarfoss

One of Iceland's most photographed waterfalls, Aldeyarfoss on Skjálfandafljót ('shivering river') lies at the northern end of the Sprengisandur Route in upper Barðadalur. It flows over a layer of interesting basalt columns. The Sprengisandur bus tours travelling between Mývatn and Reykjavík (but not the one terminating in Akureyri) make a photo stop here. More interesting basalt patterns can be seen in the shallow canyon above the falls.

Getting There & Away

There are a couple of variations on the Sprengisandur tour. Going from south to north, buses travel from Reykjavík to Akureyri on Mondays and Thursdays departing from the BSÍ terminal at 8 am. On Wednesdays and Saturdays, they end instead at Mývatn, a slightly shorter trip. From north to south, it's only possible to depart from Mývatn. The bus leaves the hotel there on Thursdays and Saturdays at 8.30 am.

The trip from Reykjavík to Akureyri costs US$110 while the Mývatn option is only US$99. With Omnibuspass, all three tours cost about US$70. Holders of the Full-Circle Passes may opt to replace the Reykjavík to Akureyri section of their pass with the Sprengisandur Route at Omnibuspass rates.

The most popular way to cross the Sprengisandur seems to be from south to north in order to return via the one-way (for bus tours, anyway) Kjölur Route.

ÖSKJULEIÐ ROUTE

The Öskjuleið Route, whose name is a confusing declination meaning 'Askja way', leads to Herðubreið and Askja, the two most popular wonders of the Icelandic desert. The route, which more or less follows the western bank of the Jökulsá á Fjöllum most of the way, meanders across tephra wasteland and then winds circuitously through several rough, tyre-abusing encounters with Ódáðahraun, Iceland's largest lava flow. The road then passes through the oasis Herðubreiðarlindir and, if you aren't greeted by an opaque wall of blowing sand as you approach, you'll be treated to a close-up view of Iceland's most distinctive mountain.

From Herðubreið, the track wanders through sand dunes and lava flows past Dreki hut and up the hill toward Askja where you'll probably be stopped by deep snowdrifts well short of the road's end.

It goes without saying that only 4WD transport applies here, and even then it can be a touch and go situation; sometimes you touch the gas and only go deeper into the sand drift. When I took the Askja tour, the 4WD bus ploughed into a dune and had to be dragged out by another vehicle.

Grafarlandaá

This tributary of the Jökulsá á Fjöllum is the first major stream to be forded along the southbound journey to Askja. It's a particularly nice place for a picnic and has the freshest and best tasting water I've ever tried.

Kollótadyngja

This 1180-metre peak, 10 km north-west of Herðubreið, is a classic example of a shield volcano – a broad shield-like cone which oozed lava gently rather than exploded violently as so many of its Icelandic counterparts have been known to do. At its base is the Ferðafélag Íslands' Braeðrafell mountain hut. It accommodates 16 people and has a coal stove but no running water. The easiest access to this hut is along the footpath that heads west from the Herðubreið circuit.

Herðubreiðarlindir

The grassy oasis at Herðubreiðarlindir was created by springs flowing out from beneath the lava. It's only about 6 km from Herðubreið itself and is a sort of mini tourist complex for visitors to the Herðubreið nature reserve. There's a tourist information office, a camping site, and the Þórsteinsskáli hut belonging to Ferðafélag Íslands. The hut, open from June to August, accommodates 40 people and has a gas stove and a coal stove but no cooking implements.

Not far from the hut is another of those Fjalla-Eyvindar shelters, this one is scarcely large enough to breathe inside. It was renovated in 1922 on the remains of the original which had long since collapsed. Eyvindar is believed to have occupied it during the hard winter of 1774-75 subsisting on angelica root and raw horse meat stored on top of the hideout to retain heat inside.

About 4 km downstream from Herðubreiðarlindir, the Jökulsá á Fjöllum is just beginning to carve out a brand new canyon. The dramatic landscape being constructed is definitely worth seeing if you're passing by or staying at the oasis. The tours stop there for a quick photo-snapping session as well.

Many travellers on BSÍ Askja tours choose to spend a couple of days at Herðubreiðarlindir before returning to Mývatn in order to more thoroughly explore the area. Southbound, the bus passes at lunchtime on Mondays, Wednesdays, and Fridays and returns to Mývatn late in the evening, normally passing through Herðubreiðarlindir sometime after 6 pm on the same days.

Herðubreið

It has been described by travellers as a birthday cake, a cooking pot and a lampshade but the more sophisticated tourist industry likes to call it the 'Queen of the Icelandic desert'. Whatever you see in its oddly symmetrical shape, you're bound to think it's a welcome view after all those km of desert just crossed.

If Herðubreið, 1682 metres in elevation, appears to have been made in a jelly mould, you're right. It's another of those móberg mountains, the result of sub-glacial volcanic eruptions. If Vatnajökull were to melt tomorrow, Grímsvötn, Öraefi, and Kverkfjöll would emerge looking just like Herðubreið.

There's a trail that will allow you to easily circumnavigate Herðubreið in a day. The mountain looks the same from all sides, so disorientation is a possibility but, if you remember Kollótadyngja is west-north-west and Herðubreiðarlindir is east, there should be no problem.

Herðubreið may be climbed from the western side but it is still very steep; snow or bad weather may render it unclimbable without mountaineering equipment. Under optimum conditions, it may be climbed (from Herðubreiðarlindir) in a very long day

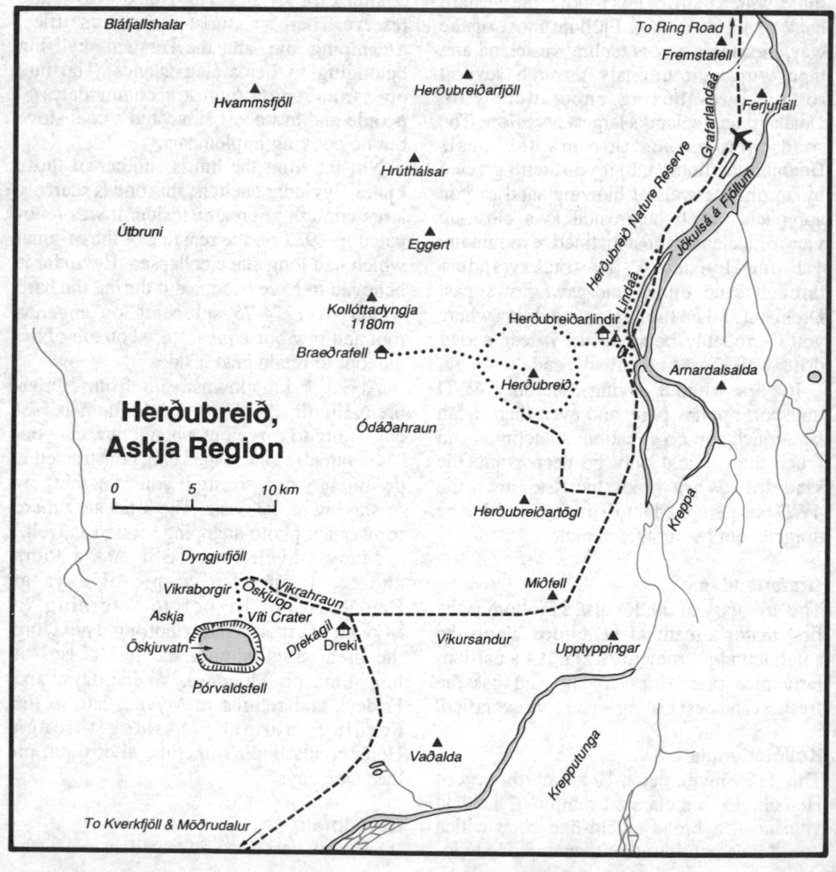

– remember daylight is irrelevant during the Icelandic summer. Common sense would dictate that you don't go alone, that you prepare for the foulest weather imaginable, and inform the attendant at the information office of your intentions before setting out.

The topo sheet applicable throughout this region is *Herðubreið 1:100,000* (1986).

Drekagil

The name of the gorge behind the Ferðafélag Íslands' Dreki hut means 'dragon ravine' after the perceived form of a dragon in the impressive rock formations that tower over the hut. The canyon behind it looks like something out of Arizona or the Sinai; the bitter wind and normally freezing temperatures just don't go with the landscape!

Dreki accommodates 20 people, and those who'd like to spend a bit more time at Askja than the tour allows, will have the option to hole up here for a couple of days if they'd like. There are no cooking facilities available but the coal stove will work at a pinch. Water is available from the river.

The price here is slightly lower than at the posh huts over at Landmannalaugar – US$5/7.75 for touring club members/non-members.

Unbelievably, there is even a small tourist information office which is attended for several hours a day. Camping is permitted as well but the wind and cold can get oppressive when you're huddled in a tent.

At Dreki is the intersection of Öskjuleið and Route F98 which goes to Kverkfjöll and the Ring Road at Möðrudalur across some fairly intimidating expanses.

Dyngjufjöll

The stark Dyngjufjöll range which contains the Askja caldera and the Drekagil gorge is what remains of a volcanic system that collapsed in on its magma chamber. At its highest point (Þórvaldsfell) along the southern rim, it rises to an altitude of over 1500 metres.

This inhospitable territory is extremely intriguing but not terribly inviting to the casual hiker. If you come to explore beyond the tracks and footpaths, make careful preparations and take due precautions.

Askja

Askja shouldn't be missed. It's a cold, windy, and forbidding place that sets one thinking about the power of nature and who's really in charge and all that. It's difficult to imagine what sort of forces combined to create this immense 50-sq km caldera. It's rather daunting to think that such events can be repeated at any time.

The deepest part of the collapsed magma chamber contains the sapphire blue (when it's liquid, anyway) lake Öskjuvatn which reaches a depth of 217 metres, the deepest in Iceland.

The cataclysm that formed the original Askja caldera happened a very long time ago (in 1875), when 2 cubic km of tephra were ejected from the volcano making a mess as far away as mainland Europe. For the next 30 years or so, subsequent activity caused another massive collapse of surface material, this time over an area of 11 sq km and 300 metres below the rim of the original. This new depression subsequently filled with water and became Öskjuvatn.

This lake is thought to have some potentially hazardous quirks, possibly odd currents or whirlpools, evidenced by the disappearance in 1907 of the two German researchers, Max Rudloff and Walther von Knebel.

Near the north-eastern corner the lake, one particularly active vent exploded and formed Víti (not to be confused with the Viti at Krafla), a tephra crater that contains a hot lake. It is, incidentally, an ideal temperature for swimming if you're so inclined. It's a bit slippery on the way down from the rim, however, and some people are put off.

Askja has erupted frequently over the last century. As recently as 1961, the vents at Öskjuop near the road entrance to the caldera went off and formed the crater row now known as Vikraborgir.

Getting There & Away The BSÍ tour to Askja departs Reykjahlíð (Mývatn) at 8.15

am on Mondays, Wednesdays, and Fridays during July and August *if* the road is passable. The 15-hour tour is fairly gruelling by Icelandic standards, but those who've travelled on some African or South American roads will be able to sit back and reminisce about journeys past. Participants who want to see Askja itself will have 1½ to 3 hours walking depending on the snow and road conditions so come prepared with strong footwear and as much warm and windproof clothing as you can muster.

The day-trip costs US$78 for transport and guide only so you'll have to bring your own food or ask the Hotel Reynihlíð in Mývatn to pack your lunch. Thanks to the popularity of this trip, Omnibuspass and Full-Circle Pass holders don't get much of a discount – they pay about US$72 per person.

As always, participants are welcome to leave the tour en route, in this case at either Herðubreiðarlindir or Drekagil, and rejoin later. Be sure to tell the driver when and where you want to be picked up so you'll have a seat going back to Mývatn.

KVERKFJÖLL ROUTE

Kverkfjöll is actually a mountain spur capped by the ice of Kverkjökull, a northern tongue of Vatnajökull. Through common usage, however, it has also come to refer to the hot spring-filled ice cave beneath the western margin of the Kverkjökull ice. Besides being the source of the roiling Jökulsá á Fjöllum, central Iceland's greatest river, it is also one of the world's largest geothermal areas. The hot river flows beneath the cold glacier ice, clouds of steam swirl over the river and melt shimmering patterns on the ice walls, and there you have it – the ideal tourist attraction. Perhaps this was the source of the overworked 'fire and ice' prose that seems to pervade everything ever written about Iceland.

The cave lies 5 km from the end of a long 4WD track which turns off the Ring Road near Möðrudalur. The road ends at the Sigurðarskáli hut so you'll have to walk from there to the ice cave. It's also possible to climb up the snowfields at the edge of the glacier to explore the Hveradalur geothermal fields amid pastel coloured sulphur hills or see the steaming crevasses higher up.

Places to Stay

Accommodation at Kverkfjöll is in Ferðafélag Íslands' 70-bunk Sigurðarskáli hut or the camping site at the end of the track, just 3 km from the glacier Kverkjökull and 5 km from the ice cave. The hut contains a coal stove suitable for cooking on but no pots and pans so, if you want a hot drink or meal, bring your own.

I've heard that there is another hut further up the edge of the glacier at a much higher altitude but I haven't seen it – if you're interested, check it out with the Ferðafélag Íslands.

Getting There & Away

Unless you have a robust 4WD vehicle, the only way to visit Kverkfjöll is to get there under your own steam or take a tour. The most popular is the one operated by BSÍ in conjunction with Ice & Fire Expeditions (tel 96-42101).

Due to the site's remoteness, the minimum tour length is 3 days from Húsavík or Mývatn. Participants are required to bring their own food and warm, wind and waterproof clothing. Hiking boots are more or less essential and crampons are recommended if you're wary of walking on ice and snow.

The tour operates on Fridays in July and August, departing Húsavík at noon and Mývatn at 1 pm. This means that if you opt to leave the group at Kverkfjöll, you'll be waiting a week before the tour comes around again. The tour cost costs US$175 or US$160 with an Omnibuspass or Full-Circle Pass. Hut fees are not included in the price of the tour so it might pay to carry a tent if you're set up for the extremely brisk temperatures you're likely to encounter at Kverkfjöll.

Hvannalindir

As an added bonus, the Kverkfjöll tour also stops at Hvannalindir where there is – you guessed it – another of good ol' Fjalla-

Eyvindar's winter hideouts! He even constructed a rather high-tech (for those days) sheep fold at this one so the sheep could visit the stream without having to face the elements. Hvannalindir is about 30 km north of the Sigurðarskáli hut.

Fjallabak Route

The Fjallabak, or 'behind the mountains', route (F22) to the north of the Mýrdalsjökull massif provides a spectacular alternative to the coastal route south of it. It begins near the Sigölduvirkjun power plant on the Tungnaá river and passes through the scenically diverse Fjallabak nature reserve to Landmannalaugar. It continues east past Kirkjufell marshes and enters the Jökuldalur valley and follows a riverbed for 10 km or so before climbing to the Herðubreið lookout and descending to Eldgjá.

For the next 40 km the road is fairly good but there are a couple of significant river fords to contend with so conventional vehicles wishing to reach Eldgjá from the east may still have problems when the water is high. At Búland, it joins with Route 208 and emerges at the Ring Road south-west of Kirkjubaejarklaustur.

Fjallabak Tour

The only public transport over the Fjallabak Route is the BSÍ tour which operates daily (river conditions permitting) between Reykjavík and Skaftafell from 15 July to 31 August. It departs from both Reykjavík and Skaftafell at 8.30 am and stops at several points of interest along the way. Both buses arrive at Landmannalaugar at about 12.30 and depart at 2.30 pm. They stop for an hour at Eldgjá as well, allowing time for a walk to the spectacular falls Ofaerufoss.

Most people who take this tour break their trip at least once, most often at Landmannalaugar. The normal one-way fare, regardless of the number of stops, is US$60. Holders of Omnibuspass pay US$32.

Cycling

Because much of this route is along rivers (*in* rivers!), it is not ideally suited to bicycles. Quite a number of people do attempt it with mountain bikes but it's not casual cycling by any means. In fact, there are places where the only way through is to wade across (or along) icy rivers carrying your gear and the bike on your back. If the weather has been very dry, it may not come to that but don't count on it.

Driving

It's a safe bet to say that a regular non-4WD vehicle wouldn't have a hope of completing this route. If the rivers are low, a conventional vehicle could possibly reach Landmannalaugar from the west and Eldgjá from the east but the route between the two would be impassable under any conditions.

LANDMANNALAUGAR

Anyone who may be tempted to do the BSÍ trip from Reykjavík to Skaftafell over the Fjallabak Route in a single day should probably resign themselves to a change of plans once they've seen Landmannalaugar. The 2 hours allowed by the bus tour isn't enough time for even a fleeting glimpse of what's there. Its magnificent rhyolite peaks, rambling lava flows, blue mountain lakes, and soothing hot springs can easily hold you captive for several days.

This area, which lies 600 metres above sea level, is the largest geothermal field in Iceland outside the Grímsvötn caldera in Vatnajökull. The activity is believed to be centred on the Torfajökull caldera, 10 km south-east of Landmannalaugar. The most recent eruption in this field, however, occurred at the Veiðivötn fissure in 1480. This north-east to south-west tending crater row includes all the lava fields between the Laugahraun and Ljótipollur craters and beyond.

The variegated peaks that are the trademark of Landmannalaugar are composed of rhyolite, a combination of minerals metamorphosed by geothermal and volcanic activity.

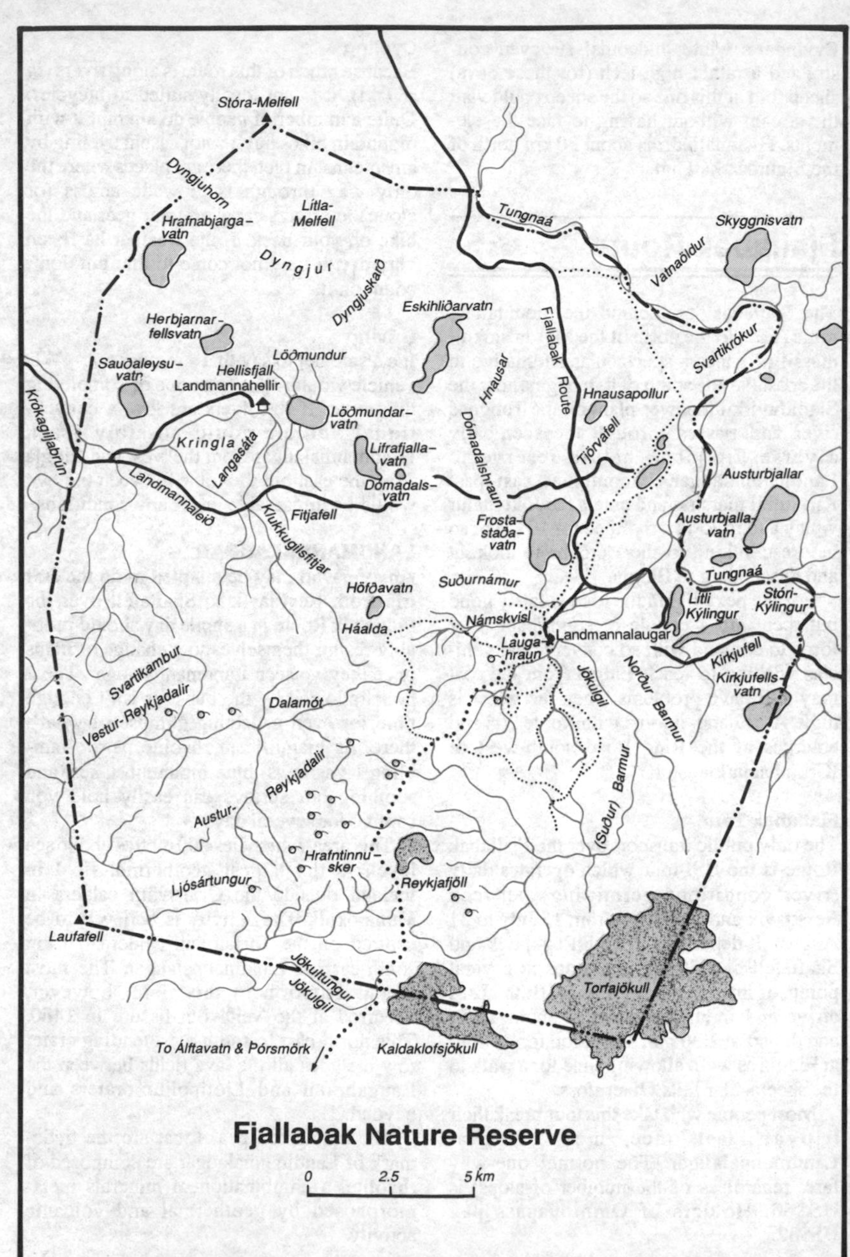
Stóra-Melfell
Dyngjuhorn
Lítla-Melfell
Hrafnabjarga-vatn
Dyngjur
Dyngjuskarð
Tungnaá
Skyggnisvatn
Vatnaöldur
Eskihlíðarvatn
Fjallabak Route
Herbjarnar-fellsvatn
Svartikrókur
Löðmundur
Hnausar
Sauðaleysu-vatn
Hellisfjall
Landmannahellir
Hnausapollur
Löðmundar-vatn
Dómadalshraun
Krókagiljabrún
Kringla
Lifrafjalla-vatn
Tjörvafell
Langasáta
Dómadals-vatn
Austurbjallar
Landmannaleið
Fitjafell
Frosta-staða-vatn
Austurbjalla-vatn
Klukkugilsfitjar
Tungnaá
Suðurnámur
Höfðavatn
Litli Kýlingur
Stóri-Kýlingur
Námskvísl
Háalda
Landmannalaugar
Lauga-hraun
Kirkjufell
Jökulgil
Norður Barmur
Kirkjufells-vatn
Svartikambur
Vestur-Reykjadalir
Dalamót
Reykjadalir
Austur-
(Suður) Barmur
Hrafntinnu-sker
Ljósártungur
Reykjafjöll
Laufafell
Torfajökull
Jökultungur
Jökulgil
To Álftavatn & Þórsmörk
Kaldaklofsjökull
Fjallabak Nature Reserve
0
2.5
5 km

Information
The coach drivers and Landmannalaugar hut warden can help you with specific advice about the area. The official information office is on Fjallabak (F22) at the Landmannalaugar turn-off, 2 km from the camping ground. It seems to be closed most of the time, however.

Weather Although the weather in the area of Landmannalaugar can be quite chilly, it is generally pretty good. When it does rain, it's more of a wind-driven horizontal mist than an actual drenching downpour. It's annoying but doesn't curtail outdoor activities and you can expect the weather to change literally from moment to moment. Interestingly enough, this is the first place I've ever experienced rain when there wasn't a cloud in the sky – presumably, it had been carried on the wind from a cloud somewhere just over the horizon!

Landmannalaugar Hot Springs
Both hot and cold water flow out from beneath Laugahraun and combine in a natural pool at Landmannalaugar to form the most ideal hot bath imaginable. It shouldn't be missed.

Places to Stay
The Ferðafélag Íslands' hut at Landmannalaugar accommodates 115 people on a first-come-first-served basis, but in July and August, it's normally booked out by tour groups and club members so individuals will have little chance of finding space.

All Ferðafélag Íslands' huts in the Fjallabak nature reserve and along the Landmannalaugar to Þórsmörk track cost US$7.75/11.50 per night for members/non-members (of Ferðafélag Íslands). Only the Landmannalaugar and Þórsmörk huts have running water (the latter has showers!) and kitchen facilities.

The camping area at Landmannalaugar is soggy and gravelly but it's free. The hut and the camping site share facilities and, in the morning, the toilet block looks like the New York subway with staggering queues on all fronts. In case of emergencies, there are primitive toilets scattered around the perimeter of the camping area.

South-east of Torfajökull at Strútslaug hot springs there is a Dick Phillips' mountain hut which is open to the public. Apart from taking one of his tours, however, there's no easy access since it involves walking in along Hólmsárlón from the 4WD track across the sandur north of Mýrdalsjökull or cross-country from the Álftavatn area. If you'd like to make your way in there independently and not risk running into a tour group, you can enquire about his schedule by contacting Dick Phillips at the address listed under Tours in the Iceland Getting Around chapter.

Day-Walks
Laugahraun & Brennisteinsalda In the time allotted on the bus tour, there's just enough time for you to dash across Laugahraun and up to Brennisteinsalda ('burning stones crest') for a quick look but you'll regret having to see it that way. There are a number of variations on this walk, all worthwhile; the star attractions, the hot vents and the peak itself, are worth more than a 10-minute glance.

The slopes of the rainbow-streaked mountain Brennisteinsalda are punctuated by steaming vents and sulphur deposits. It's possible to climb to the summit for a good view out across the rugged and variegated landscape.

Frostastaðavatn The blue lake Frostastaðavatn lies just behind the rhyolite ridge, immediately north of Landmannalaugar. It's a good walk for far-ranging views from the ridge as well as the interesting rock formations and moss-covered lava flows that flank the lake itself. Allow about 3 hours for the return trip, if you plan to walk at least one way on the road, and do some exploring at the lake. For a longer day you can walk along the shore right around the lake where you can occasionally spot loons and ducks.

Bláhnúkur The name of this big blue peak

immediately south of the Laugahraun means, strangely enough, 'blue peak'. If you don't mind scrambling around on scree, it's a fairly easy climb to the summit but it gets steep in places so watch your footing.

The route to the top of the 943-metre mountain is up the north-eastern ridge across Graenagil from Landmannalaugar. Don't try to ford the river; you'll find a plank bridge just downstream from the mouth of the ravine. The easiest return route is down to the hot vents below Brennisteinsalda and back to Landmannalaugar via Laugahraun.

Ljótipollur The route around the crater lake Ljótipollur is a good day-walk from Landmannalaugar through several types of landscape: tephra desert, lava flow, marsh, and glacial river valley. The return trip is approximately 15 km and will require a full day to complete, less if you walk on the road at least one way.

Tjörvafell & Hnausapollur Another good day-walk from Landmannalaugar is around the peak Tjörvafell and the crater lake of Hnausavatn. Tjörvafell is a low gravelly peak rising about 200 metres above the surrounding tephra desert and can be easily climbed for a good view.

Landmannalaugar to Þórsmörk Track
For travellers, the 4-day trek from Landmannalaugar to Þórsmörk (or vice versa) is the premier walk in Iceland. In fact, it wouldn't be surprising over the next few years to see it join the Milford Track and the Inca Trail as one of the great walks of the world. If you want to do it while it's still relatively unknown outside Iceland, you'd best hurry. July and August are the only months when it is passable to casual trekkers. This track can understandably become a veritable freeway, so don't expect much of a wilderness experience unless you're prepared to take side-trips away from the main route.

During the high-season, it's an easy trip and can be completed by anyone in reasonable physical condition. The Ferðafélag Íslands and several adventure tour companies offer organised trips over this route for those who'd rather not go it alone.

Due to the popularity of the trip, those planning to stay in huts will have to pay their hut fees and pick up keys in advance through the wardens in Landmannalaugar or Þórsmörk, or through Ferðafélag Íslands in Reykjavík. Any of these sources can also answer specific questions and provide advice on trail conditions. Alternatively, camping is allowed in the vicinity of any of the huts but wilderness camping inside the Fjallabak reserve is only possible with a permit.

Most people walk the track from north to south in order to take advantage of the net altitude loss and the shower at the Þórsmörk hut. Many don't stop at Þórsmörk (or stop only long enough for a shower) but continue instead along the Þórsmörk to Skógar track and make a 6-day trip out of it.

The trip begins behind the hut at Landmannalaugar and crosses the Laugahraun lava flow before climbing into the rhyolite peaks and steaming vents of the Brennisteinsalda area. It then crosses a pass and descends to Stórihver ('big hot springs') and more steaming vents. Most people spend the first night at the Hrafntinnusker hut. The second day involves passing below the small icecap of Kaldaklofsfjöll and steeply descending the Jökultungur ridge to arrive at the Álftavatn hut beside the beautiful lake Álftavatn for the second night.

At this point, the track joins up with a 4WD track and follows it on and off for 11 or so km passing en route the sheep hut at Hvanngil. After leaving the jeep track, the route passes through sand and gravel flat lands to the Botnar (sometimes known as Emstrur) hut, the destination on the third night.

The final day involves a descent to the Fremri-Emstruá river and crosses it just below where it leaves Entujökull glacier, the north-western spur of the Mýrdalsjökull icecap. From there, the track follows the gravel flats along the Markarfljót before crossing the low pass into Þórsmörk.

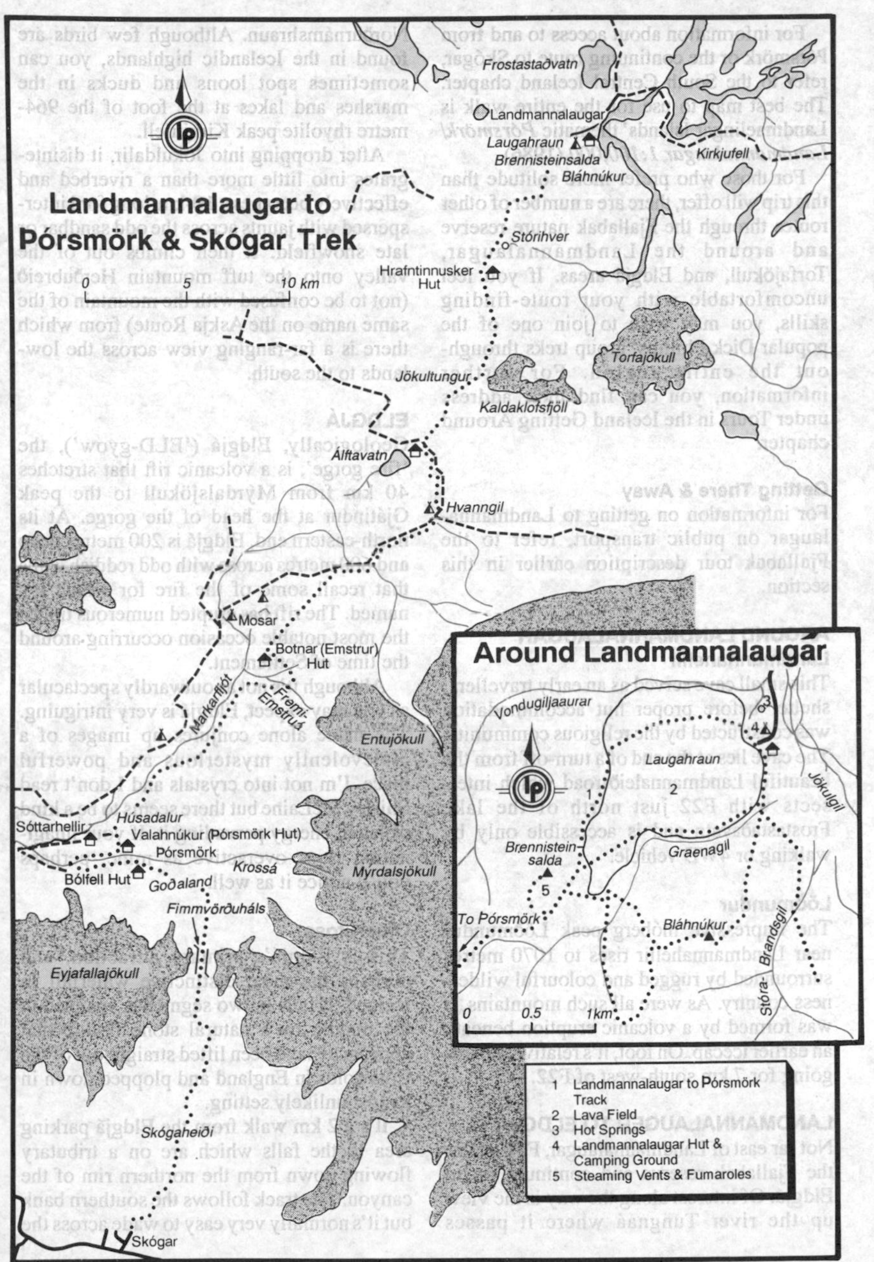
Landmannalaugar to
Þórsmörk & Skógar Trek
0
5
10 km
Frostastaðvatn
Landmannalaugar
Laugahraun
Brennisteinsalda
Kirkjufell
Bláhnúkur
Stórihver
Hrafntinnusker
Hut
Torfajökull
Jökultungur
Kaldaklofsfjöll
Álftavatn
Hvanngil
Mosar
Botnar (Emstrur)
Hut
Markarfljót
Fremi-
Emstrua
Entujökull
Húsadalur
Sóttarhellir
Valahnúkur (Þórsmörk Hut)
Þórsmörk
Krossá
Bólfell Hut
Goðaland
Mýrdalsjökull
Fimmvörðuháls
Eyjafallajökull
Skógaheiði
Skógar
Around Landmannalaugar
Vondugiljaaurar
3
4
Laugahraun
1
2
Jökulgil
Brennistein-
salda
Graenagil
5
To Þórsmörk
Bláhnúkur
Stóra-
Brandsgil
0
0.5
1km
1 Landmannalaugar to Þórsmörk Track
2 Lava Field
3 Hot Springs
4 Landmannalaugar Hut & Camping Ground
5 Steaming Vents & Fumaroles

For information about access to and from Þórsmörk or the continuing route to Skógar, refer to the South Central Iceland chapter. The best map to use for the entire walk is Landmaelingar Íslands' thematic *Þórsmörk/Landmannalaugar 1:100,000* (1986).

For those who prefer more solitude than this trip will offer, there are a number of other routes through the Fjallabak nature reserve and around the Landmannalaugar, Torfajökull, and Eldgjá areas. If you feel uncomfortable with your route-finding skills, you may wish to join one of the popular Dick Phillips' group treks throughout the entire region. For further information, you can find their address under Tours in the Iceland Getting Around chapter.

Getting There & Away

For information on getting to Landmannalaugar on public transport, refer to the Fjallabak tour description earlier in this section.

AROUND LANDMANNALAUGAR

Landmannahellir

This small cave served as an early travellers' shelter before proper hut accommodation was constructed by the religious community. The cave lies at the end of a turn-off from the beautiful Landmannaleið road which intersects with F22 just north of the lake Frostastaðavatn and is accessible only by walking or 4WD vehicle.

Löðmundur

The impressive móberg peak Löðmundur near Landmannahellir rises to 1070 metres surrounded by rugged and colourful wilderness country. As were all such mountains, it was formed by a volcanic eruption beneath an earlier icecap. On foot, it's relatively hard-going for 7 km south-west of F22.

LANDMANNALAUGER TO ELDGJÁ

Not far east of Landmannalaugar, F22 leaves the Fjallabak reserve and continues on to Eldgjá. Of interest along the way is the view up the river Tungnaá where it passes Norðurnámshraun. Although few birds are found in the Icelandic highlands, you can sometimes spot loons and ducks in the marshes and lakes at the foot of the 964-metre rhyolite peak Kirkjufell.

After dropping into Jökuldalir, it disintegrates into little more than a riverbed and effectively becomes a 10-km-long ford interspersed with jaunts across the odd sandbar or late snowfield. It then climbs out of the valley onto the tuff mountain Herðubreið (not to be confused with the mountain of the same name on the Askja Route) from which there is a far-ranging view across the lowlands to the south.

ELDGJÁ

Geologically, Eldgjá ('ELD-gyow'), the 'fire gorge', is a volcanic rift that stretches 40 km from Mýrdalsjökull to the peak Gjátindur at the head of the gorge. At its north-eastern end, Eldgjá is 200 metres deep and 600 metres across with odd reddish walls that recall some of the fire for which it's named. The rift has erupted numerous times, the most notable occasion occurring around the time of Settlement.

Although it's not as outwardly spectacular as you may expect, Eldgjá is very intriguing. The name alone conjures up images of a malevolently mysterious and powerful place. I'm not into crystals and I don't read Shirley McLaine but there seems to be a kind of latent energy pervading it. If your imagination is as overactive as mine, perhaps you'll notice it as well.

Ofaerufoss

This is Eldgjá's primary attraction, and perhaps the most distinctive waterfall in Iceland. It falls in two segments, spanned in the middle by a natural stone bridge that appears to have been lifted straight out of the Cotswolds in England and plopped down in a most unlikely setting.

It's a 2 km walk from the Eldgjá parking area to the falls which are on a tributary flowing down from the northern rim of the canyon. The track follows the southern bank but it's normally very easy to wade across the river to the falls. Those who have no problems with vertigo can then climb up and walk right across on the arch.

Hánípufit

In the green and fertile area of Hánípufit, 8 km south of the Eldgjá turn-off, the river Skaftá widens into an entanglement of cascades and waterfalls that is 500 metres across in places. It's unusual and quite beautiful.

Getting There & Away

For information on getting to Eldgjá, see the description of the Fjallabak tour earlier in this chapter.

Greenland

Facts about the Country

It's said that once you've seen the world, you can always go to Greenland which looms as a distantly mysterious destination on the travel horizon. Its appeal is more than an unusual stamp in a passport, it's a unique experience of reality.

The landscape is rugged, forbidding and, at times, even frightening. Its diversity is expressed in subtle variations on Arctic conditions: rocky, treeless mountains; dry or boggy tundra; long, winding fjords; vast ice sheets and flowing glaciers. What it lacks in range, it makes up in quality.

Coastal Greenland meets the sea in towering cliffs, walls of glacial ice, and ancient rock – the oldest on the planet. Areas away from the coast lie in the original deepfreeze beneath a 3000-metre-thick blanket of ice. The seas (near which everything set down by humans in Greenland is found) are just a degree or so above freezing. In places they're hostile or infested with mountains of floating ice. For me it's a challenge to write about this country. One can only repeat the words 'beautiful', 'spectacular', 'magnificent' so many times before they sound flat and meaningless.

Despite its small population of 50,000, Greenlanders call their home *Kalaallit Nunaat*, (Ka-LAHT-lit, although it normally comes out more like KHLAKH-let NOO-naht) the 'land of the people'. They are proud of their country – or more accurately, in love with it – and travellers will find them some of the friendliest folks around, welcoming visitors who didn't have the good fortune to inherit the place as a birthright. You need only travel by boat from village to village and watch your fellow passengers to see their fascination with their surroundings. They gaze at the shore with the sort of reverence normally reserved for a wise and respected elder. As one Greenlandic poet put it,'I get dizzy of all this beauty and shiver with happiness'.

The land has never allowed more humans than it was [illegible]
– the conc[illegible]
Greenland. [illegible]
tlement boa[illegible]
next largest [illegible]
where like [illegible]
inclusion on [illegible]

The ancien[illegible]
dence – no py[illegible]
that it has bee[illegible]
greatest achiev[illegible]
that, for many [illegible]
vived the eleme[illegible]
Arctic winters an[illegible]
casual observers [illegible]
habitable wastelan[illegible]
more than can be said for Greenlan[illegible]
colonies. They survived only a couple centuries before mysteriously disappearing from the face of the earth.

Greenland is currently in a state of transition – the product of a resourceful and independent past struggling to reconcile itself, as part of the Kingdom of Denmark, with a soft and modern European present. Today it's a country of far-flung villages, none connected by asphalt. Locals can visit their neighbours by Mercedes in the summer and dog sled in the winter. In the supermarkets they can buy pineapples from Hawaii, tomatoes from Mexico, and frozen seal steaks from the nearest fjord. They can live in a 100-unit block of flats or in a brightly painted Scandinavian bungalow and practise law, word processing, or seal hunting.

The days of the polar explorers are long past and Greenland has well and truly come into step with 20th-century Scandinavia. It does, however, remain one of the few places that hasn't been forever altered by mass tourism. Outside Kulusuk (the world's most unusual day-tripper's dream), there are few tourists; travellers will find a lot of space between rucksacks, but expect things to change. Within the next few years, Greenland could well become a popular

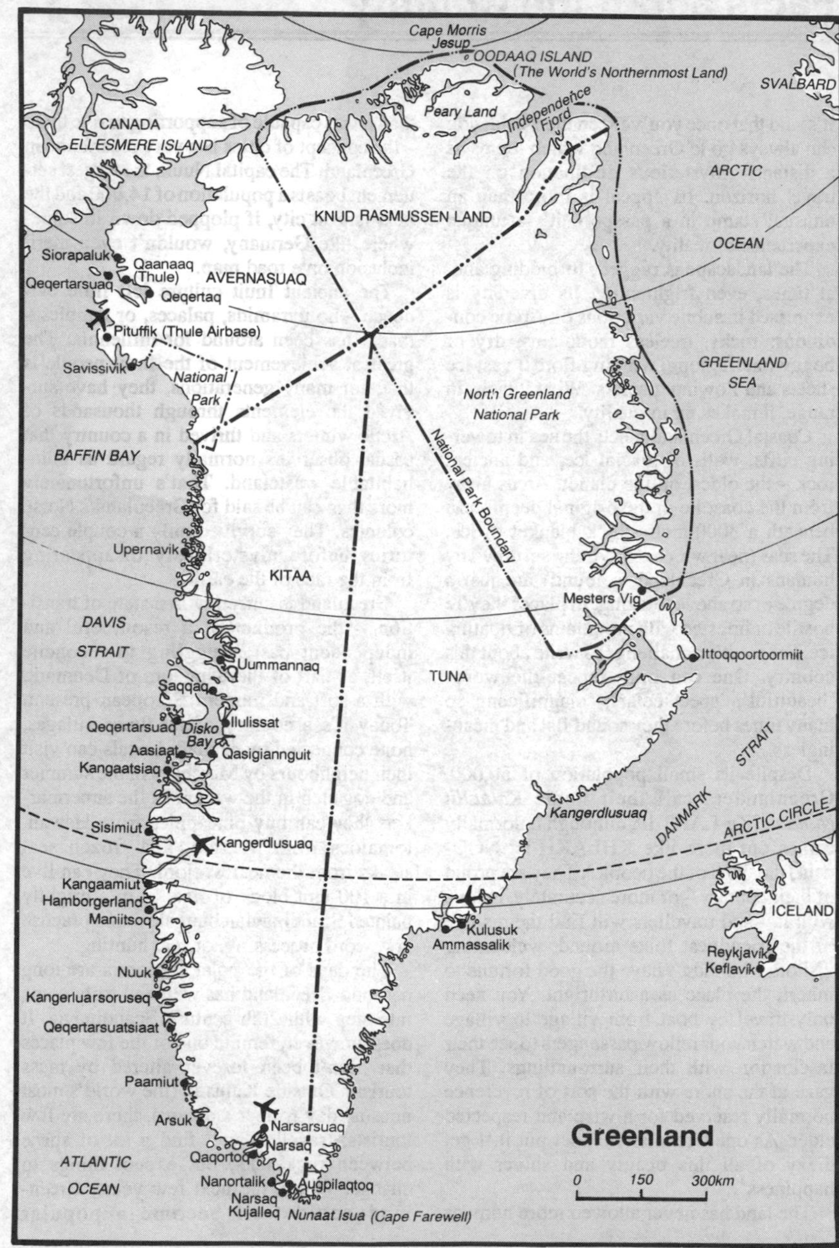
Cape Morris Jesup
OODAAQ ISLAND
(The World's Northernmost Land)
SVALBARD
Peary Land
Independence Fjord
CANADA
ELLESMERE ISLAND
ARCTIC
KNUD RASMUSSEN LAND
OCEAN
Siorapaluk
Qaanaaq (Thule)
Qeqertarsuaq
AVERNASUAQ
Qeqertaq
Pituffik (Thule Airbase)
Savissivik
National Park
GREENLAND SEA
North Greenland National Park
National Park Boundary
BAFFIN BAY
Upernavik
KITAA
Mesters Vig
DAVIS STRAIT
Uummannaq
TUNA
Ittoqqoortoormiit
Saqqaq
Ilulissat
Qeqertarsuaq
Disko Bay
Aasiaat
Qasigiannguit
Kangaatsiaq
DANMARK STRAIT
Kangerdlusuaq
ARCTIC CIRCLE
Sisimiut
Kangerdlusuaq
Kangaamiut
Hamborgerland
Maniitsoq
ICELAND
Kulusuk
Ammassalik
Reykjavík
Keflavík
Nuuk
Kangerluarsoruseq
Qeqertarsuatsiaat
Paamiut
Arsuk
Narsarsuaq
Narsaq
Greenland
Qaqortoq
ATLANTIC OCEAN
Nanortalik
Augpilaqtoq
Narsaq Kujalleq
Nunaat Isua (Cape Farewell)
0 150 300km

destination experiencing the same tourist crush that pervades formerly exotic and out-of-the-way places elsewhere. Those who are travelling the world and saving Greenland for last may arrive only to learn they've waited too long to beat the crowds.

HISTORY

The Inuit

The Inuit (pronounced 'INN-yuit') people, commonly known as Eskimos ('eaters of raw meat' in Native American languages), are the predominant population group in Greenland.

Although the American Indians are descendants of the Siberian peoples who migrated into North America across the Bering land bridge from 25,000 to 23,000 years ago, there is evidence that the Inuit first arrived in Alaska by *umiaq* or skin boat from 7000 to 8000 years ago. This was long after the land bridge had disappeared beneath the Bering Strait.

The first Greenlanders migrated from Ellesmere Island in northern Canada some 5000 years ago. This Stone-Age culture, which has been called *Saqaq* merged with the Independence I (named after Independence Fjord in Peary Land, North Greenland) by anthropologists, probably consisted of no more than 500 nomadic individuals who eked out a meagre existence at the very frontier of human endurance. These people sustained themselves by hunting polar bear, musk oxen, Arctic hares, and other animals.

Around 2500 years ago, the climate of the region turned colder and the Saqaq culture mysteriously disappeared, probably retreating westward. It was replaced by a more technologically advanced culture, the Independence II. These people lived in more communal societies than their predecessors. They carved weapons and artistic pieces from bone and ivory, used sleds to transport belongings, and burned oil from whale and seal blubber for heat and light.

Interestingly enough, this group and the similarly advanced Dorset culture of northern Canada thrived during the cooler climatic period. When a warming trend began in the early 10th century, they were either absorbed into or displaced by the Thule culture which had originated in western Alaska and quickly, in perhaps as little as 75 years, spread eastward all the way to Greenland.

It was the Thule people who made such innovations as the *qajaq* ('kayak'), the harpoon, and the dog sled, all still used in one form or another. Although another climatic shift during the 12th century forced the Thule people to migrate southward fragmenting into a number of sub-cultures, there is fairly conclusive archaeological evidence that the modern-day Inuit have descended from this group.

The Norse Colonies

There are two main sources of the history of the Norse in Greenland: the *Graenlendinga Saga* or *Tale of the Greenlanders* and the *Saga of Eirík Rauðe*. Because these were written down well after the fact, neither of them can be relied upon to tell the *whole* story. In some cases, they even contradict each other but the sagas, combined with archaeological evidence, have allowed researchers to piece together much of the tale of the Greenlandic Norse.

According to the sagas, the first European discovery of Greenland was in 900 when an Iceland-bound Norwegian, Gunnbjörn Ulfsson, was blown off course. He came ashore at Gunnbjarnar Skerries near present-day Ammassalik on the east coast then turned around and headed for Iceland.

Early Icelanders had a tendency to get caught up in vicious family feuds involving generations of vengeful killings. One so embroiled was Snaebjörn Galti, who avenged the death of a family member and then, to avoid the court system and being declared an outlaw, he decided to escape from Iceland and head for the western land reported by Gunnbjörn 78 years earlier. He gathered some companions and prepared to set off. Before they could leave, one member of their party recounted a dream he'd had of their intended venture, recorded in a passage that is one of the most poignant in the sagas:

I can see death in a dread place, yours and mine. North-west over the waves, with ice and cold and countless wonders...

Undaunted by the ominous warning, Snaebjörn and his companions set sail and landed at the icy fjord Bláserk, near Ammassalik. They built a hut just before the snows began to fall, intent on holing up for the winter. Snaebjörn, a fairly disagreeable character, took to quarrelling with his companions in their confined winter quarters. The predictable happened. The dream's prophecy came true, with only a couple of the party returning home alive.

Nearly a century later, Norwegian Eirík Rauðe Þorvaldsson, now known as Eric the Red, and his father were exiled from Norway after a rather bloody revenge killing. They fled to Iceland where they settled in the Laxdaela country of the north-west. Eirík was again convicted of outlawry in 982 when he avenged the killing of two of his slaves who had vandalised a neighbour's property. Rather than remain *persona non grata*, he left Iceland for Gunnbjörn's and Snaebjörn's land over the western horizon.

Like the others, Eirík first came ashore at Bláserk but considered the place unlucky after Snaebjörn's fiasco so he continued further down the coast. After rounding Cape Farewell, he landed on a small island naming it, not surprisingly, Eiriksey ('Eirík's island'), and settled in for the winter. The following summer, he continued further up the nearest fjord (Eiriks Fjord) and found some tolerable country reminiscent of north-west Iceland. Eirík took the best plot of land for himself, naming it Brattahlíð ('steep hillside') and built his farm.

In 986, Eirík returned to Iceland to share the news of his success and report that the new country, *Graenaland*, was rich, fruitful, and ripe for settlement. This was, of course, a bit of an overblown assessment but as the *Saga of Eirík Rauðe* puts it:

The land he discovered he called Greenland because he said it would attract people if the country had a beautiful name...

'Green' isn't exactly the first thing that springs to mind when you arrive there! He left Iceland with 25 ships loaded with prospective colonists, 14 of whom actually survived storm, doubt, and trepidation to land and settle in. People continued to arrive and, when all the available lands had been settled around Eirík's colony (the Østerbygd or 'eastern settlement'), they moved several hundred km further up the coast to present-day Nuuk, the Vesturbygd or 'western settlement'.

Eirík suffered some severe marital problems while at Brattahlíð. His wife Þjoðhild had converted to Christianity and, being a rather fervent Christian, had a church built at their farm. When Eirík refused to join the new faith, she refused to sleep with him. It was fortunate for their son Leif, who introduced his mother to the new religion, that he'd already been born at the time because Eirík never did convert and Þjoðhild never did relent. Perhaps that's how he got his nickname, 'Leif the Lucky'.

The first Norse to sight the North American coast was Bjarni Herjolfsson, an Icelander who set off to visit family in Greenland and was blown off course. He came upon a hilly and wooded land. Disgusted at having missed Greenland, he left without even disembarking. Had he set foot on solid land, perhaps a statue of Bjarni Herjolfsson would now grace the lawn of Hallgrímskirkja in Reykjavík.

As it happened, Eirík's son Leif was overcome with curiosity about the new land (and the description 'wooded' sounded particularly alluring in treeless Greenland). He set off on an expedition visiting Helluland (Baffin Island), Markland (Labrador), and Vinland. The whereabouts of Vinland has never really been determined but it became the site of the only known Norse colony in North America. It was a rather half-hearted attempt at colonisation and the Europeans just couldn't seem to get along with the American natives (they called them skraelings or 'those wrinkled by the sun') and the project was abandoned. Modern archaeological research has revealed that the

Vinland colony was probably at L'Anse aux Meadows (Newfoundland) which has recently been named a world heritage site.

At their peak, the Greenland colonies included some 300 farms with around 5000 inhabitants who, though not exactly thriving, successfully ran sheep, cattle, and hogs and hunted seals, caribou, walrus, and polar bears.

In 1261, Greenland was annexed by Norway (a year before Iceland was taken) and a trade monopoly which allowed the colonies to trade only with Norway was immediately imposed. The agreement was that two ships would visit annually to bring supplies and carry locally produced goods back to Europe. Unfortunately, during the late 13th century, there was a noticeable cooling trend in the North Atlantic climate. Glaciers advanced, animals died, and the seas choked with ice making shipping impossible. By the 15th century, the Greenland colonies were left high and dry with no link to the outside world and, just a century later, they had disappeared without a trace. The last report of life in the Østerbygd is from 1406 of a wedding at the Hvalsey church between an Icelander from a ship that went astray and a Greenlandic colonist. After their wedding, they returned to Iceland and provided a detailed account of the event.

There are several theories but very few clues about what happened to the colonies. Based on a 1379 report of a skraeling attack on the Vesturbygd, some believe the colonies were destroyed by the Inuit who saw the foreigners as threatening. It is unlikely, however, they had the means or the demeanour to totally obliterate the colonies and the theory hasn't gained much of a following. Other theories include a devastating change in the climate, a scourge of caterpillars which destroyed the grazing lands, a massive epidemic, inbreeding, emigration to North America, absorption into the Inuit community, and obliteration by English pirates.

The last seems to have several shreds of evidence to support it but they're certainly not conclusive. In 1448, Pope Nicholas sent an epistle to Irish bishops recounting a tale of the Greenland colonies being plagued by heathen barbarians and that, around 1418, some church properties had been destroyed and many inhabitants taken as slaves. This account made it fairly clear that only a portion of the colonies had been affected.

In his diary, the son of Hans Egede the 'Greenland Apostle', reported an Inuit legend about repeated raids by pirate ships. Although the Inuits and the colonists together resisted the onslaught, many people and much property were lost. It is unlikely, however, that the entire population could have been drastically reduced in this manner – the disappearance of the Greenland colonies remains one of the great mysteries of history.

The North-West Passage

In 1575, when speculation about the North-West Passage was reaching fever pitch, Martin Frobisher, outfitted by an entrepreneur named Michael Lok, sailed from London, across the Atlantic, up the west coast of Greenland, and into the Canadian archipelago. Believing that he had found the gateway to Asia on Baffin Island, he picked up a stone and returned home.

Frobisher's souvenir marked the beginning of the second great scam in the history of the North Atlantic. Lok, who hoped to attract investments, determined it contained gold-bearing ore. A second expedition resulted in three shiploads of worthless mica being carried across the Atlantic and being assayed as having high value by the unscrupulous Lok. The fraud wasn't discovered until after a third voyage, which incidentally resulted in the loss of a ship and 40 sailors.

Despite the problems, Greenland had suddenly become the flavour of the month. In 1585, John Davis, a humble but skilled navigator, set off toward the Greenland coast in two small ships, the *Sunneshine* and the *Mooneshine*. On this and his two subsequent voyages, he managed to establish rapport with the Greenlandic Inuit gaining their friendship and esteem. He observed closely their customs and lifestyles and wrote the first ethnographic study of the Arctic peoples. He also took prodigious notes on the topographic features, currents, vegetation, and wildlife of the island.

Thanks to the search for the elusive North-West Passage, later voyagers added further to the growing store of knowledge about the North Atlantic. In 1607, Henry Hudson explored the east coast of Greenland and went on to discover Jan Mayen Island. On his third voyage, in 1610, he discovered the bay that is named for him (assuming it was the Pacific Ocean) but, as a result of mutiny he was set adrift, never to be seen again.

After two more men, Thomas Sutton in 1612 and William Baffin in 1615, unsuccessfully had a go to find the North-West Passage, the British Admiralty decided to offer a £20,000 reward for its discovery. The race heated up but for 200 years no one made much headway.

In 1818, however, Lieutenant William Parry embarked on a 3-year voyage that took him further toward that prize than anyone had been before but he was turned back by impenetrable ice in McClure Strait. Many more people tried before 1854 when Robert McClure was successful. He entered the Arctic from the Bering Sea, spent 2 years beset by ice at Banks Island, walked to Dealy Island near Parry's 'furthest west', and sailed home to England with another explorer, Sir Edward Belcher, who was attempting the route from the east.

Hans Egede

Christianity & the Trade Monopoly

After the Danish absorption of Norway in 1380 and the demise of the original Norse colonies, there were no European attempts at colonising Greenland for 300 years. In fact, European awareness of the island had dwindled to practically nil after the trade monopoly failed so miserably there. Economic interest in the place was only revived after the existence of a North-West Passage to the East Indies was speculated on in the late 16th century.

Anyone who's listened to the lyrics of the beautiful song *Farewell to Tarwathie* will realise that whaling has historically been an important economic venture in Greenlandic waters. During the late 16th century, with the first rumblings of interest in a North-West Passage, whaling nations discovered the rich waters of Davis Strait between Greenland and Baffin Island. For 2 centuries, up to 10,000 men arrived on Danish, Norwegian, British, Dutch, German, and Basque whaling vessels each year to hunt in the Arctic waters. Many of them came ashore. This led to interbreeding with the Greenlandic people.

In 1605, the Danish king Christian IV sent an expedition to Greenland and officially claimed it for Denmark. The first renewed attempt at permanent European colonisation of the island, however, came in 1721 when the Danish granted Hans Egede permission to set up a trading post and Lutheran mission. Egede's original plan was to find the Norse colonies, which he was sure had reverted to paganism during the intervening years, but having no luck, he decided that Inuit souls were valuable as well.

His first mission on Håbets Ø, an island near Godthåb, established what Denmark perceived as colonial 'grandfather' rights to

Greenland. The mission was relocated to the present site of Nuuk (formerly Godthåb, meaning 'good hope') in 1728. Five years later, a rival mission (this one Moravian and led by Samuel Kleinschmidt) was also set up in Godthåb. Both were quite successful at converting the native Greenlanders to Christianity and correcting their 'mistaken notions' that hell was a cold place and that seals, rocks, shrubs, and icebergs all had immortal souls of their own.

By 1776, Denmark decided to play its hand with Greenland and impose a trade monopoly, administered by the Royal Greenland Trade Department, as it had earlier in both Iceland and the Faroes. While the other monopolies failed in the 19th century, Greenland was closed to non-Danish shipping and trade until 1950.

Samuel Kleinschmidt

Further Exploration

With the North-West Passage more or less conquered, Arctic exploration turned towards new goals: reaching the North Pole and exploring the icy interior of Greenland. More accurately, however, the primary goal of Arctic expeditions during the late 1800s was to reach a point further north ('furthest north') than the previous expedition, especially if it had been sponsored by another nation. Predictably, the Americans were the most concerned with this issue which spelt disaster on occasions.

In 1883, the USA sent Adolphus Greeley to Ellesmere Island (Canada) to set up a base at Fort Conger and carry out scientific research. Greeley, not content with such a mundane task, sent an expedition led by Lieutenant James Lockwood up the west coast of Greenland to beat the previous furthest north record held by the British. Although they broke it by 4 nautical miles, the Americans weren't satisfied with such an insignificant 'victory'. For some reason, the supply ships which were to have provisioned Lockwood failed to turn up for 2 years and 16 of his 25 men died of starvation on Ellesmere Island.

Perhaps the most renowned Arctic explorer was Robert Peary who 'discovered' the fictitious Peary Channel in north Greenland in 1900 and reached the North Pole in 1909. He was a confused and insecure man, an American who believed that self-worth came only with success and notoriety – that once achieved, success commanded respect. He went alone to the Pole, he said, because no other person he knew deserved to share in the acclaim. It was later suggested that he went alone because he never really went at all, but this issue has been fairly conclusively settled in his favour.

Peary was bothered more that Frederick Cook claimed to have reached the pole 12 months before Peary himself than by his mistake about Peary Channel. This geographical error which was corrected only at the cost of the Mylius-Erichsen expedition, a Danish-Greenlandic mapping and surveying crew, in 1907. A Greenlander from Ilulissat, Jørgen Brønlund, made his mark in history by leaving the famous note that revealed the fate of the party. It read:

> Perished 79 fjord after attempting to return across inland ice in November. I arrived here in waning moonlight and could go no further due to frost-bitten feet and darkness. The others' bodies will be found mid-fjord off glacier (about 2½ leagues). Hagen died

15 November, Mylius about 10 days later. Jørgen Brønlund.

Another sort of explorer entirely was Norwegian Fridtjof Nansen was known as the first European to cross Greenland's inland ice. Apparently not overly confident of his capabilities, Nansen decided to begin on the barren east coast and travel towards the populated west, thereby preventing himself turning back. The trip across Greenland was begun on 15 August 1888, and successfully completed on 26 September. Nansen was also known for his theory of ice drift in the Arctic which he proved by constructing a ship, the *Fram*, allowing it to freeze into the drift ice, and following its path through the Arctic Ocean. In 1922, by the way, he was awarded the Nobel Peace Prize for his work with prisoners of war and refugees after WW I.

The most beloved of all the explorers in Greenland was Knud Rasmussen. He was born in Ilulissat on the west coast in 1879 and combined his explorations of Greenland and the North American Arctic with ethnological studies of all the Inuit tribes in the region collecting their literature, songs, and mythology. He crossed the icecap by dog sled in 1912 and, in 1921, embarked on his crowning achievement – an expedition from Upernavik (Greenland) to Barrow (Alaska) – tracing in reverse the ancient Inuit migration routes and comparing the various cultures he encountered along the way. This expedition was described in the book *Across Arctic America* published in 1927. The Greenlandic people now refer to Knud Rasmussen as *Kununguaq* or 'our little Knud'. His home in Ilulissat is now a museum and the second largest KNI ferry plying the west coast of Greenland is named *Kununguak* in his honour.

Knud Rasmussen

Recent History

Although Denmark had officially claimed all Greenland in the 1600s, the issue of Danish sovereignty over the entire island was dredged up by Norway in 1924. Norway felt that by virtue of east Greenland's discovery by Icelanders prior to the Danish-Norwegian union, it still belonged to them, especially since the issue hadn't been broached at the time of confederation. The matter was taken before the international court in The Hague in the early 1930s and Denmark was given sovereignty over the entire island.

In 1940 Hitler occupied Denmark and, after the USA became involved in the war in 1941, the US military moved into Greenland and set up bases at Søndre Strømfjord (Kangerdlusuaq) and Narsarsuaq, also known as 'Blue West One' or 'Bluie West'. Ostensibly, the former served as a meteorological station but it seemed to figure more prominently as a headquarters for the destruction of German meteorological stations. The latter, however, was a horror that lasted through two American wars – WW II and Korea. Here, the US military sent its hopeless casualties – those so badly injured in battle they would have dampened the war enthusiasm of the American public had they gone home. No patient sent to Narsarsuaq ever left; families of these victims were sent a bottle of ashes and told their soldier had been killed in action.

After the Korean War, the US offered the base to Denmark free of charge, but Norway offered to pay nearly US$250,000 for salvage rights. The offer was accepted and the Norwegians took out four times their investment's worth in equipment.

In 1953, Greenland became a Danish county (an integral part of Denmark) and Greenlanders acquired full Danish citizenship. Over the next 20 years, they were ready for more autonomy and pressed for more responsibility in their domestic affairs. On 1 May 1979, the county council was replaced by the *Landsting*, the parliament and the *Landstyrre*, or Home Rule government, retaining two representatives in the Danish parliament as well. The Royal Greenland Trade Department (KGH) was replaced by Kalaallit Niuerfiaat (the ubiquitous KNI) to handle all trade matters and the government infrastructure.

GEOGRAPHY

When most people think of a typically Danish scene, they don't think of towering peaks, glaciers, and icebergs but then few realise that Greenland comprises 98% of the land area in the Kingdom of Denmark. With an area of 2,175,600 sq km and a 40,000-km coastline, Greenland is the world's largest island, over 2½ times the size of New Guinea and 52 times the size of mainland Denmark.

Although Greenland is vast, all but 341,700 sq km lie beneath a sheet of ice up to 3000 metres thick – a burden so great that the interior of the island has sunk beneath its weight into an immense concave basin which reaches a depth of 360 metres below sea level. The vast ice sheet, seen while flying over Greenland, measures 2500 km from north to south and up to 1000 from east to west. Around the edges, it spills over forming the thousands of valley glaciers that have sculpted the coast into today's deep fjords and dramatic landscapes. On the north-west coast, the face of one – the Humboldt – is 120 metres high and 80 km wide. If Greenland were to melt down, the sea level would rise an estimated 6 metres and many of the world's coastal cities would begin to look more like Venice.

Greenland is the northernmost country in the world. Its southernmost point, Cape Farewell, lies at 59° 45' north latitude while the northernmost point of the mainland, Cape Morris Jesup, is at 83° 20' north. Oodaaq Island, a 50-metre-wide scrap of rock off the north coast, is the world's most northerly land at around 83° 21' north.

All but the southern quarter of Greenland lies north of the Arctic Circle. In the far north, the sun is visible for nearly 3 months during the summer but nowhere on the island is there darkness between late May and mid-July. During mid-winter, southern Greenland experiences several hours of real daylight. On the Arctic Circle, the sun doesn't rise at all on 21 December. The far north experiences true polar night with several weeks of constant darkness and 2 months of little more than a hazy twilight before the sun returns and builds up to its summer marathon.

Greenland's nearest neighbour is Canada whose Ellesmere Island lies only 26 km away across Kennedy Channel from the north-west coast. At its nearest point, Iceland is about 300 km away across Davis Strait and Svalbard (Norway) lies about 500 km east of the north-east coast.

Geologically, Greenland and Iceland could scarcely be further apart. While Iceland's landscape is the world's most dynamic, Greenland's is the oldest yet discovered – you don't need to be a geologist to be amazed at its compressed, scraped, ground, and tortured surface. Some formations around Nuuk have been determined to be around 3.7 billion years old. When the airport was constructed at Nuuk, the tarmac was blasted and smoothed out of metamorphic rock that had been around for over 3 billion years.

CLIMATE

As would probably be expected, Greenland isn't as warm as most places. Fortunately, it enjoys the continental effect more than Iceland or the Faroes and therefore has a more stable but extreme climate. In the summer, daytime temperatures average between 10°C and 18°C in the south and perhaps between 5°C and 10°C in the north but, because of practically incessant winds, expect to need a jacket or pullover even on the warmest days.

During the winter in the far south, temperatures of -20°C can be expected but, further north and on the ice, the legendary bitter temperatures of the Arctic become reality. It's not unusual for the thermometer to hover at a chilling -50°C for weeks on end. The good news is that the coldest days are also the clearest and calmest. The seemingly unearthly beauty of such an Arctic winter day (or night!) can scarcely be described.

Sometimes, the south-western coast blocks warm air masses moving up from North America and captures storm systems which seem to hang on for days before raining themselves out. This is especially true around the Nuuk area which has a tendency toward the foulest weather in Greenland. Occasionally, south Greenland also experiences bouts of wet and windy weather. Even on clear summer days, fog is common around all the coasts, especially in the far south, but it normally lifts before noon.

Despite this rather general assessment of the Greenlandic climate, it is important to remember that this is an Arctic region and the weather could produce anything at any time, including snow in July or temperatures of 30°C.

FLORA & FAUNA

The wildlife of Greenland is diverse but necessarily sparse due to the harsh conditions. Visitors will probably not have the opportunity to see any of the larger land animals unless they are lucky. Some of the most prominent mammal species include the polar bear, Arctic fox, Arctic hare, musk ox, lemming, and the Peary caribou.

The foxes come in two colours: those living on the inland ice are white, while those around the coast have blue-grey coats.

The musk ox population reaches its greatest density in north-east Greenland. This animal looks very much like an American bison and, with some imagination, can be compared to an African Cape buffalo but its closest relatives are the Rocky Mountain goat and the European chamois.

The Peary caribou, smallest of the three caribou species found in the Arctic, are sometimes referred to in Greenland as 'reindeer'. Although they have been known to breed with domestic European reindeer in Canada, they are actually a separate species.

Although polar bears wander throughout Greenland and habitually turn up in the southern village of Nanortalik ('the place of bears'), they are without exception welcomed to the human realm with both barrels. The only polar bears I've ever seen in Greenland were a couple of future rugs lying on the floor of the Qaqortoq tannery.

Bears live in fairly large numbers in the North Greenland National Park in the north-east but access is difficult and, at last report, the park was off limits to casual visitors. Those who'd like to observe polar bears in the wild would do better visiting Churchill, Manitoba (Canada), where the world's densest and most accessible population exists.

Numerous marine mammals inhabit Greenlandic waters, among them beautiful and unusual whales: the beluga or white whale and the narwhal, known for the spiral tusk that protrudes from its upper jaw. The tusk is normally unique to the male but has also been noted in females on rare occasions. Some other whales common in Greenland are the pilot whale, the fin whale, orcas (killer whales), and the blue whale.

Common pinnipeds include walrus, sea lions, hooded seals, bearded seals, spotted seals, and harp seals. The harp seal, whose Latin name *Pagophilus groenlandicus* means 'ice-lover from Greenland' is one of the mainstays of Inuit life and is of increasing value to the Greenlandic fur industry. In many cases, harp seal skins are sold to the tannery by local people who hunt the seals for food.

Fish are abundant in both fresh and salt water. In the lakes and streams there are salmon, trout, and Arctic char and in the surrounding seas there are well over 100 species of fish and shellfish making Greenlandic waters some of the richest in the world.

More than 150 species of birds breed on or near the shores, among them cormorants, puffins, guillemots, eider ducks, sea eagles, dovekies, buntings, great skuas, kittiwakes, snowy owls and swans.

Among insects, the mosquitoes, midges, no-see-ums, and other annoyances seem the most prominent. Bring some DEET-based repellent along on summer camping trips if you want to retain your sanity. As well as these pests there's also the odd butterfly.

Arctic vegetation is fairly limited but interesting nonetheless. In sheltered areas around Qaqortoq and Narsarsuaq, there are several stands of dwarf birch, alder, juniper, and willow. During late summer, the lowland areas of the south are carpeted with the beautiful national flower, the broad-leafed willow herb which, in other parts of the Arctic, is known as dwarf fireweed. Other flowering plants that splash colour across the landscape include chamomile, dandelion, buttercup, gentian, *saxifrage*, and numerous others.

Both boggy tundra and dry tundra vegetation are found in abundance as well. Huckleberries, crowberries, lowbush cranberries, other miniature flowering plants, mosses, sedges, lichens, and grasses figure prominently.

GOVERNMENT

Before 1953, Greenland was considered a colony of Denmark, but due to a constitutional change in that year, it was given the status of county with the same relationship to Denmark that Alaska has to the USA. Greenlanders were given full Danish citizenship and all the rights and privileges of Danes on the mainland.

The Faroe Islands received home rule in 1948 and, in the 1970s, Greenland began rumbling about the possibilities of a similar setup at home. It was approved through an act of parliament which allocated powers and administrative responsibilities (in matters regarding Greenland) previously held by the Danish Folketing to the Greenlandic Landsting. The current status of Greenland, therefore, is officially 'Self-Governing Member of the Kingdom of

Denmark'. Queen Margrethe II of Denmark remains Greenland's official head of state.

The Greenlandic flag was designed by local artist Thue Christiansen, who intended it to represent the sun, the sea, the inland ice, and the icebergs. It is the first Scandinavian flag to stray from the Nordic cross motif, consisting of a half-red and half-white circle on a rectangular half-white and half-red background. It is used interchangeably with the Danish flag and may be flown in Denmark, as well.

Currently the Landstyrre or Home Rule government has jurisdiction over such matters as culture, telecommunications, housing, taxation, education, foreign trade, transport, public works, and religion.These responsibilities are divided between seven branches, each of which has an elected member. One of these branches could be rather loosely defined as an executive body whose director, Jonathan Motzfeldt, serves as the head of the Home Rule government.

Legislative responsibility belongs to the parliament, the Landsting. It consists of 27 members elected to 4-year terms by residents of individual legislative districts. It meets three times annually.

Greenland Coat of Arms

Four political parties are represented in the current Landsting. The *Siumuk* or Social Democratic party favours Greenlandic autonomy while remaining within the Kingdom of Denmark. It has 11 seats in the Landsting. The *Atassuk* or Solidarity party, which also has 11 seats, promotes a strengthening of ties with Denmark. The third party, the *Inuit Ataqatigiik* or Human Brotherhood Socialist party has two members in the Landsting, and would like to see complete independence from Denmark. With only one seat in the Landsting, the *Issittuk* or Polar party promotes minimalisation of both Danish and Home Rule government economic controls and increased privatisation of business.

In addition to the Landsting, Greenland elects two members to the Danish Folketing. It also sends a delegation to the Nordic Council in which both it and the Faroe Islands are regarded as separate from Denmark. Iceland, Greenland, and the Faroes have set up a special alliance, the West Nordic Conference, which deals with issues particularly pertinent to these three Scandinavian outliers, especially tourism. Greenland, along with Inuit Canada, Alaska, and the Soviet Union, belongs to the Inuit Circumpolar Conference, a body which deals with Inuit interests in the respective countries.

Denmark is responsible for for the court system, national defence, public health, and foreign relations. Greenland is not, however, subject to the Danish criminal code and has a unique penal system which avoids imprisonment or other negative punishment of criminal offenders. It instead subjects them to fines, counselling sessions and, in the most severe or repeated cases, reform centres. This system is based on the traditional Inuit method of child-rearing and has thus far proved relatively successful.

ECONOMY

Predictably, the vast majority of Greenland's income is derived from fishing and related industries. Approximately 200,000 tonnes of fish per year are taken from Greenlandic waters, about 25% by foreign fishing vessels. During the mid-1960s, a lowering of offshore water temperatures severely affected the cod fishery. Shrimp then provided the largest source of revenue from fisheries.

Currently, shrimp remains in the lead followed by cod, salmon, capelin, halibut, and haddock. The Home Rule government owns about a third of the trawlers operating in Greenland but most of the fishing is done from small private boats. In order to ensure the future economic viability of the fishery, each species is regulated by a quota.

Most of the Greenland's fishing takes place off the west coast inside the 200-mile zone awarded in 1977. Processing is increasingly done aboard ship or on shore prior to export.

In northern and eastern Greenland, about 80% of the economy is based on whaling, sealing, subsistence fishing, and hunting. Moving south, the proportion decreases and, in far south Greenland, subsistence activities account for only about 20% of the total income.

Other important economic activities include handicrafts, tourism, building trades, commercial sealing, and reindeer and sheep herding. In south Greenland, there are approximately 60 farms breeding sheep for both export and local consumption. There are currently two mining interests in the country: the Danish cryolite mine at Ivigtut in the south-west and the Swedish-owned lead, zinc, and silver mine at Marmorilik in the north-west. Exploration for oil and other mineral resources is ongoing.

Despite the rapid development and moves toward economic viability, Greenland's balance of trade falls far short of an actual balance. The considerable deficits are made up by subsidies from Denmark. Nearly all consumer goods are imported from Denmark and subsidised to keep prices more or less on a par with those on the mainland.

In 1985, Greenland withdrew from the European Economic Community after a referendum revealed most citizens opposed being subjected to regulations handed down from countries unfamiliar with Greenland's unique status and situation. It remains affiliated with the EEC in a way similar to which French overseas departments relate to France and Commonwealth nations relate to Britain.

POPULATION & PEOPLE

Although they're often referred to as Eskimos, the native Greenlanders prefer to be called Inuit which means in their own language, 'the people'. An alternative word is *Kalaallit* which refers specifically to the Greenlandic people.

Greenland's population currently stands at around 55,000. Of these, 80% are Inuit or mixed Danish and Inuit, and the remaining 20% are of European extraction, primarily Danish.

Most Greenlanders live on the west coast of the island although there are isolated communities on the east coast and in the far north. The capital and largest city, Nuuk, has around 14,000 people.

CULTURE

On the whole, visitors find the Greenlandic people friendly and welcoming. The Inuit enjoy life in general and appreciate interaction with other people. Often, however, they are not particularly open or talkative and this seems to cause breakdowns in communication between European and Inuit people all around the Arctic.

The Inuit, however, don't place a lot of emphasis on talk. Even at parties and on festive occasions, there is frequently a marked lack of conversation. Europeans often take this as shyness, rudeness, or standoffishness. In return the Inuit often consider Europeans too loud, forward, boisterous, or chatty. One possible explanation offered by Jean Malaurie in *The Last Kings of Thule* is that the Iniut are still afraid that they will paralyse the forces of nature with the spoken word.

Perlerorneq

Another factor which foreigners may notice, especially in the winter, is a high incidence of depression, a state which the Inuit themselves recognise and call *perlerorneq* ('the burden'). Violence or abnormal behaviour are often blamed on it but the people don't try to explain it away or make excuses. Rather, they accept it as a part of life.

It is interesting that in polar regions, among people of all cultures, winter depression is greater than in other areas. It was long believed that this stemmed from restlessness through being forced into long periods of inactivity. Recently, however, it's been determined that the condition is physiological, the result of a lack of vitamin D (obtained from natural sunlight) during the long,dark winters. In many places, this is treated with daily doses of artificial sunlight and the results have been very good.

Relation to the Land

Although the Inuit culture is rapidly adopting many European values, gadgets, and customs, its traditional outlook on the world and existence is generally very Eastern and specifically Taoist. There is an overall concern with harmony and balance with the environment and its inhabitants, which incidentally include rocks, fish, vegetation, animals, and even abstracts such as moods and misfortunes. The maintenance of this balance is particularly important for happiness and stability.

The Inuit people love the land and are comfortable with it on its own terms. They don't want to change or conquer it but rather to get along with it, fearing it, respecting it, and accepting its kindness. They are not sentimental about the death of animals or the relationship of animals with humans. They feel it's natural that animals give up their lives to sustain human life, much as humans have historically had to sacrifice theirs to the harsh elements and, at times, to the animals themselves. The interdependence is again part of the ideal balance. If the more traditional people sometimes convey reservations about their dealings with outsiders, much of it may stem from a fear of the power Europeans seem to wield over the land and the environment: power that can permanently upset the balance so important to the traditional Inuit.

Children

Greenlanders believe their children are born with complete personalities and are endowed as a birthright with the wisdom, survival instinct, magic, and intelligence of their ancestors. It is believed that a child who is out of touch with its ancestors cannot survive. Therefore, Greenlandic children are neither punished nor chastised because to do so would be construed by the ancients as a message of dissatisfaction with their gifts and may place the child in danger of losing his or her heritage.

Modern Changes

Having said all that, it's important to point out that Greenland is a developed country. Most Greenlanders are modern European citizens and few subscribe to or wish to return to the old ways. Many have been successful at adapting to European values but it's evident that others aren't entirely comfortable with the new way of life. The land and the seasons are predictable but 'success', as westerners define it, is anything but certain. The people sometimes have difficulty reconciling themselves to the changes like replacing veneration of the land with the veneration of money and the power it gives. This is one of the primary causes of the high incidence of alcoholism, suicide, and feelings of inadequacy that seem so prominent among the Arctic people today.

Most Greenlanders would agree they've been fortunate to have had the Danes in control of their country. Denmark's relatively enlightened attitude toward the traditional native culture has spared it the effects of outright plunder and exploitation, the military bases, and the mineral-related frenzies of destruction that Inuit in other countries have inherited. It has provided schools, hospitals, and housing instead. Once you've seen the immense and impersonal blocks of flats in Greenlandic towns, however, you may begin to wonder about the aesthetic values of anyone who'd create such things.

When murmurings of Home Rule surfaced back in the 1970s, the Danes were quick to leglislate for it. It's also to their credit that, whether right or wrong, they've held on for so long. To my knowledge, there's never been a European colony that's provided so little wealth and so much liability as Greenland has for Denmark, yet the Danes feel they have a responsibility to Greenland and, if they let it go, they'll do so slowly and only when it's ready to manage on its own. Many Greenlanders, however, are beginning to feel the time has come.

For those who are interested in learning more about the traditional Greenlandic culture, to my knowledge, the best treatise is *The Last Kings of Thule* by Jean Malaurie, published by the University of Chicago Press. Malaurie spent 2 years among the people of the Thule area in north-west Greenland during the early 1950s and used his experiences with them as the basis for his book. The rather tragic ending in which Malaurie returns to Thule and finds what effect the American base has had is a vivid description of today's ongoing trends in the Arctic.

Tupilaq

The popular *tupilaq*, now produced and sold as art and souvenirs, had its origins in east Greenland around the village of Ammassalik. They were made from bone, skin, and chunks of peat as a bad luck charm against an enemy. They were originally intended to bring misfortune and even death to that person, so one had to be particularly careful when casting harm with a tupilaq. If the victim's power were greater than the

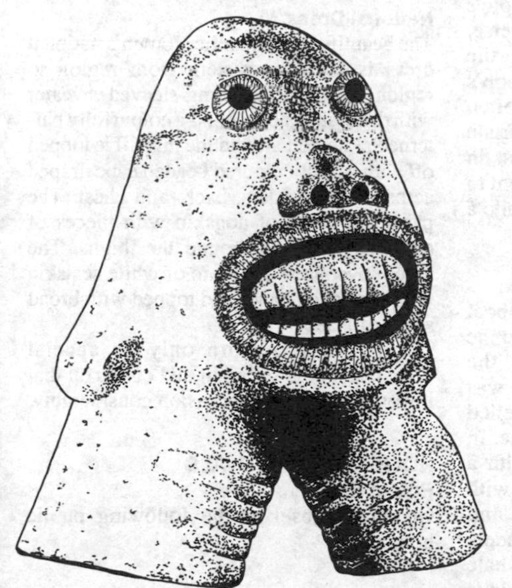

Tupilaqs

maker's, the spell would backfire and harm would return befall its maker instead.

Today, tupilaq are carved from caribou antler, soapstone, driftwood, narwhal tusk, walrus ivory, and bone. These carvings are small and meant to be held in the hand. They represent polar bears, marine mammals, and hideous imaginary beings. They are, incidentally, no longer intended to project misfortune, only to satisfy the artistic urge of and stimulate financial good fortune for the artists.

Oral Tradition

Historically, Greenlandic storytellers were held in high esteem and were believed to have a special insight into other realms. Stories were carefully passed down through generations and amazingly, weren't severely altered by embellishment or lapse of memory as so frequently occurs with oral traditions.

Collections of Inuit stories, myths, and songs reveal a great deal about the people's everyday life, the balance of the universe, their relationship with nature, and the animals they hunted. Much like Aesop's fables, Greenlandic stories were most often meant to convey a lesson or an appropriate code of behaviour in the communities. In 1919, the explorer Knud Rasmussen went to Ammassalik in east Greenland to compile a collection of these stories.

Qajaq & Umiaq

The qajaq ('kayak'), the long, narrow boat which is now used recreationally around the world was originally developed by the Greenland Inuit as a hunting boat. It was designed without a keel and was propelled and steered with a double-bladed paddle. In Greenland a qajaq was constructed with a driftwood or whalebone frame, covered with sealskin stretched tightly across it, and waterproofed with animal fat. Greenlanders used it for walrus, polar bear, and whale hunting for which it was ideally suited since it could be rolled over and then righted by the occupant without it taking on water.

Greenlandic qajaqs were longer and significantly narrower than their modern recreational counterparts. Some reached lengths of up to 7 metres yet there was little room inside – the occupants had scarcely enough room for their legs inside the hull.

A similar skin-covered boat which was used by women was called an umiaq. It was open and not specifically designed for hunting although it was sometimes used in taking whales. Its primary purpose was the transport of women, children, older people, and cargo.

Although the odd hunting qajaq is still used occasionally in the Thule area, both the qajaq and umiaq haven't really been in common use since the 1950s. They've been replaced in Greenland by the Mariner-90 powered motorboats. There is currently a qajaq club based in Nuuk which is promoting qajaq skills among younger people to preserve construction and handling skills, both significant to the Greenland's heritage.

National Dress

The beautiful Greenlandic women's national dress is fairly consistent from region to region. A bright red long-sleeved sweater with decorated sleeves and a colourfully patterned cloth belt around the midriff is topped off with a multicoloured beaded cape draped across the shoulders, back, and chest. The pants are made of dogskin with pieces of coloured fur sewn around the thighs. The lovely oversized boots are of white sealskin with appliqued bands and topped with broad strips of lace.

This dress is worn only on special occasions but is so bright and colourful that it would enliven any occasion considerably.

HOLIDAYS & FESTIVALS

Public Holidays

Greenland observes the following public holidays:

1 January
    New Year's Day
6 January
    Epiphany

March or April
Maundy Thursday
Good Friday
Easter Sunday
Easter Monday
1 May
Labour Day
11 May
Common Prayer's Day
May
Ascension Day
June
Whitsunday
Whitmonday
21 June
Ullortuneq (Longest Day)
1 November
All Saints' Day
24 December
Christmas Eve
25 December
Christmas Day
26 December
Boxing Day
31 December (afternoon only)
New Year's Eve

Festivals

In addition to the official public holidays, several local festivals are staged around the country at various times. Around Easter, villages north of the Arctic Circle hold dog-sled races which are accompanied by festivities.

Amazing as it may seem, in the summer, south Greenland towns hold a sort of 'sheep rodeo' which includes shearing, herding, and other sheep-related competitions. Aussies in particular will probably feel at home here.

In northern Greenland, a festival and (I suspect) a sigh of relief mark the end of the polar night when the sun returns after its sojourn below the horizon. In Ilulissat, this occurs in mid-January; in Upernavik it's in late January; and in Thule, early February.

Other Events

During late August or early September, the Grønlandmester national football tournament is held somewhere in the country. It includes a week-long series of play-offs to determine the best team and, although alcohol is officially forbidden to team members, spectators seem to do a lot of partying.

Another event which takes place in Greenland every couple of years is the Inuit Circumpolar Conference, a week-long cultural meeting where Inuit people from Greenland, Canada, Alaska, and the Soviet Union gather and discuss Arctic issues which affect them all. A number of cultural exhibitions and performances accompany the official proceedings and guests are welcome.

If you're visiting in late August, don't miss the first day of school. Parents and kindergarten-age children dress in national costume. The new scholars are formally introduced to academic life by their families

Greenlandic women's national dress

who parade them through the school grounds and throw fistfuls of coins into the crowd. Other children scramble to collect as much of these as they can.

Greenlanders, who don't seem to be overly concerned with the future and are happy to just have fun today, enjoy parties and get-togethers as much as anyone. These events are called *mik* and can happen at anytime someone takes the notion to provide the goodies and alcohol. They aren't normally earth-shaking affairs but they will offer a bit of insight into the local social life.

LANGUAGE

The official language of Greenland is Greenlandic, one of many Inuit dialects spoken all around the Arctic. Amazingly, it is essentially the same language spoken in northern Canada and Alaska. Within Greenland, regional variations occur and, although the different dialects are often a source of amusement for locals, all the Inuit in Greenland can essentially understand each other. The second language is Danish and is now spoken by nearly everyone. Although most Greenland residents reared in mainland Denmark have learned English at school, a very small number of the local people speak any foreign language.

Greenlandic is known as a polysynthetic language in which entire ideas are expressed in a single word by addition of prefixes and suffixes to a root subject, hence the impossible-looking mega-syllabic words which intimidate foreigners with their sheer length when written on a page. Some English speakers have pointed out that written Greenlandic, to them, resembles the result of a small child banging on a typewriter. For example, a newspaper headline announcing a harpoon throwing competition would read: *Unammineq naakkiarneqqortusaanneq toraajuneqqussaanneq*. Enough said.

Those who'd like to learn more than the following snippets of Greenlandic won't have much option but to go to Greenland and find a native speaker as a tutor. To my knowledge, the only book available for teaching yourself is *Grønlandsk for Begyndere* by Karl-Peter Anderson but you'll have to speak Danish first to get anything out of it.

Pronunciation & Spelling

I have the utmost respect for any foreigner who has learned to speak Greenlandic and so do the Inuit. Pronunciation is very difficult and can't really be demonstrated in a pronunciation guide. Consonants come from deep in the throat and the many vowels are scarcely pronounced. You'll just have to listen to get the hang of it.

Unfortunately, the spelling of Greenlandic words is hardly standardised and once you've heard the spoken language, you'll probably realise why. The spellings used in this section seem logical to me but those who speak Greenlandic well may disagree. Therefore, take this as a rough guide only and, after you've spent awhile in Greenland, things should become clearer.

Useful Words & Phrases

Here are a few words and phrases pertaining to things which may interest travellers. It may be useful to note that superlatives are constructed by adding *suaq* to the end of the root word and diminutives by adding *nnguaq*. Therefore, the word for 'ship' is *umiarsuaq*, the superlative of *umiaq*, the name of the traditional-sized boat. The word for 'house', on the other hand, is *iglu*. Therefore, a hut or small house would be called *iglunnguaq*.

hello	*kutaa*
thank you	*qujanaq*
(very much)	(*qujanasuaq*)
Cheers!	*Kasuta tamaaisa!*
yes	*aap*
no	*naaga*
maybe	*imaqaa*
expensive	*akisuvoq*
very good/beautiful	*nuuenn*
Where is...?	*Qanoq...?*
When?	*Qaqugu?*
Welcome!	*Tikilluarit!*
visitor	*takornartaq*
Mush, you huskies!	*Gamma, gamma!*

reservation	*inissanik innimi-nniineq*
ticket	*billettit*
ship	*umiarsuaq*
plane	*timmisaatit*
helicopter	*helikopterit*
motorboat	*pujortuleeraq*
dog sled	*qimussit*
weather	*silalu*
rain	*sialuk*
sun	*seqineq*
fog or cloud	*pujoq*
snow	*aput*
ice	*siko*
wind	*anoreq*
church	*oqaluffik*
school	*atuarffik*
today	*ullumi*
tomorrow	*aqagu*
winter	*uqioq*
summer	*aasaq*
water	*imeq*
man	*angut*
woman	*arnaq*
father	*ataata*
mother	*anaana*
child	*qitornaq*
house	*iglu*
party or gathering	*mik*
home-brew	*imiaq*
tent	*tupersuaq*
museum	*katersugaasivik*
post office	*allakkeriviat*
shop	*pisniarffik*
accommodation	*najugaqarfissat*
travel	*angalaneq*

Animals

Animals play a major role in Greenlandic life and frequently come up in conversation. The following are some of the ones more commonly referred to:

bear	*nanoq*
caribou	*tugtu*
cod	*saarugdlik*
dog	*qimmeq*
eagle	*nagtoralik*
guillemot	*tuugdlik*
hare	*uqaleq*
mosquito	*ippernaq*
salmon	*eqaluk*
seal	*puisi*
sheep	*sava*
whale	*arfeq*

Months

January	*Januari*
February	*Februari*
March	*Martsi*
April	*Aprili*
May	*Maji*
June	*Juni*
July	*Juli*
August	*Augusti*
September	*Septemberi*
October	*Oktoberi*
November	*Novemberi*
December	*Decemberi*

Days

Monday	*Ataasinngorneq*
Tuesday	*Marlunngorneq*
Wednesday	*Pingasunngorneq*
Thursday	*Sisamanngoneq*
Friday	*Tallimanngorneq*
Saturday	*Arfininngorneq*
Sunday	*Sapaat*

Geographical Features & Placenames

Geographic names in Greenland are by no means exclusive to one particular place. A casual glance at a large-scale map will reveal at least five or six places called *Qeqertarsuaq*, a couple called *Narsaq*, a few called *Nuusuaq*, and the odd *Kangerdlusuaq*, to list but a few. Names in Greenlandic were not given to features or areas simply to endow them with a name or to honour some famous person or event. Since maps weren't in use among the earlier hunting cultures, the names in effect *were* the map.

In order, the four previously mentioned names, which belong to commonly visited villages and towns as well as scores of other places in Greenland, mean 'big island', 'plain', 'big peninsula', and 'big fjord'.

Some other useful geographical terms include:

fjord	*kangerdluq*
hot spring	*puilassoq*
iceberg	*ilulissat*
inland ice	*sermersuaq*
island	*qeqertaq*
lake	*tasseq*
land	*nunaa*
mountain	*qaqaaq*
mountain glacier	*sermertaq*
peninsula	*nuuk*
river	*kuuk*
sea	*imiaq*
valley	*qooroq*
valley glacier	*sermeq*

Greenlandic Cities

Most Greenlandic cities are known by two names, one Danish and one Greenlandic. Throughout this book, I have used mainly the Greenlandic names. In order to alleviate some of the confusion that will inevitably arise, here is a table of the most significant ones.

Greenlandic	European
Aasiaat	Egedesminde
Alluitsup	Lichtenau
Alluitsup Paa	Sydprøven
Eqaluit	Frobisher Bay (Canada)
Igaliko	Gardar
Igaliko Kujalleq	Søndre Igaliko or Undir Høfdi
Illiminaq	Claushavn
Ilulissat	Jakobshavn
Ittoqqoortoormiit	Scoresbysund
Kangerdlusuaq	Søndre Strømfjord
Kangerluarsoruseq	Faeringahavn
Kangilinnguit	Grønnedal
Kulusuk	Kap Dan
Maniitsoq	Sukkertoppen
Narsaq Kujalleq	Frederiksdal
Nerlerit Inaat	Constable Pynt
Nuuk	Godthåb
Oqaatsut	Rødebay
Paamiut	Frederikshåb
Pituffik	Thule Airbase
Qaanaaq	Thule
Qagssiarsuk	Brattahlid
Qaqortoq	Julianehåb
Qasigiannguit	Christianshåb
Qeqertarsuaq	Godhavn
Qeqertarsuatsiaat	Fiskenaesset
Sisimiut	Holsteinsborg

Numbers

Numbers in Greenlandic only go up to 12. After that you have to use Danish numbers because after 12 there is only *passuq*, 'many'.

1	*atuaseq*
2	*mardluq*
3	*pingasuq*
4	*sisamaq*
5	*tatdlimaq*
6	*arfinigdliq*
7	*arfineq mardluq*
8	*arfineq pingasuq*
9	*qulingiluaq*
10	*quliq*
11	*arqanigdliq*
12	*arqaneq mardluq*

Danish Numbers

1	*een*
2	*to*
3	*tre*
4	*fire*
5	*fem*
6	*seks*
7	*syv*
8	*otte*
9	*ni*
10	*ti*
11	*elleve*
12	*tolv*
13	*tretten*
14	*fjorten*
15	*femten*
16	*seksten*
17	*sytten*
18	*atten*
19	*nitten*
20	*tyve*
21	*een og tyve*
22	*to og tyve*
30	*tredive*
31	*een og tredive*

40	*fyrre*	90	*halvfems*
50	*halvtreds*	100	*eet hundrede*
60	*tres*	101	*eet hundrede een*
70	*halvfjerds*	120	*eet hundrede tyve*
80	*firs*	1000	*eet tusind*

Facts for the Visitor

VISAS

Citizens of only a few countries are required to have a visa for Greenland. Among them are those from some of lesser known African countries, Poland, Hungary, Turkey, Jordan, Vanuatu, Tonga, Western Samoa, Papua New Guinea, Taiwan, the People's Republic of China, the USSR, Myanmar, India, Iraq, Pakistan, Bangladesh, Iran, Sri Lanka, Indonesia, the Philippines, Belize, Egypt, South Africa. If you have any doubts, contact the nearest Danish consulate or embassy.

Visitors from other Nordic countries – Norway, Finland, Sweden, the Åland and Faroe islands, and, of course, Denmark – only need valid identification cards. Citizens of other countries not requiring visas only need a valid passport for stays of up to 3 months.

Technically, you must be able to prove you have sufficient funds for your intended length of stay but customs and immigration formalities are normally very rudimentary, especially since the vast majority of visitors to Greenland enter from Denmark or Iceland.

US Bases

Those visiting the vicinity of the US bases in Thule (that's Pituffik, not Qaanaaq) or Kangerdlusuaq (Søndre Strømfjord) are required to obtain a permit to enter the base areas. This is necessary also for those walking into Kangerdlusuaq from Sisimiut. Danish citizens must apply to the Ministry for Greenland, Dansk Polarcenter, Hausargade 3, DK-1128 Copenhagen. Others should contact the US Air Attaché, 24 Dag Hammarskjölds Alle, DK-2100, Copenhagen, Denmark. A permit is not required by those in transit at the airports at Kangerdlusuaq or Pituffik.

Embassies & Consulates

Greenland is represented abroad by Danish embassies and consulates which can be found in the capital cities of most countries and often in other major cities as well.

Working in Greenland

Skilled Danes will have little difficulty finding work in Greenland. Often they are needed to train Greenlanders for specific jobs or to fill positions for which no qualified Greenlanders can be found but, in theory, locals always take precedence over foreigners, including Danish people.

Most Danes working in Greenland go for an initial 2-year stint (on a contract) after which they may renew their work contract or let it lapse and return to Denmark. These jobs include all sorts of cushy fringe benefits, including luxury wages, free living quarters, and regular tickets home. They are open only to persons born in Denmark (including those of Greenlandic heritage) and Greenlanders are understandably resentful. Although some Danes get caught up in Greenland's spell and opt to remain, most seem to be chaffing at the bit to get out.

Since Greenland is no longer part of the EEC, citizens of member countries aren't permitted to work there. None of the foreign job seekers I spoke with, regardless of nationality, had any luck finding work. There's no shortage of unskilled labour, so the fishing and fish-processing jobs available elsewhere in the North Atlantic aren't available in Greenland.

If you have a particularly marketable skill and are really keen to work in Greenland, about all I can suggest is that you contact a Danish consulate and see what sort of advice they have to offer. I suspect those who speak Danish and/or an Inuit dialect will have a much better chance of success.

Scientific Research

Those who are interested in carrying out scientific research or staging expeditions in Greenland should contact the Commission for Scientific Research (tel 01-13-68-25 in Copenhagen) at the Ministry for Greenland.

CUSTOMS

Travellers over 18 years of age are permitted to import duty-free 1 litre of spirits and 1 litre of wine, which must be carried personally. Anyone over 15 years of age can bring in 250 g of tobacco and 200 cigarette papers or 200 pre-rolled cigarettes. Although hunting rifles can be brought in with airline permission, pistols and fully or semi-automatic weapons are not allowed. Live animals of any kind are also prohibited. These regulations apply to Danish citizens as well as to foreigners.

MONEY

Both the Danish króna (Dkr) and Faroese króna (Fkr) are used interchangeably throughout the Kingdom of Denmark – that is on the mainland and in the Faroes and Greenland. One króna is equal to 100 øre. All other prices in the text, however, will be given in US$.

Notes come in denominations of 20, 50, 100, 500, and 1000 króna. Coins in use include 5, 10, and 25 øre and 1, 5, and 10 króna.

Foreign Exchange

Greenland has two banks, Nuna Bank and Grønlandsbanken, both of which have branches around the country. In villages without banks, KNI performs bank functions and takes care of foreign exchange. All brands of travellers' cheques, all Scandinavian currencies, and all major currencies can be exchanged for Dkr in any bank or KNI office. Eurocheques are also negotiable as are cheques drawn on Danish or Faroese banks.

Major credit cards are accepted at tourist restaurants and hotels in larger towns only (including Narsarsuaq).

The approximate exchange rates at the time of writing were:

A$1 = 4.7Dkr
C$1 = 5.0Dkr
DM1 = 3.7Dkr
Ikr1 = 0.10Dkr
US$1 = 5.8Dkr

COSTS

Thanks to massive subsidies from Denmark, costs of food and consumer goods in Greenland are unexpectedly lower than in Iceland and more or less on a par with Copenhagen. The cost of formal accommodation and restaurant meals is quite high, however, and transport is extremely expensive.

There are no highways in Greenland and towns and villages are linked only by ferry service, charter boat, or by air. There are international airports for fixed-wing aircraft in Narsarsuaq, Nerlerit Inaat, Kangerdlusuaq, Pituffik (Thule Airbase), Nuuk, and Kulusuk near Ammassalik and a domestic airport at Ilulissat. All other towns accessible by air have only a heliport.

The cost of flying anywhere in Greenland can be prohibitive. Just for shock value, to fly between Nuuk and Narsarsuaq, less than an hour's flight in a 727, will cost US$370 one way. The 10-minute flight by helicopter from Narsarsuaq to Qaqortoq by helicopter costs US$69. If you want to reach Nanortalik from Upernavik, however, plan on shelling out US$1346.

Greenland on a Shoestring

It is possible to see Greenland on a limited budget, avoiding transport and accommodation costs and limiting food costs by self-catering using food purchased from the harbour markets and supermarkets or found in the bush or the sea.

For more information on eating as cheaply as possible, see the Food and Hunting & Fishing sections in the General Information section later this chapter.

The best way to keep accommodation costs down is to bring a tent. You can camp anywhere in Greenland outside villages and, although there are no facilities available, water is normally plentiful and camping sites free. Those who prefer solid shelter can resort to youth hostels, Nuna-Tek hostels, and sheep huts. For more information, refer to the Accommodation section in the Regional Facts for the Visitor chapter at the beginning of the book.

The only way to avoid transport costs is to

walk, bring your own sea kayak, or fly into a particular region and fully explore it. Such regions correspond fairly well to the chapter divisions in this book, although north-west Greenland and any of east Greenland apart from Ammassalik will be off limits to budget travellers.

TOURIST INFORMATION

Local Tourist Offices

Tourist information offices in Greenland are mostly helpful, but not all tourism officers speak English well so communication requires a bit of effort. Most offices provide some sort of brochure or map but there's no guarantee it will always be in a language you understand. Some towns seem to stock only French brochures, others Italian, and others just Danish or Greenlandic. Nearly all, however, will manage to find something in English or German, even if it's just a soil study conducted in 1957.

There are fully fledged tourist offices in Sisimiut, Nuuk, Qaqortoq, Narsaq, Nanortalik, Maniitsoq, Ilulissat, Aasiaat, and Ammassalik. In Uummannaq, Upernavik, Kangaatsiaq, and Qasigiannguit, the town offices have desks that handle tourist enquiries. The airports in Kangerdlusuaq and Narsarsuaq open an impromptu tourist enquiry desk when international flights arrive. For addresses of individual offices, see the Information sections for the relevant town.

Hotels, seamen's homes, and youth hostels all offer tourist information as well.

Overseas Reps

Denmark maintains Danish Tourism boards in several countries. These dispense tourist information and provide commercial investment guidelines. If you have any queries prior to your trip regarding tourism or other Greenlandic topics, contact one of the following offices:

Austria
Dänisches Fremdenverkehrsamt, Ferstelgasse 3/4, A-1090 Vienna

United Kingdom
Danish Tourism Board, Sceptre House, 169-173 Regent St, GB-London W1R 8PY

Belgium
L'Office National du Tourisme de Danemark, Avenue Louise 221, B-1050 Brussels

Denmark
Danish Tourism Board, H C Andersens Boulevard 22, DK-1553, Copenhagen
Green Tours, formerly DVL Rejser (private backpackers' agency), Kultorvet 7, DK-1175 Copenhagen
Grønlands Rejsebureau, Gammel Mønt 12, PO Box 130, DK-1004 Copenhagen

Canada
Danish Tourism Board, PO Box 115, Station N, Toronto, Ontario M8V 3S4

Finland
Tanskan Matkailutoimisto, P L 836, SF-00101 Helsinki

France
Office National de Tourisme de Danemark, 142 Champs Elysées, F-75008 Paris

Germany
Dänisches Fremdenverkehrsamt, Glockengiesserwall 2, 2000 Hamburg 1

Italy
Ente Danese per il Turismo, Via Santa Orsola 3, I-20123 Milano

Japan
Scandinavian Tourist Board, Sanno Grand Building #401, 14-2 Nagatacho 2-chome, Chiyoda-ku, Tokyo

Netherlands
Deens Verkersbureau, Piet Heinstraat 3, NL-2518 CB The Haag

Norway
Danmarks Turistkontor i Norge, Karl Johansgate 1, 6 sal, N-0154 Oslo 1

Sweden
Danska Turistbyrån, Gustav Adolfs Torg 14, Box 1659, S-0111 86 Stockholm

Switzerland
Dänisches Fremdenverkehrsamt, Münsterhof 14, CH-8001 Zürich

USA
Danish Tourism Board, 655 Third Avenue, 18th floor, New York, NY 10017

When to Visit

The tourist season in Greenland begins more or less in early July and goes until the first week in September. In May the previous winter's snow hasn't yet melted and new snow remains a possibility until early June. Springtime really doesn't begin to take off until mid to late July and the best time to see wildflowers in bloom is in early to mid-August. Berries normally ripen in late August and last until early September when the tundra has a short period of bright autumn colour. During late August, expect freezing temperatures at night and increasingly cooler days. By mid-September, you can plan on experiencing new snow and extremely cold weather.

December, January, and February are absolutely beautiful in the Arctic with long black nights and normally clear but bitterly cold days with a brief time of pale red light. 'Winter' visitors for dog-sledding and skiing expeditions, however, come between late March and early May in order to avoid the extreme hours of darkness and uncomfortably low temperatures of deep winter.

The best times for viewing the northern lights in the southern half of Greenland are from mid-September to early November and from mid-February to early April. The northern lights are not normally visible in northern Greenland.

GENERAL INFORMATION

Post

Every Greenlandic town has a post office, *Kalaallit Allakkerivia*t, which offers the usual gamut of postal services as well as fax and telephone facilities. They are normally open Monday to Friday from 9 am to 12 noon and 1 to 3 pm.

The post offices also offer a range of free postcards with photographs or drawings of Greenlandic scenes and indigenous birds and wildlife.

Postal rates for postcards are Dkr3.20 within Denmark and Dkr3.40 to foreign countries. Airmail letters weighing 20 g or less to points within Denmark cost Dkr3.20 and Dkr4.40 to other countries. Fax services cost Dkr65 per page within Denmark and Dkr130 per page to other countries.

To receive mail, have correspondence addressed to you care of Poste Restante in the main village of the area you'll be visiting. For south Greenland, it's probably best to use DK-3920 Qaqortoq and, for the south-west, use DK-3900 Nuuk. For west central use DK-3952 Ilulissat and, for the east, DK-3913 Ammassalik. To speed things up, it sometimes helps to write 'Greenland via Denmark' in addition to the postal code.

Telephone

Telephone offices in Greenland are associated with the post offices and a call may be made or a fax sent to anywhere in the world. Reverse-charge calls are not accepted, however. The larger coastal ferries (*Disko* and *Kununguak*) offer radio telephone services.

Greenland's country code is (299). If you want to call out of Greenland, you must first dial (009) for international access, then the desired number.

MEDIA

Both television and radio are operated by Radio Greenland. Television, however, is only available in larger towns. Programmes are in Danish or have Danish subtitles and are essentially the same as those broadcast on the mainland. You don't normally get Greenlandic subtitles – there isn't enough room on the screen for the words!

Radio programmes are exclusively in Greenlandic and can be received nearly everywhere around the country with the aid of relays.

The press is limited to two weekly papers in Danish and Greenlandic and several small local periodicals. The larger tourist hotels will keep abreast of world news and in some cases may be able to provide foreign language newpapers, however late they may arrive.

FOOD

Self-Catering

The least expensive way to eat in Greenland is to buy supermarket food and prepare it yourself on a camping stove or in hostels. There's an amazing variety of things available although orders sometimes get mixed up and a supermarket will have three shelves of various and sundry pasta products but not a single item that can be used to make a sauce for it. Sometimes you'll find pineapples and rather sickly looking mangoes but not an onion in sight. Prices are similar to those in Copenhagen and will be a relief if you're coming from Iceland.

There are two major supermarket chains in Greenland, the government KNI and the cooperative Brug Brugsen. Both are represented at least once in all major towns but, in villages, you'll rarely find anything but a small general kiosk.

Shops are normally open weekdays from 9 or 10 am to 5 pm but close for a lunch hour. They're open for 2 or 3 hours on Saturday mornings. In most large towns, you'll be able to find smaller kiosks open until 8 or 9 pm on weekdays but prices will be higher and the selection of goods quite limited.

Every town and even a few villages will have a bakery which supplies fresh bread, cakes, doughnuts, and biscuits daily except Sunday. Most of them are excellent though it's worth making sure that what you're buying is fresh. In some towns, the bakery is associated with the Brugsen or KNI supermarket.

Restaurants

Outside of the tourist hotels, there are few actual restaurants. The hotel fare is predictably very expensive but normally of high quality. Lots of fish, mutton, and beef dishes will be available, in that order, and will normally be accompanied by the ubiquitous boiled potatoes and frozen vegies served through the North Atlantic region. Salads are normally available in restaurants but they aren't always included with meals so you may have to pay extra for a green fix.

Seamen's homes all serve acceptable cafeteria meals but, apart from that, you'll have to resort to the *grill-baren* that can be found in nearly every town. They mostly serve such quick snacks as sausages, chips, and burgers for people on the run and are commonly used as hangouts by the under-18 crowd.

Traditional Foods

Although many visitors are put off partaking in traditional Greenlandic fare for sentimental or ideological reasons, it's important to understand that whales and seals have dominated the Inuit subsistence hunting culture for several thousand years and that the entire animals are utilised including the blubber, oil, skin, and bones. They are also hunted on a very small scale and only one at a time although, the presence of the tannery in Qaqortoq may well bring about distressing changes.

Frozen seal meat is available in the supermarkets but it is also sold fresh at the braettet or harbour markets. Whenever a whale is brought in, it is accompanied by a lot of clamouring to buy the blubber and the choice cuts. Fresh whale steaks will cost around US$3 per kilo, it's rich and filling fare. Seal is a bit tough and more fishy but very good. It can be cooked by cutting it into chunks and boiling it for an hour or so.

Whale blubber, although relatively tasteless and at best difficult to chew, is rich in vitamins and fats which the body uses efficiently to retain heat. It's best sliced as thinly as possible – most people can get several hours of jaw work out of just a tiny bit.

I feel hypocritical condemning so strongly the whale slaughter in Iceland and the Faroes and yet condoning whaling among the Inuit.

This is based largely on emotional responses to the nature and attitude of the people doing the killing. The Inuit love the whales and are thankful the whales give up their lives to sustain human life. They wouldn't consider harming the species as a whole and actually revere them. If a man is accidentally killed or injured while hunting whales, they consider it more or less a fair balance.

Wild Foods

During certain summer months, you'll be able to supplement your diet with some of the natural wild foods which abound in Greenland. During August and early September, you'll find the bush carpeted with huckleberries (small blueberries). The tundra also offers a bounty of small black bearberries (also known as crowberries) which are sometimes a little bitter but improve immensely with the addition of sugar. Occasionally, you'll also find lowbush cranberries (bright red) growing alongside them. Angelica is found all over south Greenland and wild thyme is abundant too and makes an excellent tea as well as seasoning for the freeze-dried fare many people bring from Europe. In late summer, bluebells grow everywhere and the sweet, slightly fragrant flower is delicious.

Many types of edible mushrooms grow in Greenland but the most delicious is the large, chocolate-coloured one with the spongy centre which reaches its peak in early August and is found all over ice-free south Greenland. Don't worry about the vague description – Greenlanders swear that not a single poisonous mushroom grows in their country. If you are still wisely dubious ask a local to point out the best ones.

Of course, fishing will also provide nourishment. You don't even need a rod – just a lure, hook, and line will do. In the fjords, the cod snap at anything that moves. In the lakes, use a small hook to catch pan-size trout and Arctic char. For licence information, see Hunting & Fishing in the Activities section of this chapter.

At low tide, you can collect mussels in most sheltered areas. They are excellent fried with butter and garlic or just eaten steamed. Many varieties of Arctic seaweed are delicious, as well, especially the very slimy species known as 'sea lettuce'.

DRINKS

Alcohol

Although alcoholism isn't more prevalent in Greenland than in Iceland or the Faroes, its effects are more obvious. Alcohol is used more as an escape mechanism here and results more frequently in violence than in the other North Atlantic countries. I'm not trying to gloss over a very serious social problem but, before outsiders point fingers at the Greenlanders and condemn their enjoyment of alcohol, consider who introduced the alcohol in the first place and who inspired the feelings of guilt and hopelessness that invite its abuse. To cite this problem as need for strict alcohol controls is to miss the point entirely.

Regardless, visitors will probably be delighted to watch their airline crews hopping off the plane after touchdown, trotting down to the local shop, and buying relatively inexpensive and lightly regulated cases of Danish beer to take back to Iceland. Most will no doubt enjoy the option to do the same. Beer, wine, and spirits may be purchased in kiosks and supermarkets on weekday afternoons and in pubs and bars in the evening. No outside alcohol may be consumed on ferries although it is available at a premium from ships' cafeterias.

Those with a bit more gumption than most may have the urge to sample the local home-brew called *imiaq*.

BOOKS & BOOKSHOPS

All major settlements in Greenland have free public libraries and publishing in the Greenlandic language is subsidised by Denmark.

Several towns have shops where it's possible to purchase Greenlandic or Danish-language school texts and even novels but there are few places to find foreign-language books. A couple of the hotels carry a rack of pulpy English and German-language novels and the tourist office in Qaqortoq sells a few souvenir books, but the only place that has a wide selection is Atuagkat on Aqqusinersuaq, the road into the centre from the harbour in Nuuk. There you'll find a good selection of German and English-language books on Greenland and Arctic themes, history books, novels, and souvenir books.

An informative magazine dealing with Greenland-related topics in Danish, English and Greenlandic is *SULUK*. Annual subscriptions cost US$28 from Eskimo Press, PO Box 939 Nuuk, Greenland.

Modern Non-Fiction

Greenland and the Arctic have inspired some of the best travellers' and explorers' literature ever written. I've read scarcely a single work on the subject that I haven't thoroughly enjoyed. In addition to the following recommendations, the journals of the explorers like Robert Peary, Fridtjof Nansen, Knud Rasmussen provide much insight into the region and its traditions. Biographies of these men are also available in several languages.

Some books that I'd recommend are:

The Last Kings of Thule by Jean Malaurie (University of Chicago Press, 1985). This classic about the lives of Greenland's polar Inuit people prior to the arrival of the Danes is more a wonderfully human account of 2 years in the Arctic rather than an anthropological study. It's both fascinating and inspiring and should be considered required reading for every visitor to Greenland.

Arctic Dreams by Barry Lopez (Charles Scribner's Sons, 1986) and (Bantam, 1987). Apart from gaining insight into the 'spell of the Arctic', you'll be amazed at the author's facility with words and his ability to convey deep feelings for the place. Much of this book deals with Greenland although he also wanders through Canada and Alaska even touching on Siberia and northern Scandinavia. It's also highly recommended.

Last Places – A Journey in the North by Lawrence Millman (Houghton Mifflin Co, 1990). Although this book is a very entertaining work from an unusually gifted writer, a lot of the narrative is a bit too good to be true. Still, there was nothing implausible about the experiences he reports from Greenland (or anywhere else he visited in the book). I found it especially amusing to read his accounts of being sexually harrassed by Greenlandic women. Finally a man learns what women travellers deal with all over the world. Don't miss this excellent book.

Ice! by Tristan Jones (Avon Books, 1978). This is another of the intrepid sailor books by Tristan Jones and, although it's much like his others, his forays into Arctic waters make entertaining reading. Part of his journey includes a sail into Scoresbysund and up the east coast of Greenland before heading for Svalbard.

The Viking Circle by Colin Simpson (Angus & Robertson,1966). This is an easily digested account of high-speed up-market travels around Scandinavia from an Australian's perspective. The chapter on Greenland provides a good insight into that country in the early 1960s and will offer a ruler by which to measure the recent changes taking place there.

The Arctic Grail by Pierre Berton (Viking Penguin, 1988). This large, well-written volume is the last word on the Arctic explorers and the race for the north-west Passage.

Land Under the Pole Star by Helge Ingstad. This is an exhaustive compilation of information and research on the Norse movements and colonies in the North Atlantic. It deals in depth with the connection between Greenland and North America.

Travel Guides

Exclusively English speakers are probably out of luck here. The only other reliable travel-guide treatise to date is the few pages in *Frommer's Scandinavia*. Unfortunately, although it claims to be 'Greenland on $60 a day', few hotels recommended cost less than $100 per night! Unlike most such coverage, their researcher actually visited Greenland to collect his data. Especially if you're combining your Greenland trip with a visit to mainland Scandinavia, you may want to pick up a copy.

For those who speak Danish or German, there are guides available dealing exclusively with Greenland. The German *Mai's Weltführer Grönland* is better than the Danish *Grønland – en Skarv Guide*. I found it accurate and very reliable. It also provides a lot of interesting background information.

Prospective trekkers and hikers in Greenland will find the Skarv Guide *Trekking in Greenland* (1990) by Torbjoern Ydegaard a wealth of information on all the major treks and many of the more obscure routes. It's available from Green Tours in Copenhagen or through major travel bookshops in Britain and the USA. See also the Trekking section of this chapter.

Trekkers who may be able to decipher a bit of Danish may also get some use from the walking guides *Vandreruter i Sudgrønland* and *Vandreruter i Vestgrønland* by Kirsten Kempel (Udvalget, for Vandreturisme, 1978). They outline walking routes around the Narsarsuaq-Narsaq-Qaqortoq and Sisimiut-Kangerdlusuaq areas respectively, but they seem to overestimate the capabilities of even the hardiest trekkers. Some of the routes described, especially in south Greenland, require fairly technical trekking skills.

Other

The Arctic World by Fred Bruemmer (Century Publishing,1985). Despite the fact that this is mostly intended as a coffee-table photo book, it contains one of the best and most concise descriptions of the transition of the Inuit people from hunting culture to European culture to be found anywhere. The photographs, which were taken in Greenland, Canada, Alaska, Siberia, and Scandinavia, convey well the character of the Arctic landscape and people.

The Greenlanders by Jane Smiley (Collins, 1988). This is a fictionalised account of the lost Norse settlements in Greenland told in a haunting saga form. You could imagine you're reading a translated bit of ancient literature. Although it's very entertaining, it doesn't purport to be anything but a novel of 'how it could have happened'.

MAPS

Greenland's ice-free coastal areas are covered in 1:250,000 series topo sheets by the Dansk Geodaetisk Institut. Although the scale isn't particularly ideal for trekkers, they're the only maps available for most of Greenland. To order maps or catalogues, contact Dansk Geodaetisk Institut, Proviaantgaarden, Rigsdagsgaarden 7, DK-1218 Copenhagen, Denmark.

Green Tours (formerly DVL Rejser) the backpackers' travel bureau in Copenhagen, publishes four walking maps of popular areas in Greenland at a scale of 1:100,000, including Kangerdlusuaq, Sisimiut, Nuuk, and Narsarsuaq-Narsaq-Qaqortoq. The latter two cost US$16.50 each and the others US$10 each. To order, write to Green Tours, Kultorvet 7, DK-1175 Copenhagen, Denmark. These are the best walking maps available but are not without error and cannot be relied upon for serious exploration away from the main routes. In Greenland, they can be purchased through Arctic Adventure at the Hotel Arctic or at the Narsarsuaq Hostel in Narsarsuaq or at the Hotel Perlen in Narsaq.

Atuagkat in Nuuk publishes an all-Greenland atlas, *Kalaallit Nunaat Atlas*, which is extremely well done and covers the country in great detail. The text is in Danish and Greenlandic but the maps are internationally intelligible. Those interested in the finer points of the Greenlandic geography will enjoy it immensely. It costs US$50 and may be ordered from Atuakkiorfik, PO Box 840, DK-3900 Nuuk, Greenland.

ACTIVITIES

Hunting & Fishing

All visitors must purchase a non-resident licence from a police station, tourist office or hotel before hunting or fishing in Greenland. Quite a few regulations apply to hunting the larger animals which are probably best left to the locals. Polar bear, musk ox, snowy owl, falcon, and sea eagles may not be taken by foreigners under any circumstances. Many other species are protected over large areas of Greenland and some may not be removed from the country. If hunting interests you, contact the Ministry for Greenland, Hausergade 3, DK-1128 Copenhagen, Denmark, for a rundown on seasons and regulations.

If you plan to do a lot of trekking, a fishing rod and a variety of lures are highly recommended. Greenlandic lakes, particularly in the south, are rich in trout, Greenland salmon, and Arctic char while the fjords are teeming with cod that seem to snap at anything. Some regulations apply so be sure to ask for a list of them when purchasing a licence.

For non-residents, a non-commercial season fishing licence will cost US$86 (Dkr500) although some visitors I met were able to purchase a short-term licence for US$28.50. A licence for small game such as hares and small birds will cost US$143, and for larger game – fox or caribou – it will cost US$429.

Trekking

Walking in Greenland isn't much like walking anywhere else. Apart from the odd sheep track in south Greenland and the track to the inland ice at Narsarsuaq, trails are essentially non-existent and the are all cross-country or along dog-sled routes. In short, you need to be better prepared for trekking in Greenland than in most other places; you'll need to be good at reading a compass including knowing the compass deviations for the applicable latitude and at finding your way in some of the most difficult non-technical country around.

In places, the terrain (even along popular routes) can become suddenly impassable requiring long detours. Thick low-lying vegetation hides fields of ankle-cracking boulders. Mossy bogs and hidden waterholes abound and walkers must make their way along steep, rocky and slippery mountainsides, climbing and descending often to avoid the rough bits. At times, the detour will take them over lofty mountains or up boulder-choked valleys to avoid dangerous stream crossings.

At this point, you have probably realised that Greenland isn't an ideal country for casual or amateur trekkers but, having said that, it provides some of the most magnificent and rewarding walks in the world. Best of all, it's relatively undiscovered. You're not likely to run into another party, even on the 'popular' multi-day trips which, at the time of writing, were attracting, at most, 20 groups per year.

Despite the low numbers, in 1989, several trekkers went missing in Greenland and were never found. The weather can be horrendous even in the summer. Fog and freezing rain can obscure the terrain for days on end, and even the best map and compass won't help you. This isn't to put you off trekking – there is no better way to appreciate the Greenlandic wilderness – but it is a warning that careful preparation is of utmost importance.

I'll only discuss the most popular routes in this book. There are plenty of others but don't set off without carefully soliciting local advice or you will be taking significant risks. Although I've trekked all over the world and thought I had taken sufficient precautions before setting out on the popular walk from Qaqortoq to Igaliko in south Greenland, several seemingly innocent mistakes combined with horrid weather very nearly resulted in disaster on one occasion.

If you're going trekking in Greenland, even on day-hikes, it's a good idea to tell someone about your plans and estimated time of return, but don't fail to inform them when your trip is complete. Rescue helicopters cost around nearly US$6000 per hour and you will pay. If you tell someone your itinerary and change it without notifying them, you could very quickly end up poor.

One last important note – I heard from several government officials that it is against Greenlandic law to wander into the bush alone. I suspect this may be a scare tactic rather than an actual law, but keep it in mind. It *is* illegal, however, to set off on an expedition to the inland ice without first obtaining a permit and paying a hefty deposit of tens of thousands of dollars for your rescue, should it be necessary (see the following Mountaineering section). You may not be surprised to learn that when I was there, a few of the more intrepid (some would say stupid and I'm not recommending it!) explorers decided to take their chances and face the ice without the official insurance policy.

If you're planning on trekking, you'd do well to pick up a copy of the excellent Skarv Guide *Trekking in Greenland* (1990) by Norwegian Torbjoern Ydegaard. It provides up-to-date information on routes, access, and practicalities. If you can't find it in a local travel bookshop, it can be ordered from Green Tours, Kultorvet 7, DK-1175 Copenhagen, Denmark.

See also the Hunting & Fishing, Maps, and Wild Foods sections of this chapter.

Mountaineering

For mountaineers who dream of doing a first ascent, Greenland may offer them the chance but, for any serious expedition, the previously mentioned deposit keeps cropping up like a bad dream. Officials just don't like the idea of people risking their lives for the thrill of the experience. I suspect they also know the interest rate on the amount of the deposit they demand.

For what it's worth, the highest peak in Greenland is officially 3708-metre Gunnbjørn Fjeld between Ammassalik and Ittoqqoortoormiit in east Greenland. It has been climbed only three or four times. Interestingly, a Swedish expedition that climbed a nearby mountain, the Dome, claims it is higher than Gunnbjørn by 82 metres.

For those on the rock side of the climbing spectrum, one of the world's highest sea cliffs, 2012-metre Uiluit Qaqaa on Tasermiut Fjord near Nanortalik, lies in a region of granite faces that rival those of Yosemite. Uummannaq in the north-west has a most intriguing technical peak as a backdrop. There's fairly easy access to these two areas and no deposit is needed.

For further information on organising a mountaineering expedition in Greenland, contact the Commission for Scientific Research, Ministry for Greenland, Hausergade 3, DK-1128 Copenhagen, Denmark.

Kayaking

Although it was developed in Greenland, the days of the practical hunting qajaq are numbered there. These boats have been completed overwhelmed by the ubiquitous Mariner-powered speedboats that buzz around every harbour in the country and chase the coastal passenger ships like barking hounds after cars. Most visitors will only only see the sealskin-covered one-person craft that made Greenland famous in museums. In Nuuk, however, there is a Qajak Klubben ('qajaq club') whose motto is *Qajaq, Atoqqilerparput* or 'Qajaq, we are beginning to use it again'. Their efforts are aimed at a revival of the Greenlandic qajaq as a practical and even competitive and recreational craft.

Recreational kayaking (with a 'k', I'm referring to the wider fibreglass variety) is only recently been introduced into Greenland although avid sea kayakers will probably be drooling as they cruise the coastline. Currently, however, there are no kayaks for hire commercially in Greenland.

One Dutch group in 1989 managed to secure commercial sponsorship at home and merrily set off on a 4-week kayak adventure from Narsarsuaq to Paamiut but such opportunities are rare, particularly outside of sponsorship-minded Europe. There are too many adventurers and not enough adventures left. Avid kayakers will just have to lug their own equipment to Greenland by air and then set off on their own.

Taking wind, weather, technical difficulty, exposure to open seas, the interesting landscapes, and accessibility into consideration, the most suitable areas for independent kayak exploration are to be found in the Tasermiut Fjord area near Nanortalik, Kangerdlusuaq, Hamborgerland near Maniitsoq, the Narsarsuaq-Narsaq-Qaqortoq region, and Godthåbsfjord.

The area around Ilulissat is magnificent and would appear ideal to kayakers, but the danger posed by icebergs is great and must be recognised. If you choose to explore this wonderful area by small boat, steer clear of the ice. Stories of capsize and death by rolling iceberg will follow you all over Greenland like those of bears in Canada and of guerillas in Peru.

Tours If you want a lower key adventure, Trail Head/Black Feather in Toronto and Ottawa (Canada) offers organised sea-kayaking trips to Greenland. They provide the kayaks, equipment, meals, and guides as well as arranging air and land transport between Ottawa and Nuuk. Their primary areas of interest are the Nuuk Kangerdluaq (Godthåbsfjord) near Nuuk, the icefjord at Ilulissat, and the magnificent Uummannaq area in north-west Greenland. For further information or booking, contact Trail Head/Black Feather (tel 416-862-0881 or 613-722-9717, both in Canada), 40 East Wellington St, Toronto, Ontario M5E 1C7, Canada, or 1341 Wellington St, Ottawa, Ontario K1Y 3B8, Canada.

For those who may be interested in the traditional Greenlandic qajaq and its use, there's a videotape entitled *Greenland Kayaking Techniques* available for US$75 from Heath Services, Rt 1 Box 125, Damon, Texas 77430 USA.

THINGS TO BUY

Most towns in Greenland have hotels and crafts outlets where visitors can buy soapstone, reindeer bone, and walrus and narwhal-ivory carved to make jewellery or a tupilaq. The place that's been repeatedly recommended for tupilaq carvings is Paamiut in the south-west where prices are reasonable and quality is high. At some places, especially Qaqortoq where there is a tannery, you can also purchase Greenland fur products, including seal and fox. Of course, all purchases should reflect consideration of home-country import regulations and environmental impact concerns, as well.

Greenlandic music will be a real surprise for most visitors. It is exceptionally good and tapes and recordings by local artists are available in all major towns.

It should be noted that the export of artefacts, by definition anything made prior to 1940, is prohibited without a special export licence from the National Museum in Nuuk. It's also forbidden to disturb any historic or prehistoric sites or remove souvenir stones from ruins. If you discover anything that appears significant, contact the Grønlands Landsmuseum (tel 22611), PO Box 145, DK-3900 Nuuk.

Getting Around

Getting around in Greenland will probably be your biggest expense and your greatest uncertainty as well. The best advice I can give on dealing with it is to remember the word *imaaqa* 'maybe', which seems to have been invented specifically for the Greenlandic transport system. In fact, Greenlanders will tell you that the name of their national airline is actually *Grønlandsfly...imaaqa.*

AIR

Given the climatic conditions, Greenland is served very well by the national airline, Grønlandsfly (Greenlandair) which operates a fleet of Sikorsky S-61N and Bell helicopters as well as several De Havilland Dash-7 fixed-wing aircraft. The company links most of the country's settlements by scheduled air routes. The planes may operate in and out of Kangerdlusuaq, Nuuk, Ilulissat, Narsarsuaq, Pituffik (Thule), and Kulusuk (Ammassalik), but all other villages accessible by air are served by helicopter only.

The unofficial airline name 'Grønlandsfly...imaaqa' came about because the fickle and unpredictable Greenlandic weather doesn't allow flights to operate according to a schedule. Timetables are made for convenience but this will quickly become inconvenience if you rely on them.

The obvious corollary to all this is never book a flight from say, Qaqortoq to Narsarsuaq that is scheduled to arrive 2 hours before your connecting flight to Copenhagen is due to depart. The odds are against your making the connection unless, of course, the trans-Atlantic flight is also delayed. And chances are it will be, often for 24 hours or more.

I was once flying by helicopter from Narsarsuaq to Nanortalik and, as we approached the heliport to land, a sudden fog materialised and enveloped everything, forcing us to turn around and fly to Qaqortoq instead, all the while keeping only 30 metres from 'the deck' to ensure at least minimal visibility. Nanortalik remained in the fog for the next 24 hours.

If your airline ticket says you're going to Narsarsuaq, don't count on it. Flights to Greenland from Iceland and Copenhagen are often diverted between Narsarsuaq and Kangerdlusuaq due to inclement weather. Grønlandsfly doesn't pay your expenses in the wrong city if this happens, either, because it happens too often. Be prepared.

Sometimes all this works in your favour. Once, all Tuesday flights from Narsarsuaq to Qaqortoq were booked up and I had to book for the following day, which meant an expensive overnight stay awaiting the flight. I arrived in Narsarsuaq at 2 pm to discover that day's half-empty 8 am flight hadn't yet departed and I was able to get on it.

The cost of flying in Greenland is high, so budget travellers will want to do as little of it as possible. For some sample airfares, see Costs in the previous chapter.

Airline Offices

The main Grønlandsfly office (tel 24488, fax 23788) is in Nuuk; the postal address is PO Box 1012, DK-3900 Nuuk, Greenland. There are also small offices at the various airports but, in smaller towns, tickets and bookings are most easily made through KNI offices. In Copenhagen, they have an office (tel 01-11-22-41, fax (45) 01-93-22-51) at Gammel Mønt 12, Box 192, DK-1004 Copenhagen, Denmark.

BOAT

Ferry

For those into soft sightseeing and wonderful cultural experiences, I don't think you can beat the largest Greenland coastal ferries. Although they're not Caribbean cruise ships by any description, they're safe, comfortable, and cross indescribably glorious waterways past soaring peaks through seas choked with mountainous icebergs. On one particularly icy trip to the north-west, I was awakened more than once in the night by a collision with an iceberg. Although all the foreigners aboard expected to go down (literally) in history like those on the *Titanic*, the *Disko* crew wasn't even fazed.

KNI owns a fleet of five coastal ferries used to transport passengers up and down the west coast between Augpilaqtoq (near Cape Farewell) in the south and Upernavik in the north. The rumour is that they will soon purchase three more ships and increase the frequency of service, which will in turn, make travelling by ferry much more convenient for short-term visitors. If this deal doesn't materialise, plan on twice-weekly sailings around the south Greenland ports, weekly trips on the *Kununguak* between Paamiut and Ilulissat and fortnightly runs between Narsarsuaq, Narsaq or Qaqortoq and Upernavik on the *Disko*.

The two largest vessels, the *Disko* and the *Kununguak* are comfortable with private cabins, couchettes, a cafeteria, a shop, hot showers, and video rooms. Yes, you get the worst of American cinema nightly, complete with Danish subtitles.

Three smaller ferries, the *Aleqa Ittuk*, the *Taterak*, the *Tugdlik*, and the *Aviaq Ittuk* are used for shorter hauls (of up to about 12 hours) and are a bit more cramped. The *Aviaq Ittuk* operates in the area around Maniitsoq, the *Tugdlik* around Disko Bay, and the other two run from Narsarsuaq and Augpilaqtoq in south Greenland including most towns and villages in between. Children aged between 4 and 13 years pay half price on all fares.

If you'd like a copy of the sailing schedule and an update on new vessels and routes, contact KNI Trafikkontoret (tel 25211, fax 25211), Aqqusinersuaq 4, PO Box 608, DK-3900 Nuuk, Greenland, or the Grønlands Rejsebureau (tel 45-01-13-10-11), Gammel Mønt 12, PO Box 130, DK-1004 Copenhagen, Denmark.

It's wise to book all ferry trips at a KNI office at least 24 hours before sailing. Ship-capacity regulations are adhered to strictly and, without a booking, you could lose out.

For the larger ships, *Disko* and

Ferry Fares - deck class
Prices in US$

	Upernavik	Uummannaq	Ilulissat	Qasigiannguit	Qeqertarsuaq	Aasiaat	Kangaatsiaq	Sisimiut	Kangerdlusuaq	Kangaamiut
Uummannaq	78									
Ilulissat	113	82								
Qasigiannguit	124	92	20							
Qeqertarsuaq	107	77	29	31						
Asiaat	121	96	28	24	24					
Kangaatsiaq	134	108	38	34	34	19				
Sisimiut	160	133	83	78	70	62	49			
Kangerdlusuaq	231	205	159	150	142	134	126	84		
Kangaamiut	186	159	110	105	98	89	83	39	64	
Maniitsoq	201	174	124	120	112	103	95	55	80	
Nuuk	238	209	160	155	149	139	134	92	49	
Qeqertarsuatsiaat	265	238	190	184	178	169	160	120	146	
Paamiut	294	267	217	213	205	198	190	148	175	
Arsuk	324	299	249	244	237	229	220	179	206	
Qaqortoq	359	331	282	276	270	262	253	211	239	
Narsaq	363	333	285	280	273	264	256	215	241	
Narsarsuaq	372	345	295	291	283	275	267	225	252	
Nanortalik	372	345	295	291	283	275	267	225	252	

Kununguak, it's best to book as far in advance as possible, especially if you want a cabin. All the ferry fares provided in this book are deck class only. Cabin fares may be worked out by adding approximately 120% to the deck-class fare.

If you're travelling deck class on one of the larger ships, be prepared for a crush when getting on. The locals know where all the best couchettes are and these go quickly so, if you don't want a stuffy cubbyhole deep in the hull, queue up early. There are, incidentally, infrequent thefts from the couchettes but it is rather half-hearted and the culprits are easily caught. If you're concerned, however, watch your valuables.

Charter Boat

The villages and points of interest that can't be reached by ferry are normally accessible by charter boat. Nearly every Greenlandic family owns a powerboat of some description and finding someone to take you to the more out-of-the-way places shouldn't be too difficult. It will, however, be expensive unless you can find someone who's going anyway and just wants help paying for petrol. Don't count on this, however. The Home Rule government has devised a complex set of official charges for boat charter and people tend to stick by it pretty closely except on very short trips where the official charge would be ludicrous.

As a general guideline to the structure of the fee schedule, a small, open boat under 2.8 metres will cost US$17 per hour while a 9 to 10.5-metre boat will cost US$40.50 per hour. There's a big catch, however. You must pay for a minimum of 6 hours whether you use them all or not. For the first 8 hours, you must pay 50% more per hour than the official rate. What that works out to is a minimum charge of US$151 for the smallest open boat and US$364 for the larger boats. Overnight waiting hours are half-price.

If you can muster a group, however, you can bring the rate per person down to a manageable figure, although the smallest boats won't normally handle more than four people including the pilot.

DRIVING

In a country without roads, Greenlanders seem to do a fair bit of driving. Even in towns that can be crossed on foot in 5 minutes, everyone seems to own a vehicle and drives it whenever they set foot out the door. To my knowledge, however, no one has yet opened a vehicle rental agency so local drivers pretty much have the streets to themselves (pedestrians take the hint). Visitors will have to rely on taxis or, in a few cases, town buses.

DOG SLED

During the 8 or 9 months of continuous snow and frozen seas in Arctic or east Greenland, travel by dog sled is the most common method of getting around. For those visitors who have more money to spend than most, it's exciting to do a 'winter' tour of those regions as well including the most popular places Ammassalik, Uummannaq, Ilulissat, Sisimiut, Qasigiannguit, and a few other smaller places. Most dog-sled tours, with only a couple of exceptions, are arranged by the hotels in the respective towns.

25	Maniitsoq								
63	49	Nuuk							
92	81	45	Qeqertarsuatsiaat						
119	105	74	42	Paamiut					
150	136	105	74	33	Arsuk				
183	170	139	108	78	55	Qaqortoq			
187	174	143	112	186	59	16	Narsaq		
196	184	151	121	92	70	28	19	Narsarsuaq	
196	184	151	121	92	70	36	42	54	Nanortalik

Greenlandic sled dogs bear little resemblance to the drippy tongued, tail-wagging pooches most visitors probably think typical of the species. These seem to be only a generation or two removed from wolves and their penchant for snarling, howling, and their general ill-tempered demeanour should be taken seriously. To approach them or try to pat them would be to court disaster. In many Arctic villages, these dogs spend a lot of their day snoozing on the rocks and blend in quite well so you have to be particulary careful not to trip over them.

Tourist trips rarely last more than a day but you can find some that offer accommodation in a village for an overnight trip. Occasionally, longer tours are available as well. Just for example, a week-long package (from March to May) which includes 7 nights in the hotel in Ammassalik, 2 day-trips by dog sled, an optional overnight trip to a village, and food will cost US$1150. Organised ski trips are also available through the hotel.

Less expensive and touristy dog-sled trips can be arranged spontaneously in such places as Uummannaq or Qasigiannguit. You'll normally pay around US$30 per day for a far more realistic experience than will be possible on the east coast. You'll pay quite a bit more in airfares getting there because the coastal ferry does not operate during the dog-sledding season from March to May. Those who'd prefer to do a longer overnight trip the way locals do would probably have the most success in Uummannaq in the north-west.

Apart from in Ammassalik, Greenlanders are not permitted to keep sled dogs in villages south of the Arctic Circle nor can they keep ordinary domestic dogs north of the Circle. This means that you cannot have a go at dog sledding in Nuuk, Qaqortoq, or elsewhere in southern Greenland. Cross-country skiing is possible anywhere the dog sleds go but, as yet, you'll have to bring your own skis unless you go with a tour.

TOURS

Tours in Greenland are pretty convenient for everyone. Although it's possible to book a 2-week, all-inclusive race around the island, it will cost a small fortune. Fortunately for those whose tastes don't run to such extremes, it's possible to join such tours for a day or so at à la carte rates and still see the sights with relative ease without having to fork out big bucks for individual boat charters. In many towns, the tourist organisations run day-trips to accessible points of interest, normally at least once a week, charging around US$50 or US$60.

The two most prominent tour operators which offer excursions in Greenland are Green Tours, Kultorvet 7, DK-1175 Copenhagen, Denmark, and Arctic Adventure, 37 Aaboulevard, DK-1960 Copenhagen, Denmark. The latter organises both a variety of scheduled tours and excursions tailored to suit a group's interests. I've heard that larger cruising ships are planning to begin operation up the west coast in the near future as well.

South Greenland

In Greenlandic, south Greenland is sometimes known affectionately as *Sineriak Banaaneqarfik*, the 'banana coast', but don't be fooled – this area was also the source of the island's verdant-sounding name. It's not Ecuador or Bali but is, you could say, a less hostile manifestation of the Arctic than most places further north.

Most visitors to Greenland who aren't shooting over to Kulusuk for a couple of hours get their first taste of the island here in the south and it's a stunning introduction. You spiral into the airport at Narsarsuaq, see ice-choked fjords, glaciers, and stark snowy mountains and begin to realise that you're somewhere very special. South Greenland is an area of sheep farms, hundreds of Norse and Inuit ruins, tiny colourful villages, great scenery, and even a hot spring where you can bathe while watching the icebergs drift past in the fjord.

NARSARSUAQ

The name of this settlement of 180 people means 'the big plain', an apt description by Greenlandic standards, but we're not talking about the Ukraine here. It's just a small flat area (just big enough for the international airport) combined with a braided river delta that, although flat, is too silty and stream-ridden to be considered much of a 'plain' in the traditional sense.

Narsarsuaq had its beginnings as the 'Blue West One' US military base during WW II. It was constructed practically overnight and, by 1945, was Greenland's largest settlement with a population of 5000 and all the trappings of a small US town. There was a rather dark side to its history, however (see the Greenland Facts About the Country chapter), and it continued operations through the Korean War.

This was one of the bases the Americans abandoned after its 'usefulness' expired. All the military surplus was then sold to Norway and the site destroyed and abandoned. Today, an ice-monitoring station exists at the village. This was established to track drift ice after the Danish passenger ship *Hans Hedtoft* ran foul of an iceberg off Cape Farewell on its maiden voyage in 1959 and went down with no survivors.

Information

Tourist Information Arctic Adventure runs an informal information desk for arriving international flights primarily for their incoming clients. At other times, the main desk at the Arctic Hotel will be useful; Arctic Adventure has a permanent desk in the lobby where they'll help you with your travel plans.

All visitors should be prepared for the legendary Arctic mosquito encounter in Narsarsuaq so carry repellent (something with a high percentage of that bug bane, DEET). The hotel sells face nets which can be used in extreme cases.

Banks Foreign exchange is available at the Hotel Arctic desk and at the KNI office across the main road from there. This office handles all banking transactions in Narsarsuaq.

Things to See & Do

Naomi Uemura Monument The monument in the 'park' opposite the airport terminal honours Naomi Uemura, the Japanese national hero who went solo to the North Pole, crossing Greenland's inland ice. This most recent great Arctic explorer met his demise in 1985 during an attempt at a first solo winter ascent of Alaska's Denali (Mt McKinley).

Radio Tower A quick, scenic walk is up to the radio tower on top of the 240-metre hill rising from the main road. To get there, walk up the gravel track behind the Butik shop. Where several tracks intersect, turn left uphill past the ruined buildings and follow

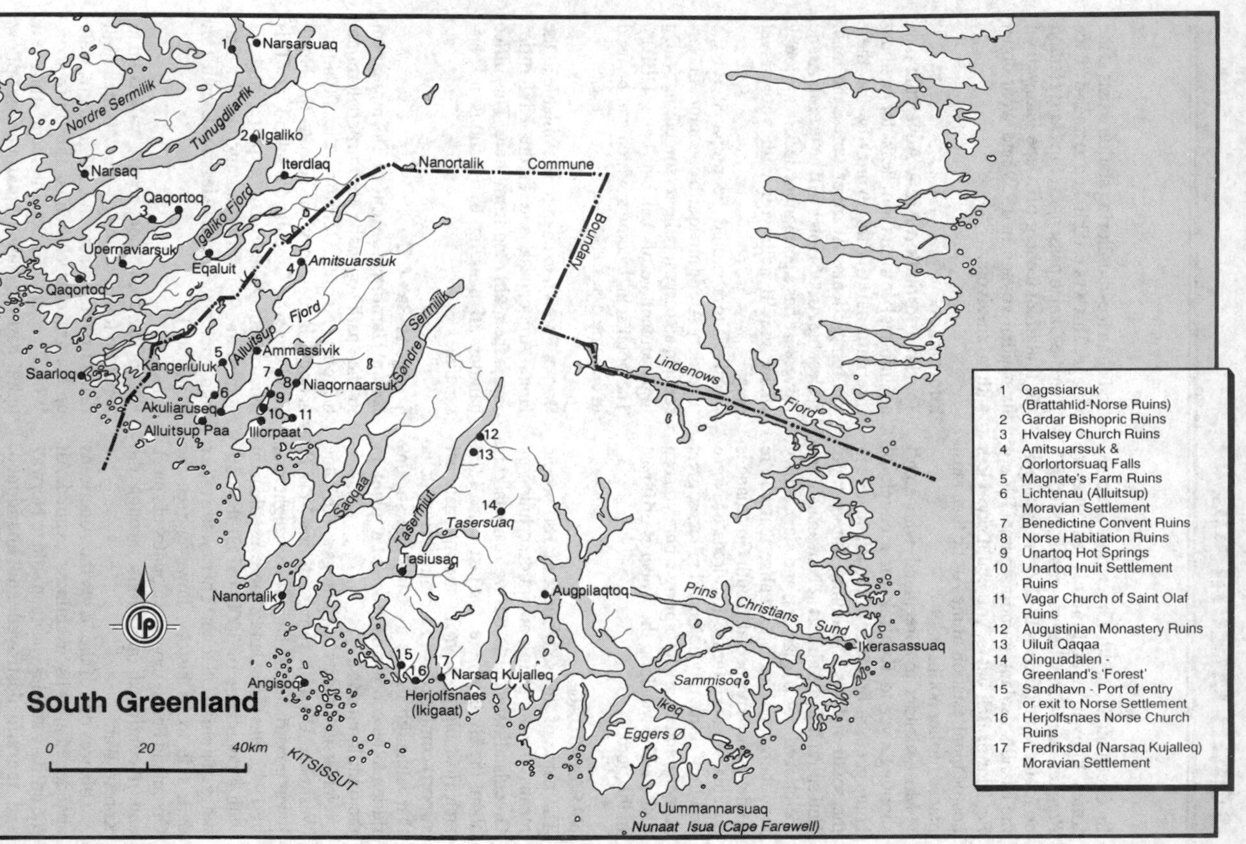
South Greenland
0 20 40km
1 Qagssiarsuk (Brattahlid-Norse Ruins)
2 Gardar Bishopric Ruins
3 Hvalsey Church Ruins
4 Amitsuarssuk & Qorlortorsuaq Falls
5 Magnate's Farm Ruins
6 Lichtenau (Alluitsup) Moravian Settlement
7 Benedictine Convent Ruins
8 Norse Habitiation Ruins
9 Unartoq Hot Springs
10 Unartoq Inuit Settlement Ruins
11 Vagar Church of Saint Olaf Ruins
12 Augustinian Monastery Ruins
13 Uiluit Qaqaa
14 Qinguadalen - Greenland's 'Forest'
15 Sandhavn - Port of entry or exit to Norse Settlement
16 Herjolfsnaes Norse Church Ruins
17 Fredriksdal (Narsaq Kujalleq) Moravian Settlement
Narsarsuaq
Nordre Sermilik
Tunugdliarfik
Igaliko
Narsaq
Iterdlaq
Nanortalik Commune Boundary
Qaqortoq
Igaliko Fjord
Upernaviarsuk
Eqaluit
Amitsuarssuk
Qaqortoq
Alluitsup Fjord
Ammassivik
Søndre Sermilik
Saarloq
Kangerluluk
Niaqornaarsuk
Akuliaruseq
Alluitsup Paa
Illorpaat
Lindenows Fjord
Saqqaa
Tasermiut
Tasersuaq
Tasiusaq
Nanortalik
Augpilaqtoq
Prins Christians Sund
Ikerasassuaq
Narsaq Kujalleq
Angisoq
Herjolfsnaes (Ikigaat)
Sammisoq
Ikeq
Eggers Ø
KITSISSUT
Uummannarsuaq
Nunaat Isua (Cape Farewell)

the track to the top for a great view over the entire area. From there, you can return to the intersection and walk up toward the waterfall (avoiding the off-limits watershed area) or continue down through the maze of trails to the youth hostel.

Hospital Valley Over the moraine from the main town, if you can call Narsarsuaq a town, is Hospital Valley. There, you'll find a lot of the detritus left behind after the USA pulled out of the place – bits of planes, machinery, and unidentified scraps interspersed with chunks of concrete, springs and debris from the ruins of insidious military buildings. The most prominent feature of the valley is a lone chimney and fireplace that stand as a monument to Narsarsuaq's unpleasant history. Almost elegiacally, two small species of orchid *(platanthera hyperborea* and *leuchorchis albida)* bloom in Hospital Valley from early to mid-August.

At the Hotel Arctic is an interesting photo of the valley at the height of operations.

Places to Stay

The *Hotel Arctic* (tel 35253) once had a bit more character than it does today – it looks like just another block of flats in the cluster – but it is the only hotel in Narsarsuaq. It's often packed with tour groups. Singles/doubles here will cost US$100/130. Extra beds can be added for US$29 each. There's also offer a restaurant, cafeteria, pub, laundry service, a small gym, and a sauna for use by guests.

The most pleasant place to stay is the *Youth Hostel* which is not only beautifully situated in a valley of blooming willow herb within earshot of a lovely waterfall but is also sparkling clean and comfortable. Since it's not yet officially part of the Danish Youth Hostels Association, there's no discount for IYHF members.

As youth hostels go, it's a bit steep at US$16 per night but, by Greenland's standards, that's a pittance for the quality. A prepared continental breakfast here will cost US$3, lunch is US$4, and dinner US$7. Be sure to book in advance, however, because they won't prepare anything otherwise. The hostel has kitchen facilities for guests, as well. Non-guests can use the shower or the kitchen for US$2 each. They sell the DVL-Rejser walking map for US$16.50.

The hostel's only drawback is that it closes down for the winter on 21 August and doesn't re-open until mid-June. At other times, budget travellers may stay in the rather awful staff quarters of the Hotel Arctic for US$23 per person.

Camping The camping site is on a moraine beside the lake near the southern end of Hospital Valley. There are no facilities but the location is pleasant enough and it's only a half-hour walk from the settlement. Arctic Adventure normally puts up a sign pointing the way.

Places to Eat

The cafeteria at the hotel serves a very limited menu of surprisingly good food between 7 and 9 am, noon and 2 pm, and 7 to 9.30 pm. A buffet breakfast, including cereal, fruit, yoghurt, rolls, and trimmings, will cost US$6.40. Set lunches and dinners will cost about US$9. For anything more extravagant you'll have to resort to the hotel restaurant where the chef prepares excellent meals costing over US$25.

When there's a reason for the airport terminal to be open, the grill bar in the lounge there serves hot dogs and plastic-wrapped microwave versions of other things. You can also get coffee or soft drinks but don't expect much.

The supermarket is inside one of the blocks of flats south of the hotel. It's marked *Butik* and sells everything from groceries to socks to ammunition for rifles. There's a fairly good selection of frozen and freeze-dried food and, at times, you can even buy fresh produce.

Getting There & Away

Air Weather permitting, Grønlandsfly with Icelandair has four flights weekly in the summer to and from Copenhagen via Iceland's Keflavík International Airport. You

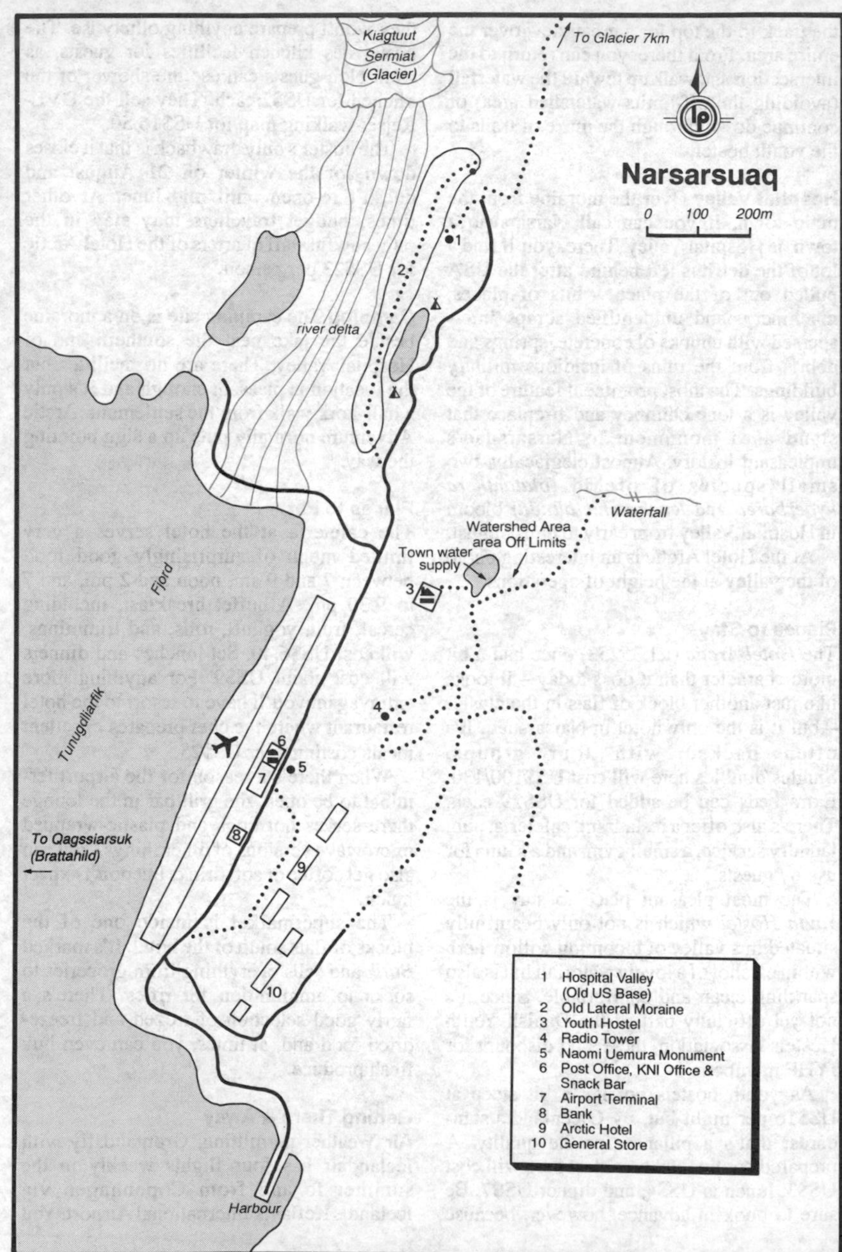
Narsarsuaq
0 100 200m
Kiagtuut Sermiat (Glacier)
To Glacier 7km
river delta
Waterfall
Watershed Area area Off Limits
Town water supply
Fjord
Tunugdliarfik
To Qagssiarsuk (Brattahild)
Harbour
1 Hospital Valley (Old US Base)
2 Old Lateral Moraine
3 Youth Hostel
4 Radio Tower
5 Naomi Uemura Monument
6 Post Office, KNI Office & Snack Bar
7 Airport Terminal
8 Bank
9 Arctic Hotel
10 General Store

can also fly by helicopter at least three times weekly to or from Paamiut for US$243 one way, to Nuuk for US$370, to Qaqortoq for US$68.50, to Narsaq for US$47, or to Nanortalik for US$113 each way.

Ferry The *Disko* calls into Narsarsuaq on an average of every 2 weeks in the summer bound for Qaqortoq, Nuuk, the Disko Bay area, and as far north as Upernavik. The *Taterak* sails twice weekly to and from Qagssiarsuk, Itivdleq (Igaliko), Narsaq, Qaqortoq, and Nanortalik (staying overnight in Qaqortoq).

Getting Around

The Arctic Hotel owns a tour bus which meets incoming flights and shuttles guests and their luggage 200 metres down the road to the hotel. The bus normally does the 1.5 km run down to the harbour when there's a ferry leaving or arriving. You can also arrange for a ride out the road north to Hospital Valley, the camping site, and the start of walks to the inland ice and Mellemlandet. The bus goes at least once a day to both the harbour and Hospital Valley so enquire at the hotel for information or arrangements.

Basically, you can walk anywhere in Narsarsuaq in a few minutes. If catching a boat, leave yourself about half an hour to walk down to the harbour with luggage although it doesn't normally take that long.

Around Narsarsuaq

Narsarsuaq Valley Walk & Inland Ice The walk out past Hospital Valley into Narsarsuaq Valley is the easiest and most pleasant in Greenland. It is also the only one which follows a proper track.

It begins at the rubbish-dumping point at the northern end of Hospital Valley and climbs a small hill for a spectacular view across Narsarsuaq Valley before descending into it. The track then passes through some areas of relatively luxuriant vegetation (trees 3 metres high in some very sheltered enclaves), over some glacier-scoured boulders, and across patches of glacial silt to the foot of a 300-metre-high cascade at the head of the valley.

Although most casual walkers turn back at this point, it's more than worthwhile to continue. The track winds steeply upward, climbing over 300 metres to a haunting prehistoric-looking lake surrounded by tundra and smooth glacier-scraped boulders.

Beyond the lake, you'll get a good view of the Kiagtuut Sermiat glacier, a tongue of the inland ice, before descending for another 1.5 km to its flank. Hikers commonly carry along a bottle of whisky or vodka and drink a toast to the 10,000 year old ice cubes they can chisel off and place in the drinks.

Taken quickly, the return walk can be completed in about 6 hours but, plan on it taking all day, if you want to stop for any length of time and contemplate the wonderful views along the way.

Mellemlandet A longer trip to the 'middle land' for more experienced trekkers begins by walking to the lake above Narsarsuaq Valley. From there, climb the ridge to the east and follow it north-east for 12 rugged km through Mellemlandet to the promontory that overlooks the vast split of the glaciers Kiagtuut Sermiat and Qoorqut Sermiat. Plan on at least 3 days for the return trip due to the nature of the country and the strong possibility of poor weather higher up.

Qooroq Fjord Most of the icebergs you see floating around Narsarsuaq were born in the glacier Qoorqut Sermiat and calved into Qooroq Fjord, which is densely choked with an unusual amount of ice. Arctic Adventure offers a 4-hour cruise through Qooroq Fjord twice weekly for US$43 per person. Arrangements can be made at the Hotel Arctic in Narsarsuaq.

QAGSSIARSUK (BRATTAHLID)

Just a half-hour by boat across Tunugdliarfik Fjord (originally Eiriks Fjord) from Narsarsuaq is the village of Qagssiarsuk. With a population of less than 100, it currently serves primarily as a sheep-raising centre. Qagssiarsuk was Eirík Rauðe's Brattahlid –

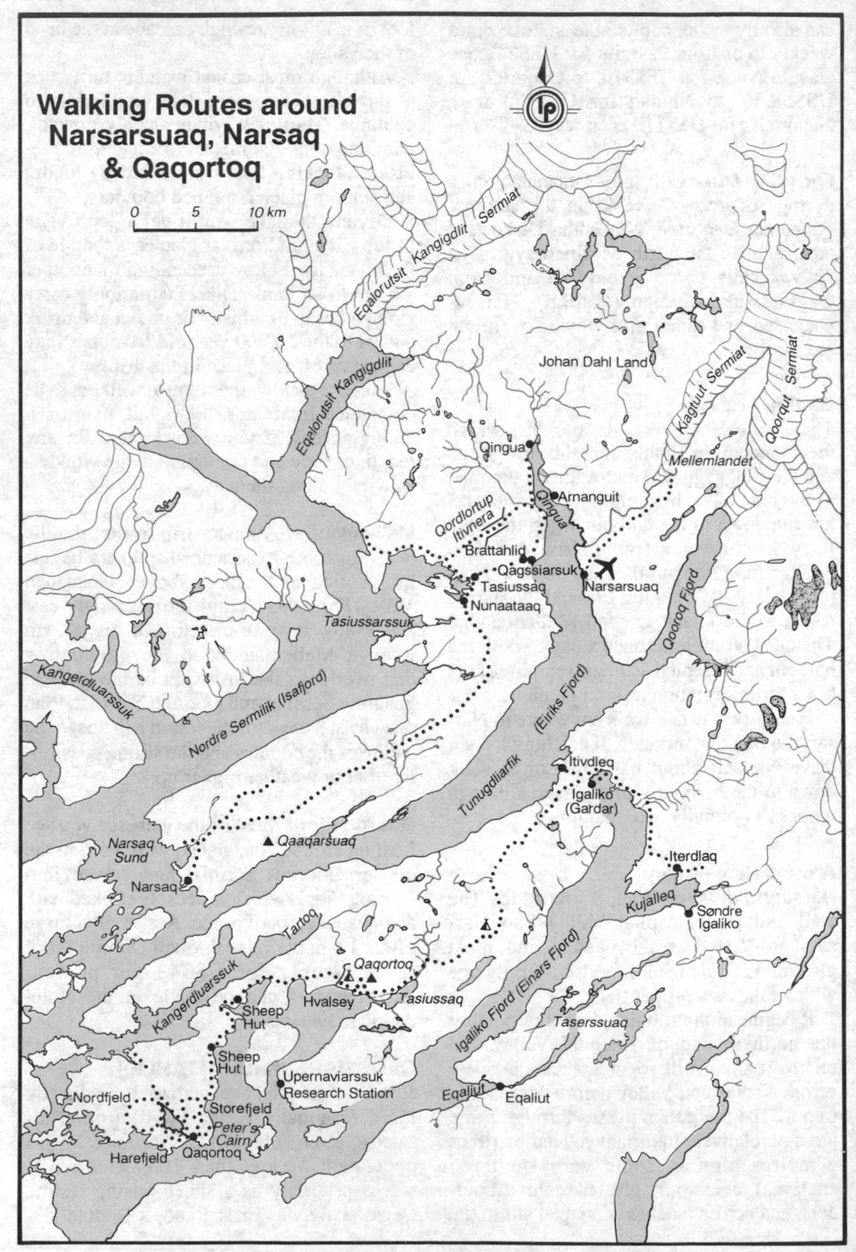
Walking Routes around Narsarsuaq, Narsaq & Qaqortoq
0 5 10 km
Eqalorutsit Kangigdlit Sermiat
Johan Dahl Land
Kiagtuut Sermiat
Qoorqut Sermiat
Mellemlandet
Eqalorutsit Kangigdlit
Qingua
Arnanguit
Qingua
Qordlortup Itivnera
Brattahlid
Qagssiarsuk
Narsarsuaq
Tasiussaq
Nunaataaq
Qooroq Fiord
Tasiussarssuk
Kangerdluarssuk
Nordre Sermilik (Isafjord)
Tunugdliarfik (Eiriks Fjord)
Itivdleq
Igaliko (Gardar)
Qaaqarsuaq
Narsaq Sund
Narsaq
Iterdlaq
Kujalleq
Søndre Igaliko
Tartoq
Kangerdluarssuk
Qaqortoq
Hvalsey
Tasiussaq
Sheep Hut
Sheep Hut
Igaliko Fjord (Einars Fjord)
Taserssuaq
Upernaviarssuk Research Station
Eqaliut
Eqaliut
Nordfjeld
Storefjeld
Peter's Cairn
Harefjeld
Qaqortoq

the place he considered the richest and best in Greenland when he arrived in 986. Today, it contains a wealth of fascinating Norse ruins.

There are no services in Qagssiarsuk except a small kiosk with opening hours that seem to depend largely upon local demand. Visitors may also want to watch out for the pack of ATV's (all-terrain vehicles) that frequently terrorises the street and everything in it.

In addition to the ruins, there are some typical Greenlandic fish-drying racks, a monument to the Norse settlers and a statue of the first sheep-breeder in the area. Both of the monuments are partially constructed of the beautiful red and white Igaliko sandstone found only in this area of Greenland. It looks vaguely edible, something like a cherry vanilla marble cake.

Norse Ruins

The tiny square foundation beside the current church is all that's left of Þjóðhilde's Church, the first Christian church constructed in the western hemisphere. It was built by Eirík Rauðe's wife Þjóðhilde, a zealous convert to Christianity, sometime around the year 1000.

Among the other ruins there is the foundation of a later church, and that of the hall of a great manor house, the home of Eirík and Þjóðhilde themselves including the remains of a fireplace and a system of running water. Beside it is the ruin of a cattle and sheep byre and evidence of a Þing or political assembly area. Down nearer the water are remains of Inuit sod dwellings – evidence of an ingenious system of retaining heat during the winter.

The fanciful copper work on the rock behind the ruins by artist Sven Havsteen Mikkelsen is also worth a look. Part of it is a map of the settlement at its height.

Church

The current village church is also good to see. It was financed and built by the local people after the Danish government in the 1930s repeatedly refused appropriations for a church catering for 90 residents. Every year, they sold their best sheep to the slaughterhouse in Narsaq to add to the fund. When the government recognised their efforts, it appropriated half the money. The church was constructed in 1936. It was used through WW II by Americans from the base who donated the hymn board which is still used. The odd interior colour scheme is said to include white for ice, blue for the sea, yellow for the sun, and red for the warmth of fire. At Christmas, there is a special children's mass held here which is said to be particularly good.

Walks

The most common walk from Qagssiarsuk is the circuit route that begins by crossing the peninsula on the small dirt track over to the sheep station at Tasiussaq, a branch of Nordre Sermilik, where there's sheep-hut accommodation for US$11.50 per night. From there, walk up the shore (for two valleys) and return to Tunugdliarfik Fjord through the valley marked on the walking map as Qordlortup Itivnera (pass). The entire trip is about 22 km and should be spread over 2 days unless you want to move flat out through the relatively hospitable, but occasionally challenging terrain.

With more time, you'd have the option of continuing south from Tasiussaq to the sheep stations of Nunaataaq and Kangerdluaq before returning to Qagssiarsuk. The popular 3 to 5-day walk along the peninsula to or from Narsaq begins or ends at Qagssiarsuk. Most people choose to walk it from north to south because supplies and transport from Narsaq are more reliable than from Qagssiarsuk. This is truly a wilderness walk, however, and shouldn't be undertaken casually. Although it's possible to stay in sheep huts along the way for US$11.50 per night, no one should set out on this walk without a tent and a warm sleeping bag because the huts cannot be relied upon to be open or available.

Getting There & Away

Twice a week, the ferry *Taterak* sails

between Narsarsuaq and Qagssiarsuk. Guided tours are available from Arctic Adventure at the Hotel Arctic for US$15 per person return and it's well worth it. Even though little time is spent in the village, you get a lot of interesting history for your money. The tour runs on an average of twice a week but, if you want to go at any other time, Arctic Adventure will try to arrange some sort of transport. If you want to stay around Qagssiarsuk, do some walking, and then return with the next tour or make your own arrangements, that's possible as well.

Since the official minimum charter rate would apply between Narsarsuaq and Qagssiarsuk, it's probably not a viable alternative to charter a boat. It shouldn't be too difficult to get a lift over from the harbour at Narsarsuaq with someone going anyway, for around US$25 to US$30.

NARSAQ

If South Greenland has an industrial centre, it's Narsaq ('the plain') which sprawls across a level area at the end of the peninsula separating Nordre Sermilik Fjord from Tunugdliarfik Fjord. Although such an invitingly flat area couldn't have been ignored by the 10th-century Norse colonists, the actual village wasn't founded until 1830. It became a Royal Greenland Trade Department station 3 years later and was given town status in 1959. Now there's a shrimp-tinning and fish-freezing plant that doubles as a slaughterhouse that means D-day for 15,000 tender new lambs each season. There's also a small woollens and fur factory, a ceramic works, and a mineral-polishing and craft shop.

Narsaq now has around 2000 inhabitants but it seems bigger because it's so spread out. It's as if the locals realised they had surplus space and built the settlement with gaps to fill in later.

Information

The Narsaq tourist office (tel 31325) in the centre offers brochures and information. If you'd like to write in advance, their address is Narsaq Turistforening, PO Box 47, DK-3921 Narsaq, Greenland. The town also has a laundrette.

Qajaq Harbour

Local sealing and whaling activities have historically been centred on the old peninsula at the north-western end of town where the hunters moored and hung their qajaqs. Sometimes there will still be a qajaq or two around, especially when tour groups are passing through.

Narsaq Harbour Museum

The town museum is in the buildings of the old trading station and printing office near the old harbour (not the ferry dock) which dates back to 1883. It doesn't seem to keep any consistent hours. If it's not open, enquire at the tourist office and they may arrange an opening for you.

Henrik Lund Museum

This museum was actually the home of priest, poet, and painter Henrik Lund and his wife, Malene. He's best known for having written the song *Nunarput* which became the Greenlandic national anthem.

Top: Nanortalik, Greenland (DS)
Bottom: Summer afternoon in Nanortalik, Greenland (DS)

Top: Traditional sod hut, Nanortalik, Greenland (DS)
Bottom: Church tower, Nanortalik, Greenland (DS)

Places to Stay

The *Hotel Perlen* (tel 31062) is the main place to stay in Narsaq. It's run by Arctic Adventure for their tour groups but it's open to anyone if there's space available. Singles/doubles with private bath cost US$72/93; they're US$54/86 without private bath. When there's space, they offer sleeping-bag accommodation for US$14.50 per person. Arctic Adventure also takes over the vocational school Inuili during the summer and uses their flats as up-market hotel rooms.

Since the Hotel Perlen is booked out by tour groups most of the season, independent travellers normally end up at the *Youth Hostel* (tel 31114). It's in an old building with two beds per room, showers, and cooking facilities. It sits on a ridge overlooking the town and has a great view but the decor is a bit odd. The unusual stripes on the walls have been known to send people to the brink. It's open from mid-June to mid-September and at US$11.50 per person, however, it's a bargain.

Camping The unofficial but most commonly used camping site is up in the bush, north-east of the Hotel Perlen. (See the map.)

Places to Eat

Narsaq has a good variety of eating places for Greenland, anyway. There are two proper restaurants, the low-key *Ujuat* near the youth hostel and the slightly more extravagant *Hønekroen*, at the end of town, which specialises in such Greenlandic fare as lamb, whale, reindeer, trout, char, salmon, halibut, and shrimp for only about US$10 per person – a very good deal.

For more casual dining, there are two *Grill-Baren* which serve standard fast food. The Hotel Perlen serves breakfast only.

For self-caterers, there's a bakery (their specialty is *fiberbrød*) and the *braettet* or harbour market which sells the catch as soon as it's brought in.

Activities

Town Tour There's a 5-hour town tour which gives details of Narsaq's history and points of interest. It includes lunch as well as some time being coerced into buying souvenirs. It's offered twice a week and costs US$19.

Glacier Excursion

The most popular trip from Narsaq is by boat across Iqersuaq (Bredefjord) to two points where the inland ice spills down and calves icebergs into the sea. The trip also stops at some beautiful bird cliffs, makes a picnic at a nice spot between the two glaciers, and briefly visits an abandoned Inuit settlement as well. The twice-weekly trip takes about 7 hours and costs US$79 per person.

Getting There & Away

Air The chopper does the 5-minute buzz over to Qaqortoq daily except Sundays for US$28.50. You can also fly to Narsarsuaq at least once daily except Sundays for US$47.

Ferry In the summer, the *Taterak* travels between Narsarsuaq and Qaqortoq via Narsaq twice a week with one extra run from Qaqortoq and Narsaq in between. The *Aleqa Ittuk* runs between Qaqortoq and Narsaq three times per week and the *Disko* runs once every 2 weeks on its way up the coast and back. The fare to Qaqortoq is US$15.50, to Narsarsuaq it's US$18.

Tour

For those in a hurry, Arctic Adventure offers a day cruise to Narsaq from Narsarsuaq including a guided tour of the village and a helicopter flight back. It's offered once a week and costs US$96.50. If you cruise both ways, it costs only US$86.

If you're in Narsaq already and would like to join the town tour or one of the other organised excursions enquire at Arctic Adventure in the Hotel Perlen.

AROUND NARSAQ

Qaqaarsuaq

Qaqaarsuaq ('big mountain') is the prominent mountain (685 metres high) behind Narsaq. The trip to the top is popular and can be made, with some difficulty, in about 1½ hours for a predictably great view (if the weather cooperates).

Dyrnaes

Dyrnaes is the ruin of a Norse church and settlement, 3 km north of Narsaq. There's really not much there to go out of your way for but the setting is nice and, if you're walking up to Kvanefjeld anyway, it's a convenient side trip.

Kvanefjeld

This mountain, about 8 km from Narsaq, is the site of as yet unexploited uranium deposits and some old exploratory diggings. Some sort of skewed reasoning regarding these deposits led Narsaq to give Danish nuclear physicist Niels Bohr honorary residency. If you have a free day in Narsaq, it's a nice trip to go up there to poke around. The locals promote excursions up to Kvanefjeld to search for the gemstone they call Tugtupit, which I suspect is a variety of garnet.

Those who prefer to walk with an organised group can take the twice-weekly Arctic Adventure tour which costs US$18 and takes about 4 hours. This trip stops briefly at Dyrnaes, as well.

QAQORTOQ (JULIANEHÅB)

With a population of 3500, Qaqortoq (the 'white place') is the hub of south Greenland, or the 'big city', if you like. It was founded by the Norwegian trader Anders Olsen in 1775 and named Julianehåb after Queen Juliana Maria of Denmark. Most visitors find it the cleanest and tidiest of all Greenlandic towns.

Information

Tourist Information Qaqortoq's tourist office (tel 38444, after hours tel 38647) is extremely friendly and helpful. It offers several excursions from town to outlying points of interest such as Unartoq hot springs, Igaliko, Hvalsey, and the agricultural research station. The address is Qaqortoq Turistforening, PO Box 128, DK-3920 Qaqortoq, Greenland. It's in the back room of the souvenir shop, opposite the harbour, and is open Monday to Friday from 10 am to 5 pm and on Saturdays from 10 am to 1 pm.

Film & Photography Kodak print and slide film, including processing, is available (US$15 for 36 exposures) at Radio Ras near the Seamen's Home.

Laundry Qaqortoq has two laundry services, one downstairs in the block of flats on the corner of Nipinngaaq and Qaava streets and the other downstairs in block 2, on Lytzensvej near the intersection of Alanngunnguaq.

Books & Bookshops The bookshop near the fountain occasionally has some English or German novels.Books on the history of Hvalsey and Herjolfsnaes as well as several other souvenir publications are available at the tourist office souvenir shop.

Things to See & Do

Museum Thanks to the efforts of archaeologist and curator Joel Berglund, the Qaqortoq museum is one of Greenland's finest. The main museum building was constructed as a blacksmith's shop in 1871. Out the back there's a traditionally furnished sod hut built around 1905. On the front lawn is a big gun from an ill-fated whaling vessel which foundered off Greenland's east coast in the 1700s and was brought to Qaqortoq in 1933 by Knud Rasmussen.

Exhibits include photos of early Qaqortoq, sealskin qajaqs and associated apparatus, and other ingenious Inuit hunting and fishing implements as well as artefacts from the Dorset, Thule, Norse, and modern Inuit cultures. Opposite the main museum is the Forstanderskabshus, the old colonial assembly hall, where local political leaders held hot-air sessions. It was constructed for that purpose in 1863 and later was a school and a bakery. It's now been taken over by the museum and turned into an exhibit of the town's political history.

From June to September, the museum is open weekdays from 2 to 4 pm.

Church The beautiful Saviour's Church is an early example of the prefabricated architecture which today characterises most

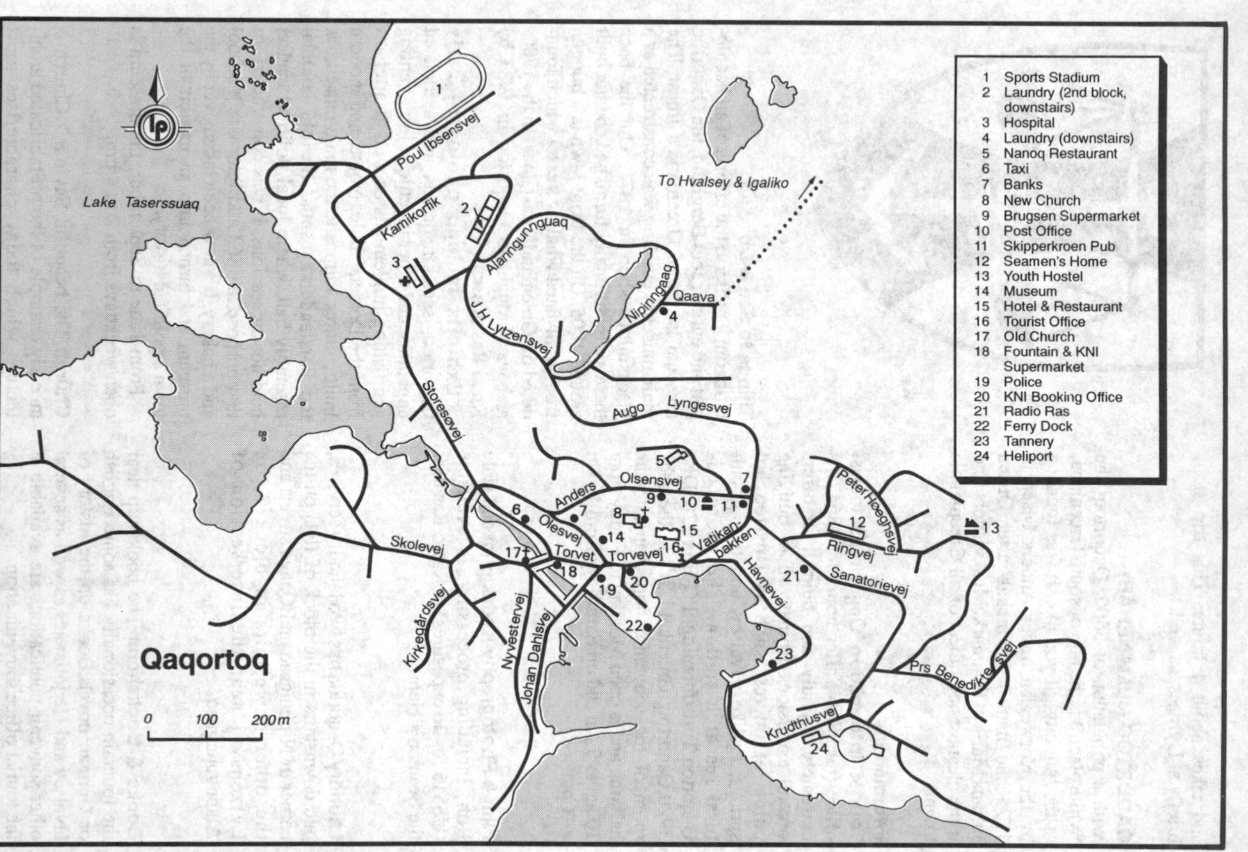
Qaqortoq
0 100 200m
Lake Taserssuaq
To Hvalsey & Igaliko
Poul Ibsensvej
Kamikorfik
Alanngunnguaq
J H Lytzensvej
Storesøvej
Nipinngaaq
Qaava
Augo
Lyngesvej
Olsensvej
Anders
Olesvej
Torvet
Torvevej
Vatikanbakken
Havnevej
Peter Høeghsvej
Ringvej
Sanatorievej
Prs Benediktesvej
Krudthusvej
Johan Dahlsvej
Nyvestervej
Skolevej
Kirkegårdsvej
1 Sports Stadium
2 Laundry (2nd block, downstairs)
3 Hospital
4 Laundry (downstairs)
5 Nanoq Restaurant
6 Taxi
7 Banks
8 New Church
9 Brugsen Supermarket
10 Post Office
11 Skipperkroen Pub
12 Seamen's Home
13 Youth Hostel
14 Museum
15 Hotel & Restaurant
16 Tourist Office
17 Old Church
18 Fountain & KNI Supermarket
19 Police
20 KNI Booking Office
21 Radio Ras
22 Ferry Dock
23 Tannery
24 Heliport

Greenlandic construction. In the early 1800s when Denmark was at war with France, the government could hardly be bothered with pleas for a church from a such a backwater post as Julianehåb. The Danish Missionary Society, however, succeeded in collecting private funds for the construction. It was prefabricated in Norway in 1826 and shipped off 2 years later. Unfortunately, the ship was wrecked at Paamiut (Frederikshåb) and it was 1932 before the salvaged timber was finally erected on its current site.

Inside you can see a life preserver from the passenger ship *Hans Hedtoft* which hit an iceberg off Cape Farewell in 1959 and sank with no survivors. On the flower-filled lawn between the church and the old white bridge is a monument to the 'Greenland Apostle' Hans Egede and his wife Gertrude Rask, who established the first Christian mission in Greenland near Nuuk in 1721.

If you want to have a look inside the church, you have to visit the priest at the new church (on the hill) between 10 am and noon weekdays. He has a key and will arrange a look around. While you're up there anyway, note the nice altarpiece in the new church.

Tannery The Kalaallit Nunaata Ammerivia tannery, between the harbour and the heliport, turns seals into fur coats and is one of Qaqortoq's economic mainstays. Tours can be arranged at the office if you're interested in the tanning process. Whether you approve of the concept or not (in Qaqortoq, you'd best appear to approve), the furs are quite beautiful but you'll be astounded by the numbers we're talking about here. For what it's worth, most of the seals are sold to the tannery by local people who shoot them for food. The polar-bear rugs produced here seem to be another story, however. Finished products are sold at the tourist office's souvenir shop.

Fountain No discussion of Qaqortoq would be complete without a mention of its fountain which, the locals are proud to point out, is the only one in Greenland. They've started engraving the names of prominent Greenlanders in its Igaliko-sandstone base but they haven't managed to fill it up yet.

KNI Office The wonderful blacktarred log building on the harbourfront was designed by the Danish Royal Architect Kirkerup and constructed in 1797 as the residence of the colonial overseer. It is now used as the KNI office.

Harbour The busy and colourful harbour is an attraction in itself. You'll find examples of anything from trawlers to derelicts to yachts moored there. Even the odd iceberg finds its way in; when I was last there, something that looked exactly like the Sydney Opera House drifted and in bottomed out. It stayed around until an unusually high tide carried it away. Expect to take lots of good, bright photos.

Taxi Office The little building which now houses the taxi office once was the public baths. It was built in 1929 of Igaliko sandstone.

City Tour

Arctic Adventure offers a 4-hour guided city tour for US$21.50 including lunch. It visits the museum, the tannery, and the fish market as well as the harbour and some of the interesting old buildings around town. The tourist office or the Hotel Qaqortoq can help with bookings and information.

Places to Stay

The up-market hotel is the *Hotel Qaqortoq* (tel 38505), a new and sparkling place that overlooks the harbour. It's architecturally one of Greenland's more interesting hotels. Singles/doubles with bath cost US$97/130.

Moving down the scale one notch, we have the *Seamen's Home* (tel 38239), the green building about midway up the hill from the harbour. For a single room with/without bath, the charge is US$57/47. Doubles cost US$72 with private bath. Potential guests should be warned that like in most seamen's homes, they're a bit over the top with the religion.

The *Youth Hostel* (tel 38444, after hours 38647) in Qaqortoq is exceptionally clean and in a beautiful location, at the foot of a waterfall which does its best to lull you to sleep at night. The hostel isn't normally attended so you have to book through the tourist office. One of their representatives normally meets incoming ferries and helicopters to fetch those who've pre-booked or to offer a lift to travellers who appear to be lost. If no one is there, stop at the tourist office to pick up a key before climbing the hill. Dorm rooms cost US$13.

Places to Eat

Those who are due for a bit of expensive elegance should splurge at the excellent hotel restaurant. You can enjoy the service and fine dining topped off with a broad glassy vista across the harbour, the iceberg studded fjord, and the distant snowy peaks. Meal prices begin at about US$25 (not including drinks or salads) and rocket straight into the ozone from there. If you're not staying at the hotel reservations (tel 38282) are recommended; wear something presentable.The restaurant is open for lunch from 11.30 am to 2 pm and for dinner from 5 to 8.30 pm. The hotel pub, if rather elegant, is a cosy candlelit up-market place.

Another option is the cafeteria at the *Seamen's Home*. It's open Monday to Friday from 7 am to 7 pm and on Sundays from 8 am to 7 pm. It's inexpensive and not too bad quality-wise.

The third restaurant is *Nanoq* which serves good meals but is best known for its pub. Another pub is the *Skipperkroen*, both pubs are popular with locals.

The old stand-by *Grill-Baren* near the fountain offers the usual hamburgers, chips, ice cream, and the like.

There are two supermarkets in Qaqortoq and one, the *Brugsen*, is an immense place stocked with anything and everything your palette could dream of. I just about fell over when I saw watermelons and pineapples. They also have an extensive bottle shop and French cabernet sells for as little as US$6 per litre bottle. The bakery which offers a wide variety of fresh bread, doughnuts, and pastries is near the fountain. Fresh fish and sometimes whale and seal are available at the harbour market.

If you're arriving late on the boat, there's a convenience shop which stays open until 8 pm, on Nipinngaaq uphill north of the centre.

Walks

The tourist office has a list of day-walks which may be done from town but, for all but the crash hottest trekkers, many of the times are underestimated. The DVL-Rejser walking map is essential for any trekking in the area. Refer to the map in this book only for basic routes.

The quickest walk is up to 220-metre Peters Varde or 'Peter's cairn', most easily reached by going up the ravine with the waterfall, behind the youth hostel. Other day-walks include the 4-hour circuit of the 'big lake' Taserssuaq. From the northern end, it's also possible to walk another 2 hours or so down to Eqaluit ('salmon') Bay on Kangerdluarsuk Fjord. Other options include the 4-hour return climb to 412-metre Størefjeld and the 3-hour return climb to the parabolic dish on Harefjeld.

A longer hike is westward along the shore of Taserssuaq to the end of the track, then west over the pass and down to the shore of Munkebugt. Follow the shore to the north-west end of the bay then climb the stream up a steep ravine to its source in a small pond. At this point, you can continue on up to the summit of 418-metre Nordfjeld, then descend its eastern slope to the northern end of Taserssuaq from where you can choose either the eastern or western shore-route back to town. This walk will require a minimum of 6 hours to complete.

For other walking possibilities, refer to the description of the Qaqortoq to Igaliko route.

Getting There & Away

Air From Qaqortoq, you can take a helicopter to Nanortalik, Narsaq, and Narsarsuaq. For information on fares and flight frequency, refer to the Getting There & Away section of your destination city.

Ferry To and from Narsaq, both the *Aleqa Ittuk* and the *Taterak* do three runs per week. Between Qaqortoq and Narsarsuaq, the *Taterak* goes twice and, to Nanortalik, both ferries do one trip each. The fare to Narsaq is US$15.50, to Narsarsuaq it's US$28, and to Nanortalik, you'll pay US$36 each way.

Once every 2 weeks, the *Disko*'s departure for Upernavik is cause for much pomp and fanfare on the docks. Even if you're not travelling, it's fun to join in as the locals gather to send it off.

Getting Around

Yes, Qaqortoq deems itself big enough to warrant a city bus system. It consists of a passenger van with bank advertising painted on the side which runs across town approximately every half- hour.

AROUND QAQORTOQ

Qaqortoq to Igaliko Walk

The 6-day trek from Qaqortoq to Igaliko, one of the two premier walks in Greenland, offers a combination of Norse history and wonderful scenery. Depite that, however, it's not easy.

The trek begins at the end of Qaava street in Qaqortoq, crosses a low pass, and then follows an arm of Julianchåbs Fjord along the shore past a grotty sheep hut (use it for accommodation only in an emergency) to a narrow isthmus with a lovely lake in the middle. This is a common first-night camping site. This is about as far as it would be possible to go in a long day-hike from Qaqortoq but plan on 12 hours or so for the return trip. (Unless you're Reinhold Messner, don't believe anyone who tells you it's possible to reach Hvalsey from Qaqortoq in a single day. Although the long hours of daylight would make it logistically possible, it would be a miserably long slog.)

To continue, walk along Tartoq, a lovely bay surrounded by peaks with a waterfall at the northern end. The route along Tartoq is steep, bouldery, and often covered with foot-entangling vegetation. It's slow-going and you'll be relieved to get up onto the pass which is rather easy walking. Unfortunately, past there the way gets worse and going on to Hvalsey ruins involves a steep climb through boulders and dense vegetation over a 350-metre pass, then down to the mouth of a nameless river that will get you good and wet if the water is high. From the river, it's an hour along a steep and difficult stretch of coast to the ruins. If you camp at Hvalsey, you must do so outside the fence.

The rest of the trip to Igaliko is a bit easier although it still involves some serious climbs and some problematic boulder fields. Follow the shore past the Qaqortoq sheep stations and along Tasiussaq lake, then up the valley at its head. From there, it's a matter of 3 or 4 days picking your way over the tundra moors and hills to Igaliko. Some suggested camping sites are marked on the map.

Hvalsey

Known to Greenlanders as Qaqortukulooq, the Hvalsey ruins are the most extensive and best preserved Norse ruins in Greenland. They lie on a level coastal strip at the head of Hvalsey Fjord, named after the 'whale island' in the middle of it. The well-preserved ruins today sit alone and abandoned in the wilderness at the foot of Mt Qaqortoq. For most visitors, they elicit a sense of timeless awe that defies description.

Although Hvalsey was first inhabited in the late 10th century, the church, which was constructed of hewn granite and lime mortar, was probably one of the last built during the Norse period. It measures 16 metres by 8 metres at the base. The church and nearby manor farm, which oversaw about 30 smaller farms in the district were first mentioned in the Icelandic annals the *Flateyjarbók*, written around 1390. Although tithes for the entire district would have been paid to the Hvalsey church, there's no evidence of a warehouse for storage of agricultural produce. A great hall, a dwelling, several barns and byres, and burial sites have all been excavated nearby.

In the early 15th century, two notable events were recorded at Hvalsey. The first was the burning at the stake in 1507 of a resident named Kolgrim. He was convicted of using sorcery to seduce Steinum, the wife of Thorgrim Søløveson and daughter of the sheriff, Hrafn. According to the annals, Steinum later went mad and died at an early age.

The second event, which was special because it was the last reference to the Norse colony before it vanished, was the wedding on (14 September 1408) of the prominent Icelander Þórstein Ólafsson of Skagafjórður and Greenlander, Sigrid Bjórnsdóttir. The ecumenical records explain that the ceremony took place over three Sundays with two priests officiating. Greenland colonists as well as many foreigners attended.

Those who'd like to read the complete scoop on Hvalsey should pick up a copy of *Hvalsø – the Church and the Magnate's Farm* by Joel Berglund, which is available at the Qaqortoq tourist office souvenir shop in English, Danish, and Greenlandic for US$6.

Upernaviarsuk Research Station

Agriculture fans will probably consider Upernaviarsuk a must to visit. It's an experimental research station dedicated to coaxing

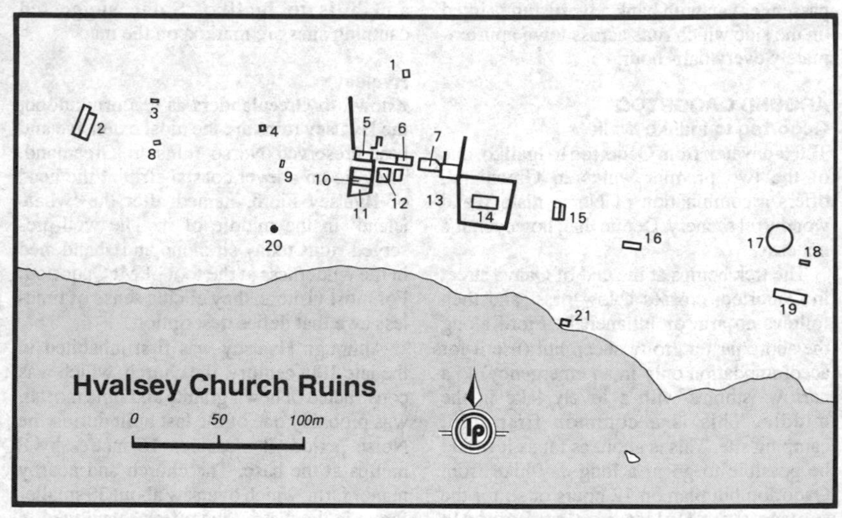

1 Storehouse
2 Byre and Barn
3 Outbuilding
4 Sheep shed*
5 The Great Hall
6 Storeroom
7 The Old Hall
8 Sheep shed*
9 Outbuilding
10 Pantry
11 Kitchen
12 Bedroom
13 Byre and Barn
14 Church
15 Sheep shed
16 Livestock Building*
17 Horse Fold
18 Gravesite*
19 Livestock Building*
20 Well
21 Storehouse

*Possible functions

the Arctic into agricultural productivity. They're also hoping to come up with a strain of sheep that will be able to withstand even the harshest climatic conditions.

Tours The Qaqortoq tourist office offers boat tours to the Hvalsey ruins and Upernaviarsuk Research Station when demand dictates. They most often go on Sundays and cost approximately US$46 for the day-trip.

Arctic Adventure also offers an à la carte tour for US$61 which includes a packed lunch. Enquiries can be made at the tourist office or the Hotel Qaqortoq.

IGALIKO (GARDAR)

The standard tourist brochure photo of Igaliko (pronounced 'ee-GOLLY-co'), portraying hayfields and a hay-raking farmer, wants you to believe that agriculture is thriving in Greenland. This tiny village with 52 residents, near the head of Igaliko Fjord, was established in 1126 as Gardar the episcopal seat of Norse Greenland, home of the bishops. In a grave which was excavated in 1926, archaeologists have found the skeleton of Bishop Jón Smyril, who was wearing an episcopal ring and holding a crosier or bishop's staff.

The present church at Igaliko is very nice, constructed of unique and seemingly edible Igaliko sandstone. The village economy today relies on sheep breeding.

St Nicolai Cathedral

Although it was once an imposing structure, to call this pathetic ruin a cathedral is really stretching the word to its limit. All that remains of the foundation, which measures 16 metres by 27 metres, are a few sandstone boulders which appear to be vaguely artificial, the result of dismantling the cathedral's building materials for more practical uses such as homes and sheds.

The cathedral was dedicated to St Nicolai, the patron saint of the seafarer and, by Greenlandic standards, it was elaborate. It's windows were of rough glass rather than stretched animal stomachs. There was a large bell to call the faithful to worship and soapstone carvings of religious themes decorating the interior. Under the church were found 25 walrus skulls and beneath the chancel were five narwhal skulls. It is believed that their significance probably dates back to pre-Christian times.

Around the church perimeter, there's also evidence of the wealthy church farms with their large byres and storehouses, a great hall for social and ecumenical events, and an elaborate irrigation system. Without a guide, little of this will be obvious.

Places to Stay & Eat

There's no hotel at Igaliko but you will find sheep-hut accommodation which is loosely described as a youth hostel. It costs only US$11 per night for basic sleeping-bag accommodation but it's best to book through a tourist office if you want to be assured of a place. The settlement also has a tiny cafeteria where you can buy snacks.

Getting There & Away

Most visitors arrive by boat at Itivdleq on Tunugdliarfik (Eiriks) Fjord, and walk the 3 km across the peninsula along the Kongevejen or 'King's Road' to Igaliko on Igaliko (Einars) Fjord. For the less energetic, you can arrange a ride from Itivdleq with a local farmer or take the infrequent ferry all the way around the peninsula to the landing in Igaliko. For those on the opposite end of the motivation spectrum, it's possible to walk from Qaqortoq to Igaliko in 6 days. For more information on this walk, refer to the Qaqortoq section.

The ferry *Aleqa Ittuk* runs between Qaqortoq and Igaliko once weekly. The *Taterak* sails between Qaqortoq and Narsarsuaq via Narsaq, Itilleq, and Qagssiarsuk twice weekly in either direction.

VATNAHVERFI DISTRICT

The Vatnahverfi district is a remote region of lakes, moors, and peaks between Igaliko Fjord and Alluitsup (Lichtenau) Fjord. This was a region heavily settled by the early Norse and it is dotted throughout with unexcavated ruins of sheep farms and dwellings. The lakes are full of trout and char. This would be an excellent destination for experienced trekkers with plenty of time who'd like to explore some wilderness.

Walks

The most popular route in the Vatnahverfi district begins or ends at Igaliko Kujalleq (Undir Høfdi or Søndre Igaliko), a tiny sheep station and Norse church ruin on the Kujalleq arm of Igaliko Fjord and Alluitsup Paa (Sydprøven) at the mouth of Alluitsup Fjord. Igaliko Kujalleq offers sheep-hut accommodation for US$11.50 per night. The most popular route is to or from Alluitsup Paa.

Since only the northernmost end of this trip appears on the DVL-Rejser walking map, you'll have to purchase the smaller scale and less suitable *Nanortalik 1:250,000* series sheet for this trip. It will be available from the tourist offices in Qaqortoq and Nanortalik. The map included in this book is to be used as a route guide only, since no suggested routes appear on the topo sheet or the walking map. A number of other walks in the Vatnahverfi district are outlined in the book, *Trekking in Greenland*, described in the Books & Bookshops section of the Greenland Facts for the Visitor chapter.

Qorlortorsuaq Greenland's largest waterfall, Qorlortorsuaq ('big waterfall') is 75 metres high. It's found between the uppermost arm of Alluitsup Fjord and the large lake Qordlortorsuk Tasia. It's a 5-km-return side trip off the route from Alluitsup Paa to Igaliko Kujalleq.

Getting There & Away

In order to reach the southern end of the Vatnahverfi walk, refer to the Alluitsup Paa Getting There & Away section. Getting to Igaliko Kujalleq can be a bit more tricky and, for that reason, most people who do the walk prefer to take it from north to south. The recommended access to Igaliko Kujalleq is to walk from Igaliko (for information on getting to Igaliko refer to the Igaliko section) to Iterdlaq and then try to privately arrange a boat trip across Kujalleq, a small arm of Igaliko Fjord. Another possibility is to arrange a boat all the way from Igaliko itself but either option can get expensive unless your charisma and bargaining skills are well-honed. Smile a lot.

If you'd rather do the shorter walk to Tasiluq, you'll have to pre-arrange transport from there back to Qaqortoq with the Qaqortoq Turistforening and of course, be sure to turn up at Tasiluq at the specified time.

For those who'd rather skip the boat ride across the Kujalleq arm there's meant to be a route from Iterdlaq up the valley Inorquaqssaap Quua to the glacier tongue Jesperson's Brae, going steeply down to another glacier, and back along the braided stream to Igaliko Kujalleq. I don't have any information on this walk, however, and haven't met anyone who's done it but it appears to be very tricky if the contour lines on the map are any indication. Don't attempt it without first seeking local advice.

ALLUITSUP PAA (SYDPRØVEN)

The village of Alluitsup Paa lies colourfully prominent on the end of the peninsula at the mouth of Alluitsup Fjord. Those who don't have time to travel further south into the magnificent country of the Nunaat Isua (Cape Farewell) region can get a tempting taste of it here. The village itself is also quite picturesque.

Alluitsup (Lichtenau)

The village of Alluitsup, originally called Lichtenau or 'light meadow', was founded in 1774 as a Moravian mission. It was the birthplace of Samuel Kleinschmidt who set up a similar mission at Nuuk and produced the first Greenlandic translation of the Bible. The settlement is now home to just a few families and serves as a YMCA camp. It's along the walking route to Søndre Igaliko, just a pleasant 5-km walk up the coast north of Alluitsup Paa.

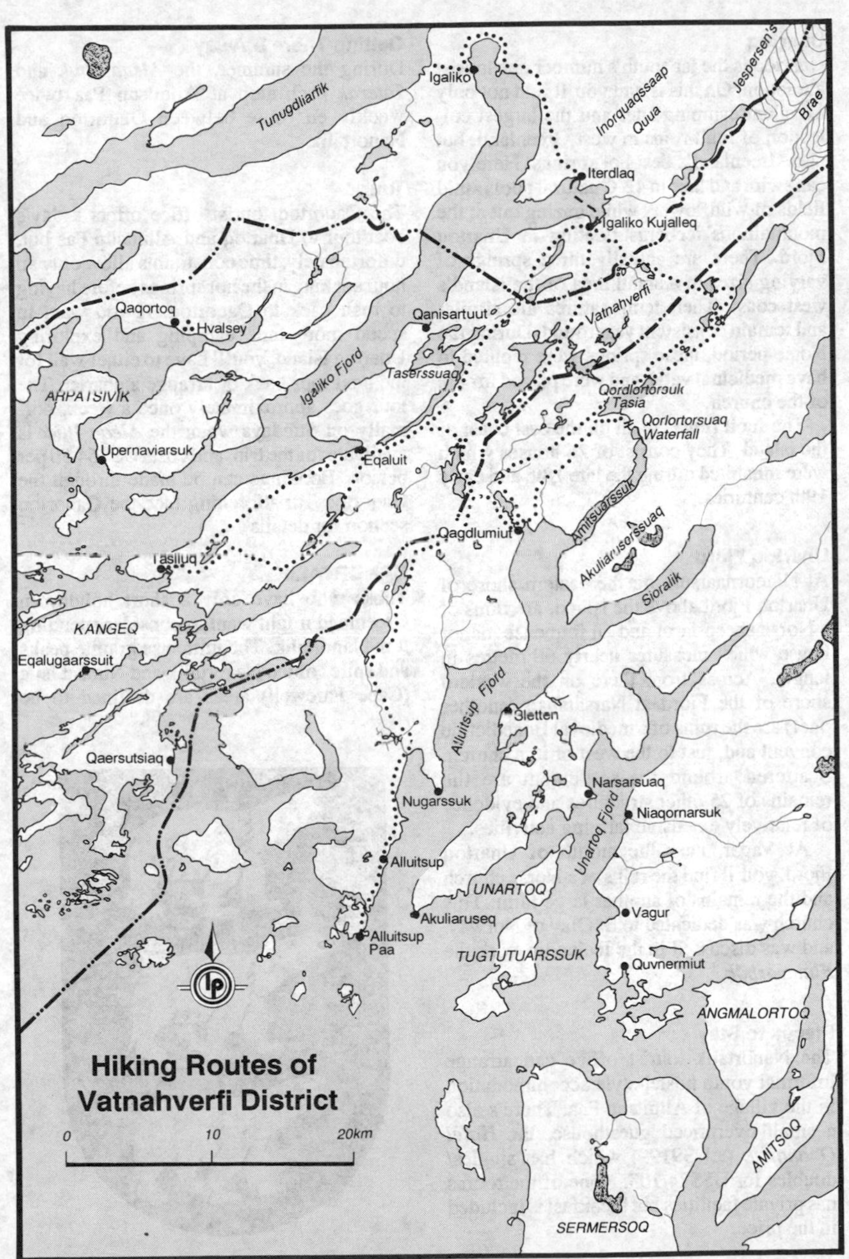
Igaliko
Tunugdliarfik
Inorquaqssaap
Quua
Jespersen's
Brae
Iterdlaq
Igaliko Kujalleq
Vatnahverfi
Qaqortoq
Hvalsey
Qanisartuut
Igaliko Fjord
Taserssuaq
ARPATSIVIK
Qorlortorsuk
Tasia
Qorlortorsuaq
Waterfall
Upernaviarsuk
Eqaluit
Amitsuarssuk
Akuliarusorssuaq
Qagdlumiut
Tasiluq
Sioralik
KANGEQ
Eqalugaarssuit
Alluitsup Fjord
Sletten
Qaersutsiaq
Narsarsuaq
Nugarssuk
Unartoq Fjord
Niaqornarsuk
Alluitsup
UNARTOQ
Akuliaruseq
Vagur
Alluitsup
Paa
TUGTUTUARSSUK
Quvnermiut
ANGMALORTOQ
Hiking Routes of
Vatnahverfi District
0
10
20km
AMITSOQ
SERMERSOQ

Unartoq

Unartoq is the far south's number one tourist attraction. On this island you'll find not only excellent camping sites and the largest collection of Inuit ruins in west Greenland, but also Greenland's best hot springs. Here you can swim and laze in 42°C natural pools amid fields of wildflowers while gazing out at the mountainous icebergs floating in Unartoq Fjord. There are actually three springs of varying sizes in a small area of the island's west coast. Their temperatures are similar and remain consistent year round. During the Norse period, these springs were reputed to have medicinal value and were placed in care of the church.

The Inuit ruins are all on the east coast of the island. They consist of 26 houses which were inhabited during the late 18th and early 19th centuries.

Unartoq Fjord

At Niaqornaarsuk, on the eastern shore of Unartoq Fjord above the island, are ruins of a Norse sheep farm and an immense manor house which measures nearly 60 metres in length. Across from there on the western shore of the Fjord at Narsarsuaq (another one!) are the ruins of a medieval Benedictine convent and, just to the west of it, a church. Scattered around the settlement are the remains of 25 other structures and evidence of relatively extensive farming activities.

At Vagar, near the mouth of Unartoq Fjord, you'll find the ruins of a Norse church and the remains of another large farm. This church was dedicated to St Olav of Norway, and was discussed in the Icelandic work the *Flateyarbók*.

Places to Stay

The Nanortalik tourist office can arrange informal youth hostel-style accommodation in the village of Alluitsup Paa. There's also a small overpriced guesthouse, the *Hotel Qaannivik* (tel 39199) which has singles/doubles for US$74/103. None of the rooms has private facilities but breakfast is included in the price.

Getting There & Away

During the summer, the *Aleqa Ittuk* and *Taterak* each stop at Alluitsup Paa twice weekly en route between Qaqortoq and Nanortalik.

Tour

The Qaqortoq tourist office offers a day's boat tour to Unartoq and Alluitsup Paa but, unfortunately, time constraints allow only an hour soaking in the hot springs before having to rush back to Qaqortoq. If you want to spend more time camping and exploring Unartoq Island, you'll have to either wait for the next tour back or arrange a charter. The tour goes approximately once a week, normally on Sundays when the *Aleqa Ittuk* is available for the trip, and costs US$64.50 per person. Bookings can be made through the Qaqortoq Turistforening (see the Qaqortoq section for details).

NANORTALIK

Those who have only a short holiday in Greenland might want to consider spending it in Nanortalik. The immense granite peaks and spires of the Nanortalik and Nunaat Isua (Cape Farewell) areas are destined to be

compared with those of Chilean Patagonia or Yosemite. Even comparisons fall short, however; this is a most spectacular place.

The name of this town with 1550 residents means, loosely translated, 'bear country'. Bears should be warned, however, that they are not welcome and any which inadvertantly wander into town won't be tolerated longer than it takes someone to grab a rifle.

Nanortalik prides itself on being the southernmost town in Greenland. It was originally founded at nearby Sigssaritoq as a trading and supply depot for Cape Farewell area communities in 1797 and was moved south-west to its current location in 1830. Although it remains off the beaten track, it should become more popular as scenery-inspired travellers discover what it has to offer.

Information

The tourist information office (tel 33398) in Nanortalik is one of the best in Greenland and, because so few travellers make it to Nanortalik, they always have time to help. You'll find them in the little office between the old harbour and the church. The person to contact is Rene Nielsen at Nanortalik Turistforening, PO Box 13, DK-3922 Nanortalik, Greenland. It's open Monday to Friday from 9 am to 5.30 pm. On weekends, ring (tel 33470) for information.

Old Harbour

The old harbour area of Nanortalik is too picturesque to be real. It resembles the archetypal New England fishing village that's been reconstructed as an artificial movie-set complete with a painted backdrop. Most of the historical buildings in the area are constructed of stone and heavy timber and date back to the 19th century. It's pleasant to stroll around at different times of the day and appreciate the hour-to-hour changes in the tide and the odd Arctic light.

Museum

The town museum, is housed in several historical buildings of the Royal Greenland Trade Department. There are many tupilaqs and photos of historical Nanortalik and some interesting old qajaqs and relics from the Greenlandic past. It's open on Wednesdays and Friday to Sunday from 2 to 4 pm.

Sod House

There's a traditional old sod house being restored just west of the old harbour area. It's intended to give visitors insight into the Greenlandic lifestyle that existed before the Danish transplanted modern Europe onto the island. Ask at the tourist office and they'll unlock the house and explain things for you.

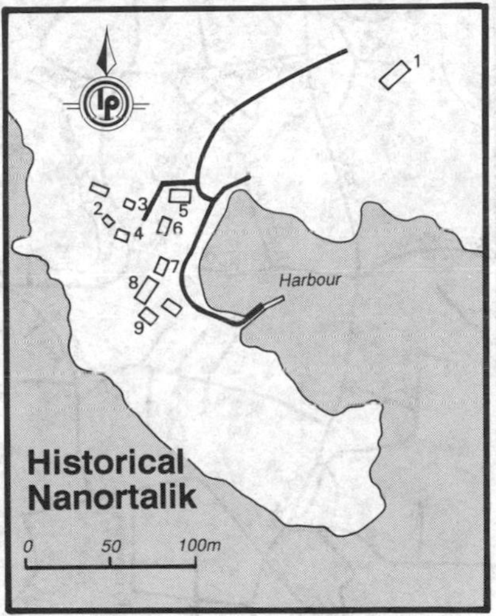

1 Timber church (1913) designed and built by Greenlandic Architect and master builder Pavia Høegh
2 Stable (1840)
3 Personnel House (1840)
4 Cooperage (1852)
5 Manager's Dwelling (1904)
6 Outlying dwelling (1820), local museum since 1982
7 General Store (1897)
8 Blubber House (1852)
9 Oil-Boiling House (1839)

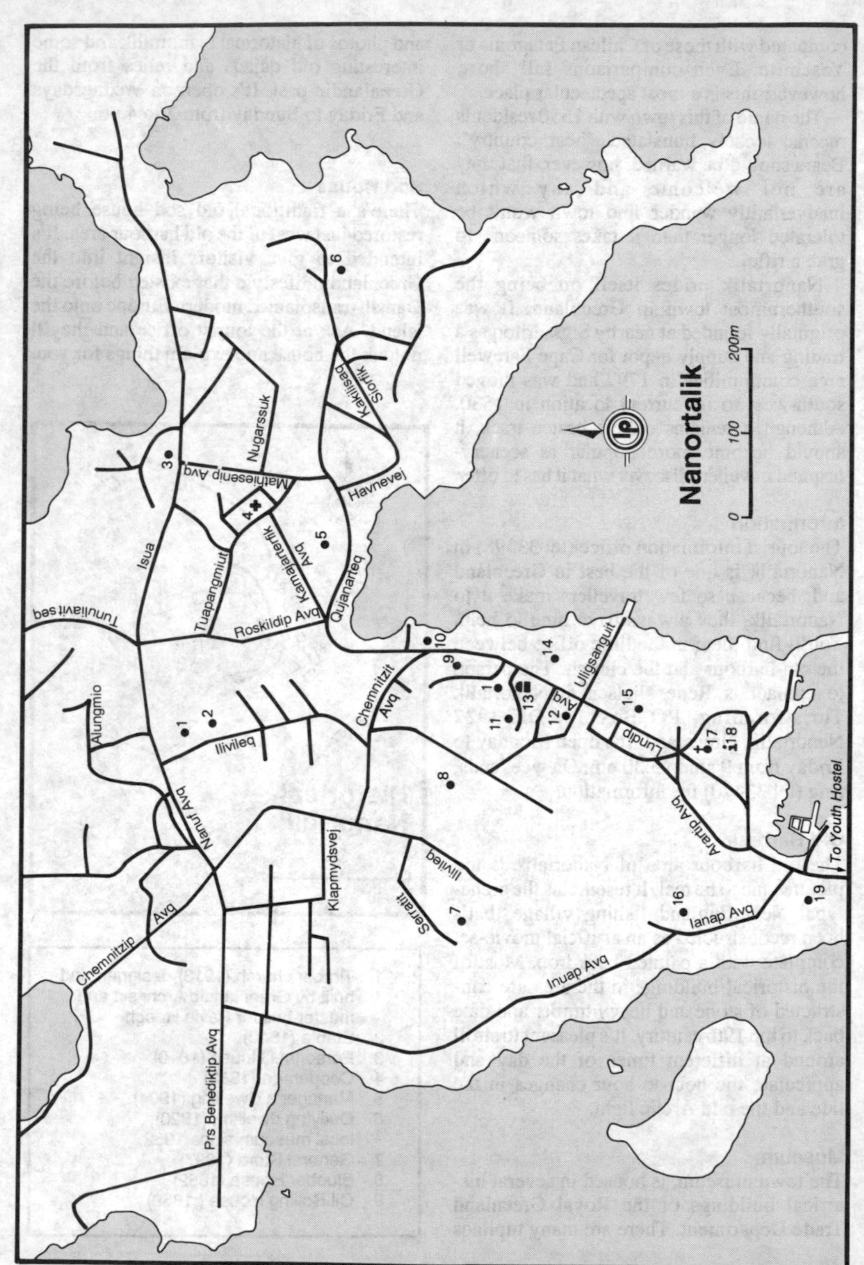
Nanortalik
0
100
200m
To Youth Hostel
Chemnitzip Avq
Prs Benediktip Avq
Naruf Avq
Alungmio
Ilivileq
Klapmydsvej
Serratit
Inuap Avq
Ianap Avq
Aratip Avq
Lundip
Uuligssanguit
Chemnitzit Avq
Tunuliavitseq
Isua
Tuapangmiut
Roskildip Avq
Qujanarteq
Kamajartefik Avq
Mathieseniip Avq
Nugarssuk
Havnevej
Kakilisaq
Sioriffik

1 KNI Stores
2 Nan-Grill
3 Hotel Kap Farvel
4 Hospital
5 Nanortalik Fish Plant
6 Heliport
7 Telephone Office
8 School
9 Hotel Tupilaq
10 Fish Market
11 City Offices
12 Brugsen Supermarket
13 Post Office
14 Bank & KNI Office
15 Police
16 Traditional Sod House
17 Church
18 Tourist Office
19 Museum

Knud Rasmussen's Face
This large boulder near the church was once called simply 'the Face' but, since Knud Rasmussen became a national hero, the locals decided that it looked an awful lot like him.

Places to Stay
There are two hotels in Nanortalik. One option is the *Hotel Kap Farvel* (tel 3294), a rather grotty little place that charges singles/doubles US$47/57 without attached bath, but including breakfast. Non-guests can use the showers for US$3. Meals are also available in the reasonably pleasant little coffee shop-cum-diningroom.

The *Hotel Tupilaq* (tel 33379), serves as a disco and place for festivities Monday to Thursday from 6 pm to midnight and on Fridays and Saturdays from 6 pm to 1 am. If you'd rather not participate in that action, there's a TV room, a video machine, and a sauna. Singles/doubles cost US$50/71, including breakfast. There are no private baths available. Incidentally, they also sell tupilaqs on the side.

Not surprisingly, Nanortalik also has a *Youth Hostel*. This one is in a cosy little house between the old harbour and the sea. It's a perfect retreat for a few days just enjoying the magical surroundings. Bookings should be made through the Nanortalik tourist office. Dormitory beds cost US$13 per night and cooking facilities are available. If you book in advance, they'll be pleased to come and fetch you at the heliport or ferry landing.

Places to Eat
Both hotels offer proper meals for similar prices but each meal is available for only 2 hours so don't miss it. The Hotel Tupilaq prefers that guests book their meals in advance.

The *Grill-Baren* offers snacks, sausages, sandwiches, and soft drinks. The small KNI affiliate just uphill from it has a pretty good range of groceries and is open until 9 pm.

The village has both KNI and Brugsen stores. The fish market at the new harbour sells whale, seal, and whatever's brought in with the catch of the day. The bakery is inside the Brugsen supermarket opposite the ferry landing.

Getting There & Away
Air You will probably notice that Nanortalik is often plagued by fog which rolls in without warning and engulfs everything in cream of mushroom soup causing frequent delays in helicopter schedules. For what it's worth, if you're going to or from Narsarsuaq, Narsaq, or Qaqortoq, there's a chance you'll be able to make the trip on any day but Sunday. The fares to those towns, respectively, are US$113, US$104, and US$89.

Ferry From Qaqortoq, the *Taterak* goes once a week to and from Narsaq Kujalleq and Augpilaqtoq via Nanortalik. The *Aleqa Ittuk* also does one run per week via the small villages of Ammassivik, Alluitsup Paa, Saarloq, and Eqalugaarsuit. This is a rather long ride, 12 hours each way, but the scenery is good. If they're not obscured by fog, notice the magnificent granite cliffs and spires on Sermersoq Island as you pass. The fare from Qaqortoq is US$36.

AROUND NANORTALIK

Nanortalik Island

There are lots of day-walks around Nanortalik Island which range from a pleasant stroll to a climb of several hours. There are a number of old stone ruins, both Inuit and early Norse, and the site of Sigssaritoq or 'old' Nanortalik. On the way down the coast, look for an odd pillar-like stone standing in a field. This is said to be the 'bear stone', an old lintel used by an Inuit boy for tying up his pet polar bear.

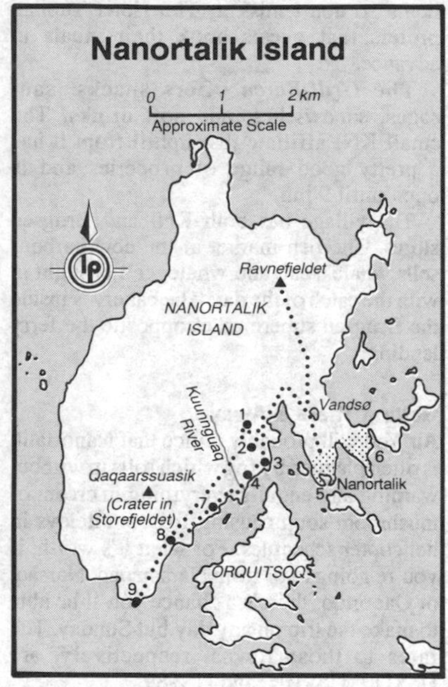

1 Nassiffik (Old Inuit Ruins & Graves)
2 Winter Provisions Cache
3 The Bear Stone
4 Norse Ruins
5 Old Harbour
6 Beach (good fishing)
7 Sigssaritoq (Old Nanortalik)
8 Pukitsit (Small Hut Ruins & Winter Provisioning Grounds)
9 Erliva Beach (good fishing)

Other longer and more challenging walks include climbs up 308-metre Ravnefjeldet ('ravens mountain') on the north end of the island or 559-metre Qaqaarssuasik, a crater peak on the island's southern end.

Tasermiut Fjord

Another wonder of far southern Greenland is the narrow 75-km-long Tasermiut Fjord which winds its way north-east from Nanortalik and ends at the face of the tide-water glacier Tasermiut spilling down from the inland ice.

Tasiussaq Tasiussaq, the village above Nanortalik on Tasermiut Fjord, can be reached by mailboat several days a week and is the logical jumping-off point for trekking trips deeper into the Tasermiut Fjord area. Youth-hostel style accommodation can be arranged through the Nanortalik tourist office but, given the rather volatile nature of the village, it's probably best to either camp in the bush or wander the relatively easy 6 km up to the hut just below the lake Taserssuaq.

The more energetic can charter a boat from Nanortalik across the north of Tasermiut Fjord to Jakobinerhven and then follow the coastline northward to Tasiussaq, a walk which will require a minimum of 2 days.

Qinguadalen Six hours walking up the valley north-east of Tasiussaq will bring you to Qinguadalen, loudly acclaimed as Greenland's only forest. This awesome arboreal fecundity boasts *trees* up to 3 metres high. If that isn't exciting enough to warrant a 12-hour return hike, prepare yourself for some of the most stunning vertical granite formations on earth as a backdrop.

Klosterdalen Base Camp Also known as Uiluit Quua, the site called Base Camp lies about 14 km from the glacier face at the head of Tasermiut Fjord. Those magnificent scenes with tents beneath soaring granite

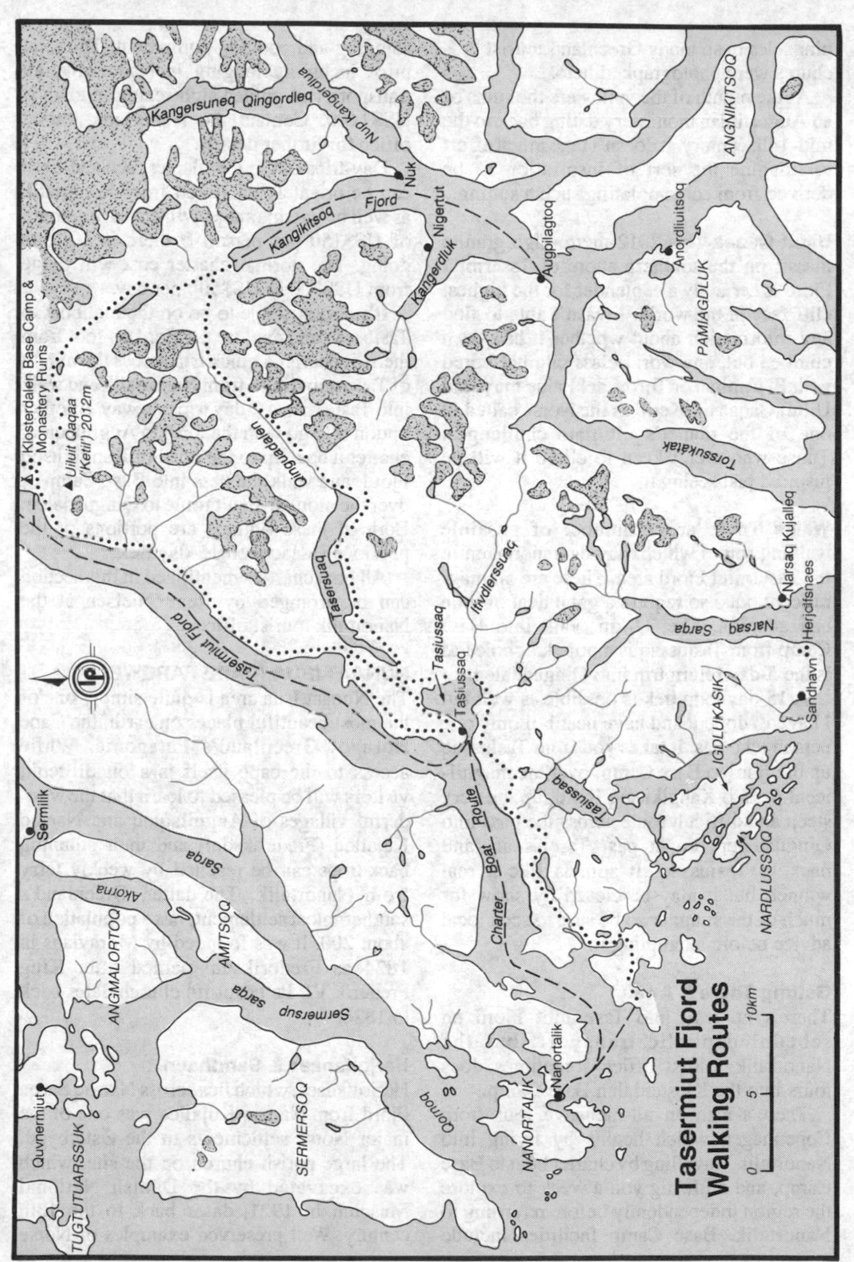
Tasermiut Fjord
Walking Routes
0
5
10km
Klosterdalen Base Camp &
Monastery Ruins
Uiluit Qaqaa
("Ketil") 2012m
Kangersuneq Qingordleq
Nup Kangerdlua
Nuk
Kangikitsoq Fjord
Nigertut
Kangerdluk
Augpilagtoq
Anordliuitsoq
ANGNIKITSOQ
PAMIAGDLUK
Torssukatak
Narsaq Kujalleq
Narsaq Sarqa
Herjolfsnaes
Sandhavn
IGDLUKASIK
NARDLUSSOQ
Qinguadalen
Tasersuaq
Itivdlerssuaq
Tasiussaq
Tasiussaq
Tasiussaq
Tasermiut Fjord
Charter Boat Route
Sermilik
Sarqa
Akorna
ANGMALORTOQ
AMITSOQ
Sermersup sarqa
Quvnermiut
TUGTUTUARSSUK
SERMERSOQ
Qornoq
NANORTALIK
Nanortalik

pinnacles in so many Greenland tourist brochures were photographed here.

At the mouth of the valley are the ruins of an Augustinian monastery dating back to the mid-14th century. It doesn't take much effort to imagine the sort of inspiration to be derived from contemplating such a setting.

Uiluit Qaqaa This 2012-metre-high granite massif on the southern shore of Tasermiut Fjord is certainly a contender for the highest cliff face in the world. I wasn't able to find any information about whether it had been climbed but, any world-class climber bored with El Capitan or Torres del Paine may find Uiluit Qaqaa or 'Ketil' as the Norse called it, one of the planet's ultimate challenges. Those who aren't keen to climb it will be inspired just seeing it.

Walks There are a number of possible walking routes which may be undertaken in the Tasermiut Fjord area. These are all magnificent but also require a great deal of time and stamina. The 37-km walk into Base Camp from Tasiussaq is a popular choice as is the 5-day return trip into Qinguadalen.

A 15-day loop trek is possible as well but I haven't done it and have heard of only one person who has. It takes you from Tasiussaq up the fjord to Base Camp, over the magnificent pass to Kangikitsoq Fjord, up the very steep and difficult route across the pass into Qinguadalen, down past Taserssuaq, and back to Tasiussaq. It sounds like a real winner, but it may be closed by snow for much of the summer so be sure to seek local advice before attempting it.

Getting There & Away

There's no way into Tasermiut Fjord on scheduled public transport, but the Nanortalik tourist office sometimes does tours into the Klosterdalen Base Camp.

There's also an all-inclusive tour from Copenhagen which begins by flying into Nanortalik, travelling by charter boat to Base Camp, and allowing you a week to explore the region independently before returning to Nanortalik. Base Camp facilities include camping and cooking equipment. The total price including lodging in Nanortalik, all transport, and guided sightseeing in town is US$1400. Contact the Nanortalik tourist office for further details.

Day-trips out to the glacier face and back can be privately chartered from Nanortalik as well but, at this stage, will cost a minimum of US$150 per person *if* there is a group going. The normal charter cost will range from US$300 to US$500 per day.

It's also possible to go on the mailboat to Tasiussaq and explore the fjord on foot from there or charter a quick trip across the mouth of Tasermiut Fjord from Nanortalik and walk into Tasiussaq, a 2-day trip one way. Another option is to go with the ferry to Augpilaqtoq, charter a boat up to the head of Kangikitsoq Fjord, and walk the pass into Base Camp or over the more difficult route to Qinguadalen. Both of these options are portions of the previously described 15-day trek.

All boat charters mentioned in this section can be arranged by Rene Nielsen at the Nanortalik tourist office.

NUNAAT ISUA (CAPE FAREWELL)

The Nunaat Isua area is quite simply one of the most beautiful places on earth, the Cape Horn of Greenland's Patagonia. While access to the cape itself is a bit difficult, visitors will be pleased to learn that the wonderful villages of Augpilaqtoq and Narsaq Kujalleq (Frederiksdal) and their stunning backdrops can be reached by weekly ferry from Nanortalik. The latter, Greenland's southernmost settlement, has a population of about 200. It was founded by Moravians in 1824 as Frederiksdal named after King Frederik VI. Its beautiful church dates back to 1826.

Herjolfsnaes & Sandhavn

Herjolfsnaes, which lies across Narsaq Sarqa Fjord from Narsaq Kujalleq was one of the major Norse settlements in the Østerbygd. The large parish church on the site, which was excavated by the Danish National Museum in 1921, dates back to the 13th century. Well preserved examples of Norse clothing have been discovered in the permafrost beneath the church.

Sandhavn was established by the Icelandic merchant Herjólfur. It was probably the first trading post in Greenland and served as a sort of entry and exit point for the country before the end of the 10th century. The ruins, which lie beside a nice sandy bay, are just an hour's walk across the peninsula from Herjolfsnaes.

There's not really enough left of either Herjolfsnaes or Sandhavn to justify bargaining for a boat trip over there from town but Norse fiends may well disagree.

Places to Stay If you'd like to spend a longer time in either village, you can camp anywhere outside the populated area. Youth-hostel style accommodation can also be arranged through the Nanortalik tourist office.

Getting There & Away The ferry *Taterak* sails between Nanortalik, Narsaq Kujalleq, and Augpilaqtoq once weekly during the summer. If you'd like to spend more than just a ferry stop in Narsaq Kujalleq, you can disembark there and look around while the boat sails on to Augpilaqtoq before returning to collect passengers and heading back to Nanortalik in the afternoon.

Norse costumes excavated at Herjolfsnaes

Those who want to see the grand cape Nunaat Isua itself will have to be either rich enough to afford a private charter or lucky enough to connect with the annual Nanortalik tourist office tour which sails right to the southern tip. If you'd like to book or want more information, write to them at the address in the Nanortalik section. The price can't be determined until they know how many people are interested.

South-West Greenland

The national capital Nuuk, Greenland's largest town with a population of 14,000, is on the south-west coast. This was the Norse Vesturbygd (the 'western settlement') that disappeared even before its neighbour to the south-east and was later the Greenland mission headquarters for the first two Christian sects to arrive on the island. Now it claims to be the metropolis of Greenland.

Unfortunately, Nuuk and the rest of the south-west seem to catch more than their share of unpleasant weather. The further north you move, the better your chances of fine weather. Sisimiut's climate is generally as good as that of the Disko Bay area further north.

The Arctic Circle cuts through Greenland between Maniitsoq and Sisimiut so the latter is not only the southernmost town permitting sled dogs, it's also the first one heading north which experiences the true midnight sun in late June. In addition, one of Greenland's longest yet least demanding walks connects Sisimiut with the US airbase and international airport at Kangerdlusuaq, which has direct connections to Copenhagen via Reykjavík.

IVIGTUT AREA

The lightly populated Ivigtut area lies midway between Qaqortoq and Paamiut. It is little visited and there are no tourist facilities to speak of. Wilderness excursions are always possible and the area is good for sea kayaking.

Arsuk

Arsuk was originally established as a trading station and survived on hunting. When fishing came into its own as the economic mainstay of Greenland, many smaller villages were doomed but Arsuk has survived by flexibly shifting to base its economy on fishing. It's only other claim to fame is that it boasts one of the longest roads in Greenland, 5km or so of gravel.

The *Disko* calls into Arsuk both northbound toward Nuuk and Disko Bay and southbound toward Qaqortoq.

Ivigtut

The village of Ivigtut ('the grassland') has a cryolite mine which is unfortunately beginning to play out. The mineral is a form of sodium crystal used in the production of aluminium and, during WW II, Ivigtut cryolite was important to the Allied war effort. There's no ferry service to Ivigtut but charter boats are available from Arsuk. I just couldn't imagine why anyone would want to visit.

Kangilinnguit (Grønnedal)

Further up Arsuk Fjord from Ivigtut is Kangilinnguit which was originally a US naval station. It is now used as the Danish naval headquarters in Greenland. Again, there are no services and you'd be hard pressed to come up with a reason to visit it.

PAAMIUT (FREDERIKSHÅB)

The original mercantile station of Frederikshåb was established in 1742 around the mouth of Praestevigen Creek as a fur and whale-product trading centre for the district between Nuuk and the far south. The village is now called Paamiut or 'those at the mouth'. It currently has a population of 2500 is informally known as Greenland's 'artist colony' noted for its high quality tupilaqs and other carvings.

Information

There is a bookshop near the harbour which also sells film, postcards, and general merchandise. There is no official tourist office in Paamiut so, for the time being, the community office is responsible for tourist information. They provide a map for those who'd like to go walking outside the village and can also arrange boat trips to the face of the massive tidewater glacier, Frederikshåbs Isblink, north of town. It's impressive and is probably Paamiut's only hope of attracting visitors.

Museum

The village museum is pretty typical displaying Inuit artefacts, qajaqs, and photos. It opens only while the ferry is in port or by private arrangement with the community office.

Church

The church in Paamiut reminded me of Dr Seuss's Boogle House – it appears to be a collection of afterthoughts. The typically Greenlandic churchyard is very colourfully decorated with bright and durable plastic blooms. A larger cemetery further inland takes the same concept to even greater extremes.

Places to Stay & Eat

The only formal accommodation in town is *Petersen's Hotel* (tel 17299) which charges singles/doubles US$47/72 without bath. Its small, grotty dining room is the extent of the restaurant scene. There's also a small grill bar for snacks.

The harbour market is the best place to buy fish and you'll find both Brugsen and KNI supermarkets. The bakery is in an unassuming building opposite the church.

The camping area is south-east of town beyond the last kiosk and colourful residential complex. The best area is on the hill where you'll find a few level dry places which is difficult to do in Paamiut. There are no facilities but a lot of space.

Getting There & Away

Grønlandsfly flies directly to Narsarsuaq four times weekly for US$242. The flight to or from Nuuk goes three times weekly and costs US$259 each way.

Paamiut is the southernmost port of call for the ferry *Kununguak* which plies the west coast as far north as Disko Bay. The *Disko* calls in twice during its 2-week run up and down the coast. It's normally 16 hours by ferry from Paamiut to Nuuk, unless the boat calls in at Qeqertarsuatsiaat, which adds about an hour. Southbound, it's 19 hours to Qaqortoq costs US$78. To or from Nuuk, the fare is US$159.

Qeqertarsuatsiaat (Fiskenaesset)

This village, 150 km south of Nuuk, was founded as Fiskenaesset by Anders Olsen who decided a settlement was needed between Paamiut and Nuuk. It sits on a small, flat peninsula near the open waters of Davis

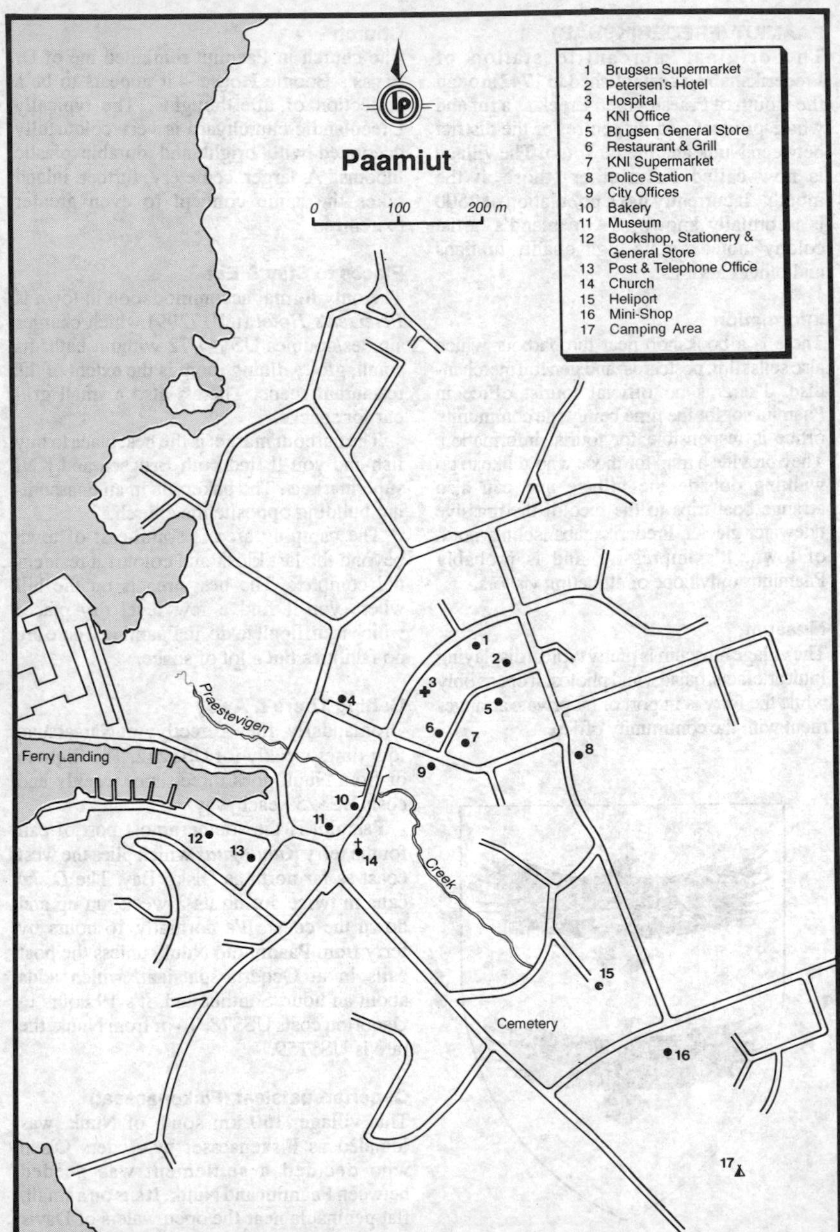
Paamiut
0
100
200 m
1 Brugsen Supermarket
2 Petersen's Hotel
3 Hospital
4 KNI Office
5 Brugsen General Store
6 Restaurant & Grill
7 KNI Supermarket
8 Police Station
9 City Offices
10 Bakery
11 Museum
12 Bookshop, Stationery & General Store
13 Post & Telephone Office
14 Church
15 Heliport
16 Mini-Shop
17 Camping Area
Praestevigen
Ferry Landing
Creek
Cemetery

Strait. It turned out to be a rich fishing ground and, at one time, the salmon were so thick in the bay of Fiskenaesset that the light reflected from their bodies was once thought to be supernatural. Just offshore, the Fiskenaes Bank was discovered to be teeming with cod.

Visitors come primarily to buy the Qeqertarsuatsiaat bags which are handmade by local women. If you're stopping, be sure to carry a tent because accommodation is difficult to arrange.

Getting There & Away

The *Kununguak* calls in weekly in each direction during the summer but, even then, it doesn't allow visitors time to disembark and look around or purchase a bag. The fare from Nuuk is US$46 each way.

KANGERLUARSORUSEQ (FAERINGAHAVN)

The Danish name of this small settlement, 52 km south of Nuuk, means 'Faroese harbour'. Faroese boats were visiting Greenlandic waters in growing numbers at a time when Denmark, struggling to shelter Greenlanders from the encroachment of modern society, limited trading rights to a government monopoly and controlled access to the large island. As citizens of the Danish realm, Faroese cod fishermen working in Davis Strait felt they were as entitled to exploit this fishery as any other Danish concern. The government refused them access to Greenlandic settlements but offered them a bit of land on which to set up a base for operations. Faeringahavn was founded in 1900. Industry today depends primarily on the prawn fishery which justifies a large Danish fish-processing plant.

Very few residents remain in Kangerluarsoruseq today but it claims the dubious honour of having Greenland's largest petrol tank complex. The old part of town, Gamla Faeringahavn, is still picturesque.

Getting There & Away

During the summer, the Nuuk tourist office runs infrequent day-tours to the settlement. If you're interested, write in advance for dates, information, and bookings.

NUUK (GODTHÅB)

Greenland's capital, Nuuk (pronounced 'nuke') is best known for the biggest and ugliest housing blocks in the country. Nuuk's original Danish name, Godthåb or 'good hope' (an assumption which some would say has been disproven) was bestowed by its founder, Hans Egede.

It's been calculated that 15% of Greenland's population lives in the Nuuk projects and that the city's social problems can at times appear overwhelming. Predictably, visitors have been known to say that the new name describes what appears to have happened to the place. Actually, the word means 'the peninsula' and the name of Nuusuaq, Greenland's only suburb, means the 'big peninsula'. Despite all the ribbing the place gets, it's really only new Nuuk that deserves it – the old Kolonichavn area is lovely.

History

Nuuk is now near the site of the Norse Vesturbygd, the western settlement. After the

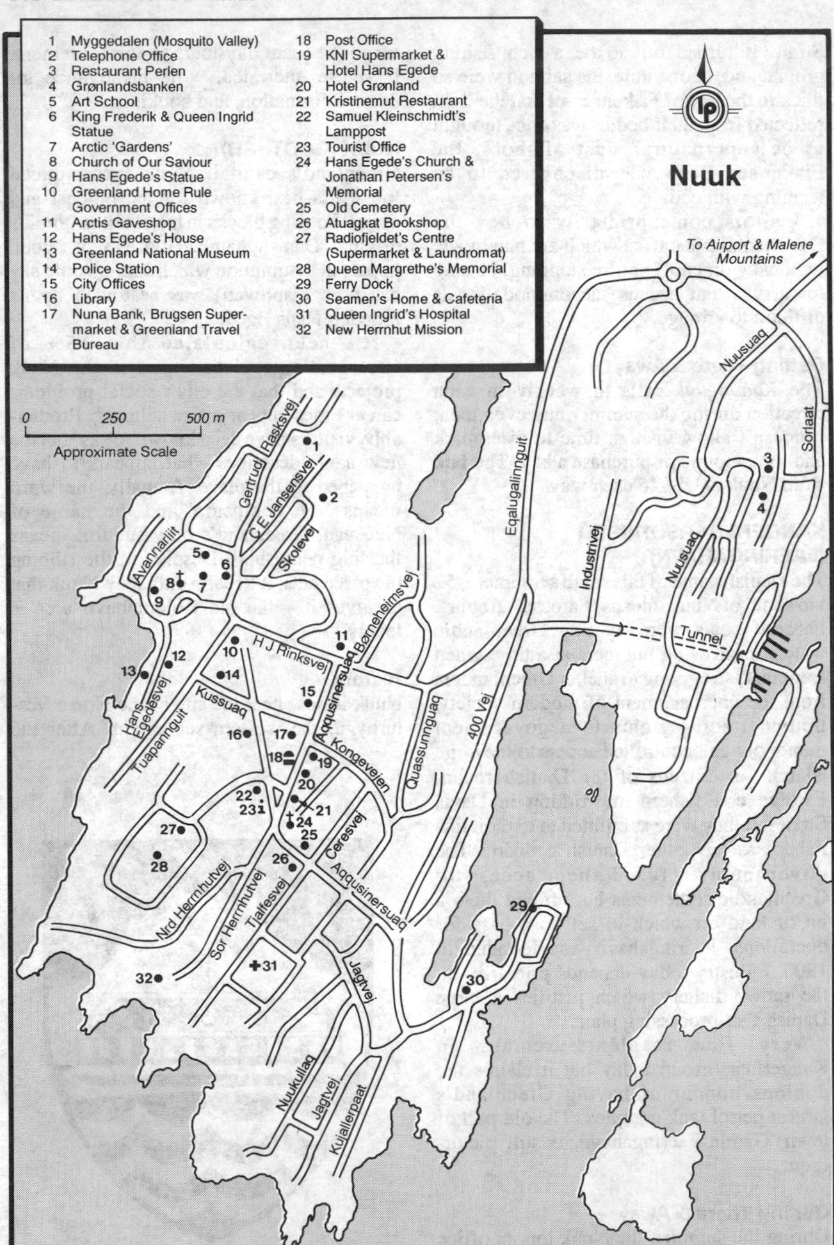
1 Myggedalen (Mosquito Valley)
2 Telephone Office
3 Restaurant Perlen
4 Grønlandsbanken
5 Art School
6 King Frederik & Queen Ingrid Statue
7 Arctic 'Gardens'
8 Church of Our Saviour
9 Hans Egede's Statue
10 Greenland Home Rule Government Offices
11 Arctis Gaveshop
12 Hans Egede's House
13 Greenland National Museum
14 Police Station
15 City Offices
16 Library
17 Nuna Bank, Brugsen Supermarket & Greenland Travel Bureau
18 Post Office
19 KNI Supermarket & Hotel Hans Egede
20 Hotel Grønland
21 Kristinemut Restaurant
22 Samuel Kleinschmidt's Lamppost
23 Tourist Office
24 Hans Egede's Church & Jonathan Petersen's Memorial
25 Old Cemetery
26 Atuagkat Bookshop
27 Radiofjeldet's Centre (Supermarket & Laundromat)
28 Queen Margrethe's Memorial
29 Ferry Dock
30 Seamen's Home & Cafeteria
31 Queen Ingrid's Hospital
32 New Herrnhut Mission
Nuuk
0 250 500 m
Approximate Scale
To Airport & Malene Mountains
Nuusuaq
Sorlaat
Industrivej
Eqalugalinnguit
Tunnel
400 Vej
Quassunnguaq
Rasksvej
Gertrud
C E Jansensvej
Skolevej
Avannarliit
Børneheimsvej
H J Rinksvej
Aqqusinersuaq
Hans Egedesvej
Kussuaq
Tuapannguit
Kongevejen
Ceresvej
Nrd Herrnhutvej
Sor Herrnhutvej
Tjalfesvej
Jagtvej
Nuukullaq
Kujallerpaat

best lands in southern Greenland were settled, other colonists sailed up the coast in search of green pastures. The Nuuk area, although not the best, seemed as good a place as any. Up the fjord, they actually found small pockets of land with grass suitable for sheep. The heart of the settlement was Amerilik Fjord, known to them as Lysefjord (the 'fjord of light') just south of present-day Nuuk.

Compared to its eastern counterpart, very little is known of the Vesturbygd. It's said the Inuit (skraelings) repeatedly attacked the settlement and eventually brought about its demise but there isn't really enough evidence to support any theory.

When Hans Egede arrived, he originally stopped at Håbets Ø, about 18 km west of present-day Nuuk. A subsequent reconnaissance of the area led him to establish his mission on a peninsula where he found meadows, nesting ducks, and 12 families of Greenlandic souls.

The mission and trading company were officially formed on 29 August 1728, and the locals, unhappy about the intrusion, headed for less congested ground. The Danish King Christian IV, dismayed at how expensive it was for Egede to carry religion and supplies all around the district, considered abandoning the whole idea. In 1733, after Egede encouraged him to reconsider, he sent three German Moravian missionaries led by Samuel Kleinschmidt to help out. There was tension between the two missions, however, and Kleinschmidt set up New Herrnhut mission across the peninsula.

Although we can assume the missions' intentions were good, the kindnesses began to cause local problems. One Greenlandic leader, Ulaajuk, was dismayed at the growing dependence of his people on the mission and decided to move them away to prevent the disastrous consequences he anticipated. What he didn't anticipate was the 1736 smallpox epidemic which decimated both the European and Inuit populations and killed Hans Egede's wife, Gertrude Rask. Hans, who came to be known as the 'Greenland Apostle', returned to Denmark and left his sons to carry on the mission.

Meanwhile, Samuel Kleinschmidt was becoming proficient with the Greenlandic language. He did the first philological study, produced a grammar and written language, and translated the Bible into Greenlandic.

Over the years, the missions and the trading companies brought more people to Godthåb. During WW II, this town established itself as the administrative centre of Greenland and, during the 1950s when the island became a full county of Denmark, the city boomed. A reservoir project brought running water, a new harbour was constructed, and a wave of Danish immigration brought technical expertise. Despite a tragic epidemic of tuberculosis, the population continued to grow. At this stage, the immense apartment blocks began to spring up. The largest of these houses 1% of Greenland's population under one roof! Between 1950 and the present, Nuuk gained 13,000 of its 14,000 inhabitants. During the 70s, the city got an international airport at the foot of Quasusuaq (Lille Malene) and it even spawned the suburb, Nuusuaq, which is today the country's second largest town with 5000 people.

Information

Tourist Information I found the Nuuk Turistforening (tel 22700) somewhat less than helpful but things change so it's probably worth dropping by anyway. They have maps and brochures and one very informative booklet *Godthåb/Nuuk* which outlines the town's history and economy in some detail.

The office is open Monday to Friday from 10 am to 4 pm all year round and, in the summer, on Saturdays from 10 am to 3 pm. They also open briefly on Sundays when the big ferries are in town. The postal address is PO Box 199, DK-3920 Nuuk, Greenland. To find them, just look for Samuel Kleinschmidt's lamppost near the centre.

Post The post office in the centre is open Monday to Wednesday from 9 am to 3 pm, on Thursdays from 9 am to 5 pm, and Fridays between 9 am and 3.30 pm.

Telephone The telephone office is at Skolevej 8, north of Koloniehavn. It's only open Monday to Friday from 9 am to 4 pm. For booking overseas calls from other telephones, dial 0012. For directory assistance, the number is 0019.

Banks Branches of both Nuna Bank and Grønlandsbanken can be found in the centre and in Nuusuaq.

Books & Bookshops Greenland's largest bookshop Atuagkat is between the new harbour and the city centre on Aqqusinersuaq. They sell souvenir books and novels in German, English, Danish, and Greenlandic They also sell the *Kalaallit Nunaat Atlas*, a few mostly Danish periodicals, and school texts. If you're looking for books on Greenland, this is the best place to find them.

Travel Agency The Grønlands Rejsebureau (tel 21205) in the centre is open Monday to Friday from 9 am to 3 pm (Thursdays until 6 pm) and on Saturdays from 9 to 11 am. They can make travel bookings all over Greenland and worldwide.

Samuel Kleinschmidt's Lamppost

For some reason, this non-attraction in front of the tourist office has a strange appeal. In the mid-1800s, Moravian missionary Samuel Kleinschmidt walked between his home and his mission at New Herrnhut. In order to light his way on dark winter mornings, he hung a lantern on this post at the mid-point of his journey and picked it up on his way home at night.

New Herrnhut Mission

This building, which was built in 1747, was the early headquarters of the Moravian Mission in Greenland, headed by Samuel Kleinschmidt. He was dispatched by King Christian IV and instructed to assist Hans Egede's efforts. This arrangement didn't work out, of course, and the Moravians established their own mission across town. The building once housed the National Museum and is now used as the National Theological Seminary.

Hans Egede's Church

Despite its being named for Greenland's first Christian missionary, Hans Egede's church was consecrated on the 250th anniversary of the founding of his mission and is a singularly uninteresting building. The oft-photographed church beside the monument of Hans himself is called the Church of our Saviour.

Koloniehavn

Most interesting things to see & do in Nuuk are centred on Koloniehavn ('colony harbour'). This old, quiet, and picturesque section of town is juxtaposed against the apartment blocks.

Koloniehavn was the centre of old Nuuk and it's possible to imagine it as the heart of the settlement prior to the construction of the new industrial harbour. It was from here that the hunters and fishermen set out in their qajaqs. It was also the 'central business district', if you like, and the place that whalers brought their victims for flensing. The headquarters of the qajaq club are beside the National Museum and, if you're there on a weekend, you may see a qajaq demonstration.

Many of the buildings in Koloniehavn date back to the 18th and 19th centuries.

Arctic Gardens If you thought Samuel Kleinschmidt's lamppost was a non-attraction, you should see the so-called Arctic Gardens. These meticulously laid-out garden boxes on the Arqaluk Plads (Koloniehavn square) appear to contain the same vegetation as the square itself. I think this project was a failure. Towards the church from the gardens is a statue commemorating the visit 1952 of King Frederik and Queen Ingrid to Nuuk.

Church of Our Saviour & Monuments The lovely little church at the edge of Koloniehavn was consecrated on 6 April 1849, with several renovations since. If it's unlocked, it's worth looking inside. The chalices date back to 1722 and bear the initials of King Christian IV, the altar has King Frederik VII's mark. You'll also find artistic marble reliefs depicting Hans Egede and Gertrude Rask.

On the stony hill beside the church is a statue of Hans Egede. From here you'll have a great view of the constrasting old and new parts of Nuuk. In front of the church is a bust of the hymnist and organist Jonathon Petersen by sculptor Hans Lynge. He's actually quite a down-to-earth looking chap.

Hans Egede's House Opposite the National Museum is the yellow house where Hans Egede lived while overseeing his mission in Nuuk. It was built in 1728 making it the oldest useful structure in Greenland and is now the home of Greenland's premier, Jonathan Motzfeldt.

Greenland National Museum The National Museum, which occupies three buildings in Koloniehavn, depicts 4500 years of Greenlandic culture. There's one entire hall filled with historical dog sleds, qajaqs, and umiaqs. The museum is working with the qajaq club to revive interest in the culture's most renowned innovation. Another area is devoted to the cultures of east Greenland, and other displays include artefacts from the earliest Greenlandic cultures, traditional hunting methods and tools, both historical and modern Greenlandic dress, geology, Inuit art, and Norse history.

The most famous items in the museum are the 15th-century Qilakitsoq mummies found near the north-western village of Uummannaq. They came to the attention of the modern world when two brothers uncovered them while on a hunt in 1972 but were content to let them rest in peace. When the director of the National Museum got wind of the discovery in 1977, Qilakitsoq was suddenly on the map. The mummies made the cover of *National Geographic* and were considered world-class archaeological finds. The museum is open between 1 June and 1 September daily except Saturdays from 1 to 4 pm. During the winter, it's open Wednesday to Saturday from 1 to 4 pm. There are sometimes special openings for tour groups so, if you're there at an odd hour, phone (tel 22611) and ask if there's a group scheduled.

Greenland Seminary

Just north of Koloniehavn is the Greenland Seminary or Illiniarfissuaq, founded in 1845. The building, constructed in 1907, is featured on Nuuk's coat of arms and is Greenland's only teacher training institution. In front is a monument to Greenlandic teacher Jørgen Brønlund who perished on the Mylius-Erichsen expedition, led astray in 1907 by Robert Peary's fateful geographical error. For more on this story, see the History sections in the Regional and Greenland Facts about the Country chapters.

Quasusuaq & Uvkusissat (Lille Malene & Støre Malene) From the airport (7 km north-east of Nuuk) or from Nuusuaq, the 430-metre peak Quasusuaq can be easily climbed, normally even in the time available while the *Disko* is in the harbour.

The most direct route up Quasusuaq is straight uphill behind the airport terminal but it can also be scaled by walking east along the shore of Malene Bay (Malenebugten) from Nuusuaq and up Quasusuaq's south-west ridge. The more energetic can continue climbing to the summit of 780-metre Uvkusissat. Between the two peaks, there's a large aquamarine lake. Descend by following the outflow from the lake nearly to Malene Bay and then cut west toward Nuusuaq. During the winter, a ski lift operates on the mountain.

The airport is best reached by taxi. Alternatively, you can wait at the bus shelter opposite the Hotel Grønland. Bus No 2 goes only as far as Nuusuaq so you'll have to walk from there. The less frequent bus No 3 goes all the way to the airport.

Places to Stay

Nuuk has two large international hotels of similar quality and price range. A single room in the new *Hotel Hans Egede* (tel 24222) will set you back US$136 while a double is a bargain at US$168 per night. Those who want to go 'business class', which I suspect means 'on an expense account', will pay US$193. Next door is the *Hotel Grønland* (tel 21533) where singles/doubles go for US$122/157. Rooms are all equipped with private bath, TV and video, radio, bar, and telephone. Luxury has arrived in Greenland.

The *Hotel Godthåb* in the centre, which used to be a popular place to stay, seems to be just a restaurant and pub these days. It was locked up tight and I never could find anyone around to ask about accommodation.

The *Seamen's Home* (tel 21029) at the (new) Atlantic Harbour is the middle-range place to stay. Singles/doubles cost US$43/68, neither with bath. For a room with bath, add 35%.

Unfortunately for budget travellers, there is no youth hostel in Nuuk although there has been talk about building one. At the moment, the *Nuna-Tek Hostel* on Kujallerpaat, south of the harbour, is the only option. Staying in a dormitory room with use of cooking facilities there costs US$20. If you opt not to use the kitchen, you can get by with paying only US$13.

Camping The recommended camping site in Nuuk is around the lake at the end of Børneheimsvej, north of the centre. It's a nice quiet area but just a few minutes' walking from the shops and restaurants.

Places to Eat

Each of the big hotels has an elegant restaurant which serves international cuisine and gourmet versions of Greenlandic specialties. Although they're over the top for budget travellers, they're not as dear as you may expect. A reindeer steak, for instance, will set you back US$26, salmon about US$22, whale will cost US$20, and beef dishes will cost between US$21 and US$27. Add alcohol, however, and the price triples.

More down-to-earth restaurants in Nuuk include the *Kristinemut* (tel 21240) near Hans Egede's Church and the *Restaurant Perlen* (tel 23040) in Nuusuaq. There's also a small cafe with a pleasant, relaxing atmosphere opposite the Hotel Grønland.

A lot of people swear by the cafeteria at the Seamen's Home which offers basic but edible fare for US$6 to US$9. In the centre, you'll find three grill bars which serve the usual, familiar range of fast food.

Self-catering is fairly easy. The central Brugsen store is well stocked and has an attached bakery. The new KNI supermarket is between the big hotels on Aqqusinersuaq and the braettet or 'board' fish market is down the hill in Koloniehavn.

Entertainment

The community assembly hall in front of the tourist office is used for films, dances, and bingo, a winning combination to be sure. Information on scheduled events will be available at the tourist office.

Nuuk has a couple of discos in pubs as well. Apart from those in the two big hotels which offer drinks and dancing (the Hotel Hans Egede has a 'super up-to-date Disco Palace'). They're rollicking dens where 'anything goes' including personal injury for alleged indiscretions. Be prepared. The rather sleazy Hotel Godthåb in the centre and the Kristinemut near Hans Egede's Church are the two most prominent.

Unaccompanied women will probably feel a bit uncomfortable but most of the attention will be slobbery and drunken and unlikely to amount to much. This is one city where men, too, can experience the sexual harassment (by women) that plagues women travellers in so many places. Those interested in enjoying the local hospitality, however, should be warned that gonorrhoea and syphilis are particularly rampant in Nuuk.

Things to Buy

Souvenirs There's a souvenir shop on nearly every street corner in the centre and a few scattered elsewhere. The dearest carvings, books, artwork, and furs will come from the hotel shops and the Arctis Gaveshop in the centre. The bookshop, tourist office, and the Seamen's Home all stock a limited supply of souvenirs. The Seamen's Home also sells film.

Getting There & Away

Air Greenlandair has direct flights going between Nuuk and Ilulissat (US$473), Kangerdlusuaq (US$266), Maniitsoq (US$123), Narsarsuaq (US$370), Paamiut (US$259), and Reykjavík, Iceland (around US$500). To Keflavík International Airport in Iceland, there are connecting flights via Kangerdlusuaq and Narsarsuaq.

First Air flies to and from Eqaluit, NWT, Canada, weekly in the summer for US$480 return with connections to and from Montreal.

Ferry If you're pressed, Nuuk isn't the best value in Greenland and your time may be better spent at Ilulissat or in the far south. Unless they want to go walking or touring around the fjords, those travelling on the *Disko* may find that the lengthy stops in Nuuk – normally between 5 and 9 hours – are enough to see just about everything of interest in the city without having to sort out accommodation. The *Kununguak* normally stops for only 3 hours, passing once weekly in either direction.

The fare between Nuuk and Paamiut is US$159. For the 20-hour trip between Nuuk and Sisimiut it's US$92. To Ilulissat, 54 hours north of Nuuk, you'll pay US$160.

Getting Around

Although its drivers have been accused of completing their training in Cairo and pedestrians should take due precautions, Nuuk has a good city bus system. Bus No 3 seems to be the most useful to travellers, connecting the Seamen's Home, the centre, and the airport in Nuusuaq. It runs once an hour between 5.30 am and 5.30 pm weekdays. Buses Nos 1 and 2 run daily four times per hour between 6.25 am and 11.30 pm. The bus costs US$1.40 (Dkr8) per ride.

If you want a taxi in Nuuk, ring Taxa Taxi (tel 22222 or 21349) or Mini Taxi (tel 21818).

NUUK KANGERDLUAQ (GODTHÅBSFJORD)

For those with time in Nuuk, the excursion up into the 120- km-long Nuuk Kangerdluaq will provide insights into village life. The terrain is gentle compared to that of south Greenland but walking is still not easy. Those who'd like to have a go at the wilderness in this area will need DVL Rejser's *Nuuk-Godthåbsfjorden 1:100,000* walking map. A detailed description of the route is given in *Trekking in Greenland.* See Books & Bookshops in the Greenland Facts for the Visitor chapter.

Kapisillit

The village of Kapisillit ('salmon') is 101 km north-east of Nuuk and is known for its salmon stream about 2 km or so north-east of town. The village is also involved in reindeer farming. The 470-metre ascent up the hill Pingo behind the village is fairly easy as is the 4-km walk across a narrow isthmus to see the Kangersuneq Icefjord (Nuuk Isfjorden). It's a long, challenging day-trip up 924-metre Nivko from where there's a view of the glacier and the Kangersuneq Icefjord. Kapisillit is also used as a base for longer walking trips up to the tidewater glacier Qassertuq Nuua, a tongue of the inland ice, and beyond.

Getting There & Away Access to Kapisillit is via charter boat, helicopter tour, or infrequent tour boat from Nuuk. Over the Whitsunday weekend, the Nuuk tourist office leads the relatively easy walk from the head of Amerilik Fjord across to Kapisillit. On the boat ride in, they visit the ruins of Sandnaes from the Norse Vesturbygd. Write for details if you're interested in participating. If you'd like to do this trip any other time, the tourist office staff can provide advice on finding transport into Amerilik Fjord.

Qoorqut

On a small sub-fjord, about 56 km from Nuuk, is Qoorqut where there is a rather quirky lodge, the Qoorqut Mountain Hotel, near an excellent freshwater fishing area. The hotel has its own boat and will provide transport if you're booked in. Bookings must be made through the Nuuk tourist office.

The geological base of the area, Qoorqut granite, is over 3 billion years old and was formed perhaps 25 km beneath the surface.

Helicopter Tour

Whenever there's sufficient interest, the Nuuk tourist office offers a helicopter tour of the fjord area for US$63 per person. It stops for about 45 minutes each at the Norse ruins (dating from around 1300) in Austmannadalen, the icecap at the head of Kangaussarssuuq Sermiaq (glacier), at Kapisillit, and at Qoorqut, before returning to Nuuk.

Kayak Tour

Black Feather/Trailhead offers 15-day sea-kayaking tours around Nuuk Kangerdluaq. They depart from Ottawa (Canada) and fly to Nuuk via Eqaluit, NWT. The trip includes 13 days paddling around the fjord and its numerous arms, hiking, and visiting settlements and ruins ashore. Kayaks and kayaking equipment are provided. If you're interested or would like further information, contact Black Feather at the address given under Kayaking in the Greenland Facts for the Visitor chapter.

MANIITSOQ (SUKKERTOPPEN)

The new name of Maniitsoq means 'the rough place'. The town is squeezed into a basin backed by cliff walls and split by canyons and low, rugged hills. The old Danish name means 'sugar loaf' after a prominent mountain that used to dominate the town. Sukkertoppen was founded by trader Anders Olsen in 1755 and relocated in 1781, the name went with it. The mountain now towers over a town called Kangaamiut, 65 km north.

The economic mainstay of the village is, of course, fishing but diets and incomes are both supplemented by hunting caribou and seals. Deposits of niobium and uranium have been discovered nearby but the locals are less than enthusiastic about messing with the environment or blighting the landscape with big machines in order to mine. Greenland's longest bridge spans the channel between the ferry landing and the main town.

Information

The tourist information office (tel 13277) in Maniitsoq, run by Ms Magdalene Pedersen, is very helpful. The office is at the town hall and its postal address is PO Box 12, DK-3912 Maniitsoq, Greenland.

The two banks, Nuna Bank and Grønlandsbanken (handled by the KNI office) are open weekdays from 10 am to 3 pm.

Church

Although the old church in Maniitsoq was built in 1864 and has historical value, the new church, dating back to 1981, is worth a look. The altar and font are made of beautiful

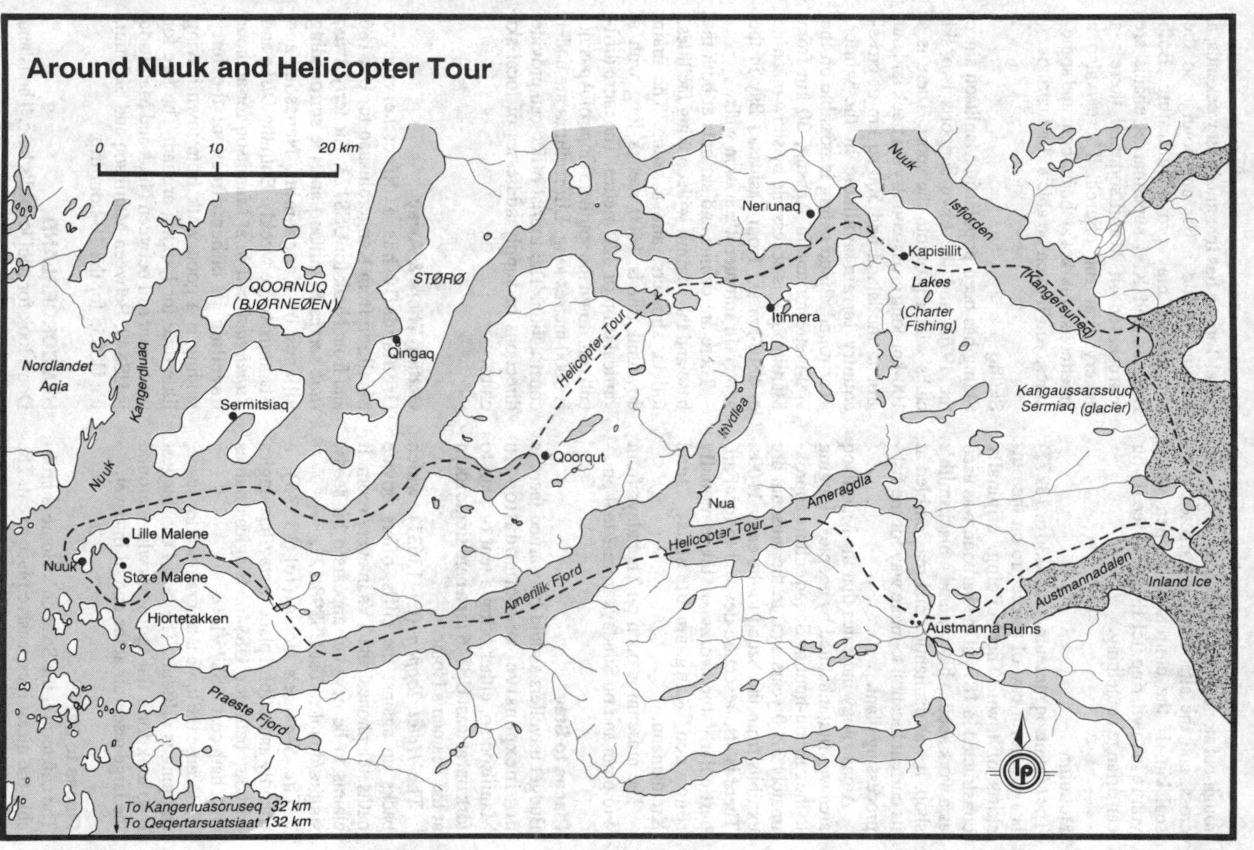
Around Nuuk and Helicopter Tour
0
10
20 km
Nordlandet
Aqia
Kangerdluaq
QOORNUQ
(BJØRNEØEN)
STØRØ
Qingaq
Sermitsiaq
Nuuk
Helicopter Tour
Qoorqut
Neriunaq
Itinnera
Kapisillit
Nuuk
Isfjorden
Lakes
(Charter
Fishing)
(Kangersuneq)
Kangaussarssuuq
Sermiaq (glacier)
Itivdlea
Nua
Ameragdla
Helicopter Tour
Lille Malene
Nuuk
Støre Malene
Hjortetakken
Amerilik Fjord
Austmannadalen
Inland Ice
Austmanna Ruins
Praeste Fjord
To Kangerluasoruseq 32 km
To Qeqertarsuatsiaat 132 km

rough-cut stone, the altarpiece is a driftwood cross, and the altar itself is carpeted with sealskin. If the church isn't open when you're in town, ring (tel 13284) to see if you can arrange something.

Museum

The Maniitsoq museum (tel 13236 or 13277) is 1 km north-east of the centre on the outskirts of town. The building, originally constructed in 1874 at the harbour, was used as a work shed, a bakery, and a blacksmith's shop. It was dismantled and reassembled at its current location to make way for the fish-processing plant.

Archaeology indicates that the Maniitsoq area was first inhabited by people belonging to the caribou-hunting Saqaq culture approximately 3200 years ago. In the museum are exhibits from the Saqaq to the early 1900s. There is also a section devoted to local art, particularly the works of the nationally renowned Kangaamiut artist, Jens Kreutzmann.

The museum is open on Thursdays from 4 to 6 pm and on Sundays from 2 to 4 pm.

Places to Stay

Budget travellers should be warned there is no inexpensive accommodation in Maniitsoq so, either bring a tent or plan to fork out at least US$46 for a bare single room at the Seamen's Home.

The *Hotel Toppen* (tel 13631), which backs up against the cliffs, offers private baths, telephones, and TVs in every room. It claims to be new but appears a bit seedy, singles/doubles cost US$98/127.

The *Seamen's Home* (tel 13535), a friendly and helpful place to stay, has singles without bath for US$46. Singles/doubles with bath cost US$75/100.

Because the town is so cramped for space, camping is difficult. The best I can suggest is to look for a flat spot somewhere around the large reservoir at the end of Imeqvej.

Places to Eat

The cafeteria at the Seamen's Home is probably the nicest inexpensive place to eat. The Hotel Toppen has live music on weekends, a restaurant, and a bar and lounge so the atmosphere may prove interesting. Both Brugsen and KNI supermarket chains are represented in Maniitsoq and there's a bakery near the church. There's also a braettet fish market at the harbour and sometimes, you'll even be able to find caribou.

Skiing

Skiing has been popular in Maniitsoq since the 1970s and the town supports two ski clubs which promote the sport. There is a 100-km-long cross-country ski track laid out around the island and 500 sq km of cross-country terrain available in the winter. Year-round alpine skiing is possible on the 900-metre mountain Apusuit, 30 km from Maniitsoq. It is accessible by snow machine or a 10-km ski from Tasiussaq Bay in the winter. In summer it's a 7-km walk.

There are cabins and ski huts at both the base and the summit with cooking facilities, toilets, showers, and a sauna. The main downhill run is 1600 metres long with a vertical drop of 320 metres. The more difficult run, down the southern slope of Apusuit, is 6000 metres long. Lift facilities are under construction. The tourist office can provide directions or supply addresses of local ski clubs.

Getting There & Away

Grønlandsfly has a direct service to Maniitsoq from Kangerdlusuaq for US$186 and from Nuuk for US$123. The ferry *Aviaq Ittuk* serves Maniitsoq and the surrounding villages of Kangaamiut, Napasoq, and Atammik twice weekly. Both the *Disko* and *Kununguak* call in at Maniitsoq for an hour travelling in either direction; the ferry landing is a good walk from town leaving little time for looking around. The fare for the 8-hour sail between Nuuk and Maniitsoq is US$49. Between Maniitsoq and Sisimiut, it's US$55 for the 10-hour trip.

HAMBORGERLAND

Don't look for McDonald's here. The island

Top: Entrance to Qooroq Fjord, Greenland (DS)
Bottom: Youth Hostel at Narsarsuaq, Greenland (DS)

Top: Along the walk to Hvalsey, near Qaqortoq, Greenland (DS)
Left: Spring flowers, Qaqortoq, Greenland (DS)
Right: Old Church, Qaqortoq, Greenland (DS)

of Hamborgerland north of Maniitsoq has nothing to do with fast food. It's simply one of the most spectacular sights along the Greenland coast: an island of sheer and jagged granite spires, tangled glaciers, and utterly forbidding terrain. Surprisingly, the waters of Hamborgersund, the channel between the island and the mainland, are well sheltered and normally calm. Sea kayakers will gaze at the shore and salivate as they sail through on the coastal ferries. If you're doing the coastal route and have fine weather, don't miss seeing it.

Getting There & Away

While you can get good close-up views of Hamborgerland from the coastal ferries, if you'd like to land on the island, you'll have to charter a boat from Maniitsoq.

SISIMIUT (HOLSTEINSBORG)

Sisimiut or 'place of the burrowers' is in the midst of rich whaling grounds. It is the southernmost extent of the walrus habitat and the northernmost ice-free port in the country, 75 km north of the Arctic Circle. These factors attracted a relatively large population and set it up as a trading centre between northern and southern Greenland even prior to the arrival of Dutch whalers and traders in the late 1600s.

After establishing his mission at Nuuk, Hans Egede came to the Sisimiut district to set up a joint mission and whaling station. Twice he set up business and twice he was burned out by the Dutch whalers who claimed he was invading their territory.

It wasn't until 1756 that the Danish successfully set up a mission there on the northern side of Ulkebugt near present-day Sisimiut. They named it Holsteinsborg after the Danish count of Holstein, a patron of the mission back in Copenhagen. In 1764, the settlement moved to its present site. The interesting church in Sisimiut, which looks slightly Oriental, was built in 1775 and Niels Egede, son of Hans, stayed on in the mission until 1782.

Although civil construction continued, the 1800s were characterised by plagues from Europe which decimated the local population. When fishing and shrimping took over the town's economy in the early 1900s, population growth resumed and, by the

mid-1950s, Sisimiut had changed from a traditional hunting and fishing community to an industrial centre – the shrimping centre of Greenland processing nearly 10,000 tonnes annually. With 4400 residents, Sisimiut is the country's third largest town after Nuuk and its suburb, Nuusuaq.

The harbour is bright and colourful, the weather is better than in most areas along the west coast. It's popular with visitors who haven't time to continue further north but still want to experience a bit of Arctic Greenland.

Information

Tourist Information The tourist information office (tel 14848) is near the old church. In the summer months, it's open Monday to Friday from 9 am to 4 pm and on Saturdays 10 am to 2 pm. Their postal address is Sisimiut Turistforening, Frederik IX's Plads 3, DK-3911 Sisimiut, Greenland.

A limited range of books is available at the central bookshop.

Laundry There are two laundry services in Sisimiut, one at each end of town (see map). They're open weekdays and Saturdays from 8 am to 8 pm and on Sundays 8 am to 4 pm. The eastern one, Blok 12, closes on Mondays and the western one, Tuapannguanut, closes on Tuesdays.

Old Town & Holsteinsborg Museum

Sisimiut's old town and historical museum, which you enter beneath a whale-jawbone arch, date back from the mid-18th to mid-19th centuries. The buildings themselves are probably of greatest interest. The Gammelhuset (meaning 'old house' in Danish), a recently restored structure originally prefabricated in Norway and first erected in Greenland around 1756, contains most of the museum. The kindergarten building beside it was built at Assimmiut in 1759 and moved to Sisimiut 8 years later where it served as the vicarage. The blue church building was consecrated in 1773. It's the oldest church in Greenland. The newer red church on the hill, which looks a bit Korean, is a relatively recent addition.

Other buildings, which will eventually be incorporated into the exhibit, include the Halvvejshuset or 'half-way house' built in 1844 and the Gamle Butik or 'old store' from 1852. The current displays include the usual Greenlandic gamut of Settlement history, hunting and fishing tools and relics, and local art and clothing. During the summer it's open Wednesdays, Thursdays, Saturdays, and Sundays from 2 to 5 pm. In the winter, it closes on Saturdays.

Places to Stay

You have three choices in Sisimiut. The *Hotel Sisimiut* (tel 14840) isn't really the nicest Greenland has to offer but it's adequate. You'll pay US$92/126 for a single/double room with bath. Meal plans are available, as well.

The second option is the *Seamen's Home* (tel 14150) which costs US$75/52 for singles with/without bath, respectively, and US$99/70 for doubles.

South of the centre is Greenland's most northerly *Youth Hostel* (tel 14848), a large and comfortable place which is open from 15 June to 31 August. They charge US$16 per person for shared rooms. There's no atten-

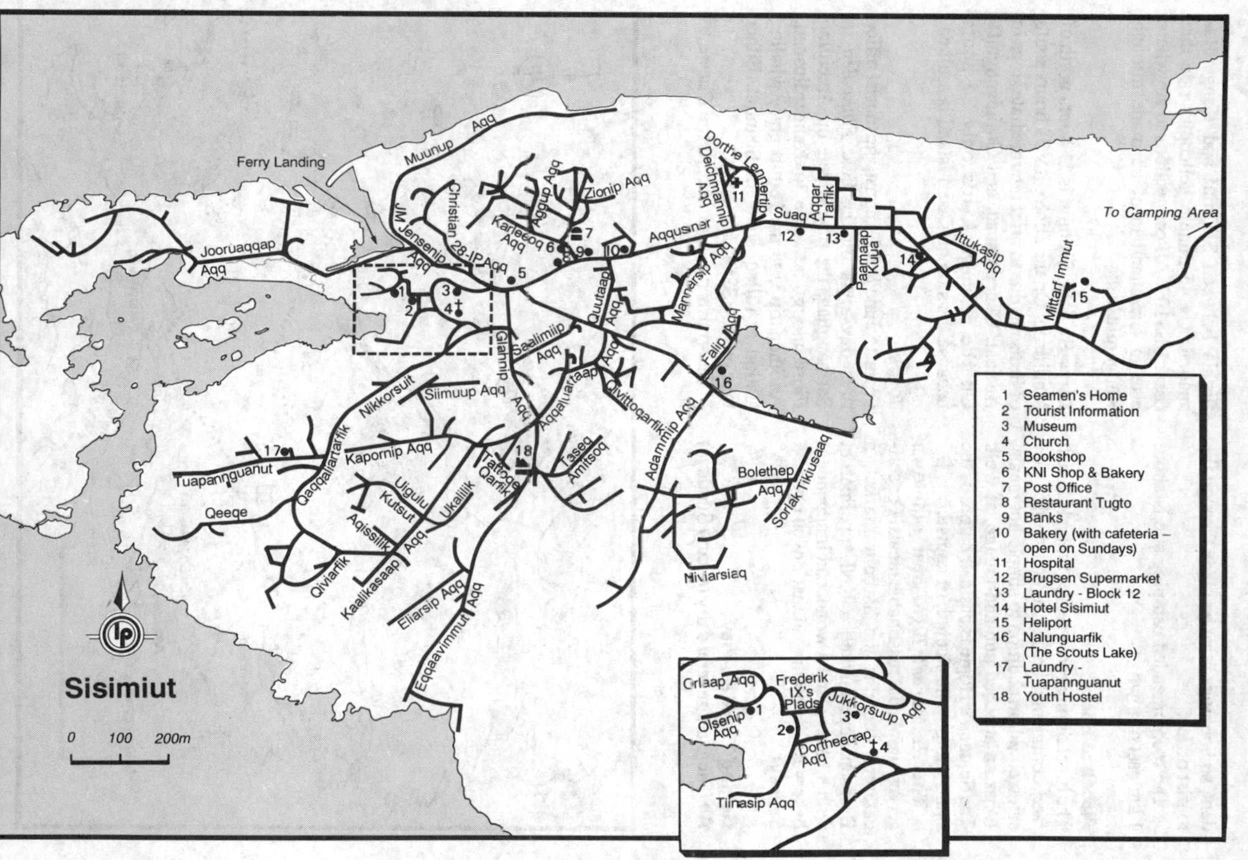
Sisimiut
0
100
200m
1 Seamen's Home
2 Tourist Information
3 Museum
4 Church
5 Bookshop
6 KNI Shop & Bakery
7 Post Office
8 Restaurant Tugto
9 Banks
10 Bakery (with cafeteria – open on Sundays)
11 Hospital
12 Brugsen Supermarket
13 Laundry - Block 12
14 Hotel Sisimiut
15 Heliport
16 Nalunguarfik (The Scouts Lake)
17 Laundry - Tuapannguanut
18 Youth Hostel
To Camping Area
Ferry Landing
Muunup Aqq
Jooruaqqap Aqq
JM Jensenip Aqq
Christian 28-IP Aqq
Karleeoq Aqq
Aqqup Aqq
Zionip Aqq
Aqqusiner
Deichmannip Aqq
Dortre Lennertip
Suaq
Aqqar Tarfik
Paamaap Kuua
Ittukasip Aqq
Mittarf Immut
Quutaap Aqq
Mannersip Aqq
Falip Aqq
Saalimiip Aqq
Glahnip Aqq
Aqqaluartaap
Qivittoqarfik
Adammip Aqq
Siimuup Aqq
Nikkorsuit
Qaqqaliartarfik
Kapornip Aqq
Tuapannguanut
Qeeqe
Uigulu
Kutsut
Aqissilik
Ukalilik
Taffoqe Qarfik
Taseq
Amitsoq
Bolethep Aqq
Sorlak Tikiusaaq
Niviarsiaq
Qiviarfik
Kaalikasaap Aqq
Eliarsip Aqq
Eqqaavimmut Aqq
Orlaap Aqq
Frederik IX's Plads
Olsenip Aqq
Jukkorsuup Aqq
Dortheecap Aqq
Tiinasip Aqq

dant, so bookings must be made through the tourist office.

The recommended camping site is about 1 km east of town

Places to Eat

The hotel dining room serves typical Danish fare: continental breakfast, cold buffet, and smørrebrød, in addition to simple hot meals. It has an attached pub and lounge, as well. The Seamen's Home is basically more of the same without the alcohol, of course.

The *Restaurant Tugto* near old town serves simple but reasonable meals. For self-caterers, there is the harbour market, a Brugsen supermarket, a KNI supermarket with a bakery, and a wonderful independent bakery on the main road that's even open on Sundays.

Getting There & Away

Air There are several daily (except Sundays) flights between Sisimiut and Kangerdlusuaq. It's a 45-minute helicopter ride that costs US$109. All connections to anywhere else in Greenland must be made through Kangerdlusuaq.

Ferry By boat, Sisimiut is 11 hours north of Maniitsoq. On the ***Disko***, it's 35 hours south of Ilulissat (due to brief intermediate stops in Aasiaat, Qeqertarsuaq, and Qasigiannguit). On the *Kununguak*, it's only 24 hours because the stop on Disko Island is omitted.

Tours

From 15 June to 15 August, the tourist office runs day-tours on the boat ***Finhvalen*** to Sarfaanguaq, the tiny village on Amerdloq Fjord along the route to Kangerdlusuaq. Another trip is to the 18th-century whaling station at Itilleq, south of Sisimiut. Either tour costs US$54 per person.

They also run trips aboard the *Carina* to

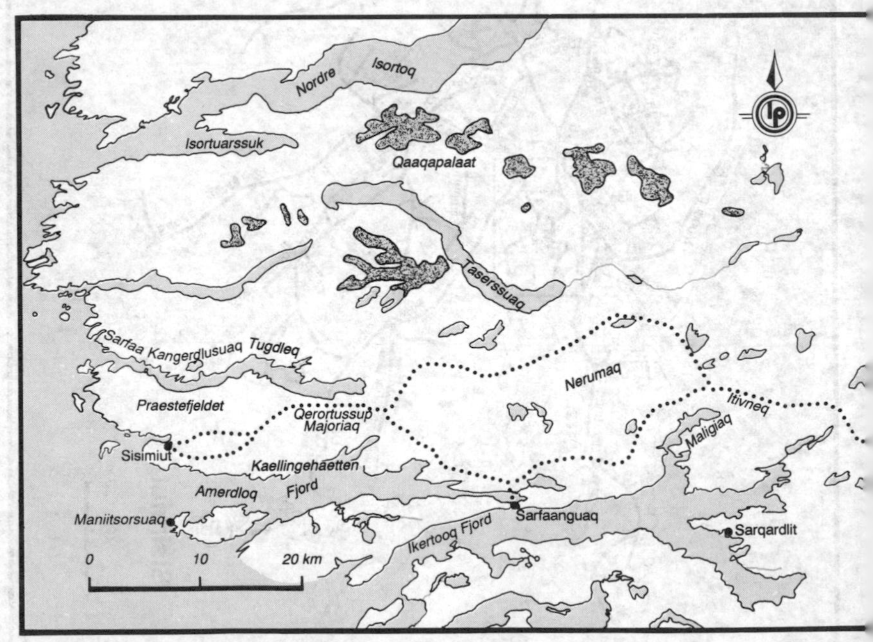

the outlying 18th-century whaling station at Nipisat and the abandoned villages of Uummannaarsuk and Assaqutaq four times during the summer, visiting centres of the Saqaq culture. They require a minimum of eight participants and charge US$104 per person for an 8-hour trip.

Other group hiking tours are available including scaling the 775-metre Kaellinge-haetten for US$11 per person (you still have to walk). For information, scheduling, and booking of any of these, write to the tourist office prior to your visit.

Dog-sled Tours The tourist office offers a range of dog-sled tours during April and May including a 5-day trip that takes you to the settlement of Isortoq and back, staying over-night in huts and tents. Participants will have to bring their own warm clothing but the tourist office provides polarguard sleeping bags and camping equipment. The trip costs about US$930 per person but is one of the best and most realistic of all the pre-organised sled tours in Greenland. Shorter tours are also available. A day-trip will cost about US$129 and a 3-hour tour to the village of Qiterlinnguit costs US$70 for one person per sled and US$77 for a double, so to speak.

Kangerdlusuaq to Sisimiut Trek

The 150-km walk between Kangerdlusuaq and Sisimiut is one of the two most popular treks in Greenland. Although it's a relatively easy trip, it will require from 10 to 12 days and some careful planning. In short, anyone not put off by the prospect of at least 10 days of walking will probably be able to handle it. The tourist offices will normally recommend a local guide. Although it can get expensive, the expertise of a local person on such a trip can open up new realms of awareness the

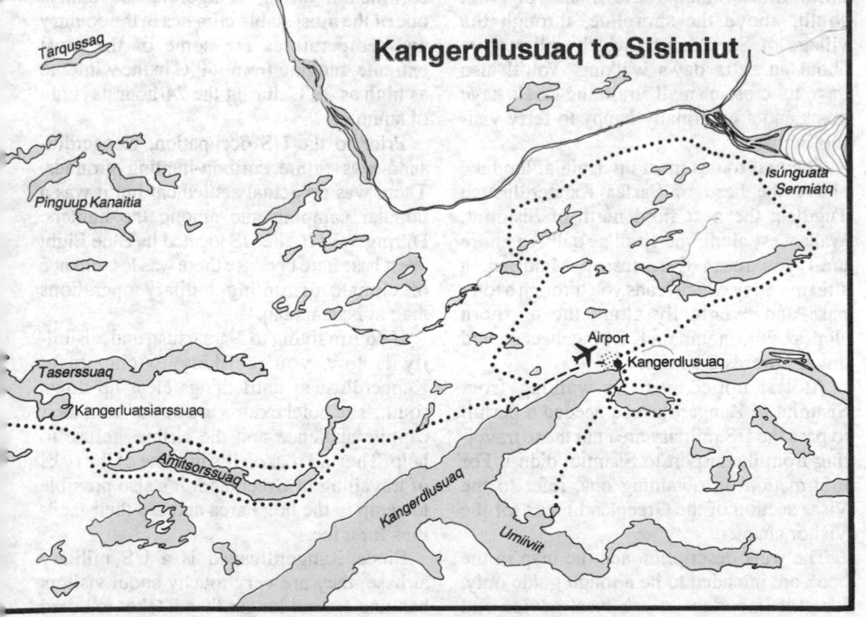

foreign trekker would otherwise probably miss.

Starting out, climb up onto the 'moors' from the airport at Kangerdlusuaq and follow the shore in a south-westerly direction. After 2 days, you should reach the lake Amitsorssuaq (Amitssuaq on the walking map). From here, you have the option to take the northern or southern route along the lakeshore, the southern being the longer but considerably easier of the two.

From the western end of Amitsorssuaq lake follow the river up stream and over the low pass to the Kangerdluatsiarssuaq bay of the lake Taserssuaq (it's about 7 km). Then bear west through the lake-studded landscape to Itivneq (the river valley connecting Taserssuaq with the fjord Maligiaq, an arm of Ikertooq Fjord which is sometimes called Sisimiut Fjord). Cross the river as soon as you can to avoid high water. The northern fork which must be crossed later, however, may still prove problematic. At this point, you have to decide whether you'll follow the northern Nerumaq route inland or walk south, above the shoreline, through the village of Sarfaanguaq which will require about an extra day's walking. You'll also have to cross a small strait; the locals have boats and are normally happy to ferry visitors across.

The two routes meet up again at the lake above the head of Sarfaa Kangerdlusuaq Tugdleq, the next fjord north of Sisimiut. Walk west along the fjord's southern shore until you reach Qerortussup Majoriaq, a stream valley which leads you through a long pass and eventually along the northern slopes of the mountain Kaellingehaetten and down towards Sisimiut.

At last notice, visitors walking from Sisimiut to Kangerdlusuaq needed a permit to pass the US military area but those travelling from the airport to Sisimiut didn't. For information on obtaining one, refer to the Visas section of the Greenland Facts for the Visitor chapter.

The walk description and the map in the book are intended to be a rough guide only. It's still important to ask local advice and you'll need to carry the DVL-Rejser walking maps *Søndre Strømfjord 1:100,000* and *Sisimiut 1:100,000*.

Several other walks are possible around Kangerdlusuaq and those who have a permit may want to spare themselves the high transport costs and spend their entire holiday thoroughly exploring the area. Route details are outlined in the essential book *Trekking in Greenland* by Torbjoern Ydegaard, published by Skarv Guides and in *Vandreruter i Vestgrønland* by Bjarne Ljungdahl. Although the latter is in Danish, the maps will make it worth the US$6 you'll pay. Order both the books and walking maps from Green Tours, Kultorvet 7, DK-1175 Copenhagen, Denmark.

KANGERDLUSUAQ (SØNDRE STRØMFJORD)

Kangerdlusuaq lies in a 200-km wide ice-free zone, the widest in Greenland, at the head of the island's longest fjord. Its means 'the big fjord'. What else? Thanks to the continental effect, Kangerdlusuaq enjoys one of the most stable climates in the country and temperatures are some of the most extreme, ranging from -50°C in the winter to as high as 28°C during the 24-hour daylight of summer.

Prior to the US occupation, Kangerdlusuaq was prime caribou-hunting grounds. There was no actual settlement but it was a popular camping site among the hunters. During WW II, the US located its Blue Eight West base here because there was less chance of climate disrupting military operations than at Narsarsuaq.

If you're flying to Narsarsuaq and visibility is low, you're likely to end up at Kangerdlusuaq until things clear up down south. The hotel extorts top bucks from their captive audience and the airlines refuse to help. They all reckon it's just one of the risks of travelling in Greenland. It's also possible to camp in the hotel area and use their facilities for a fee.

Since Kangerdlusuaq is a US military airbase, they are very touchy about visitors hanging around longer than it takes to board the first flight out. Anyone who wants to camp or spend time visiting the base's hinterland has to get permission from the appropriate authorities who'll make certain the applicant's politics check out. For more information on this process, refer to Visas in the Greenland Facts for the Visitor chapter.

Places to Stay & Eat

Across the tarmac from the base's buildings is the *Transit Hotel* (tel 11180), the name being another subtle reminder they don't want anyone hanging around too long. Additional coercion is provided by the prices. Singles/doubles without bath cost US$62/70. With private bath, singles/doubles cost US$95/120. It is, incidentally, the largest hotel in Greenland. At times, it needs to accommodate several stranded Copenhagen-bound flights and, often, several diverted Narsarsuaq-bound flights as well.

For meals, there is only the hotel restaurant and cafeteria.

Getting There & Away

Air Virtually everyone passing through Kangerdlusuaq is transiting between the SAS or Icelandair flights and the Grønlandsfly flights. SAS uses Kangerdlusuaq as its sole terminal in Greenland.

There are direct flights between Kangerdlusuaq and Ilulissat (US$208), Maniitsoq (US$186), Nuuk (US$266), and Sisimiut (US$109).

Ferry Ferry service to Kangerdlusuaq is infrequent. In an average summer, the *Disko* and the *Kununguak* call in once each.

Disko Bay

The largest island off the Greenland coast shelters Disko Bay, an iceberg crowded expanse 300 km north of the Arctic Circle. 'Bergy bits' of Disko Bay ice, that is semi-trailer-sized chunks, are towed into harbours, chipped into cubes and exported to Japan and Europe to chill drinks. That scotch you order in a Tokyo pub may contain 25,000-year-old cubes from the frozen heart of Greenland's icecap and the air that fizzes out as they melt has been trapped since long before anyone ever heard of smog alerts.

The four main towns of Disko Bay – Ilulissat, Qeqertarsuaq, Qasigiannguit, and Aasiaat – have a combined population of about 12,000. Visitors heading north up the coast normally feel they're getting their first real taste of the high Arctic here. During the winter, Disko Bay is the southern extent of the pack ice. In the summer, the world's most prolific tidewater glacier advances up to 30 metres a day and calves formidable bergs – some weighing up to 7 million tonnes – filling up the Ilulissat Kangerdluaq (Ilulissat or Jakobshavn Icefjord) and spilling them out into Disko Bay to wander for centuries around the Arctic.

If you're visiting between late May and mid-July, you'll experience the true midnight sun. For a month, there's no hint of twilight and most visitors tend to sleep restlessly as the sun circles day after day without setting.

AASIAAT (EGEDESMINDE)

Aasiaat, Greenland's fifth largest community, sits amid low, stark, and rocky islands. There are none of the rugged peaks visitors are probably used to by the time they get this far north but the flatness makes a pleasant change. For some unfathomable reason, the name of the town means 'the spiders', although no one could tell me how this came about, I doubt the climate there is suitable for the little buggers.

Although the original site of Aasiaat, south of the current town, had long been called Eqaluksuit ('salmon') by the Inuit, Niels Egede called the settlement he founded in 1759 'Egedesminde' after his father, Hans Egede. It was a fertile site but out of the way as a trading post and, in 1763, it was shifted to its present location.

Prosperity in the mercantile business alternated with repeated small pox epidemics. Four times (in 1776, 1800, 1825, and 1852) the population of Egedesminde was decimated by the disease. At one point, only 21 people remained in the once populous district. The tourist information says that the medical missionary Carl Wulff published a diary of his experiences in Aasiaat during the epidemic of 1852 under the title *Solstice in the Night* but I've never been able to find a copy.

During WW II, the USA had a small second-string base at Tupilaq near the mouth of Aasiaat harbour. When the base shut down, the local economy stagnated and, for years, primitive methods of fish salting and shrimp processing carried the meagre

economy. In the mid-1980s, however, an efficient fish and shrimp-processing plant was established and Aasiaat prospers once again.

The area is now home to 4700 people, 3200 of whom live in Aasiaat proper.

Information

The tourist information office (tel 42088) in this little-visited town is very friendly, helpful, and informative. It's in the museum and is open whenever a ferry is docked in town. The post address is Aasiaat Turistkontor, PO Box 220, DK-3950 Aasiaat, Greenland.

Things to See & Do

Colonial Old Town The older buildings in town are found around the harbour area. There you'll find the home of the whaling station manager from Kronprinsens Island. It was constructed in 1778 and moved to Aasiaat when the station was abandoned in 1826. There are also the old manager's home and a monument to Aasiaat's 'founding father' Niels Egede.

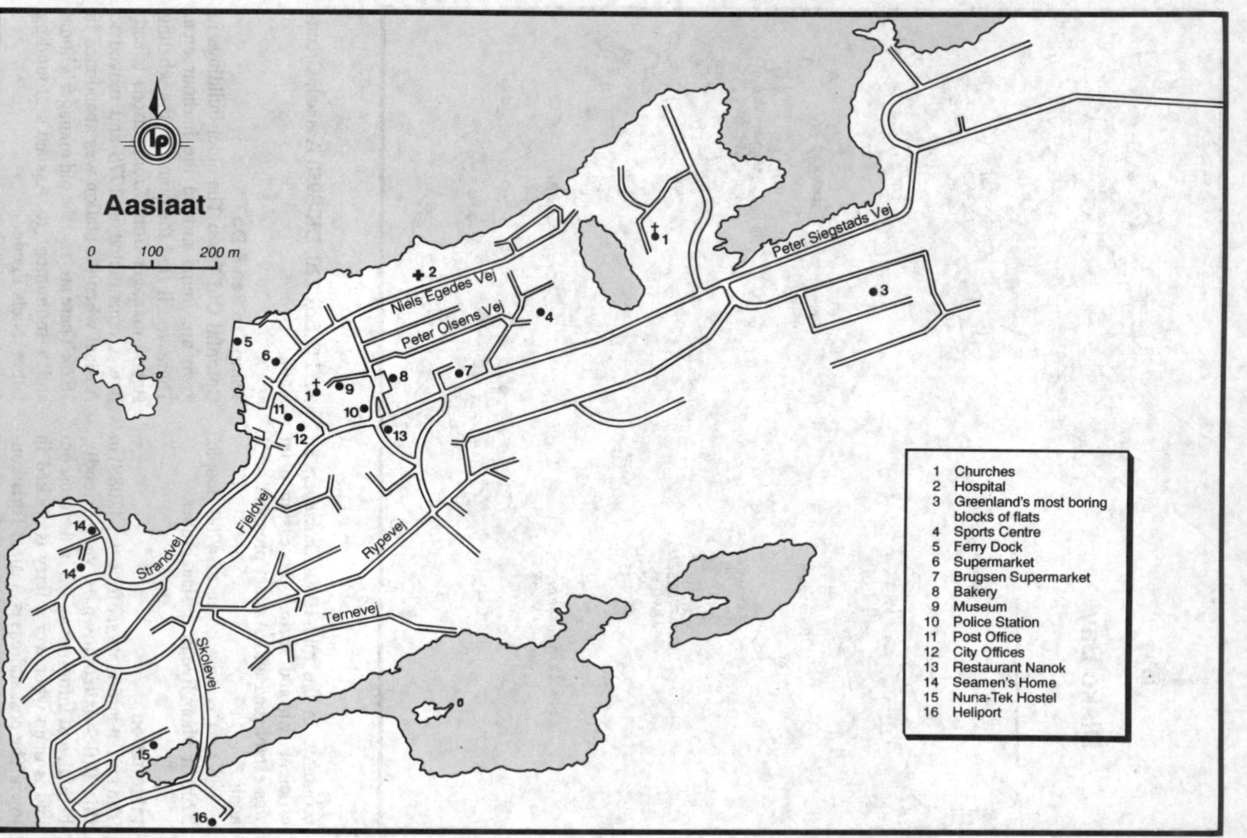
Aasiaat
0
100
200 m
1 Churches
2 Hospital
3 Greenland's most boring blocks of flats
4 Sports Centre
5 Ferry Dock
6 Supermarket
7 Brugsen Supermarket
8 Bakery
9 Museum
10 Police Station
11 Post Office
12 City Offices
13 Restaurant Nanok
14 Seamen's Home
15 Nuna-Tek Hostel
16 Heliport
Peter Siegstads Vej
Niels Egedes Vej
Peter Olsens Vej
Rypevej
Ternevej
Fjeldvej
Skolevej
Strandvej

Inuit Old Town Across the bridge east of the centre is the traditional hunters' community. It's picturesque in an odd way and well worth a walk around but beware of irritable sled dogs which are tied up everywhere.

Aasiaat Systue In 1982, Aasiaat established a leather-crafting shop which places emphasis on traditional tanning, drying, sewing, and embroidery skills. Interested foreigners can visit the workshop and learn the processes involved or just purchase a leather handbag or a festive white anorak. Visitors may also commission custom-made pieces for reasonable prices, including bits of the beautiful Greenlandic national costume.

Museum Aasiaat's museum is small but well presented and very worth visiting. It is in the residence of the poet, merchant, and parliamentarian, Frederik Lynge. There's an array of things from the area's history as well as an assortment of decomposing historical machinery lying around outside. It opens whenever a ferry is docked at Aasiaat and admission is US$1.50.

Walks The terrain around Aasiaat is relatively flat and ordinary but walkers who'd like to stroll and take it easy, rather than puff up and slip down mountains, will find it unchallengingly perfect. The low hills behind town offer some fine views of the archipelago.

Kitsissuarsuit (Hunde Island)

The name of this tiny settlement with 120 people, 21 km from Aasiaat, means 'dog island' in Dutch (named by early whalers). The Greenlandic name means 'strange island of the west'. It is renowned for its traditional arts, particularly the crafting of qajaqs and umiaqs and decoration of leather products.

The ferry *Tugdlik* sails to Kitsissuarsuit once weekly on its circuit of Disko Bay. The trip from Aasiaat takes 2 days because stops are made in Qasigiannguit, Ilulissat, and Qeqertarsuaq before reaching Kitsissuarsuit and then returning to Aasiaat. It would make a fairly tiring circuit trip since cabins are not available.

Places to Stay & Eat

Aasiaat has no hotel but there is a *Seamen's Home* (tel 42175) near the harbour tanks. Singles/doubles without bath cost US$53/79; they cost US$70/93 with attached bath. The cafeteria is open Monday to Friday from 7.30 am to 10 pm, on Saturdays from 7.30 am to 8 pm, and on Sundays from 8 am to 10 pm. Lunch specials are served from 11.30 am to 1 pm and dinner from 5.30 to 7 pm.

The budget option in Aasiaat is the *Nuna-Tek Hostel* which charges US$20 per person. The tourist office can help if you'd like to book in advance.

The *Nanok* is your only choice for proper restaurant meals in town. They're open from 6 to 11 pm Monday to Thursday and 6 pm to 1 am on Fridays and Saturdays. As you can well imagine, this becomes the town's action spot on weekends.

Camping is possible just about anywhere in the rocky tundra knolls behind the town. Brugsen and KNI both have supermarkets in Aasiaat.

Getting There & Away

Air There are helicopter services to and from Ilulissat or Qasigiannguit, both costing US$65, at least once daily except Sundays.

Ferry Aasiaat is served weekly by the *Tugdlik* from Ilulissat, Qeqertarsuaq, and Qasigiannguit as well as a number of smaller settlements around Disko Bay. The *Kununguak* stops here twice weekly, once northbound and once southbound, and the *Disko* calls in once in either direction every 2 weeks in the summer.

KANGAATSIAQ

Although it has only 450 inhabitants, Kangaatsiaq acquired town status in January, 1985, the most recent Greenlandic settlement to do so. Its name means 'the little headland'. There are few facilities yet but they are establishing a tourist office whose

postal address is Kangaatsiaq Turistudvalg, Kommunen, DK-3950 Kangaatsiaq, Greenland. The *Kununguak* makes a brief stop at Kangaatsiaq on its way up and down the west coast.

QASIGIANNGUIT (CHRISTIANSHÅB)

Qasigiannguit (the 'small spotted seals') sits at the foot of a long escarpment which rises almost vertically above its well-sheltered small boat harbour. It was founded by Poul Egede, son of Hans Egede, in 1734 and set up as a trading station by Jakob Severin, who also founded Ilulissat. The Danish name, Christianshåb or 'Christian's hope', refers to King Christian IV of Denmark. The town was moved from its original site across the bay in 1764.

The Qasigiannguit area has been inhabited for over 4000 years and remnants of the Saqaq, Thule, and Dorset cultures have all been found. The oldest evidence yet discovered of early habitation in Greenland is the skeleton of a Saqaq woman who lived around 2000 BC on the nearby island of Qeqertasugsuk.

Although the town was used briefly as a military post to protect Danish whaling interests from Dutch 'intruders' and experienced a minor trade war between Denmark and Holland in the mid-1700s, nothing really took off there for over 2 centuries. When rich shrimping grounds were found offshore in the early 1950s, the population was 245. When a shrimp-processing plant was built in 1952, however, the town began to grow and now has around 1800 residents.

Information

There isn't a tourist office per se in Qasigiannguit so the Seamen's Home fills in. Don't expect a wealth of information from them, however. As soon as the *Hotel Igdlo* is completed, I suspect it will take over the tourist information business.

Like in all Greenlandic towns north of the Arctic Circle, dog-sled trips can be arranged in March and April either individually or through the new hotel.

Banks in town close at 2 pm.

Museum

The museum (tel 45477) has an excellent collection of relics from the Saqaq through to the present Inuit culture, is open Tuesdays, Thursdays, and Sundays from 2 to 4 pm. Individuals visiting on other days can arrange private openings by contacting them in advance.

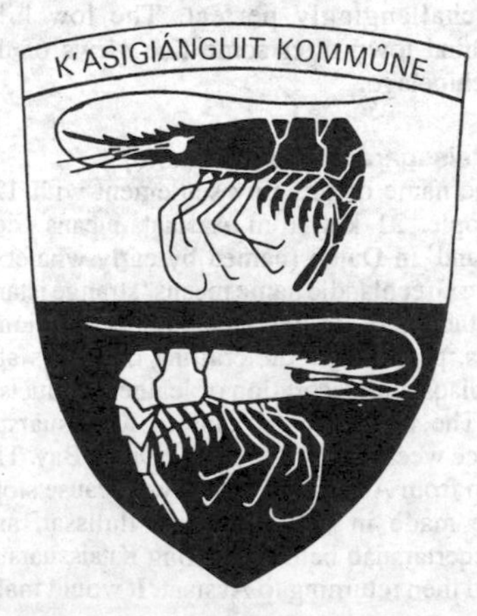

Places to Stay & Eat

The *Hotel Igdlo* (tel 45081), which was under construction when I was in Qasigiannguit, should be finished and operating by the time you read this. No specific prices have been given yet, but it will be the up-market place to stay.

For the time being, the only lodging is at the *Seamen's Home* (tel 45081) which costs singles/doubles US$58/81, including a continental breakfast. As usual, the standard but edible lunches and dinners are served in the cafeteria.

Camping is possible on top of the hill above the police station. It's reasonably private and there's an good view over Disko Bay. You may have to search for awhile, however, to find a flat area suitable for pitching a tent. You can also set up camp at Flyversø, a tidal lake north of the inlet.

Qasigiannguit has two grill bars, the *Nanok* near the museum and the small snack kiosk in the centre. The KNI shop contains a bakery, in case you're interested and, of course, the new hotel will offer a complete dining room service.

Getting There & Away

Air It's possible to fly to or from Ilulissat at least once daily except on Saturdays for US$65 but some discounted seats (US$36) are available as well. There are also five flights weekly between Qasigiannguit and Qeqertarsuaq for the same price.

Ferry During the summer, both the *Kununguak* and the *Disko* call in for an hour or so at Qasigiannguit while travelling up and down the coast. The *Kununguak* stops once weekly in each direction and the *Disko* once every 2 weeks in each direction. The *Tugdlik* passes through Qasigiannguit three times weekly connecting it with other Disko Bay towns and most of the small settlements as well.

Tours

After the Hotel Igdlo opens, it will offer 6-day holiday excursions in Qasigiannguit. The first day will include the ferry trip from Ilulissat and a sightseeing tour of the town for a total of US$65. The following day will feature a guided walk to Paradisbugten ('paradise bay'). It's a 6-hour return walk and costs US$11. Next is an 8-hour boat tour to the settlement of Ikamiut and the Saqaq excavations at Qeqertasugsuk which will cost US$72. On the 4th day there's a fishing tour for US$18 with tackle supplied, and on the 5th day is a visit to the museum and dinner at the hotel for US$30. The final day is free but, at this point, I expect you'll have have seen all you want of Qasigiannguit.

All these day-trips are available à la carte as well and may be booked through the hotel.

QEQERTARSUAQ (GODHAVN)

The Greenlandic name of both Disko Island and its town mean 'big island'. Most visitors comment that the landscape, particularly Qeqertarsuaq's backdrop which is 1.5 billion years old, resembles something you'd expect in a warmer desert clime. The Danish name Godhavn means simply 'good harbour'. The town itself is of very limited interest and the main attraction is the walking available in the valleys between the high, striated, mesa-like mountains of the island.

Qeqertarsuaq was a European whaling port long before the town was actually founded in 1773. Over the years, it slowly grew into the trading centre of northern Greenland and remained the most important village north of Nuuk right up to 1950.

After Qeqertarsuaq began declining relative to other Disko Bay communities, it sank quickly into its present obscure position as a scientific base. The Arctic Research Station, founded by the University of Copenhagen in 1906, carries out field work and classes on the island and the Meteorological Institute Ionosphere Station does meteorological and climatic studies. There was once a small coal mining operation at Qullissat on the north coast of Disko Island but it was closed down in 1969 leaving Qeqertarsuaq, with its population of about 1200, as the island's only habitation.

The village has an odd-looking church (North Atlantic churches always have good curiosity value) that dates back to 1915. Ostensibly, this one, which was designed in by Danish architect Boisen-Møller, is meant to emulate the Viborg church in Denmark but, to me, it looks more like a squared-off

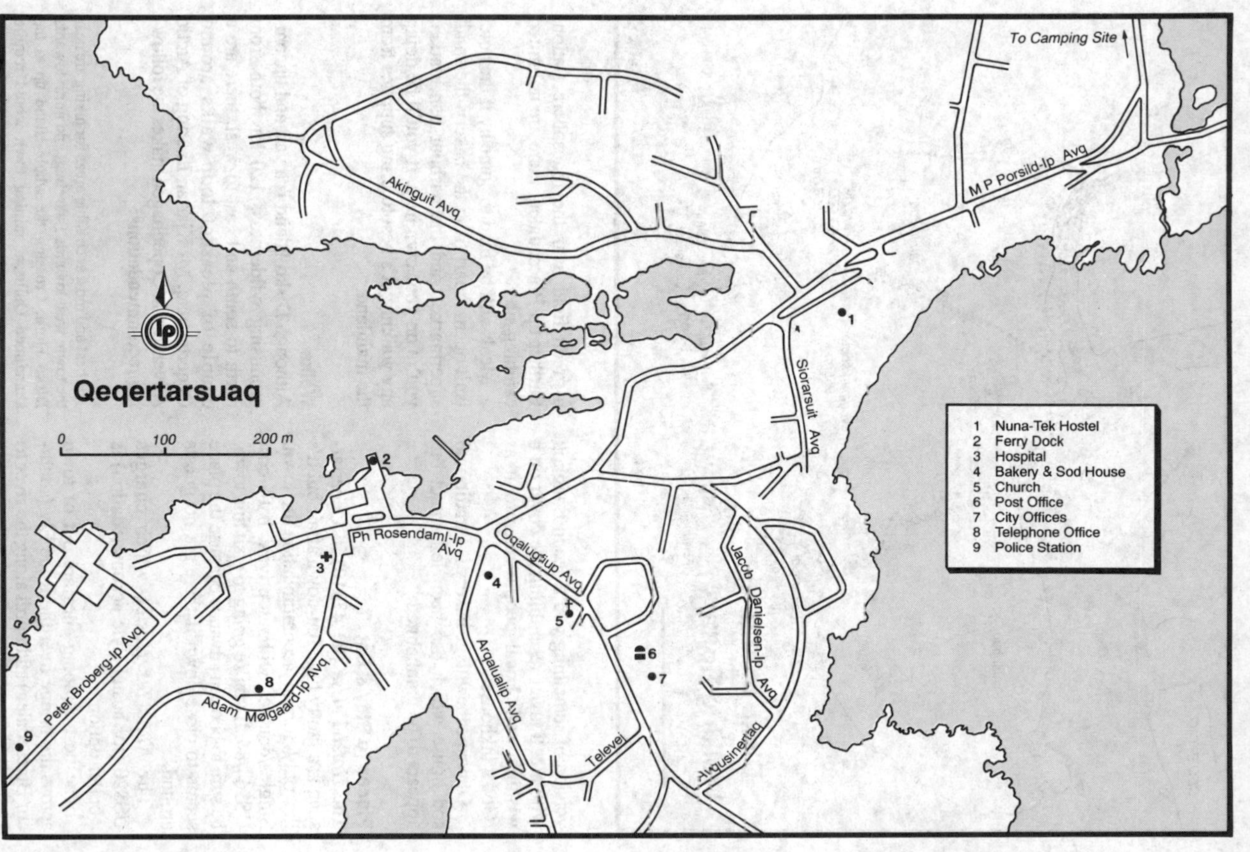
Qeqertarsuaq
0
100
200 m
1 Nuna-Tek Hostel
2 Ferry Dock
3 Hospital
4 Bakery & Sod House
5 Church
6 Post Office
7 City Offices
8 Telephone Office
9 Police Station
To Camping Site
M P Porsild-Ip Avq
Akinguit Avq
Siorarsuit Avq
Ph Rosendaml-Ip Avq
Oqalugfiup Avq
Jacob Danielsen-Ip Avq
Arqalualip Avq
Televej
Avqusinertaq
Adam Mølgaard-Ip Avq
Peter Broberg-Ip Avq
1
2
3
4
5
6
7
8
9

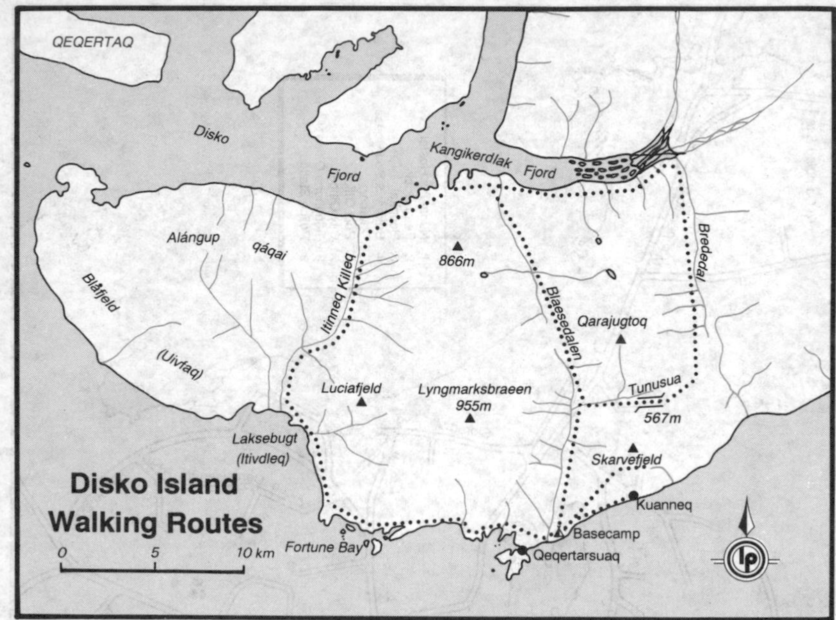

version of something you'd see in Bangkok with a bell tower resembling the cover on a wishing well. Local people refer to it as 'God's inkhouse'.

Opposite the village bakery is a traditional sod house which has been left intact but appears to be uninhabited.

Places to Stay & Eat

The *Hotel Puisse* (tel 47310) in Qeqertarsuaq is a grotty little run-down affair but it's the only formal accommodation in town. Singles/doubles without private bath cost US$64/85. If you're going to visit this town, be sure to book in advance because the place seems to close down if there are no guests around.

The *Nuna-Tek Hostel*, which charges US$20 (for hostel-style accommodation) is a better option.

The best camping sites are out of town across the bridge over the Røde Elv (southern Blaesedalen) and north along the river to a green field near the ionosphere station. Further up Blaesedalen, there are unlimited camping sites.

Meals will be hard to come by if the hotel isn't open. Apart from the bakery, the small supermarket, and the harbour fish market, you're on your own here. If you'll be doing any walking, it's best to bring supplies from the mainland.

Walks

Although Disko Island is a vast and uncompromising wilderness, 120 km both from north to south and east to west, there are a couple of pleasant loop-walks around Qeqertarsuaq. Mr Kjartan Lauring of Arctic Adventure in Copenhagen makes the following recommendations:

> The best and most accessible areas for hiking are near the town; west towards Laksebugt and north towards Disko Fjord. Crossing the whole island up to the abandoned Qullissat mining town would require

extremely good hiking skills and an expedition permit from the Greenlandic government so it's not recommended.

Kuanneq There is a fine 3-km walk east along the beautiful coastline to Kuanneq where there's an impressive outcrop of basalt columns. It is impossible to continue further east because the mountains drop right into the sea. Nor is it possible to continue east by walking around the mountain Skarvefjeld because it's closed off by a big ravine that cannot be crossed on foot.

Skarvefjeld From Qeqertarsuaq, you can climb to the top of the peak Skarvefjeld which is visible from the Blaesedalen camping site. You have only to follow the south-west ridge up the mountain to the flat summit. It's important to go in clear weather or the return route could be obscured by fog.

Laksebugt & Disko Fjord Loop This is another good walk which will require 5 days or longer. The coastline west of town is easier walking although, at times, you'll have to divert to a route higher up the mountainside. Soon you'll come to the beach at Fortune Bay. Follow the steep but negotiable coast line north from there to Laksebugt and then turn inland and walk through the broad and easy pass Itinneq Killeq. Look for the well-formed basalt columns on the mountain Luciafjeld east of the valley.

After you reach the coast again at Disko Fjord, turn east and follow the easy route along the shore to the foot of Blaesedalen pass. From there, it's a reasonably easy walk through the pass back to Qeqertarsuaq. The eastern side of the valley is easier going than the western side.

Along this route, there will be many opportunities for day-trips into side valleys but remember that the basalt mountains are too soft for climbing.

Brededal Alternative From the northern end of Blaesedalen, it's possible to walk east along the shore of Disko Fjord to the head of Kangikerdlak Fjord and then through Brededal valley. When you reach the mouth of the Tunusua valley, branching off to the west, turn up it and cross the 567-metre pass back to Blaesedalen, then turn south and return to Qeqertarsuaq.

Adding this segment to the Laksebugt and Disko Fjord loop trip will add approximately 3 days to the total journey.

Getting There & Away

Air You can fly between Ilulissat and Qeqertarsuaq daily from Monday to Thursday in the summer for US$65. A couple of seats on each flight are sold for a special discount fare of US$36.

Ferry The *Disko* calls in briefly twice fortnightly, once northbound and once southbound. It stops for only an hour carrying passengers to shore and back in a launch. If you want just a quick look around, try to go in with the first run or you won't have enough time for even a superficial look around. On rare occasions, the *Kununguak* calls in briefly. The *Tugdlik* does one weekly trip to Qeqertarsuaq from Ilulissat and continues on to Aasiaat and Qasigiannguit before returning to Ilulissat.

ILULISSAT (JAKOBSHAVN)

Ilulissat ('the icebergs') is an unkempt sort of place whose harbour turns its worst face toward the arriving visitor. If location is everything, however, then Ilulissat is *the* destination in Greenland. This is the Arctic you came to see – a cold and mirror-like sea crowded with icebergs and floes, an often unrelenting grey sky, and a disorderly spirit noticeably missing from the tidier towns further south.

History

The area was inhabited by the ancestors of today's Inuit people, the Saqaq and the Inde-

pendence I and II cultures, between 3500 and 4000 years ago. The abandoned village of Sermermiut, beside the icefjord, dates back perhaps 3500 years and is one of over 120 archaeological sites in the Ilulissat district. When the Norwegian missionary Poul Egede arrived in 1737, Sermermiut was the largest Inuit village in Greenland with 200 people living in 20 or more houses.

The first Europeans to visit Ilulissat were the Norse who undoubtedly sailed up the coast from the Vesturbygd to hunt seals and walrus. The next contact didn't come until the late 17th century when Dutch whalers worked off the coast to provide train oil and whalebone for growing European markets. They named the place Maklykkout and traded European beads, wood, guns, and iron with the Inuit, but took advantage of the locals at every turn. The Dutch government became so upset with their practices, it officially placed mistreatment of the Greenlanders in the same category as piracy and determined it would attract the same stiff penalties.

Whaling continued in the area until 1780 when Greenland's only naval battle took place just outside the present harbour. The Danish king decided monopoly trade would be an appropriate economic setup for Greenland and that the Dutch were getting in the way of his plans. Denmark was successful in ousting the competitors and the Dutch were put out of the picture.

The town of Ilulissat was founded on 12 January 1742, by missionary Poul Egede who intended using it as a summer mission and trading centre. They called it Jakobshavn after Jakob Severin, the influential merchant who controlled much of the trade on Greenland's west coast.

Because the religious mission proved successful, the local Inuit began moving into the European settlement and, by 1782, Ilulissat had become a colony. Today the city is the fourth largest in the country and supports itself primarily with its fleet of over 70 fishing boats and two shrimp and fish-processing plants. It is the hometown of Arctic explorer Knud Rasmussen and also of Jørgen Brønlund, who wrote the note that described the awful fate of the Mylius-Erichsen expedition in north-east Greenland.

Information

The Ilulissat tourist office (tel 43079) is open Monday to Friday from 8.30 am to 4 pm and on Saturdays from 9 to 11 am. Their postal address is Ilulissat Turistforening, PO Box 272, DK-3952 Ilulissat, Greenland. The attached Grønlands Rejsebureau travel agency is open from 9 am to 3 pm Monday to Friday. At other times, the Hotel Hvide Falk and the Hotel Arctic can provide basic information.

The tour company Arctic Adventure offers several tours around the Ilulissat area. Either hotel will be able to set you up with one of their tours or, if you'd rather go with a longer package tour, contact them at the Copenhagen address listed in the Tours section of the Greenland Getting Around chapter.

Boat charters to outlying settlements or to the mouth of the icefjord can be arranged through any of those organisations or by phoning Kaj Madsen (tel 43340).

Things to See & Do

Knud Rasmussen Museum The lovely red house in the centre of Ilulissat once served as the town vicarage. It was here that Greenland's favourite son Arctic explorer, anthropologist, and author Knud Rasmussen was born on 7 July 1879. The building is now a village museum dedicated to Kununguaq or 'little Knud' whose philosophy of life seems typically Greenlandic; he once said, 'Give me winter, give me dogs, and you can have the rest'.

One room of the museum is devoted to his expeditions, and his anthropological and linguistic studies throughout the Arctic. Other exhibits are devoted to traditional Greenlandic life, early Danish life in Greenland, and ancient Inuit artefacts and history. It's open Monday to Friday from 2 to 4 pm.

Cold Museum The Cold Museum, in the oldest building in town (the 'black warehouse' near the harbour) was built when

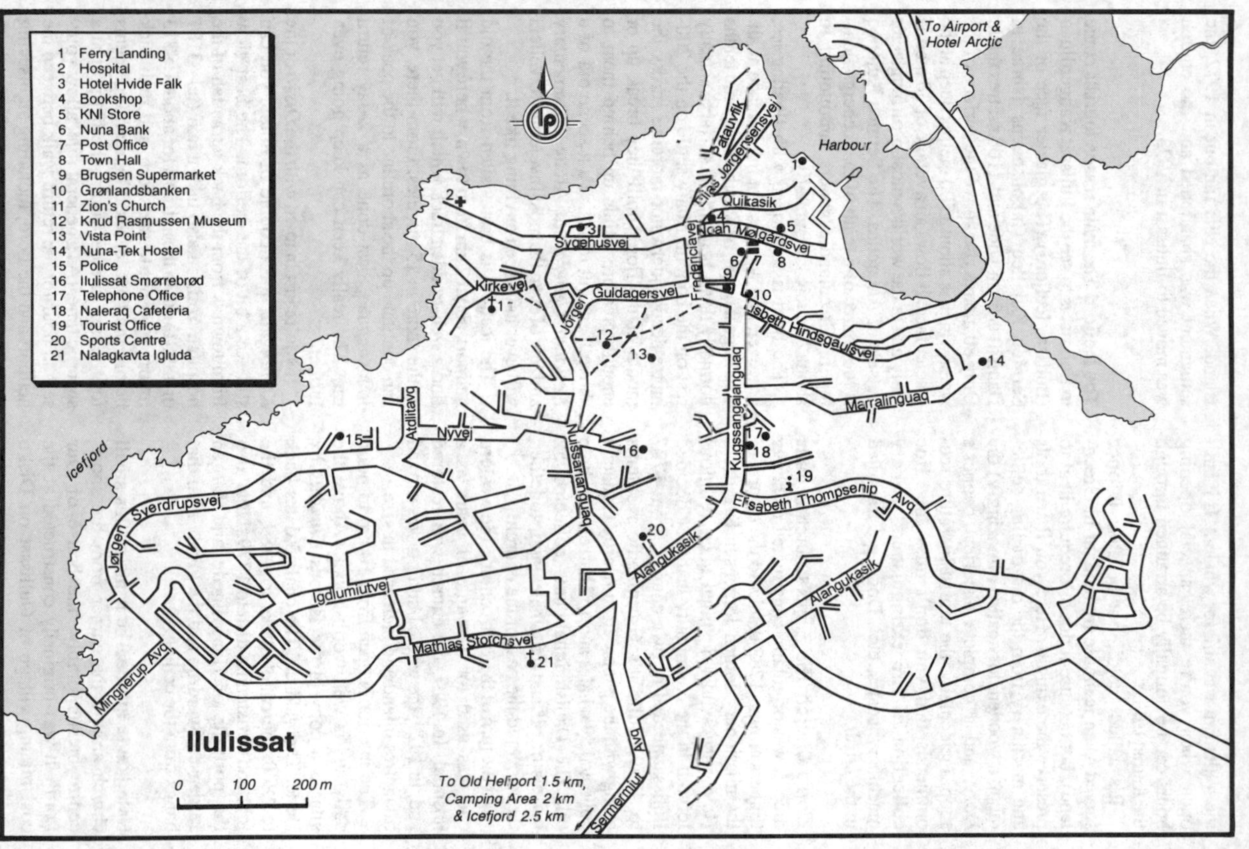
1 Ferry Landing
2 Hospital
3 Hotel Hvide Falk
4 Bookshop
5 KNI Store
6 Nuna Bank
7 Post Office
8 Town Hall
9 Brugsen Supermarket
10 Grønlandsbanken
11 Zion's Church
12 Knud Rasmussen Museum
13 Vista Point
14 Nuna-Tek Hostel
15 Police
16 Ilulissat Smørrebrød
17 Telephone Office
18 Naleraq Cafeteria
19 Tourist Office
20 Sports Centre
21 Nalagkavta Igluda
To Airport & Hotel Arctic
Harbour
Icefjord
Ataavik
Elias Jørgensensvej
Quikasik
Noah Mølgårdsvej
Fredericiavej
Sygehusvej
Kirkevej
Guldagersvej
Jørgen
Isbeth Hindsgaulsvej
Marralinguaq
Kugssangajanguaq
Nuissarianguaq
Atdlitavq
Nyvej
Elsabeth Thompsenip Avq
Alangukasik
Alangukasik
Jørgen Sverdrupsvej
Igdlumiutvej
Mathias Storchsvej
Mingnerup Avq
Sermermiut Avq
Ilulissat
0
100
200 m
To Old Heliport 1.5 km,
Camping Area 2 km
& Icefjord 2.5 km

the settlement was still for whalers. If it isn't open when you're there, special opening hours can be normally be arranged through the tourist office.

It's called 'cold', not because it once served as an icehouse (redundant in Greenland), but because it doesn't require heat to preserve the exhibits. Here you'll see tools and machinery from the old trading settlement, a wooden dory called (amazingly) the *Dory*, and a complete historical cooper's shop. Incidentally, the tourist literature recommends that you don't miss the 'fine collection of fire extinguishers, bakery machinery, scales, etc'. Don't get trampled in the crush.

Zion's Church The Zion's Church is quite nice. It was originally constructed of heavy timbers around 1782 thanks to the efforts of the missionary Jørgen Jørgensen Sverdrup. He'd successfully instilled such religious fervour in the community that they decided Ilulissat needed its own church. From 1777 to 1779, Ilulissat's Greenlandic residents along with the people from nearby Oqaatsut collected 59 whales and 157 barrels of whale oil. The Danish inhabitants collected 52 barrels of oil and 25 whales and, together, they covered the cost of the church.

At the turn of the 20th century, the western end was used for a couple of years as a hospital. In 1907, the church was restored and, in 1929, the whole building was moved 50 metres inland and increased in size.

The interior is open from 10 am to noon daily and is well worth a look. Above the altar is a copy of the famous *Christus* by Bertel Thorvaldsen. The chalice dates back to 1840, the candlesticks to 1789, and the font and christening dish to 1779. Note also the portraits of Hans Egede and Jørgen Jørgensen Sverdrup and the lovely ship that hangs from the ceiling.

Nalagkavta Igluda The name of this small church around the corner from the sports centre means simply 'the house of Our Lord'. It was originally constructed at the coal mining village of Qullissat on Disko Island. When the coal ran out in 1972, the settlement was abandoned and the church was moved to Ilulissat in 1973.

The Icefjord The main reason tourists come to Ilulissat is to see the Ilulissat Kangerdluaq (Ilulissat Icefjord). The glacier face of the Sermeq Kujalleq (Jakobshavns Isbrae in Danish) is 5 km wide and 1100 metres thick. Only 80 metres rise above the surface of the water which is about 1500 metres deep at the glacier face. It flows an average of 30 metres daily and is the world's most prolific glacier outside of Antarctica. The Sermeq Kujalleq is the source of a tenth of the icebergs floating in Greenlandic waters, amounting to about 20 cubic km annually.

The fjord is so choked with floating ice, however, that water is not in evidence at all. The largest bergs, of which about nine tenths normally floats beneath the surface, actually rest on the bottom. Many settle on the 200-metre-deep underwater moraine across the mouth of the fjord, until they break up or enough pressure builds up behind them to shove them out to sea. It's a scene out of a *National Geographic* Arctic documentary and few of even the most inveterate travellers will ever have seen anything like it.

The icefjord is best visited from the old heliport, about 2 km from town, where you'll find a well-trodden track which will get you to the shore in 15 minutes. From there, you can continue up the shoreline to the peak of Inugsunguaq, best done as a 2-day return trip. The really keen can keep going even further.

If you're just in town with the *Disko* or the *Kununguak* for a couple of hours, you can still see a bit of the icefjord. The best view from town is from the back verandah of the hospital. You can also take a taxi (tel 43181 or 43981) out to the heliport for about US$13 return, rush out to the shore, and rush back before the boat leaves. Make arrangements for the taxi to meet you at the heliport at a specific time. (As a general rule, allow yourself an hour for the return walk between the heliport and the fjord, including sightseeing time.) Meet the taxi on time because the driver won't wait and neither will the ferry.

Places to Stay

The new *Hotel Arctic* (tel 44153, fax 43924) is away from traffic and enjoys an excellent view of the icebergs floating in the sea below the promontory. It has conference facilities, free shuttle service between the port or the airport and the hotel, a dining room, a bar with live music and dancing, a souvenir shop, and a billiard room. For all this 'luxury in the Arctic', they charge singles/doubles US$100/128.

The *Hotel Hvide Falk* (tel 43343, fax 43924)) is less pretentious but nearly as expensive. The biggest advantage is that it's convenient to town. There's a bar with live music on weekends, a dining room overlooking the mouth of the icefjord, and a small souvenir shop. Singles/doubles cost US$93/113.

The *Naleraq Cafeteria* (tel 44040) is also a guesthouse, a small and cosy place with only six beds and a common bath.

The *Nuna-Tek Hostel* costs US$20 per night and offers showers, cooking facilities, a sauna, and a TV room. If you book it through Green Tours, you can stay for US$17 per person but that often ends around 21 August when all their staff head back to Denmark. It's also possible to stay at the *Ilulissat Sportshallen* (tel 43459) at hostel prices but you must book in advance.

Camping The two most popular and convenient sites are on the promontory near the Hotel Arctic and along the track between the old heliport and the icefjord. The latter is more secluded but is less convenient to town. Toilets and washing facilities have been set up for campers at the heliport. Camping in the Sermermiat Valley is prohibited.

Places to Eat

For fine dining, you'll have to resort to the hotel dining rooms. Both hotels offer good views but the Hvide Falk's dining room actually overlooks the mouth of the icefjord. It's a good splurge but plan on paying dearly for the view.

For good cafeteria meals or nice but reasonably priced restaurant fare, nothing beats the homely *Naleraq Cafeteria* in the centre. In the residential area behind the museum is *Ilulissat Smørrebrød*, a nice little place that specialises, of course, in smørrebrød concoctions.

The bakery and the KNI and Brugsen supermarkets are all in the centre, convenient to the harbour.

Entertainment

The Naleraq Cafeteria engages Greenlandic bands and offers live music and dancing several nights weekly. Even more of a cultural experience can be had at the Hotel Jakobshavn, just out of town, where locals go to drink and dance to the sounds of Ilulissat musicians. This place doesn't really advertise itself and it's been described as 'a bit odd'. If you go unaccompanied, be prepared for some attention.

Activities

City Tour The tourist office conducts a walking and bus tour for an hour around the highlights of Ilulissat including a drive out along the coastline north of town, the harbour, and Knud Rasmussen Museum, and both churches. How all this can be done in an hour is a mystery, but they manage.

Arctic Adventure also offers a town tour for US$29 including lunch. It visits the same sights as the tourist-office tour except for the drive north but spends more time at each place.

Getting There & Away

Air Ilulissat is the transport hub of northern Greenland and it now has an airport that can handle fixed-wing aircraft including 727s. There are direct flights to all the Disko Bay towns (US$65) as well as to Kangerdlusuaq (US$208), Nuuk (US$473), Uummannaq (US$163), and Upernavik (US$390).

Ferry Most visitors arriving by ferry are aboard the northbound *Disko*. They stay in

Ilulissat while the ship pops off to Uummannaq and Upernavik further north. Then they catch it southbound to Sisimiut where they spend a couple of days before flying to Kangerdlusuaq and on to Iceland or Denmark. Of course it's also possible to travel north on the *Kununguak* and remain in Ilulissat for a week until that ferry returns or await the next arrival of the *Disko* either on its way north or south. Ilulissat is currently the northernmost port on the *Kununguak's* route.

The *Tugdlik* sails from Qasigiannguit twice weekly but returns via a roundabout circuit through Disko Bay.

Tours

Icefjord Tours The tourist office offers 2-hour boat trips around the mouth of the icefjord for US$53 per person. They also do 1-hour helicopter tours up the icefjord to the icecap for US$140 per person. Although the helicopter lands and spends 20 minutes there, the organisers reckon it's too dangerous to do any real looking around. For anyone who must prove they've put out the dough and endured the strain of climbing aboard a helicopter, they'll provide a signed certificate.

Dog-sled Tours From March to May, Ilulissat is one of the best places in Greenland for individually arranged dog-sled tours. They're customised and can last from a couple of hours to several days. You stay in hunters' huts. Possible destinations will include Inugsunguaq peak beside the icefjord, Oqaatsut village, Illiminaq village, and the 'big valley' – Qoororsuaq. It's also possible to go further afield, even as far as Qasigiannguit if you wish. To make advance arrangements, write to the tourist office for further information.

In April, Arctic Adventure conducts prearranged dog-sled tours departing from Copenhagen for US$2450. Although the tour lasts a week, you get only 3 days dog sledding, that is one day-trip and one overnight trip. The rest of the time you get the Hotel Arctic. Most tourist dog-sled tours offer a largely artificial perspective of the experience but this one seems to go to extremes to pamper you.

Kayak Tour Trail Head/Black Feather of Toronto (Canada) offers 27-day kayak tours including 17 days of kayaking around Ilulissat as well as around Nuuk and Uummannaq. The tour spends 7 days in the Ilulissat area kayaking and camping around the mouth of the icefjord and visiting the settlement of Illiminaq to the south. For further information, contact the company at one of the addresses provided in the kayaking section of the Greenland Facts for the Visitor chapter.

AROUND ILULISSAT

Walks from Ilulissat

The map in the book is intended as a guide only. For any of these walks, carry the Dansk Geodaetisk Institut's *Jakobshavn 1:250,000* topo sheet.

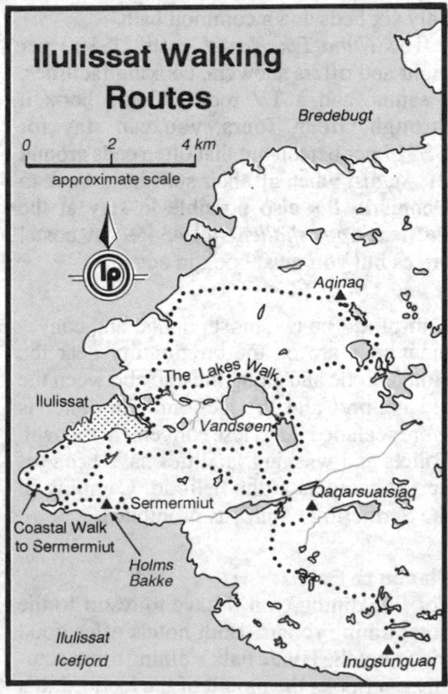

Sermermiut The most popular walk from Ilulissat is out to the abandoned settlement of Sermermiut, to the icefjord, and up the hill Holms Bakke. Begin by walking or taking a taxi out to the old heliport in the huckleberry-carpeted valley about 2 km from the edge of town. Follow the well-worn track out past the cemetery and down to the shore where you'll find the remains of Sermermiut, an abandoned Inuit settlement over 3500 years old.

An alternative route to Sermermiut takes you along the shoreline south of town. This way is a bit rougher but it provides continuous views of the icefjord along the way. At the site you'll find a 4-metre-high slope where archaeologists have uncovered layers of the Saqaq, Dorset, and Independence I and II cultures.

From Sermermiut, continue out along the peninsula which juts into the icefjord for a great view of the densely packed bergs. At the cape is the site where Sermermiut residents once tossed the dead into the sea. Continuing up the fjord from there, you'll reach Holms Bakke where the entire village gathers on 13 January to welcome the sun back after its 5-week sojourn below the horizon.

To return to town, follow the track back to the cemetery and the heliport. The coastal route is the longer of the two but it won't take more than half a day in any case.

The previously mentioned Sermermiut walk can be done with a guide. It costs US$18 and can be arranged on demand through the tourist office or through Arctic Adventure when they have a pre-booked group in town. They also arrange 5-hour walks north of town to Bredebugt and, during the summer, there is a 3-hour midnight-sun walk to Sermermiut and Holms Bakke.

Vandsøen The 7-hour circuit across the Ilulissat plain and past the five Vandsøen lakes is pleasant and not too physically demanding for the average trekker although the ground can be quite soggy in places. Begin by crossing the bridge north-east of town and continue on to the reservoir where you should turn east and follow its southern shore. Cross the river connecting the reservoir with the next lake upstream then again turn east and continue up past three tiny ponds to a larger lake, Vandsø No 4. Walk around the north-east shore, where you'll cross the inflow stream, then turn south and continue to Vandsø No 5.

From there, you can either turn west and return to town or continue south along the eastern shore to the southern end of the lake. Then follow the dog-sled track south over the hill to a long, narrow lake. Walk west, above its northern shore, then bear north to climb a 208-metre hill where there's a great view across the Ilulissat plain and all the Vandsøen. At this stage, the route back to town should be obvious.

Aqinaq A more challenging all-day trip to the 395-metre peak of Aqinaq follows the Vandsøen walk as far as Vandsø No 4. After crossing the inflow, head upstream for less than 1.5 km to the next lake. Pass south of it and around the eastern shore, then turn west and ascend the hill Aqinaq. From the top, you'll have a view all the way north to Oqaatsut and to Ilulissat in the south-west. On the return, walk straight west to the shore where you'll find a track leading south towards town. Again, be prepared for soggy conditions.

Other More walking routes will take you along the dog-sled tracks up the 234-metre peak of Inugsunguaq from which you'll have a commanding view of the icefjord. A good side trip from this route is a climb up 300-metre Qaqarsuatsiaq which offers a great view across the icefjord and the Vandsøen area. The return trip to Inugsunguaq alone will require about 9 hours. Therefore, if you'd like to climb Qaqarsuatsiaq as well, it's best to camp somewhere along the way. Longer trips from Ilulissat are outlined in *Trekking in Greenland* see Books & Bookshops in the Greenland Facts for the Visitor chapter.

Oqaatsut (Rødebay)
Just 20 km walk north of Ilulissat, a long day-hike up the coast, is Oqaatsut. The name of the village means 'cormorants' – the birds which inhabit the nearby cliffs. It first served as a trading post for Dutch whalers during the 1700s. Today it has a population of about 80.

Getting There & Away The 20-km walk to Oqaatsut from Ilulissat isn't too difficult and can be done in a long day. The village is known for its friendly inhabitants and hikers should have no trouble hitching a ride back to Ilulissat that way. Be prepared to pay something, however, and carry a tent anyway. In Greenland, poor weather can disrupt anyone's plans.

The tourist office in Ilulissat offers day-trips to Oqaatsut aboard the *Niga*, a lovely wooden ship built to transport the doctor around the Uummannaq district further north. The Hotel Arctic in Ilulissat also organises weekly 6-hour tours to Oqaatsut and Illimanaq. Advance enquiries should be made to the address listed under Illiminaq at the end of this chapter.

Saqqaq
Saqqaq is probably the nicest settlement in the area. Its name means the 'sunny side' and was apparently given in the same spirit as 'Greenland'. Who could resist a place called Sunny Side, Greenland?

Saqqaq is famous for the gardens of its modern benefactor Hannibal Fencker, a Danish Greenlander dedicated to improving living conditions there. He supplied its electrical generator, grew vegetables in the 24-hour Arctic daylight without fertiliser or artificial means, reared village orphans, and promoted secondary education for the local people. His garden is still a tourist attraction of sorts.

The surroundings are lush compared to those at Ilulissat. The village church, which was built in 1908, is particularly nice. Most of the village income is derived from a meat and fish-processing plant.

Getting There & Away The ferry *Tugdlik* travels between Ilulissat and Saqqaq weekly and stops for 2 hours, enough for a quick look around this beautiful, clean, and successful village.

Illiminaq (Claushavn)
This tiny community with a population of only 70 was probably named after the Dutch whaling captain Claus Pieter Thop who operated in Disko Bay in the early 1700s. Its more beautiful Greenlandic name means 'hopeful place'. It's a good place to visit if you'd like to see the icefjord from the southern perspective. Walk 2 hours north along the shore for the view. You can also visit the three ancient ruined settlements of Iglumiut, Avangnardliit (Nordre Huse), and Eqe along the way.

You can also walk for an hour inland to the two big Taserssuaq lakes or another hour beyond them to the convoluted bay Tasiusaq which is cut off from Disko Bay by the icefjord itself.

Getting There & Away In 5 days, it is possible to walk between Illiminaq and Qasigiannguit but, thanks to the icefjord, you'll have to take a boat from Ilulissat. The *Tugdlik* normally stops at Illiminaq twice weekly on its run from Qasigiannguit to Ilulissat, part of its twice weekly route through Disko Bay, so arranging a return trip from either city may prove problematic.

The Hotel Arctic in Ilulissat does a weekly 6-hour guided tour of both Illiminaq and Oqaatsut. Enquire at the front desk if you're interested or make advance enquiries to the Hotel Arctic (tel 44153, fax 43924), PO Box 501, DK-3952 Ilulissat, Greenland.

North-West Greenland

As yet, few visitors make it to north-west Greenland. It's not due to a lack of interest but rather to transport schedules and the expense required to get there. The *Disko* heads north to Uummannaq and Upernavik once a fortnight in the summer but there is no reliable transport to Qaanaaq (Thule) or villages beyond.

The fact is, most visitors would agree the Arctic paradise of Knud Rasmussen and Jean Malaurie is nearly lost. The Danish brought education together with a new language, economic dissatisfaction, and social changes. The US base at Pituffik brought – the US. What remains is a very confused group of people who only 40 years ago still lived and hunted as their ancestors had for thousands of years. Today they have junk food, alcohol, video, snow machines, speed boats, prefab housing, and all the trappings of what some would call the worst of Europe and North America combined.

UUMMANNAQ

If South Greenland is the country's 'banana coast', Uummannaq with its incredible setting is its Rio de Janeiro. Uummannaq's crowning feature is the wonderful and imposing 1175-metre red gneiss mountain. The way the town rambles over striated gneiss hills at its feet, anchored to the rocks with pipes and cables, you wonder if a big wind might not send it all tumbling into the sea.

The town sits at 70° north latitude, the same as North Cape, Norway, and Prudhoe Bay (Alaska) yet nearly half of Greenland is still north of it!

Although the Uummannaq district has been a seasonally inhabited hunting ground for several millennia and Dutch whalers worked in the area during the 17th century, the first settlement was founded on the Nuusuaq peninsula in 1758 and moved to the present site of Uummannaq in 1763. It developed over the years into a sealing district and service centre to the mines in the Marmorilik and Qaarsut areas.

In the 1960s, a shrimp-processing plant was built at Uummannaq and the area is slowly making the transition from a hunting to a fishing district. The current population is around 1300 but everyone lives in single family dwellings because, thankfully, there is too little level space and too much solid rock to anchor the characterless blocks of flats so common in other towns.

Information

The friendly and enthusiastic tourist office (tel 48277) is upstairs in the community building. It's open from 8.30 am to 2 pm weekdays. The postal address is Uummannaq Turistudvalg, PO Box 70, DK-3961 Uummannaq, Greenland.

Both the tourist office and the hotel can arrange dog-sled trips or suggest drivers to those who'd like to make organise their own trips. The Hotel Uummannaq has a boat which is used for excursions around the district. If you're interested in visiting the villages, enquire at the hotel.

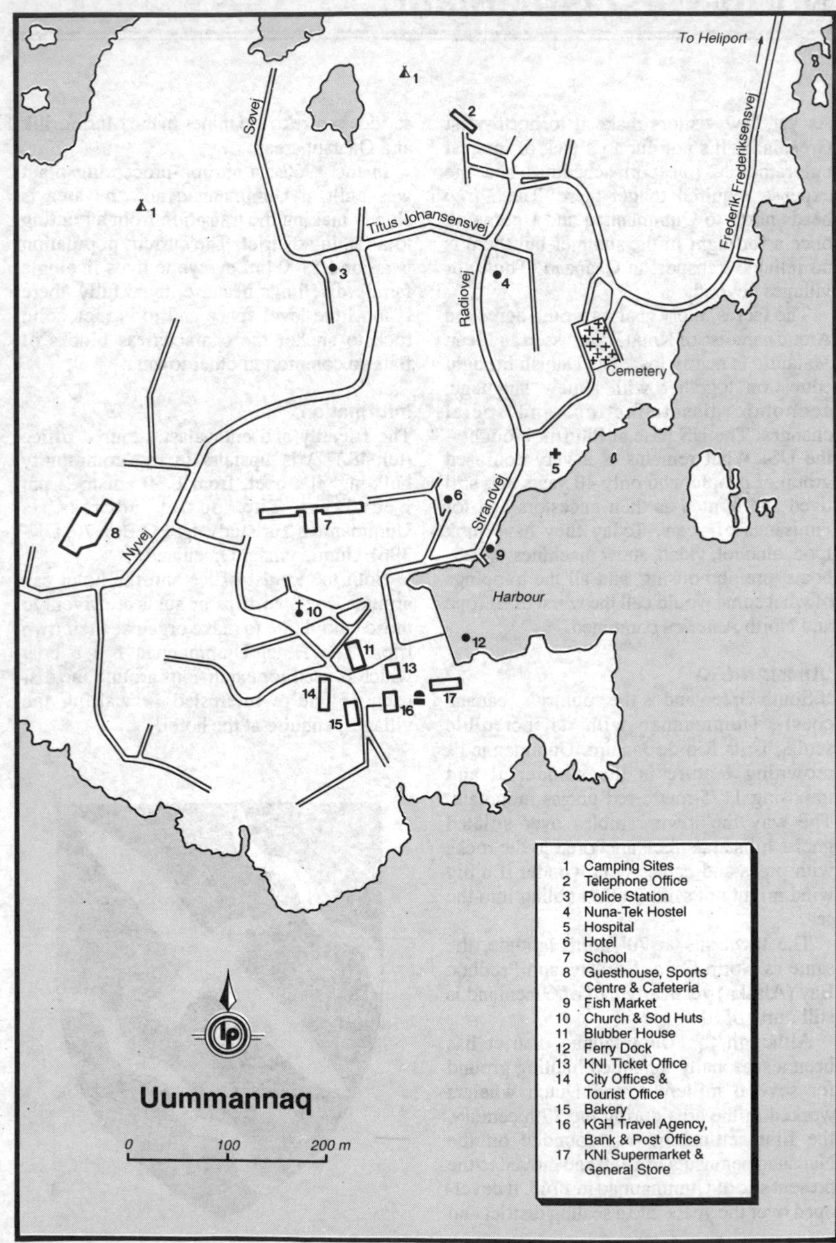
To Heliport
Søvej
Titus Johansensvej
Radiovej
Frederik Frederiksensvej
Cemetery
Strandvej
Nyvej
Harbour
Uummannaq
0
100
200 m
1 Camping Sites
2 Telephone Office
3 Police Station
4 Nuna-Tek Hostel
5 Hospital
6 Hotel
7 School
8 Guesthouse, Sports Centre & Cafeteria
9 Fish Market
10 Church & Sod Huts
11 Blubber House
12 Ferry Dock
13 KNI Ticket Office
14 City Offices & Tourist Office
15 Bakery
16 KGH Travel Agency, Bank & Post Office
17 KNI Supermarket & General Store

Things to See & Do

Church & Sod Huts The Uummannaq church is unique in Greenland, constructed of granite boulders chipped from the nearby hillside. It was consecrated in 1935. When the ferry is in port, the church opens and it's possible to climb the bell tower.

On the church lawn are three old sod huts which are marked for preservation as national historical buildings. The largest one was constructed in 1925 and once housed two families. Another, also built in 1925, was not inhabited until 1982. The third, built in 1949, served as a potato storage shed.

Museum The northern end of the building was constructed in 1880 as the home of the Royal Greenland Trade Department's clerk. It was enlarged 9 years later and converted into a hospital and, in 1921, further additions were made. It went through various stages, finally becoming a museum in 1988. The nearby yellow houses were built in 1907, one as the home of the clergy and the other as the doctor's residence.

There's an entire room devoted to the ill-fated expedition of German scientist Alfred Wegener on the inland ice in 1930. There's also information about the Marmorilik mine, Greenlandic archaeology and history, the Qilaqitsoq mummies, the whaling era, and the history of the museum itself. It's one of the better museums in Greenland .

The museum (tel 48104) is open from 8 am to 4 pm Monday to Friday. If you're there at any other time, phone and they'll arrange special opening hours for you.

Blubber House The yellow-washed boulder house opposite the sod huts was built in 1860 and served as a whale-oil warehouse. The blubber wasn't actually boiled down there because the smell would have driven everyone out of town.

Ship's Welcome It's an Uummannaq tradition to heartily welcome the first ship to sail into the harbour each spring. Lookouts are posted on the hill Nasiffik west of town. When they call out 'Umiarssuit!' or 'Ship!' the entire village gathers on the hill to await the arrival. From the fort hill, south of the harbour, three old cannons are fired in welcome not only to the ship but also to the springtime. The cannons are fired again for the departure of the season's last ship, but with considerably less fanfare.

Dog-sled Tours Uummannaq is the best place in Greenland to enjoy a traditional winter dog-sledding experience with local seal hunters who offer tours during the slack hunting period from March to May. The seas around Uummannaq are permanently frozen through the winter and provide a level and comfortable sledding surface between villages normally accessible only by boat. During the sledding season, dog-sled races occur around the district and some visitors may be fortunate enough to join in the festivities.

The prices are about half those of individually organised expeditions in Ilulissat and the number of villages in the area will ensure that tourists who'd like to sleep indoors can do so. Villages rent out their community halls to sledding parties for around US$60 per night and the driver's fee normally works out to about US$30 per person per day.

Kayak Tours Again, Black Feather/Trail Head does organised kayak trips around the Uummannaq area in conjunction with their package tour to Ilulissat. It includes kayaking back and forth to Qilaqitsoq and travelling by charter boat to the outlying settlement of Ukerasaq and exploring the area (by kayak). The highlight is the 7-day paddling and camping trip from the settlement of Ukkusissat back to Uummannaq. For further information, see Ilulissat in the Disko Bay chapter.

Around the Island

Since Uummannaq is on a small island, walking opportunities from town are limited. It is possible to walk into the hills above the reservoir and up to the shoulder of Uummannaq Mountain. The geology in these areas is fascinating and it's a safe bet you'll see nothing like it anywhere else.

Santa Claus House It seems that Danes and Greenlanders have declared Uummannaq the official residence of Santa Claus. The Finns have him living in Rovaneimi (Finland) and the Swedes in Kiruna (Sweden). Well, I've always been told he was a fellow Alaskan. I guess the guy is probably wealthy enough to maintain residences all around the Arctic.

His home in Uummannaq is a traditional Greenlandic sod house beneath the slopes of Uummannaq Mountain. It's about a 3-hour return walk from town. You can visit, if you'd like, but you probably already realise that Santa is a very busy man so don't expect to find any one home.

Uummannaq Mountain Wonderful Uummannaq Mountain, one of the most unusual and colourful sights in the Arctic, provides both a backdrop and a source of entertainment for those looking up at it. Like Australia's Ayers Rock, it can change dramatically from moment to moment, passing through any combination of colours from dull cloud-wrapped grey to pastel rose to carrot orange, back to sepia and pale violet to grey.

The mountain and the entire island is composed of a geological formation known as basement gneiss, a type of granite which has been deformed by intense pressure and heat into a wildly striped and swirled surface which could make some very interesting photos.

An unlikely story has it that the precipitous peak has been climbed only twice: the first time by a Swiss expedition which planted its flag on the summit and the second time by an Inuit who tramped up there to remove the 'debris' they'd left behind. The truth is, it has been climbed several times but it's a highly technical trip. Most visitors are content to just tramp around the base and marvel at the black, white, and rose swirls, whorls, and stripes that characterise the island's bizarre granite formations.

Places to Stay

The new *Hotel Uummannaq* (tel 48518) is the most northerly hotel in Greenland. Singles/doubles cost US$86/107 and, if you want a luxury suite (Arctic style), you'll pay US$138. All rooms have private bath, colour TV, radio, and telephone.

Other accommodation is available at the *Sports Centre* which charges US$29 per person for a comfortable room. The *Nuna-Tek Hostel* charges the usual US$20.

Camping is possible around the reservoir above town. You'll find a few level places but there's a lot of trash lying around.

Places to Eat

For those craving something elegant with an iceberg-studded view, go to the restaurant at the Hotel Uummannaq. Otherwise, try the *Grill-Baren* by the harbour or the typical cafeteria at the Sports Centre. The braettet harbour market is also near the hotel opposite the ferry landing site.

Just above the harbour area, you'll find the KNI supermarket which also sells postcards, shoes, clothing, and sports equipment. Across the parking lot is a wonderful bakery.

Getting There & Away

Air There are helicopter departures daily except Sundays between Ilulissat and Uummannaq for US$163 each way. You can also fly on to Upernavik three times weekly in the summer for US$227 each way.

Ferry The *Disko* calls into Uummannaq (for 5 or 6 hours on both its northbound and southbound journeys) once a fortnight during the summer. Those who'd like to spend a couple of days in Uummannaq can arrive on the northbound ferry, wait while it does the 2-day run up to Upernavik and back, and then return with the boat to Ilulissat.

AROUND UUMMANNAQ

Qilaqitsoq Qilaqitsoq was catapulted to international fame in 1977 when the National Museum in Nuuk – and through them the world – learned of the 1972 discovery of eight Inuit mummies in a cave there.

National Geographic did a cover story on the find and, suddenly, people everywhere were captivated by the haunting face of the 6-month-old boy on the cover who lived and died in 15th-century Greenland.

They were originally found by ptarmigan hunters Hans and Jokum Grønvold from Uummannaq. They photographed the site and made reports to government authorities but nothing was done about the discovery until 1977 when Jens Rosing took over the director's post at the National Museum.

One mummy was the 6-month-old baby, another was a 4-year-old, apparently a victim of Down's Syndrome and, one of the six adults (all women) suffered from debilitating disease. According to Greenlandic custom, the bodies were dressed in heavy clothing suitable for the long, cold journey to the land of the dead. There was no evidence of violence, famine, accident, or epidemic which may have caused the deaths of these people and several theories have arisen about their fate. Food poisoning is postulated, as are drowning and hypothermia. It is most probable, however, that they were considered burdens on the society and sent out to die of exposure.

Although several of the mummies may now be seen in the National Museum in Nuuk, the Uummannaq tourist office still organises tours to Qilaqitsoq and the mummies' cave while the *Disko* is in port. It will cost about US$170 for up to three people, a bit steep unless you're extremely keen to visit.

You can read more about the discovery and subsequent researching of the find in the *National Geographic* (February 1985). The museum in Nuuk also sells the booklet *Qilakitsoq – the Mummy Cave* available in English, Danish, and Greenlandic for US$1.

Qilaqitsoq Mummy

Qaarsut

This village's name means 'naked mountains'. It sits in a broad valley on the Nuusuaq peninsula, just 21 km west of Uummannaq, and is home to over 200 people. It supports itself with seal hunting, fishing, and seal-leather working at the Neriunaq Cooperative. Until 1924, the first coal mine in Greenland operated in Qaarsut and supplied the district with inexpensive fuel. This mine was the site of the country's first labour strike during which the foremen and the village priest had to go to work as miners! The Uummannaq tourist office can arrange trips by charter boat across the strait for visits to Qaarsut's sandy beach and for climbing or hiking around the distinct 1900-metre cone-shaped peak Qilertinnguit which rises nearby.

Ukerasaq

Ukerasaq ('the sound') lies on an island of the same name, 40 km east of Uummannaq.

On the island, at the abandoned village of Uummannatsiaq, is a school camp for Uummannaq district students. Although I haven't done it, the tourist office recommends a relatively easy day-walk from Uummannatsiaq to Ukerasaq. They can arrange transport to the island and back and sometimes lead guided trips along the route.

Marmorilik

Marmorilik, a mining village, 30 km north of Uummannaq, is run by the Danish and Canadian venture Greenex employing 300 workers. Its name means 'place of marble' because marble was quarried there and exported to Europe until that was no longer profitable. The mine today produces lead, zinc, and silver. The ore is extracted from a 1000-metre mountain called 'the black angel' due to a dark ore deposit on the rock wall. It is transported from the rock face at 600 metres to the processing area on a 1.5-km-long suspension cable, processed on site and exported to Europe in powder form.

Marmorilik isn't currently open to visitors and few miners are even permitted to take their families there. Eight million tonnes of ore have been extracted since mining began in 1972. The supply is rapidly running out, however, and the site will probably open up to visitors after it's abandoned, which is likely to happen soon.

UPERNAVIK

Upernavik, a community of 900 people, is the most northerly ferry terminal in Greenland. A few travellers ride the boat up there just for the curiosity value. Its economy is based on sealing and polar-bear hunting but is currently diversifying with some fishing.

At this point, you're more than 700 km north of the Arctic Circle at a latitude of 72° 50' north and the average summer temperature is 5°C. It's really not a terribly interesting village but the geology of Upernavik Island is fascinating and worth a day of exploration. It's small and, since the *Disko* normally anchors in the harbour for 9 hours, energetic visitors will have plenty of time to explore the entire island on foot.

Information

Although the tourist information office upstairs in the city offices is marginally helpful, the best information is found at the museum office opposite the museum itself.

Museum

Upernavik's museum is a real surprise. It's hopelessly disorganised but has a lot of cosy character and was one of my favourites. The visitors' book was started 60 years ago and still isn't full.

Perhaps the most interesting display is the original qajaq ensemble complete with harpoon, throwing stick, bird skewer, knife, seal-stomach float (to prevent seals diving after being hit), and line made of leather thong. The curator, Mr Peter Bendtzen, will explain their use in as much detail as you have time for. He's also the best tourist officer in town and can tell you anything you'd like to know about getting around the outlying areas of the Upernavik district.

You'll also see lots of other assorted historical paraphernalia including a collection of Greenlandic money which was in use until the Danish notes became the standard currency in the 1950s. One beautiful 100 krona note bears a portrait of Knud Rasmussen and a drawing of the Thule mountains.

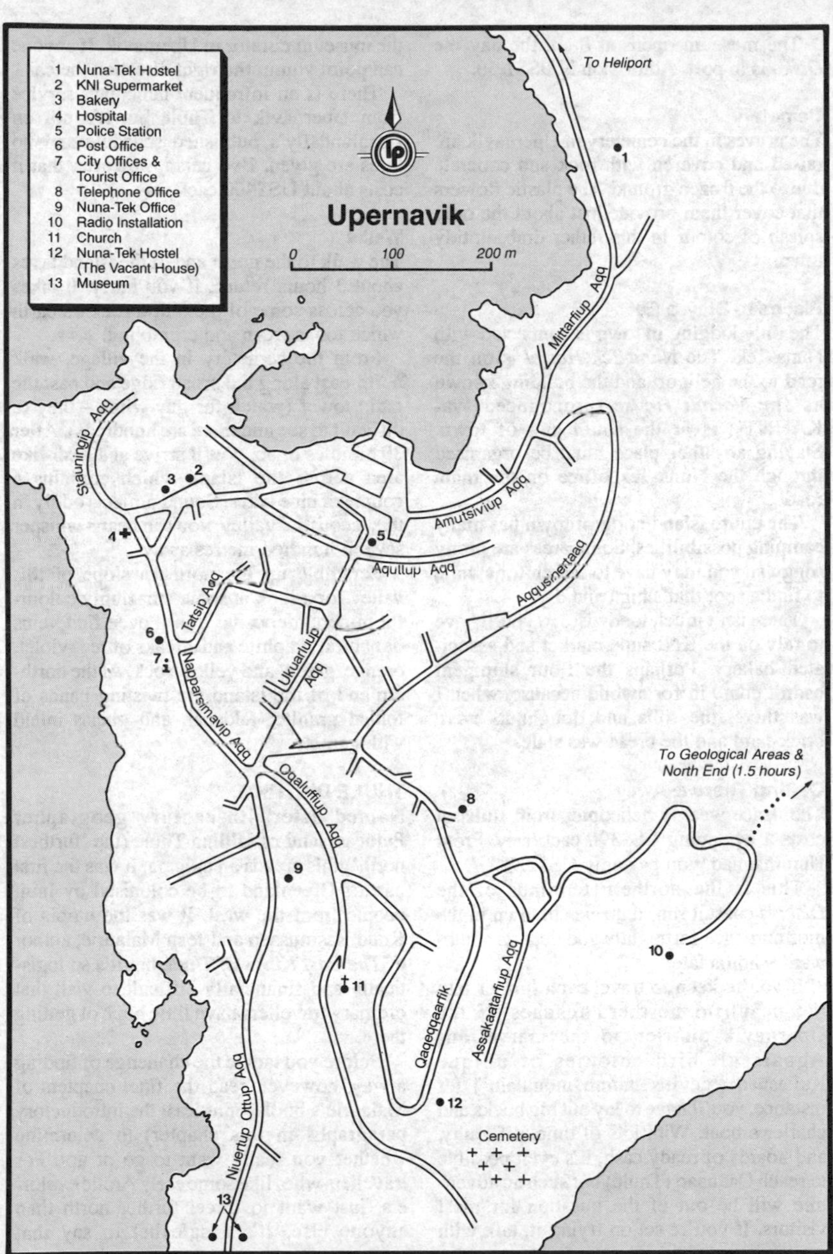

1 Nuna-Tek Hostel
2 KNI Supermarket
3 Bakery
4 Hospital
5 Police Station
6 Post Office
7 City Offices & Tourist Office
8 Telephone Office
9 Nuna-Tek Office
10 Radio Installation
11 Church
12 Nuna-Tek Hostel (The Vacant House)
13 Museum
Upernavik
0
100
200 m
To Heliport
Mittarfiup Aqq
Stauningip Aqq
Amutsiviup Aqq
Aqqusinertaaq
Aqullup Aqq
Tatsip Aqq
Ukuarluup Aqq
Napparsimavip Aqq
Oqaluffiup Aqq
To Geological Areas & North End (1.5 hours)
Qaqeqqaarfik
Assakaatarfiup Aqq
Niuertup Ottup Aqq
Cemetery

The museum opens at 8 am the day the *Disko* is in port. Admission is US$1.50.

Cemetery

The graves in the cemetery in Upernavik are raised and covered with rock and concrete due to the frozen ground. The plastic flowers that cover them provide just about the only splash of colour in this rather drab, untidy town.

Places to Stay & Eat

The only lodging in town is connected with Nuna-Tek. The *Nuna-Tek Hostel* is on the road to the heliport and the building known as the *Vacant House* (pronounced 'va-KAHNT') is at the south end of town. Staying at either place must be organised through the Nuna-Tek office on the main road .

The entire island north of town has many camping possibilities. Some areas are pretty soggy so you may have to search for awhile to find a spot that's high and dry.

There isn't much foodwise, so you'll have to rely on the KNI supermarket and associated bakery. Perhaps the flour shipment hadn't come in for awhile because, when I was there, the rolls and doughnuts were brick-hard and the bread was stale.

Getting There & Away

The thrice weekly helicopter from Ilulissat costs a whopping US$390 each way. From Uummannaq, you pay only US$228.

This is the northern terminus of the *Disko*'s coastal run. It arrives in town in the morning once fortnightly and departs southward 9 hours later.

If you're keen to travel even further into the beautiful northern reaches of the Upernavik district, to the marvellous Agparssuit bird colonies or unique Kullasuaq ('devil's thumb mountain') for instance, you'll have to lay out big bucks and charter a boat. With lots of time, difficulty, and hoards of ready cash, it's even possible to reach Qaanaaq (Thule) but such an adventure will be out of the question for most visitors. If you're set on trying it, talk with the museum curator in Upernavik. If anyone can point you in the right direction, he can.

There is an infrequent helicopter service from Upernavik to Thule but it's not on Grønlandsfly's published schedule and no fares are given. I've heard, however, that it costs about US$400 each way.

Walks

The walk to the north end of the island takes about 3 hours return, if you hurry. It takes you across some of the oldest rock on earth which looks worn and crumbling.

From the cemetery in the village, walk north-east along the broad ridge and past the radio tower (watch for guy wires – they're difficult to see and there are hundreds). After 30 minutes or so, you'll arrive at a gash-like area across the island which contains a couple of nice lakes. Sound projects oddly in this 'acoustic' valley; you can hear a whisper several hundred metres away!

Scramble up the northern slope of this valley for a look at some amazingly colourful mineral deposits. You'll even find veins of natural graphite and streaks of red, violet, orange, green, and yellow rock. At the northern end of the island are twisting bands of folded granite, feldspar, and gneiss inlaid with garnets.

THULE DISTRICT

Named after 4th-century geographer Pytheas' land of Ultima Thule (the 'furthest north') this area is an enigma. It was the first part of Greenland to be colonised by Inuit people from the west. It was the utopia of Knud Rasmussen and Jean Malaurie, author of *The Last Kings of Thule* but it's so logistically and financially difficult to visit that ordinary travellers have little hope of getting there.

Before you tackle the challenge of finding a way, however, read the final chapters of Malaurie's book (or at least the introductory paragraphs in this chapter) to determine whether you really want to go or not. For travellers who, like some early Arctic explorers, just want to travel further north than anyone else, it's a safe bet to say that

Hot springs, Unartoq Island, Greenland (DS)

Top: Harbour at Qeqertarsuaq, Disko Island, Greenland (DS)
Bottom: Hvalsey ruins, 2 day's walk from Qaqortoq, Greenland (DS)

Upernavik is already further north than anyone you know has ever been and is infinitely easier to visit!

Qaanaaq (Thule)

The village of Qaanaaq, the world's most northerly palindrome, was moved 200 km north of its original site to its present location in 1953 after being displaced by the US airbase at Pituffik. It currently has a population of about 400. There's no hotel but visitors can find lodging at the Nuna-Tek hostel or camp out. The only place to eat is the Polar Grill which serves fast food but there is a KNI Supermarket which is stocked whenever the flight comes in.

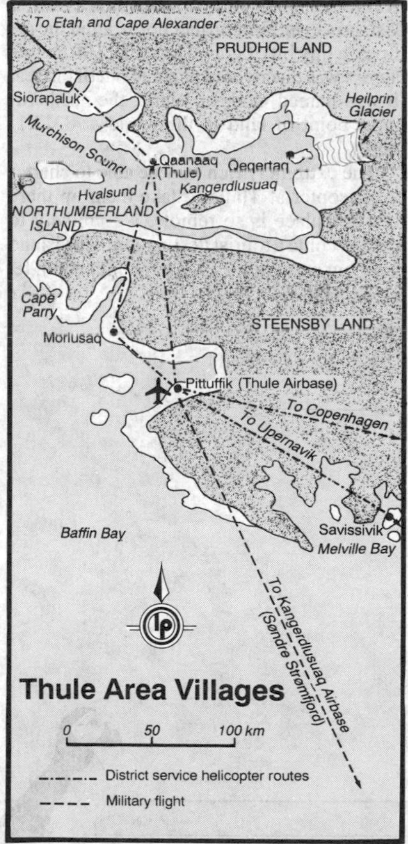

Siorapaluk

The northernmost civilian village in the world (Alert on Canada's Ellesmere Island is further north but it's a scientific post), Siorapaluk, has neither electricity nor running water. In the winter, water is made by melting ice. The locals survive by halibut fishing and seal, narwhal, and polar-bear hunting. Winter temperatures reach -50°C and lower. Siorapaluk is accessible by private boat or helicopter from Qaanaaq.

Getting There & Away

Those who manage to fly into Pittuffik (Thule Airbase) must secure a permit similar to the one necessary for the Kangerdlusuaq base. It is possible every few weeks to fly to the airbase (with a permit, of course) from Copenhagen and Kangerdlusuaq for around US$600 each way. From there, you can reach the other villages by helicopter or private boat.

In early 1989, when KNI announced a special 25th anniversary cruise of the *Kununguak*, commemorating the ship's inauguration and Knud Rassmussen's overland expeditions to Greenland's far north, the trip was booked out in an hour. It's unlikely that KNI will ever begin a regular ferry service to the far north (the lucky few who laid out the bucks for the 25th anniversary cruise certainly seemed hostile to the idea, anyway) but, if they do, look for this remote outpost district to become *the* destination in Greenland.

For other more complicated options, see the Upernavik Getting There & Away section. Incidentally, visitors are not permitted to bring alcohol of any kind into the Thule district.

Tour

Those who have an extra US$4600 may be happy to know that 'the adventure of a lifetime' is now available from Grønlands Rejsebureau. Once a year they offer 16-day dog-sled tours to the Thule district in late winter. The tour includes the flight to the Thule Airbase and journeys by helicopter to Qaanaaq and by dog sled to Siorapaluk, some time at the Neqit hunting camp, and returns to Qaanaaq. The grand finale is a 4-day hunting trip by dog sled (with accommodation in hunting huts and tents) to Northumberland Island and back. Considering what you get, the price isn't really all that exorbitant. Address enquiries to Grønlands Rejsebureau, Gammel Mønt 12, Box 130, DK-1004 Copenhagen, Denmark.

OODAAQ ISLAND

For many years, geography books told us the northernmost point of land in the world was Cape Morris Jesup (Greenland) at 83° 20' north latitude. Then, a small island was discovered off the north coast – a speck of land way up north of Peary Land named Kaffeklubben Ø ('coffee club island') presumably because someone decided to pass a thermos around while looking at it. Kaffeklubben Ø's day in the sun was not to last, however. Still further north, amid the ice floes, a tiny bit of gravel less than 100 metres across was discovered peeping out of the sea. It was named Oodaaq Island, the northernmost point of land in the world at 83° 21' north.

The extremely rich may be able to charter a helicopter at Thule to take them up there but this place is so remote, it's unlikely to ever become a tourist destination. This island isn't big enough for even a mountain hut, let alone a hotel.

East Greenland

Culturally, the isolated eastern coast of Greenland is significantly different to the western coast. It's known to the Greenlanders as *Tuna* or 'the back door'.

It is believed that the Independence I culture migrated via Peary Land in the extreme north and the Saqaq culture came from the west coast. They met somewhere around the present site of Ittoqqoortoormiit but their settlement on the east coast lasted only briefly. During the 15th and 16th centuries another migration took place, this time from the Thule region of north-west Greenland. The people settled in several places along the coast but, in 1800, all but Ammassalik had been abandoned.

It was in this area that Gunnbjörn, the lost sailor from Iceland, ended up in 875. He called the coastal islets Gunnbjörn's Skerries and left posthaste for his original destination. After the Østerbygd had been settled, Europeans undoubtedly sailed up the eastern coast of Greenland on hunting trips.

Until 1884, many historians mistakenly believed the Østerbygd had been on the east coast but several hundred years of searching had proved unfruitful. In that year, when the Danish Umiaq expedition which had set out in search of evidence of Norse habitation came back empty handed, it was decided the Østerbygd was actually Eirík Rauðe's settlement on the west coast. Led by Dane Gustav Holm, this expedition found 416 Inuit people in the Ammassalik area and took home some 500 artefacts (these relics are now being returned to Greenland for display in

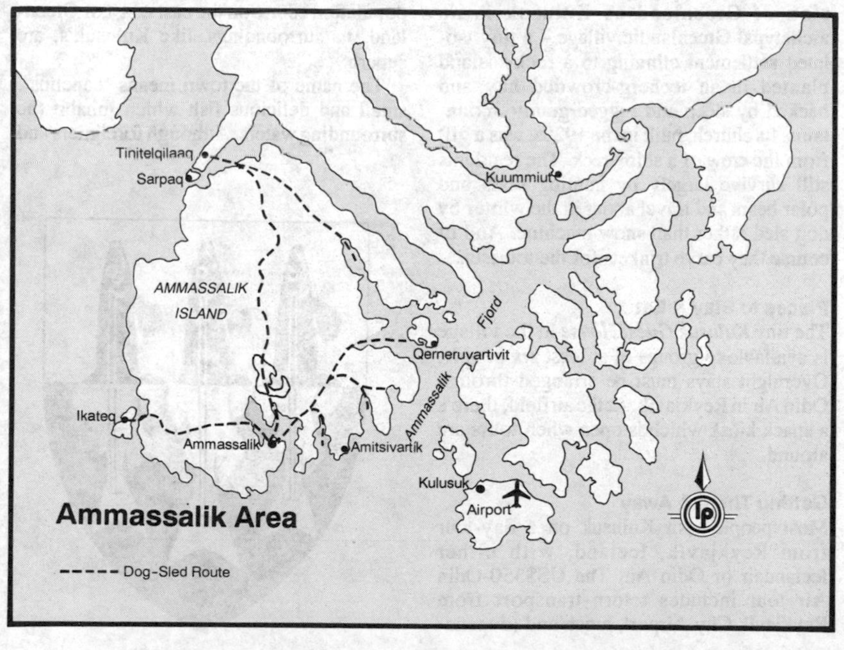

museums). In 1894, the first Royal Greenland Trade Department trading post was established on Ammassalik Island.

Today, east Greenland remains dependent on hunting and subsistance fishing. The place has a noticeably different feel to it than the more populous west coast and, although tourism is big business in the Ammassalik area, there is still time before radical changes come to this beautiful area.

KULUSUK (KAP DAN)

Tourism in Greenland has so far been well contained. One could safely estimate that 80% of foreign visitors see only the small island village of Kulusuk, where the airport serving Ammassalik was built by an American crew setting up a radar station in 1958. Most people stay only 3 hours; it's rare for anyone to stay longer than 3 days. These short-term visits mean that Kulusuk hasn't been overwhelmingly affected by easy access from the outside world.

These day-trippers get a splendid impression of Greenland as Kulusuk is an archetypal Greenlandic village – a tiny isolated settlement clinging to a rocky island planted in an iceberg-crowded bay and backed by steep and rugged granite mountains. Its church, built in the 1920s, was a gift from the crew of a shipwreck. The residents still survive largely by hunting seals and polar bears and travel about in the winter by dog sled rather than snow machine. And of course they carve trinkets for the tourists...

Places to Stay & Eat

The tiny *Kulusuk Guest House* in the village is available to groups of at least six people. Overnight stays must be arranged through Odin Air in Reykjavík. At the airfield, there's a snack kiosk which is open when tours are around.

Getting There & Away

Most people visit Kulusuk on a day-tour from Reykjavík, Iceland, with either Icelandair or Odin Air. The US$350-Odin Air tour includes return transport from Reykjavík City Airport, lunch and (depending on the season) a jeep or dog-sled tour around the island. Icelandair charges US$332 for a similar trip. These tours have been described as '1-day jaunts to another planet'. If you'd rather not get such an impression of Greenland, which is very much a part of planet Earth, give the tour a miss.

If you want to go to Ammassalik and extend your stay up to 3 days, the price rises to US$500 per person. Since Icelandair is not permitted to carry transit passengers, if you arrive in Kulusuk with them, you are not permitted to remain in Greenland longer than 3 days and may not leave the Kulusuk-Ammassalik area.

Grønlandsfly has twice-weekly flights between Kulusuk and Kangerdlusuaq for US$277 each way.

AMMASSALIK (TASIILAQ)

Ammassalik lies on an island of the same name just across the mouth of the fjord from Kulusuk. With 5000 residents, it is the main population centre on the east coast of Greenland. Its surroundings, like Kulusuk's, are superb.

The name of the town means 'capelins', small and delicious fish which inhabit the surrounding waters. Although foreigners and

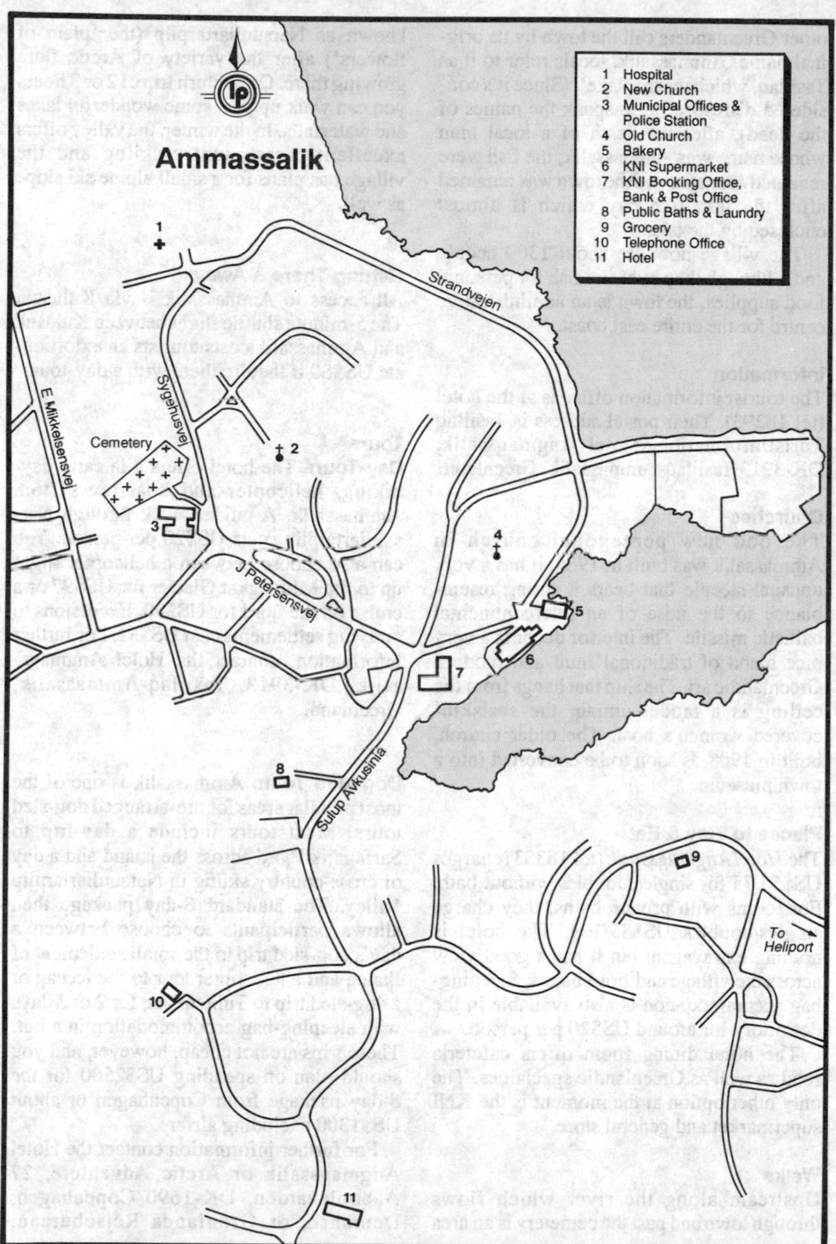
Ammassalik
1 Hospital
2 New Church
3 Municipal Offices & Police Station
4 Old Church
5 Bakery
6 KNI Supermarket
7 KNI Booking Office, Bank & Post Office
8 Public Baths & Laundry
9 Grocery
10 Telephone Office
11 Hotel
Strandvejen
Sygehusvej
E Mikkelsensvej
Cemetery
J Petersensvej
Sulup Avkusinia
To Heliport
1
2
3
4
5
6
7
8
9
10
11

other Greenlanders call the town by its original name, Ammassalik, locals refer to it as Tasiilaq, which means 'lake'. (Since it's considered disrespectful to speak the names of the dead), after the death of a local man whose name was Ammassalik, the fish were renamed *kersaqat* and the town was renamed after the lake-like bay which is almost enclosed by the island.

The village now has about 1300 people and, although they hunt and fish for personal food supplies, the town is an administrative centre for the entire east coast.

Information

The tourist information office is at the hotel (tel 18293). Their postal address is Tasiilaq Turistinformation, Hotel Angmagssalik, DK-3913 Tasiilaq-Ammassalik, Greenland.

Churches

The odd new pentagonal church in Ammassalik was built in 1985. It has a very unusual steeple that bears a strong resemblance to the nose of an intercontinental ballistic missile. The interior decor is a very nice blend of traditional Inuit and modern Greenlandic art. The ship that hangs from the ceiling is a model umiaq, the sealskin-covered women's boat. The older church, built in 1908, is soon to be converted into a town museum.

Places to Stay & Eat

The *Hotel Angmagssalik* (tel 18383) charges US$55/75 for singles/doubles without bath. For rooms with private baths, they charge singles/doubles US$85/104. The hotel is nothing extravagant but it has a good view across the village and fjord below. Sleeping-bag accommodation is also available in the dormitory for around US$20 per person.

The hotel dining room offers cafeteria food as well as Greenlandic specialties. The only other option at the moment is the KNI supermarket and general store.

Walks

Upstream along the river which flows through town and past the cemetery is an area known as Narsuuliartarpiip (the 'plain of flowers') after the variety of Arctic flora growing there. On a return trip of 2 or 3 hours you can walk up past some wonderful lakes and waterfalls. In the winter, the valley offers excellent cross-country skiing and the village has plans for a small alpine ski slope as well.

Getting There & Away

All access to Ammassalik is via Kulusuk. The 5-minute shuttle flight between Kulusuk and Ammassalik costs tourists an extortionate US$80 if they're there with a day-tour.

Tours

Day-Tours The hotel offers à la carte day-hiking, helicopter and boat tours from Ammassalik. A guided walk through Narsuuliartarpiip costs US$20 per person. You can also choose between a helicopter flight up to the Mitivagkat Glacier for US$97 or a cruise on the fjord for US$30. Excursions to outlying settlements cost US$51. For further information, contact the Hotel Angmagssalik, DK-3913, Tasiilaq-Ammassalik, Greenland.

Dog-sled Tours Ammassalik is one of the most popular areas for pre-arranged dog-sled tours. Most tours include a day-trip to Sarfagajik Fjord across the island and a day of cross-country skiing in Narsuuliartarpiip Valley. The standard 8-day package then allows participants to choose between a day's dog-sled trip to the small settlement of Ikateq and a helicopter tour to the icecap or a dog-sled trip to Tiniteqilaaq for 2 or 3 days with sleeping-bag accommodation in a hut. These trips are not cheap, however, and you should plan on spending US$2500 for the 8-day package from Copenhagen or about US$1300 excluding airfare.

For further information contact the Hotel Angmagssalik or Arctic Adventure, 27 Aaboulevarden, DK-1690 Copenhagen, Denmark, or Grønlands Rejsebureau,

Gammel Mønt 12, Box 130, DK-1004 Copenhagen, Denmark.

ITTOQQOORTOORMIIT (SCORESBYSUND)

Ittoqqoortoormiit, with a population of about 350, is in one of the finest hunting districts in the country and musk oxen, seals, and polar bears are plentiful. Access is via the airfield at Nerlerit Inaat (Constable Pynt) although there's little reason to visit unless you're very keen to get out and see the animals or go climbing in the area of Gunnbjörns Fjeld.

Reports are that drunken and murderous violence erupts with some frequency in Ittoqqoortoormiit; visitors are normally warned to stay away or remain as unobtrusive as possible. There is no accommodation so those who are still keen to venture in should bring a tent but this might make you conspicuous.

Getting There & Away

All flights to Ittoqqoortoormiit are via Nerlerit Inaat and all flights to Nerlerit Inaat are via either Keflavík or Reykjavík City Airport in Iceland. This makes the cost of a flight from anywhere else in Greenland prohibitive. From Nuuk, for instance, you'll pay US$720 one-way. From Uummannaq, the nearest west coast city, the fare is US$1100 one-way! If you're coming from Iceland, however, you can probably get by paying less than US$500 for the return flight.

MESTERS VIG & NORTH GREENLAND NATIONAL PARK

The world's largest national park takes in all of north-east Greenland or approximately 25% of the island's total area. It's a haven for musk oxen, polar bears, Arctic wolves, and Peary caribou in vast untouched expanses of tundra. Most of the park, however, is on the inland icecap.

Although it was long closed to visitors, it's now opening up for limited tourism. There are no facilities and access is difficult so most park visitors are professional botanists, biologists, and Arctic researchers. The Stauning Alps do attract a few climbers seeking challenging new terrain.

Future visits will depend largely on the fate of Mesters Vig airfield at the southern end of the park. Access will be thwarted or prevented altogether if the US is successful in its bid to build yet another military base on the site.

In the far north-east of the park at Danmarkshavn and Daneborg, respectively, are a weather station and a small Danish military installation where the Sirius Sled Patrol rescue rangers are stationed.

It's possible to charter an Odin Air 5-passenger Piper Navajo from Reykjavík to Mesters Vig for as little as US$3500. A 15-passenger jet charter will cost about US$5400. For further information, contact Odin Air (international tel 354-1-610880, fax 354-1-10858), Reykjavík City Airport, Reykjavík (Iceland).

The Faroe Islands

Facts about the Country

An old Faroese legend says that when the earth was created, the foreman in charge cleaned his nails and what he discarded plopped into the North Atlantic to become the Faroe Islands. Those are romantic beginnings, to say the least!

This is one of those mysteriously remote sort of places, akin to the Aleutians or the Falklands, that most would be hard-pressed to find on a map let alone aspire to visit. These 18 spots of land in the North Atlantic seem to get very little press and, although they're a stone's throw from mainland Europe, few Europeans ever think much about them.

Therefore, visitors are normally not prepared for the undeniable beauty of the Faroese landscape. From the sea on a fine day (which in the Faroes includes anything from patchy cloud cover right down to a medium drizzle), the first view of the towering cliffs, layer-cake mountains, crashing surf, and millions of circling and squawking sea birds dive-bombing the colourful Faroese fishing boats is likely to produce an aesthetic jolt. It's just as you'd imagine the 'stormy North Atlantic' to look. Add the odd tidy lighthouse on a craggy headland and you've got the stuff of paintings.

Even under scrutiny, the scene remains inspiring. The Faroes are islands of green grass and grey gravel, splashes of white or yellow flowers, patches of snow at high altitudes, herds of sheep grazing on the hillsides, cascading waterfalls, and villages of colourful modern homes.

Many Danes maintain the islands are as much a part of the their country as is Copenhagen. The Faroese, however, like to believe that they're actually an independent nation under the protection of mother Denmark. The truth is, the Faroes remain in a sort of political limbo between Danish control and complete independence. Although they receive 600 million Danish króna from Denmark annually, most of the current Home Rule government functions are supported by locally collected taxes. The Faroes have a flag and their own stamps and currency, but matters of defence and foreign relations are handled by Denmark. Faroese citizens, however, don't pay taxes to the Kingdom of Denmark and refuse to join the motherland in the EEC.

It may be surprising to learn that the national language is not Danish but Føroyskt (pronounced 'FEHR-wish'), a close relative of Icelandic. Although nearly everyone learns Danish at school and a few go on to learn English and German. The people have successfully resisted, wherever possible, the encroachment of foreign languages into everyday life.

Most visitors travelling independently to the Faroes aren't there by choice but are on the obligatory 2-day stopover imposed by Smyril Line which requires those travelling from Denmark to Iceland to wait in Tórshavn while the ferry goes to collect passengers in Norway and the Shetlands. Consequently, most visitors to the Faroes turn up with little idea of what to do, where to go, or what the place is all about. It is, however, quite easy to get around. The road system is well maintained and the Faroese have tunnelled like

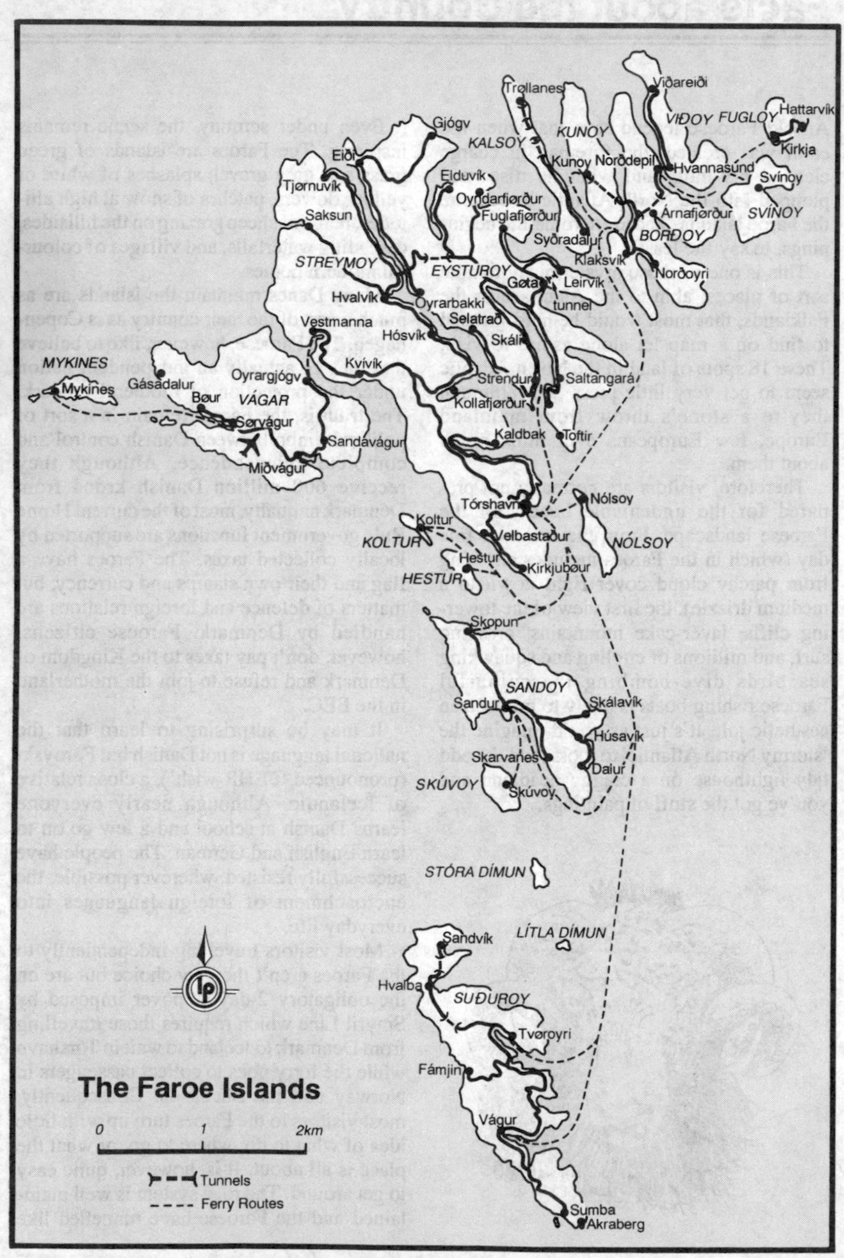
The Faroe Islands
Viðareiði
Trøllanes
Hattarvík
VIÐOY
FUGLOY
KUNOY
KALSOY
Gjógv
Kirkja
Eiði
Kunoy
Norðdepil
Hvannasund
Svínoy
Elduvík
Tjørnuvík
Oyndarfjørður
Árnafjørður
SVÍNOY
Fuglafjørður
Saksun
Syðradalur
BORÐOY
STREYMOY
EYSTUROY
Klaksvík
Norðoyri
Gøta
Leirvík
Hvalvík
Oyrarbakki
tunnel
Vestmanna
Selatrað
Hósvík
Skáli
MYKINES
Kvívík
Oyrargjógv
Strendur
Saltangará
Mykines
Gásadalur
Bøur
VÁGAR
Kollafjørður
Sørvágur
Sandavágur
Kaldbak
Toftir
Miðvágur
Tórshavn
Nólsoy
Koltur
Velbastaður
NÓLSOY
KOLTUR
Hestur
Kirkjubøur
HESTUR
Skopun
SANDOY
Sandur
Skálavík
Húsavík
Skarvanes
Dalur
SKÚVOY
Skúvoy
STÓRA DÍMUN
LÍTLA DÍMUN
Sandvík
Hvalba
SUÐUROY
Tvøroyri
Fámjin
Vágur
0
1
2km
Tunnels
Ferry Routes
Sumba
Akraberg

moles through the roughest bits. In addition, there's an excellent transport network with bus, ferry, and helicopter routes connecting all parts of the country with the capital, Tórshavn.

Those who are visiting on the 2-day stopover will probably be happy to learn that some of the Faroes' most magnificent landscapes lie within a couple of bus-hours from the capital. If you have more time, you'll want to venture out to some of the more remote islands, each offers something unique and more of those magnificent scenes that send your senses into overload.

HISTORY

The Monks – 500 to 800

Like Iceland, the Faroes were uninhabited when they were first stumbled upon by Europeans. It's possible that these islands were discovered as early as the 6th century when St Brendan, on his 7-year cruise through then unknown parts, saw the Faroes although there's no evidence or tradition indicating he made a stop there. He did, however, run across two islands several days' sailing from Scotland, one of which he named the Island of Sheep and the other the Paradise of Birds. Some modern-day historians speculate that the Island of Sheep is somewhere in the Faroes (*Føroyar*, pronounced 'FER-ya', which is derived from *faar oy* in old Norse, means 'the islands of sheep') and that the Paradise of Birds is, in fact, Mykines, the westernmost of the Faroes. It has an unusually dense bird population and a voyager trying to avoid the narrow and potentially hazardous channels between the islands would have passed by here.

Frequently obscured by rain and mist and lying in a distant, inhospitable corner of the Atlantic, it isn't surprising that the Faroes remained neglected and uninhabited until at least the late 600s. The first settlers were Irish monks who were searching, no doubt, for lands populated by pagans 'awaiting' Christianity or quiet countries where they could live out their lives of devotion in peace. In the Faroes the monks encountered only the latter.

Unfortunately, we have very little information about their stay. It's likely that they were responsible for the herds of sheep that were roaming the islands when the first Norse arrived in the early 9th century and were inspired to call the place Føroyar. Although new breeds of sheep have been introduced over the ages since then, it is assumed that these first sheep were similar to those which are still raised on the Scottish island of St Kilda.

The Norse Period – 800 to 1400

The first Norse peoples probably arrived in the Faroes in the early 9th century from southern Norway and the Orkneys. Contrary to popular legend, they weren't Vikings in the true sense of the word but were, like Iceland's early settlers, farmers and pastoralists in search of an independent country where they could live peacefully away from the pirates and tyrants who were ravaging the mainland.

Unlike early Icelanders, the Faroese didn't carefully record the history of their exploits so comparatively little is known about life in the Faroes prior to the 14th century. The most reliable work available, ***Faereyingar Saga*** was written in Iceland during the 1200s. Although most of it isn't regarded as factual, a few points are accepted as historical probabilities. It faithfully reports the acceptance of Christianity in the Faroes around the year 1000, which is most likely true, and outlines the structure of early relationships between Norway and the Faroes. According to the saga, in 1035, inevitably the Faroes became a constitutional part of the Kingdom of Norway when the Faroese chiefs conceded to pay tribute to the Norwegian king.

From very early on, the government of these islands lay in the hands of the *Alting* or 'peoples' assembly' which was a parliamentary body, more or less the Faroese equivalent of the renowned Icelandic Alþing. It convened at Tinganes, the 'assembly peninsula' in Tórshavn and was the ultimate authority in the islands until 1035. From then until 1380, the Alting retained limited power.

With the Union of Kjalmar , when Norway

became part of Denmark, the Faroes became a Danish rather than a Norwegian province adopting a system of law and justice that was a Danish version of Norwegian King Magnus' code. A couple of other documents reveal the nature of the earlier legal system, giving some idea which issues islanders deemed most important. One document, which originated in Iceland but was adopted in the Faroes, defined punishments for offences against the church's standards of morality. In 1298, the *Seyðabraevið* or 'sheep letter', a sort of constitution regarding division of pastureland, common grazing lands, and other ovine issues, was drawn up and remained in effect right up to 1866.

After 1380, parliamentary procedures ceased and the Alting converted into little more than a royal court. The parliament was renamed *Løgting*, after similar bodies that functioned in what was formerly southern Norway. At that time, the real power in the Faroes rested on the king's bailiff who controlled royal interests there.

Unfortunately, the history of the early Christian church in the Faroes has been obscured by time. It is known that the ecumenical centre of the islands was Kirkjubøur, the Faroese bishopric, near the southern tip of the island Streymoy. From the time of its establishment in the early 12th century until 1535 when the Reformation took effect, there were 33 bishops.

At the height of its influence in the late 13th century, the church held about 40% of the islands' territory. One particularly motivated 13th-century bishop, Erlendur, single-handedly set about alleviating, at the expense of his parishioners, any financial worries the church may have had. As a result, several church buildings at Kirkjubøur were destroyed by arsonists and the grand 'unfinished cathedral' still stands roofless as a monument to the numerous skirmishes between supporters and detractors of this church leader.

The Reformation & the Trade Monopoly

Early trade regulations required that all commerce between the European mainland and the Faroe Islands passed through Bergen in Norway, where customs taxes would be collected. During the mid-14th century, however, a group of north German cities formed the Hanseatic League, a mercantile association destined, over the next century, to effectively take control of commerce throughout the continent.

Norwegian regulations, however, forbade the league's entry into mainland Scandinavia, including Iceland, and the Faroes until 1361, when Norway, whose population was being decimated by the Black Plague, realised it was powerless to resist economic encroachment from the south. Competition was therefore healthy and the Faroes enjoyed a predominantly favourable and consistent mercantile atmosphere for nearly 200 years.

During the civil war launched by King Christian III of Denmark in order to wrest power from Christian II, the powerful German trading companies in Lübeck supported the soon-to-be-deposed king. Having backed the loser, they were expelled from the Scandinavian commercial scene. In 1535, King Christian III granted Thomas Köppen of Hamburg exclusive trading rights in the Faroe Islands, an arrangement which would remain in effect for the next 300 years.

Also in 1535, Denmark decided to bring religious enlightenment in the form of the protestant Lutheran church to its provinces which, up until then, had languished under what it considered was the yoke of Catholicism. The Reformation, lasting 5 years, effected the transfer of church properties into state hands and replaced Latin with Danish as the language used in ecclesiastical matters. These events, tightened Denmark's grip on the Faroes and its other offshore provinces.

After Köppen, the monopoly passed through various hands but it didn't have such devastating effects on the Faroes as the similar Danish Trade Monopoly of 1602 had on Iceland.

Ironically, the Icelandic Company, which was responsible for so much suffering in that country, probably served the Faroes better than any other establishment had or would.

The worst time was during the mid-1600s when Denmark was fighting with Sweden and wartime prices forced the Icelandic Company out of the Faroese markets.

The stipulations laid out for Köppen (and subsequent monopolists) included requirements that he only provide quality goods in a quantity commensurate with the market, that prices reflect the true market value of the goods delivered, and that traders conduct themselves in a friendly and honest manner in all their dealings with the islanders. Most of the goods exported from the Faroes – wool stockings, meat, sheepskins, and fish – were sent to Holland and, under the terms of the monopoly agreement, traders were obligated to purchase at pre-determined prices as many of these items as the Faroese could produce for sale.

In theory, it sounded like an equitable deal for everyone, but in practice, greed and dishonesty often meant the guidelines were ignored by the wayside and the Faroese faced shortages and delays while both they and the traders found themselves forced to accept inferior goods. Occasionally, the market for the Faroese goods (which the trading company was required to accept) declined and the monopolists often lost money on the deal. Smuggling and piracy became rampant and the entire system began to collapse.

In 1655, the Danish government presented the Faroes to Christoffer von Gabel and subsequently his son, Frederick, as a personal feudal estate. The oppressive reign brought little more than hardship to the islanders who were severely exploited by the overlords. In 1709, the Danish government nipped the 54-year-old von Gabel dynasty in the bud and seized control of the Faroes and the trade monopoly. Like governments everywhere, they proved hopelessly inept at market economics. Throughout the 18th century, they and the merchants operated at a loss over the deal and, on 1 January 1856, the whole project was finally abandoned as a failure.

Modern History

During the 19th century, Denmark's association with the Faroes was characterised by its increasing domination over the islands and their conversely decreasing autonomy. In 1816 the Løgting, still a psychological link with the Faroes' long lost independence though it had long since been stripped of its original power, was abolished and replaced by a Danish judiciary. The use of the Faroese language was discouraged and Danish became the language of official proceedings. In 1849, the Danish *Rigsdag* officially incorporated the Faroes with Denmark, thereby allowing the islands two seats in the legislative body.

The obstinate Faroese re-established their Løgting in 1852 as a county council which was merely an advisory body, reasoning that having done this, the following years would see them gaining momentum along the road to independence.

The next major step was taken in the 1890s. Thanks especially to economic prosperity, many islanders were becoming increasingly obsessed with the idea of Home Rule. Only the wealthy opposed the proposal because it would result in their being taxed to support local government.

In the early 20th century, the two viewpoints polarised into those expressed by the Unionist Party promoting full association with Denmark and the Home Rule Party looking towards slowly gaining complete independence under the guidance of Faroese statesman Jóannes Patursson.

Concurrent to these developments was the growth of the Faroese economic viability. As time passed the population grew and, of necessity, the economy expanded to include fishing as well as the traditional shepherding and agriculture. By right of their Danish citizenship, the Faroese were allowed to fish throughout the Danish-controlled North Atlantic region. In 1872 they replaced their low, open fishing boats with more seaworthy English wooden ships and, in turn, replaced these by steam trawlers. The fishery developed rapidly into a thriving enterprise.

During WW II, the British occupied the Faroes in order to secure the strategic North Atlantic shipping lanes and prevent the islands following the rest of Denmark into German occupation. This political separation from Denmark resulted in the upgrading of the Løgting to a legislative body with the Danish prefect retaining executive power. Some factions were prepared to take advantage of Denmark's extreme vulnerability and declare complete independence at this stage, but others expressed reservations.

On 23 March 1948, the *Act on Faroese Home Rule* was passed – a variation on a proposal made by the Danish government immediately following the war. The Faroes' official status had been changed from 'county of Denmark' to 'self-governing community within the Kingdom of Denmark'. When Denmark joined the EEC, the Faroes refused to follow. Over the locally hot issue of fishing rights, the Faroe Islands maintain their claim to a 200-mile exclusion limit.

The islands now have their own official flag, currency, and stamps and oversee their own affairs inasmuch as Denmark is not affected by their decisions. Føroyskt has been declared the official language of Home Rule or *Landsstýri* proceedings but Faroese children must learn Danish at school.

Denmark retains control of and financial responsibility for insurance and banking, defence, foreign relations, and justice. The Home Rule government is entirely responsible for economic, cultural, and communications issues administering health, education, and social programmes. It seems very likely that, before long, the Faroes will follow Iceland along the path to complete independence, a goal to which they seem to fervently aspire.

Faroese flag

Currently, the islands' most pressing problem is their relationship to the EEC now that Denmark has joined. While the Faroese do not want to jeopardise their position in the Kingdom as regards fishing rights off the Danish mainland and Greenland, neither do they want to open up their own territorial waters to EEC interests and competition. What's more, if they don't join, traditional markets such as Germany and Britain will be required to buy fish from Norway and Denmark (which has the right to fish in Faroese waters) effectively cutting the Faroes out of the competition. It seems a no-win situation unless the Faroese can convince the EEC to let them into the fold without requiring them to relinquish their territorial waters.

GEOGRAPHY

Geologically, the Faroe Islands are eroded remnants of the Thulean plateau, a mid-Atlantic continent built up volcanically after North America, Greenland, and Europe tectonically went their separate ways. Other bits of this long-disappeared Atlantis include the Westfjords of Iceland, County Antrim in Northern Ireland, bits of southern Greenland, and the rugged territory north of Glasgow in Scotland.

The rock strata of the Faroes are quite interesting. Their terraced or 'layer-cake' appearance is derived from four stages of basalt-building vulcanism separated by substantial periods of inactivity. Small seams of coal between two of the basalt layers provide evidence that life had time to take hold during that intermediate stage. The final volcanic stage was one of intrusion in which molten material forced its way into vertical and horizontal cracks in the existing rock, forming erosion-resistant dykes and sills.

During the great ice age, the Faroes and all of what is now their continental shelf were blanketed with ice. Towards the end of that era after the icecap had begun to melt, its remnants gouged out the cirques, valleys, sounds, and fjords that characterise the islands today. The resulting landscape is primarily a series of mountain ridges and arêtes separated by textbook cirques. The best examples can be found on the north-eastern islands of Kalsoy, Kunoy, and Borðoy.

The strata of the Faroes dip slightly toward the south-east. Therefore, the northern and western coasts, whose layers are more resistant to the onslaught of the waves, meet the sea in steep cliffs which reach 750 metres at Enniberg on the island of Viðoy. The southern and eastern shores, which are far more susceptible to wave erosion, have more gently sloping coastlines and less dramatic drop-offs.

The 18 islands of the Faroes cover a land area of 1399 sq km. The compact archipelago is shaped like a southward pointing arrow that appears to be threatening Scotland 300 km away. The islands lie 600 km west of Norway and about 450 km south-east of Iceland. The greatest distance from east to west is about 75 km and from north to south, 115 km.

The islands can be divided roughly into four major geographical areas. At the heart of the country are Streymoy and Eysturoy, the first and second most populated islands. The capital city of Tórshavn lies near the southern tip of Streymoy in one of the country's most climatically vulnerable situations. Also clustered around the southern tip of Streymoy are the small but beautiful islands of Koltur, Hestur, and Nølsoy.

West of Streymoy are Vágar (the only island with enough level land suitable for an airport) and magnificent Mykines, the westernmost island in the group renowned for its poor climate and diverse bird life.

North-east of Eysturoy are the rugged fingerlike northern islands Kalsoy, Kunoy, Borðoy, Viðoy, Svínoy, and Fugloy. Apart from Klaksvík on Borðoy, the Faroes' second largest community, these islands are well off the beaten tourist track even though they offer the most spectacular walking and the most dramatic scenery in the country.

Finally, the southern group of islands – Suðuroy, Sandoy, Skúvoy, Stóra Dímun, and Lítla Dímun – forms the tip of the Faroe arrow. The climate here is the generally the best in the archipelago. Lítla Dímun is the only major island that is not inhabited and once you've seen it, you'll probably be able to work out why.

CLIMATE

The climate is similar to Iceland's, only a bit warmer and, if you can believe it, stormier. Rain in some form – drizzle, mist, downpours – can be expected about 280 days of the year. Fortunately, weather is somewhat localised – it could be bucketing down in Tórshavn while Suðuroy basks in the sun. Those who are interested in timing excursions to take advantage of the best weather, should tune into Útvarp Føroya radio which broadcasts weather information in English daily at 8.05 am.

Thanks to the tropical current the Gulf Stream which sweeps past the islands, the water temperatures remain about 10°C year-round providing an ideal environment for fish and plankton and moderating the climate. The annual average temperature range is only 8°C – from 3°C in January to 11°C in July.

FLORA & FAUNA

Although the Faroes are home to several species of introduced pests – rats, mice, and rabbits – the bird life is most prolific. Thanks to the profusion of plankton and therefore fish and other sea life, the Faroese maintain that their bird population is the densest in the world. Whether or not this is true, it isn't difficult to believe. The high nest-covered cliffs teem with activity.

Forty-nine species of birds breed regularly in the Faroes and nearly 30 more do so occasionally. Among them, the comical puffins, which are netted and eaten in large quantities, are the most profuse. Other common species include guillemots, fulmars, great skuas (these become health hazards if you imprudently wander too close to their eggs!), razorbills, gannets, cormorants, and kittiwakes. Most of these feast on herring, crayfish, and small eels although the larger birds have been known to take larger fish, as well.

Inland you'll find great colonies of eider ducks, golden plovers, snipe, rock doves, and the avian symbol of the Faroes, the oystercatcher or *tjaldur*. In addition, about 200 more species are occasional visitors to the islands. The only bird of prey in residence is the merlin – a small, dark-plumed falcon.

The best time to observe the birds is in the summer, roughly between April and August. All species in the Faroes are protected and tourists aren't permitted to net them or collect eggs. In addition, fulmar chicks are often afflicted with psittacosis, a contagious pneumonia-like disease that can also affect humans, so it's best to just leave them alone.

In the sea around the Faroes are found large pods of pilot whales or *grind* (pronounced *grint*) the unfortunate victims of the *grindadráp*, bloody massacres of 1500 to 2000 of these creatures annually – a Greenpeace sympathiser's nightmare.

Other whale species, which inhabit the Faroes and are fortunately spared the horrors of grindadráp, include bottlenose whales, fin whales, killer whales (orcas), dolphins, and porpoises. The only pinniped which breeds along the Faroese coast is the grey seal which inhabits sea-level caves and is rarely seen.

Merlin

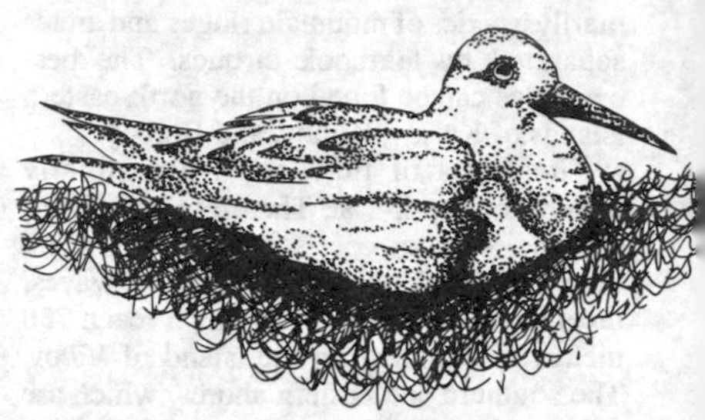

Oystercatcher

There are only five species of freshwater fish found in the Faroes – the Arctic char, salmon, eel, river trout, and stickleback. Saltwater species include Atlantic halibut, sand eel, redfish, haddock, lemon sole, blue whiting, lobster, and scallops. Cod is also present but not in the quantities that are encountered further north and west.

Domestic animals include cattle and sheep, sheep, and more sheep. There are twice as many Faroese sheep as there are people.

As for vegetation, although there are no trees and the entire landscape seems to be cast out of some uniformly green material; there are actually 1600 species of plants growing in the Faroes. Most of these are grasses, sedges, mosses, lichens, and fungi. The most complex vegetation found is flowering species and ferns, usually growing in ravines where the sheep aren't likely to venture.

Historically, driftwood was so valuable a commodity that its collection was strictly controlled. Any tree or bit of uncut wood that drifted ashore belonged automatically to the farmer on whose property it landed. If the wood were cut or altered by humans in any way, it would revert to the Crown and be put up for auction by the local authorities. The finder would receive a third of the auction price.

GOVERNMENT

As previously mentioned, up until 1948, the Faroes like Greenland were a county of Denmark. In a referendum held in 1946, however, the islands voted for a Home Rule government, one which provided for an independently functioning government within the Kingdom of Denmark.

The Home Rule government or Landsstýri is headed by a *Løgmaður* ('lawman'), with three to six subordinates, and a bureaucratic jumble of committees, boards, and councils. Danish interests in joint affairs are overseen by a representative known as *Rigsombudsmand.* Conversely, the Faroese elect two representatives to the Danish Parliament or Folketing.

The legislative duties are covered by the Løgting, a 27-member parliament which opens its annual session on the Faroese national holiday, Ólavsøka, on 29 July. Elections to the Løgting are held every 4 years. Most of the seats are currently occupied by four major political parties representing both liberal and conservative views as well as both Unionist (pro-Danish) and nationalist leanings. The Home Rule majority leader is currently Jógvan Sundstein elected in 1988.

The Seal of the Leader of the Faroese Government

The Faroese finance their own government which is responsible for all domestic issues while the Danish mainland handles matters relating to foreign relations, banking, and defence. In matters of insurance and banking regulations, the penal code, and civil law, any legislation originating on the Danish mainland must be passed through the Faroese Løgting before it can be put into effect in the Faroe Islands.

Although Faroese defence is technically the responsibility of Denmark, it seems to rest predictably on Yankee shoulders in the form of an American-controlled NATO base north of Tórshavn.

Individual communities often have their own government authorities in charge of local issues including education. Due to the remote nature of many communities, these officials actually have a great deal of control over local affairs.

ECONOMY

You probably won't be surprised to learn that the economy of the Faroe Islands is based almost entirely upon fishing and fish processing. Up until the mid-1800s, subsistence farming was the primary economic activity. Householders raised sheep for wool, milk, and mutton; they also cultivated potatoes – some even kept cattle for beef and chickens for eggs. When the population began to increase,the economy had to diversify. Fishing, already a significant economic factor elsewhere in the North Atlantic, seemed the obvious answer.

Initially, most fishing took place far offshore around Greenland, Svalbard or Spitsbergen (Norway), Canada, and Iceland. Most of these had waters rich in shrimp and cod while Iceland offered coalfish and haddock, as well. From the nearby North Sea, the Faroese took mackerel and whiting. Although a small majority of the Faroese annual catch still comes from foreign or international waters, since the extension of the exclusion limit to 200 miles in 1977, domestic fishing has increased. Nearly 50%

of the annual catch is currently made in Faroese waters. Dried or salted fish and fish meal comprise just about all exports and nearly 25% of all employment in the Faroes is related in some way to fishing or fish processing. Another 10% involves manufacturing equipment for the fishing industry.

A relatively new economic venture is fish farming and, at the time of writing, there were nearly 100 fish farms in the Faroe Islands raising primarily roe, fry, and mussels as well as trout and salmon.

Unemployment in the country is insignificant and the standard of living ranks among the world's highest. In fact, from time to time, the Faroes suffer a labour shortage and foreign labour must be imported in order to satisfy the market. Most foreigners working in the Faroes are, of course, involved in the fishing industry.

In addition to fishing, there is a small woollens industry and tourism is on the increase. The Faroes, however, don't seem to aspire to worldwide recognition as a tourist destination and, apart from participating in the West Nordic Tourism Conference (along with Iceland and Greenland), they aren't putting much effort into promoting themselves.

Outside Tórshavn, many people supplement other incomes with agriculture, raising a few sheep and cultivating potatoes for personal consumption.

POPULATION & PEOPLE

In 1989, about 49,000 people lived in the Faroes, 15,000 of them in the capital, Tórshavn, and 5000 more in the second city, Klaksvík. There are approximately 100 other communities of varying size throughout the country. Up to now, migration into Tórshavn from the countryside hasn't caused any significant decline in the rural population.

The majority of the Faroese are of Nordic origin and have descended from the early Norwegian settlers who arrived during the Viking Era. There are quite a few Danes most of whom live in the capital.

The birth rate is 1.6% with a net annual growth of 0.8% – one of the highest in Western Europe.

CULTURE

Most of the elements that normally characterise Western European arts and culture have historically never been important in the Faroes. Individual artistic expression there has actually only been obvious during this century. As far as poetry and literature are concerned, much of this can be attributed to the status of the Faroese language as a 'peasant' dialect with no written form. Lack of musical tradition or classical composition is largely due to the absence of any sort of musical instrument other than the human voice until the end of the 1800s.

Artistic endeavours, at least as far as a national heritage was concerned, were thwarted by a general lack of time in the subsistence households. The visual arts didn't mature on the Faroese scene until fishing replaced agriculture as the economic mainstay.

Music & Dance

Early Faroese music would be considered rather bland by modern standards so it may be surprising that it still survives in its original form. Rather than having everyday air play, it is now dredged out only on special or festive occasions that emphasise traditional events or national identity.

The historical music was designed to accompany the Faroese chain dance (see the following) and the *kvaeði*, a massive body of late medieval poetry. Danish songs, poems, and ballads were also set to music and danced as were humorous and teasing anecdotes about everyday life.

The music was nearly always written in 6/4 time, primarily in order to best accompany the chain dance. Melodies, commonly sung in a minor key, were very simple and repetitive. Accompaniment was with voice only, since no musical instruments were present in the Faroese tradition.

The very simple Faroese chain dance was once popular all over Scandinavia but has survived intact only in the Faroes. It's a fairly slow and repetitive series of steps, mimicking perfectly the music that accompanies it; the dancers themselves are expected to take the feelings behind the words and interpret them in their dancing. Although the steps remain the same, a sad text is danced in one way and a gleeful text in another. When everyone is moving on the same wavelength, so to speak, and conveying the emotion behind the song, then the effort is considered a success.

The dances are led by a choir leader who sets the mood for the occasion. It begins with leader and several dancers forming a circle on the dance floor, with hands and elbows joined. At this point, everyone present is welcome and expected to participate. As more people join in, the circles grow and when they can no longer be contained in the room, they develop into serpentine rows that wind their way through the room and allow everyone to dance close to everyone else sometime during the song.

National Costume

The Faroese national costume is worn only on special occasions, including religious functions and high school graduations – young men and women both consider it important to acquire this get-up for use at festivities.

Although the costume is distinctive in style, there's a lot of room for individual variation and a festive group of Faroese so dressed can really be quite colourful. The men's costume includes a lavishly embroidered vest over a white shirt. Over this they wear a dark wool embroidered waistcoat with closely spaced silver buttons and matching calf-length homespun trousers with decorative buttons on the knees. This is topped off with a reddish cap with black stripes for young men and dark blue ones for older men.

Women's dress includes an ankle-length red skirt with a uniquely patterned red and black bodice, gathered in front with a laced silver chain. Over the top, they wear a patterned apron and a beautiful cape embroidered with the family's unique design. This is often accompanied by a large ribbon around the neck. Both men and women wear the same Welsh-style black shoes.

Literature

The first Faroese literature was passed on orally, for there was no written language to record it. During the Middle Ages, people occupied themselves through long winter nights with recitations of stories and poetry that had been handed down for generations. Those stories purported to be historical were called *sagnir* but it's not difficult to imagine that after several generations of retelling, they lost some of their original credibility. Fictitious stories, those designed to become more interesting over the years, were known as *aevintýr*. The ballads, presented in verse and often set to music and dance, were called the kvaeðl. All these forms were carried over into the 19th century when what remained of them was collected and written down lest it be lost forever.

In the early 1800s, the first modern Faroese poet, Nølsoyar-Poul Poulson, composed brilliant politically inspired ballads dealing with the corruption and troubled economics of the day. His most famous work is the 229-verse *Fuglakvaeði,* which compared political leaders and monopolistic traders to birds of prey. Poul himself was portrayed as the tjaldur or oystercatcher, whose job was to warn the ordinary citizens – the smaller, weaker birds – to beware of those in power.

The best known Faroese writer during the short history of literature in the country is Heðin Brú whose books are incredibly popular in the Faroes and have gained acceptance abroad as well. Like many eminent authors in small nations, his work deals primarily with the struggle between forces that would modernise and homogenise the world and those which value preserving the uniqueness of the smaller societies. His most renowned work is *The Old Man and his Sons* published during WW II.

Other Faroese authors include Jørgen-

Frantz Jacobsen and William Heinesen who both got around the lack of a written language by using Danish rather than Faroese. They are fairly well known outside the islands but aren't as popular in their homeland due to their unusual humour and their dealing with uncomfortable topics disconcertingly close to home.

Apart from the lyrics which accompanied the early chain-dance music, the first Faroese poetry wasn't written until the early 20th century when J Djurhuus published a collection of his work, thereby exposing the need for some sort of standardised written language. His brother, Hans, took up poetry as well, much of his work extolling the grandeur of the Faroese landscape.

Rói Patursson, a more recent poet has turned to modern lyrical constructions and minimalist language. He's becoming recognised throughout Scandinavia as a literary force.

Art

Again, the visual arts are very young in the Faroes and haven't yet had time to develop into any sort of national tradition. Several painters have come forth during this century with some interesting interpretations of the inspiring landscape and harsh environment. Up to now, the most renowned has been Sámal Joensen Mikines (Faroese sometimes tack the name of their home island onto their surname as a patronymic, of sorts) who was inspired to surrealism by the gloomy magnificence of Mykines.

Somewhat more faithful to reality is Ingálvur Reyni, who emphasised colour as a means of expressing a more positive aspect of the landscape than Joensen Mikines had. Another landscape painter, Ruth Smith, was particularly adept at conveying the overall mood of the country by capturing the clear and unusual light that characterises the higher latitudes.

The best of Faroese art is displayed in an annual national exhibition during the Ólavsøka or St Olav's Day festivities in Tórshavn in late July. Those visiting at other times can see the permanent exhibition at the National Gallery, also in Tórshavn.

Grindadráp

Although most foreigners consider the Grindadráp an abomination rather than anything remotely resembling culture, to most Faroese it's as much a part of life as Christmas is.

Here's how it works. Upon sighting a pod of migrating pilot whales ('grind'), a fisherman hoists a flag as a signal that whales are present and the hunt is to begin. Someone on shore yells the war cry 'grind' and mayhem ensues. The islands effectively shut down as everyone runs to their boats to join in. The pod is surrounded by the boats, herded toward the shore, and eventually forced up onto the beach. Once they're too close to shore to escape by sounding, the men attack them with knives, hooks, and harpoons and struggle to get them onto the beach, turning the water red with blood.

In order to justify all this, they maintain that the whales, once beached, are killed as quickly as possible and not allowed to suffer unduly. Often over 100 whales are taken in 15 minutes, the largest one going to the fisherman who first sighted the pod and the rest being divided between all residents of the participating district. After the bodies are carved up and distributed, everyone goes off to a party singing the *Grindevise*, a traditional song that goes something like 'We are strong men and killing whales is our greatest joy...'

The islanders have been put under extreme pressure from Greenpeace and other international environmental organisations to abandon this morbid tradition. Predictably, T-shirts advocating the equivalent of a 'greenie-*dráp*' appeared and, what's more, one of the Faroes' most faithful customers McDonald's (it can't be true – I've never seen a single square fish around those parts!) has threatened to boycott Faroese fish if the grindadráp continues.

Despite the threats, in 1989 an article was published in the West Norden Tourism Conference newspaper under the headline: 'The Faroese will not Stop their Pilot Whale Hunt'. Full Stop.

The Faroese claim that they aren't breaking any International Whaling Commission regulations because it's a recreational (and, they claim, 'subsistence') rather than commercial hunt and that they are not severely depleting the whale population. They also claim that boycotts on Faroese products and other foreign efforts to curtail the hunt are violations of the United Nations Covenants of 1966.

The grindadráp takes place in the summer as the pilot whales are migrating past the islands. Anyone who's around to witness this event will need to have a strong stomach and keep reminding themselves that it's a tradition carried over from the Viking days. It may well be the most graphic remaining example of what that culture must have been like.

HOLIDAYS & FESTIVALS

Public Holidays

The Faroes recognise an unusually large number of public holidays including:

1 January
New Year's Day
6 January
Epiphany
March
Gregorius' Day
March or April
Maundy Thursday
Good Friday
Easter Sunday
Easter Monday
25 April
Flag Day
1 May
Labour Day
11 May
Common Prayer's Day
May
Ascension Day
June
Whitsunday
Whitmonday
5 June
Constitution Day
28 & 29 July
Ólavsøka (Faroese National Day)
1 November
All Saints' Day
24 December
Christmas Eve
25 December
Christmas Day
26 December
Boxing Day
31 December (afternoon only)
New Year's Eve

Ólavsøka

Ólavsøka or Faroese National Day is the earth-shaking festival of the year in the islands. Conveniently at the height of summer, on 28 and 29 July, the normally reserved Faroese cut loose and celebrate St Olav's Day.

The festival is named in honour of St Olav, or Olav Haraldsson II, patron saint of Norway, who pressed for acceptance of Christianity in Scandinavia and devised Norway's religious code in the year 1024. It is likely, however, that the festival actually dates back to pagan times and adopted St Olav's name as a convenient way of giving it Christian sanction.

One of the highlights of this 2-day (often dragging on into a 3-day) festival is the rowing competition in which several villages at a time participate. The locals practice throughout the year for this event in their traditional craft which are shaped like small Viking ships. (These are still in everyday use in the Faroes, primarily for fishing.)

Other events associated with Ólavsøka include horse races, art exhibitions, chain dancing, and a variety of sporting competitions and, of course, the obligatory religious services. Despite the difficulty of obtaining alcohol in the Faroes, the people seem to manage especially during Ólavsøka; it's fairly obvious that they enjoy themselves immensely.

Local Festivals

Many smaller towns stage local festivals, some of which get pretty exciting. They all follow more or less the same agenda as Ólavsøka with rowing competitions, sports matches, both chain and modern dances, religious meetings, feasting, and alcohol. Approximate dates and locations will be outlined in the sections on the separate towns.

LANGUAGE

Faroese is a Germanic language derived from old Norse and significantly influenced by Gaelic. It is related most closely to Icelandic and some Norwegian dialects.

The original language of all Scandinavia (except Finland) was old Norse and only after the period of migration and Settlement had passed did individual areas begin to develop their own linguistic characteristics. Although some medieval manuscripts exist, the Faroese dialect ceased to be a written language after Norway was absorbed by Denmark and the Danish version replaced the Faroese as the written language of the islands.

In 1781, the scholar Jens Christian Svabo travelled to the Faroes to research and preserve, what remained of the Faroese language. He collected stories, songs, and as much vocabulary as he could muster, then set about creating an orthography so he could record it all.

Subsequent researchers followed his example and suddenly Faroese had many orthographies but none that stood out as a feasible standard. Several disputes arose and it wasn't until 1890 that a standard written version of Faroese was adopted. It wasn't long before the first Faroese literature began to appear and in 1948, the language Føroyskt was made official and given equal status with Danish in public and government affairs.

As in Icelandic, new words to describe new ideas and inventions are not merely borrowed from Danish or English, but are either taken directly from the local language or created from already existing words.

Pronunciation

In most cases, Faroese words are stressed on the first syllable. Grammar is very similar to that of Icelandic but pronunciation is another matter entirely. A lot of Icelandic, Danish, and even Gaelic influences come in to play. For example, the name of the Eysturoy's village Eiði is inexplicably pronounced 'OY-yeh'. The nearby village of Gjógv is referred to as 'Jag'. The name of the capital, Tórshavn, gets the more or less Danish pronunciation, 'TORSH-hown'. As you can see, it can get a bit complicated and unusual.

Unless you're one of those lucky people who can pick up the general tone and pronunciation of a language just by listening, it may be a good idea to show the text in the following vocabulary section to a local and ask for the correct pronunciation before attempting or slaughtering it.

If you still have problems, quite a few Faroese speak at least some English. Everyone speaks Danish and therefore they can handle Norwegian and Swedish as well.

Some Basic Vocabulary

The Faroese will not only be surprised if a foreigner makes an attempt to struggle through a word or two of their language, they will be proudly shocked. They've struggled for years trying to preserve it and its successful restoration as an official language is a matter of national pride. That an outsider would recognise it as unique, let alone bother to use it, will inspire them even more.

Greetings & Civilities

hello	*ey, hallo, goðan dag*
good morning	*goðan morgun*
good-bye	*bay-bay* or *farvael*
How's it going?	*Hvussu gongur ta tað*?
What is your name?	*Hvussu eitar tú?*
please	*ger so vael*
thank you	*takk fyri*
thank you very much	*stóra tøkk*
welcome	*vaelkomin*
excuse me	*orsaka*

Useful Phrases

Do you speak English?
Tala tygum enskt?
What would you like?
Hvat vilja tygum hava?
What time is it?
Hvat er klokkan?
It is...minutes to/past...
Klokka er...Minuttier i/yvir...
How much is this?
Hvussu nógv kostar tað?
Where is the...?
Hvar er...?

Useful Words

bus	*bussur*
boat	*bátur*
plane	*flogfar*
bank	*banki*
post office	*posthús*
youth hostel	*ferðafuglaheim*
supermarket	*keypsamtøkan*
restaurant	*matstova*
cafe	*kaffistova*
tourist office	*ferðaskrivstova*
road	*vegur*
street	*gøta*
village	*bygd*
map	*vegakort*
rucksack	*ryggsekkur*

Geographical Features

bay	*vágur*
bird cliffs	*fuglaberg*
coast	*strond*
harbour	*havn*
island	*oy* or *oyggj*
lake	*vatn*
mountain	*fjall*
mountain pass	*fjalladskarð*
ravine	*gjógv*
river or stream	*á*
slope	*brekka*
valley	*dalur*

Food & Drink

bread	*breið*
butter	*smör*
cheese	*ostur*
chocolate	*sukurlátu*
egg	*egg*
fish	*fiskur*
fruit	*frukt*
lamb	*lamb*
meat	*kjót*
milk	*mjólk*
mutton	*seyðakjöt*
pork	*grisur*
potato	*jördepli*
salmon	*laksur*
sausage	*pýlsa*
sugar	*sukur*

Days & Months

Sunday	*sunnudag*
Monday	*mánadag*
Tuesday	*týsdag*
Wednesday	*mikudag*
Thursday	*hósdag*
Friday	*friggjadag*
Saturday	*leygardag*
January	*januar*
February	*februar*
March	*mars*
April	*april*
May	*mai*
June	*juni*
July	*juli*
August	*august*
September	*september*
October	*oktober*

November	*november*
December	*desember*

Numbers

1	*eitt*
2	*tvey*
3	*trý*
4	*fýra*
5	*fimm*
6	*seks*
7	*sjey*
8	*átta*
9	*níggju*
10	*tíggju*
11	*ellivu*
12	*tólv*
13	*trettan*
14	*fjúrtan*
15	*fimtan*
16	*sekstan*
17	*seytjan*
18	*átjan*
19	*nítjan*
20	*tjúgu* (pronounced 'CHEW-wah')
21	*ein og tjúgu*
30	*tredivu*
40	*fjøriti*
50	*hálvtrýs*
60	*trýs*
70	*hálvfjers*
80	*fýrs*
90	*hálvfems*
100	*hundrað*
101	*hundrað og eitt*
121	*hundrað ein og tjúgu*
200	*tvey hundrað*
1000	*túsund*

Facts for the Visitor

VISAS

Citizens of only a very few countries are required to have a visa for Denmark, the Faroes, and Greenland. Among them are some of the lesser known African countries, Poland, Hungary, Turkey, Jordan, Vanuatu, Tonga, Western Samoa, Papua New Guinea, Taiwan, the People's Republic of China, the Soviet Union, Myanmar, India, Iraq, Pakistan, Bangladesh, Iran, Sri Lanka, Indonesia, the Philippines, Belize, Egypt, South Africa, and a handful of others. If you have any doubts, refer to the nearest Danish consulate or embassy.

When visiting the Faroes from other Scandinavian countries – Norway, Finland, Sweden, the Åland Islands, Iceland, Greenland, and Denmark – you only need valid identification cards. Citizens of those countries not requiring visas need only a valid passport for stays of up to 3 months.

Technically, you must be able to prove you have sufficient funds for your intended length of stay in the Faroes but customs and immigration formalities are normally very rudimentary, especially for those entering from another Scandinavian country. All the officials are really looking for is alcohol which, for some reason, they're quite touchy about.

Embassies & Consulates

The Faroes are represented abroad by Danish embassies and consulates which can be found in the capital cities of most countries and often in other major cities as well.

Working in the Faroes

Quite a few foreigners come to the Faroes to take advantage of the marginally high wages offered by the fishing industry. Nearly every town has its cannery or processing plant and at very least a harbour full of fishing boats. There are normally job vacancies during the summer season to be filled by temporary overseas labour. Citizens of Scandinavian countries need only turn up at the plant and, if work is available, they can start immediately.

Although Denmark is in the EEC, the Faroes are not; citizens of EEC countries, and those from other countries, must officially obtain permission to work in the islands. First they must find a job – in the cannery, on a fishing boat, on a construction site, or whatever – then apply to the police in Tórshavn for permission to work. Unless the potential employer can convey a sense of urgency to the powers that be, you could find yourself waiting several months before the decision is forthcoming.

Those who choose to work illegally are beyond protection of the law and may be taken advantage of by unscrupulous employers – so use good judgement.

It is significant to note that most canneries do not provide accommodation for workers and housing must be arranged individually. In Tórshavn, this normally means the camping site or renting a flat. In other villages, you will have to convince youth hostel management to let you stay long-term or find a local family willing to rent out an extra room. Ask individual employers for suggestions.

Some of the larger and more popular processing plants where there'll be a reasonable chance of finding work include:

Bacalao (tel 11360), Tórshavn
Stranda FIskavirki PF (tel 48057), Strendur
Norðis (tel 23055), Eiði
Fuglafjarðar Ísvirki (tel 44577), Fuglafjørður
Handils og Frystivirkið (tel 44125), Fuglafjørður
Nykur (tel 47423), Toftir
Fiska Virkið PF (tel 41002), Syðrugøta
PF Ísvirkið (tel 44503), Oyndarfjørður
Frostvirkið (tel 52022), Norðdepil
Flakavirkið á Kosini (tel 55690), Klaksvík
Føroya Utróðrarvirki (tel 56433), Klaksvík
Skálavíkar Frystivirki (tel 61234), Skálavík
Borgin (tel 61440), Sandur
Solarris (tel 61316), Skopun
Vestmanna Fiskivirki (tel 24140), Vestmanna

Klivar (tel 27091), Nólsoy
Flakavirkið (tel 32017), Sørvágur
Norðurfisk (tel 56915), Árnafjørður
PF Frost (tel 43049), Leirvík

Incidentally, those who may have an interest in visiting any of these places and getting the low-down on the fate of Faroese fish can either contact these businesses in advance or visit the tourist office to arrange a tour.

If you're interested in working on a fishing boat, lucrative employment will be hard to come by, but those who'd just like a cultural experience can ask around the villages and will probably be able to find work on one of hundreds of small family boats that fish for personal supplies.

CUSTOMS

Visitors over 18 years of age are permitted to bring 3 kg of chocolate, 50 g of perfume, and a quarter of a litre of eau de toilette. They may also import 200 cigarettes, 50 cigars, or 250 g of tobacco.

Alcohol is strictly and puritanically controlled in the Faroes. Those over 20 years of age may bring in 1 litre of wine, 1 litre of spirits (from 22 to 60% proof), and 2 litres of beer (less than 4.6%). Under normal circumstances, 2 additional litres of spirits may be imported upon payment of duties. Non-recyclable containers are forbidden in all cases.

Animals may not be brought into the Faroes under any circumstances. Those who wish to bring in firearms must have an export licence from the country of origin and written permission from the Faroese government and police in order to carry weapons in the country. Otherwise, transit passengers will have to leave firearms in care of customs and collect them upon departure from the Faroes.

MONEY

Although the Faroes issues its own currency, the Faroese króna (Fkr) is tied to the Danish one; the two are used interchangeably throughout the Kingdom of Denmark, that is on the mainland and in the Faroes and Greenland. The Faroes don't mint coins and so all coins in use are Danish. One króna is equal to 100 aurar. Prices in the text will mostly be given in US$.

Notes come in denominations of 20, 50, 100, 500, and 1000 króna. Coins in use include 5, 10, and 25 aurar and 1, 5, and 10 króna.

Foreign Exchange

Foreign currency may be exchanged at any Faroese bank during regular hours, from 9.30 am to 4 pm Monday to Friday and until 6 pm on Thursdays. The exchange bank at the Vágar airport is open during regular banking hours and for arriving flights at other times. Normally a small commission is charged for exchange services. During their off-hours, hotels will also normally exchange money as will tourist information offices and travel agencies. All brands of travellers' cheques and all major currencies are accepted.

Post offices in Tórshavn, Vestmanna, Vágur, Tvøroyri, Klaksvík, and Saltangará will exchange postal cheques from France, the Netherlands, Luxembourg, and the UK, and postal savings bank cheques from Norway, Finland, Sweden, and Germany.

Major credit cards – Eurocard, MasterCard, Visa, American Express, and so on – are widely accepted in the Faroes, particularly by tourism-oriented establishments. Banks will issue cash advances on credit cards and also cash Eurocheques.

The Faroese króna (Fkr) is always equal and interchangeable with the Danish króna (Dkr). The approximate exchange rates at the time of writng were:

A$1	=	4.7Dkr
C$1	=	5.0Dkr
DM1	=	3.7Dkr
Ikr1	=	0.10Dkr
US$1	=	5.8Dkr

TOURIST INFORMATION

Local Tourist Offices

National tourist information is available at

the Aldan tourist office on Tinganes peninsula in Tórshavn. The city tourist office handles enquiries about the city and environs but they seemed to be overstressed to the point of irritability. The best they were normally prepared to offer was a finger pointing at the rack of brochures.

A word of warning: the tourist offices, for some unfathomable reason, will officially try to discourage you trying anything even slightly adventurous – hiking, camping, kayaking, seeking employment, visiting more remote islands, etc – and will try to steer you toward more up-market activities such as helicopter and bus tours, and hotels. While warnings about generally misunderstood dangers and private land ownership are absolutely warranted, those who wish to enjoy the outdoors on its own terms shouldn't be put off by the tourist-office line or they may find the Faroes a pretty dull place.

The following are the addresses of the various offices and private bureaux where you'll be able to glean information:

Aldan (Central Information Office (tel 12277), Reynagøta 17, PO Box 368, FR-100 Tórshavn
Kunningadiskurinn (Airport Office) (tel 33200), Vágar airport, FR-380 Sørvágur
Klaksvík Ferðamannastovan (tel 56939), Nólsoyar Pállsgøta, PO Box 58, FR-700 Klaksvík
Tora Tourist Traffic (private agency) (tel 15505), Niels Finsensgøta 21, FR-100 Tórshavn
Kunningastovan (City Office) Vaglið, FR-100 Tórshavn

Overseas Reps

The Faroes, Denmark, and all other Scandinavian countries have several offices which dispense tourist information and guidelines for commercial ventures. If you have any queries prior to your trip regarding tourism and other Faroese topics, contact one of the following offices or refer to the Greenland Facts for the Visitor chapter for addresses of Danish Tourism boards worldwide:

United Kingdom
Faroese Commercial Attaché (tel 244-592777), 150 Market St, Aberdeen, Scotland AB1 2PP

Denmark
Faerøernes Repraesentationskontor (tel 33-140866), Højbroplads 7,2, DK-1200 Copenhagen
Danish Tourism Board, H C Andersens Blvd 22, DK-1553 Copenhagen
Green Tours (private backpackers' agency), Kultorvet 7, DK-1175 Copenhagen
Føroyahúsið (Faroes House), Vesterbrogade 18 mezz, DK-1620 Copenhagen

Foreign Consulates

Most consular representation in the Faroes is of the honorary variety although there are some official representatives based in Tórshavn. A few of the most useful ones are:

Finland
Torolf Björklund (tel 13631)
France
Valdemar Lutzern (tel 11020)
Germany
Jógvan á Dul (tel 12094)
Iceland
Moul Mohr (tel 11155)
Norway
Leif Wagsteinn (tel 12317)
Spain
Hans Hansen (tel 11161)
Sweden
Aksel Hansen (tel 11360)
United Kingdom
Johan Mortensen (tel 13510)

GENERAL INFORMATION

Post

The postal service in the Faroes is called *Postverk Føroya*. Post offices can be found in most towns and villages around the islands but opening hours will vary widely. The central post office in Tórshavn is open Monday to Friday from 9 am to 5 pm and on Saturdays between 10 am and noon.

The postal rate for letters and postcards weighing less than 20 g to destinations within the Kingdom of Denmark is Fkr3.50. To other European countries via airmail, it's Fkr5 for letters and Fkr3.50 for postcards. To other countries it costs Fkr6 to send a letter and Fkr4 to send a postcard. Post offices provide fax services as well which cost Fkr60 per page within Denmark and Fkr120 per page to overseas destinations. A fax service is available at the post offices in Tórshavn, Klaksvík, and Tvøroyri.

Post Restante services are available in Tórshavn. To receive mail, have it addressed to you at Poste Restante, Central Post Office, FR-100 Tórshavn, Faroe Islands. It will help with filing if the surname is capitalised or underlined.

The Faroes became a separate postal zone on 30 January 1975, and have since issued a variety of interesting and collectable stamps. Philatelists interested in a catalogue of Faroese stamps should write to Postverk Føroya, Frimerkjadeildin, FR-159 Tórshavn, Faroe Islands. See also the Things to Buy section of this chapter.

Telephone

Overseas calls may be booked at the central telephone office at Tinghúsvegur 76, Tórshavn. It's open Monday to Friday from 8 am to 9 pm and weekends from 8 am to 2 pm.

If you'd like to make a reverse-charge call, you must first ascertain whether Denmark (and therefore the Faroes) has a reciprocal agreement with the destination country. You can book operator-assisted calls of any kind by dialling (0013) from anywhere in the Faroes. For telephone information and directory assistance, ring (54) in the north-eastern islands and (0033) everywhere else.

The Faroes' international country code is (298). To dial out of the Faroes, you must dial (009) and then the destination country code, area or city code, and phone number. To ring Denmark, however, you don't need to use (009). For calls to destinations within the Faroes, you need only dial the telephone number since there are no area codes to worry about.

Left-Luggage

All Faroese youth hostels will store luggage for guests at a nominal fee. There is a left-luggage service primarily for the benefit of Smyril Line stopover passengers at Kioskin á Steinatúni at the intersection of Winthers Gøta and Niels Finsensgøta in central Tórshavn. It is open Monday to Friday from 7 am to 11 pm, Saturdays from 9 am to 11 pm, and Sundays from 2 to 11 pm. They charge US$1.50 per day for a maximum of 3 days.

MEDIA

There are eight local newpapers, all in Føroyskt, which are issued from one to four times per week. Copenhagen, Frankfurt, London, and New York papers are also flown in, but they're often quite late appearing and can be several days old by the time they hit the stands. Several international news magazines, including *Time*, *Newsweek*, and *Der Spiegel* are available in Tórshavn.

Sjónvarp Føroya, the Faroes rather hopeless attempt at television production, broadcasts on weekends and Tuesdays, Thursdays and Fridays. It first hit the scene in 1984 and it seems they're still getting the bugs out of it. Films are broadcast in the original language with Danish or Faroese subtitles.

During the summer months, Útvarp Føroya, the local radio station broadcasts weekdays from 7.15 am to 1 pm and 6 to 8 pm, Saturdays from 7.15 am to 5 pm, and Sundays from 10 am to 7 pm. The English-language news programme goes to air at 8.05 am from Monday to Saturday.

FOOD

Self-Catering

Supermarkets and cooperatives in Tórshavn are, on the whole, as well stocked as their counterparts in Copenhagen. Most towns and villages have at least a kiosk (something like a US 7 Eleven or an Aussie milk bar) where you can buy basic groceries. Kiosks are normally open until 11 pm on weeknights and for varying hours on Saturdays and Sundays.

You'll also find bakeries and butcher shops open during normal shopping hours. For details about fish, see the following section on traditional foods.

Restaurants & Cafeterias

If you're coming from Europe, Faroese restaurants will seem quite expensive but, if you're coming from Iceland, you'll probably consider them a bargain. For a continental buffet breakfast, plan on spending about US$6 and about US$11 for lunch or dinner. Meals will typically consist of some sort of meat and potatoes accompanied by a pathetically small and precious pile of steamed frozen vegies and possibly even soup. Since lettuce is treated like green gold in these northern climates, salads must usually be ordered separately and will cost around US$6. One wonderful little pizza restaurant in Tórshavn has an American-style salad bar which is very appealing, especially if you've gone without them for awhile.

Cafeterias offer the closest thing to fast food available in the Faroes. You'll find a variety of small and decorative salads and Danish-style smørrebrød open-faced sandwiches containing a variety of fish, lunch meat, and colourful vegetables plastered together with butter and mayonnaise or tartar sauce. There'll also be a selection of cold desserts and cakes and a hot-meal counter where you can get sausages, fish & chips, chicken, and maybe some sort of daily special.

In a country dependent on fish, it's amazing that cafeterias seem to serve only reconstituted and frozen fish patties imported from Denmark. They're invariably cold once they hit the display case and, after a couple of hours, become downright disagreeable. Likewise, the burgers normally consist of a few grams of beef mince patted into burger-size globs mixed with cereal to make them go further, an even more unappealing option. Petrol stations in the countryside also have snack bars and there are a couple of coffee shops around Tórshavn and Klaksvík.

Traditional Foods

The first thing visitors notice about the traditional Faroese diet is the marked lack of green vegetables to accompany the ubiquitous meat and potatoes. Those hailing from more fertile countries and more agriculturally amenable climates may even find some of it rather unappealing.

First of all, meat in one form or another is the basis of every meal. One of the most popular treats is *skerpikjøt*, well-aged, wind-dried mutton which requires a hefty knife and powerful jaws to appreciate. New batches of skerpikjøt are prepared at Christmas time and are intended to last through the following Christmas. Things may begin to get a bit green around November, but I don't think that has much effect on the taste. In fact, this is one Faroese delicacy that grows on you. In addition to mutton, fish and puffin meat are also dried. The drying shed, a necessity in the Faroes, is called a *hjallur*.

Another meat variation is *rast kjót* or boiled mutton. Similarly boiled fish is called *rastan fisk*. After a grindadráp, a very popular meal with the locals will consist of *grind og spik* or 'whale and blubber'. Whale meat is not fishy at all and tastes very much like a rich filet mignon but those who've witnessed a grindadráp will almost certainly be put off trying it.

Several varieties of sausage are also common. One which is made of offal, trimmings, and spices is called *Føroyskt rollipylsa.* A slightly more interesting variety is called *blóð pylsa* and you can probably work out what its main ingredient would be.

The Faroese version of the Icelandic svið is called *seyðar høvd* here and that's just what it is – sheep's head.

Of course, fresh fish figures prominently in the diet but commercially caught fish all seem to end up on the export market. If the Faroese want to enjoy freshly caught fish, they have to arrange this themselves as the supermarkets only sell it dried and frozen. If you're keen on a meal straight from the North Atlantic, just ask around the harbour in any village and see who has some extra to sell. Alternatively, see 'Fishing' in the Activities section later this chapter.

The Faroese are also particularly fond of sea birds and their eggs and go to great lengths to collect them. The birds are normally collected in long-handled nets known as *fleygustong* which are commonly described as resembling lacrosse rackets. The clumsy little puffins are most trusting and vulnerable and therefore fall victim more frequently than some others.

The Faroese are permitted to gather eggs for 9 days each June, allowing the birds to produce another egg before the mating season's over. Egg collectors lower themselves over cliffs to gain access to the nests of the prospective parents who probably assumed their precariously placed homes were inaccessible to such dangers. The eggs are, by the way, very good.

Puffins are sometimes eaten stuffed with sweet dough and baked or roasted. Gannets and guillemots are also netted and eaten in large quantities. Oily fulmars used to be eaten frequently as well, but now they've been discovered to carry psittacosis, or 'parrot fever' and have declined in popularity.

DRINKS

Alcohol

The Faroese government's attitude toward alcohol borders on the paranoid. For travellers, it's one of those topics that's good for many hours of amusement. It's just as well because there aren't any colourful watering holes where folks can get together and while away the hours over a jug or two of the Faroes' finest. In fact, there aren't any pubs of any kind in the Faroes.

The paranoia all began back in the darkest 1800s when destitute farmers habitually bartered bits of land with grocers in exchange for foodstuffs. You can imagine what happened when the grocers realised they could stock alcohol, as well. Farmers would awaken from a euphoric stupor to find themselves former farmers and shopkeepers found themselves suddenly in the real estate business. At that stage, alcohol was banned as an undesirable influence.

Top: Dog sled, Ammassalik, Greenland (KL)
Bottom: Clothesline, Alluitsup Paa, Greenland (DS)

Top: Sumba, Suðuroy, Faroe Islands (DS)
Left: Harbour at Fuglafjørður, Eysturoy, Faroe Islands (DS)
Right: Uummannaq, Greenland (DS)

Although the total ban was later lifted, local religious forces have, in effect, kept control in the form of rationing. Through a long and tedious process, prospective imbibers are required to provide proof that they're up-to-date on their tax payments before being eligible for the quarterly distribution of alcohol allotments which must be ordered from Copenhagen. You can imagine the condition of the country immediately following the arrival of these anxiously awaited supplies!

Visitors who wish to partake will find that getting themselves into the rationing scheme will prove a time consuming experience. If you just want to buy a beer, you may be happy to learn that you can be chug-a-lugging in less than week. The local brewery (yes, there really is one) issues the following instructions:

BRYGGJARÍ
MINERALVATNSVIRKI

v/ Einar Waag

Telefon +298 5454 - Telefax +298 56544 - Telex 81395 fabeer fa

How to buy beer on the Faroes:

They brew an exellent beer on the Faroes, the problem is how to get it, because you can only buy a light beer (2.25% alc. by weight) at the grocers and in the hotels.

Here is the long and troublesome way you have to go:
First of all you have to be 20 years old.

1. At LANDSFÓLKAYVIRLITIÐ (National Register). Adress: Yviri við Strond 19, FR-100 Tórshavn, Phone 17530, you ask for a touristrationcard (Rúsdrekkaskamtunarkort). You have to present identification card or passport.
   If you read this letter before you leave home, you may write to LANDSFÓLKAYVIRLITIÐ, state your year & date of birth and they will send you, to your address in the Faroes or Poste restante, the rationcard.
   If you happend to be outside Tórshavn when you want a beer, the local town council will arrange point 1 for you, but it takes some days.
   If you only want lager, you just need to prove your age, as lager is not rationed.
2. Now you can *order your beer on phone 13434* in Tórshavn or another depot in the list below, if it is closer. *Next day* you will receive a postal cheque form on your address or Poste Restante in a post office of your choise.
3. You pay your beer at the postoffice, and at the same time you have to give up the license, if you order export beer.
4. Now you can get your beer at one of our depots by handing over the postal cheque receipt. Minimum sale 1 case á 30 bottles. The address in Tórshavn.: Akranesgöta 10.

Föroya Bjór depots:

Tórshavn,	phone: 13434, fax: 10934
Leirvík,	phone: 43038,
Klakksvík,	phone: 55454, fax: 56544
Skálavík,	phone: 61231, fax: 61731
Tvöroyri,	phone: 71025.

If you think this is not worth while, you can still buy a light beer at your hotel or the grocers.

Spirits and wine you have to order from a wine-merchant in Copebhagen. Time of delivery is about a week. Quantities up to 6 liters will be mailed. You have to get the same certificate as mentioned above for export beer. The quantities of spirits and strong wine (Port etc.) is restricted to 3 liters of each.

FÖROYA BJÓR - POSTBOX 4 - FR-700 KLAKKSVÍK/FAROES

If you want to save yourself the effort, drink up in one of the Faroes-bound ferry's three bars and stock up with the maximum allowance in their duty-free bottle shop before disembarking. Otherwise, resign yourself to drinking the 2.2% brew that tastes more like mountain spring water than anything else. It's pleasant but doesn't pack much of a punch.

Despite all this fuss about alcohol, you'll soon notice that a significant percentage of Faroese manage to spend a great deal of time in varying states of consciousness. It seems the ultimate paradox that one of the world's rainiest countries is officially nearly as dry as Saudi Arabia, and yet it has one of the highest rates of alcoholism in the world. Perhaps it also provides the world's best commentary on prohibition.

BOOKS & BOOKSHOPS

All the bookshops of any consequence in the Faroes are in Tórshavn where there are two very good ones in the city centre and a couple of others scattered elsewhere. While most publications are understandably in Danish or Faroese (Føroyskt), there are some foreign-language titles available at Hjalmar Jocobsens Bókahandil on the Niels Finsensgøta pedestrian mall and at H N Jacobsens Bókahandil at Húsagarður 2 near the harbour church.

Apart from this book and a few pages coverage in several overall Scandinavia guides, there are no English-language guidebooks dealing with the Faroe Islands. The one most people use if they can understand it at all is the German book *Färöer Reisehandbuch* by Ulrich Kreuzenbeck and Hans Klüche and published by Nordis Verlag of Düsseldorf. It's a bit dry and outdated but most of the information is useful. For the benefit of Danish travellers, this book has been translated into Danish and marketed as the *Skarv Guide*.

There is the usual gamut of coffee-table publications extolling the Faroese landscape in brilliant glossy colour (primarily green). These are available in several languages at the previously mentioned shops. There you can also purchase a Føroyskt-English dictionary.

Although it was written in Iceland, you may want to read the English translation of *Faereyringar Saga* which outlines in saga form the settlement of the Faroes and the misadventures of their early characters. There's an English version, *The Faroese Saga*, translated by G V C Young and Cynthia Clewer. It was published in Belfast in 1973.

A brief, but wonderfully clever, account of travelling in the Faroes is included in the North Atlantic travelogue *Last Places – A Journey in the North* by Lawrence Millman, published by Houghton-Mifflin (Boston, 1990). Another light and positive account of life in the Faroes is *The Atlantic Islands* (1970) by Kenneth Williamson who was there during WW II.

The best and most thorough historical treatise on the islands is *Faroe – the Emergence of a Nation* by John F West, published by C Hurst & Co (London, 1972).

A few works of modern Faroese literature have found their way into English translation, most prominently the works of William Heinesen (*Neils Peter*, *Tower at the Edge of the World*) and Heðin Brú (*The Old Man and his Sons*) which can be found at both Jacobsen bookshops in Tórshavn and the shop upstairs in the SMS Shopping Centre as well.

MAPS

The Dansk Geodaetisk Institut publishes topographic sheets at a scale of 1:100,000 which cover the Faroe Islands in two sheets. The northern section includes Streymoy, Eysturoy, the north-eastern islands, the western islands as well as Koltur, Hestur, and Nólsoy. The southern section includes Suðuroy, Sandoy, Skúvoy, Stóra Dímun, and Lítla Dímun. These maps were last updated in 1985 and are therefore a bit outdated as regards tunnels, causeways, and ferry routes, but you'll get a good idea of what you can expect, anyway. They cost US$5.70 each and are available at tourist offices and bookshops in the Faroes and some places in Denmark.

There is also a 1:20,000 series of 53 topo sheets covering the entire archipelago. If you're planning any serious walking, these are by far the most useful and detailed. If you'd like to study the maps before you go, you can write for a catalogue or order them directly from Dansk Geodaetisk Institut (tel 45-1-92-33-30), Proviaantgaarden, Rigsdagsgaarden 7, DK-1218 Copenhagen, Denmark.

The best map of Tórshavn I could find was in the tourist office handout *Around the Faroe Islands*. It's fairly pathetic especially in its coverage of the city centre (the locator numbers clustered there obscure the street plan) but, to my knowledge, there's nothing else available.

ACTIVITIES

Fishing

If you're planning to spend a lot of time camping and walking through thc highlands, you may want to bring along a rod and reel so you can supplement your diet. In the Faroes, fishing is less restricted and more reasonably priced than in Iceland.

Salmon and sea trout inhabit the lakes Saksunarvatn and Leynavatn on Streymoy. A full-year licence for Saksunarvatn costs about US$40 and one for Leynavatn costs US$64. One-day licences sell for US$7 and US$11 for these lakes, respectively, and can be purchased at the Tórshavn tourist offices, the Esso petrol station in Kollafjørður, or the Shell petrol station in Oyrarbakki. The Saksunarvatn licence covers only the northern shore of the lake. The shore beside the road is owned by Mr Jakup Hansen who will permit fishing from his property for an additional fee.

In the case of other lakes and streams, fishing is permitted upon payment of a fee to the landowner. Sea trout, brown trout, Arctic char, and salmon are all available in Faroese lakes. Fishing for saltwater species from the shore is free and you don't need a licence. Stream fishing is permitted only between 1 May and 31 August but lake fishing continues all year round. Fishing around stream mouths and fish farms is subject to special regulations. These are updated annually can can be obtained from the tourist offices.

Deep-sea fishing trips for cod, haddock, halibut, and herring can be arranged through the tourist offices but they are likely to be quite dear. They can also help you arrange boat rentals from individuals in several outlying villages.

Trekking

For those who have webbed feet or a high tolerance for wet and stormy conditions, the Faroes have some superb trekking country. Before the road system existed, routes between villages followed the shortest distances along ridges and over passes. They crisscrossed the country and were marked by cairns placed closely enough to be seen from one to the next in a moderate fog or misty drizzle, both common weather conditions.

Although they're little used today and many of the cairns have been long destroyed, these routes still provide excellent opportunities for visitors to get out and travel on foot through the astonishing 'vertical' scenery that is the Faroes' trademark.

As always in the North Atlantic, weather is changeable. A warm sunny day may quickly turn into a cold and wet or blustery day so be prepared with a range of suitable clothing for all eventualities. A waterproof and windproof outer layer will be of utmost importance to prevent hypothermia. Even though the temperature may be well above freezing, wet and/or windy weather can rob the body of heat faster than it can be produced, and without proper protection, the results can be life-threatening.

In addition to appropriate clothing, trekkers should carry a compass and, if possible, 1:20,000 scale topo sheets for the area you're crossing. The 1:100,000 maps will be sufficient for experienced trekkers but, if you have any doubts about your ability to pick your way through rugged and often fog-bound mountains, you're better off with the larger scale maps. Although it's best to travel in groups or at least in pairs, those with wilderness common sense who prefer the hermit experience shouldn't encounter any serious problems.

All the old buildings, stone fences, cairns, and relics which dot the landscape are officially protected in the Faroes and trekkers aren't permitted to damage them. Pile a nearby rock on the cairn, if you'd like to, but don't remove any.

Camping

Bush camping is possible throughout the islands but, if you plan to set up in a farmer's sheep pasture, you're officially required to obtain permission before doing so. Also, take care not to trample fields planted for hay and remember to close any gates you may open when crossing private land.

If you'll be doing any cooking, it's important to carry a stove and sufficient fuel for the duration of your intended trip. Open fires are forbidden and there isn't any wood, anyway. Purchasing stove alcohol in the Faroes isn't as frustrating as buying beer but it's just as ludicrous. To buy methylated spirits, you must be over 20 years of age, present ID, and fill out a police form with your name, address, and the purpose for which the fuel is intended. When I was last there, you were limited to half a litre at a time.

Surface water is potable anywhere outside settled areas and I had no problems drinking it directly from streams. If there are sheep on the slopes higher up and you're concerned about giardia, you may want to use some sort of purification method (see the Health section in the Regional Facts for the Visitor chapter). Make sure toilet areas are kept well clear of the water, this will ensure the water stays clean – if possible, bury these areas.

When your're camping you can also do some fishing – see the previous page for details.

THINGS TO BUY

As in Iceland, the most popular souvenirs are locally knitted woollens. Faroese designs are slightly different to the Icelandic ones. The woollens factory Tøtingarvirkið is in Góta on south-eastern Eysturoy. Locally handknitted garments can be purchased at the outlets Føroyskt Heimavirki at Kongabrúgvin in Tórshavn or Norðoya Heimavirki at the head of the harbour in Klaksvík. Prices of all woollens in the Faroes are comparable to those in Iceland at around US$55 for a traditional pullover.

Faroese stamps are also an interesting commodity. Since the islands stopped using Danish stamps and began printing their own in January 1975, more Faroese stamps, seem to be ending up in collections than stuck on envelopes and postcards. The *frímerkjadeildin* or philatelic bureau is at Tradagøta 38 in Argir, just a km or so down the coast from Tórshavn.

On Suðuroy, a superior stoneware shop has sprung up at the village of Hvalba. The product isn't strictly Faroese, however, since it's crafted by resident Danes. They do excellent work and the clay that goes into it is 100% Faroese. It's certainly worth a stop if you're passing though those parts.

Finally, for those whose tastes run a bit higher, the Faroes offer what is undoubtedly one of the world's great kitsch finds – stuffed birds. Yes, there are Faroese who spend their lives netting and skinning puffins, filling them with sawdust, and selling them to discerning tourists who want to take a bit of that island charm home with them. Before you buy, consider the sort of industry you're supporting and check import restrictions in your home country or in those countries you'll be passing through en route. Understandably, quite a few people can't appreciate the urge to own such things.

Getting Around

It won't take you long to discover that the transport system in the Faroes is superb, easily the equal of that in any other northern European country. The roads are surfaced and the difficult or twisting sections have been by-passed by tunnelling through the mountains. In fact, although there were quite a few isolated villages in the islands just 20 years ago, the only remaining village not connected to the highway system is Gásadalur on the island of Vágar. It's been listed to receive its tunnel in the very near future. Streymoy and Eysturoy are connected by a 226-metre-long bridge across Sundini, the channel that separates them. Hvannasund between Borðoy and Viðoy is also bridged and Haraldssund between Borðoy and Kunoy is crossed by an earth-dam causeway.

All but two of the islands, one uninhabited, are connected to Tórshavn by the ferry system and many have helicopter service as well. Buses run frequently to most accessible parts of the islands and travellers who are in a hurry will find several tours, albeit rather expensive, available to make excursions away from the capital even easier.

If you're stopping over for just a brief visit, it's a good idea to remember the word *kanskar*, 'maybe'. The Faroes' nickname the 'islands of maybe', was coined by occupying British soldiers during WW II in reference to the weather's final say in just about everything. Don't wander off to Mykines or Fugloy, for example, it you have to catch the ferry to Iceland the following day – you could become the next victim of kanskar.

AIR

Since the Faroes have only one airport, the international terminal on Vágar, all inter-island air travel is by helicopter (*tyrlan* pronounced TOOR-lan) – it's a remarkably inexpensive way to get around. Several days a week, helicopters connect Tórshavn with the islands of Koltur, Skúvoy, Stóra Dímun (the only access to this island), and with Klaksvík. There are also routes from Vágar to Mykines and Gásadalur and from Klaksvík to Svínoy and Fugloy. Like the ferry system, helicopter services are operated by Strandfaraskip Landsins Tyrluavgreiðslan (tel 16450) at Yviri við Strønd, PO Box 88, FR-100 Tórshavn. The Tórshavn heliport is about 500 metres north of the camping ground along the coast.

Some sample one-way fares are:

Tórshavn to Skúvoy or Dímun – US$25.70
Tórshavn to Klaksvík – US$25.70
Tórshavn to Koltur – US$10
Vágar to Gásadalur or Mykines – US$10
Klaksvík to Svínoy or Fugloy – US$10

BUS

The Bygdaleiðir inter-city bus service is excellent. They follow a strict and convenient schedule and, when combined with the ferry services, connect virtually every corner of the country with every other corner, including some fairly remote outposts like Akraberg on Suðuroy, Dalur on Sandoy, and Bøur on Vágar. (See also the helpful map *Ferðakort* from Samferðsluskrivstovan, R C Effersøesgøta 1, 3800 Tórshavn (tel 14366).

Bus fares are fairly steep and will add up quickly if you're doing a lot of running around. Fortunately, those who are staying awhile can opt to buy the Bygdaleiður Ferðamannakort which allows 14-days unlimited travel on inter-city buses for US$40 (Fkr280). It is well worth the money and can pay for itself in just 4 or 5 days, especially if you're doing excursions into remoter areas. The passes are available at tourist information offices, at the Auto and Bíl taxi stands, and at LFÚ-Ferðir (Student Travel office) in Tórshavn.

The main terminal in Tórshavn is actually just a long bus stop beside the harbour. Buses also stop at Auto and Bíl taxi stands on Niels

Finsensgøta and in Gundadalur, respectively, to pick up passengers before leaving Tórshavn. The one exception is the Kirkjubøur bus which stops on its way out of town.

Some inter-city buses only go to certain destinations on request. When you board the bus, tell the driver where you want to go so he or she will know when to stop or can radio ahead for a connecting bus to meet you at the appropriate junction.

Airport Bus Since the Faroes international air terminal is on Vágar, a bus ride, a ferry ride, and another bus ride away from Tórshavn (it's an even more complicated connection from Klaksvík) there is a through bus to the airport from both towns leaving 3 hours before flight departures. For information and bookings, make arrangements at the tourist office or phone (tel 12626).

BOAT

All the islands in the Faroes except Stóra Dímun and Lítla Dímun are connected by the ferry system. Some routes are travelled by car-ferries but some ferries carry passengers only. The table below is a rough guide to routes, approximate frequency of sailings, and one-way fares in US$ for passengers and for passenger cars (with driver). Students, children under 13, and people over 65 receive a 20% to 50% discount.

Some ferry trips, especially those to Mykines, Svínoy, and Fugloy, require navigation through open seas in small boats and are frequently cancelled if the weather warrants it. If you're planning to do either of these trips, try to remain as flexible as possible.

DRIVING

Driving in the Faroes is easy. There are few unsurfaced roads and most of the islands which have roads are connected to Tórshavn by car-ferry. The greatest hazards while driving are fog, sheep, and significant drop-offs which become even more significant in the presence of the typically distracting Faroese scenery. It's possible to bring a vehicle from the Europe on one of several ferries: the *Nörrona* from Hanstholm (Denmark), Lerwick (the Shetlands), Seyðisfjörður (Iceland), or Bergen (Norway); the *Smyril* from Scrabster (Scotland); and the *Winston Churchill* from Esbjerg (Denmark).

Renting a Car

You must be at least 20 years of age to rent a car in the Faroes. As you'd expect, it's a

routes	*frequency of sailing (w–weekly d–daily)*	*one-way fares ($US)* *passengers*	*passenger cars (with driver)*
Tórshavn-Tvøroyri (Suð)	13 *w*	10.00	17.50
Tórshavn-Skópun (Sandoy)	3 *d*	3.50	8.50
Tórshavn-Klaksvík	1 *w*	8.50	13.00
Tórshavn-Toftir (Eysturoy)	5 *d*	3.50	8.50
Tórshavn-Strendur (Eysutroy)	5 *d*	3.50	8.50
Tórshavn-Vágur (Suð)	2 *w*	10.00	17.50
Vestmanna-Oyrargjógv (Vágar)	10 *d*	3.50	8.50
Leirvík (Eysturoy)-Klaksvík	10 *d*	3.50	8.50
Sørvágur (Vágur)-Mykines	5 *w*	3.50	
Sandur-Skúvoy	2 *d*	3.50	
Hvannasund-Svínoy	1 *d*	3.50	
Hvannasund-Fugloy	1 *d*	3.50	
Klaksvík-Kalsoy	3 *d*	3.50	
Tórshavn-Nólsoy	2 *d*	3.50	
Tórshavn-Hestur	1 *d*	3.50	
Tórshavn-Koltur	3 *w*	3.50	

fairly expensive proposition but a much better deal than in Iceland because there is no per km charge and the daily rate decreases the longer you keep the car.

For a sedan, the first day will cost between US$50 and US$60 while the seventh will be only US$35 or so. Normally, a deposit of about US$150 is required against liability; tax and petrol are not included. A couple of companies will allow you to keep the vehicle over the weekend for the price of a single day. Some rental agencies are:

Car Hire Á Heygnum Mikla (tel 16190), Á Heygnum Mikla, FR-110, Tórshavn
Wenzel Petersen (tel 13873 Tórshavn or tel 32765 Vágar Airport), Oyggjarvegur, Tórshavn
Inter-Rent Norrøna (tel 15354), Vegurin Langi, Hoyvík
Bilverkstaðið (tel 13375), Eyðbjørn Hansen, Varðagøta 75, Tórshavn

Driving Regulations

For those hiring a vehicle or driving their own vehicle, third party insurance is compulsory. Rental agencies will normally tack it onto the hire costs but, if you're travelling with your own vehicle on the ferry, you'll need proof of third party insurance or be required to purchase it from the customs department. Seat belt use is also compulsory in the Faroes.

It also important to note that the country is mostly open-range and animals may wander onto the road just about anywhere. Be particularly alert in heavy fog because motorists must take financial responsibility for anything they hit, be it accidental or not.

The speed limit on open highways is 80 km per hour and 50 km per hour through villages.

In Tórshavn, you must place a parking disc in the front window set to the time you parked your car. These discs are available free at the tourist office and at local banks. Legal parking spaces are marked with a *P* followed by a number and the word *tíma*, indicating the length of time you're permitted to park there.

People in the Faroes drive on the right-hand side of the road.

Tunnels

The Faroe Islands look as if very large rabbits have been busy at work; I wouldn't be surprised if they had densest concentration of highway tunnels anywhere outside the Alps. Given the impossibly steep and rugged landscape, however, many villages would be utterly cut off from the outside world were it not for the local facility with tunnel technology. Now that most settlements are tied in, however, they're still not satisfied. Now they're boring in order to straighten out some of the inconvenient bends in their highway system.

A number of the tunnels, especially those in the north-eastern islands, are wide enough for only one vehicle to pass but there are bays every few hundred metres. If they are marked with a *V*, you are to pull in and allow the other car to pass. If they're marked with an *M*, the other car is to give way.

If you're driving a large vehicle, you may be interested to know that the tunnel between Hvalba and Tvøroyri on Suðuroy is only 3.2 metres high and both the Borðoy tunnels are 3.3 metres high.

As a matter of interest, the longest tunnel currently in use is between Haraldssund and Kunoy on Kunoy island at 3310 metres, soon to be outdone by the new one between Kollafjørður and Kaldbaksfjørður on Streymoy which will be 3500 metres long. The latter will by-pass the high mountain road between Tórshavn and Kollafjørður and make the trip to Eysturoy considerably less interesting.

BICYCLE

Although there are lots of steep hills, tunnels as well as wind and rain to contend with, cycling in the Faroes is still better than cycling in Iceland because the highways are generally wide and surfaced and you don't have to contend with the sandstorms and the gravel-tearing motorists from hell that plague Iceland's generally basic roads.

Even so, cycling shouldn't be taken too lightly in the Faroes. Suitable windproof and waterproof clothing is essential and you'll need more than just a light jacket to keep you warm on all but the few finest days of the year. Warm gloves, a muffler, and a good warm hat will also be appreciated on most days. If the weather gets too wretched, keep in mind that all the buses accept bicycles as luggage.

If you plan to be riding though any of the numerous tunnels on the Faroes, you'll need a good bicycle light both front and back which can be seen in a dark tunnel several km away. Under certain conditions, toxic gases can be trapped in the more congested tunnels so it's wise to get through them as quickly as possible. It's also a good idea to be sure your brakes are in excellent working order. The hills are quite steep, highways are wet most of the time, and the drop-offs are severe.

Bicycle hire is available from André Andréson (tel 11829) at Varðagøta 9, Tórshavn; Thomas Dam (tel 11403) at Niels Finsensgøta 4, Tórshavn; and John W Thomsen (tel 55858), Nólsoyar Pállsgøta, Klaksvík. All three charge US$7.50 per day for the first 2 days, US$5.75 for the third day, and US$4.25 for each day thereafter.

TOURS

Although the Faroe Islands are ideal for leisurely independent exploration using the public transport system, those who are pressed for time or who'd like to do a boat trip to remote bird cliffs may want to join a tour. There are, however, a couple of problems associated with them.

Firstly, compared to making your own arrangements, they are fairly expensive. Secondly, and more importantly, scheduled tours are quite often cancelled due to lack of interest and/or foul weather, two very real possibilities in the Faroes. If you haven't reserved your tour abroad and paid in advance, and neither the *Nörrona* nor the *Winston Churchill* is in port at the time you want to go, the chances of your tour being cancelled are quite good unless you can muster enough interest to keep it going. This may change, of course, as tourism in the Faroes continues to expand. Some of the more prominent agencies specialising in North Atlantic travel include:

Tora Tourist Traffic (tel 15505), Niels Finsensgøta 21, FR-100 Tórshavn

LFÚ-Ferðir (tel 15037), Dokta R A Jacobsensgøta 16, FR-100 Tórshavn, specialising in student and budget travel

Green Tours, Kultorvet 7, DK-1175 Copenhagen, Denmark

Arctic Adventure, 37 Aaboulevard, DK-1960 Copenhagen, Denmark

Skandinavisches Reisebüro GMBH, Kurfürstendamm 206, D-1000 Berlin 15, Germany

Abroad, you can also get help planning trips as well as tour rundowns at offices of the Danish Tourism Board. Addresses are listed in the Tourist Information section of the Faroe Islands Facts for the Visitor chapter.

Tórshavn

Despite being the capital and by far the largest community of the Faroes, Tórshavn – like Reykjavík – is not your typically vibrant European capital. If you thrive on round-the-clock action (or action of any kind) you'll shrivel up and fade away here. In his study of North Atlantic life, *Last Places*, Lawrence Millman writes that in the worldwide sweepstake for the most boring town, Tórshavn would lose out only to an Ecuadorian village where most of the entertainment was attributed to the wasp colony nesting in the armpits of the town statue. Enough said.

Whatever it lacks in thrills, however, Tórshavn makes up in picturesque charm. Just a stroll around Tinganes, the small peninsular headland where the town began nearly a thousand years ago, is enough to endear this quiet and rainy little place to just about anyone.

The rest of the town, a mixture of quiet but pleasant harbour areas, colourfully painted residential sections, and even a city park boasting, proudly but rather pathetically, that forests have finally made their debut in the Faroes, all have a peculiar appeal. Faroese writer William Heinesen writes that Tórshavn for him was, as Cuzco was for the Incas, the 'navel of the universe'. Few Faroese would argue with that but visitors will have to come to their own conclusions about this oddly intriguing place.

History

The name of the Faroese capital means 'Thor's harbour' after the slow-witted and relatively innocuous god best liked by the settlers fleeing the wrath and tyranny of Oðinn's gang on the European mainland.

It was far from the best harbour in the Faroes and its position on an exposed headland did nothing to shelter it from the weather. Furthermore, it had poor soil and no cliffs teeming with edible birds and their eggs. It wasn't conducive to traditional settlement but it was central and therefore became the site of the early parliament, the Alting.

The Alting was organised around the time of Settlement in the early 9th century and was first mentioned in the 13th-century Icelandic work *Faereyingar Saga.* Around the year 1000, it accepted Christianity as the official religion of the islands. The Alting was dissolved with the Faroes' incorporation into Norway in 1035 and was re-formed in 1380 as the Løgting when Norway was absorbed into Denmark. At that time, it was almost completely deprived of power and remained little more than a council until modern times. The Løgting continued to function, nonetheless, and official records of its annual conventions on Tinganes each 29 July, St Olav's Day, have been preserved since 1615.

Because Tórshavn was an official meeting place, a market sprang up to accommodate the representatives and visitors. It seemed to follow naturally that foreign monopoly traders would also eventually set up business there. Debtors and poor islanders were

Tórshavn City Seal

impressed into service to fortify the trading area.

During the early 1800s, Faroese genius Nølsoyar Poul Poulson attempted to rid the Faroes of what he perceived was its greatest inequity and threat to prosperity, the monopoly trading scheme. Smuggling and piracy was out of control in Tórshavn and officials had become hopelessly corrupt. He felt that something should be done about it before the system collapsed leaving the islands destitute.

Poulson salvaged a wrecked ship from the island of Suðuroy, which became the only sea-going vessel in the Faroes, and he sailed to Europe to plead his case in Denmark which had, by the way, just engaged itself in a war with the British who had blockaded the North Sea, cutting off Faroes-bound trade. Poulson managed to carry a bit of grain back to Tórshavn but his efforts were otherwise unsuccessful and he found himself embroiled in legal battles with the Danish government and the trading companies as well. Although he was unsuccessful in his struggle to abolish the monopolies, he became quite a hero with the Faroese and aroused a bit of healthy speculation about their centuries old economic system.

When monopoly trading was finally abolished for economic reasons in 1856, the Faroese took to fishing and bought up larger sea-going British fishing boats so they could fish further offshore than their tiny open boats would allow. Tórshavn, although it was the capital, had very marginal harbour facilities and was being left behind the rest of the country economically. In 1927, the harbour was upgraded; it remains the centre of the fishing industry, commerce, transport, and trade in the islands.

By 1950, Tórshavn had a population of 5600, having grown by 1000% since the early 19th century. Since then, the population has tripled and migrants continue to arrive from the countryside to this, the Faroes' closest approximation to a big city.

Information & Orientation

Tórshavn, a small city, is easily negotiated on foot. The older section surrounds the two harbours, which are separated by Tinganes, the original site of the Løgting and the trading settlement. The eastern harbour is the ferry terminal and all inter-island and mainland ferries dock here. The western harbour is used primarily for commerce.

The modern centre of Tórshavn is now just up the hill from the harbour areas between Tinganes and Winthers Gøta. There you'll find most of the shops, restaurants, and services. The SMS Shopping Centre on R C Effersøesgøta is an indoor shopping mall with a supermarket, cafeteria, bookshop, snack bar, and numerous other shops. Surrounding areas are primarily residential with the exception of Gundadalur where you'll find the city park, the sports complex, and a few businesses. On the hill between Gundadalur and the camping site is the central industrial zone.

Tourist Offices The Faroes tourist office, Ferðamannastovan, has now been closed permanently. It has been replaced by Aldan, an office of the Faroe Islands Tourist Board, at Reynagøta 17, Tinganes.

The Kunningarstovan tourism authority and the Tórshavn city tourist office also handle enquiries. The city office, on the town square near the central post office, is open Monday to Friday from 8 am to 5 pm and on Saturdays from 10 am to 2 pm. They have a few useful brochures to hand out and also sell topographic maps and postcards.

Tora Tourist Traffic (tel 15505), at Niels Finsensgøta 21, is also very helpful.

Banks Tórshavn's banks are open weekdays from 9 or 9.30 am to 4 pm. On Thursdays they remain open until 6 pm. All banks do foreign exchange. Outside banking hours, the tourist office will exchange money and, in a pinch, you can try the Hotel Hafnia between Vaglið, the town square, and the harbour. They'll charge a higher commission but are open evenings and Sundays.

Post The central post office is found on Vaglið behind the Ráðhús or city hall. It's

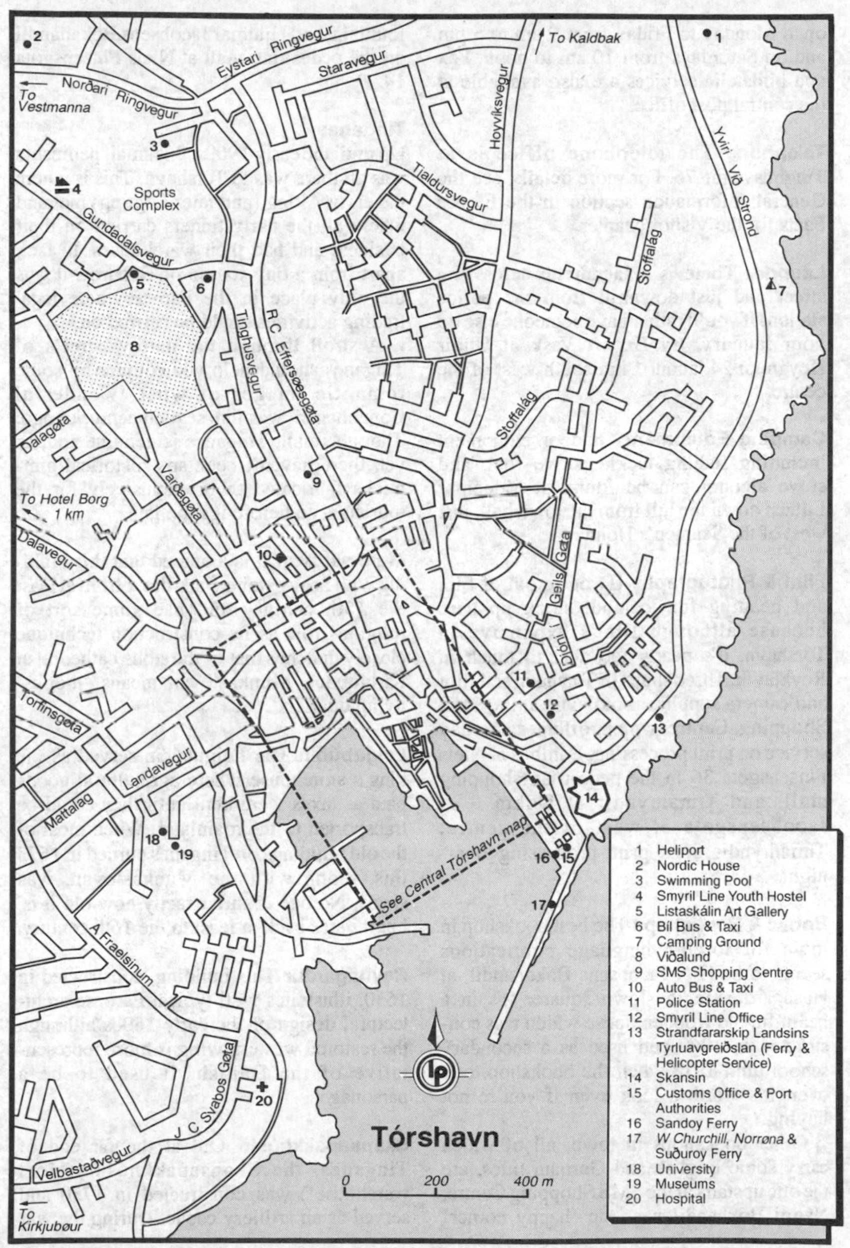
Tórshavn
To Kaldbak
To Vestmanna
Norðari Ringvegur
Eystari Ringvegur
Staravegur
Hoyviksvegur
Yviri Við Strond
Tjaldursvegur
Sports Complex
Gundadalsvegur
Stoffalág
Tinghusvegur
R C Effersøesgøta
Dalagøta
Vardagøta
To Hotel Borg 1 km
Dalavegur
Geils Gøta
Dìðni
Torfinsgøta
Landavegur
Mattalag
See Central Tórshavn map
A Fraelsinum
J C Svabos Gøta
Velbastaðvegur
To Kirkjubøur
0 200 400 m
1 Heliport
2 Nordic House
3 Swimming Pool
4 Smyril Line Youth Hostel
5 Listaskálin Art Gallery
6 Bíl Bus & Taxi
7 Camping Ground
8 Viðalund
9 SMS Shopping Centre
10 Auto Bus & Taxi
11 Police Station
12 Smyril Line Office
13 Strandfararskip Landsins
Tyrluavgreiðslan (Ferry & Helicopter Service)
14 Skansin
15 Customs Office & Port Authorities
16 Sandoy Ferry
17 W Churchill, Norrøna & Suðuroy Ferry
18 University
19 Museums
20 Hospital

open Monday to Friday from 9 am to 5 pm and on Saturdays from 10 am to noon. Fax and philatelic services are also available at the central post office.

Telephone The telephone office is at Tinghúsvegur 76. For more details, see the General Information section in the Faroes Facts for the Visitor chapter.

Laundry There is a laundrette across the street and just downhill from the police station. If you'd rather have someone else do your laundry, try Expert Vask at Undir Heygnum 24, about 1 km south-west of the centre.

Camping Equipment Outdoor equipment including fishing tackle, stove fuel, and stove alcohol can be found at Valdemar Lützen down the hill from the town hall, just west of the Seamen's Home.

Film & Photography If you're out of film and heading for Iceland, stock up here because although film's expensive in Tórshavn, it's nearly too dear to touch in Reykjavík. Three shops in Tórshavn sell film and camera supplies: Fotobúðin at the SMS Shopping Centre which offers same-day service on print processing, Bambus at Niels Finsensgøta 36 in the pedestrian shopping mall, and Tímamyndir at Dokta R A Jacobsensgøta 3, west of the centre. Tímamyndir does print-processing overnight.

Books & Bookshops The best bookshop in town for foreign language publications seems to be H N Jacobsens Bókahandil, at Húsagardur on the town square. It's in a beautiful old wooden house which was constructed in 1860 and used as a secondary school until 1918 when the bookshop took over. It's worth a look even if you're not buying.

Other bookshops in town, all of which carry some English and German titles, are the one upstairs at the SMS Shopping Centre, Nýggi Bókhandil near the 'happy corner' fountain, and Hjalmar Jacobsens Bókahandil on the pedestrian mall at Niels Finsensgøta 14.

Tinganes

Up until the early 1900s, this small peninsula was all there was to Tórshavn. This is where the early Alting (and later Løgting) met and where all the early traders carried on their business and had their warehouses. In fact, apart from a tiny station on Suðuroy, it was the only place in the Faroes where legal trading activities could be carried on.

A stroll through the narrow streets of Tinganes should help you conjure up some romantic images of what 'wonderful Copenhagen' was like several centuries ago. Though small, Tinganes is genuine and, as yet, there haven't been any historical gimmicks fabricated there exclusively for the tourists – go before it's too late.

Munkastovan It is assumed that this building with heavy stone walls dates from at least the 15th century and had some sort of religious role as its construction technique closely matches that of the stone cathedral at Kirkjubøur. Munkastovan means 'monks' living quarters'.

Leigubúðin The Leigubúðin served as the king's storehouse where agricultural goods paid as taxes were kept until they could be transported to the mainland. When most of the old buildings on Tinganes burned in 1673 this, along with the Munkastovan, was saved. No one is sure exactly how old it is, but it dates back at least to the 16th century.

Reynagarður This building, constructed in 1630, illustrates well typical Faroese architectural design of the early 1600s although the restored western wing is more representative of the Danish. It used to be a parsonage.

Skansapakkhúsið Out at the far end of Tinganes, the Skansapakkhúsið ('fort warehouse') was constructed in 1750 and served as an artillery cache. During the war

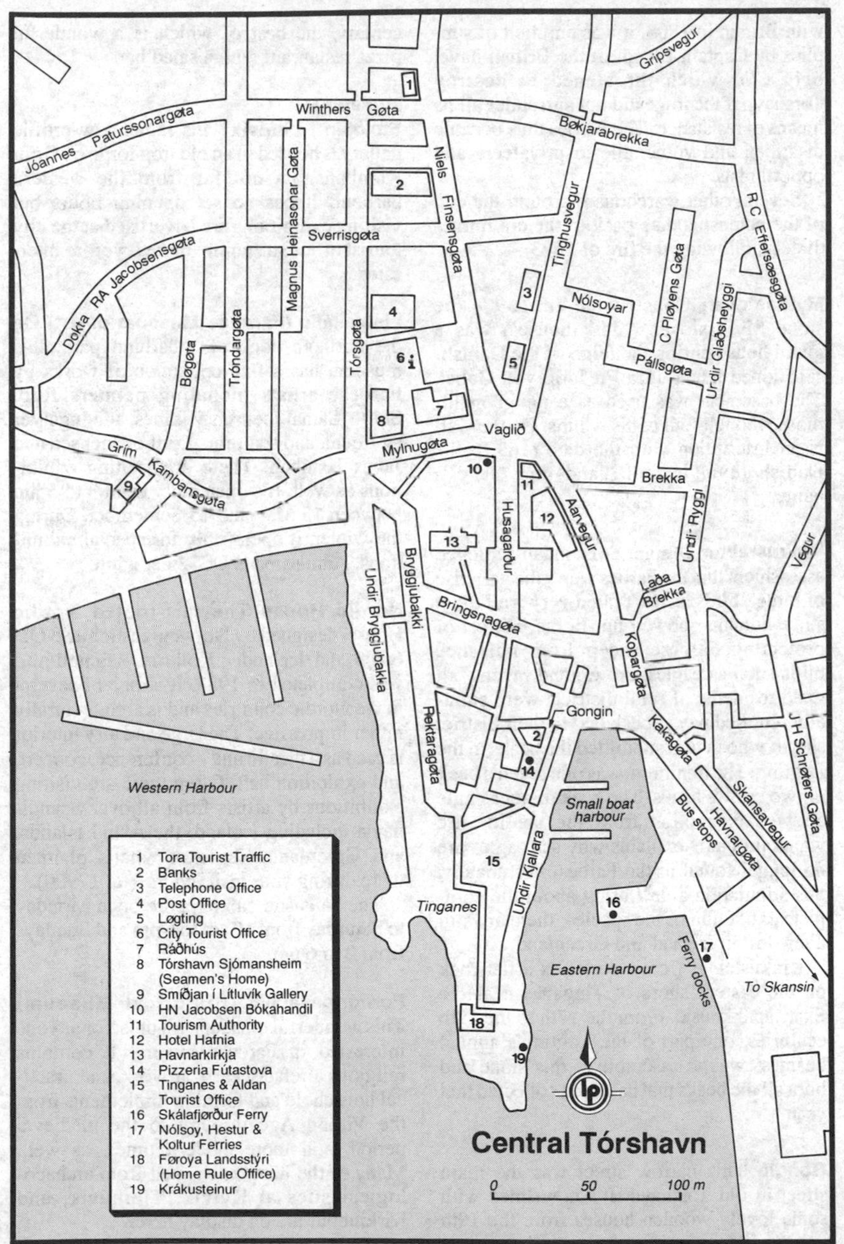

Central Tórshavn

with Britain in 1808, it was emptied of supplies by Captain Baugh of the British naval brig *Clio* which threatened to destroy Tórshavn if the town did not surrender all its means of resistance. The Faroes thus became disarmed and vulnerable to privateers and opportunists.

Several other warehouses around the end of the peninsula date back to the era immediately following the fire of 1673.

Myrkastovan Constructed in 1693, the stone Myrkastovan ('dark house') was a guard house during the reign of the Danish-sanctioned feudal lord Frederik von Gabel. The basement was used as a dungeon for those who fell foul of his whims. On the wall is an inscription with the date (1693), the Danish royal insignia, and von Gabel's name.

Krákusteinur Despite St Brendan's alleged assessment that the Faroes were 'the paradise of birds', birds haven't fared very well there since humans showed up. In the interest of protecting Faroese sheep from nuisance birds such as eagles, crows, and ravens, all male residents of rural districts were annually required pay a 'beak tax' to their district sheriff who in turn submitted the beaks to the Løgting. The minimum was one raven's beak or two crow's beaks. The beak of a sea eagle allowed exemption from the tax for life which probably explains why sea eagles are no longer found in the Faroes. Fortunately, this stipulation didn't bring about the complete extinction of the species; there are still a few left in Iceland and Greenland.

Krákusteinur ('crow rock') is a flat rock on the eastern shore of Tinganes near the Skansapakkhúsið. From the 17th to the 19th centuries, one part of the Løgting's annual business was to assemble at this stone and burn all the beaks that had been collected that year.

Gongin This narrow street was the main street in old Tórshavn. It's now lined with some lovely wooden houses from the 19th century, the best of which is a wonderful pizza restaurant with a salad bar.

Museums

Smiðjan í Lítluvík This rather low-profile gallery is housed in an old iron forge on Grim Kambansgøta not far from the western harbour. It has no set opening hours but visiting exhibitions are advertised at the city tourist office so enquire there if you're interested.

Listaskálin (Faroese Museum of Art) On the northern edge of Viðarlund park, this museum has a fine collection of works by Faroese artists including painters Ruth Smith, Sámal Joensen Mikines, and Ingálvur av Reyni, and sculptors Fridtjof Joensen and Janus Kamban. There are visiting exhibitions as well. It's open daily from 3 to 5 pm between 15 May and 15 September. During the winter, it opens only for special exhibitions. Admission is US$2 per adult.

Nordic House The turf-roofed Nordic House, designed by Norwegian architect Ola Steen and Icelander Kolbrún Ragnardóttir, was completed in 1983. It is one of several in the Nordic countries and is architecturally rather impressive. The large and airy interior is used as a theatre and a conference, concert, and exhibition hall. Often there are visiting exhibitions by artists from all over Scandinavia including Iceland, the Åland Islands, and Greenland. To learn what's planned there during your visit, phone (tel 17900).

The halls and cafeteria are open Monday to Saturday from 10 am to 6 pm and Sundays from 2 to 6 pm.

Forngripasavnið (Historical Museum) This wonderful museum is a must for anyone interested in Faroese history. It contains religious artefacts, early artwork, and practical household and farming implements from the Viking Age through to the medieval period, and more modern times, as well. Many of the items excavated from archaeological sites at Kvívík, Tjørnuvík, and Kirkjubøur are on display here.

During the summer (from 15 May to 15 September), the museum is open Monday to Friday from 10 am to noon and 2 to 4 pm and on weekends from 3 to 5 pm. At other times of the year, it's only open on Sundays from 3 to 5 pm. Admission is free. Foreign-language handouts with a rundown on the exhibits are available for US$0.80.

Bátasavnið (Maritime Museum) This museum, next door to the Historical Museum, displays typical Faroese boats and artefacts relating to navigation and fishing in the islands. The most interesting exhibit is the 150-year-old *fýramannafar* or 'five-man conveyance' from Hvalvík whose design is believed to have evolved from the early Viking ships.

This museum is open during the same hours as the Historical Museum.

Náttúrugripasavn(Natural History Museum) The exhibits in this museum seem to revolve primarily around the Faroese fascination with marine mammals. There are skeletons of a grey seal, a pilot whale, a bottle-nosed whale, and a killer whale. And, of course, this wouldn't be complete without all the instruments of destruction that got them into skeleton form. There's also a fairly comprehensive collection of stuffed Faroese birds and a display of the geology of the North Atlantic region. Perhaps the most interesting item in the museum is the stuffed giant squid – nearly 6 metres of giant squid from the top of its head to the tip of the tentacles. The museum brochure is quick to point out that their giant squid isn't the largest ever found. One that beached in eastern Canada measured 16.6 metres long! Another section of the museum deals with the North Atlantic food chain from plankton and algae right up to man and the toothed whales.

Opening hours are the same as those for the Historical Museum.

Viðarlund

The Viðarlund park in Gundadalur is a nice place for a stroll. There are several paths across grassy lawns, stands of scrubby birch, a couple of pleasant duck ponds and the archetypal babbling brook. Tórshavn's seamen's monument is also found there.

Most visitors want to see the park because it's said to contain the Faroes' only 'forest'. Unfortunately, some of the trees (er – shrubs) have been ill of late and many of them have been reduced to so much kindling heaped on the ground. Many of those that remain upright are brown and dead. These islands, it seems, were just not meant to be forested. If you're craving trees, much larger and healthier specimens can be found in sections of central Tórshavn which are sheltered by buildings.

Churches

Havnarkirkja The white 'harbour' church with the interesting clock-tower, at the base of Tinganes, was consecrated way back in 1788. In 1865 it was renovated and enlarged but the original pulpit remains. It's surrounded by beautiful flowering gardens and inside there's a font (1601) and a crucifix from the early 1700s. If you'd like to have a look inside, visit the parish office (open Monday to Friday from 4.30 to 6 pm) in the grounds and someone will unlock the church for you.

Vesturkirkjan The Vesturkirkjan or 'west church' was consecrated in 1975 and is architecturally Tórshavn's most interesting modern building (the SMS Shopping Centre is a close runner up). The church probably seems more obtrusive than it should because it sits rather alone on the western outskirts of town where there are otherwise only box-like houses. Its high vaulted roofs are unusual and worth seeing, if you're wandering out that way. The interior is open to the public on weekdays from 3 to 5 pm between 1 June and 1 September.

Løgting

The modern Løgting is no longer held on Tinganes but across the pedestrian street from Vaglið. This distinctive building was originally constructed in 1856 and has since been expanded.

Skansin

The fort Skansin, now in ruins beside the lighthouse above the eastern harbour, was ostensibly constructed to keep privateers and smugglers from upsetting the local monopoly trade. It was built by Magnus Heinason a year after he was given the trade monopoly by the Danish King Frederik II in 1579. After losing a considerable sum in a pirate raid, he was also granted a ship and a licence to pursue anyone believed to be illicitly trading or plundering in the North Atlantic region.

Heinason turned out to be not only a crooked monopolist but also a pirate himself, using his privilege to do as he pleased. After several bungled court cases against him, he was beheaded for raiding an innocent English ship. Faroese today, however, believe the conviction was the work of his enemies and lately he has been elevated to the status of a national hero.

In 1677, Tórshavn was attacked and sacked by the French, with whom Denmark was at war. Skansin was destroyed and not rebuilt until 1780. During the British occupation of the Faroes in WW II, it was used as the allied naval headquarters.

You can still see several old bronze guns from 1782 and two British guns from WW II. In my opinion, Skansin is the most pleasant spot to relax in Tórshavn. There's a good view out to sea and it's a perfect vantage point for watching the goings-on in the harbour below.

Statues & Monuments

Niels R Finsen Memorial Niels R Finsen was the Faroese physician who won the Nobel Prize for medicine around the turn of the century. He is considered the father of radiology. As a child, he carved his initials into the rock in what is now a pleasant but tiny city park. The plaque there reads 'On this rock Niels R Finsen carved his name as a youth. His achievement has etched it into the hearts of all'.

Kamban Sculpture Beside the bank on Niels Finsensgøta is a sculpture by Faroese artist Janus Kamban who was born in 1913 and studied at the Copenhagen Academy of Art. His favourite subjects deal with everyday life in the Faroes; this one portrays a Faroese couple.

Kongaminnið This basalt obelisk in the park, above the intersection of Hoyvíksvegur and R C Effersøesgøta, commemorates the 1974 visit of King Christian IX of Denmark to the Faroe Islands. There are some other surprisingly interesting sculptures in this park.

R C Effersøe Monument In front of the Løgting building is a bust of the poet Rasmus Cristoffer Effersøe who lived from 1857 to 1916. He was a newspaperman who worked actively for the revival of the Faroese language. He also was an early advocate of strict controls on alcohol. The monument was completed in 1933.

Ráðhús

This imposing stone building on Vaglið was constructed of basalt in 1894. It served as a school until 1955 and, 20 years later, was renovated and converted into the city hall.

Places to Stay – bottom end

Smyril Line has recently opened a private youth hostel, *Vallaraheimið* (tel 19750), in Gundadalur. IYHF members/non-members pay US$12/13.50 and breakfast costs US$4.50. It's open between 4 June and 31 August.

A local couple, Ruth & Billy Olsen (tel 10310) have turned part of their home, at Skrivaragøta 3, into dormitory-style accommodation and charge US$11.50 per night per person. Groups of over 10 persons pay US$10 per person, and those who'd like a private room pay US$43 for a double.

You'll find their house on the western end of town about 1500 metres from the centre. From the northern end of the pedestrian mall, turn left and walk five blocks to Torfinsgøta.

There, turn right. Skrivaragøta is the fourth street.

The tourist office and Tora Tourist Traffic both keep lists of local families willing to open extra rooms to tourists. Most of these rooms are clean and pleasant and offer an excellent way to get to know the Faroese lifestyle. Prices for single rooms begin at US$36 per night. Double rooms will cost from US$65; entire houses or flats for three to five people, may be rented occasionally for US$75. They also keep listings of such accommodation throughout the Faroes Islands. If you're interested, enquire at Tora Tourist Traffic or the tourist office.

Places to stay – middle

From the end of June to the middle of August, it's possible to stay at *Undir Fjalli* (tel 18900 or 15900), at Vesturgøta 15 at the extreme south-western end of Tórshavn. It's a students' dormitory during the school year but, during summer holidays, is taken over by Smyril Line as a mid-range hotel.

All rooms are doubles with private bath and shower. Breakfast is available in the dining room and guests have access to the coin-operated laundry machines. Singles/doubles cost US$49/57. Extra beds can be put in the rooms for US$17 each.

In the centre, just downhill from Vaglið square, is the popular *Tórshavn Sjómansheim* or Seamen's Home (tel 13515) at Tórsgøta 4. Like all seamen's homes, it subscribes to a fairly strict code of behaviour although the alcohol restrictions aren't as relevant in the Faroes as in Greenland. Singles/doubles without bath cost US$35/55. Three meals are available for an extra US$22 per day.

Places to Stay – top end

Tórshavn has two up-market hotels. The most popular seems to be the *Hotel Hafnia* (tel 11270) just up the street from the harbour. It's central, clean, and pleasant but not at all pretentious. Singles/doubles with private bath begin at US$114/143. Extra beds are available for US$29 each.

The *Hotel Borg* (tel 17500) is also a convention centre. In a beautiful location, on the hillside above Tórshavn about 2.5 km from the centre, it's probably one of the most expensive views you'll come across anywhere. The cheapest single is US$115 and doubles cost from US$142 to US$190. Meal prices are equally astronomical. A cold lunch, for instance, costs US$17 but they make a point to tell you that this price excludes coffee. And get this – those who are attending conventions at the hotel can actually wash their lunch down with a glass of beer in the conference room. The price? – a mere US$9.25!

Camping

Must budget travellers in Tórshavn end up at the camping ground about 1500 metres north along the coast from the centre. It costs US$1.50 per tent and US$3 per person to set up there. If you bring a caravan, add US$2 and another US$2 if there's a car attached to it. It costs yet another US$2 per motorbike you dare to park on the property. For this you get a wet spot on the grass and use of the toilet and shower facilities.

A word of warning – the camping ground is in a flood-prone area. While I was staying there, about 80% of the campers found themselves surrounded by water in the middle of the night and had to shift to the loo, rendering the shower and facilities inaccessible. It's essential to pitch your tent on the highest ground you can find (I awoke that fateful morning to find myself on a tent-sized island). It may also help to sleep on an air mattress and dig a trench around your tent if the weather appears particularly threatening.

Places to Eat

Self-Catering The largest and best stocked supermarket is the one at the SMS Shopping Centre on R C Effersøesgøta. You'll also find a small supermarket on Aarvegur just across the street from the Hotel Hafnia. The cooperative supermarket in the industrial area is pretty good value as well, but it's not exactly convenient. When they're not open, you'll find plenty of kiosks around town which sell basic groceries. They have slightly higher prices than the supermarkets but stay open during the evenings and weekends.

You can buy freshly baked goods just down the hill from there at the *Frants Restorff* bakery outlet on Tórsgøta or from the bakery itself up in the industrial area north-east of the centre.

Snacks The nicest, but far from cheapest, place for a snack is the cosy *Konditarlið* on Niels Finsensgøta opposite the end of the pedestrian mall. It's open weekdays from 9 am to 6 pm and on Saturdays between 9 am and 2 pm.

For sausages, burgers, and chips, try the *City Burger*, at Tórsgøta 17, or the generically labelled *Restaurant* across the street from the ferry docks.

At the SMS Shopping Centre, there's an irresistible ice cream and cappuccino shop which serves an excellent product.

Cafeterias *Tórs Cafeteria* at Niels Finsensgøta 38, a couple of blocks up from the pedestrian mall, is convenient and fairly good for typical cafeteria food. You can eat lunch for less than US$10.

A bit better is *Perlan* in the SMS Shopping Centre where you can get a wide variety of salads, smørrebrød, desserts, hot snacks, or a daily special for fairly reasonable prices. The special costs US$6 and normally includes some meat dish, boiled potatoes, and a few vegies. It nearly always works out a better deal than making up a meal from the separate dishes available there.

The *Sjómansheimið* cafeteria (in the Seamen's Home) is open from 7 am to 9.30 pm. They offer à la carte salads and smørrebrød as well as set specials. A continental breakfast costs US$5.70, lunch and dinner are each US$9, and a late snack will cost US$7. The food is consistently pretty good.

In addition, there are two cafeterias in the industrial area north-east of the centre: one above the cooperative supermarket which is open during supermarket hours (Monday to Friday from 9 am to 6 pm and Saturdays 9 am to noon) and *Idé Cafe* above the furniture shop (also closed Sundays). In the same area, at the *Restorff Bakery* there is a coffee and snack shop where you can buy baked goods straight from the oven. All of these places are a bit out of the way, but their prices are more reasonable than at more convenient places. It's pretty easy to get lost in the complex up there, however, so resign yourself to asking directions at some stage.

Pizza Highly recommended is the *Pizzeria Fútastova* at Gongin 3 on Tinganes. For about US$11, you can feast on a small pizza and salad from an endless salad bar. In my opinion, it's the best place to eat in the Faroe Islands and the atmosphere there in the narrow streets of old Tórshavn is superb.

Fine Dining Both of the top-end hotels have relatively elegant dining rooms and offer complete meals. At the *Hotel Hafnia* you can get a buffet breakfast including coffee, juice, cereal, fruit, bread, and cold meats and cheeses for only US$8.50. At the *Hotel Borg*, the same fare goes for US$10. Two-course lunches at the hotels will cost about US$17 and dinners, which may include such Faroese specialties as puffin, whale, or lamb will be about US$22 to US$25 per person. In most cases, the dinner will include soup but salads will cost extra.

Entertainment

Theatre The Tórshavn theatre company is called Sjónleikarfelag but they perform only in the winter and most visitors won't have the chance to catch them. They use the Sjónleikarhúsið at Hoydalsvegur 2 which operates as a cinema whenever there isn't a play on. Visiting theatre groups perform from time to time at the Nordic House. Contact the tourist office for programme information.

Sport The large city sports centre in Gundadalur has a football pitch, badminton courts, and a swimming pool. It's open weekdays from 6.45 to 9 am and 3 to 8 pm (except Wednesdays). On Saturdays, it's open from 7 to 10 am and 2 to 5 pm. On

Sundays, you've got only 2 hours (from 8 to 10 am) to have your swim.

For information on scheduled sporting activities, contact the Faroese Sports Association (tel 12606) at the Gundadalur centre.

Getting There & Away

For a concise schedule of inter-city buses and inter-island ferries and helicopters, pick up a free copy of the booklet *Ferða Aetlan* from the tourist office or from Strandfaraskip Landsins (see following).

Helicopter The Tórshavn heliport is just north of the camping ground along the coast road. For information and booking, contact Strandfaraskip Landsins Tyrluavgreiðslan (tel 16450) at Yviri við Strønd, PO Box 88, FR-100 Tórshavn. For a rundown on flights and fares, refer to the Faroes Getting Around chapter.

Bus All inter-city buses depart from the bus stops in front of the eastern harbour and all (except the Kirkjubøur bus) stop at the Auto and Bíl taxi stands on their way out of town.

Numerous buses (No 100) go daily to Vestmanna via Kvívík. Several of these connect with the ferry across to Oyrargjógv and the Vágar Airport terminal. Bus services to and from Tórshavn include these:

bus nos	*destination*	*number of services daily*
101	Kirkjubøur	3-5
102	Kaldbak	4-5
104	Norðradalur	2-3
105	Syðradalur	2-3
400	Fuglafjørður	3
400	Leirvík	6-9

From these terminals, you'll find connecting buses to all corners of Streymoy and Eysturoy.

Ferry Both international and inter-island ferries leave from the ferry dock at the eastern harbour. For information about the international routes, see the general Getting There chapter at the beginning of the book. Inter-island routes to and from Tórshavn and applicable fares are outlined in the Faroes Getting Around chapter.

Getting Around

Airport Transport The airport for Tórshavn and the rest of the Faroes is in a windy pass on Vágar island. The airport bus (No 300) leaves from the harbour bus stops approximately 3 hours before international flights depart. Make bookings at the tourist office or through your hotel or phone (tel 12626).

Bus The red Bussleiðin city buses cover just about any place you'd like to go in tiny Tórshavn They do the cycle half hourly on weekdays and once every hour in the evening.

Taxi Taxis can be found at the Auto and Bíl stands which double as inter city bus stops, and at the Ráðhús. You can also call a taxi by phoning the Tórshavn taxi service (tel 11234 or 11444).

Bicycle Tórshavn is pretty good for cycling due to its relatively sparse traffic but it's small enough for you to go anywhere on foot as well.

During the summer the Tórshavnar Súkkufelag (Tórshavn Cycling Club) offers cycling tours which depart Wednesdays at 7 pm from the Teachers' College parking area on A Fraelsinum in south-west Tórshavn. Buses cost US$1.10 per ride. A city bus pass is available from several kiosks around town.

Tour

Tora Tourist Traffic offers a guided excursion around Tórshavn which includes a walk around the old town, a visit to the museums and the Nordic House, and lunch at the Perlan cafeteria in the SMS Shopping Centre. After this, it goes to Kaldbaksfjørður north of town for a look at the fish farming there. The tour leaves on Thursdays at 10 am and lasts 5 hours. It costs US$27 and must be booked at Tora Tourist Traffic or the tourist office no later than Wednesday afternoon.

Streymoy & Eysturoy

The two largest islands of the Faroese archipelago, Streymoy and Eysturoy, are the geographical and economic centre of the Faroes. The island of Streymoy, shaped a bit like a horse's head when viewed from the north-east, covers 374 sq km and makes up 25% of the land area and has over a third of the population of the Faroes. The island's name means 'island of currents', in reference to both the ocean waters around it and the numerous streams and waterfalls that cascade from its peaks.

Far less romantic is the name of Eysturoy ('eastern island') which refers only to its position relative to Streymoy. It's an oddly shaped island divided into two parts by the fjords Funningsfjørður and Skálafjørður. The western part is a long dagger-shaped chunk, while the eastern side is a rambling mixture of fjords and headlands. Eysturoy covers 266 sq km and has around 10,000 inhabitants in its 30 villages, many of which are strung out monotonously along southern Skálafjørður.

Around Streymoy

KIRKJUBØUR

Historically, Kirkjubøur was the largest and wealthiest farm in the Faroes. During medieval times its land area was much larger than now because the islet Kirkjubøhólmur was once connected to Streymoy. Excavations have revealed that at one stage, the settlement had several hundred inhabitants.

Its position was probably chosen because the Gulf Stream deposited large chunks of driftwood and beds of seaweed there. Driftwood was important for fuel and construction in the treeless Faroes and the seaweed was dried to make fertiliser, which allowed grain to grow in the poor climate and scanty soil.

There is speculation that the site was also occupied by Irish monks prior to Norse colonisation. The small bay just south of the settlement is known as Brandansvík after St Brendan who reputedly wandered through these parts in the 6th century. Ruins of small stone houses and fireplaces have been discovered just south of the farmhouse and, although they haven't yet been excavated, it is supposed they were once inhabited by the Irish friars.

Perhaps Kirkjubøur's most renowned resident was Sverri Sigurdsson, the illegitimate son of King Sigurd of Norway whose mother was a Norwegian milk maid named Gunnhild. The child was born in the Faroes in 1149 and, in 1151, the girl brought him to Kirkjubøur. The religious community of the day wouldn't have taken kindly to a young unmarried mother, so she hid the child in a cave above the village and cared for him there.

One day a Faroese man whom she'd known in Norway arrived and before long they were married, agreeing to rear the boy as their own. After the wedding they went to Norway but remained only a couple of years. On their return to the Faroes, they placed Sverri in the care of the Kirkjubøur Bishop, Hrói, who saw to it that the heir to the Norwegian throne received a proper education.

In 1174, after his mother had disclosed his royal lineage, Sverri again left the Faroes, this time to claim his father's throne. The interesting account of his entire life is related in *Sverrir Saga* which was recorded in Iceland shortly after his death in 1202.

Magnus Cathedral

The largest and most impressive ruin at Kirkjubøur is the 'unfinished cathedral', a grand Gothic church originally intended to be dedicated to St Magnus of the Orkney Islands. It was begun by Bishop Erlendur of the Faroes in the late 13th century but, thanks to his ruthless collection of funds for this pet project, disputes ensued among his constituents regarding his worthiness, while arson and vandalism of church property thwarted its completion even more effectively.

On 6 February 1772, an avalanche came roaring down the slopes behind Kirkjubøur and destroyed the western wall of the cathedral as well as a spiral staircase that wound up towards the unfinished bell tower. Surprisingly, however, quite a lot of the cathedral remains – probably due to its cementing with a mortar called *skilp*, a combination of powdered bone and shells that has held up well with age.

At several of the windows there are reliefs of Håkon V of Norway and in the western and one of the southern windows, of Bishop Erlendur himself. Outside on the eastern wall is a relief of the crucifixion with Mary Magdalene, the Virgin Mary, and two angels in attendance. A small cache of seven religious artefacts was discovered beneath this panel but only four of them were legibly identifiable. Two of them were bone fragments from the remains of St Magnus of the Orkneys and St Þorlákur of Iceland. Two others were reputed to be a shred of cloth from the Virgin Mary's dress and a sliver of the cross on which Christ was crucified. These objects have again been replaced in the wall behind the relief panel.

St Olav's Church

The mere age of St Olav's church is enough to set it apart. It was originally constructed in 1111 and dedicated to St Olav, the king who had formulated Norway's religious code during the previous century. Due to the failure of the St Magnus cathedral project, this unassuming church served as the religious centre of the Faroes and was used right through to the Reformation.

It was restored in 1874, after which it bore little resemblance to the original building, and again in 1966. During the first makeover, most of the valuables were carted off to Copenhagen and placed in the National Museum and the windows were altered to appear artificially Gothic. The second restoration went a bit better, but was still bungled when some debris was dropped on the tomb of Bishop Hilarius (who was buried beneath the chancel) destroying his original tombstone.

Perhaps the most interesting part of the church is the bricked-over window behind the pulpit. When leprosy was still a problem in the Faroes, the afflicted weren't permitted to enter the church but could sit outside and hear mass through this window. It remained open until 1744.

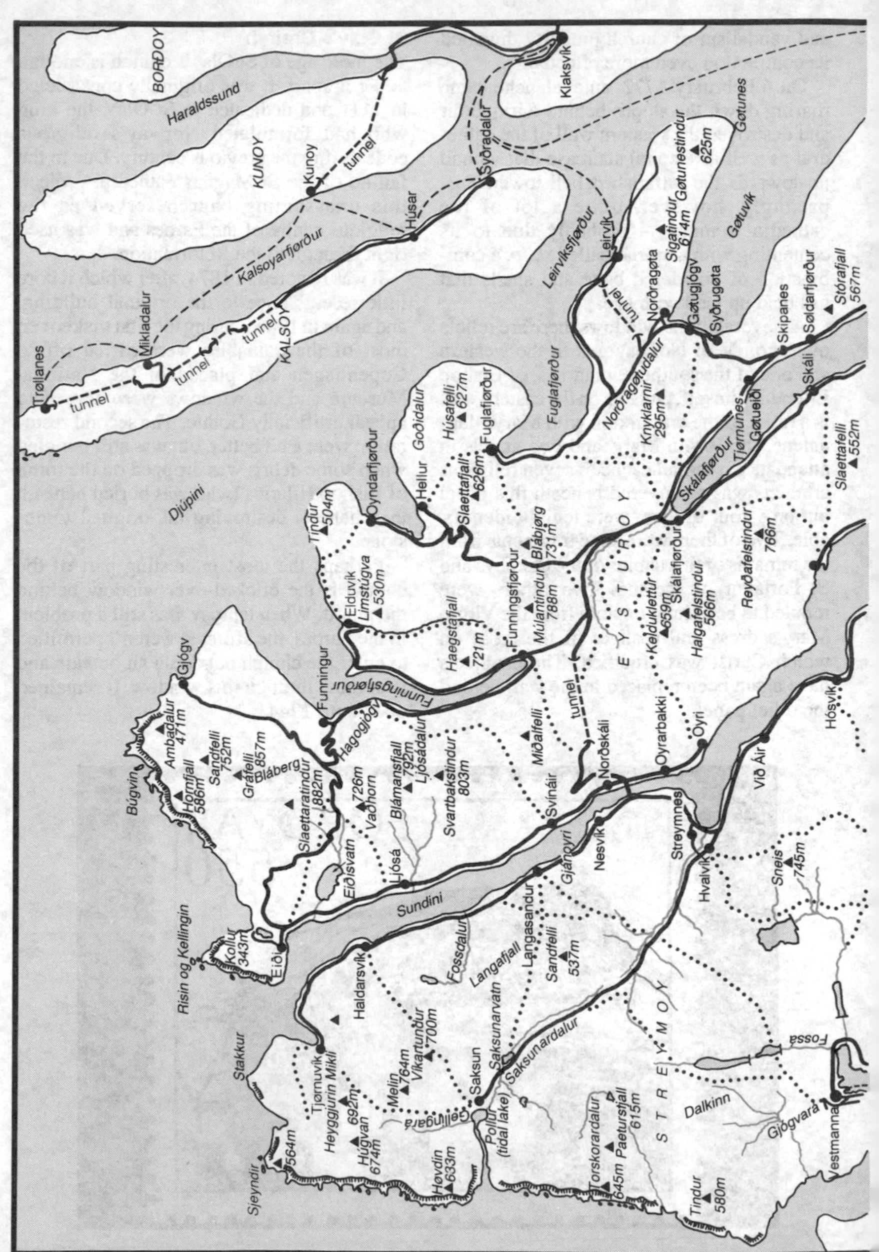

BORÐOY
Haraldssund
KUNOY
Kunoy
tunnel
Klaksvík
Syðradalur
Húsar
Kalsoyarfjørður
KALSOY
Mikladalur
Trøllanes
tunnel
Djúpini
Gøtunes
Gøtuvík
Gøtunestindur 625m
Sigatindur 614m
Leirvík
Leirvíksfjørður
Norðragøta
Gøtugjógv
Syðrugøta
Skipanes
Søldarfjørður
Stórafjall 567m
Fuglafjørður
Húsafell 627m
Goðidalur
Hellur
Oyndarfjørður
Slættafjall 626m
Tindur 504m
Blábjørg 731m
Norðragøtudalur
Knyklarnir 295m
Skálafjørður
Tjørnunes
Gøtueiði
Skáli
Slættafelli 552m
EYSTUROY
Elduvík
Límstúgva 530m
Funningsfjørður
Múlantindur 788m
Haegstafjall 721m
Funningur
Gjógv
Keldukléttur 659m
Halgafelstindur 566m
Reyðafelstindur 766m
Ambadalur 471m
Sandfelli 752m
Gráfelli 857m
Bláberg
Hornfjall 586m
Búgvin
Slættaratindur 882m
Vaðhorn 726m
Hagogjógv
Blámansfjall 792m
Ljósádalur
Svartbakstindur 803m
Miðafelli
tunnel
Norðskáli
Oyrarbakki
Oyri
Svínáir
Eiðisvatn
Ljósá
Sundini
Eiði
Kollur 343m
Risin og Kellingin
Gjánoyri
Nesvík
Streymnes
Hvalvík
Sneis 745m
Við Áir
Hósvík
Haldarsvík
Fossdalur
Langafjall
Langasandur
Sandfelli 537m
Stakkur
Tjørnuvík
Heyggjurin Mikli 692m
Melin 764m
Víkartundur 700m
Saksunarvatn
Saksunardalur
Saksun
Gellingará
Pollur (tidal lake)
Húgvan 674m
Høvdin 633m
564m
Sjeyndir
Torskorardalur 645m
Pæturstjall 615m
STREYMOY
Dalkinn
Fossá
Gjógvará
Vestmanna
Tindur 580m

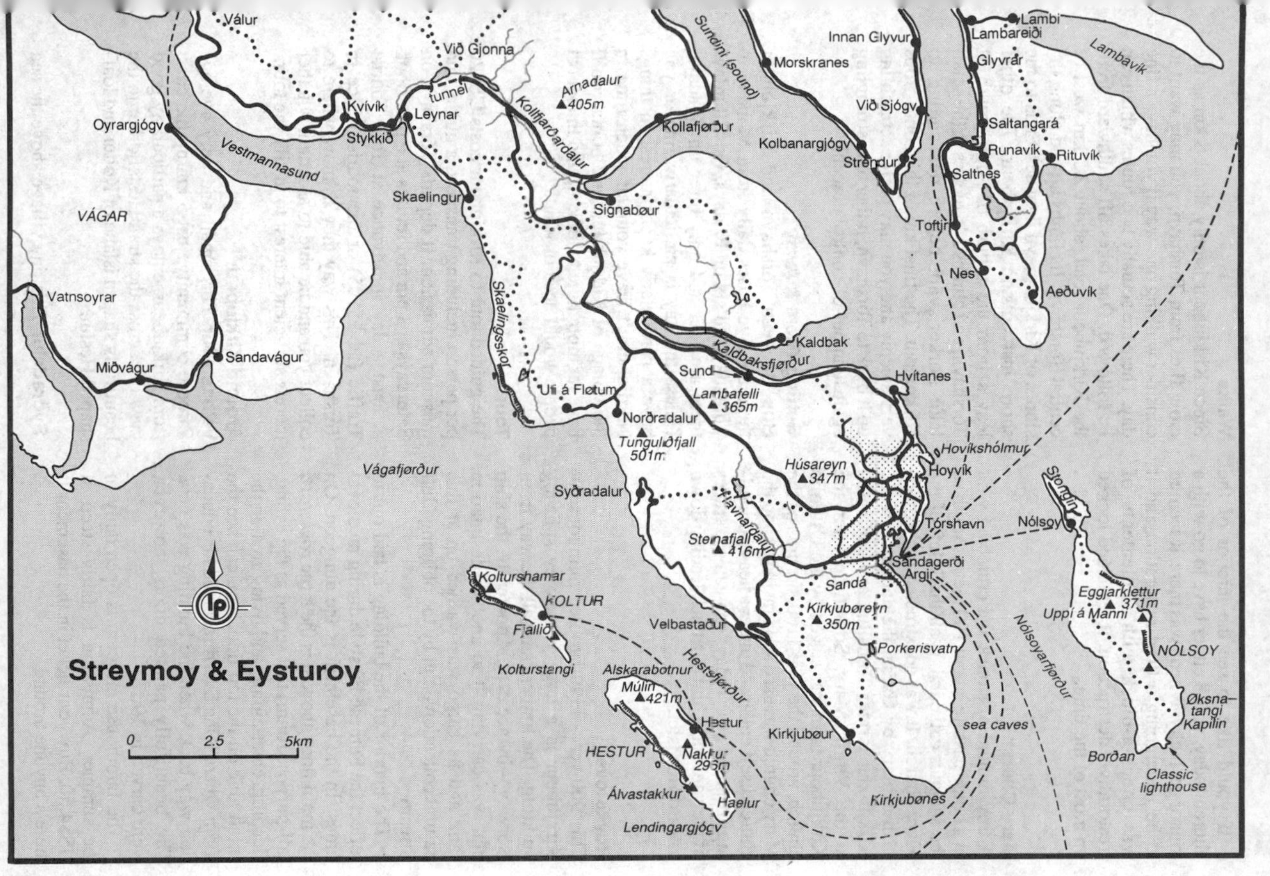
Streymoy & Eysturoy
0
2.5
5km
Válur
Við Gjonna
tunnel
Árnadalur
405m
Kvívík
Leynar
Stykkið
Oyrargjógv
Vestmannasund
Kollfjarðardalur
Kollafjørður
Skaelingur
Signabøur
VÁGAR
Vatnsoyrar
Sandavágur
Miðvágur
Skaelingsskor
Úti á Fløtum
Norðradalur
Tunguliðfjall
501m
Vágafjørður
Syðradalur
Sundini (sound)
Innan Glyvur
Morskranes
Við Sjógv
Kolbanargjógv
Strendur
Lambi
Lambareiði
Lambavík
Glyvrar
Saltangará
Runavík
Rituvík
Saltnes
Toftir
Nes
Aeðuvík
Kaldbak
Kaldbaksfjørður
Sund
Lambafelli
365m
Hvítanes
Hovíkshólmur
Hoyvík
Húsareyn
347m
Havnardalur
Steinafjall
416m
Tórshavn
Nólsoy
Stongin
Sandagerði
Argir
Sandá
Kirkjubøreyn
350m
Velbastaður
Porkerisvatn
Kirkjubøur
Kirkjubønes
sea caves
Nólsoyarfjørður
Eggjarklettur
371m
Uppí á Manni
NÓLSOY
Øksna-
tangi
Kapilin
Borðan
Classic
lighthouse
Koltursham ar
KOLTUR
Fjallið
Kolturstangi
Alskarabotnur
Múlin
421m
Hestsfjørður
Hestur
HESTUR
Nakkur
293m
Álvastakkur
Haelur
Lendingargjógv

If you'd like to see the interior of the church today, you'll either have to go with a tour or get lucky. When I was there, it seemed to be undergoing a third restoration and it was chock-a-block with implements of 'restorative' destruction. It remained locked up most of the time.

Mary Church

A tiny mound of stones and crumbled wall in a horse pasture, about 100 metres south of the Magnus cathedral, is all that's left of the Mary church. It was constructed in the mid-11th century by Gaesa, the daughter of the Kirkjubøur farmer Tórhallur, and dedicated to the Virgin Mary. Sometime after the Kirkjubøur farm was seized by the Catholic church, around the year 1100, the area of the Mary church was used as a graveyard and the church itself collapsed under a heavy pounding from the sea. Today, you can see traces of the yard and a hint of a track leading down towards the islet.

Roykstovan

This 900-year-old turf-roofed farmhouse at Kirkjubøur is a large two-storey split-log building. The timber came all the way from Norway – by accident. Apparently, the ship that was carrying it to another destination sank and its cargo was washed up at this natural collection point by the obliging Gulf Stream.

The interior of the building is laid out to reflect the Faroese lifestyle during medieval times. In the basement is the dungeon. On the main floor above it is the large *roykstova* (all-purpose room) that served as the eating, sleeping, entertaining, and living area. In the small attic on the top floor, you can see the room where King Sverri received his education way back when the building was new. The beautifully painted doors, however, were carved in 1907.

The farmhouse museum is open daily in the summer. Admission is fairly steep at US$4.50. Buy your ticket in the basement if there's anyone around.

Walks

Since Kirkjubøur is only about 8 km as the crow flies from Tórshavn, you may want to consider walking one-way if you have a fine day. There are actually two routes which can be followed. One takes off southward from the Kirkjubøur road, about 2.5 km west of central Tórshavn. It climbs up and along the slopes of Kirkjubøreyn then descends to the shore just outside Kirkjubøur. The other leaves from the suburb of Argir, south of Tórshavn, and climbs 245 metres to the small lake Þorkerisvatn before descending to Kirkjubøur. The final km of this route drops very steeply and you may prefer scrambling up it back to Tórshavn, rather than struggling against an out-of-control descent.

Getting There & Away

Bus Between Tórshavn and Kirkjubøur there are five buses daily from Monday to Thursday and six on Fridays. On Saturdays there are four and only three on Sundays. Unless the day is particularly fine or you have a particularly keen interest in things Nordic, don't leave yourself much time in the village of Kirkjubøur. In 2 hours you'll have far more time to look around than most people would need or want.

Tour

The guided tour to Kirkjubøur costs US$20 per person including transport, a guide, and museum admission. It departs Tórshavn on Saturdays at 3 pm and returns at 6 pm. Book at least a day in advance at Tora Tourist Traffic (tel 15505) or the tourist office in Tórshavn. This way they'll know where to collect you and be able to ascertain whether there's sufficient interest to justify the tour.

Around Kirkjubøur

Velbastaður This small and very average Faroese community, just 5 km up the coast from Kirkjubøur, enjoys a particularly good view out across the strait Hestsfjørður to the beautifully shaped island of Koltur and loaf-shaped Hestur.

Syðradalur This tiny village above the sea

lies 12 km north of Kirkjubøur. It's the best vantage point for the odd profile view of Koltur island. There's also a nice cirque valley up behind it. There are two or three buses (bus No 105) daily between Syðradalur and Tórshavn.

It's possible to walk between Tórshavn and Syðradalur. The road takes off from the western side of Route 10, less than 1 km above the Hotel Borg in Tórshavn, climbs over the moors to the dam on the river Sandá and then descends in two steep steps to Syðradalur. It's about an 8-km walk each way measured from the Hotel Borg.

KALDBAK

The small village of Kaldbak lies on the northern shore of the magnificent fjord Kaldbaksfjørður with its numerous wispy waterfalls and impossibly steep cliffs. When the wind is howling up the fjord, a fairly common occurrence, the water actually falls upwards.

In the village itself, the only item of interest is the cosy wooden turf-roofed church which was built in 1835. It has a small wooden steeple and is surrounded by a rambling stone wall. The carvings in the choir screen are unique in the Faroes – hearts, fiddles, and shamrocks – and are particularly nice. As usual, however, you may have trouble visiting the church on any day besides Sundays.

Getting There & Away

Bus No 102 does the quick run back and forth from Tórshavn five times daily on weekdays and four times daily on Saturdays and Sundays.

KVÍVÍK

Kvívík on Vestmannasund is one of the lushest parts of the Faroes and, on a fine day, its fields glow a bright green. The coast provides good views across the strait to Vágar island and southward to Koltur.

Kvívík is the site of an 11th-century farm which is currently being excavated.

Farm Ruins

The house apparently belonged to a family of high social standing because by Faroese standards it is immense – 22 metres long and nearly 6 metres wide. The walls were constructed of double rows of stone, which were insulated with a layer of mud and gravel between them, altogether forming a 1.5-metre-thick obstacle to the wind and cold.

In traditional Faroese style, the living quarters consisted of the large roykstova where the occupants cooked, ate, slept, and entertained. In the centre of the room is a large fireplace, 7 metres long and 1 metre wide, which was used for both heating and cooking. Around it, the floor is clay (pounded solid over a base of flat stones) reminiscent of modern linoleum on cement.

Outside the great house there's a cow byre, the only such ruin that's been found in the Faroes. It measures 10 metres by 3.5 metres and it was apparently more luxurious than many of the commoners' dwellings on the islands.

There isn't really very much to look at but archaeologists and other ruin buffs may be interested in seeing it. Across the bridge from the ruins, near the village church, is an old turf-roofed vicarage constructed in the traditional Faroese manner.

Getting There & Away

To reach Kvívík from Tórshavn, take bus No 100 from the harbour. It departs for Vestmanna 11 or 12 times daily and passes through Kvívík, so it's an easy and convenient day-trip from town.

VESTMANNA

Although it's the second largest town on Streymoy, Vestmanna itself is of little interest. There are, however, several walks in the area as well as a tour to the remote bird cliffs of north-western Streymoy. The ferry to Vágar also leaves from here.

Places to Stay & Eat

If for some reason you have a hankering to stay in Vestmanna, the *Vestmanna Holiday Centre* (tel 24243) will be happy to accommodate you. From 27 June to 12 August, they operate a private *Youth Hostel* in the local school, offering dormitory beds for US$14 per night and camping sites for US$5 per person. There's a gymnasium and swimming pool which are available to guests. A continental breakfast is included in the price of the hostel but campers will have to pay an extra US$5.75. Bookings should be made through Tora Tourist Traffic in Tórshavn.

There's a coffee shop and cafeteria, *Kaffistovan á Keiini*, which is open from 8 am to 7 pm daily.

Activities

Walks There are roads from the village through Fonsdal or Heygjadal valleys, past their respective power plants, to the dams which form four reservoirs (two in each valley) and provide the Faroes with hydroelectric power. After the Fonsdal road passes between two dammed lakes, it wanders over a low pass and disappears. From this road, there are several walking routes over to Saksunardalur, any of which can be easily done in a day.

Another option is to walk up the river Gjógvará from the top of the village, to the ridge of Dalkinn and around its eastern slope, past the upper Fonsdal reservoir, and then down into Saksunardalur. This trip takes about 5 hours each way. It's best, however, to take an entire day and allow time for side trips and rests along the way.

From the head of the first reservoir on the Heygjadal side, the road makes a loop up to the dam on the second lake and then returns. This is about a 4-hour return trip from Vestmanna.

Bird Cliffs Tour You'll have to be lucky if you want to do the magnificent boat trip up to the wild and little-visited bird cliffs of north-western Streymoy. First of all, if the tour isn't cancelled due to lack of interest, it's often cancelled due to inclement weather which can play havoc with the small, open boats used for the trip. When things work out, you sail from Vestmanna up the west coast of Streymoy to the towering north-western cliffs which teem with bird life. If the seas are calm, the tour also visits some caves at sea level beneath the cliffs.

The tour departs Wednesdays and Sundays at 1 pm and costs US$38.50 per person including transport from Tórshavn or Vestmanna and a tour guide. Book in advance through Tora Tourist Traffic or the tourist offices.

Getting There & Away

Between Vestmanna and Tórshavn, there are 11 or 12 buses daily. The ferry to Oyrargjógv on Vágar island leaves the harbour at Vestmanna 14 or 15 times a day. The first daily departure is at 7.50 am and the last trip back is at 10.40 pm (summer only).

KOLLAFJORÐUR

The village of Kollafjørður, at the southern entrance to Sundini (the sound between Streymoy and Eysturoy) is of little interest except for its turf-roofed church which was described by a German scientist in 1828 as 'the most miserable house of God in the whole of Christendom'. Well, it's not all that bad now – it was completely rebuilt in 1837 – although it certainly isn't very inspiring.

The interior is wooden, typical of 19th-century Faroese churches, and the roof is covered with turf. Unfortunately, those who'd like to have a look inside will either have to peer through the windows or turn up on a Sunday because most of the time, it's locked up. The door has particularly nice and unusual carvings.

Kollfjðardalur

Beyond the head of the fjord from Kollafjørður is the deep and lovely valley of Kollfjarðardalur where a new tunnel is being bored through the mountain to Kaldbaksfjørður. At the Statoil petrol station you'll find a pretty good snack bar and coffee shop which is open from 8 am to 8.30 pm daily.

Getting There & Away

The Kollafjørður area is best reached from Tórshavn by taking bus No 400 which travels between Tórshavn and Oyrarbakki or Leirvík (both on Eysturoy island) six to 10 times daily.

VIÐ AÍR

Við Aír, on the Streymoy shore of Sundini, was the last commercial whaling station in the Faroes. Its primary quarry was the blue whale and, in the first 2 decades of this century, 178 were harpooned and boiled down. Over the next score of years, only a third of that was taken, indicating that stocks were being depleted. The whalers then turned their attentions to the more plentiful (and therefore more profitable) fin whales. Commercial whaling from Við Aír was abandoned in 1959 but was resumed in 1962. In 1966, the station closed down and hasn't been used since.

At Hvalvík, just north of Við Aír near the bridge, is another of those old turf-roofed churches, this one was reconstructed in 1829 after being destroyed by a storm. It is supposed that the original was built sometime during the 18th century.

Once upon a time there was a youth hostel at Streymnes, next to Hvalvík, but it has been closed down. If the tourism scene changes perhaps it will re-open, so it may pay to check this out.

SAKSUN

The setting of this village is quite scenic and unusual. It sits in two parts on the steep hillsides above the beautiful and almost perfectly round tidal lake Pollur ('pond'). It's a wonderful walk above its southern bank and the outlet, which is appropriately called Ósin or 'mouth', to the open sea. The church in Saksun was built in 1858 and overlooks Pollur. Today, the village is home to less than 30 people.

Saksunardalur

Just 1 km above the village, along the river Dalsá ('valley river') is the lake Saksunarvatn – good for trout and salmon fishing and a nice camping site.

Dúvugarður Museum

Near the end of the northern branch of the road in Saksun is the 19th-century turf farmhouse Dúvugarður. It has been converted into a folk museum which attempts to convey what the rigours of Faroese were like life in earlier times, from the medieval era to the 1800s. The building in which the museum is housed contains the usual roykstova, a guest bedroom, a bedroom for visiting clergy, and a cow byre. The building was inhabited as recently as WW II. It's open daily in the summer from 2 to 6 pm. Admission is US$2.15.

Walks

There are a couple of nice walking routes around Saksun. The easiest one merely follows the river through Saksunardalur, but it's also possible to walk over to Vestmanna, on the west coast, from near the mouth of the river Heljardalsá in Saksunardalur via the Fossá hydroelectric project. Another option is to walk from Saksun village up the very steep hillside above the river Gellingará and over the narrow pass between the cirques down into Tjørnuvík. Any of these walks can be completed in a day.

Getting There & Away

Bus To get to Saksun from Tórshavn take bus No 400 to Oyrarbakki (Eysturoy) and change to bus No 204 which runs between there and Saksun at 6.50 am, 2.10 and 6.45 pm from Monday to Saturday. It returns from Saksun to Oyrarbakki, where you can connect with a bus back to Tórshavn at 7.20 am, 4 and 7.30 pm. On Sundays, there are only two buses in either direction.

Tour

On Tuesdays at 1 pm, there's a Tora Tourist Traffic tour from Tórshavn which visits Saksun and its museum, as well as the village of Eiði on the neighbouring island of Eysturoy. At US$35 per person it's pretty steep considering that it includes only a tour guide and transport, but it will be convenient if you're in a hurry. Again, be sure to book the previous day.

TJØRNUVÍK

Like Saksun, Tjørnuvík enjoys a beautiful location. It's wedged tightly between two headlands and has a wide and appealing sandy beach. In bright and calm weather, of which there is precious little in Tjørnuvík, it's a good place to sit and watch the surf or read a book. More than likely though, you'll be huddled in the chilly wind for just as long as it takes to snap a photo. The view out to sea includes the impressive sea stacks called Risin og Kellingin, the remnants of a bungled attempt to tow the Faroes to Iceland (see the Eiði section).

The most interesting site in Tjørnuvík is where a medieval farm and grave site has been evacuated near the eastern entrance to the town. Like the farmhouse at Kvívík, this one also had thick stone walls. Rather than one large all-purpose room, however, it had two major rooms, one for sitting and one for sleeping, as well as a gabled roof, and a wooden floor which rested on joists. Wood was scarce and damage to this floor was repaired with the more traditional stamped clay.

During medieval times, hazelnuts were a common folk cure for hangovers and a great many hazelnut shells were found in the boards and clay in front of one of the sitting benches that line the walls of the living room. One can only imagine the rollicking drunken parties that must have taken place there.

Fossdalur

About 6 km south-east of Tjørnuvík along Sundini, the road crosses the Fossá or 'falls river', which has the highest waterfall in the Faroes, falling 140 metres in several steps. The best view is available down the slope from the road.

Getting There & Away

Bus If you're coming from Tórshavn, begin this trip as you would heading for Saksun, that is, by first taking bus No 400 to Oyrarbakki. From there, three to five buses (bus No 202) run daily back and forth to Tjørnuvík.

Tour

The only tour to Tjørnuvík is the one that replaces Tora Tourist Traffic's Vestmanna bird cliffs tour on Wednesdays and Sundays when the weather is too foul to do the boat tour. This seems to happen more often than not, but don't expect any miracles from the weather in Tjørnuvík either. This tour also visits the picturesque village of Elduvík on Eysturoy. The prices and times of this tour are the same as for the bird cliffs one (see the Vestmanna section).

Eysturoy

OYRARBAKKI

Just about everyone who uses the bus system around the Faroes ends up spending some time at the petrol station in Oyrarbakki thanks to the bottleneck caused by the bridge across Sundini between Streymoy and Eysturoy. All the buses stop here, exchange passengers, and continue on their merry ways.

As far as I know, there's absolutely nothing special to see or do here while you're waiting for your bus but go for a bite in the petrol station snack bar or change money at the bank next door.

Places to Stay

At Norðskáli, north of Oyrarbakki, is the new *Sunda Motel* (tel 18183) which offers accommodation in four-berth caravans for US$72 per day. Camping is permitted for US$5.

SKÁLAFJØRÐUR

Skálafjørður is the name given to both the long sheltered fjord enclosed by the southernmost peninsulas of Eysturoy, and the village at its head. It's probably one of the most uninteresting areas in the country. The western shore villages of Strendur, Við Sjógv, Innan Glyvur, Skáli; and on the eastern shore, Nes, Toftir, Saltnes, Runavík, Saltangará, Glyvrar, Lambareiði, Søldarfjørður, Skipanes, and Gøtueiði, are combining into an increasingly congested conurbation – a sort of Faroese megalopolis.

History

Skálafjørður is the best harbour in the Faroes. Carl Emil Dahlerup, governor of the Faroes in the mid-1800s, worked towards shifting the commercial and political centre of the country from Tórshavn to Toftir or Strendur. It was a good idea, but it never took hold. During the German occupation of Denmark in WW II, Skálafjørður became a British naval base

Festivals

Skálafjarðarstevna This is an annual local festival that takes place in Runavík sometime around mid-June. Expect the athletic contests and chain-dance-till-you-drop sort of entertainment that always accompanies Faroese festivals.

Places to Stay & Eat

In Runavík there is a *Seamen's Home* (tel 47420) which charges US$52/38 for single rooms with/without bath. Doubles with/without bath are US$66/55. There's an attached cafeteria which has snacks, an à la carte menu, and set meals. A continental breakfast costs US$5.70 while lunch and dinner cost about US$8 each.

Alternatively, try the cafeteria in Toftir or the *Ólavstova* in Saltangará.

Getting There & Away

The ferry *Dúgvan* travels between Tórshavn, Toftir, and Strendur six times daily on weekdays and four times daily on weekends. The trip takes 35 minutes between Tórshavn and Toftir, and about 15 minutes from there to Strendur.

GØTA

The Gøta area, which is actually divided into the villages of Norðragøta, Gøtugjógv, and Syðrugøta, has another of those wonderfully scenic and dramatic settings. On both shores of Gøtuvík, the broad fjord on which the villages sit, the mountains rise steeply straight out of the sea. The northern shore ascends to 614 metres and the southern, to 516 metres.

At Syðrugøta, there are ruins which reveal the settlement patterns of the early Faroese. Five small and simple farmhouses have been excavated, as well as a central churchyard and cemetery. It's expected that a large central landowner's home will be discovered somewhere near the church to complete the *bygd* or settlement.

Interestingly, the current parish church, which was rebuilt in 1833, isn't anywhere near this medieval site but is now in Norðragøta. This was the home village of Trondur Gøtuskegg, the hero of *Faereyingar Saga*, and part of the tale takes place in Norðragøta.

A nice walk is up the chasm Gøtugjógv behind the town, and up to the relatively easy summit of 295-metre-high Knyklarnir. From here there is a good view out over the magnificent surroundings.

Tøtingarvirkið

In Syðrugøta is the spinning and woollens mill Tøtingarvirkið where Faroese wool becomes Faroese yarn and pullovers. Those who are interested can have a look around the place, or visit the outlet where wool, yarn, and knitwear are sold.

Blásastova

This old farmhouse serves as a local museum and has a lot of character. Openings must be pre-arranged through the tourist office in Tórshavn.

Getting There & Away

Bus No 400 between Tórshavn and Leirvík or Fuglafjørður passes through Gøta nine times daily on weekdays in either direction. On Saturdays, there are eight buses and six on Sundays.

FUNNINGUR

The road to Funningur makes a serpentine descent of 400 metres in only 3 km, with magnificent views all the way. Above the village rises Slaettaratindur, the Faroes' highest point. Funningur provides the best view of the rugged, serrated ridges and cliffs of Kalsoy island across the strait Djúpini.

The village church has a traditional turf roof. The current building was consecrated in 1847. The old wooden figure of Christ inside is battered and showing some age, but it's quite beautiful.

With a bit of a struggle the surrounding mountains can be climbed. There's a fairly hazardous route across to the west coast as well. It takes off from the village, heads south and skirts the coastline, climbs above the road, then wanders inland and over the pass Kvígandalsskarð before it descends quickly to Svínáir on the shore of Sundini. It's less than 10 km walking and could be negotiated in a full day, but 2 days would be far more comfortable given the sometimes rough terrain.

Getting There & Away

Bus No 205 between Oyrarbakki and Gjógv stops in Funningur – sometimes winding its way down from the heights and sometimes travelling along the basic unsurfaced road from Funningsfjørður.

GJÓGV

The village of Gjógv (pronounced 'jag') is named after its harbour, which is an impressive sea-filled gorge. Although it's probably the most pleasant village in the Faroes, there really isn't anything here of overwhelming interest. Take a look at the tidal pools out on the mussel-covered rocks. Visit the churchyard with the local seamen's memorial or walk through the old, narrow streets and along the stream Dalá which tumbles through the village.

The view over to northern Kalsoy is superb and the grassy hillside above the harbour's northern precipice makes an excellent place to laze on a nice day (I've spent a fair bit of time there, myself).

Also, notice the geological oddity along the shore where the horizontal strata of the waterfront is broken by an intrusion of basalt 'posts' lying stacked on their sides. They've resisted erosion better than the surrounding materials and form a natural staircase from the sea up to the grassy bluffs.

The grass-roofed youth hostel may also be of interest. It's a new building, constructed to resemble a traditional Faroese farmhouse, but has ended up looking more like a Swiss chalet. This is probably the best base to use if you want to climb mounts Slaettaratindur or Gráfelli.

Slaettaratindur

From the road, which reaches an altitude of about 400 metres at the three-way pass between Eiði, Funningur, and Gjógv, the climb up 882-metre Slaettaratindur isn't too difficult. The best way to the top is up the eastern ridge which begins at the road less than 1 km north of the three-way junction. Be sure to go on a nice day, however, as finding the way can be difficult in heavy cloud cover (which becomes fog at this altitude). The view is predictably wonderful.

The mountain immediately north of Slaettaratindur is 857-metre Gráfelli, another impressive peak which may be climbed up its south-east pointing ridge.

Ambadalur

An excellent day-walk from Gjógv is over the pass immediately west of town and down into Ambadalur on the other side. There, you'll see the pinnacle Búgvin. At 188 metres, it's the highest sea stack in the Faroes.

Places to Stay

The *Gjáargarður Youth Hostel* (tel 23175) is quite nice, although it's a bit more of a child-minding service than many people will be comfortable with. It seems to serve as an out-of-the-way repository for school groups, and the management can sometimes go over the top with rules and regulations. If you're put off, be sure to bring a tent.

Aesthetically, the building is very nice, with its grassy roof and balconies on all four storeys. The top one is arranged like an old Faroese roykstova.

Family rooms with six beds and a kitchen, bath, and toilet cost US$51.50 per night.

Single/double private rooms are US$50/71. Dorm beds cost US$11.50/14 for IYHF members/non-members.

Camping is permitted in the hostel grounds and costs US$5 per person, but those who'd like more privacy should have no problem finding a suitably serene camping site above the shore or in the hills around the village.

Places to Eat

Meals are available at the youth hostel and there's a small snack shop next door. In the village are two rustic old general stores which date back to the late 1800s. They stock only very basic supplies so it may be wise to bring groceries from Tórshavn.

Getting There & Away

To get to Gjógv from Tórshavn, you must first take bus No 400 to Oyrarbakki. From Monday to Thursday and on weekends there are two buses daily in either direction, from here. On Fridays the bus goes four times daily.

ELDUVÍK

Elduvík is another village at the end of the road. It's got a lovely setting, surrounded by green fields and peaks, but there's not much else. A lot of people like to visit Elduvík on special occasions and eat at the country restaurant Lonin, which serves nice but expensive fare.

A good walk from Elduvík is across the low pass to Oyndarfjørður. Another option is to take the 6-km mountain route to Funningsfjørður. Make your way up the Stórá river valley behind the town and over the moors to the pass from where it's a quick, steep descent to Funningsfjørður. A third trip, which offers spectacular views across to Kalsoy island, is up the ridge south-west of Elduvík to the summit of 721-metre-high Haegstafjall.

There's no place to stay in Elduvík so those who'd like to visit for more than the day will need to have camping equipment.

Getting There & Away

Bus No 441 to and from Skálabotnur connects with bus No 400 to and from Tórshavn) does the run five times each weekday and twice daily on weekends.

EIÐI

At the head of Skálafjørður, Eiði is on a pass between the Eysturoy mainland and the hulking Kollur peninsula (which makes up what it's lacking in area with sheer bulk). The word *eiði* (pronounced 'OY-yeh') refers to just this sort of pass, a low windy chute which lies between highlands and connects two bodies of water. The small lake to the north of town is stocked with fish and the village church is one of the nicest in the country. As in most Faroese churches, model sailing ships hang from the ceiling as a petition for the safety of sailors far from home.

Eiðisvatn

The lake Eiðisvatn sits on the plateau about 130 metres higher than its namesake village. It's quite beautiful and merits a day-hike. The lake is reputed to offer some fairly good trout fishing as well.

Risin og Kellingin

These two sea stacks, whose names mean 'the giant and the witch', are featured on quite a few Faroese tourist brochures and are worth a photo or two if you're in the area.

The story goes that an Icelandic giant thought he'd like to drag the Faroes a bit closer to home, so he took a heavy rope and secured it around the most solid thing he could find which turned out to be the rock Kollur. He and his wife (who happened to be a witch or a hag, depending on your translation) splashed into the sea and began to tug on the load but, of course, it failed to budge.

They struggled all through the night (everyone knows giants and witches are only permitted to be abroad at night) and scarcely noticed the time passing. When the sun appeared, they attempted to flee underground where they had to remain by day but they were too late and were turned to stone on the spot. For the best view of the rocks, follow the road to the northern end of the small lake at Eiði, then turn east and head out to the coast. After a few hundred metres they should begin to come into view. Other pretty good but distant views are from the village of Tjørnuvík on the island of Streymoy, and from the road that enters Eiði from the east.

Places to Stay & Eat

The only formal accommodation in town is the *Hotel Eiði* (tel 23456). It seems a rather sterile and impersonal place but you'd be hard pressed to find a North Atlantic hotel that doesn't. There's a wonderful view from this one, overlooking the lake below town. Singles/doubles with attached bath go for US$68/84, both prices include a continental breakfast. Lunch and dinner in the hotel dining room cost US$13.50 per person.

The hotel also has a camping ground. Campers may use their facilities – showers, toilets, and kitchen – for US$5 per person.

Getting There & Away

Bus To reach Eiði from Tórshavn, you first have to take bus No 400 to Oyrarbakki. From there, bus No 200 goes to and from Eiði six times daily from Monday to Friday, three times on Saturdays, and four times on Sundays.

Tours

In summer, Tora Tourist Traffic (tel 15505) in Tórshavn does a tour to Eiði and Saksun every Tuesday at 1 pm. It visits Risin og Kellingin and the church as well as the sights mentioned in the Saksun section earlier in this chapter. The price is US$35.70 including transport and a tour guide. The tour lasts approximately 5 hours.

A boat tour which departs from Eiði daily at 3 pm will take you around Risin og Kellingin and the bird cliffs at Eiðiskollur as well as the large pinnacle Búgvin, near the remote northern tip of Eysturoy. The tour costs US$17 per person and may be booked through the Hotel Eiði or through the tourist office in Tórshavn.

FUGLAFJØRÐUR

With nearly 2000 inhabitants, Fuglafjørður is the fourth largest city in the Faroes. It has a magnificent setting but is not extremely interesting unless you want to walk across the pass to Oyndarfjørður (see the Oyndarfjørður section) or up the steeper route to 731-metre high Blábjørg. From the top there are good views that encompass most of Eysturoy and a few other islands – weather permitting, of course.

The harbour of Fuglafjørður is particularly colourful and the town is one of the primary fish-processing centres in the Faroes.

Varmakelda

Varmakelda is the only hot spring in the Faroes. It lies near the shore of fjord Fuglafjørður, about midway between the town of Fuglafjørður and Leirvík. Unfortunately, it is only 'hot' relative to the sub-Arctic seawater, a few metres away. (The spring water issues from the earth at a chilly 18° C.) If you'd like to see it anyway, it's near the shore, just 1 km north-east of the intersection between the coastal route to Leirvík and the Fuglafjørður turn-off.

Getting There & Away

Bus No 400 travels between Tórshavn and Fuglafjørður three times daily. Before you hop on, however, be sure that the bus is bound for Fuglafjørður. Far more often, it goes only to Leirvík, necessitating a 5-km walk from the intersection for anyone going to Fuglafjørður.

LEIRVÍK

This village, which lies on the other side of a tunnel from Norðragøta, faces the southern ends of the rugged islands Kalsoy and Borðoy. Most people who visit are on their way to Klaksvík, the Faroes' second city.

Places to Stay & Eat

The small guesthouse *Gistingarhúsið Laðangarður* (tel 43021) is, by Faroese standards, quite good value. Singles/doubles with shared bath go for US$31/47 including breakfast. Other prepared meals will cost you around US$8 each.

The petrol station across the highway from the ferry landing has a basic snack bar and coffee shop. There's a kiosk in the centre which serves quick snacks. It's open until 10 pm nightly and this is where the local younger crowd hangs out.

Getting There & Away

Bus Bus No 400 does nine trips daily from Monday to Friday, between Leirvík and Tórshavn. The bus and ferry coordinate quite well making a convenient connection to Klaksvík, where it is presumed everyone is headed anyway. On Saturdays there are eight runs and on Sundays only six.

Ferry The ferry trip between Leirvík and Klaksvík must be one of the loveliest 20-minute rides on earth. It passes beneath the towering peaks of southern Kalsoy, and between the beautiful headlands of Kunoy and south-western Borðoy, before chugging into Klaksvík's well-sheltered harbour.

On Mondays, Wednesdays, and Fridays the ferry *Ternan* does 11 trips from Klaksvík to Leirvík starting at 5.20 am. On Tuesdays, Thursdays and Saturdays, the first trip departs at 6.35 am. On Sundays they don't get started until 7.50 am. Going the other way, the first crossing is at 7.10 am daily except on Sundays when they sleep in and don't leave until 8.50 am. There's a crossing approximately every 2 hours in either direction until 8.40 pm westbound, and 10.30 pm eastbound.

Amazingly, this ferry connects like clockwork with the bus system, that in turn connects Leirvík with Tórshavn.

OYNDARFJØRÐUR

Oyndarfjørður is prime walking country and, because it has a very pleasant youth hostel, many people on the 2-day stopover en route to Iceland rush up here straight from the ferry dock in Tórshavn.

Although it's not nearly as charming a village as Gjógv, it's a nice enough community. Oyndarfjørður's hostel is more casual and therefore generally more pleasant for adult travellers. What's more, it apparently hasn't yet been discovered by school groups.

The shabby little church in Oyndarfjørður appears not to have seen much attention since it was built in 1838. The turf roof is in sore need of replacement and the churchyard is rather unkempt, but it's somehow more appealing that way.

The real 'attraction' in this tiny village is the mildly entertaining Rinkurssteinar or 'rocking stone'. On the shoreline, below the entrance to the village, is an immense underwater boulder (about 8 metres by 6 metres by 3 metres) that moves back and forth with the wave action. Asmall stone attached to a rope, which is in turn attached to the boulder, bobs up and down as the big rock rocks. How this bizarre phenomenon was ever discovered is a complete mystery to me.

Places to Stay & Eat

The *Fjalsgarður Youth Hostel* (tel 44522) is the only place to stay in Oyndarfjørður. It sits on a rise at the far end of town. The price for IYHF members/non-members is US$10/13. If you plan to visit on the ferry*Norröna* en route to Iceland, it may be wise to book in advance. If you'd like to camp in the hostel grounds and use their facilities, they charge US$5.70 per person.

Meals are available from the hostel at US$4.25 for breakfast or lunch and US$6 for dinner, but they must be ordered in advance – on the previous day if possible. Alternatively, you can use their kitchen facilities and rustle up your own grub.

There's a kiosk in the village where you can purchase basic groceries but it's probably better to bring your own supplies, if you plan to cook your own meals.

Walks

The most popular day-walk from Oyndarfjørður is up the track to the north-west, past the great swampy cirque of Vatnsdalur, through the low pass between the 500-metre peaks of Limstúgva and Tindur, and down along the coastline to the village of Elduvík on Funningsfjørður. From there, you can return to Oyndarfjørður by bus (with some difficulty) or return the way you came.

Another great walk is up the winding road past the Hellur intersection to the highest hairpin bend and then diagonally up the slopes to the boggy pass between Hellur and Fuglafjørður. If you scramble up to the ridge, east of the pass, you'll get fine views across to the fingerlike north-eastern islands. From the pass you can continue down to the village of Fuglafjørður and work out the rather involved bus schedule back to Oyndarfjørður. (It's 5 km walking and 28 km by bus with a change at Skálabotnur) or, just walk back the way you came.

Getting There & Away

Bus No 481 to and from Skálabotnur (which connects with bus No 400 to and from Tórshavn) runs six times each weekday, three times on Saturdays, and twice on Sundays.

Around the Faroes

Those with a bit more time than the 2-day stopover affords, may want to do some exploring beyond the main islands. The dramatically scenic north-eastern islands are made up of narrow fingerlike ridges protruding above the surface of the water. Their centre is the town of Klaksvík.

The southernmost island of Suðuroy has a combination of precipitous cliffs, gentle hills and, best of all, a tendency towards the finest weather in the country.

The smaller islands of Sandoy, Vágar, and Nólsoy show what village life is like on the more isolated, outer islands while Mykines, Skúvoy, Hestur, Koltur, and Stóra Dímun, though inhabited at least part of the year, are not only isolated, but quite rural as well. Each has only a handful of people living in a single village or settlement. Lítla Dímun, the smallest of the major islands, is uninhabited and practically inaccessible.

North-East Faroes

The six islands that comprise the north-eastern Faroes are Borðoy, Viðoy, Svínoy, Fugloy, Kunoy, and Kalsoy. They are among the most beautiful in the North Atlantic but, unlike such enigmatic places as Jan Mayen, St Kilda or Svalbard (Spitsbergen), they are easily accessible.

Except for Klaksvík, the north-eastern Faroes are very sparsely settled. There are no harbours, the weather is harsh, the wind is cold and fierce, and life can be difficult. Level (or relatively level) land is greatly valued and, for the most part, the islands' few villages cling precipitously to steep hillsides which threaten to heave them into the sea.

All the villages are now connected by tunnel or ferry but, instead of encouraging residents to remain in their no-longer isolated homes, the new infrastructure has inspired many to use them as escape routes. One way trips to Tórshavn or Klaksvík are growing more commonplace and some villages like Skálatoftir on Borðoy have been abandoned altogether.

KLAKSVÍK ON BORÐOY

Klaksvík, which makes a perfect U-turn around its sheltered harbour, is the Faroes' second largest city with over 5000 inhabitants. Like most Faroese towns, its economy is based primarily on fishing and fish processing. One of the interesting sights in

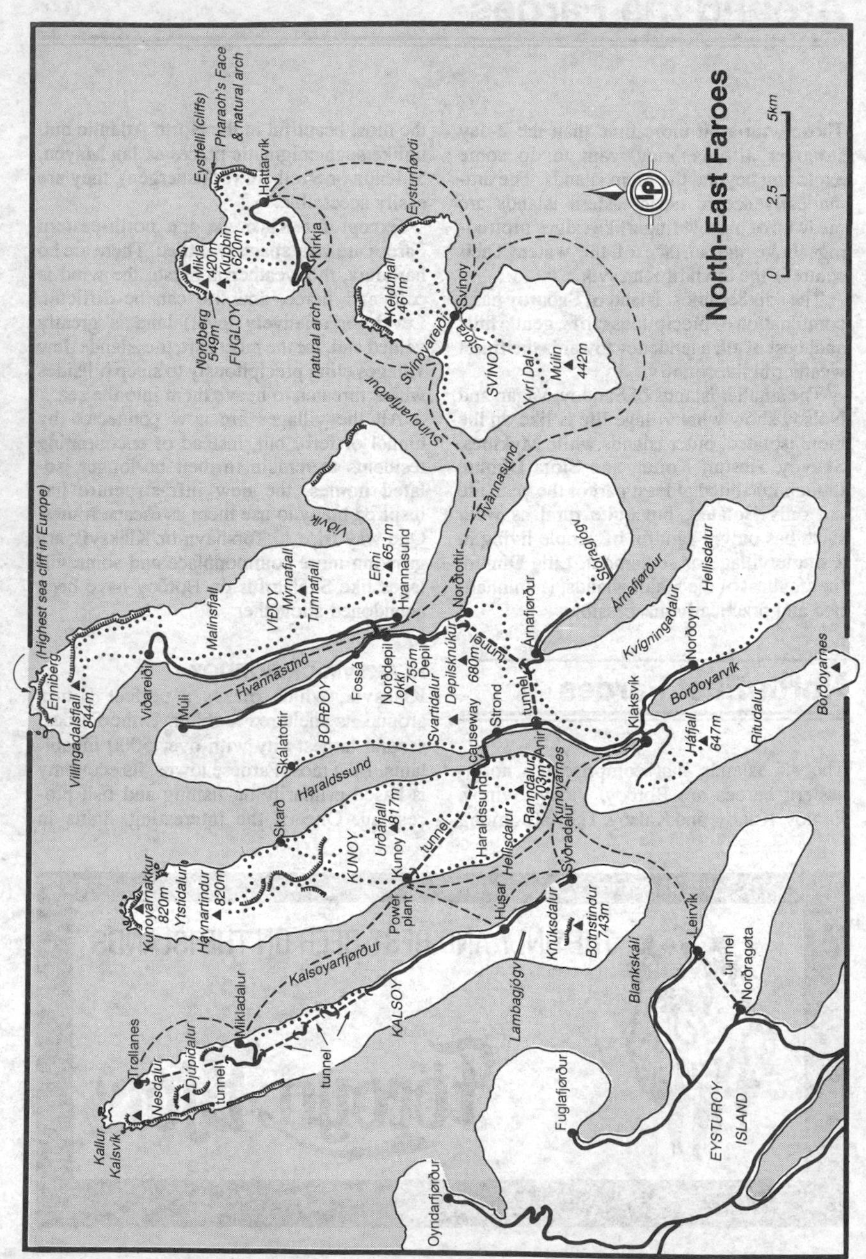
North-East Faroes
0
2.5
5km
FUGLOY
Eystfelli (cliffs)
Pharaoh's Face & natural arch
Hattarvík
Kirkja
Mikla 420m
Klubbin 620m
Norðberg 549m
natural arch
Eysturhøvdi
Keldufjall 461m
Svínoy
Svínoyareiði
Stóra
SVÍNOY
Yvri Dal
Múlin 442m
Svínoyarfjørður
Hvannasund
Viðvík
VIÐOY
Enni 651m
Mýrnafjall
Tunnafjall
Malinsfjall
Enniberg
(Highest sea cliff in Europe)
Villingadalsfjall 844m
Viðareiði
Múli
Fossá
Norðdepil
Lokki 755m
Depil
Norðtoftir
Depilsknúkur 680m
Svartidalur
BORÐOY
Skálatoftir
Haraldssund
Strond
causeway
tunnel
Árnafjørður
Storagjógv
Kvígningadalur
Hellisdalur
Norðoyri
Borðoyarvík
Klaksvík
Háfjall 647m
Ritudalur
Borðoyarnes
Ánir
KUNOY
Skarð
Urðafjall 817m
Kunoy
Kunoyarnes
Syðradalur
Húsar
Power plant
Kunoyarnakkur 820m
Ystidalur
Havnartindur 820m
Kalsoyarfjørður
Knúksdalur
Botnstindur 743m
Lambagjógv
Blankskáli
Leirvík
Norðragøta
KALSOY
Mikladalur
Trøllanes
Nesdalur
Djúpidalur
Kallur
Kalsvík
EYSTUROY ISLAND
Fuglafjørður
Oyndarfjørður

Klaksvík is the harbour itself which boasts just about every type of high-tech fishing craft ever conceived.

Those who are interested in the Faroes' *raison d'être* can arrange to tour a fish-processing plant. It's also possible to take a tour of the Føroya Bjór brewery, but don't expect a free sample of the real thing unless you can cough up a ration card.

Rumour has it that there's a push to build an architectural oddity here, a kind of see-through structure over the harbour which would connect both shores and prove to the world that Klaksvík is the Faroes' technological front-runner. It is also hoped that this will put the town on the tourist circuit and who knows...it may improve the weather as well. Apparently, plans have already been drawn up and Klaksvík is waiting for enough financial backing to make the project happen. No one seems to be holding their breath, however.

Information

Tourist Office The KF-Stovan tourist office (tel 56939) is on Nólsoyar Pállsgøta on the eastern bank of the harbour. The staff can provide you with a few leaflets and some advice regarding your travels around the north-east islands.

Post & Telephone The post office in Klaksvík is at the head of the harbour. It's open weekdays from 9 am to noon and 2 to 5 pm. On Saturdays it opens from 9 am to noon only.

The telephone office is just east of the post office on Biskupsstøðgøta.

Banks There are four banks around Klaksvík which exchange foreign currency and travellers' cheques. Most of them are on or near Klaksvíksvegur, on the western side of the harbour.

Christianskirkja

Christianskirkja, the Lutheran church, was built in 1963 and, although not old, is worth seeing. The best time to visit is on a Sunday, on any other day you'll have to find someone to let you in. The altarpiece is entitled *The Great Supper* and was painted in 1901 by the Danish artist Joakim Skovgaard. It was originally intended for the altar of the Viborg church in Denmark but somehow ended up in Klaksvík.

The font is noteworthy as well. This granite relic is around 4000 years old and was originally used as a sacrificial bowl in a pagan temple in Denmark.

In the church, you'll also find a full-sized Faroese rowing boat that, until the present century, was used by the clergy for transport between the islands. It hangs from the ceiling in the traditional Faroese manner.

North Islands Museum

Norðoya Fornminnissavn or the North Islands Museum is on the western shore of the harbour in Klaksvík. It's housed in both an old Danish Trade Monopoly building, constructed in 1838, and its extension. In 1919 the latter was used as a general store. Inside are a number of photographs, tools and household relics from earlier days. The most interesting exhibit, however, is in the old apothecary which was used from the early 1930s to 1961. This room has been maintained pretty much as it was when it closed and all the original implements and bottles are still on display. It's fairly rustic for 1961, to say the least.

The museum is open on Tuesdays and Thursdays from 2 to 4 pm and on Sundays from 4 to 6 pm.

Háfjall & Hálgafell

A popular trip from town is the steep climb up the 647-metre peak Háfjall ('high mountain'), or up 503-metre high Hálgafell. Begin by walking from the end of the harbour to the top of the eiði. Then turn right and follow Niðan horn and Åstarbreytin to the base of the pass Brúnaskarð. Scramble your way up to the point between Háfjall and Hálgafell. Then choose your peak, either one can be climbed fairly easily in half a day.

Festivals

Norðoyastevna This 2-day annual festival

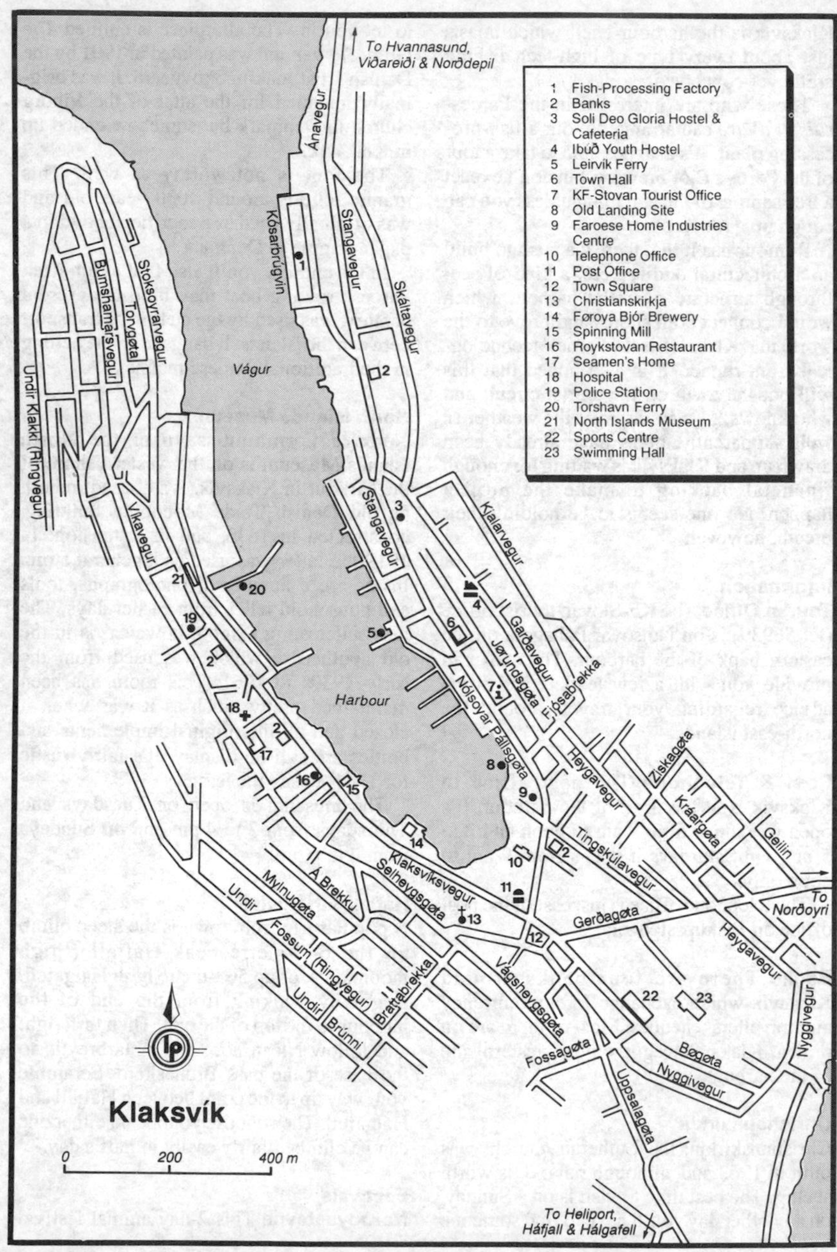
To Hvannasund, Viðareiði & Norðdepil
1 Fish-Processing Factory
2 Banks
3 Soli Deo Gloria Hostel & Cafeteria
4 Ibúð Youth Hostel
5 Leirvík Ferry
6 Town Hall
7 KF-Stovan Tourist Office
8 Old Landing Site
9 Faroese Home Industries Centre
10 Telephone Office
11 Post Office
12 Town Square
13 Christianskirkja
14 Føroya Bjór Brewery
15 Spinning Mill
16 Roykstovan Restaurant
17 Seamen's Home
18 Hospital
19 Police Station
20 Torshavn Ferry
21 North Islands Museum
22 Sports Centre
23 Swimming Hall
Ánavegur
Kósarbrúgvin
Stangavegur
Skálatavegur
Stoksoyrarvegur
Bumshamarsvegur
Torvgøta
Undir Klakki (Ringvegur)
Vágur
Víkavegur
Kjalarvegur
Garðavegur
Jørundsgøta
Nólsoyar Pállsgøta
Fíggjabrekka
Harbour
Heygavegur
Ziskagøta
Kráargøta
Geilin
Tingskúlavegur
To Norðoyri
Klaksvíksvegur
Selheygsgøta
Gerðagøta
Heygavegur
Mylnugøta
Á Brekku
Undir Fossum (Ringvegur)
Undir Brúnni
Brattabrekka
Vágsheygsgøta
Fossagøta
Bøgøta
Nyggivegur
Nyggivegur
Uppsalagøta
To Heliport, Háfjall & Hálgafell
Klaksvík
0
200
400 m

takes place in Klaksvík during the first week of June. In typical Faroese style, it's normally characterised by rowing competitions, sports matches, dancing, and feasting. During that weekend, extra ferries are rostered between Leirvík and Klaksvík.

Places to Stay – bottom end

Klaksvík has a very nice (if a bit quirky) youth hostel, the *Ibúð* (tel 55403) on Garðavegur. Although it's only three short blocks uphill from the ferry landing, it seems more like seven due to the circuitous route you have to take. It costs US$10/13 for IYHF members/non-members.

The private hostel *Soli Deo Gloria* (tel 56528) is found above the cafeteria on Stangavegur, near the ferry landing on the east side of the harbour. This one, whose name means something like 'to God only the glory', is extremely unusual, so be warned. Singles/doubles cost US$32/57 and dormitory beds cost US$14. Meals are also available, if arranged in advance.

Places to Stay – middle

Klaksvík also has a *Seamen's Home* (tel 55333), across the harbour from the ferry landing. They charge US$57/36 for single rooms with/without bath. Doubles cost US$78.50/54.25 with/without bath. Cafeteria meals and daily specials are available and, even if you're staying elsewhere, the Seamen's Home is a good place to eat in Klaksvík.

There's also a private guesthouse in Klaksvík known as *Gistingarhúsið við Vikina* (tel 55739). It is on the same street as the youth hostel but a few blocks further south, beyond the point where Garðavegur changes its name to Heygavegur. It's open only in July. Singles/doubles cost US$46.50/57. All rooms have private baths and the restaurant is open from 8 am to 11 pm daily.

Places to Eat

Apart from the previously mentioned cafeterias in the Seamen's Home, Soli Deo Gloria and the guesthouse dining room, there's also a proper restaurant called the *Roykstovan*. This is on the western side of the harbour on the corner of Klaksvíksvegur and Kommunubrekka.

You'll find excellent gooey concoctions at *Eilar Samuelsen's Bakari* near the tourist office.

Activities

Swimming At the head of the harbour is Svimjið, the swimming hall. There is a pool, sauna, swim jets, and showers.

Things to Buy

The Heimavirkið (the Faroese Home Industries Centre) sells handmade pullovers, socks, gloves, hats, and other woollen goods, all of generally high quality. Their outlet is on the seaward side of Biskupsstøðgøta, near the top of the harbour. If you'd like to have a look around the woollens mill and see the spinning, washing, and dyeing processes, it's on the harbour side of Klaksvíksvegur.

Getting There & Away

Bus On weekdays, bus No 500 does nine daily runs to and from Viðareiði, on Viðoy island, stopping in Norðdepil and Hvannasund en route. On Saturdays, there are only two runs and on Sundays, just one. Bus No 503 goes to Norðdepil and Norðtoftir five times daily from Monday to Friday. Twice a day it continues on to Múli. Again, it runs twice on Saturdays and once on Sundays.

To Haraldssund and Kunoy on Kunoy island, bus No 504 goes five times daily from Monday to Thursday, six times on Fridays, and twice daily on weekends.

If you want to travel to Kalsoy island, you must take the ferry *Barskor* to Húsar. From there, bus No 506 goes to Mikladalur and Trøllanes three times daily from Monday to Thursday, four times on Fridays, twice on Saturdays, and three times on Sundays.

Ferry The frequency of the *Ternan* ferry between Leirvík (Eysturoy) and Klaksvík is outlined in the section on Leirvík in the Streymoy & Eysturoy chapter.

The ferry *Barskor* connects Klaksvík to Syðradalur and Húsar on Kalsoy daily from Monday to Thursday at 6.40 and 9.20 am, and 5.30 pm. On Fridays, it does an additional trip at 8 pm. On Saturdays, it departs at 8.15 am and 3.30 pm and on Sundays at 9.20 am, 3.30 and 6.40 pm. Upon arriving in Húsar, it turns around and returns to Klaksvík.

From Monday to Friday the ferries *Teistin* and *Smyril* do one or two trips daily between Tórshavn and Klaksvík. On Sundays, there's one trip each way.

Getting Around

For taxi service, ring Ásmundur Poulsen (tel 56222).

AROUND BORÐOY

Outside of Klaksvík, Borðoy has the standard scenery expected in the north-eastern islands: steep cliffs, sharp ridges, and a couple of tiny villages clinging to the steep hills above the shores.

Árnafjørður

Árnafjørður ('eagle fjord') is the village between the two Borðoy tunnels. It's a scenic and secluded little place but, between the time your bus emerges from one tunnel and delves into the next, you won't catch much more than a fleeting glimpse of the view. Of course, you can get off here if you'd like, but there's really no point.

Norðdepil

This tiny settlement, at the western end of the Borðoy-Viðoy bridge, dates back to 1866. It's the site of the Hotel Bella (tel 52040) and the Youth Hostel Todnes (tel 52021). You can't miss them – their buildings are all painted a shade of yellow not normally found in nature.

Both establishments and their associated restaurant are under the management of 'Bella' Johan Petersen who comes from Fugloy. He has been around enough to pick up more odd and interesting anecdotes than you'd ever have time to listen to. He's an excellent chef as well, and the hotel restaurant is one of the best in the Faroes.

Singles/doubles without private bath cost US$32/50. With bath, they cost US$36/57. In the youth hostel, a private room is US$21.50 and dorm rooms are US$14. Meals in the restaurant should be ordered in advance. Breakfast costs about US$5.50 and lunch and dinner are US$11 each. Camping is available too for US$5 per person.

Fossá

The abandoned village of Fossá, north of Norðdepil, was bought in 1969 by the museum society of Klaksvík to turn into a typical medieval Faroese village. More than 20 years later, however, nothing has been forthcoming. The place is currently used as a camping site for boy scouts and school groups.

Múli

This village, near the northernmost tip of Borðoy, lies at the end of a poor unsurfaced road from Norðdepil. Múli has 154 inhabitants, (150 of which are sheep). It's one of the remotest villages in the country and subject to fierce winds that howl through the eiði, of Viðoy. It's only a 7-km walk one way from Norðdepil, so if you're staying at the Hotel Bella or the youth hostel there, it would be an easy full day's walk out to Múli and back.

KALSOY

In my opinion, Kalsoy has the most enigmatically rugged form of any of the Faroe Islands. The western coast consists only of steep cliffs, while on the eastern slopes there are four tiny settlements – Syðradalur, Húsar, Mikladalur and Trøllanes, whose combined populations add up to about 150.

Walks

Ridge-walking on Kalsoy is pretty difficult and quite a few visitors simply choose to walk from the ferry landings at Syðradalur or Húsar up to Trøllanes. There are four unlit tunnels along the way – none, however, sees enough traffic to pose problems with noxious gas. The last tunnel, which is 3 km long, seems the narrowest and darkest and, since it serves a village with only 20 inhabitants, is rarely used by vehicles. Walking through it is quite an eerie experience; the cold damp darkness in the heart of the mountain is rather out of the ordinary. Those who take this route should remember to carry a torch and a warm jacket.

Getting There & Away

From Klaksvík, the ferry *Barskor* sails to Syðradalur and Húsar three times daily from Monday to Thursday. On Fridays, it does an additional trip at 8 pm and, on Saturdays, it departs at 8.15 am and 3.30 pm. There are three runs on Sundays. Upon arriving in Húsar, it turns around and goes back to Klaksvík.

KUNOY

Kunoy, which covers only 36 sq km and has around 130 residents, has recently become accessible by road. Since the building of an earth-dam causeway, from Strond on Borðoy to Haraldssund, and a 3-km tunnel through the heart of the island to the western village of Kunoy, these two remote villages now have easy access to and from Klaksvík.

Skarð

This remote field on north-eastern Kunoy was once a village. It was abandoned in 1913 when all seven men of the community went fishing together, were caught in a storm and not a single one returned. The women couldn't make a go of it alone and everyone decided to move down to Haraldssund.

Although there's nothing of interest remaining at Skarð, if you have the time, it's a nice walk out there from Haraldssund.

Walks

The ridge-walk along Kunoy's spine is difficult in places, but can be negotiated on foot as far north as Havnartindur, where an immense gunsight notch puts an abrupt end to your progress. To get past it, technical expertise would be required.

Access to the ridge is roughly up the Glyuvursá stream from Haraldssund to the 703-metre peak of Ranntindur. From there, follow the ridge northwards for 9 km past Galvskorrarfjall to the notch. The most difficult and dangerous part of the trip is the descent from the ridge down Miklidalur to the shore. From there it's an easy matter of walking back along the coast past Skarð to Haraldssund. If you're daunted by it, turn around and go back the way you came. You could also do the trip in the opposite direction.

This is quite a long journey over difficult terrain, so either allow a very long day or plan to camp somewhere on the way. Weather should be a major consideration since the ridge is completely exposed and there is no shelter if it gets unpleasant.

VIÐOY

Viðoy ('wood island') is shaped like an upright vacuum cleaner (or a smoker's pipe, depending on how your imagination is working). It is the northernmost of the Faroe Islands. Although it hasn't a single tree, lots of driftwood floats in on the Gulf Stream from North America.

Viðoy is separated from northern Borðoy by Hvannasund, a channel which is severely constricted at the Norðdepil-Hvannasund bridge. Consequently, at times, it can experience tidal bores over half a metre high. The same thing happens to a lesser extent in Svínoyarfjørður, south of Viðoy. When the two currents collide in southern Hvannasund, boating through the resulting pools and eddies can be quite interesting.

Although it's accessible by bus from Klaksvík, Viðoy seems a world apart. From the bridge at Hvannasund an 8-km unsurfaced track hugs the western coastline to Viðareiði. From there, a path leads a short way down the exposed eastern coastline to the valley Dalur.

Hvannasund

The only reason to visit the village of Hvannasund is to catch the ferry *Másin* to the islands of Svínoy and Fugloy. Beyond the previously mentioned tidal quirks, this is normally a very rough ride. Those who choose to remain up top will need to hold the rails tightly, to avoid being catapulted into the sea. Those who choose to ride below will more than likely be sick and not appreciate the great views along the way.

Theoretically, this ferry calls in at both sides of the Svínoy eiði, as well as at Hattarvík and Kirkja on Fugloy. In fact, this is rarely possible. Neither island has a harbour and landing entails pulling alongside the concrete wharfs, loading and unloading passengers and freight, while avoiding being smashed to bits or washed away by the surf. If the situation appears hazardous, the ferry will not dock. The obvious corollary is that, once there, visitors may not be able to leave as quickly as they'd planned. If you go, be prepared for this eventuality or bring enough cash to fly back on the chopper.

On Mondays, the boat leaves Hvannasund at 8.15 am and 4 pm, and from Tuesday to Sunday, daily at 9.45 am. On Fridays, there's an additional trip at 6 pm. On Sundays, there's a Fugloy trip at 2.30 pm and a Svínoy one at 6 pm. There is no real arrival timetable for these boats as their movements are completely dependent upon which direction the wind and waves are moving, which stops can be made, and which way the boat travels around Svínoy.

Viðareiði

The Faroes' northernmost village, Viðareiði, lies in a low and windy pass between the Enniberg headland and the main body of Viðoy. The view, west from the village, to the headlands at the northern tips of Borðoy, Kunoy, and Kalsoy is spectacular.

Walks

Enniberg Although many tourist brochures claim that 750-metre-high Enniberg is the highest sea cliff in the world, I suspect it is more accurately the highest in Europe. In southern Greenland the one that rises 2012 metres above Tasermiut fjord is more likely to be a 'highest-in-the-world' contender.

But you'll still be impressed by Enniberg. From below, it looms formidable. From the top, it defies description; it will be one of the most memorable sights you'll ever see.

To get there, take the road leading north-west out of Viðareiði and, after it ends, continue up along the stream. Pass to the south-west of 844-metre Villingadalsfjall and north along the ridge to what appears to be the end of the world at Enniberg. If you'd like to keep the drama coming, return to Villingadalsfjall and follow the crest of the cliffs to its north, down the east coast of the island back to Viðareiði. If you stop to appreciate all the incredible views on the way, plan on taking an entire day for the walk.

Ridge Walk Another trip from Viðareiði begins with a climb up the ridge, south of town, to the summit of 751-metre Malinsfjall. From there, continue south along the obvious ridge for 8 km until you're level with Hvannasund. Then there's a steep and difficult descent to the village. If this sounds daunting, you can do the trip in the opposite direction, although the Malinsfjall descent is nothing to sneeze at either. Some worthwhile side trips along this route are up 687-metre Mýrnafjall and 651-metre Enni, above Hvannasund. This trip can be done in a full day but would be better appreciated in two. Just watch the weather though because the ridge is quite exposed.

Places to Stay & Eat

The *Hotel Norð* (tel 51061) in Viðareiði is an ideal remote retreat, especially if you want to do some walks through spectacular surroundings but come back to a hot shower and restaurant meal afterwards. A single/double room costs US$48.50/60 with private bath, both include a continental breakfast. Set lunches and dinners cost US$13 each.

If you want to stay or eat there, be sure to book in advance. When guests are not lined up, the management doesn't seem to stick around and you're liable to find the place deserted.

Getting There & Away

Bus On weekdays, bus No 500 does nine

daily runs to and from Klaksvík stopping in Norðdepil and Hvannasund en route. On Saturdays, there are only two runs and on Sundays, just one.

Tours

On Fridays at 8 am, Tora Tourist Traffic operates a weekly tour to Viðareiði from Tórshavn. It's an all-day trip that includes lunch at the Hotel Norð and, on the way back, stops in the village of Gøta for some souvenir shopping. The tour (including transport, a guide, and lunch) costs US$61 per person.

There is also a daily boat tour at 3 pm which departs from Klaksvík. This sails up the strait between Kunoy and Kalsoy, past the northern headlands of Kunoy and Borðoy to Enniberg, the northernmost point of Viðoy. Weather permitting, it then sails around the north end of Kalsoy to see the bird cliffs at the small bay Kalsvík before returning via Kalsoyarfjørður. This tour costs US$23 per person, a very good deal, and may be booked through the KF-Stovan tourist office (tel 56939) in Klaksvík.

SVÍNOY

Svínoy could well be the least visited of the easily accessible islands. Wherever it's described, it's always referred to as being relatively flat (once you've seen this island, 'flat' is not the first word that springs to mind) and uninteresting. For those of you who like places the tourist industry pans as flat and uninteresting, here's your opportunity. Personally, I think they just want to put visitors off and keep it for themselves!

With the exception of a couple of broad valleys and the eiði, which divides the island into two unequal parts, Svínoy's coastline is surrounded by high cliffs reaching 587 metres at Havnartindur, on the southern portion of the island. On the northern peninsula, which resembles a penguin's profile, is the sheerest precipice I've seen anywhere in the Faroes. You'll have a good view of it as you sail between Hvannasund or Svínoy and Fugloy.

Walks

From the village of Svínoy, where all the island's 100 or so residents live, there are several interesting walking routes. One is up the 461-metre peak Keldufjall, above the cliffs on the north-eastern coast. From here you'll have a good view of Fugloy and of Viðoy's entire remote eastern coast.

Another is to the end of the jeep track and east up the slope to Eysturhøvði, the 345-metre cliff, (the tip of the penguin's beak). It's also possible to walk up one of these routes and down the other in a single day.

The third option is to walk south from Svínoy village up the valley of the Stórá, and from its headwaters across the moors and down the steep valley Yvrí Dal to the shore. The only realistic route back to the village, in this case, is the way you came.

Lastly, from the western end of the eiði you can walk up the track going off to the south until it eventually peters out altogether on the cliffs. Again, you'll have to return the way you came.

Getting There & Away

The ferry between Hvannasund and Svínoy will only stop on the island if weather and surf conditions allow. Stops may be made at either or both ends of the eiði. If you're waiting to be collected here, you might have to run the 1.5 km over the eiði to catch the boat wherever it docks.

For information about the ferry to and from Svínoy, refer to Hvannasund in the Viðoy section.

There's a helicopter service between Klaksvík, Svínoy, and Fugloy on Mondays, Wednesdays, and Fridays. On Mondays, there are two trips, one departing the heliport in Klaksvík at noon and the second at 4.20 pm. After leaving Svínoy, the helicopter stops at both Hattarvík and Kirkja, on Fugloy, before returning to Klaksvík.

FUGLOY

'Bird island' not only has some breathtaking nest-covered cliffs complete with residents, but also the island itself is shaped like a small, fat, ordinary bird.

Places to Stay & Eat

As would be expected, there's really no formal accommodation on Fugloy, but you can camp anywhere away from the villages. If you'd rather sleep indoors, the best source of information regarding private accommodation is at the *Hotel Bella* (tel 52040) in Norðdepil on Borðoy. The proprietor, 'Bella' Johan Petersen, is a native of Fugloy and he'll know if anything is available. You're likely to get a few good Fugloy stories out of the deal as well.

As far as food is concerned, the village of Kirkja has a tiny general store which is open for several hours on weekday afternoons.

Walks

If you don't dawdle, you can explore just about all of Fugloy on foot in a day-trip from Hvannasund. This will include trips up to the 448-metre cliffs at Eystfelli (the bird's head), the 620-metre cliffs at Klubbin (the bird's tail), and both the island's villages, Hattarvík and Kirkja (the bird's neck and feet, respectively).

Since you never really know which village you'll be arriving at, there's no recommended itinerary. Just try not to miss either of the cliffs because they are spectacular. The wild vistas across all the other northern islands are nearly as impressive.

The Klubbin cliffs descend from a plateau-like ridge which is high enough to be covered with tundra tussocks and boreal vegetation rather than grass. On the other side of the island at Eystfelli, there's a natural broad amphitheatre which sweeps upward towards oblivion before reaching a cresting and wholeheartedly dropping into it.

It's only logical that somewhere in the Faroes, one should find at least one pharaoh, and it seems he's turned up on Fugloy. From the cliffs, near the lighthouse at Eystfelli, is a protruding rock shaped like an ancient Egyptian head and face. Nearby, there's a natural stone arch as well.

Getting There & Away

For information on the ferry to and from Fugloy, refer to Hvannasund in the Viðoy section. For information about the helicopter, see the Svínoy Getting There & Away section.

Western Faroes

West of Streymoy are the two islands of Vágar and Mykines. Vágar is shaped a bit like some non-descript carnivore threatening to eat Mykines. It also lies in the path of most of the weather sweeping in from the southwest and, with Tórshavn, has a reputation for the most consistently disagreeable weather in the country.

Mykines experiences similar conditions and, since the strait between the two isn't well protected, the wrath of the wind and sea can cut the smaller island off for days. The concept of kanskar (see the Faroe Islands Getting Around chapter) is perhaps best illustrated here. So great is Mykines' appeal, however, that many visitors opt to take a chance on being marooned there for a while rather than miss it.

It's ironic that inclement Vágar is also the only island in the Faroes with a level expanse large enough for the international airport. It sits in a broad windswept valley between the island's two main villages, Miðvágur and Sørvágur. It goes without saying that kanskar has been known to plague international flight schedules as well.

VÁGAR

Apart from the airport, of primary interest to Vágar's visitors are its precipitous western and southern coasts and its mountain lakes – good for fishing in and camping near. The island is also known for the largest and bloodiest grindadráps in the Faroes. The village of Miðvágur seems especially adept at bringing in the pilot whales that migrate past the southern coast of the island.

Vágar is known for being a bit more aloof than the other islands – perhaps it's the weather – and, on the whole, only longer term visitors spend any time there.

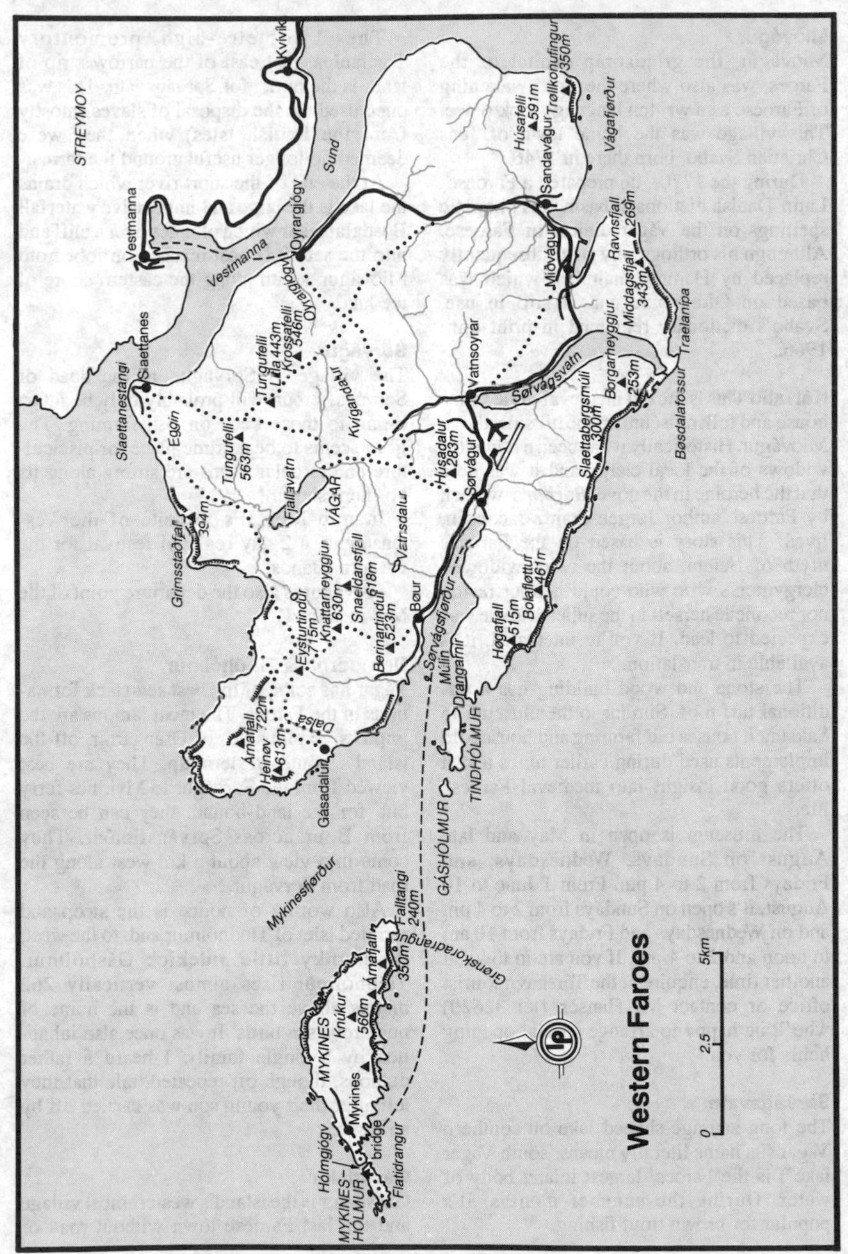

Western Faroes
0
2.5
5km
STREYMOY
Vestmanna
Kvívík
Vestmanna
Sund
Oyrargjógv
Sandavágur
Húsafelli
591m
Trøllkonufingur
350m
Vágafjørður
Miðvágur
Ravnsfjall
269m
Middagsfjall
343m
Traelanípa
Vatnsoyrar
Sørvágsvatn
Borgarheyggjur
253m
Slaettabergsmúli
300m
Bøsdalafossur
Sørvágur
Húsadalur
283m
Slaettanes
Slaettanestangi
Egin
Tungufelli
563m
Turgufelli
Lítla 443m
Krossafelli
546m
Kvígandalur
Fjallavatn
VÁGAR
Vetrsdalur
Grímsstaðfall
394m
Eysturtindur
715m
Knattarheyggjur
630m
Snaeldansfjell
618m
Bøur
Beinartindur
523m
Sørvágsfjørður
Múlin
Drangarnir
TINDHÓLMUR
Bolafløttur
461m
Høgafjall
515m
Árnafjall
722m
Heinav
613m
Dalsá
Gásadalur
Mykinesfjørður
GÁSHÓLMUR
MYKINES
Mykines
Knúkur
560m
Árnafjall
350m
Falltangi
240m
Grønskoradrangur
Hólmgjógv
MYKINES-HÓLMUR
bridge
Flatidrangur

Miðvágur

Miðvágur, the grindadráp capital of the Faroes, was also where the first awakening of Faroese as a written language took place. This village was the home town of Jens Christian Svabo, born there in 1746.

During the 1770s, he prepared a Faroese-Latin-Danish dictionary, basing his phonetic spellings on the Vágar dialect of Faroese. Although his orthography was subsequently replaced by Hammershaimb's, which was based on Old Norse and is still in use, Svabo's dictionary remained in print until 1966.

Kálvalíd This is the old medieval-style farmhouse and folk museum on the hillside above Miðvágur. Historically it has been a home for widows of the local clergy and it was here that the heroine in the novel *Barbara*, written by Faroese author Jørgen-Frantz Jacobsen, lived. This story is based on the Faroese myth of Beinta, about the twice-widowed clergymen's wife who could neither resign nor reconcile herself to the sullen life she was expected to lead. If you're interested, it is available in translation.

The stone and wood building has a traditional turf roof. Similar to the museum in Saksun, it houses old farming and household implements used during earlier times and it offers good insight into medieval Faroese life.

The museum is open in May and late August on Sundays, Wednesdays, and Fridays from 2 to 4 pm. From 1 June to 10 August, it's open on Sundays from 2 to 4 pm and on Wednesdays and Fridays from 10 am to noon and 2 to 4 pm. If you are in town at another time, enquire at the Tórshavn tourist office or contact Mr Hansen (tel 32620) who'll be happy to arrange special opening hours for you.

Sørvágsvatn

The long sausage-shaped lake on southern Vágar (its name literally means 'south Vágar lake') is the Faroes' largest inland body of water. During the summer months, it's popular for brown trout fishing.

The 146-metre-high promontory Traelanípa, just east of the narrow strip of land, is the outlet for Sørvágsvatn. This was once used for the disposal of slaves (mostly from the British Isles) when they were deemed no longer useful around the farms.

At the end of the short river which drains the lake is the large and impressive waterfall Bøsdalafossur which plunges over a cliff and into the sea. It is best reached on foot from Miðvágur, south along the eastern shore of the lake.

Sørvágur

The village of Sørvágur, at the head of Sørvágsfjørður, will probably only be interesting to those keen on fish farming. The fjord seems to be a prime place for pisciculture and circular farms are strung along its northern shore.

In mid-July, it's the site of the Vestanstevna, a 2-day regional festival for the western islands.

Sørvágur is also the departure point of the Mykines ferry.

Drangarnir & Tindhólmur

Vágar has some of the best sea-stack formations in the Faroes. The most famous are the impressive pinnacles of Drangarnir, off the island's south-western tip. They are best viewed from the Sørvágur to Mykines ferry but, for the land-bound, they can be seen from Bøur across Sørvágsfjørður. They come into view about a km west along the road from Sørvágur.

Also worthy of notice is the steep and serrated islet of Tindhólmur and, to the west, its chunky little sidekick Gáshólmur. Tindhólmur rises almost vertically 262 metres above the sea and is the home of numerous sea birds. It was once also inhabited by a single family. I heard a rather dubious, though oft-repeated, tale that they left after their young son was carried off by an eagle.

Gásadalur

Gásadalur is the island's westernmost village and the last Faroese town without road or ferry connections. It's due to receive its tunnel in the very near future but, until then, the residents only have access to the rest of the country by helicopter, foot, or private boat. The village has a population of about 25.

Walks

Vágar is quite hilly and crisscrossed by walking routes that will take you up and down valleys, past lakes, and to steep cliffs that plunge hundreds of metres to the sea. If you'd like to spend some time wandering away from civilisation and aren't overly concerned with weather, Vágar is the best place to do it. The entire northern half of the island is wild country and there are no roads north of the ferry landing at Oyrargjógv.

Fjallavatn Such imagination and creativity goes into the naming of Faroese features. The name of this beautiful and rather haunting body of water in north-western Vágar means 'mountain lake'. It's a pleasant and relatively easy day-walk (10 km return) from the road. There's a route in from Sørvágur and another from Vatnsoyrar where a small road leads about halfway up to the lake. The lake shore can get a bit muddy so appropriate footwear for bog slogging is advised.

Gásadalur Loop There is a longer and more challenging loop variation of the Fjallavatn trip. Begin by walking from Bøur (4 km west of Sørvágur) across the steep and marginally treacherous coastal route to Gásadalur, then up the valley Dalsá, eastwards along the line of cliffs at its head – down to Fjallavatn. From there, it's an easy and level walk to the road at Vatnsoyrar. This trip can also be started by climbing Berinartindur, behind Bøur, and then following the ridge to connect with the previously mentioned route near 715-metre Eysturtindur.

Large-scale topographic sheets and a compass are essential for either of these walks. Bring camping equipment and allow 2 days for the return trip.

Other walking routes around Vágar are outlined on the map in this book and on the *Føroyar 1:100,000* topographic sheet as well.

Places to Stay & Eat

The only place to stay on Vágar is the *Hotel Vágar* (tel 32955) at the airport. Its rather stark appearance (it looks like a government research station) matches the surroundings perfectly. Single/double rooms with attached bath cost US$84/108 including a continental breakfast. Lunch and dinner each cost US$13.50. The restaurant is open from 7 am to 8.30 pm daily.

There's a cafeteria at the airport but it's only recommended if you're desperate. They seem to realise they have a captive clientele and the food and service reflect this well. It's open from 8 am to only 5 pm daily.

Down in Sørvágur there's a combination coffee shop and grill bar. Here you can get coffee and a snack from 9 am to 11 pm Monday to Friday and on weekends from 2 to 11 pm. The grill is open daily in the evenings only.

Getting There & Away

Air There is helicopter service between Tórshavn and the international airport, via the island of Koltur, on Mondays, Wednesdays, Fridays, and Sundays. From Vágar airport to Gásadalur and Mykines, there is one trip each way on Mondays, Wednesdays, and Sundays. On Fridays there are two flights to facilitate day-trips to Mykines.

For information on international flights to and from Reykjavík and Copenhagen, refer to the general Getting There chapter at the beginning of the book.

Bus The most convenient way to reach Vágar from Tórshavn or Klaksvík is probably on the airport bus which connects with the Vestmanna-Oyrargjógv ferry.

Getting Around

All the buses which run from Tórshavn to the airport continue on to Sørvágur. From there, bus No 300 does the run out to Bøur five times daily from Monday to Friday and twice a day on weekends. After the Gásadalur tunnel is finished, it's likely that the schedule will be altered for buses to run out there too.

MYKINES

Mykines, the Faroes' westernmost island, isn't like the rest. Mention it to someone who's been there and you're likely to elicit a nostalgic sigh. Those who visit nearly always reckon it's their favourite island and no wonder – it's the greenest, the friendliest, the most independent, and among the most beautiful of the islands. Its single village is magical, with bright turf-roofed houses and turf streets, as well.

The island's moods are manifold and from a distance, it can remind you of Michener's Bali Hai or Rachmaninoff's Island of the Dead. Perhaps it's nicest to believe, however, that Mykines really is the 'paradise of birds' described by St Brendan in the 6th century.

The island's star attractions are the little puffins that inhabit it in overwhelming numbers. In German their name means 'diving parrots' and in Spanish, 'little fathers' – both are apt descriptions of these endearingly comical characters. It seems there's no-one who doesn't like puffins in one way or another: the Faroese like them stuffed with sweet dough and baked, Icelanders like them roasted and doused in gravy, visitors normally just like them on film.

The weather is another matter. Like Vágar, this island in the path of North Atlantic weather systems seems to catch and delay a few passing storms. If you have a bit of time and want to see the island at its best, you'll probably have to hole up and wait for a fine day. Bring a tent, food, a stove, and a few good books and settle in somewhere until the sun emerges. It will be worth it.

Places to Stay & Eat

This one is easy: there aren't any. If, due to bad weather, you get stuck without a tent on Mykines, you'll somehow find accommodation, but there's no formal arrangement for those who just fancy spending a few days on the island. Occasionally, however, private households take in visitors. The tourist office and Tora Tourist Traffic in Tórshavn both keep current lists of these homes. Expect to pay between US$35 and US$70 per night.

The best option is, of course, to bring a tent. Except for the weather, there's no problem camping on Mykines. There are, however, no restaurants on the island and the availability of groceries is unpredictable, so bring food with you. Again, when packing for the trip, be sure to consider the possibility of being on the island for longer than you'd bargained.

Walks

Mykines is ideal walking country. Thanks to the ferry schedules, however, visitors often have little choice but to follow the same rushed route out to Lundaland (the 'land of puffins') on the islet of Mykineshólmur, which is connected to Mykines by a small bridge.

This trip is considered by many to be the most beautiful in the Faroes. Walk out to the lighthouse, on the westernmost cape, which is surrounded by great sea stacks. Occasionally you can see locals on the cliffs catching puffins in a fleygustong, the bird net that resembles a large lacrosse racket.

For visitors with more than a few hours, the trip up the island's summit, 560-metre-high Knúkur, is also worthwhile. Although it's less than 3 km from the village, it's a hefty climb and it would be difficult to do both the Mykineshólmur walk and this trip in a single day (ie between ferries).

East of Knúkur, things get pretty precipitous. It is possible to pick your way through to this end of the island but it's difficult. Try walking down the steep north-east ridge of Knúkur.

Getting There & Away

Air From the international airport, there's helicopter service to Gásadalur (Vágar) and Mykines on Mondays at 9 am, Wednesdays at 9.10 am, Fridays at 11.20 am and 6 pm, and on Sundays at 5 pm. The round trip only takes 18 minutes.

Ferry From Sørvágur on Vágar island, the ferry *Súlan* goes to Mykines daily at 10 am. On Fridays, it also runs at 4 and 7.30 pm. On Saturdays and Sundays, there's an extra trip at 2 pm and, on Sundays only, the ferry goes at 5.30 pm too. The journey is normally rough and takes about an hour. After dropping and collecting passengers, the ferry returns to Sørvágur. This schedule is valid only between 26 May and 28 August. During the winter, it operates only a couple of times a week.

Southern Faroes

The southern islands form the point of the Faroese 'arrow' and include the relatively large islands of Suðuroy and Sandoy as well as the three smaller islands of Skúvoy, Stóra Dímun, and Lítla Dímun. Suðuroy is the most visited of the lot and has a youth hostel, two hotels, and a guesthouse.

The scenery is good but, best of all, the weather is reputedly the clearest and warmest in the islands. Don't bother carrying sun block or a swimming costume, but if you've been rained out of Tórshavn, Mykines, and the north-east, you can always resort to Sandoy or Suðuroy and hope for the best.

SANDOY

Although Sandoy is the least rugged of the Faroes, it's not without natural interest. It boasts the country's only sand dunes (hence the name 'sand island') and the cliffs on the western side are quite impressive. The island covers an area of 112 sq km and has a population of around 1800 in five villages.

Skopun

The quickest ferry route from Tórshavn is into Skopun. This village of about 700 was founded in 1836 and is the site of a fish-processing plant. The village itself is of little interest but the surroundings are nice. On the pass above town, there are two beautiful lakes, Norðara Hálsavatn and Heimara Hálsavatn, which are popular with trout anglers and offer excellent camping sites. They are reached by the oldest road in the Faroes which connects Skopun with Sandur, across the pass.

From Skopun, it's a wonderful walk up the track west of town and on past its end to the 269-metre cliffs of Djúpaberg. If you have time, pick your way south along a fairly rough 5 km of coastal cliffs to Søltuvík, then take the road into Sandur. Ideally, this trip should be done in 2 days.

Getting There & Away Bus No 600 operates seven or eight times daily, to and from the ferry landing at Skopun. It connects with all ferries to and from Tórshavn.

Sandur

Sandur sits on a small peninsula surrounded by two lakes, Sandsvatn and Gróthúsvatn, and two bays, Sandsvágur and Grótvík. At the head at Sandsvágur, between the village and the mountain, is an area of sand dunes (which looks quite out of place there), and a very nice black basalt sand beach. On the hill between Sandur and Grótvík is an area of greenhouse agriculture.

From the village, an easy half-day walk will take you around the lake Sandsvatn. Alternatively, walk out to the bay Søltuvík on the west coast. From there, it's possible to continue up to the cliffs which extend to the northern tip of the island.

Church The history of the Sandur church is one of the most interesting in the country. The site has been used as the parish centre since the 11th century and archaeology has revealed that at least six consecutive churches have existed there since.

The first one was constructed in the 11th century, most likely very soon after the conversion to Christianity. It was a stave structure about 9 metres long and probably not too comfortable during bad weather. The second church was built less than 200 years later, this time enclosed in heavy stone masonry, and was much stronger and resisted the climate better than its predecessor. The

Leabharlanna ... Cliath

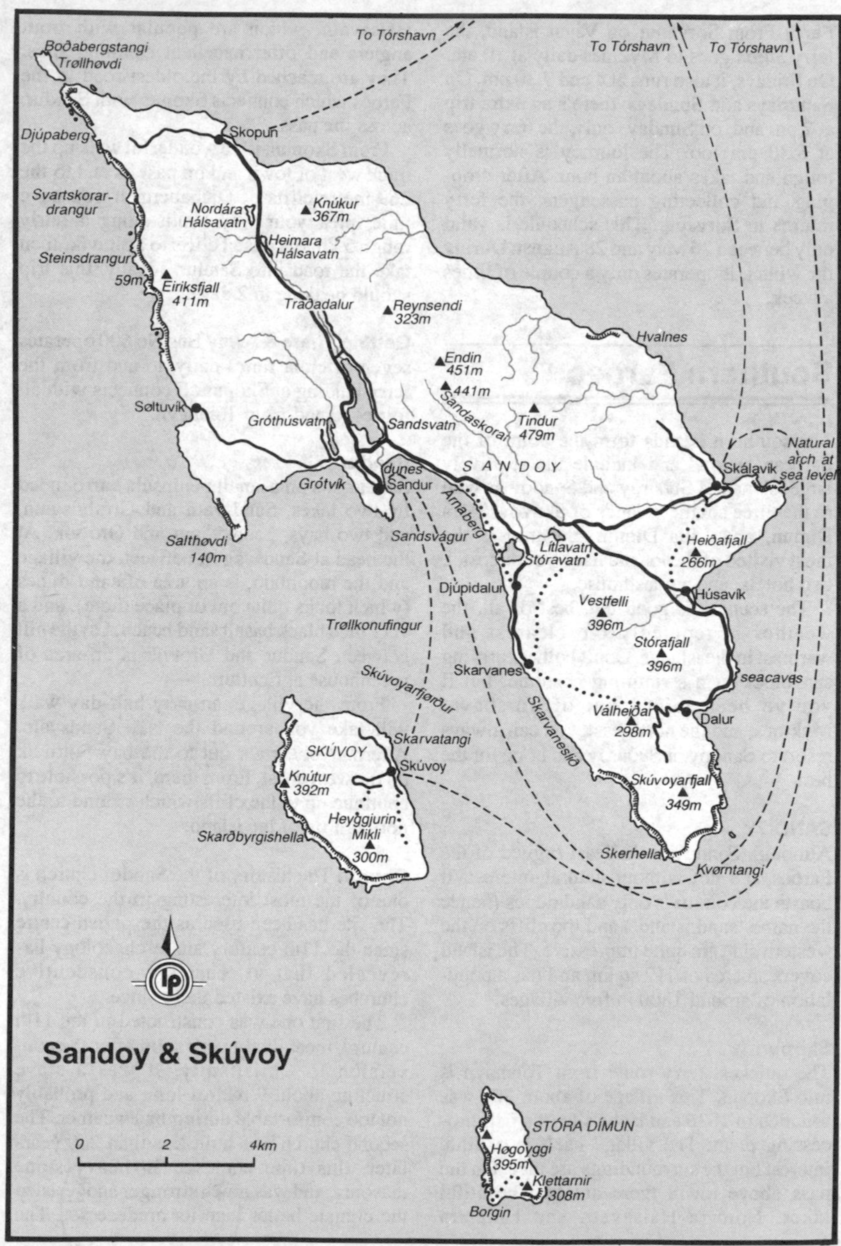
To Tórshavn
To Tórshavn
To Tórshavn
Boðabergstangi
Trøllhøvdi
Djúpaberg
Skopun
Svartskorar-
drangur
Nordára
Hálsavatn
Knúkur
367m
Heimara
Hálsavatn
Steinsdrangur
59m
Eiriksfjall
411m
Traðadalur
Reynsendi
323m
Hvalnes
Endin
451m
441m
Sandaskorar
Tindur
479m
Søltuvík
Gróthúsvatn
Sandsvatn
Natural
arch at
sea level
SANDOY
Skálavík
dunes
Sandur
Grótvík
Árnaberg
Sandsvágur
Lítlavatn
Heiðafjall
266m
Salthøvdi
140m
Stóravatn
Djúpidalur
Húsavík
Vestfelli
396m
Trøllkonufingur
Stórafjall
396m
Skarvanes
seacaves
Skúvoyarfjørður
Skarvanesliö
Válheiðar
298m
Dalur
Skarvatangi
SKÚVOY
Skúvoy
Knútur
392m
Skúvoyarfjall
349m
Heyggjurin
Mikli
Skarðbyrgishella
300m
Skerhella
Kvørntangi
Sandoy & Skúvoy
STÓRA DÍMUN
0
2
4km
Høgoyggi
395m
Klettarnir
308m
Borgin

third church came in the mid-17th century and the next in 1711. In 1762, the fifth church was constructed on the site. The current building, a typical black wood structure with a turf-roof and small white steeple, was built in 1839. If you manage to get inside, notice the lathe-turned columns in the choir screen which are unique in the Faroes.

Although the site is accessible to anyone who wants to have a look, its layered history is neither evident nor interpreted for visitors – so don't go expecting a Faroese version of Troy. Perhaps it's better to appreciate the fact that they haven't bothered to make a fuss about such things anywhere in the country.

Trollkonufingur

The 'troll woman's finger' or Trollkonufingur is the much-photographed rock pinnacle, north of the tiny settlement of Skarvanes. There's no public transport to the rock but it's an easy 4-km walk each way along the coastal track from the bus route (Nos 600 and 601) to Skálavík. You can also return to Sandur by walking the 4 km from Skarvanes across the 300-metre-high moor to Dalur on the east coast, and take the bus back from there.

Skálavík

This village is known only as the home town of the Faroes' most renowned writer, Heðin Brú. The one reason I can think of for visiting Skálavík would be to do the pleasant walk over the mountain Heiðafjall to the village of Húsavík, which has some interesting ruins. The walk offers some good views too.

At the point, east of Skálavík, there's a great, natural rock arch at sea level but it can only be seen from offshore. If you're travelling between Sandur or Suðuroy and Tórshavn on the ferry, take notice of it as you pass. Between Húsavík and Dalur are some large sea caves which are also worth seeing.

Getting There & Away Bus No 600 goes from Sandur to Skálavík seven or eight times daily on weekdays, and four times daily on weekends. Bus No 601 connects with it at the Lítlavatn intersection and runs out to Húsavík and Dalur with the same frequency.

Húsavík

The name of this tiny village, with only 100 people, means 'bay of houses'. It was settled very early in Faroese history but, after the pestilence that ravaged all of Europe in the 14th century, its population was drastically reduced. There are a couple of interesting sights in Húsavík, not least of which is its lovely dark, sand beach.

Longhouse Ruins Just north of the village's main road is the ruin of a Viking longhouse. It is believed to have been owned by the wealthy and influential Gudrun Sjurdardóttir of Shetland, during the 14th century. It was built, however, around the same time as the first 11th-century stave church in Sandur.

This manor house was similar in layout to the farmhouses excavated at Kvívík and Tjørnuvík (Streymoy) but was a much more sophisticated structure. Rather than the stamped mud floors typical in these longhouses, the floor of this one consisted of flagstone mosaics. It had a wooden roof overlain by the usual insulating layer of turf.

Museum There is also a museum in the restored Á Breyt farmhouse, but its opening hours are irregular and chances are it won't be open unless you make prior arrangements through the tourist office in Tórshavn.

Places to Stay & Eat

The island has one hotel, the *Ísansgarður* (tel 61004) in Sandur. It appears a bit run-down but the prices aren't outrageous. Singles/doubles with/without bath, cost US$41.50/36 and US$70/54. A continental breakfast is included in the price.

Meals are available at the hotel as well. The village has a couple of small grocery kiosks where you can buy limited supplies.

Getting There & Away

Air On weekdays in the summer, a helicopter service operates between Vágur (Suðuroy), Skopun and Tórshavn. It leaves Vágur at

7.30 am, Skopun at 8.17 am and Tórshavn at 8.28 am, and is back in Vágur at 8.40 am. Unfortunately, you can't use this service to reach Sandoy from Tórshavn in a single day. You'll have to stay overnight in Vágur.

Ferry The most popular way to visit Sandoy is to take the ferry *Tróndur* to Skopun, on the northern end of the island. The trip takes an hour and can get rough, although it's normally relatively smooth. It operates five times daily from Monday to Friday with one extra crossing on Fridays. On Saturdays and Sundays there are four crossings each day.

There is no ferry service between Sandoy and Suðuroy that doesn't first pass through Tórshavn.

SKÚVOY

Skúvoy, a tiny island of only 10 sq km and 100 residents, is worth visiting if you have the time. There is a set of steps leading from the harbour up to the island's single village. According to *Faereyingar Saga*, the entire island could never be captured as long as there were 10 men to defend these steps.

The island is named after the ubiquitous great skua. These raucous gull-like birds have a habit of attacking (like Hitchcock's birds) anyone perceived to be intruding on their territory.

Sigmund Bresterson's Grave

Skúvoy was the adopted home of Sigmund Bresterson, the hero of *Faereyingar Saga*. While in Norway he was coerced into accepting Christianity by the tyrant king Ólaf Tryggvason, and sent to the Faroes to convert the locals from paganism. After proclaiming the islands a Christian nation, sometime around the year 1000, he settled on Skúvoy.

Sigmund proceeded to get himself into all sorts of local religious scrapes, the last of which resulted in a swim for his life from Skúvoy to Suðuroy. To make matters worse, he had to carry his friend Thorer who had, in mid-channel, weakened to the point of exhaustion. Unfortunately Thorer ended up drowning.

Upon arriving in Suðuroy, Sigmund was welcomed and promptly murdered by greedy Thórgrim the Evil, who fancied some of the trinkets Sigmund was carrying. Thorer's body washed up beside Sigmund's, and Thórgrim hid them both on his farm near Sandvík. Years later, Sigmund's relatives discovered the bodies and carried them home to Skúvoy where they were buried in the churchyard above the village.

If you'd like to see the graves, walk up the staircase from the landing site at Skúvoy, through town up to the cemetery.

Egg Collection

On the 300 to 400-metre cliffs of the west coast, there is an immense guillemot colony. Those visiting Skúvoy during early June may be lucky enough to witness the collection of the eggs. Collectors are lowered over the cliff's edge in slings, on a 150-metre length of rope. They use a bag attached to a long pole to pluck the eggs from the nests. This is done only during the first week or so of the mating season to allow the birds to produce another egg to perpetuate the colony. Of course, the procedure isn't entirely safe but the collectors who survive do receive a great deal of respect.

Places to Stay & Eat

There are no restaurants or accommodation on Skúvoy so you'll need to make private arrangements through the tourist office or bring a tent and all the food you'll be needing on your visit.

Walks

This small and compact island can easily be explored on foot in one day. Climb to the summit of 392-metre Knútur for an impressive view down the magnificent line of cliffs along the west coast – you can walk along them as well.

Getting There & Away

Air For information about helicopter access to Skúvoy, refer to the Getting There & Away section for Sandoy island.

Ferry The ferry *Sildberin* operates between Sandur and Skúvoy from Monday to Saturday at 7 am daily, from Monday to Friday at 5.30 pm daily, and on Tuesdays, Thursdays, and Saturdays at 9.30 am and 2.30 pm. On Fridays, there's an additional trip at 8 pm and, on Sundays, between March and October there's one at 5.20 pm. The trip takes about 30 minutes to reach Skúvoy where it drops offs and collects passengers before returning to Sandur.

On Tuesdays, the ferry *Ritan* does one trip to Skúvoy directly from Tórshavn, departing at 1 pm and returning the same day.

STÓRA DÍMUN

During the Viking Age, the steep and rather forbidding island of Stóra Dímun was the home of several prominent characters in *Faereyingar Saga*. Until 1920, the ruins of a wretched church from the earlier days of Faroese Christianity still stood on the island.

Stóra Dímun has an area of 2.5 sq km and reaches an altitude of 395 metres. Today it is inhabited by a single family which stays there only part of the year.

By sea, the island can only be reached in clear and calm weather, but there is a helicopter service on Mondays, Wednesdays, and Fridays. If you'd like to visit this remote island, however, you must first have permission from the farmer. Those who are interested must apply at the tourist office in Tórshavn.

LÍTLA DÍMUN

Lampshade-shaped Lítla Dímun is the smallest of the Faroes' 18 major islands. With an area less than a sq km, it is rather intriguing. Its summit looms dauntingly 414 metres above the sea. The lower third of the island is sheer cliff. You can reach the slightly more inviting summit either by helicopter or after a very rough boat landing and an intimidating climb to the steep grassy slopes above.

Lítla Dímun is reputed to have been inhabited. When the first Norse people arrived, they found on the island a strain of dark brown Soay sheep from St Kilda island, west of the Hebrides. It is suspected they were introduced by the Irish monks who arrived in the Faroes during the late 6th century, but no one is certain. It is interesting, however, that around this time St Brendan, who is reputed to have been the first Irishman to visit these parts, happened along this way and found a place that he called the 'island of sheep'.

In *Faereyingar Saga*, Lítla Dímun is the site of a battle between Thrand of Gøta and his men and Sigmund Bresterson, the saga's hero. Two of the Gøta men were killed before Sigmund managed to escape on his ship.

During the summer, Lítla Dímun is still inhabited by sheep (the white variety) which happily nibble on its grassy summit, but there are no human residents.

A visit to this island, by the way, is essentially out of the question unless you have a particularly good reason to go (and some particularly good connections to get you there). You can have a good look at it, however, from the ferry between Tórshavn and Suðuroy.

SUÐUROY

This is the Faroes' southernmost island and is marginally drier and warmer than the more northerly ones. In addition, it boasts all the amenities of Tórshavn but has less traffic and is generally more congenial than the capital.

Jóansøka

Suðuroy's big annual festival, Jóansøka (St John's Day) or Midsummerfest, is held on the weekend nearest to 24 June.

Sandvík

Situated on a peninsula that on a map looks like Pac-man hellbent on gobbling up the Dímuns, Sandvík is Suðuroy's northernmost village. It is also the place where *Faereyingar Saga* tells us Sigmund Bresterson swam ashore and was murdered by Thórgrim the Evil (see the Skúvoy section for further details).

In the centre of Sandvík, just below the church, is a traditional Faroese house which dates back to 1860.

Behind the village, there's a road leading

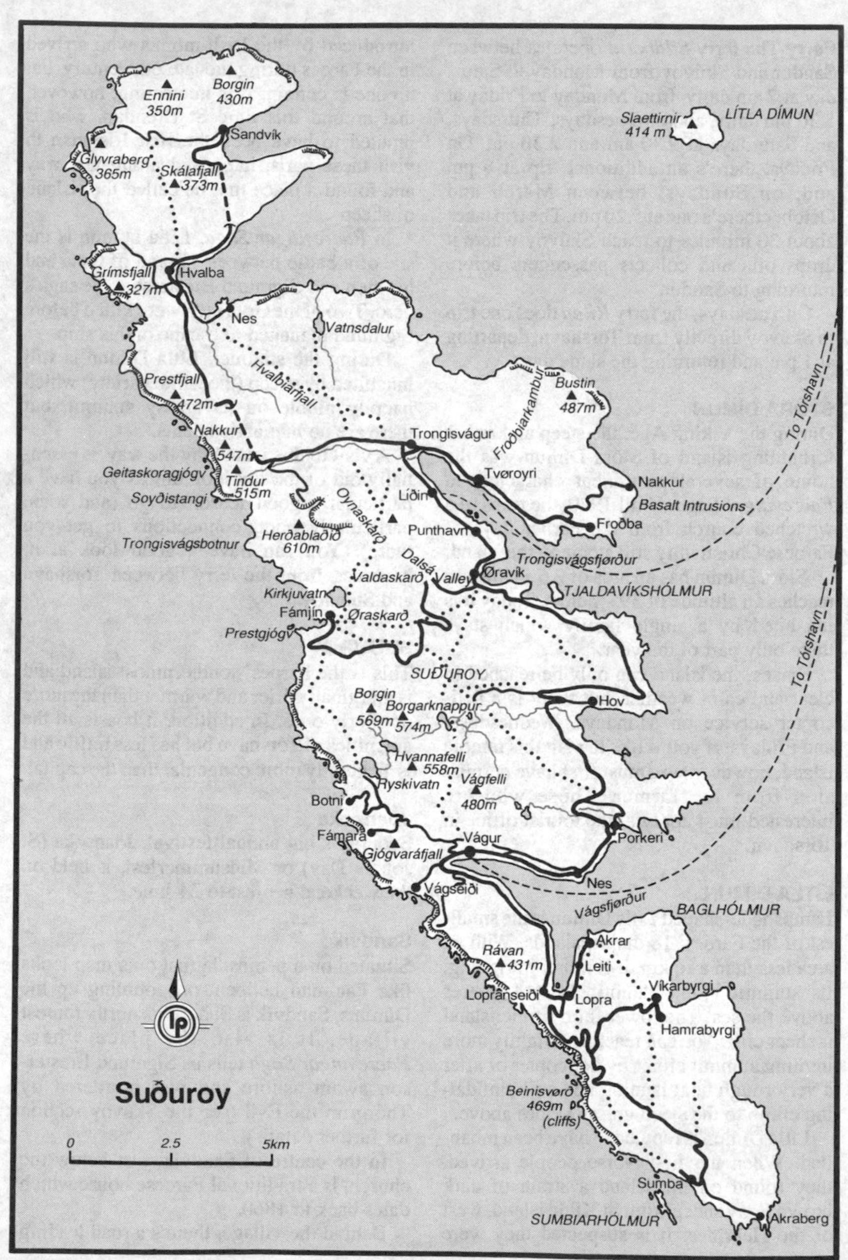
Borgin
430m
Ennini
350m
Sandvík
Glyvraberg
365m
Skálafjall
373m
Slaettirnir
414 m
LÍTLA DÍMUN
Grímsfjall
327m
Hvalba
Nes
Vatnsdalur
Hvalbiarfjall
Prestfjall
472m
Froðbiarkambur
Bustin
487m
Nakkur
547m
Geitaskoragjógv
Tindur
515m
Soyðistangi
Trongisvágsbotnur
Trongisvágur
Tvøroyri
Líðin
Nakkur
Basalt Intrusions
Froðba
Punthavn
Herðablaðið
610m
Oynaskarð
Dalsá
Valley
Valdaskarð
Trongisvágsfjørður
Øravík
TJALDAVÍKSHÓLMUR
To Tórshavn
Kirkjuvatn
Fámjin
Øraskarð
Prestgjógv
SUÐUROY
To Tórshavn
Borgin
569m
Borgarknappur
574m
Hov
Hvannafelli
558m
Ryskivatn
Vágfelli
480m
Botni
Fámara
Gjógvaráfjall
Vágur
Porkeri
Vágseiði
Nes
Vágsfjørður
BAGLHÓLMUR
Akrar
Rávan
431m
Leiti
Víkarbyrgi
Lopranseiði
Lopra
Hamrabyrgi
Suðuroy
Beinisvørð
469m
(cliffs)
0
2.5
5km
Sumba
SUMBIARHÓLMUR
Akraberg

up the valley to some of Suðuroy's many sea cliffs. Mid-way along this road, an old route takes off steeply up the mountain to the south to the summit of 373-metre Skálafjall before descending into the heart of Hvalba.

Hvalba

From the first available records of the Faroese Løgting, we learn that Hvalba was ravaged in 1629 by three shiploads of Barbary pirates and 30 of its inhabitants were kidnapped. Although a ransom was demanded for their return, the town couldn't raise the money and the poor victims were carried away to slavery in North Africa.

During the first Faroese election of representatives to the Danish parliament, Hvalba was the polling headquarters for Suðuroy island. Just as voting was about to start, the cry of 'grind' went up, signalling whales off the coast, and all interest in the election was summarily abandoned in favour of the grindadráp. Voting was resumed later, on the spot where the kill took place.

Hvalba is near the only coal mine in the Faroes. To the west of town, through the eiði, is the rugged old landing site which is fortunately no longer in use.

Most visitors who make it up to Hvalba do so to shop for locally made ceramics at the friendly Føroya Steintoy. Their products, made from Faroese clay and finished with natural glazes, are becoming quite popular souvenirs.

Tvøroyri

Although Tvøroyri has the largest population on Suðuroy, this overgrown village is really of little interest except as a transit point between the northern and southern halves of the island. If you find yourself pacing up and down the main street in search of something to do while awaiting bus connections, I'm afraid all I can suggest is a walk around the harbour and fish-processing area. Failing that, try a good book or splurge on a meal at the hotel.

The post office is open Monday to Friday from 9 am to noon and 3 to 5 pm. On Saturdays, it's open from 9 am to 5 pm.

Froðba This was Suðuroy's original settlement and pre-dates Tvøroyri by a few centuries. At the end of the peninsula, east of the village, are more basalt columns. You'll get a good view of the cliffs and the fjord by walking up the winding road behind Froðba to the radio tower.

Places to Stay & Eat The *Hotel Tvøroyri* (tel 71171), just uphill from the main street near the eastern end of town, is clean and comfortable. Doubles/singles with shared bath cost about US$62/46 including breakfast. Lunch and dinner will each cost about US$12 in the attached dining room, which is the only restaurant in town.

Tvøroyri has a bakery and two supermarkets, all along the main street. Near the harbour, there's also a rather temporary-looking fast food grill.

Walks From Trongisvágur (the part of Tvøroyri at the head of the fjord) there's a nice walk, north over the ridge, to a secluded camping and fishing lake in Vatnsdalur which is popular with locals. From Trongisvágur, the trip will take 1 to 2 hours each way.

From the southern end of the tunnel between Trongisvágur and Hvalba there's a short but very good walk to some cliffs which provide an impressive view of the roiling cove Trongisvágsbotnur. The walk from Tvøroyri to Fámjin is described in the Fámjin section, later in this chapter.

Øravík

Øravík is so tiny it can scarcely even be called a settlement, but, thanks to its central location, its youth hostel and guesthouse, I wouldn't be surprised if it's the most visited place on Suðuroy. It has a nice setting opposite a beach and is conveniently close to some good walking country.

The Áargardur Youth Hostel (tel 71157) is clean and exceptionally friendly. The staff are also very helpful with tourist information. Dorm beds cost US$13 per night and breakfast will cost an extra US$4.25.

In the same building is the Gistingarhúsið

við Á (tel 71157) which has an attached dining room and the same friendly service as the hostel. Singles/doubles without bath cost US$28.50/40.

Fámjin

From Øravík, a winding road leads across the pass Øraskarð to Fámjin, arguably the most charming village on Suðuroy.

According to a story from the trade monopoly days, Fámjin has a French connection. Once upon a time in the 1700s, two local fishermen rowed out to sell part of their catch to a French merchant ship anchored offshore. Two discerning women on board demanded they be permitted to inspect the catch before agreeing to buy. They were lowered into the rowboat and the fishermen, aware of a shortage of females on shore, decided this was an opportunity too good to pass up. They kidnapped the women and, realising that an impending storm would prevent the French taking any action, forced them back to the village where they were all married.

Fámjin is important to the Faroese as the home of the Faroes' first flag. Prior to 1920, the flag used at public gatherings portrayed the ram and tjaldur (the cheeky oystercatcher of Nølsoyar-Poul Poulson's famous ballad *Fuglakvaeði*). After Finland and Iceland gained independence and adopted flags bearing Scandinavian crosses, a group of Faroese students at Copenhagen University designed the red, white, and blue cross flag that was adopted by the Faroes in 1920. Jens Oliver Lisberg, a native of Fámjin, is given full credit for the design because he died of influenza shortly afterwards. The original flag is now housed in the church at Fámjin.

Just 15 minutes' walk from the church is the excellent trout lake Kirkjuvatn near which you can camp.

Getting There & Around

Walks For those with a bit of energy, it's a nice walk from either Tvøroyri or Øravík across the ridge to Fámjin. From the former, begin at the head of Trongisvágsfjørður and climb the slope up the 260-metre pass Oyrnaskarð. From there, the view improves as you traverse the Dalsá valley and cross 249-metre Valdaskarð before descending past Kirkjuvatn to Fámjin.

From Øravík, the trip is much more straightforward. Just head up the hill towards the point where you see the road going through the pass Øraskarð, then take the most direct descent to the village. This will be obvious (if it's not foggy).

Porkeri

The church at Porkeri, just east of Vágur, is another in the traditional turf-roofed style. This one was built in 1847. In the hillsides around Porkeri are some exposed examples of columnar basalt. At the village of Hov, 5 km north of Porkeri along the road, there are more basalt intrusions which form a procession of posts along the slopes.

Vágur

Vágur is Suðuroy's second village and has a nicer and more rustic appearance than Tvøroyri. Around 1700 people live in this fishing and fish-processing centre.

Nølsoyar-Poul Poulson Monument Near the main road through Vágur, there's a memorial to the efforts of Nølsoyar-Poul Poulson, the 19th-century Faroese hero, poet, and genius. He led the earliest opposition to the trade monopolies which he believed were crippling the potential economic viability of the Faroe Islands and the ingenuity of the people.

After purchasing the remains of a wrecked ship from the Hvalba district auction, Poul went to Vágur and set about refurbishing it. From the efforts of Poul and his brothers, emerged the *Royndin Friða*, the only ocean-going schooner in the Faroes.

After the ship was launched on 6 August 1804, Poulson and his crew plied the waters between the Faroes and the mainland carrying much-needed food and vaccines to the Faroese people, working all the while to muster resistance to the trade monopolies. Unfortunately, he only succeeded in getting caught up in litigation and becoming unpopular in high and powerful places. The *Royndin Friða* was seized in a naval confrontation with a British warship off Denmark in 1808 and was inadvertently destroyed while being towed into harbour.

Walks From Vágur, it's an easy walk through the eiði to the west coast, where there is a good view of some relatively low cliffs.

Only slightly more challenging is the walk up the Fámara road north-west of town – from here you can walk down to the lighthouse on the beautiful coast at Fámara. Another option is to continue along the track another 1.5 km to Ryskivatn, the lake which feeds the small Botni power plant found on the steep winding road. Twice daily from Mondon to Friday bus No 707 connects Vágur and Fámara around commuting hours.

Places to Stay & Eat The choice of hotels is simple in Vágur; there's only one. The *Hotel Bakkin* (tel 73196) looks a bit seedy from the outside but it's not too bad. They charge US$36/50 for singles/doubles with shared bath, including breakfast. Other meals will cost between US$10 and US$12. The supermarket in Vágur is tucked away near the harbour just off the main road.

Down the road south of Vágur, in the village of Lopra, is *Frítíðaríbúðirnar Í Lopra* (tel 73910), a block of flats where units are rented by the day. Each flat has four beds, television, attached bath and phone for US$65 per day. If you have a group, this will prove an economical option.

Beinisvørð

The 469-metre cliffs of Beinisvørð lie only a few hundred metres walk from the road between Lopra and Sumba. They provide a magnificent and easily accessible view up and down Suðuroy's incredible western coast. From Beinisvørð, it's possible to walk down the steep slope into Sumba. The road passes close to the cliffs at Lopranseiði, just 2 km above Lopra, at Suðuroy's narrowest point where there is a large puffin colony.

Sumba

There's nothing special to see or do in Sumba except gaze at the view from the cliffs to the north, and appreciate that the next landfall to the south is Scotland. The trip from Vágur to Sumba on bus No 704, which departs seven times daily on weekdays and three times daily on weekends, is worthwhile in itself with good views over the pass. These will be curtailed, however, when work is completed on the tunnel between Lopra and Sumba.

If you'd like to continue on the unsurfaced road to Akraberg, the southernmost settlement in the country, bus No 705 departs Sumba daily from Monday to Friday at 7.15 am and 4.15 pm and returns immediately upon arrival.

Getting There & Away

Air There is a helicopter service between Tórshavn and Froðba (near Tvøroyri) on Mondays, Wednesdays, and Fridays stopping en route at Skúvoy and Stóra Dímun. Daily from Monday to Friday there is also one that departs Vágur at 7.30 am, stops at Froðba, departing at 8 am, and arrives in Tórshavn at 8.25 am, stopping at Skopun (Sandoy) on the way. It then returns to Vágur from Tórshavn at 8.28 am.

Ferry During the summer, there is at least one ferry daily between Tórshavn and Líðin (across Trongisvágsfjørður from Tvøroyri) and one in each direction between Tórshavn and Vágur on Tuesdays, Thursdays, and Fridays. The trip takes about 2 hours.

Getting Around

Tvøroyri is basically the transport hub of Suðuroy. From here, buses go south to Øravík, Vágur and Sumba and also north to Hvalba and Sandvík. The heliport is at nearby Froðba and the main ferry terminal is across the fjord at Líðin.

Bus No 700 runs between Tvøroyri, Hvalba, Nes, and Sandvík about eight times daily from Monday to Friday and four times daily on weekends.

Bus No 701 connects Øravík with Tvøroyri and Froðba several times daily. In addition, bus No 700 does the run every 1 to 2 hours between 7 am and 8 pm.

Between Fámjin, Tvøroyri, and Øravík, bus No 703 runs five or six times daily from Monday to Saturday. On Sundays, it goes twice from Øravík and once from Tvøroyri.

There are 10 buses daily from Monday to Friday between Tvøroyri and Vágur which stop at all settlements in between. On Saturdays, there are six in each direction and four on Sundays. Southbound to Akrar and Sumba, bus No 704 runs seven times daily on weekdays and three times daily on weekends.

Other Islands

The three small islands of Nólsoy, Koltur, and Hestur lie clustered around the southern tip of Streymoy. They offer easy day-trips from Tórshavn or off-the-beaten-track destinations for camping and exploration on foot.

NÓLSOY

Just a stone's throw from Tórshavn, Nólsoy lies low on the capital's horizon like a crouching panther, sheltering it from the full wrath of the Atlantic. It's just a half-hour ferry ride from Tórshavn to Nólsoy – an excellent day-trip. The island's proximity to the city also makes it a particularly appealing option for campers who'd like to escape the Tórshavn swamp that serves as its camping grounds.

Nólsoy's picturesque little village and harbour lie just north of the island's isthmus which is just a few metres wide. From here, cairns mark the 6.5 km route southwards around 371-metre Eggjarklettur (the island's highest point), and along the slopes to Øksnatangi, Nólsoy's beautiful south-eastern cape with a classic lighthouse on top. From there, you can also visit the south-western cape, Borðan, but its lighthouse is less interesting. Nólsoy lighthouses were originally built in the late 1700s to aid smugglers running goods into Tórshavn during the days of the failing trade monopoly.

Places to Stay & Eat

There's no formal accommodation due to the island's proximity to Tórshavn and only a small shop in the village for food. Those who are keen on staying here should check on home-stay possibilities at the tourist office or Tora Tourist Traffic in Tórshavn. You can camp just about anywhere outside the village and the best site, in my opinion, is near the lighthouse at Øksnatangi.

Getting There & Away

From Monday to Thursday, there are ferries from Tórshavn to Nólsoy at 6.45 am, noon, 3.10, and 6 pm. The schedule is the same on Fridays except the last ferry departs Tórshavn at 7 pm. There are two runs on Saturdays at 6.45 am and 2 pm and on Sundays at 11 am and 8.30 pm. Ferries which depart at noon return to Tórshavn at 1 pm and the rest return as soon as they arrive in Nólsoy.

Tour

A guided boat tour on the *Amadeus*, which includes circumnavigating Nólsoy and a cruise below the bird cliffs of Hestur's west coast, departs Tórshavn on Tuesdays and Thursdays at 2 pm and on Saturdays at 11 am. The tour is a bargain at a mere US$14.25 per person and can be booked through the tourist office in Tórshavn.

HESTUR

The island of Hestur ('the horse') lies about 4 km off the south-west coast of Streymoy, about an hour by ferry from Tórshavn. Its single village, also called Hestur, clings to the eastern shore of the island and has about 60 inhabitants.

The seas around Hestur are particularly rich in fish and seals and the western coast has a large guillemot colony. Life has never been particularly easy there, however. In 1919, two fishing boats were sunk in a storm and a third of the island's men were drowned. Since then, the island has never really recovered its liveliness.

Oddly enough, the tiny village does have

a new swimming pool which can be used by visitors.

Walks

Near the northern end of the island are Hestur's two highest points – Múlin and Eggjarrók – which both rise to 421 metres and can be reached by going up the steep valley behind the village. If you climb the valley and bear south, rather than towards the mountains, you'll reach lovely moorland with four smallish lakes. The name of the largest is Fagradalsvatn ('beautiful lake'). Around any of these lakes are good camping sites.

On the rather forbidding western coast, about 1.5 km north of the lighthouse and below the cliffs just south-west of Fagradalsvatn, is the unusually-shaped pinnacle Álvastakkur ('elf stack'). It can be viewed from the cliffs above or from the sea, but to climb down to it seems nearly impossible.

From the village, there's an easier walk south along the coast road to the lighthouse at Haelur, on Hestur's southern tip. This trip is less than 3 km each way.

Places to Stay & Eat

There is no formal accommodation on the island so you'll have to bring a tent or make home-stay arrangements through the tourist office in Tórshavn. The village has a small shop but it's best to carry your own supplies.

Getting There & Away

From Monday to Saturday the ferry *Ritan* goes to Hestur from Tórshavn at 8 am. On Wednesdays and Fridays, there's a second trip at 4 pm and on Saturdays at 3.10 pm. On Fridays, there's a third trip at 8 pm. During the summer, it departs at noon and 5.30 pm on Sundays as well. The ferry returns to Tórshavn 1 or 2 hours after these departures, depending on whether it stops at Koltur on the way.

Tour

For tour information, see the Nólsoy section.

KOLTUR

The name of this uniquely-shaped island means 'the colt', because it seems to be trotting along just behind Hestur, 'the horse'. It is inhabited only in the summer by sheep farmers whose animals graze on the southern half of the island.

From the relatively flat plateau of the southern end, Koltur sweeps magnificently skyward, ending at 478-metre Koltürshamar. This conical mountain is quite steep and, although I've heard that climbing it is possibie, but it wouldn't be easy.

Places to Stay & Eat

There are no shops or services on Koltur although home-stays may sometimes be arranged through the tourist office in Tórshavn. Otherwise, you'll have to visit the tourist office to secure permission to camp on the island.

There is helicopter service to Koltur from both Vágar and Tórshavn on Mondays, Wednesdays, Fridays, and Sundays.

Getting There & Away

En route to Hestur, the ferry *Ritan* stops briefly at Koltur (weather permitting) several times a week. If you just want to have a quick look around, which is all that will be necessary for the 2.7-sq km island, it's best to go on Sunday. During the summer, the ferry departs Tórshavn at noon and returns in the evening.

Index

ABBREVIATIONS

(F) Faroe Islands
(G) Greenland
(I) Iceland

MAPS

TEXT

For placename derivation, the 'Geographical Features' lists in the Language sections are useful: (I) pp 59-60, (G) pp 311-312, (F) p 425.

Map references are **bold** type.

Guides to Europe

Trekking in Spain
Aimed at both overnight trekkers and day hikers, this guidebook includes useful maps and full details on hikes in some of Spain's most beautiful wilderness areas – the Sierra Nevada, Las Alpujarras, Western and Central Gredos in Castilla, the High Pyrenees, Picos de Europa and Mallorca.

Eastern Europe on a shoestring
This guide opens up a whole new world for travellers: East Germany, Poland, Czechoslovakia, Hungary, Romania, Bulgaria, Yugoslavia, Albania and western USSR.

'...a thorough, well-researched book. Only a fool would go East without it.'
– *Great Expeditions*

Lonely Planet Guidebooks

Lonely Planet guidebooks cover every accessible part of Asia as well as Australia, the Pacific, South America, Africa, the Middle East and parts of North America and Europe. There are four series: *travel survival kits*, covering a single country for a range of budgets; *shoestring guides* with compact information for low-budget travel in a major region; *walking guides*; and *phrasebooks*.

Australia & the Pacific
Australia
Bushwalking in Australia
Islands of Australia's Great Barrier Reef
Fiji
Micronesia
New Caledonia
New Zealand
Tramping in New Zealand
Papua New Guinea
Papua New Guinea phrasebook
Rarotonga & the Cook Islands
Samoa
Solomon Islands
Tahiti & French Polynesia
Tonga

South-East Asia
Bali & Lombok
Burma
Burmese phrasebook
Indonesia
Indonesia phrasebook
Malaysia, Singapore & Brunei
Philippines
Pilipino phrasebook
South-East Asia on a shoestring
Thailand
Thai phrasebook
Vietnam, Laos & Cambodia

North-East Asia
China
Chinese phrasebook
Hong Kong, Macau & Canton
Japan
Japanese phrasebook
Korea
Korean phrasebook
North-East Asia on a shoestring
Taiwan
Tibet
Tibet phrasebook

West Asia
Trekking in Turkey
Turkey
Turkish phrasebook
West Asia on a shoestring

Travel with Children

Indian Ocean
Madagascar & Comoros
Maldives & Islands of the East Indian Ocean
Mauritius, Réunion & Seychelles

Mail Order

Lonely Planet guidebooks are distributed worldwide and are sold by good bookshops everywhere. They are also available by mail order from Lonely Planet, so if you have difficulty finding a title please write to us. US and Canadian residents should write to Embarcadero West, 112 Linden St, Oakland CA 94607, USA and residents of other countries to PO Box 617, Hawthorn, Victoria 3122, Australia.

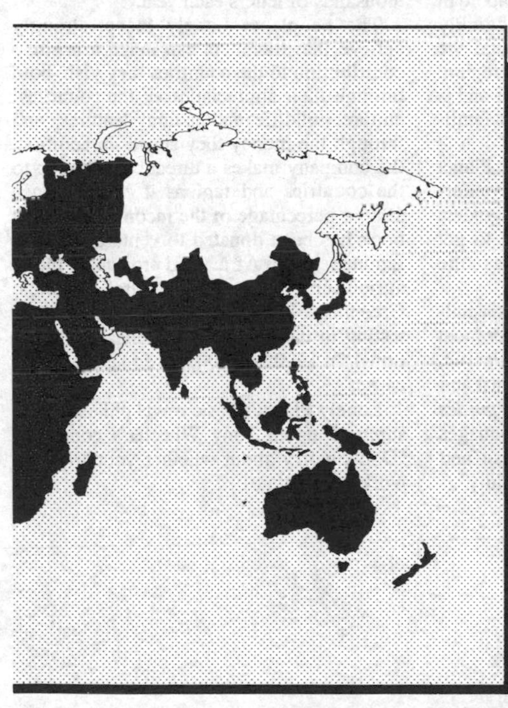

Europe
Eastern Europe on a shoestring
Iceland, Greenland & the Faroe Islands
Trekking in Spain

Indian Subcontinent
Bangladesh
India
Hindi/Urdu phrasebook
Trekking in the Indian Himalaya
Karakoram Highway
Kashmir, Ladakh & Zanskar
Nepal
Trekking in the Nepal Himalaya
Nepal phrasebook
Pakistan
Sri Lanka
Sri Lanka phrasebook

Africa
Africa on a shoestring
Central Africa
East Africa
Kenya
Swahili phrasebook
Morocco, Algeria & Tunisia
Moroccan Arabic phrasebook
West Africa

North America
Alaska
Canada
Hawaii

Mexico
Baja California
Mexico

South America
Argentina
Bolivia
Brazil
Brazilian phrasebook
Chile & Easter Island
Colombia
Ecuador & the Galápagos Islands
Peru
Quechua phrasebook
South America on a shoestring

Middle East
Egypt & the Sudan
Egyptian Arabic phrasebook
Israel
Jordan & Syria
Yemen

The Lonely Planet Story

Lonely Planet published its first book in 1973 in response to the numerous 'How did you do it?' questions Maureen and Tony Wheeler were asked after driving, bussing, hitching, sailing and railing their way from England to Australia.

Written at a kitchen table and hand collated, trimmed and stapled, *Across Asia on the Cheap* became an instant local bestseller, inspiring thoughts of another book.

Eighteen months in South-East Asia resulted in their second guide, *South-East Asia on a shoestring*, which they put together in a backstreet Chinese hotel in Singapore in 1975. The 'yellow bible' as it quickly became known to backpackers around the world, soon became *the* guide to the region. It has sold well over ½ million copies and is now in its 6th edition, still retaining its familiar yellow cover.

Today there are over 80 Lonely Planet titles – books that have that same adventurous approach to travel as those early guides; books that 'assume you know how to get your luggage off the carousel' as one reviewer put it.

Although Lonely Planet initially specialised in guides to Asia, they now cover most regions of the world, including the Pacific, South America, Africa, the Middle East and Eastern Europe. The list of *walking guides* and *phrasebooks* (for 'unusual' languages such as Quechua, Swahili, Nepalese and Egyptian Arabic) is also growing rapidly.

The emphasis continues to be on travel for independent travellers. Tony and Maureen still travel for several months of each year and play an active part in the writing, updating and quality control of Lonely Planet's guides.

They have been joined by over 50 authors, 40 staff – mainly editors, cartographers, & designers – at our office in Melbourne, Australia, and another 10 at our US office in Oakland, California. Travellers themselves also make a valuable contribution to the guides through the feedback we receive in thousands of letters each year.

The people at Lonely Planet strongly believe that travellers can make a positive contribution to the countries they visit, both through their appreciation of the countries' culture, wildlife and natural features, and through the money they spend. In addition, the company makes a direct contribution to the countries and regions it covers. Since 1986 a percentage of the income from each book has been donated to ventures such as famine relief in Africa; aid projects in India; agricultural projects in Central America; Greenpeace's efforts to halt French nuclear testing in the Pacific and Amnesty International. In 1990 $60,000 was donated to these causes.

Lonely Planet's basic travel philosophy is summed up in Tony Wheeler's comment, 'Don't worry about whether your trip will work out. Just go!'